Chapter Correlation Guide for Feenstra/Taylor, *Inte*[illegible]
Second Edition, and Three Versio[illegible]

International Economics		*International Trade*	*International Macro -economics*	*Essentials of International Economics*	*Online*
Chapter number	**Chapter title**	**Chapter number**	**Chapter number**	**Chapter number**	**Chapter number**
1	Trade in the Global Economy	1			
1	The Global Economy *(Essentials)*	[illegible]		1	
2	Trade and Technology: The Ricardian Model	[illegible]		[illegible]	
3	Gains and Losses from Trade in the Specific-Factors Model	[illegible]		3	
4	Trade and Resources: The Heckscher-Ohlin Model	[illegible]		4	
5	Movement of Labor and Capital between Countries	5		5	
6	Increasing Returns to Scale and Monopolistic Competition	6		6	
7	Offshoring of Goods and Services	7			ONLINE
8	Import Tariffs and Quotas under Perfect Competition	8		7	
9	Import Tariffs and Quotas under Imperfect Competition	9		8	
10	Export Subsidies in Agriculture and High-Technology Industries	10			
11	International Agreements: Trade, Labor and the Environment	11		9	
12	The Global Macroeconomy		1		
13	Introduction to Exchange Rates and the Foreign Exchange Market		2	10	
14	Exchange Rates I: The Monetary Approach in the Long Run		3	11	
15	Exchange Rates II: The Asset Approach in the Short Run		4	12	
16	National and International Accounts: Income, Wealth, and the Balance of Payments		5	13	
17	Balance of Payments I: The Gains from Financial Globalization		6		
18	Balance of Payments II: Output, Exchange Rates, and Macroeconomic Policies in the Short Run		7	14	
19	Fixed Versus Floating: International Monetary Experience		8	15	
20	Exchange Rate Crises: How Pegs Work and How They Break		9		
21	The Euro		10		ONLINE
22	Topics in International Macroeconomics		11		

Z4

second edition

international trade

ROBERT C. FEENSTRA
University of California, Davis

ALAN M. TAYLOR
University of California, Davis

WORTH PUBLISHERS

Senior Publisher: Catherine Woods
Executive Editor: Charles Linsmeier
Senior Acquisitions Editor: Sarah Dorger
Development Editors: Jane Tufts and Bruce Kaplan
Media and Supplements Editor: Jaclyn Castaldo Ferry
Executive Marketing Manager: Scott Guile
Associate Managing Editor: Tracey Kuehn
Project Editor: Anthony Calcara
Art Director: Babs Reingold
Senior Designer: Kevin Kall
Photo Editor: Cecilia Varas
Photo Researcher: Dena Betz
Production Manager: Barbara Anne Seixas
Composition: TSI Graphics
Printing and Binding: RR Donnelley

Cover Photo Credits: *Globes:* Fusion/Getty Images; *Apple factory:* © Bobby Yip/Reuters; *Trucks:* David McNew/Getty Images; *Picking coffee:* Courtesy TransFair USA © 2007; *787 plane:* Kyodo/AP Images; *Protestors:* © Hagerty Patrick/Corbis Sygma

Library of Congress Cataloging in Publication Data: 2010935912

ISBN-13: 978-1-4292-4104-5
ISBN-10: 1-4292-4104-7

Printed in the United States of America

Fifth printing

Worth Publishers
41 Madison Avenue
New York, NY 10010
www.worthpublishers.com

About the Authors

Robert C. Feenstra and **Alan M. Taylor** are Professors of Economics at the University of California, Davis. They each began their studies abroad: Feenstra received his B.A. in 1977 from the University of British Columbia, Canada, and Taylor received his B.A. in 1987 from King's College, Cambridge, U.K. They trained as professional economists in the United States, where Feenstra earned his Ph.D. in economics from MIT in 1981 and Taylor earned his Ph.D. in economics from Harvard University in 1992. Feenstra has been teaching international trade at the undergraduate and graduate levels at UC Davis since 1986, where he holds the C. Bryan Cameron Distinguished Chair in International Economics. Taylor has been teaching international macroeconomics, growth, and economic history at UC Davis since 1999, where he directs the Center for the Evolution of the Global Economy.

Both Feenstra and Taylor are active in research and policy discussions in international economics. They are research associates of the National Bureau of Economic Research, where Feenstra directs the International Trade and Investment research program. They have both published graduate-level books in international economics: *Offshoring in the Global Economy* and *Product Variety and the Gains from Trade* (MIT Press, 2010), by Robert C. Feenstra, and *Global Capital Markets: Integration, Crisis and Growth* (Cambridge University Press, 2004), by Maurice Obstfeld and Alan M. Taylor. Feenstra received the Bernhard Harms Prize from the Institute for World Economics, Kiel, Germany, in 2006, and delivered the Ohlin Lectures at the Stockholm School of Economics in 2008. Taylor was awarded a Guggenheim Fellowship in 2004 and was a visiting professor at the American University in Paris and London Business School in 2005–06.

Feenstra lives in Davis, California, with his wife, Gail, and has two grown children: Heather, who is a genetics counselor, and Evan, who recently graduated from Pitzer College. Taylor also lives in Davis, with his wife, Claire, and has two young children, Olivia and Sebastian.

To our parents

Brief Contents

Contents

Preface

The twenty-first century is an age of unprecedented globalization. In looking at existing texts, we saw that the dramatic economic developments of recent years had not been incorporated into a newly written undergraduate text, and felt the time was ripe to incorporate fresh perspectives, current topics, and up-to-date approaches into the study of international economics. With this book, we have expanded the vision of international economics to encompass the latest theory and events in the world today.

In decades past, international economics was taught differently. There was a much greater emphasis on theory and a strong focus on the advanced countries. Policy analysis reflected the concerns of the time, whether strategic trade policy or the Bretton Woods system. Today, the concerns are not the same. In addition to new theoretical developments, there is a much greater emphasis on empirical studies. A wave of applied research in recent years has proved (or refuted) existing theories and taught us important new lessons about the determinants of trade, factor flows, exchange rates, and crises. Trade and capital flows have been liberalized and allowed to grow, and more attention is now devoted to emerging markets and developing countries, regions that now carry substantial weight in the global economy.

Covering new and expanding ground is part of the challenge and excitement of teaching and learning the international economics of the twenty-first century. Our goal is to provide new material that is rigorous enough to meet the challenge yet approachable enough to nurture the excitement. Many of the new topics stand apart from conventional textbook treatments and in the past have been bypassed in lectures or taught through supplementary readings. In our view they deserve a more prominent place in today's curriculum.

We have taught the chapters of this book ourselves a number of times, and have benefited from the feedback of professors at colleges and universities in the United States and throughout the world. Like us, they have been enthusiastic about the response from students to our fresh, accessible, and up-to-the-minute approach, and we hope that you also will enjoy the book.

Features

Each chapter includes several features that bring the material alive for the students:

- **Applications,** which are integrated into the main text and use material that has been covered to illuminate real-world policies, events, and evidence
- **Headlines,** which show how topics in the main text relate directly to media coverage of the global economy
- **Side Bars,** which include topics that, while not essential, are nonetheless of interest
- **Net Works,** provided at the ends of the chapters with homework problems, which provide an opportunity for the students to explore chapter concepts on the Internet

The book is issued in a combined edition *(International Economics)* and in two split editions *(International Trade* and *International Macroeconomics)*, allowing greater flexibility for instructors to assign their preferred text and keep costs down for students.

In addition, in response to the needs and feedback of those instructors who teach a one-semester course that combines international trade and macroeconomics, our text now comes in a one-semester version called ***Essentials of International Economics***. We include fifteen chapters most relevant to that setting. There is more information on this one-semester version later in the Preface.

New in the Second Edition

In this second edition we have updated the text (including most of the Headline features) to reflect the rapid changes in international economic news during the last three years. The world financial crisis which started in 2008 and its aftermath are covered in many chapters: the abrupt fall in international trade and its partial recovery are discussed in Chapter 1; the increased pressures for protectionist trade policy, including U.S. tariffs against China, are discussed in Chapter 8; and the ongoing challenges to the European Union and the Euro currency are discussed in Chapter 22. Other new topics include the offshoring of service jobs and the expansion of Trade Adjustment Assistance to cover these workers (Chapters 3 and 7); an assessment of NAFTA after 15 years (Chapter 6); General Motors' recent experience in the China market (Chapter 9); the failure of the 2009 Copenhagen Climate Summit (Chapter 11); how central banks can face difficulties with interest rate policies in the presence of market risk premiums or at the zero bound (Chapters 14 and 18); how countries have used creative accounting to disguise their economic problems (Chapter 16); and how some countries have used foreign reserves to cushion the effects of shocks (Chapter 21). In addition to updating the text to cover these new topics, we have benefited from the comments of faculty using the book and from our own experiences in teaching from it. From this feedback, we have rearranged some material to make a more natural flow in teaching. For example, the Heckscher-Ohlin material (Chapter 4) has been streamlined to present an easier resolution of the Leontief Paradox, which relies on differing productivities of labor across countries; and the material on dumping is now discussed along with trade policy under imperfect competition (Chapter 9). In international macroeconomics, the presentation of the national and international accounts in Chapter 16 has been streamlined, as has the treatment of the gains from financial globalization in Chapter 17.

Topics and Approaches

Reviewers and class testers have been enthusiastically supportive of the topics we have included in our presentation. Topics covered in *International Economics* or *International Trade* include the offshoring of goods and services (Chapter 6); tariffs and quotas under imperfect competition (Chapter 9); and international agreements on trade, labor, and the environment (Chapter 11). These topics are in addition to core chapters on the Ricardian model (Chapter 2), the specific-factors model (Chapter 3), the Heckscher-Ohlin model (Chapter 4), trade with increasing returns to scale and imperfect competition (Chapter 6), import tariffs and quotas under perfect competition (Chapter 8), and export subsidies (Chapter 10).

Chapters in *International Economics* or *International Macroeconomics* include the gains from financial globalization (Chapter 17 in the combined edition, or Chapter 6 in the *International Macroeconomics* split edition), fixed versus floating regimes (Chapter 19/Chapter 8), exchange-rate crises (Chapter 20/Chapter 9), and the euro (Chapter 21 or Chapter 10). These topics are in addition to core chapters on foreign exchange markets and exchange rates in the short run and the long run (Chapters 13–15/ Chapters 2–4), the national and international accounts (Chapter 16/Chapter 5), the open economy IS-LM model (Chapter 18/Chapter 7), and a chapter on current important issues (Chapter 22/Chapter 11).

In writing our chapters we have made every effort to link them analytically. For example, although immigration and foreign direct investment are sometimes treated as an afterthought in international economics books, we integrate these topics into the discussion of the trade models by covering the movement of labor and capital between countries in Chapter 5. Specifically, we analyze the movement of labor and capital between countries in the short run using the specific-factors model, and explore the long-run implications using the Heckscher-Ohlin model. Chapter 5 therefore builds on the models that the student has learned in Chapters 3 and 4, and applies them to issues at the forefront of policy discussion.

In the macroeconomics section from *International Economics* or *International Macroeconomics* this analytical linking is seen in the parallel development of fixed and floating exchange rate regimes from the opening introductory tour in Chapter 12 (Chapter 1 in the split edition), through the workings of exchange rates in Chapters 13–15 (Chapters 2–4), the discussion of policy in the IS-LM model of Chapter 18 (Chapter 7), to the discussion of regime choice in Chapter 19 (Chapter 8). Many textbooks discuss fixed and floating regimes separately, with fixed regimes often treated as an afterthought. But given the widespread use of fixed rates in many countries, the rising macro weight of fixed regimes, and the collapse of fixed rates during crises, we think it is more helpful for the student to grapple with the different workings and cost-benefit tradeoffs of the two regimes by studying them side by side. This approach also allows us to address numerous policy issues such as the implications of the trilemma and the optimal choice of exchange rate regime.

In addition to expanding our coverage to include up-to-date theory and policy applications, our other major goal is to present all the material—both new and old—in the most teachable way. To do this, we ensure that all of the material presented rests on firm and up-to-the-minute empirical evidence. We believe this approach is the right way to study economics, and it is our experience, shared with many instructors, that teaching is more effective and more enlivened when students can see not just an elegant derivation in theory but, right next to it, some persuasive evidence of the economic mechanisms under investigation.

The Arrangement of Topics: International Trade

Part 1: Introduction to International Trade

The opening chapter sets the stage by discussing global flows of goods and services through international trade, of people through migration, and of capital through foreign direct investment. The chapter includes maps depicting these flows, so the student can get a feel for which countries have the greatest flows in each case. Historical examples of trade and barriers to trade are also provided. This chapter can serve as a full introductory lecture.

Part 2: Patterns of International Trade

The core models of international trade are presented here: the Ricardian model (Chapter 2), the specific-factors model (Chapter 3), and the Heckscher-Ohlin model (Chapter 4). Some of the topics conventionally included in the specific-factors and Heckscher-Ohlin model, like the effects of changing the endowments of labor or capital, are not covered in those chapters but are instead examined in Chapter 5, which deals with the movement of labor and capital between countries. For example, the "factor price insensitivity" result is deferred to Chapter 5, as is the Rybczynski theorem. By discussing those two results in Chapter 5, we keep the discussion of the Heckscher-Ohlin model more manageable in Chapter 4, which focuses on the Heckscher-Ohlin theorem, the Stolper-Samuelson theorem, and empirical testing of the model. In summary, the ordering of topics among Chapters 3, 4, and 5, as well as many of the applications, is new, and these chapters are linked together tightly in their pedagogical approach.

Part 3: New Explanations for International Trade

In this section we cover two new explanations for international trade: increasing returns to scale (Chapter 6), and offshoring (Chapter 7).

Formal models of trade with increasing returns to scale and monopolistic competition have been popular since the early 1980s, but there is no standardized method for presenting this topic in undergraduate textbooks. In Chapter 6, we use the original, graphical discussion from Edward Chamberlin, who introduced the *DD* and *dd* curves (which we label in Chapter 6 as simply *D* and *d*). The *D* curve represents the share of the market going to each firm and traces out demand if all firms charge the same prices. In contrast, the *d* curve is the demand facing a firm when other firms keep their prices constant. The distinction between these two demands is crucial when analyzing the impact of trade liberalization: the *d* curve clearly shows the incentive for each individual firm to lower its price after trade liberalization, but the steeper *D* curve shows that when all firms lower prices, then losses occur and some firms must exit.

Chapter 7 is devoted to offshoring, and we have found that students enjoy learning and readily understand this new material. The model used illustrates a piece of intuition that students grasp easily: the movement of one student from, say, a physics class to an economics class can raise the average grade in *both* classes. Likewise, offshoring can raise the relative wage of skilled workers in both countries. The chapter deals with Paul Samuelson's 2004 critique that offshoring to China or India might be harmful to the United States. That argument is shown to depend on how offshoring affects the U.S. terms of trade: if the terms of trade fall, the United States is worse off, though it still gains overall from international trade. In fact, we argue that the U.S. terms of trade have been rising in recent years, not falling, so Samuelson's argument is hypothetical so far.

Part 4: International Trade Policies

The concluding part of the trade portion of the book deals is devoted to trade policy: tariffs and quotas under perfect competition (Chapter 8), under imperfect competition (Chapter 9), export subsidies (Chapter 10), and a discussion of international agreements on trade, labor, and the environment (Chapter 11). Our goal is to present this material in a more systematic fashion than found elsewhere, using both very recent and historical applications.

Chapter 8, dealing with tariffs and quotas under perfect competition, is the "bread and butter" of trade policy. We adopt the partial-equilibrium approach, using import demand and export supply curves, along with consumer and producer surplus. Our experience is that students feel very comfortable with this approach from their microeconomics training (so they can usually label the consumer surplus region, for example, in each diagram before the labels are shown). The chapter uses the tariffs applied by President George W. Bush on U.S. steel imports and by President Barack Obama on imported tires from China as motivating cases, which we analyze from both a "small country" and a "large country" perspective.

Chapters 9 and 10 bring in some of the insights from the literature on the strategic role of trade policy, which was developed in the later 1980s and 1990s. Whereas that literature focused on oligopoly interactions between firms, we simplify the analysis in Chapter 9 by focusing on home or foreign monopoly cases. Chapter 10 then presents the duopoly case in the analysis of export subsidies. Most of the theory in these chapters is familiar, but the organization is new, as are many of the applications, including infant industry protection in Chapter 9 and a detailed discussion of agricultural subsidies in Chapter 10.

Chapter 11 begins by drawing upon tariffs under perfect competition (from Chapter 8), and showing that large countries have a natural incentive to apply tariffs to move the terms of trade to their advantage. That creates a prisoner's dilemma situation that is overcome by rules in the WTO. The chapter then moves on to discuss international rules governing labor issues and the environment. Students are especially interested in the environmental applications.

The Arrangement of Topics: International Macroeconomics

Part 5 (Part 1 in *International Macroeconomics*): Introduction to International Macroeconomics

This part consists only of Chapter 12 (Chapter 1 in the split edition), which sets the stage by explaining the field and major items of interest, with an elementary survey of the three main parts of the book: money and exchange rates, the balance of payments, and the role of policy.

Part 6 (Part 2): Exchange Rates

We depart from the traditional presentation by presenting exchange rates before balance of payments, an approach that we and our students find more logical and appealing. We begin the core macro material with exchange rates because (for macroeconomics) the exchange rate is the key difference between a closed economy and a world of open economies. Our approach, supported by our own experience and that of our reviewers and class testers, first treats all price topics together in one part, and then moves on to quantity topics.

Chapter 13 (Chapter 2) introduces the basics of exchange rates and the foreign exchange (forex) market (including the principles of arbitrage) and exposes students to real-world data on exchange rate behavior. It describes how the forex market is structured and explains the principles of arbitrage in forex markets. It ends with interest parity conditions, which are then covered in more detail in Chapter 15 (Chapter 4).

Chapter 14 (Chapter 3) presents the monetary approach to the determination of exchange rates in the long run. We cover the long run before the short run because long-run expectations are assumed to be known in the short-run model. Topics include goods market arbitrage, the law of one price, and purchasing power parity. We first develop a simple monetary model (the quantity theory) and then look at the standard monetary model, the Fisher effect, and real interest parity. The chapter ends with discussion of nominal anchors and their relationship to monetary and exchange rate regimes.

Chapter 15 (Chapter 4) presents the asset approach to the determination of exchange rates in the short run. Uncovered interest parity, first introduced in Chapter 13 (Chapter 2), is the centerpiece of the asset approach, and the expected future exchange rate is assumed to be given by the long-run model. Short-run interest rates are explained using a money market model. We show how all the building blocks from the monetary and asset approaches fit together for a complete theory of exchange rate determination. Finally, we explain how the complete theory works for fixed as well as floating regimes, and demonstrate the trilemma.

Part 7 (Part 3): The Balance of Payments

Chapter 16 (Chapter 5 in the split edition) introduces the key macroeconomic quantities: the national and international accounts and the balance of payments (BOP). The BOP is explained as the need for balancing trade on goods, services, and assets (with allowances for transfers). We also introduce external wealth and valuation effects, which are of increasing importance in the world economy.

Chapter 17 (Chapter 6) links the balance of payments to the key question of the costs and benefits of financial globalization, an increasingly important topic. The chapter begins by explaining the significance of the long-run budget constraint and then examines the three key potential benefits of financial globalization: consumptions smoothing, efficient investment, and risk sharing.

Chapter 18 (Chapter 7) presents the short-run open economy Keynesian model, which links the balance of payments to output, exchange rates, and macroeconomic policies. We use IS-LM and forex market diagrams, with the interest rate on a common axis. With this presentation, we use tools (IS-LM) that many students have already seen, and avoid inventing new ways to present the same model with new and challenging notation. In this chapter we also discuss fixed and floating rate regimes side by side, not in different chapters. We think it helpful throughout the book to study these regimes in parallel and at this point this presentation leads naturally to the next chapter.

The ordering of Part 7 (Part 3) echoes that of Part 6 (Part 2): we start with definitions, then cover long-run topics (the gains from financial globalization), then move to short-run topics (IS-LM). This ordering of topics allows a smooth transition from some key definitions in Chapter 16 (Chapter 5) to their application at the start of Chapter 17 (Chapter 6), a link that would be impossible if the balance of payments chapter were placed before the coverage of exchange rates.

Part 8 (Part 4) Applications and Policy Issues

Chapter 19 (Chapter 8 in the split edition) confronts one of the major policy issues in international macroeconomics, the choice of fixed versus floating exchange rates. The analysis begins with the two classic criteria for two regions to adopt a fixed exchange rate—high levels of integration and symmetry of economic shocks. The chapter then goes on to consider other factors that could make a fixed exchange rate desirable, especially in developing countries—a need for a credible nominal anchor and the "fear of floating" that results from significant liability dollarization. Empirical evidence is provided for all of these influences. A brief section summarizes the debate over the desirability and possibility of coordination in larger exchange rate systems. Finally, a historical survey uses the uses the tools at hand to understand the evolution of international monetary arrangements since the nineteenth century.

Chapter 20 (Chapter 9) studies exchange rate crises. Before explaining how pegs break, we spend some time studying how pegs work. We begin by focusing on reserve management and the central bank balance sheet, when an economy faces shocks to output, interest rates, and risk premiums. We then extend the framework to consider lender of last resort actions, a structure that allows for more realism. This presentation allows us to discuss recent controversies over reserve accumulation in China and other emerging markets, and also suggests how pegs can fail. The chapter concludes by looking at two models of crises: a first-generation model with ongoing monetized deficits with fixed output and flexible prices, applying the logic of the flexible-price model of Chapter 14 (Chapter 3); and a second-generation model featuring an adverse shock with flexible output and fixed prices, applying the IS-LM-FX model of Chapter 18 (Chapter 7).

Chapter 21 (Chapter 10) discusses common currencies, with particular focus on the euro. We develop the basic Optimal Currency Area (OCA) criteria as an extension of the fixed versus floating analysis of Chapter 19 (Chapter 8). This framework allows us to consider additional economic and political reasons why countries might join a common currency area. We then present empirical evidence to show the differences between the United States and the Eurozone with respect to the OCA criteria and to explain why so many economists believe that the Eurozone currently is not an OCA. A complete explanation of the euro project requires an examination of other forces, which are considered in the remainder of the chapter: the possible endogeneity of the OCA criteria and the role of noneconomic factors. Thus, we examine the essential history, politics, and institutional details of the euro.

Chapter 22 (Chapter 11) is a collection of four "minichapters" that tackle important topics in macroeconomics. In this edition, these topics are the failure of UIP and exchange rate puzzles in the short run (including the carry trade and limits to arbitrage); the failure of PPP and exchange rates in the long run (including transaction costs and the Balassa-Samuelson effect); the debate over global imbalances (including the savings glut hypothesis and the role of exchange rate adjustments); the problem of default (including a simple model of default as insurance and a discussion of triple crises). Each of these topics is presented in a self-contained block that can be taught as is or in conjunction with earlier material. The UIP material could be added to Chapter 13 or 15 (Chapter 2 or 4). The PPP material would nicely augment Chapter 14 (Chapter 3). The global imbalances material could be presented with Chapter 16, 17, or 18 (Chapter 5, 6, or 7). The default topic could be paired with the discussion of currency crises in Chapter 20 (Chapter 9).

Alternative Routes through the Text

Because this book is available as a combined edition and as split volumes, it can be used for several types of courses, as summarized below and in the table on the next page.

A semester-length course in international trade (say, 15 weeks) would start at Chapter 1, but for a shorter, quarter-length course (say, 10 weeks), we suggest skipping Chapter 1 and going straight to the Ricardian model (Chapter 2). Chapters 2, 3 (the specific-factors model), and 4 (the Heckscher-Ohlin model) form the core of trade theory. The movement of labor and capital between countries (Chapter 5) builds on these chapters theoretically, and summarizes the empirical evidence on immigration and foreign direct investment.

The new approaches to international trade covered in Chapters 6 (economies of scale and imperfect competition) and 7 (offshoring) can be taught independently of each other. (A quarter course in international trade may not have time for both chapters.) The final four chapters in international trade deal with trade policy. Chapter 8 (tariffs and quotas under perfect competition) should be discussed in any course regardless of its length. Tariffs and quotas under imperfect competition (Chapter 9) digs more deeply into the effects of trade policy, and is followed by a discussion of export subsidies (Chapter 10). Some or all topics in the final chapter on international agreements can be covered as time permits.

A semester course in international macroeconomics (say, 15 weeks) would start at Chapter 12 in the combined edition (Chapter 1 in the *International Macroeconomics* split edition), but for a shorter quarter-length course (say, 10 weeks), we recommend skipping Chapter 12 (Chapter 1) and going straight to the foreign exchange market presented in Chapter 13 (Chapter 2). Core material on exchange rate theory then follows, with the long run in Chapter 14 (Chapter 3) followed by the short run in Chapter 15 (Chapter 4). Next come the core definitions of the national and international accounts and the balance of payments, presented in Chapter 16 (Chapter 5). After this point a course with a macro emphasis would cover the costs and benefits of globalization in Chapter 17 (Chapter 6) and IS-LM in Chapter 18 (Chapter 7). To allow time to cover crises in Chapter 20 (Chapter 9), treatment of regime choice in Chapter 19 (Chapter 8) might be combined with a discussion of the euro in Chapter 21 (Chapter 10). Topics from Chapter 22 (Chapter 11) can be selected as time permits: a more finance-oriented course might focus on the first two exchange rate topics; a more macro-oriented course might focus on global imbalances and default. In a semester-length course, there should be time for almost all the topics to be covered.

We recognize that many schools also offer a combined one-semester course in international trade and macroeconomics, sometimes to students outside the economics major. Because of the wealth of applications, we have found that our chapters on trade or macroeconomics serve those students very well. The one-semester version of our textbook, ***Essentials of International Economics,*** available for the first time with the second edition, brings together the chapters that are the most important for such a course. The one-semester *Essentials* edition has an introduction in Chapter 1 that incorporates both international trade and macroeconomic issues. It then moves to Chapters 2–6, the basic trade chapters, followed by two chapters on tariffs and quotas under perfect competition and under imperfect competition. The international trade section concludes with the chapter on trade agreements and the environment. An extra chapter on offshoring is available online. These chapters offer students a solid

Suggested Course Outlines

Chapter Titles	Course Type and Length: Trade or Macroeconomics in one term		International Economics in two terms	International Economics in one term
	Chapter numbers from *International Trade* version		Chapter numbers from *International Economics*	Chapter numbers from *Essentials of International Economics*
	10 week quarter	13–15 week semester		
Trade in the Global Economy (*Essentials:* The Global Economy)	—	1	1	1 (introduces trade and macroeconomics)
Trade and Technology: The Ricardian Model	2	2	2	2
Gains and Losses from Trade in the Specific-Factors Model	3	3	3	3
Trade and Resources: The Heckscher-Ohlin Model	4	4	4	4
Movement of Labor and Capital between Countries	Choose two from 5, 6, 7	5	5	5
Increasing Returns to Scale and Monopolistic Competition		6	6	6
Offshoring of Goods and Services		7	7	Available online
Import Tariffs and Quotas under Perfect Competition	8	8	8	7
Import Tariffs and Quotas under Imperfect Competition	9	9	9	8
Export Subsidies in Agriculture and High-Technology Industries	10	10	10	—
International Agreements: Trade, Labor, and the Environment	As time permits	11	11	9
	Chapter numbers from *International Macroeconomics* version			
	10 week quarter	13–15 week semester		
The Global Macroeconomy	—	1	12	—
Introduction to Exchange Rates and the Foreign Exchange Market	2	2	13	10
Exchange Rates I: The Monetary Approach in the Long Run	3	3	14	11
Exchange Rates II: The Asset Approach in the Short Run	4	4	15	12
National and International Accounts: Income, Wealth, and the Balance of Payments	5	5	16	13
The Balance of Payments I: The Gains from Financial Globalization	6	6	17	—
The Balance of Payments II: Output, Exchange Rates, and Macroeconomic Policies in the Short Run	7	7	18	14
Fixed Versus Floating: International Monetary Experience	Combine with Chapter 8	8	19	15
Exchange Rate Crises: How Pegs Work and How They Break	9	9	20	—
The Euro	Combine with Chapter 10	10	21	Available online
Topics in International Macroeconomics	1 or 2 topics (as time permits)	3 or 4 topics (as time permits)	22	—

perspective on international trade and trade policy. These chapters are followed in the one-semester *Essentials* edition by six chapters dealing with the core concepts and models in international macroeconomics: the foreign exchange market, the monetary and asset approaches to exchange rates, national income and the balance of payments, short-run macroeconomic policy, and fixed-versus-floating exchange rates. An extra chapter on the euro is available online. This coverage will give students a basic grounding in international macroeconomics.

Supplements and Media Package

In addition to all its pedagogical innovations, our book brings to the market an innovative supplement and media package. These supplements were given the same careful thought, time, and preparation as the text. We are happy to provide a full suite of teaching materials for instructors along with a complete set of resources to aid students in reviewing the key concepts presented in the text.

aplia™ The Aplia/Worth course for Feenstra/Taylor is the only fully integrated Aplia solution in International Economics. It enhances students' experiences through Aplia's interactive problem sets, news analyses, and tutorials—all in a format that saves time for professors while encouraging students in their learning.

The Feenstra/Taylor Aplia course includes a full eBook as well as offering:

- **Homework sets correlated to the text.** Online homework is easy to assign, and it grades automatically. The course gradebook quickly puts results at your fingertips.
- **Algorithmic problem sets.** All homework problem sets offer Grade It Now. Students can attempt any problem set up to three times with variables that randomize on each attempt..
- **Multiple purchase options.** Aplia access can be packaged with any version of the text, or purchased separately online as a less expensive alternative to the book because it includes an eBook. Students who purchase online access can also buy a physical textbook directly from Aplia at a significant discount.

Instructor Supplements

Instructor's Manual with Solutions Manual

Instructor's Manuals for each portion of the book, prepared by UC Davis students and graduates Philip Luck (University of California, Davis), and Alyson Ma (University of San Diego), are available. The Instructor's Manual manual is available on the Book Companion Site, and provide the following for each chapter in the textbook:

- *Notes to the instructor:* notes that include a chapter summary with additional comments
- *Lecture notes:* a complete set of notes, including a detailed outline of the chapter for aid in preparing class lectures
- *Teaching tips:* 4 or 5 activities per chapter that instructors can utilize in lectures, for in-class group work, or as take-home assignments

- *In-class problems:* 10 to 15 problems per chapter, including in-depth suggested answers.
- *Solutions to textbook problems:* detailed solutions to all end-of-chapter problems.

Printed Test Bank

The test bank provides a wide range of creative and versatile questions ranging in levels of difficulty and format to assess students' comprehension, interpretation, analysis, and synthesis skills. Averaging over 170 questions per chapter, the test bank offers a variety of multiple-choice, true/false, and short-answer questions. All questions have been checked for continuity with the text content and reviewed extensively for accuracy. The test bank was coordinated by Ron Davies (University College, Dublin) with the help of contributing authors Terry Monson (Finlandia University) and Millicent Taylor (Carson-Newman College).

Computerized Test Bank

The test bank is also available in CD-ROM format, powered by Brownstone, for both Windows and Macintosh users. With this Diploma software, instructors can easily create and print tests as well as write and edit questions.

Student and Instructor Supplements

Study Guide with Worked Examples

Students' economic thinking will be challenged and extended by a creative new Study Guide with Worked Examples prepared by Stephen Yeaple of Pennsylvania State University. This study guide complements the textbook by providing students with additional opportunities to develop their knowledge of international economics through active learning. This innovative resource reinforces the topics and key concepts covered in the text. For each key section of each chapter, the Study Guide with Worked Examples provides:

- *Key themes:* detailed discussions of key concepts
- *Key terms:* a summary of important vocabulary within the chapter, with space for students to make their own notes
- *Review questions with tips:* detailed, thorough problems for students to test their comprehension, along with tips to help students work through the problems. To identify common mistakes and to demonstrate common features of different types of economic problems, tips are provided immediately following questions that delve into particularly important or difficult topics.
- *Worked-out solutions:* including solutions to all Study Guide review questions.

Companion Website for Students and Instructors

The companion site http://www.worthpublishers.com/feenstrataylor_2 is a virtual study guide for students and an excellent resource for instructors. For each chapter in the textbook, the tools on the site include:

Student Tools

- *Practice quizzes:* A set of questions with feedback and page references to the textbook. Student answers are saved in an online database that can be accessed by instructors.

- *Key-term flashcards:* Students can test themselves on key vocabulary with these pop-up electronic flashcards.
- *Web exercises*
- *Web links* to relevant research and demonstrations with related questions for applied practice

Instructor Resources

- *Quiz gradebook:* The site gives instructors the ability to track students' interaction with the practice quizzes via an online gradebook. Instructors may choose to have student results emailed directly to them.
- *PowerPoint lecture presentations:* These customizable PowerPoint slides, prepared by Fernando Quijano (Dickinson State University) are designed to assist instructors with lecture preparation and presentation by providing original animations, graphs from the textbook, data tables, key concepts, and bulleted lecture outlines.
- *Image gallery:* A complete set of figures and tables from the textbook in JPEG and PowerPoint formats
- *Instructor's Manual*
- *Solutions Manual*
- *Answers to Web Link Questions*

CourseSmart eBooks

All four versions *(International Economics*, *International Trade*, *International Macroeconomics*, and *Essentials of International Economics)* are available as CourseSmart eBooks. Students who purchase the Feenstra/Taylor CourseSmart eBooks have instant access to their textbooks on any computer or handheld device with an Internet connection. CourseSmart eBooks offer an earth-friendly and wallet-friendly option for students.

CourseSmart eBook features include:

- Copy and paste text:

  Easy integration with word processing programs
- Textbook Search:

  Find words or topics fast within your online eTextbook
- Print what you need:

  From any printer connected to the computer
- Highlighting and Note-Taking:

  Highlight relevant sections or take notes on important topics
- Same "Everything Else":

  Online eTextbooks share the same page layout and numbering as the print version
- No Connection Necessary:

Once you download the eBook and save it to your computer, you don't need the Internet. Just start reading.

Course Management System

The Feenstra Course Cartridge allows you to combine your Course Management System's most popular tools and easy-to-use interface with text-specific, rich Web content, including preprogrammed quizzes, links, activities, and a whole array of other materials. The result: an interactive, comprehensive online course that allows for effortless implementation, management, and use. The Worth electronic files are organized and prebuilt to work within your CMS software and can be easily downloaded from the CMS content showcases directly onto your department server. You can also obtain a CMS formatted version of the book's test bank.

Acknowledgments

A book like this would not be possible without the assistance of many people, which we gratefully acknowledge.

First, the renowned team at Worth has spared no effort to help us; their experience and skill in publishing economics textbooks were invaluable. Numerous individuals have been involved with this project, but we must give special mention to four: the project has been continually and imaginatively guided by acquisitions editor Sarah Dorger, now joined by executive editor Chuck Linsmeier and development editor Bruce Kaplan, and by marketing manager Scott Guile, who successfully brought the book to market. Through it all, the manuscript was improved endlessly by our primary development editor, Jane Tufts. We are greatly in their debt.

We have also relied on the assistance of a number of graduate students in collecting data for applications, preparing problems, and proofreading material. We would like to thank Leticia Arroyo Abad, Chang Hong, David Jacks, Alyson Ma, Ahmed Rahman, Seema Sangita, Radek Szulga, and Yingying Xu for their assistance. We are especially grateful to Benjamin Mandel, who has worked on many of the international trade chapters in the first edition, and to Philip Luck, who worked on all the chapters in this second edition. Thanks also to Christian Broda, Colin Carter, Michele Cavallo, Menzie Chinn, Sebastian Edwards, Ann Harrison, Mervyn King, Philip Lane, Karen Lewis, Christopher Meissner, Gian Maria Milesi-Ferretti, Michael Pakko, Ugo Panizza, Giovanni Peri, Eswar Prasad, Andrés Rodríguez-Clare, Jay Shambaugh, and Martin Wolf for providing data used in the applications.

We have taught the chapters of this book ourselves a number of times, and have benefited from the feedback of colleagues. The book has also been class-tested by a number of individuals.

For the second edition, we benefited from the suggestions of the following reviewers:

Bradley Andrew, *Juniata College*
Damyana Bakardzhieva, *George Washington University*
Mina Baliamoune, *University of North Florida*
Valerie Bencivenga, *University of Texas at Austin*
Emily Blanchard, *University of Virginia*
Nicola Borri, *Boston University*
Drusilla Brown, *Tufts University*
Vera Brusentsev, *University of Delaware*
Colleen Callahan, *American University*
Geoffrey Carliner, *Boston University*
Ron Cronovich, *Carthage College*
Firat Demir, *University of Oklahoma*
Asim Erdilek, *Case Western Reserve University*
John Gilbert, *Utah State University*
William Hauk, *University of South Carolina*
David Hummels, *Purdue University*
Hakan Inal, *Virginia Commonwealth University*
Alan Isaac, *American University*
Robert Jerome, *James Madison University*
Grace Johnson, *Oklahoma State University—Tulsa*
Kathy Kelly, *University of Texas at Arlington*
Bill Kosteas, *Cleveland State University*
Ricardo Lopez, *Indiana University*
Volodymyr Lugovskyy, *Georgia Tech*
Nicolas Magud, *University of Oregon*
Keith Malone, *University of North Alabama*
Maria Muniagurria, *University of Wisconsin—Madison*
Catherine Mann, *Brandeis University*
Steven J. Matusz, *Michigan State University*
Fabio Mendez, *University of Arkansas*
William Mertens, *University of Colorado at Boulder*
Rebecca Neumann, *University of Wisconsin—Milwaukee*
Emanuel Ornelas, *London School of Economics*
Perry Patterson, *Wake Forest University*
Masha Rahnama, *Texas Tech University*
Michael Rinkus, *Walsh College*
Sheikh Shahnawaz, *University of Southern California*
David Sobiechowski, *University of Michigan—Dearborn*
Steve Steib, *University of Tulsa*
Nicholas Stratis, *Florida State University*
Edward Tower, *Duke University*
Elizabeth Wheaton, *Southern Methodist University*
Peter Wylie, *University of British Columbia—Okanagan*

We would like to thank the following instructors for sharing their ideas with us in the development of the first edition. These colleagues have been enthusiastic about the reception of their students to our fresh approach.

Joshua Aizenman, *University of California, Santa Cruz*
Scott Baier, *Clemson University*
Paul Bergin, *University of California, Davis*
Matilde Bombardini, *University of British Columbia—Vancouver*
Drusilla Brown, *Tufts University*
Avik Chakraborty, *University of Tennessee—Knoxville*
Gordon Hanson, *University of California, San Diego*
James Harrigan, *University of Virginia*
Takeo Hoshi, *University of California, San Diego*
David Hummels, *Purdue University*
Samuel Kortum, *University of Chicago*
John McLaren, *University of Virginia*
Marc-Andreas Muendler, *University of California, San Diego*
Robert Murphy, *Boston College*
Constantin Ogloblin, *Georgia Southern University*
Kevin O'Rourke, *Trinity College, Dublin*
Sanjay Paul, *Elizabethtown College*
Priya Ranjan, *University of California, Irvine*
Andrés Rodriguez-Clare, *Pennsylvania State University*
Katheryn Russ, *University of California, Davis*
Stephen Stageberg, *University of Mary Washington*
Bruce Wydick, *University of San Francisco*
Stephen Yeaple, *Pennsylvania State University*

A huge number of colleagues were very helpful in reviewing the first-edition manuscript. We wish to thank the following reviewers:

Joshua Aizenman, *University of California, Santa Cruz*
Mohsen Bahmani-Oskooee, *University of Wisconsin—Milwaukee*
Scott Baier, *Clemson University*
Richard Baillie, *Michigan State University*
Joe Bell, *Missouri State University*
Paul Bergin, *University of California, Davis*
Robert Blecker, *American University*
Roger Butters, *University of Nebraska—Lincoln*
Francisco Carrada-Bravo, *Arizona State University*
Menzie Chinn, *University of Wisconsin—Madison*
Richard Chisik, *Florida International University*
Ann Davis, *Marist College*
Robert Driskill, *Vanderbilt University*
James Fain, *Oklahoma State University*
David H. Feldman, *The College of William & Mary*
Diane Flaherty, *University of Massachusetts, Amherst*
Jean-Ellen Giblin, *Fashion Institute of Technology*
Bill Gibson, *University of Vermont*
Thomas Grennes, *North Carolina State University*
Gordon Hanson, *University of California, San Diego*
Mehdi Haririan, *Bloomsburg University*
James Harrigan, *University of Virginia*
Takeo Hoshi, *University of California, San Diego*
Douglas Irwin, *Dartmouth College*
Michael Klein, *Tufts University*
Kala Krishna, *Pennsylvania State University*
Maria Kula, *Roger Williams University*
Ricardo Lopez, *Indiana University*
Mary Lovely, *Syracuse University*
Barbara Lowrey, *University of Maryland*
Steven J. Matusz, *Michigan State University*
Jose Mendez, *Arizona State University*
Shannon Mitchell, *Virginia Commonwealth University*
Farshid Mojaver Hosseini, *University of California, Davis*
Marc-Andreas Muendler, *University of California, San Diego*
Maria Muniagurria, *University of Wisconsin—Madison*
Robert Murphy, *Boston College*
Ranganath Murthy, *Bucknell University*
Kanda Naknoi, *Purdue University*
Constantin Ogloblin, *Georgia Southern University*
Kevin O'Rourke, *Trinity College, Dublin*
Kerry Pannell, *DePauw University*
Jaishankar Raman, *Valparaiso University*
Raymond Robertson, *Macalester College*
Andrés Rodriguez-Clare, *Pennsylvania State University*
Hadi Salehi-Esfahani, *University of Illinois at Urbana-Champaign*
Andreas Savvides, *Oklahoma State University*
Till Schreiber, *The College of William & Mary*
Gunjan Sharma, *University of Missouri, Columbia*
John Subrick, *James Madison University*
Mark P. Taylor, *University of Warwick*
Linda Tesar, *University of Michigan, Ann Arbor*
Geetha Vaidyanathan, *University of North Carolina at Greensboro*
Kristin Van Gaasbeck, *California State University, Sacramento*
Gary Wells, *Clemson University*
Mark Wohar, *University of Nebraska, Omaha*
Susan Wolcott, *SUNY Binghamton*
Bin Xu, *China Europe International Business School*
Stephen Yeaple, *Pennsylvania State University*

We received useful feedback from focus group participants. We would like to thank the following individuals:

Mohsen Bahmani-Oskooee, *University of Wisconsin—Milwaukee*
Roger Butters, *University of Nebraska—Lincoln*
Francisco Carrada-Bravo, *Arizona State University*
Mitchell Charkiewicz, *Central Connecticut State University*
Menzie Chinn, *University of Wisconsin—Madison*
Carl Davidson, *Michigan State University*
Ann Davis, *Marist College*
Robert Driskill, *Vanderbilt University*
Eric Fisher, *California Polytechnic State University, San Luis Obispo*
Diane Flaherty, *University of Massachusetts, Amherst*
Bill Gibson, *University of Vermont*
Thomas Grennes, *North Carolina State University*
Mehdi Haririan, *Bloomsburg University*
Andreas Hauskrecht, *Indiana University*
Andrew Hughes-Hallett, *George Mason University*
Eckhard Janeba, *University of Mannheim*
Mary Lovely, *Syracuse University*
Marc Melitz, *Harvard University*
Norman Miller, *Miami University of Ohio*
Shannon Mitchell, *Virginia Commonwealth University*
Ranganath Murthy, *Bucknell University*
Rebecca Neumann, *University of Wisconsin—Milwaukee*
Constantin Ogloblin, *Georgia Southern University*
Lucjan Orlowski, *Sacred Heart University*
Jeff Pliskin, *Hamilton College*
Francisca Richter, *Cleveland State University*
Hadi Salehi-Esfahani, *University of Illinois at Urbana-Champaign*
Bin Xu, *China Europe International Business School*

We would like to thank the following instructors who have provided feedback on the initial preliminary version of the first edition of our text:

Scott Baier, *Clemson University*
Paul Bergin, *University of California, Davis*
Luisa Blanco Raynal, *Pepperdine University*
James Cassing, *University of Pittsburgh*
Ted Fu, *Stanford University*
James Harrigan, *University of Virginia*
David Hummels, *Purdue University*
Farshid Mojaver Hosseini, *University of California, Davis*
Maria Muniagurria, *University of Wisconsin—Madison*
Kanda Naknoi, *Purdue University*
Raymond Robertson, *Macalester College*
Andrés Rodriguez-Clare, *Pennsylvania State University*
Jeffrey Rosensweig, *Emory University*
Jennifer Steele, *University of Texas at Austin*
Asha Sundaram, *Syracuse University*
Kristin Van Gaasbeck, *California State University, Sacramento*
Wolfgang Keller, *University of Colorado at Boulder*

We would like to thank the following individuals who have aided us in the preparation and extensive review of the ancillary package.

Francis Ahking, *University of Connecticut*
Ron Davies, *University College, Dublin*
Philip Luck, *University of California, Davis*
Alyson Ma, *University of San Diego*
Terry Monson, *Michigan Technological University*
Robert Murphy, *Boston College*
Sanjay Paul, *Elizabethtown College*
Jaishankar Raman, *Valparaiso University*
Millicent Sites, *Carson-Newman College*
Marie Truesdell, *Marian College*
Kristin Van Gaasbeck, *California State University, Sacramento*
Stephen Yeaple, *Pennsylvania State University*

We would also like to thank our families, especially Claire and Gail, for their sustained support during the time we have devoted to writing this book.

Finally, you will see an accompanying picture of children in Ciudad Dario, Nicaragua, with their teacher, in the classroom of a small schoolhouse that was built for them by Seeds of Learning (www.seedsoflearning.org), a nonprofit organization dedicated to improving educational opportunities in rural Latin America. A portion of the royalties from this book go toward supporting the work of Seeds of Learning.

ROBERT C. FEENSTRA

ALAN M. TAYLOR

Davis, California
June 2010

Sixth-grade class with their teacher in La Carreta #2 school in Ciudad Darío, Nicaragua.

James Hall

1

Trade in the Global Economy

The emergence of China, India, and the former communist-bloc countries implies that the greater part of the earth's population is now engaged, at least potentially, in the global economy. There are no historical antecedents for this development.

Ben Bernanke, chairman of the U.S. Federal Reserve, 2006

The main losers in today's very unequal world are not those who are too much exposed to globalization. They are those who have been left out.

Kofi Annan, former secretary general of the United Nations, 2000

On April 14, 2010, the Eyjafjallajökull volcano in Iceland roared to life after being dormant for more than two centuries. A plume of ash erupted 7 miles into the atmosphere, disrupting air travel in Northern Europe and beyond. An event like this has dramatic consequences for **international trade,** the movement of goods and services across borders. Roughly 100,000 flights to and from Northern Europe were canceled, and billions of dollars in air freight and millions of travelers were delayed, canceled, or re-routed.

The air freight that was disrupted included products as diverse as auto parts being sent from factories from Europe and flowers being shipped from Africa. In Kenya 10 million roses that could not be delivered to Europe had to be thrown away, and as a result, 5,000 Kenyan workers were laid off.[1] Estimates of revenue lost because of this disruption in air freight for two weeks range from $16 to 27 billion of goods imported to the United States from Europe, and $20 to 26 billion of goods exported from the United States to Europe.

In addition to the disruption to international trade in goods, there were also canceled passenger fights, which is an example of international trade in services. The

[1] See Carley Petesch and Karoun Demirjian, "10 Million Roses Ruined, 5K Kenya Workers Laid Off," *The New York Times*, April 19, 2010, p. A1.

In April 2010 the ash from Iceland's Eyjafjallajökull volcano disrupted air travel in Northern Europe and beyond.

canceled flights between the United States and Europe over two weeks in April 2010 translated into roughly $3.2 billion of lost services trade between the United States and Europe. In this book, we will study international trade in goods and services and will learn the economic forces that determine what that trade looks like: what products are traded; who trades them; at what quantities and prices they are traded; and what the benefits and costs of trade are. We will also learn about the policies that governments use to shape trade patterns among countries.

Let's begin by looking at a very broad picture of international trade. What country was the world's largest exporter of goods in 2009? If you guessed China, you are right: in that year it overtook Germany as the top exporter, selling some $1.3 trillion in goods to other countries, slightly ahead of the $1.17 trillion exported by Germany. The third largest exporter of goods is the United States, which exported $1.05 trillion in goods in 2009.

These numbers reveal only part of the trade picture, however, because in addition to exporting goods, countries also export services. In 2009 the United States exported $0.5 trillion in services (including business services, education of foreign students, travel by foreigners, etc.). If we combine exports in goods and services, then in 2009 the world's largest exporter was the United States at $1.55 trillion, followed by Germany, China, Japan, the United Kingdom, and France.

Nations trade goods for many reasons, the most obvious of which is that they can get products from abroad that are cheaper or of higher quality than those they can produce at home. The fact that Germany was the largest exporter of goods up until 2009 reflects its world-class technologies for producing high-quality manufactured goods, such as cars like the BMW and Mercedes-Benz. China, on the other hand, can produce goods more cheaply than most industrial countries. The United States has both the technology to produce high-quality manufactured goods and the ability to produce agricultural goods very cheaply (because of its abundant land resources as well as government policies).

In the first part of this book, we develop a number of models that help us understand the reasons that countries trade goods and services. In addition, we investigate **migration,** the flow of people across borders as they move from one country to another, and **foreign direct investment (FDI),** the flow of capital across borders when a firm owns a company in another country. All three types of flows between countries—of products (goods and services), people, and capital—are so common today that we take them for granted. When you go into a store to purchase an item, for example, it is possible that it was made in another country, the store itself might be foreign-owned, and the salesperson who assists you may be an immigrant. Why are these international flows so common? What are the consequences of these flows for the countries involved? And what actions do governments take to make their countries more or less open to trade, migration, and foreign direct investment? These are the questions we address.

1 International Trade

This section begins our study of international economics by defining some important terms and summarizing the overall trends in world trade.

The Basics of World Trade

Countries buy and sell goods and services from one another constantly. An **export** is a product sold from one country to another, and an **import** is a product bought by one country from another. We normally think of exports and imports as goods that are shipped between countries, but for services that is not necessarily the case. Construction services, for example, are performed on-site in the importing country rather than being shipped. Travel and tourism are large categories of service exports that also occur on-site: the money spent by a U.S. visitor to the Eiffel Tower is a service export of France, and a Chinese visitor to the Grand Canyon adds to U.S. service exports.

A country's **trade balance** is the difference between its total value of exports and its total value of imports (usually including both goods and services). Countries that export more than they import, such as China in recent years, run a **trade surplus,** whereas countries that import more than they export, such as the United States, run a **trade deficit.** In addition to keeping track of the overall trade balance for a country with the rest of the world, we often see reported in the newspaper the **bilateral trade balance,** meaning the difference between exports and imports between two countries. The U.S. trade deficit with China, for example, was more than $200 billion every year between 2005 and 2009.

In the models developed to understand international trade, we are not concerned with whether a country has a trade deficit or surplus but just assume that each country has balanced trade, with exports equal to imports. There are two reasons why we make this assumption. First, economists believe that an overall trade deficit or surplus arises from macroeconomic conditions, the overall levels of spending and savings in an economy—countries with high spending and low savings will run a trade deficit. (Macroeconomic conditions are studied in the second half of this book that deals with international macroeconomics.)

Second, the interpretation of a trade deficit or surplus is problematic when we focus on the bilateral trade balance between two countries, such as the United States and China. To see what the problem is, think about the U.S. import of a particular good from China, such as the iPod (see **Headlines: An iPod Has Global Value. Ask the (Many) Countries That Make It).**

The iPod is valued at about $150 when it leaves the dock in China en route to the United States, and it eventually sells for $299 in the United States, but only $4 of that amount reflects the value of Chinese labor used in the assembly. The rest of the $150 export value was actually imported into China from other countries, including $73 for the hard drive, $20 for the display module, $13 for various chips, and so on. Nevertheless, the entire $150 is counted as an export from China to the United States. This example shows that the bilateral trade deficit or surplus between countries is a slippery concept. It doesn't really make sense to count the entire $150 iPod as a Chinese export to the United States, as is done in official trade statistics, when only $4 is the **value-added** in China; that is, the difference between the value of the iPod when it leaves China and the cost of parts and materials purchased in

©Bobby Yip/Reuters

Workers in China assemble products like the Apple iPod.

China and imported from other countries. That shortcoming of official statistics gives us a good reason to not focus on the bilateral trade deficit or surplus between countries, even though that number is often reported in the media.

The iPod example illustrates how the manufacturing required for a single final product is often spread across many countries: the iPod and its components are produced in facilities in China, Taiwan, Thailand, Malaysia, Singapore, South Korea, the Czech Republic, Philippines, and the United States. That so many countries are involved in manufacturing a final product and its components is a new phenomenon that illustrates the drop in transportation and communication costs in the modern world economy. In the past, trade occurred in more standardized goods (such as raw materials) that were shipped long distances, but were not shipped back-and-forth between countries during the manufacturing process. This new feature of world trade and production, often called **offshoring,** is discussed later in the book; here, we present the idea by looking at how trade patterns have changed over time.

APPLICATION

Is Trade Today Different from the Past?

Is the type of trade today different from that in the past? The answer to this question is yes. Not only is there more international trade today than in the past, but the type of trade has also changed. We can see the changes in the type of trade by organizing imports and exports into five categories, depending on their use in the economy: (1) foods, feeds, and beverages; (2) industrial supplies and materials (raw materials like chemicals and petroleum and basic processed goods such as steel, newsprint, textiles, etc.); (3) capital goods (durable goods including aircraft, cars, computers, machinery, etc.); (4) finished consumer goods (all finished household goods, except cars and computers, but including the iPod). The percentage of U.S. imports and exports accounted for by these five categories from 1925 to 2009 is shown in Figure 1-1, with U.S. imports in panel (a) and exports in panel (b).

In Figure 1-1(a), we see that U.S. trade has shifted away from agriculture and raw materials and toward manufactured goods, as shown by the declining shares of foods, feeds, and beverages and industrial supplies and materials. Together, these two categories of traded goods accounted for 90% of imports in 1925 but only about 35% in 2009. Figure 1-1(b) shows that the export share of these same categories fell from about 80% to 40% over that time.

HEADLINES

An iPod Has Global Value. Ask the (Many) Countries That Make It.

Although the iPod sold in the United States is assembled in China, most of its value comes from parts made in other countries.

Who makes the Apple iPod? Here's a hint: It is not Apple. The company outsources the entire manufacture of the device to a number of Asian enterprises, among them Asustek, Inventec Appliances and Foxconn. But this list of companies isn't a satisfactory answer either: They only do final assembly. What about the 451 parts that go into the iPod? Where are they made and by whom?

The retail value of the 30-gigabyte video iPod . . . was $299. The most expensive component in it was the hard drive, which was manufactured by Toshiba and costs about $73. The next most costly components were the display module (about $20), the video/multimedia processor chip ($8) and the controller chip ($5). . . . [T]he final assembly, done in China, costs only about $4 a unit.

One approach to tracing supply chain geography might be to attribute the cost of each component to the country of origin of its maker. So $73 of the cost of the iPod would be attributed to Japan since Toshiba is a Japanese company, and the $13 cost of the two chips would be attributed to the United States, since the suppliers, Broadcom and PortalPlayer, are American companies, and so on.

But this method hides some of the most important details. Toshiba may be a Japanese company, but it makes most of its hard drives in the Philippines and China. So perhaps we should also allocate part of the cost of that hard drive to one of those countries. The same problem arises regarding the Broadcom chips, with most of them manufactured in Taiwan. So how can one distribute the costs of the iPod components across the countries where they are manufactured in a meaningful way?

To answer this question, let us look at the production process as a sequence of steps, each possibly performed by a different company operating in a different country. At each step, inputs like computer chips and a bare circuit board are converted into outputs like an assembled circuit board. The difference between the cost of the inputs and the value of the outputs is the "value added" at that step, which can then be attributed to the country where that value was added. . . .

This value added calculation illustrates the futility of summarizing such a complex manufacturing process by using conventional trade statistics. Even though Chinese workers contribute only about 1 percent of the value of the iPod, the export of a finished iPod to the United States directly contributes about $150 to our bilateral trade deficit with the Chinese.

Ultimately, there is no simple answer to who makes the iPod or where it is made. The iPod, like many other products, is made in several countries by dozens of companies, with each stage of production contributing a different amount to the final value.

The real value of the iPod doesn't lie in its parts or even in putting those parts together. The bulk of the iPod's value is in the conception and design of the iPod. That is why Apple gets $80 for each of these video iPods it sells, which is by far the largest piece of value added in the entire supply chain. Those clever folks at Apple figured out how to combine 451 mostly generic parts into a valuable product. They may not make the iPod, but they created it. In the end, that's what really matters.

Source: Hal R. Varian, "Headlines: An iPod Has Global Value. Ask the (Many) Countries That Make It," Economic Scene, The New York Times, *June 28, 2007, electronic edition.*

FIGURE 1-1

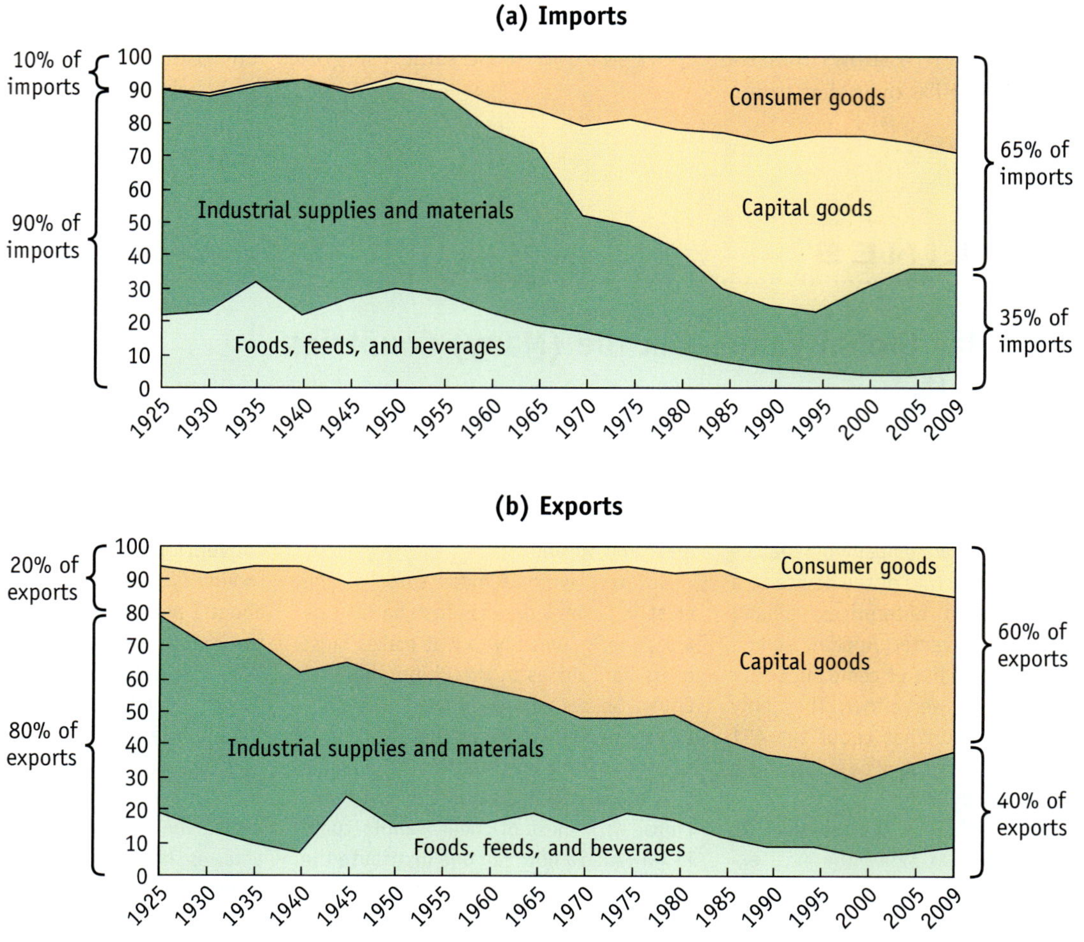

The Changing Face of U.S. Import and Export Industries, 1925–2009 The types of goods imported and exported by the United States have changed drastically over the past century. Foods, feeds, and beverages and industrial supplies were 90% of imports in 1925, but represented only 35% in 2009. These categories' shares of exports have also fallen from 80% in 1925 to 40% in 2009. Capital plus consumer goods plus automobiles have increased from 10% of imports in 1925 to 65% of imports in 2009. Exports of these goods have increased from 20% in 1925 to more than 60% in 2009.

Source: Bureau of Economic Analysis.

Figure 1-1(a) also shows that the imports of capital goods plus consumer goods have increased from 10% in 1925 to 65% in 2009. In Figure 1-1(b), we see that the export of capital plus consumer goods has increased from about 20% of exports in 1925 to about 60% of exports in 2009. Capital goods and consumer products (including the iPod) are the types of goods that are most likely to have a portion of their production process sent overseas through offshoring. The fact that the share of trade in these products has increased shows that the type of trade today has changed greatly from the past. ■

Map of World Trade

To show the flow of exports and imports around the world, we use the map in Figure 1-2, which shows trade in billions of dollars for 2006. That year about $11.6 trillion in goods crossed international borders. (Because trade in services is harder to measure between countries, we do not include it in Figure 1-2.) The amount of trade in goods is illustrated by the width of the lines, with the largest trade flows having the heaviest lines and the smallest having dashed lines. For large trade flows, we usually draw two lines indicating the direction of each trade flow. For smaller amounts of trade, we draw a single dashed line, with the amount of the trade flows shown on each arrow. The trade flows within certain regions, such as Europe, are described by a circle, with the total amount of trade shown.

European and U.S. Trade The largest amount of trade shown in Figure 1-2 is the flow of goods within Europe, which was $3.7 trillion in 2006, or nearly one-third (31%) of world trade! This fact is shown in Table 1-1 as internal trade within Europe.

FIGURE 1-2

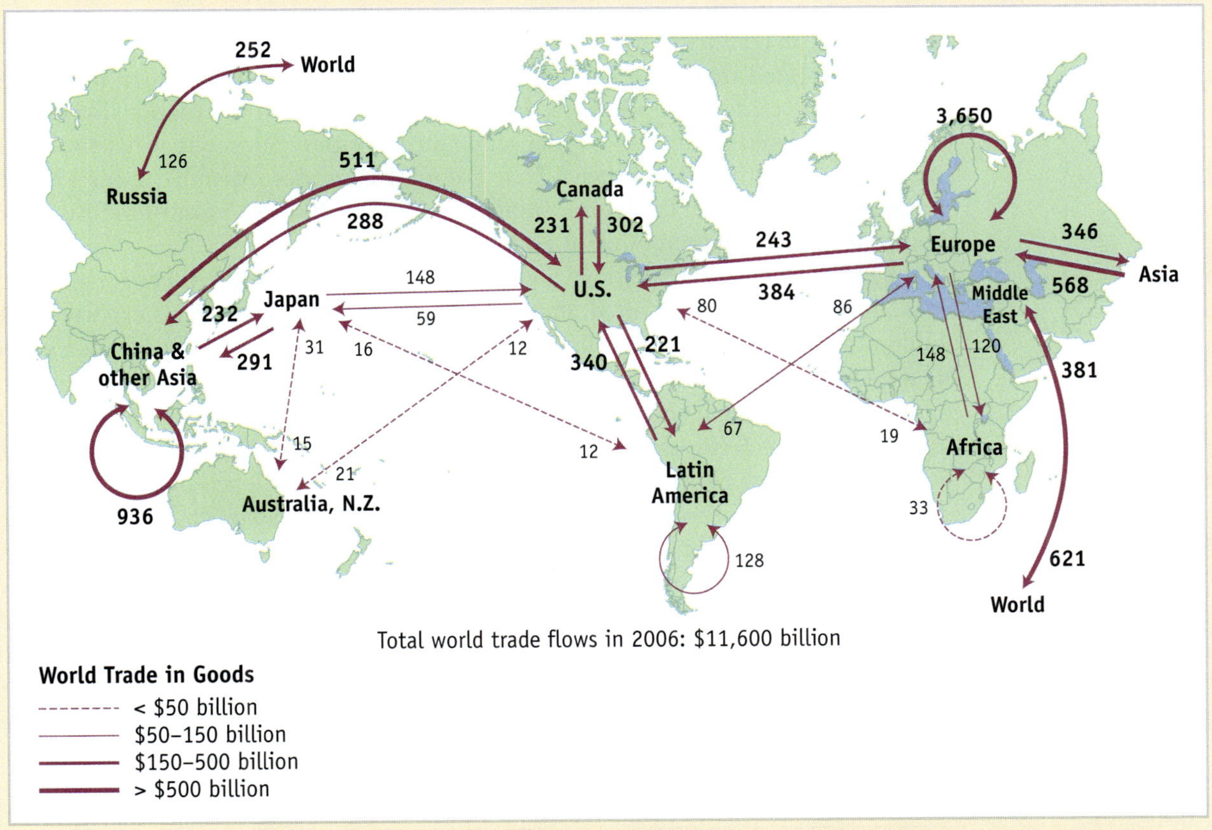

World Trade in Goods, 2006 ($ billions) This figure shows the trade in merchandise goods between selected countries and regions of the world for 2006 in billions of dollars. The amount of trade in goods is illustrated by the width of the lines, with the largest trade flows having the heaviest lines and the smallest having dashed lines.

Source: United Nations trade data.

TABLE 1-1

Shares of World Trade, Accounted for by Selected Regions, 2006 This table shows the share of trade within each region, or the share of exports from each region, as a percentage of total world trade in 2006. Europe and the Americas combined account for over one-half (60%) of world exports, and Asia accounts for another one-quarter of world exports.

	Share of World Trade (%)		Share of World Trade (%)
Europe (internal trade)	31	Asia (exports)	27
Europe (internal) plus trade with the U.S.	37	Middle East and Russia (exports)	9
Americas (internal trade)	11	Africa (exports)	3
Europe and the Americas (exports)	60	Australia and New Zealand (exports)	1.4

Note: The shares of world trade are calculated from Figure 1-2, as explained in the text. The Americas includes North, Central, and South America and the Caribbean. Exports for the Middle East and Russia also include exports for the Commonwealth of Independent States, which consists of Azerbaijan, Armenia, Belarus, Georgia, Kazakhstan, Kyrgyzstan, Moldova, Russia, Tajikistan, Turkmenistan, Uzbekistan, and Ukraine.

Source: United Nations trade data.

The European countries trade a great deal with each other because there are so many countries located there and because it is easy to ship from one country to another. Furthermore, trade is high because **import tariffs** (taxes on international trade) are low. The European Union is a group of countries within Europe that have zero tariffs on imports from each other.[2] That group of countries expanded from 15 to 25 members in 2004, with two more countries joining in 2007, so most of the European countries trade with each other at zero tariffs.

In addition to large trade flows among the European countries, there are also large trade flows between the United States and Europe. The United States exported $243 billion of goods to Europe in 2006 and imported $384 billion of goods from Europe. If we add those flows to the trade flow within Europe, we find that Europe and the United States account for about $4.3 trillion, or 37%, of the $11.6 trillion in world trade flows. This fact is also recorded in Table 1-1, and it shows that a large amount of world trade occurs between countries that are similar in their levels of advanced industrialization and great wealth. Why do these countries trade so much with each other?

The many differences among European countries and between Europe and the United States explain, in part, the trade between them. The first model of trade we study in the next chapter, called the Ricardian model, was initially used to explain trade between England and Portugal based on their difference in climate. Despite such differences, however, industrialized countries like the United Kingdom and the United States have many similarities in their consumption patterns and in their ability to produce goods and services. Why, then, do "similar" countries trade so much with one

[2] Prior to 2004 the European Union consisted of 15 countries: Belgium, France, Germany, Italy, Luxembourg, and the Netherlands (founding members in 1952); Denmark, Ireland, and the United Kingdom (added in 1973); Greece (added in 1981); Portugal and Spain (added in 1986); and Austria, Finland, and Sweden (added in 1995). On May 1, 2004, 10 more countries were added: Cyprus, the Czech Republic, Estonia, Hungary, Lithuania, Latvia, Malta, Poland, Slovakia, and Slovenia. In January 2007 Bulgaria and Romania joined. In addition to zero tariffs, countries within the European Union have many common economic regulations, and some of them share a currency (the euro).

another? We try to answer that question in a later chapter, by arguing that even similar countries have enough variety in the goods they produce (such as different models of cars or types of cheese) that it is natural for them to trade with one another.

Trade in the Americas There is also a large amount of trade recorded within the Americas; that is, between North America, Central America, South America, and the Caribbean. The United States exported $231 billion to Canada in 2006 and imported $302 billion from Canada. In addition, the United States exported $221 billion to Latin America (which consists of Mexico, Central and South America, and the Caribbean) and imported $340 billion from Latin America. If we add together these trade flows, plus the amounts that Canada trades with Latin America and Latin America trades internally, we get $1.3 trillion as the total trade in goods within the Americas in 2006, or another 11% of world trade.

So trade within the Americas is about one-third of trade within Europe, and the vast majority of that trade is within the North American Free Trade Area, consisting of Canada, the United States, and Mexico. There have been proposals to extend this free trade area further by including Central and South America in a Free Trade Area of the Americas. But the economic incentives for this extension are not that great because the distances between North and South America are large and the amount of trade is relatively small. Thus, we should not expect the Free Trade Area of the Americas to be embraced by these nations in the near future, if at all. This stands in contrast to the recent expansions of the European Union.

If we add the trade flows within the Americas to those within Europe and also include all other exports of these two regions to the rest of the world, we find that these combined regions account for $7.0 trillion in exports, or more than one-half (60%) of the $11.6 trillion in world trade. This finding is also recorded in Table 1-1.

Trade with Asia The next largest trade flows shown in Figure 1-2 are those with Asia. For example, Europe exported $346 billion to the Asian countries in 2006 and imported $568 billion. The United States exported $59 billion to Japan and $288 billion to the rest of Asia and imported about twice as much from each of these regions.

If we break up Asian exports to the United States, the largest exporting country is China (selling $288 billion in 2006), followed by Japan ($148 billion), South Korea ($46 billion), and Taiwan ($38 billion). India, Indonesia, Thailand, Vietnam, and the other Asian countries export smaller amounts. The exports from all of Asia to the United States totaled $659 billion in 2006.

All the exports from Asia totaled about $3.1 trillion in 2006, or more than one-quarter (27%) of world trade, as shown in Table 1-1. Remember that this total includes only trade in goods and omits trade in services, which is becoming increasingly important. India, for example, performs a wide range of services such as accounting, customer support, computer programming, and research and development tasks for firms in the United States and Europe. Because these services are performed for U.S. and European firms in another country, they are considered service exports from the country in which the services are performed. In the quote at the beginning of the chapter, Ben Bernanke, the chairman of the U.S. Federal Reserve, points out that the entrance of China, India, and the former Communist-bloc countries into the world economy has led to a level of globalization that exceeds anything we have seen in the past.

Why does Asia trade so much? There are many answers to this question. One answer is that wages in many Asian countries are much lower than in the industrialized world.

China's low wages allow it to produce goods cheaply and then export them. But why are Chinese wages so low? One explanation is that Chinese workers are less productive (the Ricardian model presented in a later chapter explains wages in that way). Low wages cannot explain why Japan exports so much, however. Japan's wages are very high because its workers are very productive; it exports a great deal to Europe and the United States because its highly skilled workforce and large amount of capital (factories and machines) make it possible for Japan to produce high-quality goods in abundance. Conversely, its scarcity of raw materials explains why it imports those goods from resource-rich countries such as Australia, Canada, and the United States. Trade patterns based on the amounts of labor, capital, and natural resources found in each country are explained by the Heckscher-Ohlin trade model, the topic of a later chapter.

Other Regions The Middle East sells oil to many countries, earning $621 billion in export revenues and spending $381 billion on imports. Like the Middle East, Russia also has reserves of oil and natural gas, which countries in Europe rely on and are an important source of export revenue for Russia. In 2006 Russia earned $252 billion in its export sales and spent $126 billion on imports. The exports of the Middle East and Russia combined (together with countries around Russia like Azerbaijan, Kazakhstan, etc.) total $1.0 trillion, or another 9% of world trade.

And then there is Africa. The European nations have the closest trade links with Africa, reflecting both their proximity and the former colonial status of some African countries. Europe exported $120 billion and imported $148 billion from Africa in 2006, as compared with African trade with the United States, which totaled $99 billion, mostly in U.S. imports. Internal trade within Africa is also small: only $33 billion in 2006. Adding up all its exports, the continent of Africa accounts for only 3% of world trade, a very small number given Africa's huge land mass and population.

In the quote at the start of the chapter, Kofi Annan, former secretary general of the United Nations, expresses the view that Africa's growth out of poverty will depend on its developing greater linkages with the world economy through trade. A thorough treatment of the difficulties faced by African and other least developed countries is beyond the scope of this book, and we recommend that the interested reader consult a textbook in development economics. But the lessons we draw from our examination of international trade and trade policy will still hold for the African countries.

The export percentages shown in Table 1-1 add up to 100% (being careful not to add Europe and the Americas twice), once we include trade at the bottom of the world: Australia and New Zealand export $157 billion (accounting for 1.4% of world exports) and import $148 billion. You do not need to know all the specific percentages shown in Table 1-1, but an understanding of the broad picture (such as which regions trade the most) will be useful as we undertake our study of international trade.

Trade Compared with GDP

So far, we have discussed the value of trade crossing international borders. But there is a second way that trade is often reported, and that is as a ratio of trade to a country's **gross domestic product (GDP),** the value of all final goods produced in a year. For the United States, the average value of imports and exports (for goods and services) expressed relative to GDP was 15% in 2008. Most other countries have a higher ratio of trade to GDP, as shown in Table 1-2.

At the top of the list are Hong Kong (China) and Malaysia, where the amount of trade exceeds their GDP![3] These two countries are important shipping and processing centers, so they are importing goods, processing them, and then exporting the final product to other countries. As in our iPod example, the value-added involved in the exports ($4 for each iPod) can be much less than the total value of exports ($150). That explains why the total amount that countries trade can be greater than their GDP. At the bottom of the list are the United States and Japan, which are very large in economic size; Pakistan, which is only starting to engage in international trade; and Brazil and Argentina, which are far away from other importing countries.

So even though the United States is among the world's largest exporters and importers, it is nearly the smallest trading nation of the countries shown in Table 1-2 when trade is measured as a percent of a country's GDP. What is the reason for this inverse relationship? Very large countries tend to have a lot of trade among states or provinces *within* their borders, but that trade is not counted as part of international trade. Other countries that are not quite as large as the United States but are close to their major trading partners, such as Germany, the United Kingdom, Italy, and Spain, and Canada and Mexico, tend to appear in the middle of the list in Table 1-2. Smaller countries with close neighbors, such as Hong Kong, Malaysia, and the smaller European nations, will have more trade spilling across their borders and have the highest ratios of trade to GDP.

Barriers to Trade

Table 1-2 shows the differences across countries in the amount of trade relative to GDP, but this ratio changes over time. There are many reasons, aside from country size, for the amount of trade to change. Those reasons include import tariffs, taxes that countries charge on imported goods; transportation costs of shipping from one country to another; events, such as wars and natural disasters, that lead to reduced trade; and so on. The term **trade barriers** refers to all factors that influence the amount of goods and services shipped across international borders. To see how these trade barriers have changed over time, Figure 1-3 graphs the ratio of trade in goods and services

TABLE 1-2

Trade/GDP Ratio in 2008 This table shows the ratio of total trade to GDP for each country, where trade is calculated as (Imports + Exports)/2, including both merchandise goods and services. Countries with the highest ratios of trade to GDP tend to be small in economic size and are often important centers for shipping goods, like Hong Kong (China) and Malaysia. Countries with the lowest ratios of trade to GDP tend to be very large in economic size, like Japan and the United States, or are not very open to trade because of trade barriers or their distance from other countries.

Country	Trade/GDP (%)	GDP ($ billion)
Hong Kong, China	207	215
Malaysia	116	222
Hungary	81	155
Thailand	75	272
Switzerland	65	492
Austria	56	414
Denmark	54	341
Sweden	50	479
Germany	44	3,649
Norway	38	452
South Africa	37	276
Canada	33	1,501
China	33	4,327
United Kingdom	30	2,674
Indonesia	29	511
Italy	29	2,303
Mexico	29	1,088
Spain	29	1,604
Greece	28	356
France	28	2,857
Turkey	26	735
Russian Federation	26	1,679
Venezuela	25	314
India	25	1,159
Argentina	23	328
Pakistan	18	165
Japan	16	4,911
United States	15	14,093
Brazil	14	1,575

Source: World Development Indicators, The World Bank.

[3] Hong Kong (China) has been a part of the People's Republic of China since July 1, 1997, but its trade statistics are measured separately, so we list Hong Kong in Table 1-2 as a distinct region.

FIGURE 1-3

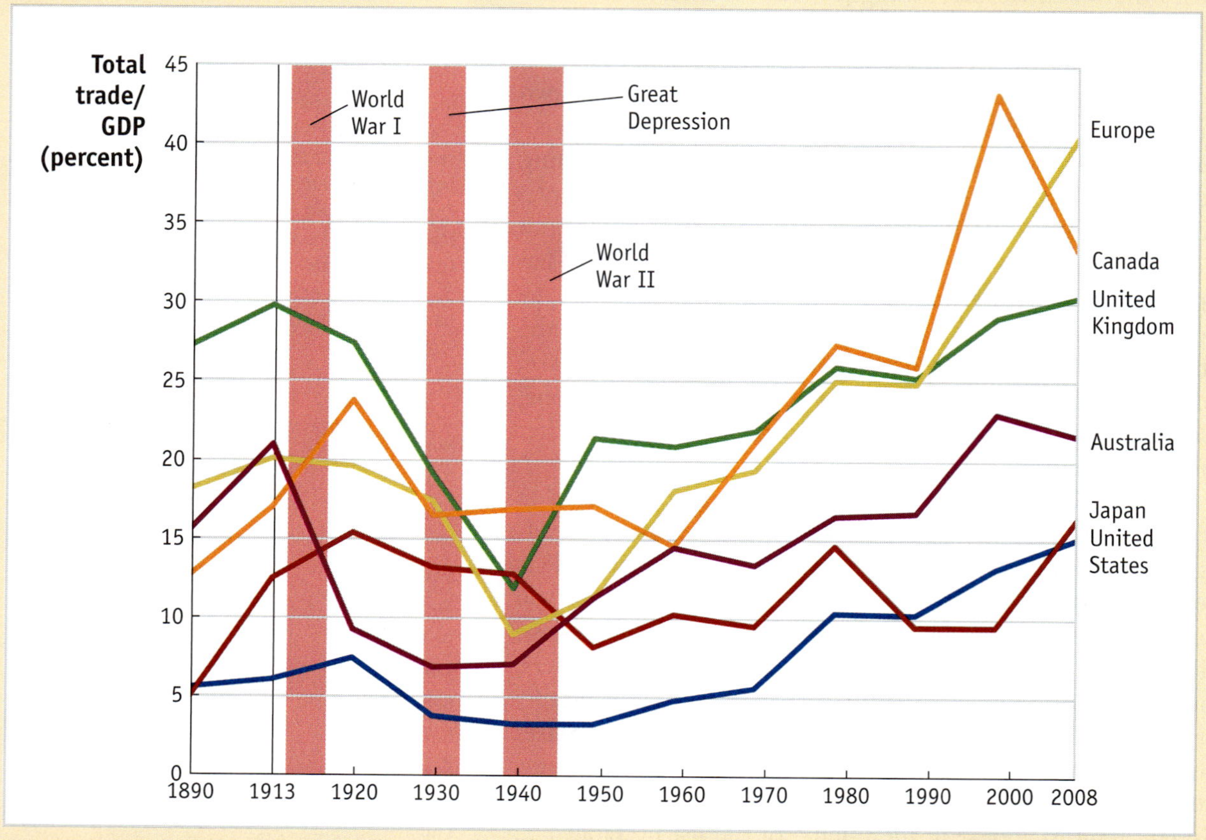

Trade in Goods and Services Relative to GDP This diagram shows total trade in merchandise goods and services for each country (i.e., the average of imports and exports) divided by gross domestic product (GDP). There was a considerable increase in the ratio of trade to GDP between 1890 and 1913. This trend ended by World War I and the Great Depression, and it took many years to regain the same level of trade. Most of the industrial countries shown did not reach the level of trade prevailing in 1913 until the 1970s. Some countries—such as Australia and the United Kingdom—did not reach their earlier levels until the end of the century.

Source: Revised from Robert C. Feenstra, Fall 1998, "Integration of Trade and Disintegration of Production in the Global Economy," Journal of Economic Perspectives, *31–50.*

to GDP for a selection of countries for which historical data are available: Australia, Canada, Japan, the United Kingdom, the United States, and an average of countries in continental Europe (Denmark, France, Germany, Italy, Norway, and Sweden).[4]

"First Golden Age" of Trade

The period from 1890 until World War I (1914–1918) is sometimes referred to as a "golden age" of international trade. Those years saw dramatic improvements in transportation, such as the steamship and the railroad, that allowed for a great increase in the amount of international trade. Figure 1-3 shows this increase in the ratio of trade to GDP between 1890 and World War I. The United Kingdom reached the highest ratio of trade to GDP (30%), while Australia, Canada, and the average of European

[4] Because historical data on trade in services are not available, in Figure 1-3 we include trade in services starting in 1950.

countries all exceeded 20% at their peaks (shown in 1913 or 1920). Japan reached a ratio of trade to GDP of 15%, while the United States achieved 7.5%, which was low in comparison with other countries (as expected for a large country) but still high by the United States' historical standards.

Interwar Period In the aftermath of World War I, the ratio of trade to GDP fell in all countries, a decline that was made worse by the Great Depression, which began in 1929, and World War II, which began in Europe in 1939. During the Great Depression, the United States adopted high tariffs called the Smoot-Hawley tariffs, named after Senator Reed Smoot from Utah and Representative Willis C. Hawley from Oregon. Signed into law in June 1930, the Smoot-Hawley Tariff Act raised tariffs to as high as 60% on many categories of imports.

These tariffs were applied by the United States to protect farmers and other industries, but they backfired by causing other countries to retaliate. Canada retaliated by applying high tariffs of its own against the United States; France used **import quotas,** a limitation on the quantity of an imported good allowed into a country, to restrict imports from the United States; Britain gave preferences to goods available from its former colonies; and other countries reacted, too. As reported by one economic historian:[5]

> A groundswell of resentment spread around the world and quickly led to retaliation. Italy objected to duties on hats and bonnets of straw, wool-felt hats, and olive oil; Spain reacted sharply to increases on cork and onions; Canada took umbrage at increases on maple sugar and syrup, potatoes, cream, butter, buttermilk, and skimmed milk. Switzerland was moved to boycott American typewriters, fountain pens, motor cars, and films because of increased duties on watches, clocks, embroidery, cheese and shoes. . . . Retaliation was begun long before the [Smoot-Hawley] bill was enacted into law in June 1930.

The response of these countries, initially against the United States and then against each other, led to a dramatic increase in worldwide tariffs during the interwar period. The average worldwide tariff for 35 countries from 1860 to 2000 is shown in Figure 1-4. We see that the average tariff fluctuated around 15% from 1860 to 1914. After World War I, however, the average tariff rose because of the Smoot-Hawley Tariff Act and the reaction by other countries, reaching about 25% by 1933. The high tariffs led to a dramatic fall in world trade in the interwar period, with large costs to the United States and the world economy. These costs are one reason that the Allied countries met together after World War II to develop international agreements to keep tariffs low, such as the General Agreement on Tariffs and Trade, now known as the World Trade Organization. Later in this book, we study tariffs and other trade policies in more detail and the international institutions that govern their use. The lesson from the interwar period is that high tariffs reduce the amount of trade and impose large costs on the countries involved.

"Second Golden Age" of Trade

It took many years for the world economy to regain the same level of global integration that existed before World War I. From Figure 1-3, we can see that some countries (the United Kingdom, Europe, and Australia) began increasing trade

[5] Charles Kindleberger, 1989, "Commercial Policy between the Wars." In P. Mathias and S. Pollard, eds., *The Cambridge Economic History of Europe*, Vol. VIII (Cambridge, UK: Cambridge University Press), p. 170.

FIGURE 1-4

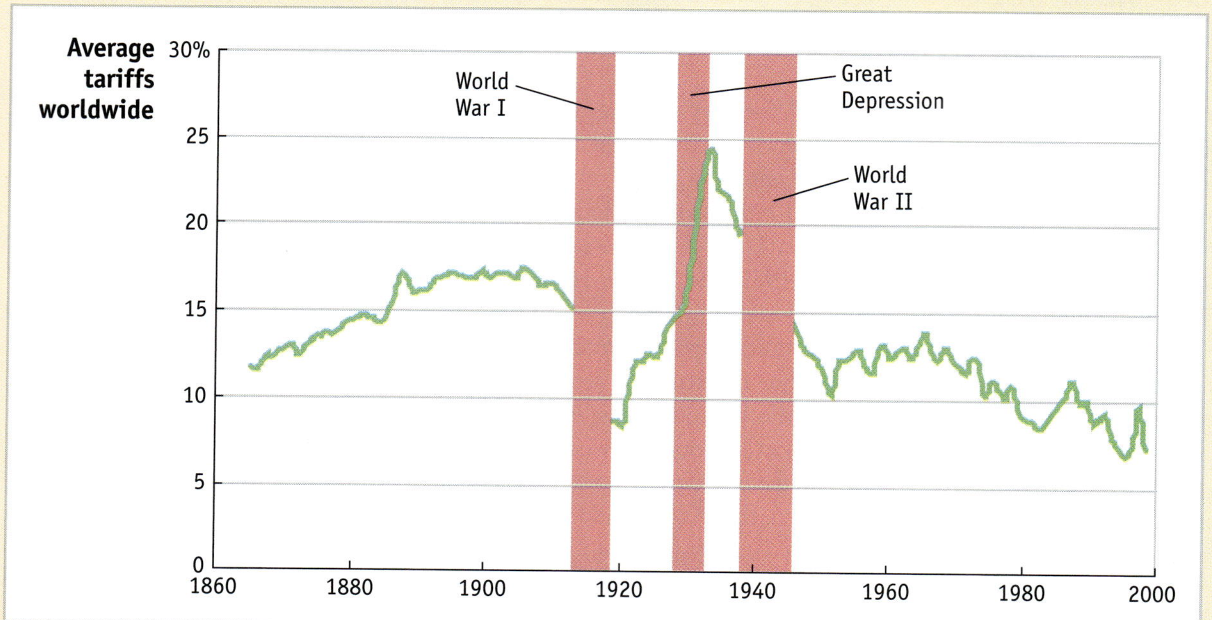

Average Worldwide Tariffs, 1860–2000 This diagram shows the world average tariff for 35 countries from 1860 to 2000. The average tariff fluctuated around 15% from 1860 to 1913. After World War I, however, the average tariff rose sharply because of the Smoot-Hawley Tariff Act in the United States and the reaction by other countries, reaching 25% by 1933. Since the end of World War II, tariffs have fallen.

Source: Michael A. Clemens and Jeffrey G. Williamson, 2004, "Why Did the Tariff-Growth Correlation Change after 1950?" Journal of Economic Growth, *9(1), 5–46.*

immediately after the end of World War II in 1945, so their ratio of trade to GDP was much higher in 1950 than it was in 1940. Some countries did not show an increase until after 1950 and others not until after 1960. In addition to the end of World War II and tariff reductions under the General Agreement on Tariffs and Trade, improved transportation costs contributed to the growth in trade. The shipping container, invented in 1956, allowed goods to be moved by ship, rail, and truck more cheaply than before (see **Headlines: A Sea Change in Shipping 50 Years Ago**). As a result of all these factors, world trade grew steadily after 1950 in dollar terms and as a ratio to GDP. For this reason, the period after 1950 is called the "second golden age" of trade and globalization.

Many of the countries shown in Figure 1-3 have substantially exceeded the peak levels of trade relative to GDP that prevailed just before or after World War I. Canada's trade ratio grew from 24% in 1920 to 33% by 2008, while the average of European countries increased from 20% in 1913 to 41% in 2008. Likewise, the United States' ratio grew from 7.5% in 1920 to 15% by 2008. A few countries, such as Australia and the United Kingdom, have only recently achieved the level of trade relative to GDP that they had prior to World War I and are now in a position to surpass that level. For the world as a whole, the ratio of trade to GDP in 2008 was about 30%, up from 20% in 1980 and 12% in 1970. But near the end of the decade, in 2008, we see a fall in the ratios of trade to GDP for some countries, such as Canada and Australia. What happened to cause this slow-down in trade?

HEADLINES

A Sea Change in Shipping 50 Years Ago

The following article discusses the invention of the shipping container 50 years ago, which allowed goods to be shipped between countries at a much lower cost.

Globalization is having an anniversary. It was 50 years ago that Malcom McLean, an entrepreneur from North Carolina, loaded a ship with 58 35-foot containers and sailed from Newark, N.J., to Houston. He wasn't the only one to suggest that containers might make shipping more efficient. But he was the first to design a transportation system around the packaging of cargo in huge metal boxes that could be loaded and unloaded by cranes.

Container shipping eventually replaced the traditional "break-bulk" method of handling crates, barrels and bags, and stowing them loose in a ship's hold, a system in use since the days of the Phoenicians. Replacing break-bulk with cargo containers dramatically reduced shipping costs, reinvigorating markets and fueling the world economy. . . .

In 1959, according to Matson Research, the industry was loading and unloading 0.627 tons per man hour. By 1976, with container shipping well established, the figure was 4,234 tons per man hour. A ship's time in port shrank from three weeks to 18 hours. In 1950, an average commercial vessel could carry 10,000 tons at a speed of 16 knots. With container shipping, the average commercial vessel carried 40,000 tons at a speed of 23 knots, Matson says. The numbers are even larger today. A vessel capable of carrying 6,600 20-foot containers can carry 77,000 tons at up to 24.8 knots.

"Containerization has transformed global trade in manufactured goods as dramatically as jet planes have changed the way we travel and the Internet has changed the way we communicate," said Joseph Bonney, editor of the *Journal of Commerce,* the bible of the shipping industry. "The Asian economic miracle of the last two decades could not have happened without the efficient transportation that containerized shipping provides."

Banana Stock/Jupiter Images

A fully loaded container ship can carry thousands of containers.

Source: Excerpted from George Raine, "A Sea Change in Shipping: 50 Years Ago, Container Ships Altered the World," San Francisco Chronicle, *February 5, 2006, electronic edition.*

The Financial Crisis

In the fall of 2008 there was a financial crisis in the United States that quickly spread to other countries. The full, detailed story of the financial crisis is beyond the scope of this book. Here, we present a highly simplified description of the crisis that allows us to show how and why the crisis affected international trade. The reason this crisis occurred was that the prices for homes rose from 1997 to 2005, and then fell substantially from 2006 up to the present time. As a result, many homeowners started to default (i.e., stop paying) their mortgages, and banks begain foreclosing on and taking possession of the homes. Mortgage defaults meant that the loans made by the banks became worth much less—they became worth only the value at which the house could be sold, which was often far less than the price for which the house had been purchased. Banks making mortgages therefore lost a great deal of money, and these losses spread throughout the whole financial system in the United States and abroad.

From this brief description of the banking crisis, it is apparent that international trade was not the cause of the crisis. Nevertheless, the crisis had a substantial impact on the amount of international trade, because it sent many countries into recessions that led to a fall in both exports and imports. This fall in trade is illustrated in Figure 1-5, where we show the percentage change in value of trade (the average of exports and imports for each country) from the first quarter (January–March) of 2007 to the fourth quarter (October–December) of 2009. For all the countries shown, the pattern is similar: at the

FIGURE 1-5

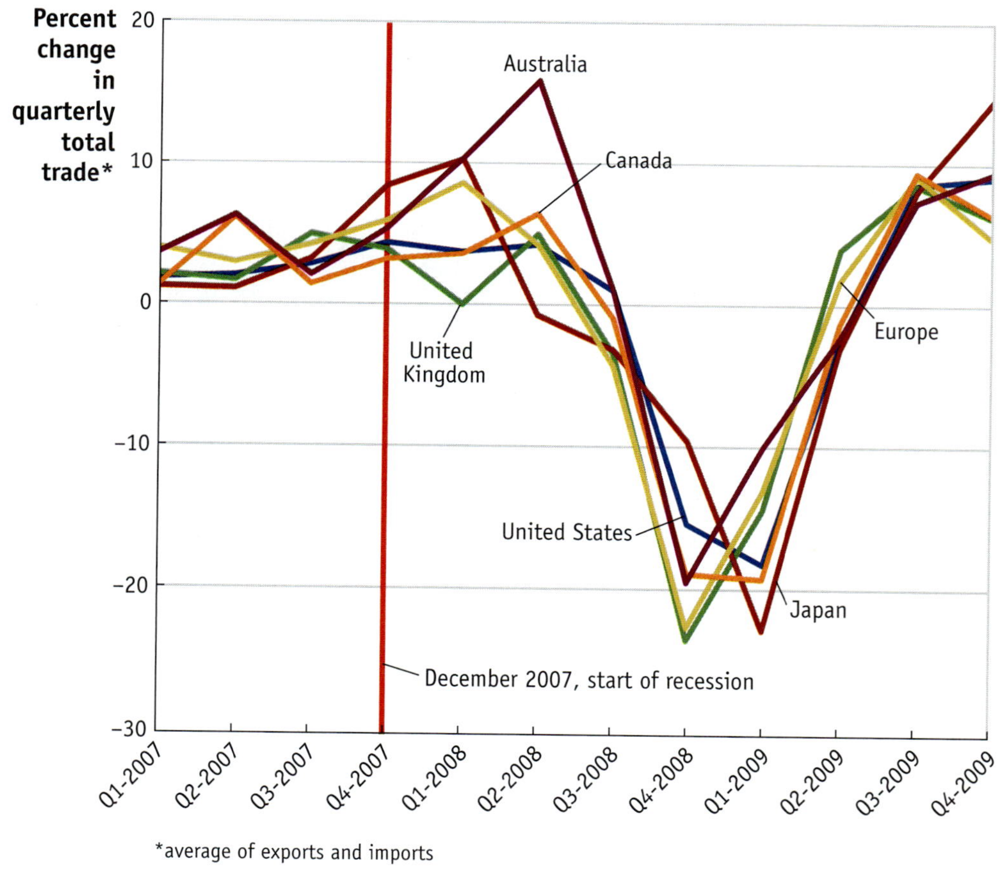

Change in the Value of Trade, 2007–2009 (percent) As a result of a worldwide financial crisis and economic recession, the value of trade plummeted between early 2008 and early 2009. The value of trade was still falling in the first two quarters of 2009, and then began to grow.

Source: Organisation for Economic Co-operation and Development (OECD) website http://www.stats.oecd.org/index.aspx.

end of 2007 or early in 2008 trade began to fall, reaching a quarter-to-quarter fall of about 20% by the end of 2008 or early in 2009. By the last quarter of 2009 trade was expanding by about 10% as compared with the previous quarter, but that was still not enough to return trade to its pre-crisis level. It will take some years for the world economy to again reach a level of trade, or ratio of trade to GDP, that is as high as what it has achieved in the past.

2 Migration and Foreign Direct Investment

In addition to examining the reasons for and effects of international trade (the flow of goods and services between countries), we will also analyze migration, the movement of people across borders, and foreign direct investment (FDI), the movement of capital across borders. All three of these flows affect the economy of a nation that opens its borders to interact with other nations.

Map of Migration

In Figure 1-6, we show a map of the number of migrants around the world. The values shown are the number of people in 2005 who were living (legally or illegally) in a country other than the one in which they were born. For this map, we combine two different sources of data: (1) the movement of people from one country to another, reported for just the Organisation for Economic Co-operation and Development (OECD) countries and shown by arrows from one country to another[6], and (2) the number of foreign-born located in each region (but without knowing their country of origin), shown by the bold arrows from World into Asia, Africa, and Latin America.[7]

In 2005 there were 62 million foreign-born people living in the OECD countries. But that is less than one-third of the total number of foreign-born people worldwide, which was 195 million. These figures show that unlike trade (much of which occurs between the OECD countries), the majority of immigration occurs *outside* the OECD between countries that are less wealthy. Asia, for example, was home to 53.1 million migrants in 2005, and Africa was home to 17.1 million migrants. Latin America has 6.9 million foreign-born people living there. We expect that many of these immigrants come from the same continent where they are now living but have had to move from one country to another for employment or other reasons such as famine and war.[8]

Given the choice, these migrants would probably rather move to a high-wage, industrial country. But people cannot just move to another country as can the goods and services that move in international trade. All countries have restrictions on who can enter and work there. In many OECD countries, these restrictions are in place because policy makers fear that immigrants from low-wage countries will drive down the wages for a

[6] The Organization for Economic Cooperation and Development (OECD) consists of 30 member countries, including most European countries as well as Australia, Canada, Japan, Mexico, South Korea, and the United States. See the complete list of countries at http://www.oecd.org.

[7] Data on total immigration for major regions are available from the United Nations at http://www.esa.un.org/migration.

[8] The United Nations data on migrants include refugees, so other reasons for moving include wars and famines. Of the 50.3 million migrants in Asia in 2000, 8.8 million were refugees; of the 16.5 million migrants in Africa, 3.6 million were refugees; and of the 6.3 million migrants in Latin America, 500,000 were refugees.

FIGURE 1-6

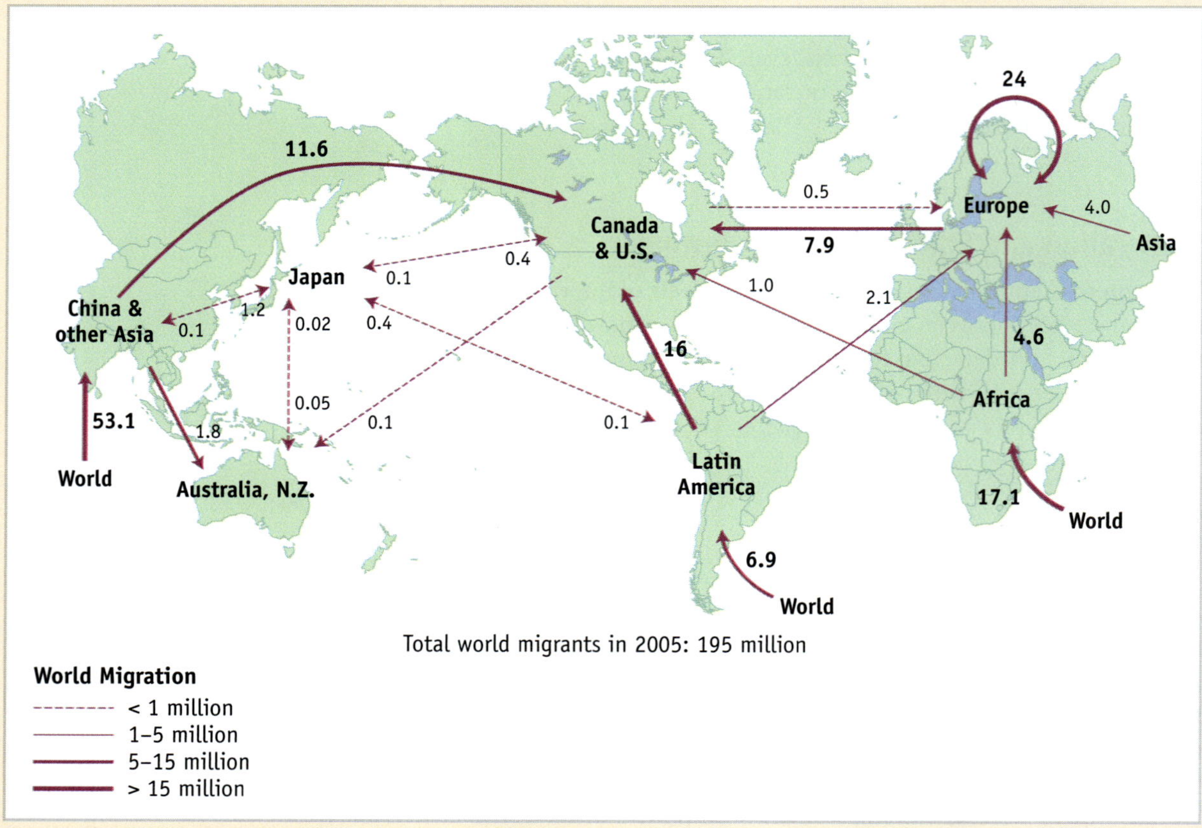

Foreign-Born Migrants, 2005 (millions) This figure shows the number of foreign-born migrants living in selected countries and regions of the world for 2005 in millions of people. The level of migration is illustrated by the width of the lines, with the largest migrant numbers having the heaviest lines and the smallest having dashed lines.

Source: OECD and UN migration data.

country's own less skilled workers. Whether or not that fear is justified, immigration is a hotly debated political issue in many countries, including Europe and the United States. As a result, the flow of people between countries is *much less* free than the flow of goods.

The limitation on migration out of the low-wage countries is offset to some extent by the ability of these countries to export products instead. International trade can act as a *substitute* for movements of labor or capital across borders, in the sense that trade can raise the living standard of workers in the same way that moving to a higher-wage country can. The increased openness to trade in the world economy since World War II has provided opportunities for workers to benefit through trade by working in export industries, even when restrictions on migration prevent them from directly earning higher incomes abroad.

European and U.S. Immigration We have just learned that restrictions on migration, especially into the wealthier countries, limit the movement of people between countries. Let us see how such restrictions are reflected in recent policy actions in two regions: the European Union and the United States.

Prior to 2004 the European Union (EU) consisted of 15 countries in western Europe, and labor mobility was very open between them.[9] On May 1, 2004, 10 more countries of central Europe were added: Cyprus, the Czech Republic, Estonia, Hungary, Latvia, Lithuania, Malta, Poland, Slovakia, and Slovenia. These countries had per capita incomes that were only about one-quarter of the average per capita incomes in those westerm European countries that were already EU members. This large difference in wages created a strong incentive for labor migration. In principle, citizens from these newly added countries were permitted to work anywhere in the EU. As shown in Figure 1-6, in 2005 there were 24 million people from Europe living in an EU country in which they were not born. In practice, however, fears of this impending inflow of labor led to policy disagreements among the countries involved.

Germany and Austria, which border some of the new member countries, argued for a seven-year moratorium on allowing labor mobility from new members, if desired by the host countries. Britain and Ireland, on the other hand, promised to open up their countries to workers from the new EU members. In January 2007 two more countries joined the EU: Romania and Bulgaria. Legal immigration from these countries in the expanded EU, together with legal and illegal immigration from other countries, has put strains on the political system in Britain. All major political parties spoke in favor of limiting immigration from outside the EU, and this issue may have contributed to the ousting of the Labour Party in Britain in the election of May 2010. A second example of recent migration policy is from the United States. As shown in Figure 1-6, there were 16 million people from Latin America living in the United States and Canada in 2005, and the largest group of these migrants is Mexicans living in the United States. It has been estimated that in 2005 close to 12 million Mexicans were living in the United States, about half legally and half illegally. This number is more than 10% of Mexico's population of 111 million. The concern that immigration will drive down wages applies to Mexican migration to the United States and is amplified by the exceptionally high number of illegal immigrants. It is no surprise, then, that immigration policy is a frequent topic of debate in the United States.

There is a widespread perception among policy makers in the United States that the current immigration system is not working and needs to be fixed. In 2007 President George W. Bush attempted an immigration reform, but it was not supported by the Congress. When he was campaigning as a presidential candidate, Barack Obama also promised to pursue immigration reform. But that promise had to wait for other policy actions, most notably the health-care reform bill, which gained approval in the House of Representatives on March 21, 2010. On that same day, there was a large rally in Washington, D.C., for immigration reform, with tens of thousands of demonstrators filling the Washington Mall. President Obama spoke to the crowd by video screen, saying, "I have always pledged to be your partner as we work to fix our broken immigration system, and that's a commitment that I reaffirm today."[10] But the acrimonious debate over the health-care reform bill has made some members of

---

[9] Those 15 countries were Belgium, France, Germany, Italy, Luxembourg, and the Netherlands (founding members in 1952); Denmark, Ireland, and the United Kingdom (added in 1973); Greece (added in 1981); Portugal and Spain (added in 1986); and Austria, Finland, and Sweden (added in 1995).

[10] Quoted in Julia Preston, "At Rally, Call for Urgency on Immigration," *The New York Times*, March 21, 2010, from which this paragraph draws.

Congress reluctant to pursue immigration reform, especially in a midterm election year. In addition, the debate over reform of the financial system in 2010 has delayed the discussion of immigration. It remains to be seen whether any immigration bill will be enacted during President Obama's administration.

Map of Foreign Direct Investment

As mentioned earlier in the chapter, foreign direct investment (FDI) occurs when a firm in one country owns (in part or in whole) a company or property in another country. Figure 1-7 shows the principal stocks of FDI in 2006, with the magnitude of the stocks illustrated by the width of the lines. As we did for migration, we again combine two sources of information: (1) stocks of FDI found in the OECD countries that are owned by another country, shown by arrows from the country of ownership to the country of location, and (2) FDI stocks from anywhere in the world found in Africa, Asia, Europe, and Latin America.

FIGURE 1-7

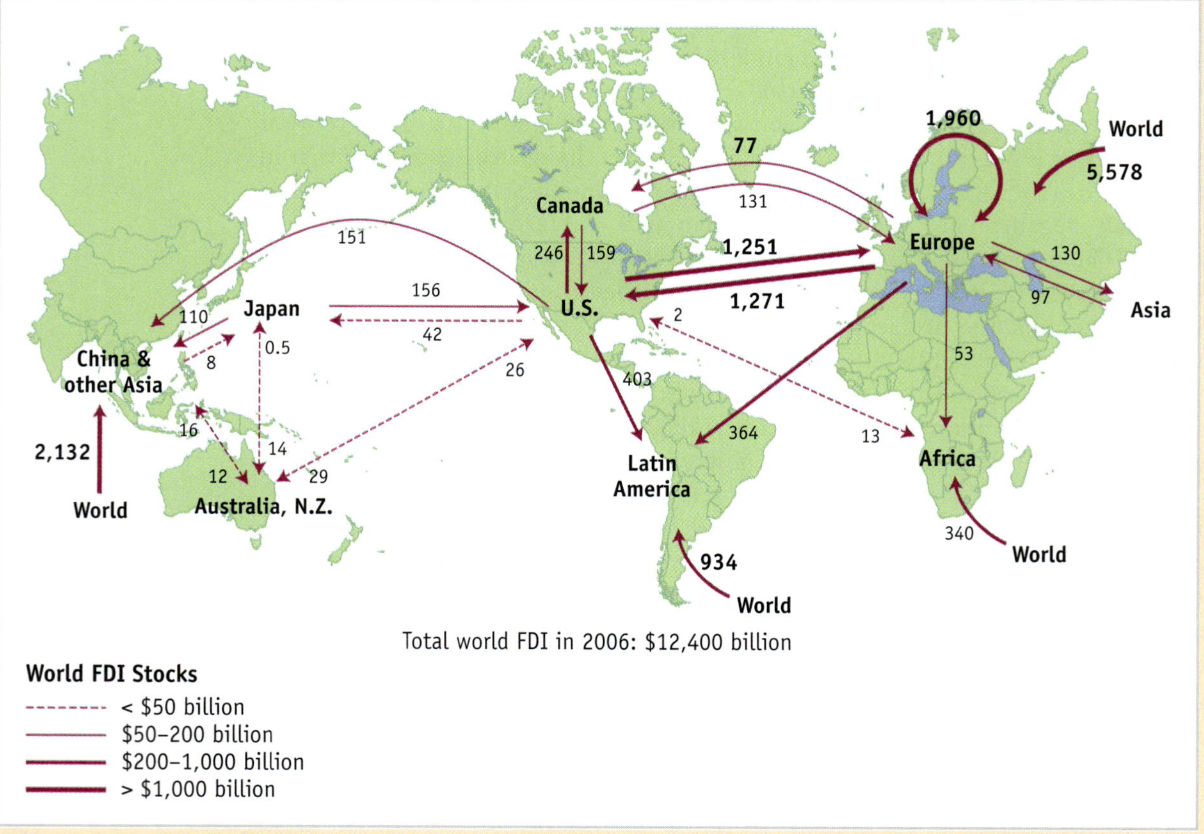

Stock of Foreign Direct Investment, 2006 ($ billions) This figure shows the stock of foreign direct investment between selected countries and regions of the world for 2006 in billions of dollars. The stock of investment is illustrated by the width of the lines, with the largest stocks having the heaviest lines and the smallest having dashed lines.

Source: OECD and UN foreign investment data.

In 2006 the total value of FDI stocks located in the OECD countries or owned by those countries was $11.4 trillion. That value is more than 90% of the total world stock of FDI, which was $12.4 trillion in 2006. So unlike our findings for immigration, the vast majority of FDI is located in or owned by firms in the OECD countries. The concentration of FDI among wealthy countries is even more pronounced than the concentration of international trade flows. The FDI stock in Africa ($340 billion) is approximately one-third of the stock in Latin America ($934 billion), which in turn is less than one-half of the FDI into China and other Asian countries ($2,132 billion). Most of this FDI is from industrial countries, but Chinese firms have begun to acquire land in Africa and Latin America for agriculture and resource extraction, as well as purchase companies in the industrial countries, as we discuss below.

Foreign direct investment can be described in one of two ways: horizontal FDI or vertical FDI.

Horizontal FDI The majority of foreign direct investment occurs between industrial countries, when a firm from one industrial country owns a company in another industrial country. We refer to these flows between industrial countries as **horizontal FDI.** Recent examples have occurred in the automobile industry, such as the 2009 purchase of Chrysler by Fiat, an Italian firm.

There are many reasons why companies want to acquire firms in another industrial country. First, having a plant abroad allows the parent firm to avoid any tariffs from exporting to a foreign market because it can instead produce and sell locally in that market. For example, as early as the 1950s and 1960s, American auto manufacturers produced and sold cars in Europe to avoid having to pay any tariffs. In the 1980s and 1990s many Japanese auto firms opened plants in the United States to avoid U.S. import quotas (restrictions on the amount imported). Today, more Japanese cars are built in the United States than are imported from Japan.

Second, having a foreign subsidiary abroad also provides improved access to that economy because the local firms will have better facilities and information for marketing products. For example, Toyota Motor Sales U.S.A. is a wholly owned subsidiary of Toyota Motor Corporation in Japan and markets Toyota cars and trucks in the United States. Many other foreign firms selling in the United States have similar local retail firms. Third, an alliance between the production division of firms allows technical expertise to be shared and avoids possible duplication of products. Examples are the American and Canadian divisions of General Motors, Ford, and Chrysler, which have operated plants specializing in different vehicles on both sides of the border (in Detroit, Michigan, and Windsor, Ontario) for decades. There are many reasons for horizontal FDI, which is really just a way for a firm to expand its business across international borders.

Vertical FDI The other form of foreign direct investment occurs when a firm from an industrial country owns a plant in a developing country, which we call **vertical FDI.** Low wages are the principal reasons that firms shift production abroad to developing countries. In the traditional view of FDI, firms from industrial economies use their technological expertise and combine this with inexpensive labor in developing countries to produce goods for the world market. This is a reasonable view of FDI in China, although as we have already seen, much of worldwide FDI does not fit this traditional view because it is between industrial countries.

In addition to taking advantage of low wages, firms have entered the Chinese market to avoid tariffs and acquire local partners to sell there. For example, China formerly had high tariffs on automobile imports, so many auto producers from the United States, Germany, and Japan established plants there, always with a Chinese partner, enabling them to sell more easily in that market. China joined the World Trade Organization in 2001, which means that it has reduced its tariffs on nearly all imports, including automobiles. Nevertheless, the foreign automobile firms are planning to remain and are now beginning to export cars from China.

European and U.S. FDI Turning back now to Figure 1-7, the largest stocks of FDI are within Europe; these stocks amounted to $5.6 trillion in 2006, or nearly one-half of the world total, with $2.0 trillion coming from other European countries. In addition, the horizontal FDI from Europe to the United States and that from the United States to Europe were almost identical in 2006 ($1.3 trillion in each direction). An example of a European direct investment in the United States was the merger of the German company Daimler-Benz (which produces the Mercedes-Benz car) and Chrysler Corporation in 1998, resulting in the firm DaimlerChrysler. That deal lasted for less than 10 years, however, and in May 2007 DaimlerChrysler sold the Chrysler firm back to an American financial company, Cerberus Capital Management, so Chrysler returned to American ownership. Then, in 2009, Chrysler was again sold to a European automobile firm, Fiat. An example of American direct investment in Europe was Ford Motor Company's acquisition of the British firm Jaguar (in 1989) and the Swedish firm Volvo (in 1999). The United States consistently ranks as the top country for both inbound and outbound FDI stocks ($1.8 trillion and $2.4 trillion in 2006, respectively), followed by France and then the United Kingdom.

Adding up the stocks within Europe and between Europe and the United States, we find that they total $4.5 trillion, or more than one-third (36%) of the world total. That share is very close to the 37% share of worldwide trade that occurs within Europe and between Europe and the United States (see Table 1-1). This finding illustrates that the greatest amount of FDI is horizontal FDI between the industrial countries.

FDI in the Americas There are also substantial amounts of FDI shown in Figure 1-7 among the United States, Canada, and Latin America. The United States had a stock of direct investments of $246 billion in Canada in 2006, and Canada invested $159 billion in the United States. The United States had a stock of direct investments of $403 billion in Latin America, principally in Mexico. Brazil and Mexico are two of the largest recipients of FDI among developing countries, after China. In 2006 Mexico had a FDI stock of $226 billion, and Brazil had a stock of $222 billion, accounting for about one-half of the total $934 billion in FDI to Latin America. These are examples of vertical FDI, prompted by the opportunity to produce goods at lower wages than in the industrial countries.

FDI with Asia The direct investments between the United States and Japan and between Europe and Japan are horizontal FDI. In addition to Japan, the rest of Asia shows a large amount of FDI in Figure 1-7. The United States had direct investments of $151 billion in the rest of Asia, especially China, while Europe had a direct investment of $130 billion in Asia. These stocks are also examples of vertical FDI, foreign direct investment from industrial to developing countries, to take advantage of low wages.

China has become the largest recipient country for FDI in Asia and the fourth largest recipient of FDI in the world (after the United States, France, and the United Kingdom). The FDI stock in China and Hong Kong was $742 billion in 2006, which accounts for 35% of the total FDI into China and the rest of Asia ($2.1 trillion). There is some "double counting" in these numbers for China and Hong Kong because Hong Kong itself has direct investment in mainland China, which is funded in part by businesses on the mainland. This flow of funds from mainland China to Hong Kong and then back to China is called "round tripping," and it is estimated that one-quarter to one-half of FDI flowing into China is funded that way.

Notice in Figure 1-7 that Asia has direct investment into the United States and Europe, or what we might call "reverse-vertical FDI." Contrary to the traditional view of FDI, these are companies from developing countries buying firms in the industrial countries. Obviously, these companies are not going after low wages in the industrial countries; instead, they are acquiring the technological knowledge of those firms, which they can combine with low wages in their home countries. A widely publicized example was the purchase of IBM's personal computer division by Lenovo, a Chinese firm. What expertise did Lenovo acquire from this purchase? According to media reports, Lenovo will acquire the management and international expertise of IBM and will even hire IBM executives to run the business. Instead of using FDI to acquire inexpensive labor, Lenovo has engaged in FDI to acquire expensive and highly skilled labor, which is what it needs to succeed in the computer industry.

Another recent example of reverse-vertical FDI from China is the 2009 purchase of Volvo (formerly a Swedish company) from Ford Motor Company, by the Chinese automaker Geely. In a later chapter, we will discuss how automobile companies from the United States, Europe, and Japan entered the automobile industry in China by buying partial ownership in Chinese firms, which allowed the Chinese firms to learn from their foreign partners. That process of learning the best technology continues in the case of Geely purchasing Volvo from Ford, but now it is the Chinese firm that is doing the buying rather than the American, European, or Japanese firms.

3 Conclusions

Globalization means many things: the flow of goods and services across borders, the movement of people and firms, the spread of culture and ideas among countries, and the tight integration of financial markets around the world. Although it might seem as if such globalization is new, international trade and the integration of financial markets were also very strong in the period before World War I. The war and the Great Depression disrupted these global linkages. Since World War II world trade has grown rapidly again, even faster than the growth in world GDP, so that the ratio of trade to world GDP has risen steadily. International institutions established after World War II have promoted the growth in trade: the General Agreement on Tariffs and Trade (now known as the World Trade Organization), the International Monetary Fund, the United Nations, and the World Bank were all established in the postwar years to promote freer trade and economic development.

Migration across countries is not as free as international trade, and all countries have restrictions on immigration because of the fear that the inflow of workers will drive down wages. That fear is not necessarily justified. We argue in a later chapter that immigrants can sometimes be absorbed into a country with no change in wages.

Foreign direct investment is largely unrestricted in the industrial countries but often faces some restrictions in developing countries. China, for example, requires approval of all foreign investments and usually requires that foreign firms have a local partner. Typically, firms invest in developing countries to take advantage of lower wages in those countries. Investments in developing countries and industrial countries enable firms to spread their business and knowledge of production processes across borders. Migration and foreign direct investment are further aspects of the globalization that has become so widespread today.

KEY POINTS

1. The trade balance of a country is the difference between the value of its exports and the value of its imports, and is determined by macroeconomic conditions in the country.
2. The type of goods being traded between countries has changed from the period before World War I, when standardized goods (raw materials and basic processed goods like steel) were predominant. Today, the majority of trade occurs in highly processed consumer and capital goods, which might cross borders several times during the manufacturing process.
3. A large portion of international trade is between industrial countries. Trade within Europe and between Europe and the United States accounts for over one-third of world trade.
4. Many of the trade models we study emphasize the differences between countries, but it is also possible to explain trade between countries that are similar. Similar countries will trade different varieties of goods with one another.
5. Larger countries tend to have smaller shares of trade relative to GDP because so much of their trade occurs internally. Hong Kong (China) and Malaysia have ratios of trade to GDP that exceed 100%, whereas the United States' ratio of trade to GDP in 2008 was 15%.
6. The majority of world migration occurs into developing countries as a result of restrictions on immigration into wealthier, industrial countries.
7. International trade in goods and services acts as a substitute for migration and allows workers to improve their standard of living through working in export industries, even when they cannot migrate to earn higher incomes.
8. The majority of world foreign direct investment occurs between industrial countries. In 2006 more than one-third of the world stock of FDI were within Europe or between Europe and the United States, and 90% of the world stock of FDI was into or out of the OECD countries.

KEY TERMS

international trade, p. 1
migration, p. 3
foreign direct investment (FDI), p. 3
export, p. 3
import, p. 3
trade balance, p. 3
trade surplus, p. 3
trade deficit, p. 3
bilateral trade balance, p. 3
value-added, p. 5
offshoring, p. 5
import tariffs, p. 8
gross domestic product (GDP), p. 10
trade barriers, p. 11
import quotas, p. 13
horizontal FDI, p. 21
vertical FDI, p. 21

PROBLEMS

1. Figures 1-2 and 1-7 rely on data from 2006, and Figure 1-6 relies on data from 2005, to map worldwide trade, migration, and foreign direct investment. Updated data for migration and foreign direct investment were not available at the time this chapter was written, but it is available for worldwide trade. In this question, you are asked to update the numbers for world trade shown in Table 1-1.

   a. Go to the World Trade Organization website at http://www.wto.org, and look for its trade data under "Resources" and "Statistics."[11] Look for the most recent edition of its *International Trade Statistics* publication, go to "Trade by region," and find the Excel spreadsheet with "Intra- and inter-regional merchandise trade." Print out this table.

      If you cannot find the website or spreadsheet, use the 2008 table for "Intra- and Inter-Regional Merchandise Trade" that appears below:

   b. From this table, what is the total amount of trade within Europe? What percentage of total world trade is this?

   c. What is the total amount of trade (in either direction) between Europe and North America? Add that to the total trade within Europe, and calculate the percentage of this to the world total.

   d. What is the total amount of trade within the Americas (i.e., between North America, Central America, South America, and within each of these regions)? What percentage of total world trade is this?

   e. What is the total value of exports from Europe and the Americas, and what percentage of the world total is this?

   f. What is the total value of exports from Asia, and what percentage of the world total is this?

   g. What is the total value of exports from the Middle East and the Commonwealth of Independent States,[12] and what percentage of the world total is this?

   h. What is the total value of exports from Africa, and what percentage of the world total is this?

   i. How do your answers to (b) through (h) compare with the shares of worldwide trade shown in Table 1-1?

Intra- and Inter-Regional Merchandise Trade, 2008 ($ billions)

	Destination							
Region of Origin	**North America**	**South and Central America**	**Europe**	**CIS**	**Africa**	**Middle East**	**Asia**	**World**
World	2,708	583	6,736	517	458	618	3903	15,717
North America	1,015	165	369	16	34	60	376	2,036
South and Central America	169	159	121	9	17	12	101	600
Europe	475	96	4,695	240	186	189	487	6,447
Commonwealth of Independent States (CIS)	36	10	406	135	11	25	77	703
Africa	122	19	218	2	53	14	114	558
Middle East	117	7	126	7	37	122	569	1,021
Asia	775	128	801	108	121	196	2181	4,353

Source: WTO, International Trade Statistics 2009.

[11] The trade statistics are available at http://www.wto.org/english/res_e/statis_e/its2009_e/its09_world_trade_dev_e.htm.

[12] The Commonwealth of Independent States consists of Azerbaijan, Armenia, Belarus, Georgia, Kazakhstan, Kyrgyzstan, Moldova, Russia, Tajikistan, Turkmenistan, Ukraine, and Uzbekistan.

2. The quotation from Federal Reserve Chairman Ben Bernanke at the beginning of the chapter is from a speech that he delivered in Jackson Hole, Wyoming, on August 25, 2006, titled "Global Economic Integration: What's New and What's Not?" The full transcript of the speech is available at http://www.federalreserve.gov/newsevents/speech/2006speech.htm. Read this speech and answer the following questions:
   a. List three ways in which international trade today is not that different from the trade that occurred before World War I.
   b. List three ways in which international trade today does differ from the trade that occurred before World War I.

NET WORK

The World Trade Organization is a good source for international trade statistics. Go to its website at http://www.wto.org, and look for trade data under "Resources" and "Statistics." Look for the most recent edition of its *International Trade Statistics* publication, and find the value for world trade in goods and in services for the most recent year provided.

2

Trade and Technology: The Ricardian Model

England exported cloth in exchange for wine, because, by so doing her industry was rendered more productive to her; she had more cloth and wine than if she had manufactured both for herself; and Portugal imported cloth and exported wine, because the industry of Portugal could be more beneficially employed for both countries in producing wine. . . .

It would therefore be advantageous for [Portugal] to export wine in exchange for cloth. This exchange might even take place, notwithstanding that the commodity imported by Portugal could be produced there with less labour than in England.

David Ricardo, *On the Principles of Political Economy and Taxation*, 1821

Comparative advantage is the best example of an economic principle that is undeniably true yet not obvious to intelligent people.

Paul Samuelson, "The Way of an Economist," 1969[1]

Pick any manufactured product, and you will most likely find that it is traded among a number of countries. Let's choose snowboards as an example. In 2005 the United States **imported** (i.e., purchased from other countries) \$59 million of snowboards from 20 different countries; Table 2-1 identifies the 12 countries with the highest dollar amount of snowboard sales to the United States. In 2009 the value of snowboard imports to the United States had fallen to \$38.5 million. This fall occurred because the U.S. recession led to a large drop in imports for many products, including snowboards.

At the top of the list in Table 2-1 is China, **exporting** (i.e., selling to another country) more than \$18 million worth of snowboards to the United States in 2005 and \$21 million in 2009. The second largest exporter to the United States is Austria, selling

[1] Samuelson, Paul A. 1969. "The Way of an Economist." In *International Economic Relations: Proceedings of the Third Congress of the International Economic Association*, edited by Paul A. Samuelson (London: Macmillan), pp. 1–11.

TABLE 2-1

U.S. Imports of Snowboards, 2005 and 2009

Rank	Country	Value of Imports 2005 ($ millions)	Value of Imports 2009 ($ millions)	Quantity of Snowboards 2009 (thousands)	Average Price 2009 ($/board)
1	China	18.15	21.30	365.0	58
2	Austria	17.77	11.04	104.0	106
3	Canada	9.11	3.94	51.8	76
4	Mexico	4.96	0.00	0.0	na
5	Spain	2.17	0.57	6.6	85
6	Poland	1.90	0.04	0.5	71
7	Tunisia	1.29	0.15	4.3	34
8	France	1.12	0.07	0.6	127
9	Germany	1.00	0.02	0.1	227
10	Taiwan	0.49	1.14	37.4	31
11	Bulgaria	0.30	0.00	0.0	na
12	Switzerland	0.18	0.08	0.7	113
13-20	All other countries	0.29	0.18	1.49	123
	Total	58.76	38.51	572	67

Source: U.S. Department of Commerce and the U.S. International Trade Commission.

AP Photo/David Zalubowski

Where did Shaun White's snowboard come from?

just under $18 million in 2005 and $11 million in 2009. Thus, although China was able to increase its exports even during the U.S. recession, exports from Austria fell. These two countries sell considerably more than the next country on the list, Canada (which sold $3.9 million of snowboards to the United States in 2009). The fourth largest exporter in 2005 was Mexico, selling $5 million of snowboards to the United States, but by 2009 this country does not appear on the list at all: it has been entirely replaced by sales from other countries, most likely China.

Then, a group consisting of mostly European countries—Spain, Poland, France, and Germany, as well as Tunisia, a country on the north coast of Africa that is a former colony of France—sold between $1 million and $2 million each to the United States in 2005. These countries sold less in 2009, and of the other countries shown only Taiwan (in addition to China) managed to increase its sales between these two years.[2] Table 2-1 shows that the value of imports to the United States has fallen in recent years and, in snowboards at least, has become more focused on exports from China and Taiwan. This pattern raises a question: With all the manufacturing capability in the United States, why does it purchase snowboards from these countries at all instead of producing them domestically?

[2] Two other countries not shown in Table 2-1, South Korea and the Ukraine, were able to export snowboards to the United States in 2009 even though they did not in 2005.

The first chapters of this book look at various reasons why countries trade goods with one another. These reasons include:

- Differences in the **technology** used in each country (i.e., differences in each country's ability to manufacture products)
- Differences in the total amount of **resources** (including labor, capital, and land) found in each country
- Differences in the costs of **offshoring** (i.e., producing the various parts of a good in different countries and then assembling it in a final location)
- The **proximity** of countries to each other (i.e., how close they are to one another)

In this chapter, we focus on the first of these reasons as an explanation for trade—technology differences across countries. This explanation is often called the **Ricardian model** because it was proposed by the nineteenth-century economist David Ricardo. This model explains how the level of a country's technology affects the wages paid to labor, such that countries with better technologies have higher wages. This, in turn, helps to explain how a country's technology affects its **trade pattern,** the products that it imports and exports.

1 Reasons for Trade

Besides technology differences across countries, which is the focus of the Ricardian model, there are many other reasons why countries trade goods. Before we get into the details of the Ricardian model, let's briefly explore the other reasons for trade.

Proximity

The proximity of countries is a reason for trade primarily because it affects the costs of transportation. Countries that are near one another will usually have lower shipping costs added to the cost of their traded goods. The proximity of countries to one another helps to explain why Canada is among the top exporters of snowboards to the United States and why Canada is the United States' largest trading partner overall. There are many other examples of how the closeness of countries affects trade partners. The largest trading partner of many European countries is another European country, and the largest trading partner of many Asian countries is Japan or China. Sometimes neighboring countries take advantage of their proximity by joining into a **free-trade area,** in which the countries have no restrictions on trade between them.

Resources

Proximity is only a partial explanation for trade patterns. As you can see in Table 2-1, Austria sells at least twice the value of snowboards to the United States as does Canada, despite being farther away, and Mexico went from selling one-half the value as Canada in 2005 to exporting none in 2009, even though it is just as close to the United States as Canada is. Why do Austria and Canada rank higher than Mexico in their sales of snowboards to the United States? Among other reasons, Austria and Canada have cold climates and mountains, making skiing and snowboarding very popular, in contrast to Mexico. In many cases, the local production of (and expertise for) ski and snowboard equipment develops as a result of being in a place where snow sports are common. This local production occurs because of either high demand for equipment or the ready supply of a complementary good (such as a snowy mountain). This is an example of how the geography of a country (mountains and climate, in this case) affects its exports. Ski resorts can also be found in many of the other countries listed in Table 2-1, including France, Switzerland, Spain, and Bulgaria.

Geography includes the **natural resources** (such as land and minerals) found in a country, as well as its **labor resources** (labor of various education and skill levels) and **capital** (machinery and structures). A country's resources are often collectively called its **factors of production,** the land, labor, and capital used to produce goods and services. In the next two chapters, we study how the resources of a country influence its trade patterns and how trade leads to economic gains or losses for different factors of production.

In some cases, a country can export a good without having any advantage in the natural resources needed to produce it. One example is "icewine," which is a type of wine invented in Germany but now also produced in the Niagara Falls region of Canada and the United States (see **Side Bar: Can Comparative Advantage Be Created? The Case of "Icewine"**). For snowboards, having mountains with ski resorts obviously does not apply to Mexico, Tunisia, and Taiwan, which are included among the top twelve sellers of snowboards to the United States in one year or the other. What explains these exports? A hint is provided by noticing that the wholesale price of a snowboard purchased by the United States from these countries is very low: in 2009 Tunisia and Taiwan sold snowboards to the United States for $34 and $31, respectively, and in 2005 Mexico's wholesale price was just $9. These prices are very low compared with the highest-priced countries shown, which are Germany ($227), France ($127), and Switzerland ($113). The very low prices from Mexico, Taiwan, and Tunisia indicate that the snowboards they sell to the United States are not finished products but unfinished boards imported into the United States for further processing. This type of trade in unfinished goods is an example of *offshoring*, a process in which a company spreads its production activities across several countries and trades semifinished products among them.

Absolute Advantage

We've now explained some possible reasons for many countries to export snowboards to the United States, but we haven't yet explained the imports from China, the largest exporter of snowboards to the United States, and from Germany, the ninth largest exporter in 2005 (and having the highest wholesale price in 2009). Germany has the Alps on its southern border, so natural resources are one reason it exports snowboards. Many people, however, may think the primary reason is that Germany has the world's best *technology* for producing snowboards. In fact, Germany is recognized as a world leader in the methods to produce many goods, including chemicals, machine tools, motor vehicles, and steel products. When a country has the best technology for producing a good, it has an **absolute advantage** in the production of that good. Germany has an absolute advantage in many industries, and it produces high-quality goods. But if Germany has an absolute advantage in producing snowboards, why does the United States import so many more snowboards from China, which uses less advanced technologies than Germany in most industries?

SIDE BAR

Can Comparative Advantage Be Created? The Case of "Icewine"

In Ricardo's original example of trade between Portugal and England, he gave Portugal an absolute advantage in both wine and cloth, based on its favorable climate. England would find it very difficult to grow grapes for wine and not so difficult to produce cloth, so it had a comparative advantage in cloth. This raises the question: What if a new technology could be discovered that would allow England to produce world-class grapes and wine? Would it be possible for it to create a new comparative advantage in wine?

Something like this occurred in the Niagara Falls region of Canada, which sells a product called "icewine." First developed in Germany in 1794 (when Ricardo was 21 years old), icewine is produced by allowing grapes to freeze on the vine. Freezing concentrates the sugars and flavors of the grapes, which are picked by hand and then processed into a sweet dessert wine. In 1983 several wineries in the Niagara Falls region of Canada experimented with producing this wine, and it has since taken off to become a local specialty. The cold climate of Niagara Falls offers an advantage in producing icewine, because the temperature should be –10°C to –13°C before picking. The yield from this process is very low—an entire vine might make only one bottle—which is why it is sold in half-bottles. But demand is high because of the unique flavor of this wine, and the half-bottles often sell for $50 or more. Icewine is now also being produced in the Okanagan Valley region of British Columbia, Canada, which similarly enjoys a climate warm enough in the summer to grow grapes and cold enough in the winter to freeze them. Will England ever be able to develop this wine? If so, the comparative advantage between England and Portugal in Ricardo's original model might be reversed!

AP Photo/Julie Jacobson

Harvesting frozen grapes to make icewine.

Furthermore, although Germany is a world leader in many technologies, so is the United States. So why should the United States import snowboards from Germany or China at all? Why doesn't it just produce all the snowboards it needs with U.S. technology and factors of production?

Comparative Advantage

These questions indicate that absolute advantage is not, in fact, a good explanation for trade patterns. This is one of the key lessons from this chapter. Instead, **comparative advantage** is the primary explanation for trade among countries. To get an idea of what comparative advantage means, let us consider the example of trade between Portugal and England, as described by David Ricardo (see **Side Bar: David Ricardo and Mercantilism**).

To keep things simple, Ricardo considered just two commodities: wine and cloth. Ricardo allowed Portugal to have an absolute advantage in the production of both goods. Portugal's absolute advantage may reflect, for example, its more favorable climate for growing grapes and raising sheep. Even though Portugal can produce wine and cloth more easily than England, England is still able to produce both cloth and wine, but it is *relatively more difficult* to produce wine in England than cloth—as any visitor to England will know, it lacks the regular sunshine needed to produce good grapes! Based on these assumptions, Ricardo argued that England would have a

SIDE BAR

David Ricardo and Mercantilism

David Ricardo (1772–1823) was one of the great classical economists, and the first model we study in this book is named after him. At the time that Ricardo was writing, there was a school of economic thought known as *mercantilism.* Mercantilists believed that exporting (selling goods to other countries) was good because it generated gold and silver for the national treasury and that importing (buying goods from other countries) was bad because it drained gold and silver from the national treasury. To ensure that a country exported a lot and imported only a little, the mercantilists were in favor of high *tariffs* (taxes that must be paid at the border when a good is imported). The mercantilist school of thought was discredited shortly after the time that Ricardo wrote, but some of these old ideas are still advocated today. For example, the United States sometimes insists that other countries should buy more from its companies and sometimes restricts import purchases from other countries; proponents of these ideas are called "mercantilists."

Ricardo was interested in showing that countries could benefit from international trade without having to use tariffs and without requiring exports to be higher than imports. He considered a case that contrasted sharply with what mercantilists believed to be best for a nation: in his writings about trade, Ricardo assumed that the value of exports equaled the value of imports (a situation called *balanced trade*) and that countries engaged in *free trade,* with no tariffs or other restrictions to limit the flow of goods across borders. Under these assumptions, can international trade benefit every country? Ricardo showed that it could. All countries gain from trade by exporting the goods in which they have comparative advantage.

David Ricardo.

Ricardo's ideas are so important that it will take some time to explain how and why they work. It is no exaggeration to say that many of the major international institutions in the world today, including the United Nations, the World Bank, and the World Trade Organization, are founded at least in part on the idea that free trade between countries brings gains for all trading partners. This idea comes from the writings of David Ricardo (and Adam Smith, a great classical economist of the eighteenth century).

comparative advantage in producing cloth and would export cloth to Portugal, whereas Portugal would have comparative advantage in producing wine and would export wine to England.

From this example, we can see that a country has comparative advantage in producing those goods that it produces best *compared with* how well it produces other goods. That is, Portugal is better at producing wine than cloth, and England is better at producing cloth than wine, even though Portugal is better than England at producing both goods. This is the idea behind the quotation from Ricardo at the start of the chapter—it will be advantageous for Portugal to import cloth from England because England has a comparative advantage in cloth. In our snowboard example, we would expect that China has a disadvantage compared with Germany or the United States in producing many manufactured goods, but it is still better at producing snowboards than some other goods, so it is able to export snowboards to the United States.

It will take us most of the chapter to explain the concept of comparative advantage and why it works as an explanation for trade patterns. As indicated by the other quotation at the beginning of the chapter, from Nobel laureate Paul Samuelson, this concept is far from obvious, and students who master it will have come a long way in their study of international trade.

2 Ricardian Model

In developing the Ricardian model of trade, we will work with an example similar to that used by Ricardo; instead of wine and cloth, however, the two goods will be wheat and cloth. Wheat and other grains (including barley, rice, and so on) are major exports of the United States and Europe, while many types of cloth are imported into these countries. In our example, the home country (we will call it just "Home") will end up with this trade pattern, exporting wheat and importing cloth.

The Home Country

To simplify our example, we will ignore the role of land and capital and suppose that both goods are produced with labor alone. At Home, one worker can produce 4 bushels of wheat or 2 yards of cloth. This production can be expressed in terms of the **marginal product of labor (MPL)** for each good. Recall from your study of microeconomics that the marginal product of labor is the extra output obtained by using one more unit of labor.[3] In Home, one worker produces 4 bushels of wheat, so $MPL_W = 4$. Alternatively, one worker can produce 2 yards of cloth, so $MPL_C = 2$.

Home Production Possibilities Frontier Using the marginal products for producing wheat and cloth, we can graph Home's **production possibilities frontier (PPF)**. Suppose there are $\overline{L} = 25$ workers in the home country (the bar over the letter L indicates our assumption that the amount of labor in Home stays constant). If all these workers were employed in wheat, they could produce $Q_W = MPL_W \cdot \overline{L} = 4 \cdot 25 = 100$ bushels. Alternatively, if they were all employed in cloth, they could produce $Q_C = MPL_C \cdot \overline{L} = 2 \cdot 25 = 50$ yards. The production possibilities frontier is a straight line between these two points at the corners, as shown in Figure 2-1.

The straight-line PPF, a special feature of the Ricardian model, follows from the assumption that the marginal products of labor are *constant*. That is, regardless of how much wheat or cloth is already being produced, one extra hour of labor yields an additional 4 bushels of wheat or 2 yards of cloth. There are *no diminishing returns* in the Ricardian model because it ignores the role of land and capital.

Given this property, the slope of the PPF in Figure 2-1 can be calculated as the ratio of the quantity of cloth produced to the quantity of wheat produced at the corners, as follows:

$$\text{Slope of PPF} = -\frac{50}{100} = -\frac{MPL_C \cdot \overline{L}}{MPL_W \cdot \overline{L}} = -\frac{MPL_C}{MPL_W} = -\frac{1}{2}$$

Ignoring the minus sign, the slope equals the ratio of marginal products of the two goods. The slope is also the **opportunity cost** of wheat, the amount of cloth that must be given up to obtain one more unit of wheat.[4] To see this, suppose that Q_W is increased by 1 bushel. It takes one worker to produce 4 bushels of wheat, so

---

[3] A special assumption of the Ricardian model is that there are no diminishing returns to labor, so the marginal product of labor is constant. That assumption will no longer be made in the next chapter, when we introduce capital and land, along with labor, as factors of production.

[4] Notice that the slope of the PPF is the opportunity cost of the good on the *horizontal* axis—wheat, in this case.

FIGURE 2-1

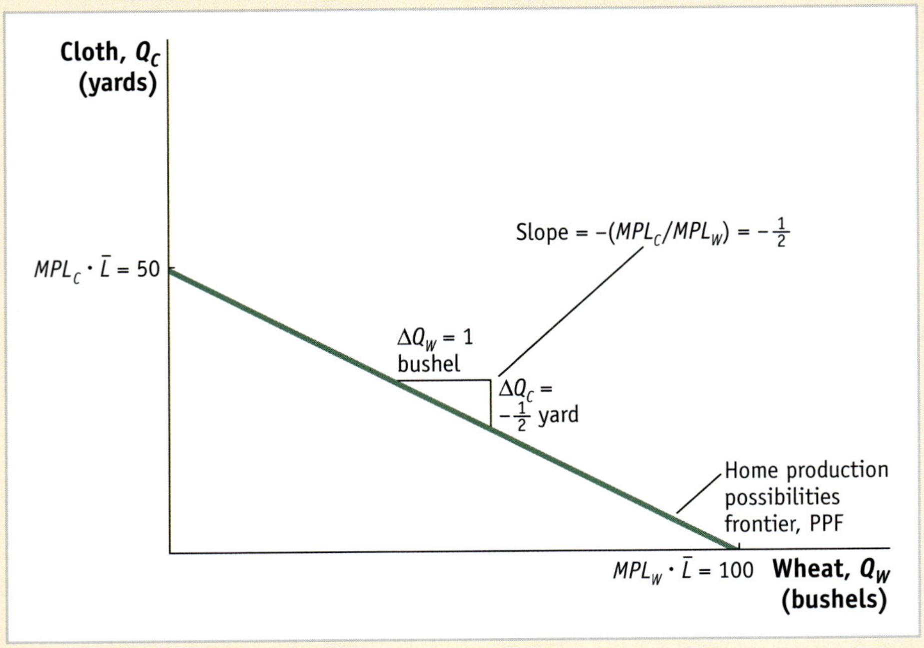

Home Production Possibilities Frontier The Home PPF is a straight line between 50 yards of cloth and 100 bushels of wheat. The slope of the PPF equals the negative of the opportunity cost of wheat; that is, the amount of cloth that must be given up ($\frac{1}{2}$ yard) to obtain 1 more bushel of wheat. Equivalently, the magnitude of the slope can be expressed as the ratio of the marginal products of labor for the two goods.

increasing Q_W by 1 bushel means that one-quarter of a worker's time must be withdrawn from the cloth industry and shifted into wheat production. This shift would reduce cloth output by $\frac{1}{2}$ yard, the amount of cloth that could have been produced by one-quarter of a worker's time. Thus, $\frac{1}{2}$ yard of cloth is the opportunity cost of obtaining 1 more bushel of wheat and is the slope of the PPF.

Home Indifference Curve With this production possibilities frontier, what combination of wheat and cloth will Home actually produce? The answer depends on the country's demand for each of the two goods. There are several ways to represent demand in the Home economy, but we will start by using **indifference curves.** Each indifference curve shows the combinations of two goods, such as wheat and cloth, that a person or economy can consume and be equally satisfied.

In Figure 2-2, the consumer is indifferent between points A and B, for example. Both of these points lie on an indifference curve U_1 associated with a given level of satisfaction, or **utility.** Point C lies on a higher indifference curve U_2, indicating that it gives a higher level of utility, whereas point D lies on a lower indifference curve U_0, indicating that it gives a lower level of utility. It is common to use indifference curves to reflect the utility that an individual consumer receives from various consumption points. In Figure 2-2, we go a step further, however, and apply this idea to an entire country. That is, the indifference curves in Figure 2-2 show the preferences of an entire country. The combinations of wheat and cloth on U_0 give consumers in the country lower utility than the combinations on indifference curve U_1, which in turn gives lower utility than the combinations of wheat and cloth on U_2.

FIGURE 2-2

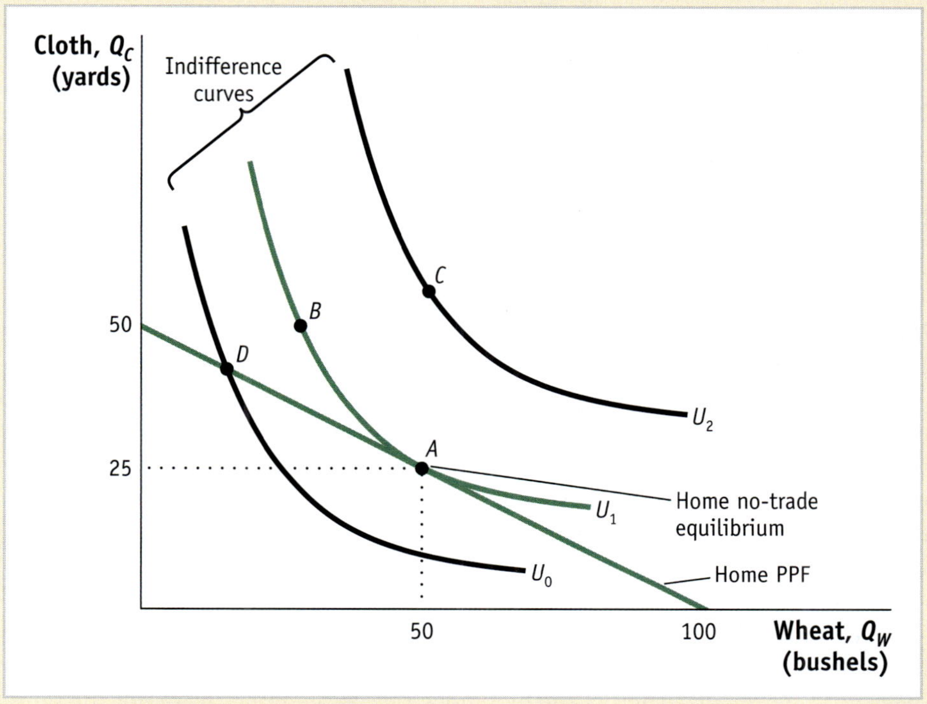

Home Equilibrium with No Trade Points *A* and *B* lie on the same indifference curve and give the Home consumers the level of utility, U_1. The highest level of Home utility on the PPF is obtained at point *A*, which is the no-trade equilibrium. Point *D* is also on the PPF but would give lower utility. Point *C* represents a higher utility level but is off of the PPF, so it is not attainable in the absence of international trade.

Home Equilibrium In the absence of international trade, the production possibilities frontier acts like a budget constraint for the country, and with perfectly competitive markets, the economy will produce at the point of highest utility subject to the limits imposed by its PPF. The point of highest utility is at point *A* in Figure 2-2, where Home consumes 25 yards of cloth and 50 bushels of wheat. This bundle of goods gives Home the highest level of utility possible (indifference curve U_1) given the limits of its PPF. Notice that Home could produce at other points such as point *D*, but this point would give a lower level of utility than point *A* (i.e., point *D* would offer lower utility because U_0 is lower than U_1). Other consumption points, such as *C*, would give higher levels of utility than point *A* but cannot be obtained in the absence of international trade because they lie outside of Home's PPF.

We will refer to point *A* as the "no-trade" or the "pre-trade" equilibrium for Home.[5] What we really mean by this phrase is "no *international* trade." The Home country is able to reach point *A* by having its own firms produce wheat and cloth and sell these goods to its own consumers. We are assuming that there are many firms in each of the wheat and cloth industries, so the firms act under perfect competition and take the market prices for wheat and cloth as given. The idea that perfectly competitive markets lead to the highest level of well-being for consumers—as illustrated by

[5] We also refer to point *A* as the "autarky equilibrium," because "autarky" means a situation in which the country does not engage in international trade.

the highest level of utility at point A—is an example of the "invisible hand" that Adam Smith (1723–1790) wrote about in his famous book *The Wealth of Nations*. Like an invisible hand, competitive markets lead firms to produce the amount of goods that results in the highest level of well-being for consumers.

Opportunity Cost and Prices Whereas the slope of the PPF reflects the opportunity cost of producing one more bushel of wheat, under perfect competition the opportunity cost of wheat should also equal the relative price of wheat, as follows from the economic principle that price reflects the opportunity cost of a good. We can now check that this equality between the opportunity cost and the relative price of wheat holds at point A.

Wages We solve for the prices of wheat and cloth using an indirect approach, by first reviewing how wages are determined. In competitive labor markets, firms hire workers up to the point at which the cost of one more hour of labor (the wage) equals the value of one more hour of production. In turn, the value of one more hour of labor equals the amount of goods produced in that hour (the marginal product of labor) times the price of the good (P_W for the price of wheat and P_C for the price of cloth). That is to say, in the wheat industry, labor will be hired up to the point at which the wage equals $P_W \cdot MPL_W$, and in the cloth industry labor will be hired up to the point at which the wage equals $P_C \cdot MPL_C$.

If we assume that labor is perfectly free to move between these two industries and that workers will choose to work in the industry for which the wage is highest, then wages must be equalized across the two industries. If the wages were not the same in the two industries, laborers in the low-wage industry would have an incentive to move to the high-wage industry; this would, in turn, lead to an abundance of workers and a decrease in the wage in the high-wage industry and a scarcity of workers and an increase in the wage in the low-wage industry. This movement of labor would continue until wages are equalized between the two industries.

We can use the equality of the wage across industries to obtain the following equation:

$$P_W \cdot MPL_W = P_C \cdot MPL_C$$

By rearranging terms, we see that

$$P_W / P_C = MPL_C / MPL_W$$

The right-hand side of this equation is the slope of the production possibilities frontier (the opportunity cost of obtaining one more bushel of wheat) and the left-hand side of the equation is the **relative price** of wheat, as we will explain in the next paragraph. This equation says that the relative price of wheat (on the left) and opportunity cost of wheat (on the right) must be equal in the no-trade equilibrium at point A.

To understand why we measure the relative price of wheat as the ratio P_W/P_C, suppose that a bushel of wheat costs \$3 and a yard of cloth costs \$6. Then \$3/\$6 = $\frac{1}{2}$, which shows that the relative price of wheat is $\frac{1}{2}$, that is, $\frac{1}{2}$ of a yard of cloth (or half of \$6) must be given up to obtain 1 bushel of wheat (the price of which is \$3). A price ratio like P_W/P_C always denotes the relative price of the good in the numerator (wheat, in this case), measured in terms of how much of the good in the denominator (cloth) must be given up. In Figure 2-2, the slope of the PPF equals the relative price of wheat, the good on the *horizontal axis*.

The Foreign Country

Now let's introduce another country, Foreign, into the model. We will assume that Foreign's technology is inferior to Home's so that it has an absolute *disadvantage* in producing both wheat and cloth as compared with Home. Nevertheless, once we introduce international trade, we will still find that Foreign will trade with Home.

Foreign Production Possibilities Frontier Suppose that one Foreign worker can produce 1 bushel of wheat ($MPL^*_W = 1$), or 1 yard of cloth ($MPL^*_C = 1$), whereas recall that a Home worker can produce 4 bushels of wheat or 2 yards of cloth. Suppose that there are $\bar{L}^* = 100$ workers available in the Foreign country. If all these workers were employed in wheat, they could produce $MPL^*_W \cdot \bar{L}^* = 100$ bushels, and if they were all employed in cloth, they could produce $MPL^*_C \cdot \bar{L}^* = 100$ yards. Foreign's production possibilities frontier (PPF) is thus a straight line between these two points, with a slope of –1, as shown in Figure 2-3.

You might find it helpful to think of the Home country in our example as the United States or Europe and the Foreign country as the "rest of the world." Empirical evidence supports the idea that the United States and Europe have the leading technologies in many goods and an absolute advantage in the production of both wheat and cloth. Nevertheless, they import much of their clothing and textiles from abroad, especially from Asia and Latin America. Why does the United States or Europe import these goods from abroad when they have superior technology at home? To answer this question, we want to focus on the *comparative advantage* of Home and Foreign in producing the two goods.

FIGURE 2-3

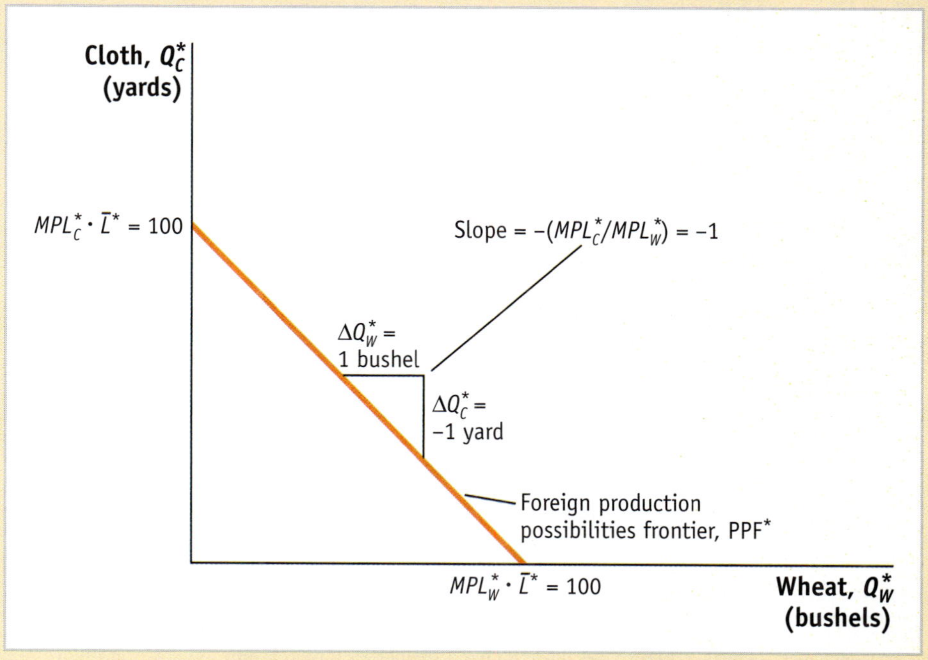

Foreign Production Possibilities Frontier The Foreign PPF is a straight line between 100 yards of cloth and 100 bushels of wheat. The slope of the PPF equals the negative of the opportunity cost of wheat; that is, the amount of cloth that must be given up (1 yard) to obtain 1 more bushel of wheat.

Comparative Advantage In Foreign, it takes one worker to produce 1 bushel of wheat or 1 yard of cloth. Therefore, the opportunity cost of producing 1 yard of cloth is 1 bushel of wheat. In Home, one worker produces 2 yards of cloth or 4 bushels of wheat. Therefore, Home's opportunity cost of a bushel of wheat is $\frac{1}{2}$ a yard of cloth, and its opportunity cost of a yard of cloth is 2 bushels of wheat. Based on this comparison, Foreign has a *comparative advantage in producing cloth* because its opportunity cost of cloth (which is 1 bushel of wheat) is *lower* than Home's opportunity cost of cloth (which is 2 bushels of wheat). Conversely, Home has a *comparative advantage in producing wheat* because Home's opportunity cost of wheat (which is $\frac{1}{2}$ yard of cloth) is lower than Foreign's (1 yard of cloth). In general, a country has a comparative advantage in a good when it has a lower opportunity cost of producing it than does the other country. Notice that Foreign has a comparative advantage in cloth even though it has an absolute disadvantage in both goods.

As before, we can represent Foreign's preferences for wheat and cloth with indifference curves like those shown in Figure 2-4. With competitive markets, the economy will produce at the point of highest utility for the country, point A^*, which is the no-trade equilibrium in Foreign. The slope of the PPF, which equals the opportunity cost of wheat, also equals the relative price of wheat.[6] Therefore, in Figure 2-4,

FIGURE 2-4

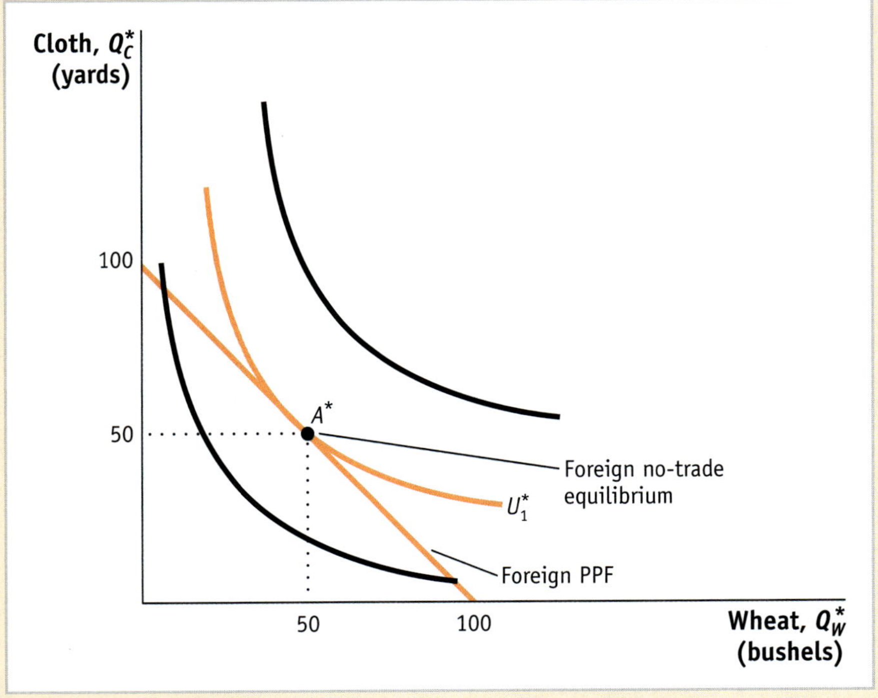

Foreign Equilibrium with No Trade The highest level of Foreign utility on the PPF is obtained at point A^*, which is the no-trade equilibrium.

[6] Remember that the slope of the PPF (ignoring the minus sign) equals the relative price of the good on the *horizontal* axis—wheat in Figure 2-4. Foreign has a steeper PPF than Home as shown in Figure 2-2, so Foreign's relative price of wheat is higher than Home's. The inverse of the relative price of wheat is the relative price of cloth, which is lower in Foreign.

Foreign's no-trade relative price of wheat is $P^*_W/P^*_C = 1$. Notice that this relative price *exceeds* Home's no-trade relative price of wheat, which is $P_W/P_C = \frac{1}{2}$. This difference in these relative prices reflects the comparative advantage that Home has in the production of wheat.[7]

APPLICATION

Comparative Advantage in Apparel, Textiles, and Wheat

The U.S. textile and apparel industries face intense import competition, especially from Asia and Latin America. Employment in this industry in the United States fell from about 1.5 million people in 1990 to less than 1 million in 1999. An example of this import competition can be seen from one U.S. fabric manufacturer, Burlington Industries, which announced in January 1999 that it would reduce its production capacity by 25% because of increased imports from Asia. Burlington closed seven plants and laid off 2,900 people, about 17% of its domestic force. After the layoffs, Burlington Industries employed 17,400 people in the United States. With 1999 sales of \$1.6 billion, this means that its sales per employee were \$1.6 billion/17,400 = \$92,000 per worker. This is exactly at the average for all U.S. apparel producers, as shown in Table 2-2. The textile industry, producing the fabric and material inputs for apparel, is even more productive, with annual sales per employee of \$140,000 in the United States.

In comparison, the average worker in China produces \$13,500 of sales per year in the apparel industry and \$9,000 in the textile industry. Thus, a worker in the United

TABLE 2-2

Apparel, Textiles, and Wheat in the United States and China This table shows sales per employee for the apparel and textile industries in the United States and China, as well as bushels per hour in producing wheat. The United States has an absolute advantage in all these products (as shown by the numbers in the right-hand column of the table), but it has a comparative advantage in producing wheat (as shown by the numbers in the bottom rows of the table).

	United States	China	Absolute Advantage
	Sales/Employee	*Sales/Employee*	*U.S./China Ratio*
Apparel	\$92,000	\$13,500	7
Textiles	\$140,000	\$9,000	16
	Bushels/Hour	*Bushels/Hour*	*U.S./China Ratio*
Wheat	27.5	0.1	275
	Comparative Advantage		
Wheat/apparel ratio × 1,000	0.3	0.01	
Wheat/textile ratio × 1,000	0.2	0.01	

Note: Data are for years around 1995.

Source: Wheat data from Colin Carter, University of California, Davis; apparel/textiles data from various sources.

[7] Taking the reciprocal of the relative price of wheat in each country, we also see that Foreign's no-trade relative price of cloth is $P^*_C/P^*_W = 1$, which is less than Home's no-trade relative price of cloth, $P_C/P_W = 2$. Therefore, Foreign has a comparative advantage in cloth.

States produces \$92,000/\$13,500 = 7 times more apparel sales than a worker in China and \$140,000/\$9,000 = 16 times more textile sales. This ratio is shown in Table 2-2 in the column labeled "Absolute Advantage." It illustrates how much more productive U.S. labor is in these industries relative to Chinese labor. The United States clearly has an absolute advantage in both these industries, so why does it import so much of its textiles and apparel from Asia, including China?

The answer can be seen by also comparing the productivities in the wheat industry. The typical wheat farmer in California devotes only 1.35 hours per acre to growing a crop of wheat, and an acre provides 37 bushels of wheat, a marginal product of 37/1.35 = 27.5 bushels per hour of labor. In comparison, the typical wheat farmer in China obtains only one-tenth of a bushel per hour of labor, so the U.S. farmer is 27.5/0.1 = 275 times more productive! The United States clearly has an *absolute advantage* in all these industries.

But China has the *comparative advantage* in both apparel and textiles, as illustrated by the rows labeled "Comparative Advantage." To keep the calculations simple, suppose that a farmer spends 1,000 hours per year growing a crop of wheat. Multiplying the marginal product of an hour of labor in wheat by 1,000, to obtain the marginal product of labor per year, and dividing by the marginal product of labor in apparel give us the *opportunity cost of apparel*. In the United States, for example, this ratio is 27,500/92,000 ≈ 0.3 bushels/\$, indicating that 0.3 bushels of wheat must be foregone to obtain an extra dollar of sales in apparel. In textiles, the U.S. ratio is 27,500/140,000 ≈ 0.2 bushels/\$, so that 0.2 bushels of wheat must be foregone to obtain an extra dollar in textile sales. But these ratios are much smaller in China: only 100/13,500 or 100/9,000 ≈ 0.01 bushels of wheat must be foregone to obtain \$1 of extra sales in either textiles or apparel. As a result, China has a lower opportunity cost of both textiles and apparel than the United States, which explains why it exports those goods, while the United States exports wheat, just as predicted by the Ricardian model. ■

3 Determining the Pattern of International Trade

Now that we have examined each country in the absence of trade, we can start to analyze what happens when goods are traded between them. We will see that a country's no-trade relative price determines which product it will export and which it will import when trade is opened. As we have shown earlier, the no-trade relative price in each country equals its opportunity cost of producing that good. Therefore, the pattern of exports and imports will be determined by the opportunity costs of production in each country, or by each country's pattern of comparative advantage. This section examines why this is the case and details each country's choice of how much to produce, consume, and trade of each good.

International Trade Equilibrium

The differences in no-trade prices across the countries create an opportunity for international trade between them. In particular, producers of cloth in Foreign, where the relative price of cloth is $P^*_C/P^*_W = 1$, would want to export cloth to Home, where the relative price, $P_C/P_W = 2$, is higher. Conversely, producers of wheat in Home, where the relative price of wheat is $P_W/P_C = \frac{1}{2}$, would want to export wheat to Foreign, where the relative price of $P^*_W/P^*_C = 1$ is higher. The trade pattern that we expect to arise, then, is that *Home will export wheat*, and *Foreign will export cloth*. Notice that both countries export the good in which they have a comparative advantage, which is what the Ricardian model predicts.

To solidify our understanding of this trade pattern, let's be more careful about explaining where the two countries would produce on their PPFs under international trade and where they will consume. As Home exports wheat, the quantity of wheat sold at Home falls, and this condition bids up the price of wheat in the Home market. As the exported wheat arrives in the Foreign wheat market, more wheat is sold there, and the price of wheat in the Foreign market falls. Likewise, as Foreign exports cloth, the price of cloth in Foreign will be bid up and the price of cloth in Home will fall. The two countries are in an **international trade equilibrium,** or just "trade equilibrium," for short, when the relative price of wheat is the same in the two countries, which means that the relative price of cloth is also the same in both countries.[8]

To fully understand the international trade equilibrium, we are interested in two issues: (1) determining the relative price of wheat (or cloth) in the trade equilibrium and (2) seeing how the shift from the no-trade equilibrium to the trade equilibrium affects production and consumption in both Home and Foreign. Addressing the first issue requires some additional graphs, so let's delay this discussion for a moment and suppose for now that the relative price of wheat in the trade equilibrium is established at a level between the pre-trade prices in the two countries. This assumption is consistent with the bidding up of export prices and bidding down of import prices, as discussed previously. Since the no-trade prices were $P_W/P_C = \frac{1}{2}$ in Home and $P^*_W/P^*_C = 1$ in Foreign, let's suppose that the world relative price of wheat is between these two values, say, at $\frac{2}{3}$. Given the change in relative prices from their pre-trade level to the international trade equilibrium, what happens to production and consumption in each of the two countries?

Change in Production and Consumption The world relative price of wheat that we have assumed is higher than Home's pre-trade price ($\frac{2}{3} > \frac{1}{2}$). This relationship between the pre-trade and world relative prices means that Home producers of wheat can earn more than the opportunity cost of wheat (which is $\frac{1}{2}$) by selling their wheat to Foreign. For this reason, Home will shift its labor resources toward the production of wheat and produce more wheat than it did in the pre-trade equilibrium (point *A* in Figure 2-5). To check that this intuition is correct, let us explore the incentives for labor to work in each of Home's industries.

Recall that Home wages paid in the wheat industry equal $P_W \cdot MPL_W$, and wages paid in the cloth industry equal $P_C \cdot MPL_C$. We know that the relative price of wheat in the trade equilibrium is $P_W/P_C = \frac{2}{3}$, that the marginal product of labor in the Home wheat industry is $MPL_W = 4$, and that the marginal product of labor in the Home cloth industry is $MPL_C = 2$. We can plug these numbers into the formulas for wages to compute the *ratio* of wages in the two industries as

$$\frac{P_W \cdot MPL_W}{P_C \cdot MPL_C} = \left(\frac{2}{3}\right)\left(\frac{4}{2}\right) = \frac{8}{6} > 1, \text{ so that } P_W \cdot MPL_W > P_C \cdot MPL_C$$

---

[8] Notice that if the relative price of wheat P_W/P_C is the same in the two countries, then the relative price of cloth, which is just its inverse (P_C/P_W), is also the same.

FIGURE 2-5

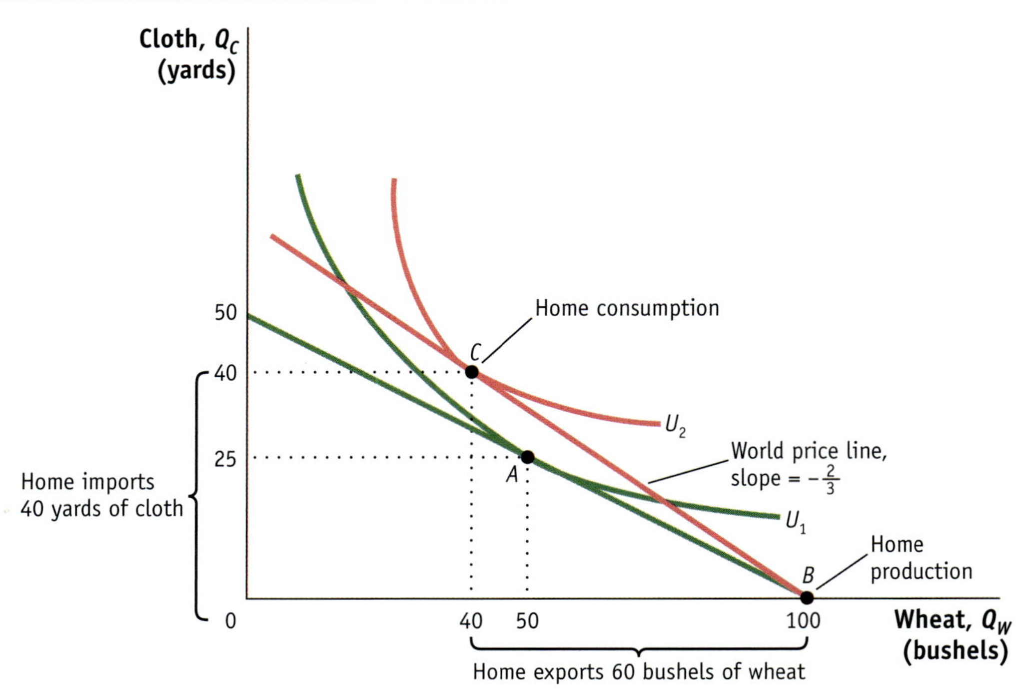

Home Equilibrium with Trade With a world relative price of wheat of $\frac{2}{3}$, Home production will occur at point *B*. Through international trade, Home is able to export each bushel of wheat it produces in exchange for $\frac{2}{3}$ yard of cloth. As wheat is exported, Home moves up the world price line, *BC*. Home consumption occurs at point *C*, at the tangent intersection with indifference curve, U_2, since this is the highest possible utility curve on the world price line. Given these levels of production and consumption, we can see that total exports are 60 bushels of wheat in exchange for imports of 40 yards of cloth and also that Home consumes 10 fewer bushels of wheat and 15 more yards of cloth relative to its pre-trade levels.

This formula tells us that with the world relative price of wheat of $\frac{2}{3}$, wages paid in Home's wheat industry ($P_W \cdot MPL_W$) are greater than those paid in its cloth industry ($P_C \cdot MPL_C$). Accordingly, all of Home's workers will want to work in the wheat industry, and no cloth will be produced. With trade, the Home economy will be fully specialized in wheat production, as occurs at production point *B* in Figure 2-5.[9]

International Trade Starting at the production point *B*, Home can export wheat at a relative price of $\frac{2}{3}$. This means that for 1 bushel of wheat exported to Foreign, it receives $\frac{2}{3}$ yard of cloth in exchange. In Figure 2-5, we can trace out its international trades by starting at point *B* and then exchanging 1 bushel of wheat for $\frac{2}{3}$ yard of cloth, another bushel of wheat for $\frac{2}{3}$ yard of cloth, and so on. From point *B*, this traces out the line toward point *C*, with slope $-\frac{2}{3}$. We will call the line starting at point *B* (the

[9] The fully specialized economy (producing only wheat) is a special feature of the Ricardian model because of its straight-line production possibilities frontier.

production point) and with a slope equal to the negative of the world relative price of wheat, the **world price line,** as shown by *BC*. The world price line shows the range of *consumption possibilities* that a country can achieve by specializing in one good (wheat, in Home's case) and engaging in international trade (exporting wheat and importing cloth). We can think of the world price line as a new budget constraint for the country under international trade.

Notice that this budget constraint (the line *BC*) lies *above* Home's original PPF. The ability to engage in international trade creates consumption possibilities for Home that were not available in the absence of trade, when the consumption point had to be on Home's PPF. Now, Home can choose to consume at any point on the world price line, and utility is maximized at the point corresponding to the intersection with the highest indifference curve, labeled *C* with a utility of U_2. Home obtains a higher utility with international trade than in the absence of international trade (U_2 is higher than U_1); the finding that Home's utility increases with trade is our first demonstration of the **gains from trade,** by which we mean the ability of a country to obtain higher utility for its citizens under free trade than with no trade.

Pattern of Trade and Gains from Trade Comparing production point *B* with consumption point *C*, we see that Home is exporting 100 – 40 = 60 bushels of wheat, in exchange for 40 yards of cloth imported from Foreign. If we value the wheat at its international price of $\frac{2}{3}$, then the value of the exported wheat is $\frac{2}{3} \cdot 60 = 40$ yards of cloth, and the value of the imported cloth is also 40 yards of cloth. Because Home's exports equal its imports, this outcome shows that Home's trade is balanced.

What happens in Foreign when trade occurs? Foreign's production and consumption points are shown in Figure 2-6. The world relative price of wheat ($\frac{2}{3}$) is less than Foreign's pre-trade relative price of wheat (which is 1). This difference in relative prices causes workers to leave wheat production and move into the cloth industry. Foreign specializes in cloth production at point B^*, and from there, trades along the world price line with a slope of (negative) $\frac{2}{3}$, which is the relative price of wheat. That is, Foreign exchanges $\frac{2}{3}$ yard of cloth for 1 bushel of wheat, then $\frac{2}{3}$ yard of cloth for another 1 bushel of wheat, and so on repeatedly, as it moves down the world price line B^*C^*. The consumption point that maximizes Foreign's utility is C^*, at which point 60 units of each good are consumed and utility is U_2^*. Foreign's utility is greater than it was in the absence of international trade (U_2^* is a higher indifference curve than U_1^*), as is true for Home. Therefore, both countries gain from trade.

Foreign produces 100 yards of cloth at point B^*: it consumes 60 yards itself and exports 100 – 60 = 40 yards of cloth in exchange for 60 bushels of wheat imported from Home. This trade pattern is exactly the opposite of Home's, as must be the case. In our two-country world, everything leaving one country must arrive in the other. We see that Home is exporting wheat, in which it has a comparative advantage (Home's opportunity cost of wheat production is $\frac{1}{2}$ yard of cloth compared with 1 yard in Foreign). Furthermore, Foreign is exporting cloth, in which it has a comparative advantage (Foreign's opportunity cost of cloth production is 1 bushel of wheat compared with 2 bushels in Home). This outcome confirms that *the pattern of trade is determined by comparative advantage*, which is the first lesson of the Ricardian model. We have also established that there are *gains from trade for both countries*, which is the second lesson.

FIGURE 2-6

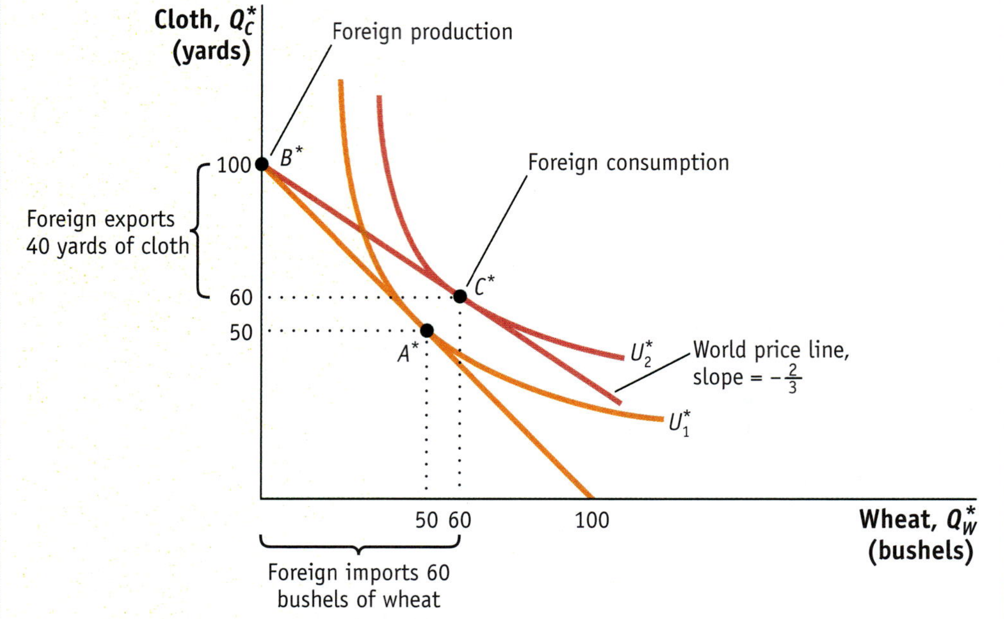

Foreign Equilibrium with Trade With a world relative price of wheat of $\frac{2}{3}$, Foreign production will occur at point B^*. Through international trade, Foreign is able to export $\frac{2}{3}$ yard of cloth in exchange for 1 bushel of wheat, moving down the world price line, B^*C^*. Foreign consumption occurs at point C^*, and total exports are 40 yards of cloth in exchange for imports of 60 bushels of wheat. Relative to its pre-trade wheat and cloth consumption (point A^*), Foreign consumes 10 more bushels of wheat and 10 more yards of cloth.

These two conclusions are often where the Ricardian model stops in its analysis of trade between countries, but the story is incomplete because we have not yet determined the level of wages across countries. We have seen that with trade, the relative price of each good converges to a single equilibrium price in both countries. Does the same occur with wages? As we now show, this is not the case. Wage levels differ across countries with trade, and wages are determined by *absolute* advantage, not *comparative* advantage. This is a third, less emphasized lesson from the Ricardian model, which we explore next.

Solving for Wages across Countries

To understand how wages are determined, we go back to microeconomics. In competitive labor markets, firms will pay workers the value of their marginal product. Home produces and exports wheat, so we can think of Home workers being paid in terms of that good: their real wage is $MPL_W = 4$ bushels of wheat. We refer to this payment as a "real" wage because it is measured in terms of a good that workers consume and not in terms of money. The workers can then sell the wheat they earn on the world market at the relative price of $P_W/P_C = \frac{2}{3}$. Thus, their real wage in terms of units of cloth is $(P_W/P_C) \cdot MPL_W = \frac{2}{3} \cdot 4 = \frac{8}{3}$ yard. Summing up, the Home wage is[10]

$$\text{Home wage} = \begin{cases} MPL_W = 4 \text{ bushels of wheat} \\ \text{or} \\ (P_W/P_C) \cdot MPL_W = \frac{8}{3} \text{ yard of cloth} \end{cases}$$

What happens to Foreign wages? Foreign produces and exports cloth, and the real wage is $MPL_C^* = 1$ yard of cloth. Because cloth workers can sell the cloth they earn for wheat on the world market at the price of $\frac{3}{2}$, their real wage in terms of units of wheat is $(P_C^*/P_W^*) \cdot MPL_C^* = (\frac{3}{2}) \cdot 1 = \frac{3}{2}$ bushel. Thus, the Foreign wage is[11]

$$\text{Foreign wage} = \begin{cases} (P_C^*/P_W^*) \cdot MPL_C = \frac{3}{2} \text{ bushels of wheat} \\ \text{or} \\ MPL_C = 1 \text{ yard of cloth} \end{cases}$$

Foreign workers earn less than Home workers as measured by their ability to purchase either good. This fact reflects Home's absolute advantage in the production of both goods.

Absolute Advantage As our example shows, wages are determined by absolute advantage: Home is paying higher wages because it has better technology in both goods. In contrast, the pattern of trade in the Ricardian model is determined by comparative advantage. Indeed, these two results go hand in hand—the only way that a country with poor technology can export at a price others are willing to pay is by having low wages.

This statement might sound like a pessimistic assessment of the ability of less developed countries to pay reasonable wages, but it carries with it a silver lining: as a country develops its technology, its wages will correspondingly rise. In the Ricardian model, a logical consequence of technological progress is that workers will become better off through receiving higher wages. In addition, as countries engage in international trade, the Ricardian model predicts that their real wages will rise.[12] We do not have to look very hard to see examples of this outcome in the world. Per capita income in China in 1978, just as that nation began to open up to international trade, is estimated to have been \$779, whereas 29 years later in 2007, per capita income in China had risen by more than 10 times to \$8,510. Likewise for India, per capita income more than doubled from \$1,430 in 1978 to \$3,826 in 2007.[13] Many people believe that the opportunity for these countries to engage in international trade has been crucial in raising their standard of living. As our study

---

[10] Recall that without international trade, Home wages were $MPL_W = 4$ bushels of wheat or $MPL_C = 2$ yards of cloth. Home workers are clearly better off with trade because they can afford to buy the same amount of wheat as before (4 bushels) but more cloth ($\frac{8}{3}$ yards instead of 2 yards). This is another way of demonstrating the gains from trade.

[11] Without international trade, Foreign wages were $MPL_W^* = 1$ bushel of wheat or $MPL_C^* = 1$ yard of cloth. Foreign workers are also better off with trade because they can afford to buy the same amount of cloth (1 yard) but more wheat ($\frac{3}{2}$ bushels instead of 1 bushel).

[12] That result is shown by the comparison of real wages in the trade equilibrium as compared with the no-trade equilibrium in each country, as is done in the previous two footnotes.

[13] These values are expressed in 2005 dollars and are taken from the Penn World Table version 6.3, http://pwt.econ.upenn.edu.

of international trade proceeds, we will try to identify the conditions that have allowed China, India, and many other developing countries to improve their standards of living through trade.

APPLICATION

Labor Productivity and Wages

The close connection between wages and labor productivity is evident by looking at data across countries. Labor productivity can be measured by the *value-added per hour* in manufacturing. Value-added is the difference between sales revenue in an industry and the costs of intermediate inputs (e.g., the difference between the value of a car and the cost of all the parts used to build it). Value-added then equals the payments to labor and capital in an industry. In the Ricardian model, we ignore capital, so we can measure labor productivity as value-added divided by the number of hours worked, or value-added per hour.

In Figure 2-7, we show the value-added per hour in manufacturing in 2001 for several different countries. The United States has the highest level of productivity and Taiwan has the lowest for the countries shown. Figure 2-7 also shows the wages per hour paid in each country. These are somewhat less than value-added per hour because value-added is also used to pay capital, but the general ranking of countries—from highest to lowest—in terms of labor productivity is the same as the ranking in terms of wages: countries with higher labor productivity pay higher wages, just as the Ricardian model predicts. The close connection between productivity and wages is also evident if we look at countries over time. These graphs are shown in Figure 2-8. We can see that the general upward movement in labor productivity is matched by upward movement in wages, as the Ricardian model predicts. ■

FIGURE 2-7

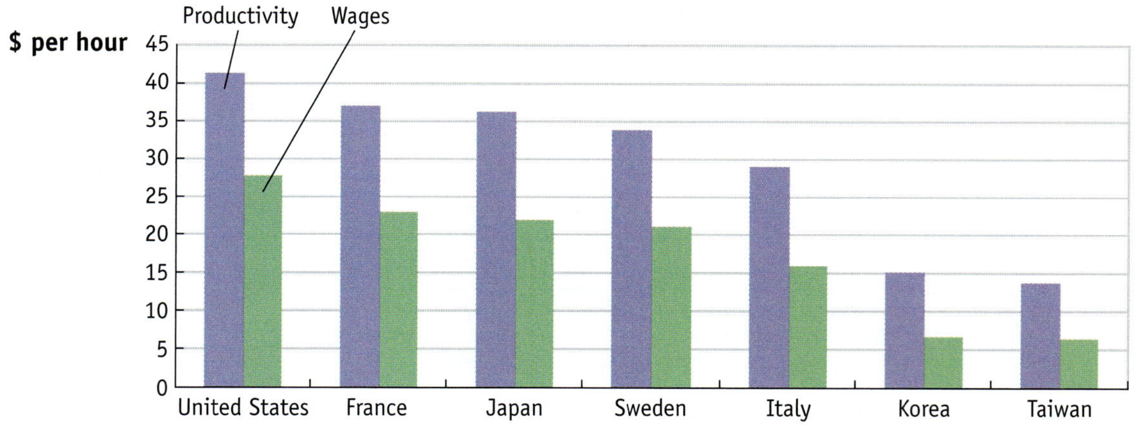

Labor Productivity and Wages, 2001 Labor productivity is measured by value-added per hour of work and can be compared with the wages paid in manufacturing in various countries. The general ranking of countries—from highest to lowest—in terms of labor productivity is the same as the ranking in terms of wages: countries with higher labor productivity pay higher wages, just as the Ricardian model predicts.

Source: U.S. Department of Labor, Bureau of Labor Statistics.

FIGURE 2-8

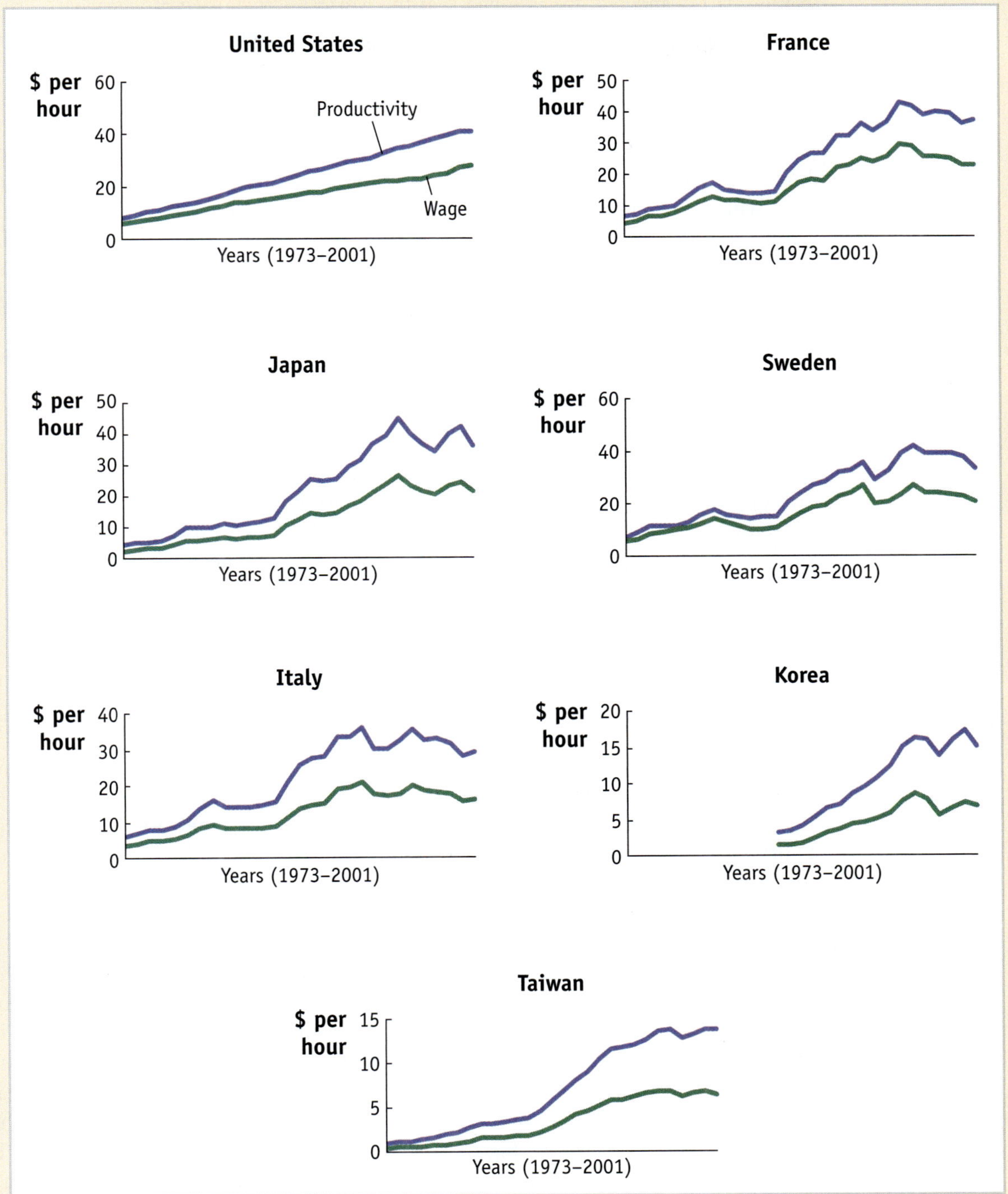

Labor Productivity and Wages over Time The trends in labor productivity and wages can also be graphed over time. The general upward movement in labor productivity is matched by upward movements in wages, as predicted by the Ricardian model.

Source: U.S. Department of Labor, Bureau of Labor Statistics.

4 Solving for International Prices

In Figures 2-5 and 2-6, we assumed that the world relative price of wheat was $\frac{2}{3}$ and that at this level Home's exports of wheat just equaled Foreign's imports of wheat (and vice versa for cloth). Now we will dig a little deeper to show how the world price is determined.

To determine the world relative price of wheat, we will use supply and demand curves. Home exports wheat, so we will derive a Home **export supply curve,** which shows the amount it wants to export at various relative prices. Foreign imports wheat, so we will derive a Foreign **import demand curve,** which shows the amount of wheat that it will import at various relative prices. The international trade equilibrium is the quantity and relative price at which Home exports equal Foreign imports of wheat. This equality occurs where the Home export supply curve intersects the Foreign import demand curve.

Home Export Supply Curve

In panel (a) of Figure 2-9, we repeat Figure 2-5, which shows the trade equilibrium for Home with production at point *B* and consumption at point *C*. At the world relative price of $P_W/P_C = \frac{2}{3}$, Home exports 60 bushels of wheat (the difference between wheat production of 100 and consumption of 40). We can use these numbers to construct a new graph, the Home export supply curve of wheat, shown in panel (b). The vertical axis in panel (b) measures the relative price of wheat and the horizontal axis measures the exports of wheat. The points *B* and *C* in panel (a), with the relative price of $P_W/P_C = \frac{2}{3}$ and Home exports of 60 bushels of wheat, now appear as point *C′* in panel (b), with $P_W/P_C = \frac{2}{3}$ on the vertical axis and Home wheat exports of 60 bushels on the horizontal axis. This is our first point on the Home export supply curve.

To derive other points on the export supply curve, consider the no-trade equilibrium in panel (a), which is shown by production and consumption at point *A*. The no-trade relative price of wheat is $\frac{1}{2}$ (the slope of Home's PPF), and Home exports of wheat are zero because there is no international trade. So the point *A* in panel (a) can be graphed at point *A′* in panel (b), with a relative price of $P_W/P_C = \frac{1}{2}$ and zero Home exports of wheat. This gives us a second point on the Home export supply curve.

To get a third point, let us keep the relative price of wheat at $P_W/P_C = \frac{1}{2}$, as in the no-trade equilibrium, but now allow Home to export some wheat in exchange for cloth at this price. Home consumption remains at point *A* in panel (a), but production can shift from that point. The reason that production can shift to another point on the PPF is that, with the relative price $P_W/P_C = \frac{1}{2}$, the wages of workers are equal in wheat and cloth. This result was shown in our earlier discussion. With wages equal in the two industries, workers are willing to shift between them, so any point on the PPF is a possible production point. Consider, for example, production at point *B* in panel (a), where all workers have shifted into wheat and no cloth is produced. With the relative price $P_W/P_C = \frac{1}{2}$, consumption is still at point *A*, so the difference between points *A* and *B* is the amount of wheat that Home is exporting and the amount of cloth Home is importing. That is, Home exports 50 bushels of wheat (the difference between production of 100 and consumption of 50) and imports 25 yards of cloth (the difference

FIGURE 2-9

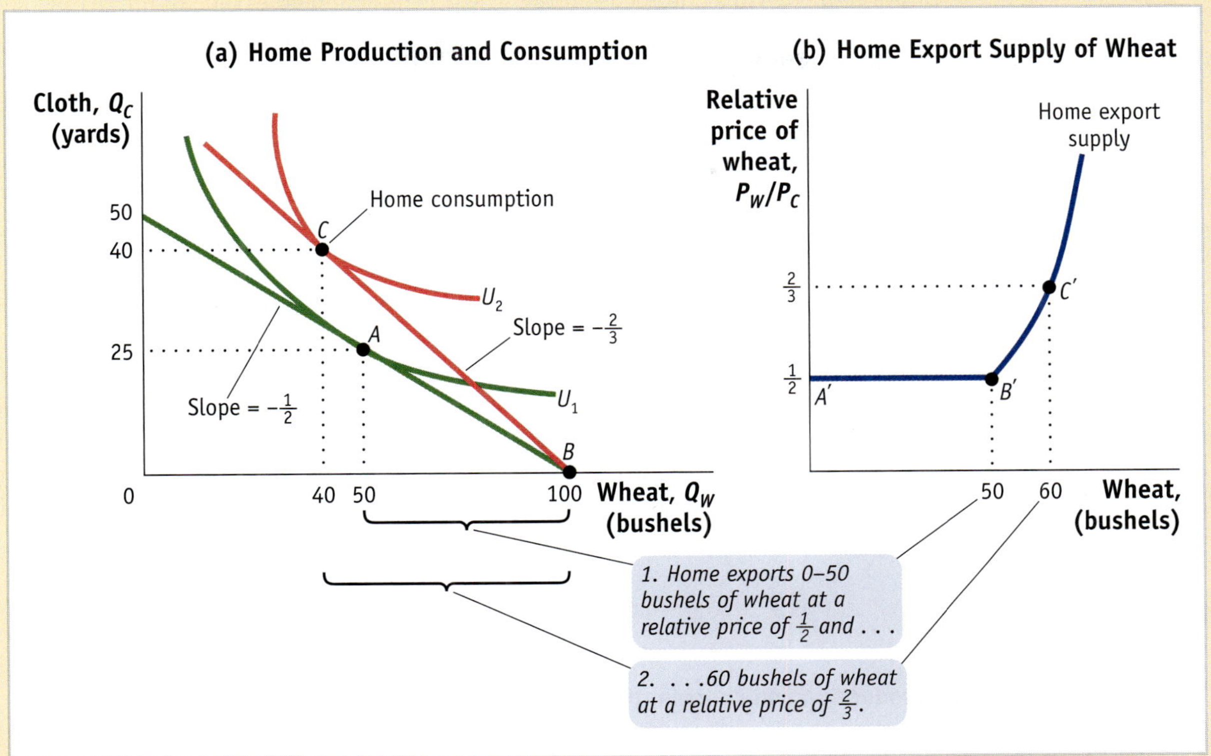

Home Export Supply Panel (a) repeats Figure 2-5 showing the trade equilibrium for Home with production at point *B* and consumption at point *C*. Panel (b) shows the Home export supply of wheat. When the relative price of wheat is $\frac{1}{2}$, Home will export any amount of wheat between 0 and 50 bushels, along the segment *A′ B′* of the Home export supply curve. For relative prices above $\frac{1}{2}$, Home exports more than 50 bushels, along the segment *B′ C′*. For example, at the relative price of $\frac{2}{3}$, Home exports 60 bushels of wheat.

between production of 0 and consumption of 25). Therefore, the relative price of $P_W/P_C = \frac{1}{2}$, with wheat exports of 50, is another point on the Home export supply curve, shown by *B′* in panel (b).

Joining up points *A′ C′*, *B′*, and *C′*, we get a Home export supply curve that is flat between *A′* and *B′*, and then rises between *B′* and *C′* and beyond. The flat portion of the export supply curve is a special feature of the Ricardian model that occurs because the PPF is a straight line. That is, with the relative price of $P_W/P_C = \frac{1}{2}$, production can occur anywhere along the PPF as workers shift between industries; meanwhile, consumption is fixed at point *A*, leading to all the export levels between *A′* and *B′* in panel (b). As the relative price of wheat rises above $\frac{1}{2}$, production remains fixed at point *B* in panel (a), but the consumption point changes, rising above point *A*. With the relative price $P_W/P_C = \frac{2}{3}$, for example, consumption is at point *C*. Then Home exports of wheat are calculated as the difference between production at *B* and consumption at *C*. Graphing the various relative prices above $\frac{1}{2}$ and the bushels of wheat exported at each price, we get the upward-sloping Home export supply curve between *B′* and *C′* in panel (b).

Foreign Import Demand Curve

In Foreign we will again focus on the wheat market and construct an import demand curve for wheat. In panel (a) of Figure 2-10, we repeat Figure 2-6, which shows the Foreign trade equilibrium with production at point B^* and consumption at point C^*. At the world relative price of $P_W/P_C = \frac{2}{3}$, Foreign imports 60 bushels of wheat (the difference between wheat consumption of 60 and production of 0). These numbers are graphed as point $C^{*\prime}$ in panel (b), where we have the relative price of wheat on the vertical axis and the Foreign imports of wheat on the horizontal axis.

Other points on Foreign's import demand curve can be obtained in much the same way as we did for Home. For example, the no-trade equilibrium in Foreign is shown by production and consumption at point A^* in panel (a), with the relative price of wheat equal to 1 (the slope of Foreign's PPF) and zero imports (since there is no international trade). This no-trade equilibrium is graphed as point $A^{*\prime}$ in panel (b). Keeping the relative price of wheat fixed at 1 in Foreign, production can shift away from point A^* in panel (a). This can occur because, as we argued for Home, wages are the same in Foreign's wheat and cloth industries when the relative price is at its no-trade level, so workers are willing to move between industries. Keeping Foreign consumption fixed at point A^* in

FIGURE 2-10

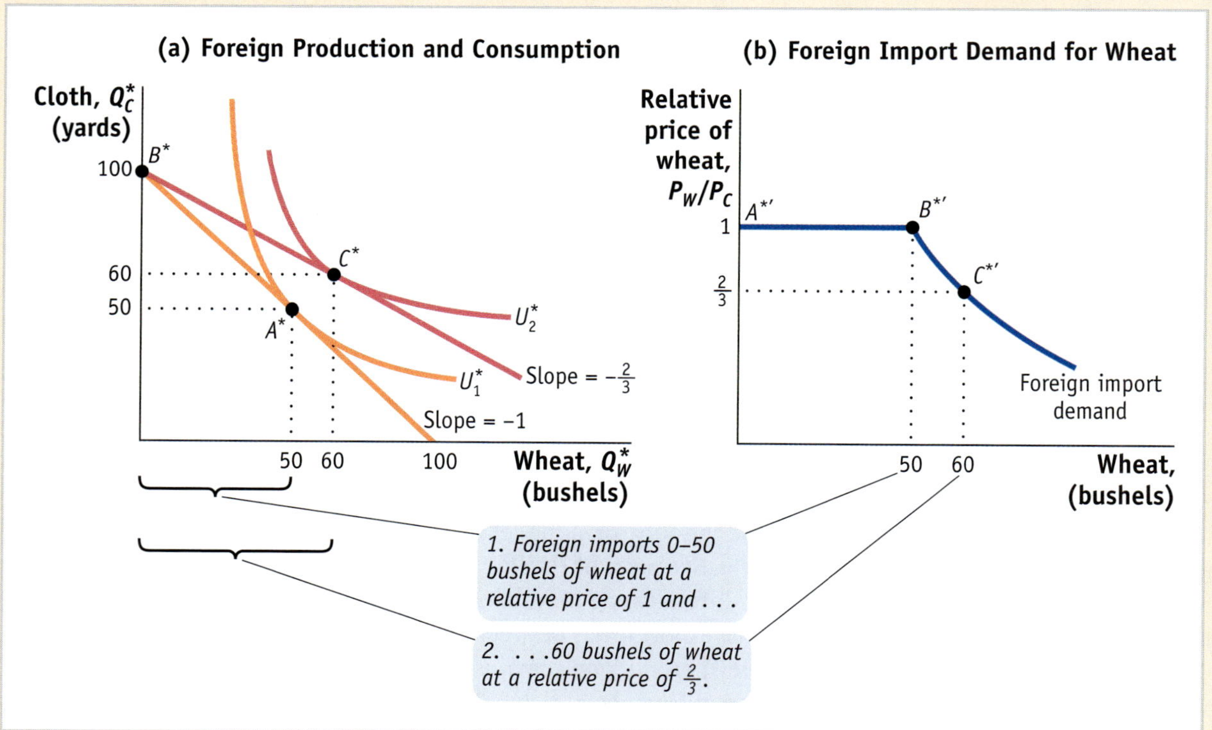

Foreign Import Demand Panel (a) repeats Figure 2-6, showing the Foreign trade equilibrium with production at point B^* and consumption at point C^*. Panel (b) shows Foreign import demand for wheat. When the relative price of wheat is 1, Foreign will import any amount of wheat between 0 and 50 bushels, along the segment $A^{*\prime}B^{*\prime}$ of the Foreign import demand curve. For relative prices below 1, Foreign imports more than 50 bushels, along the segment $B^{*\prime}C^{*\prime}$. For example, at the relative price of $\frac{2}{3}$, Foreign imports 60 bushels of wheat.

panel (a), suppose that all workers shift into the cloth industry, so that production is at point B^*. Then Foreign imports of wheat are 50 bushels (the difference between Foreign consumption of 50 and production of zero), as shown by point $B^{*\prime}$ in panel (b).

Joining up points $A^{*\prime}$, $B^{*\prime}$, and $C^{*\prime}$, we get an import demand curve that is flat between $A^{*\prime}$ and $B^{*\prime}$ and then falls between $B^{*\prime}$ and $C^{*\prime}$ and beyond. The flat portion of the Foreign import demand curve is once again a special feature of the Ricardian model that occurs because the PPF is a straight line. As we investigate other trade models in the following chapters, in which the production possibilities frontiers are curved rather than straight lines, the export supply and import demand curves will no longer have the flat portions. A general feature of these export supply and import demand curves is that they begin at the no-trade relative price for each country and then slope up (for export supply) or down (for import demand).

International Trade Equilibrium

Now that we have derived the Home export supply curve and the Foreign import demand curve, we can put them together in a single diagram, shown in Figure 2-11. The intersection of these two curves at point C' gives the international trade equilibrium, the equilibrium relative price of wheat at which the quantity of Home exports just equals Foreign imports. In Figure 2-11, the equilibrium relative price of wheat is $P_W/P_C = \frac{2}{3}$. This graph looks just like the supply = demand equilibria that you have seen in other economics classes, except that Figure 2-11 now refers to the *world* market for wheat rather than the market in a single country. That is, Home's export supply of wheat is the *excess* of the total Home supply over the quantity demanded by Home consumers, whereas Foreign import demand is the excess of total Foreign demand over the quantity supplied by Foreign suppliers. The intersection of these excess supply and demand curves, or export supply and import demand curves in

FIGURE 2-11

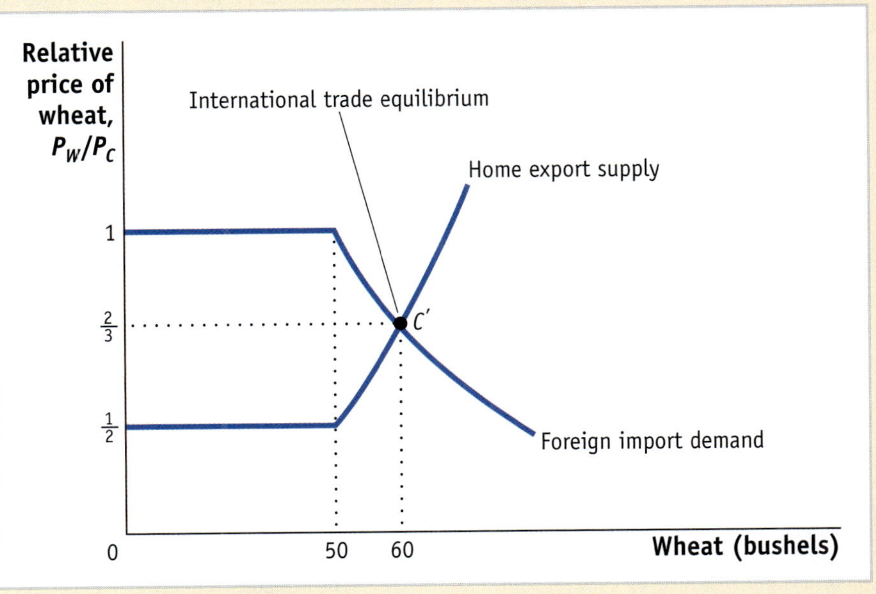

World Market for Wheat Putting together the Home export supply curve and the Foreign import demand curve for wheat, the world equilibrium is established at point C', where the relative price of wheat is $\frac{2}{3}$. At this price, Home exports of 60 bushels just equal Foreign imports of wheat.

Figure 2-11, determines the relative price of wheat that clears the world market, that is, at which the desired sales of Home equal the desired purchases by Foreign.

The Terms of Trade The price of a country's exports divided by the price of its imports is called the **terms of trade.** Because Home exports wheat, (P_W/P_C) is its terms of trade. Notice that an increase in the price of wheat (Home's export) or a fall in the price of cloth (Home's import) would both *raise* its terms of trade. Generally, an increase in the terms of trade is good for a country because it is earning more for its exports or paying less for its imports, thus making it better off. Foreign exports cloth, so (P_C/P_W) is its terms of trade. In this case, having a higher price for cloth (Foreign's export) or a lower price for wheat (Foreign's import) would make the Foreign country better off.

APPLICATION

The Terms of Trade for Primary Commodities

What has happened over time to the terms of trade? Writing in the 1950s, the Latin American economist Raúl Prebisch and the British economist Hans Singer each put forward the hypothesis that the price of *primary commodities* (i.e., agricultural products and minerals) would decline over time relative to the price of manufactured goods. Because primary commodities are often exported by developing countries, this would mean that the terms of trade in developing countries would decline over time.

There are several reasons why the Prebisch-Singer hypothesis might be true. First, it is well known that as people or countries become richer, they spend a smaller share of their income on food.[14] This means that as world income grows, the demand for food will decline relative to the demand for manufactured goods. Therefore, the price of agricultural products can also be expected to decline relative to manufactured goods. Second, for mineral products, it may be that industrialized countries continually find substitutes for the use of minerals in their production of manufactured products. For example, much less steel is used in cars today because automobile producers have shifted toward the use of plastic and aluminum in the body and frame. We can think of the substitution away from mineral products as a form of technological progress, and as it proceeds, it can lead to a fall in the price of raw minerals.

However, there are also several reasons why the Prebisch-Singer hypothesis may not be true. First, technological progress in manufactured goods can certainly lead to a fall in the price of these goods as they become easier to produce (e.g., think of the reduction in prices of many electronic goods, such as MP3 and DVD players). This is a fall in the terms of trade for industrialized countries rather than developing countries. Second, at least in the case of oil exports, the Organization of Petroleum Exporting Countries (OPEC) has managed to keep oil prices high by restricting supplies on the world market. This has resulted in an increase in the terms of trade for oil-exporting countries, which includes developing and industrialized nations.

Data on the relative price of primary commodities are shown in Figure 2-12.[15] This study considered 24 primary commodities from 1900 to 1998 and measured their

[14] This relationship is known as Engel's law after the nineteenth-century German statistician Ernst Engel. It is certainly true for purchases of food eaten at home but might not hold for dining out. As your income rises, you might spend a constant or even increasing share of your budget on restaurant food.

[15] These results are provided by Neil Kellard and Mark E. Wohar, 2006, "Trends and Persistence in Primary Commodity Prices," *Journal of Development Economics*, 79, February 146–167.

FIGURE 2-12

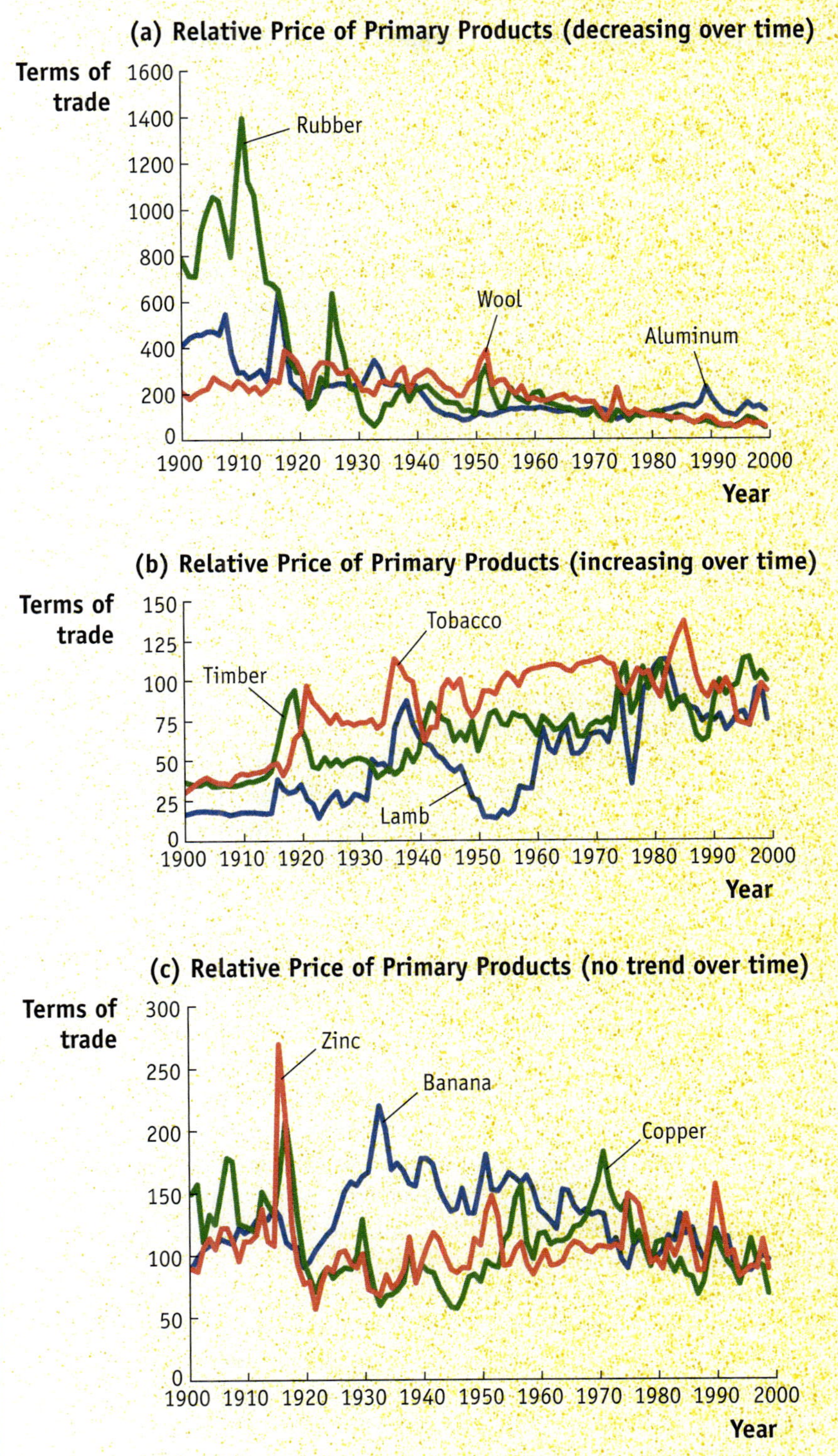

Relative Price of Primary Commodities Many developing countries export primary commodities (i.e., agricultural products and minerals), whereas industrial countries export manufactured products. Shown here are the prices of various primary commodities relative to an overall manufacturing price, from 1900 to 1998. The relative prices of some primary commodities have fallen over time (panel a), whereas other commodities have had rising relative prices (panel b). Other commodity prices show no consistent trend over time (panel c).

world price relative to the overall price of manufactured goods. Of the 24 commodities, one-half of them showed a decline in their relative price for 50% or more of the time period, including aluminum, cotton, hides, palm oil, rice, sugar, rubber, wheat, and wool. This evidence provides some support for the Prebisch-Singer hypothesis. Several examples of these commodities, with declining relative prices, are shown in panel (a) of Figure 2-12.

However, there are also a number of primary commodities whose prices increased for significant periods of time, or showed no consistent trend over the century. Commodities that had increasing relative prices for 50% or more of the time period include beef, lamb, timber, tin, and tobacco. Several of these commodities are shown in panel (b) of Figure 2-12. Finally, commodities that had no consistent trend in their relative prices between the beginning and end of the century include bananas, coffee, copper, and zinc. Several of these are shown in panel (c) of Figure 2-12. From these results for different commodities, we should conclude that there are some that follow the pattern predicted by Prebisch and Singer, with falling prices relative to manufacturing. This is not a general rule, however, and other primary commodities have had increasing or no consistent change in their prices. ■

5 Conclusions

The Ricardian model was devised to respond to the mercantilist idea that exports are good and imports are bad. Not so, said David Ricardo, and to prove his point, he considered an example in which trade between two countries (England and Portugal) is balanced; that is, the value of imports equals the value of exports for each country. The reason that England and Portugal trade with each other in Ricardo's example is that their technologies for producing wine and cloth are different. Portugal has an absolute advantage in both goods, but England has a comparative advantage in cloth. That is, the opportunity cost of producing cloth in England (measured by how much wine would have to be given up) is lower than in Portugal. Based on this comparative advantage, the no-trade relative price of cloth is also lower in England than in Portugal. When trade is opened, cloth merchants in England export to Portugal, where they can obtain a higher price, and wine vintners in Portugal export to England. Thus, the pattern of trade is determined by comparative advantage, and both countries gain from trade.

For simplicity, the Ricardian model is presented with just a single factor of production—labor. We have used a lesson from microeconomics to solve for wages as the marginal product of labor times the price of each good. It follows from this relationship that the ratio of wages across countries is determined by the marginal product of labor in the goods being produced and by the prices of those goods. Because wages depend on the marginal products of labor in each country, we conclude that wages are determined by absolute advantage—a country with better technology will be able to pay higher wages. In addition, wages depend on the prices prevailing on world markets for the goods exported by each country. We have defined the "terms of trade" as the price of a country's exports divided by the price of its imports. Generally, having higher terms of trade (because of high export prices or low import prices) will lead to higher real wages and therefore will benefit workers.

The fact that only labor is used in the Ricardian model makes it special. Because of this assumption, the PPF in the Ricardian model is a straight line, and the export supply and import demand curves each have a flat segment. These special properties do not occur in other models we consider in the following chapters, where in addition to labor, industries will use capital and land. Once we allow for the more realistic assumption of several factors of production, the gains from trade become more complicated. Even if there are overall gains for a country, some factors of production might gain as other factors of production lose due to opening trade. That is the topic we explore in the next chapter.

KEY POINTS

1. A country has comparative advantage in producing a good when the country's opportunity cost of producing the good is lower than the opportunity cost of producing the good in another country.
2. The pattern of trade between countries is determined by comparative advantage. This means that even countries with poor technologies can export the goods in which they have comparative advantage.
3. All countries experience gains from trade. That is, the utility of an importing or exporting country is at least as high as it would be in the absence of international trade.
4. The level of wages in each country is determined by its absolute advantage; that is, by the amount the country can produce with its labor. This result explains why countries with poor technologies are still able to export: their low wages allow them to overcome their low productivity.
5. The equilibrium price of a good on the world market is determined at the point where the export supply of one country equals the import demand of the other country.
6. A country's terms of trade equal the price of its export good divided by the price of its import good. A rise in a country's terms of trade makes it better off because it is exporting at higher prices or importing at lower prices.

KEY TERMS

import, p. 27
export, p. 27
technology, p. 29
resources, p. 29
offshoring p. 29
proximity, p. 29
Ricardian model, p. 29
trade pattern, p. 29
free-trade area, p. 29
natural resources, p. 30
labor resources, p. 30
capital, p. 30
factors of production, p. 30
absolute advantage, p. 30
comparative advantage, p. 31
marginal product of labor (MPL), p. 33
production possibilities frontier (PPF), p. 33
opportunity cost, p. 33
indifference curves, p. 34
utility, p. 34
relative price, p. 36
international trade equilibrium, p. 41
world price line, p. 43
gains from trade, p. 43
export supply curve, p. 48
import demand curve, p. 48
terms of trade, p. 52

PROBLEMS

1. At the beginning of the chapter, there is a brief quotation from David Ricardo; here is a longer version of what Ricardo wrote:

> England may be so circumstanced, that to produce the cloth may require the labour of 100 men for one year; and if she attempted to make the wine, it might require the labour of 120 men for the same time. . . . To produce the wine in Portugal, might require only the labour of 80 men for one year, and to produce the cloth in the same country, might require the labour of 90 men for the same time. It would therefore be advantageous for her to export wine in exchange for cloth. This exchange might even take place, notwithstanding that the commodity imported by Portugal could be produced there with less labour than in England.

   Suppose that the amount of labor Ricardo describes can produce 1,000 yards of cloth or 1,000 bottles of wine, in either country. Then answer the following:

   a. What is England's marginal product of labor in cloth and in wine, and what is Portugal's marginal product of labor in cloth and in wine? Which country has absolute advantage in cloth, and in wine, and why?
   b. Use the formula $P_W/P_C = MPL_C/MPL_W$ to compute the no-trade relative price of wine in each country. Which country has comparative advantage in wine, and why?

2. Suppose that each worker in the Home country can produce three cars or two TVs. Assume that Home has four workers.

   a. Graph the production possibilities frontier for the Home country.
   b. What is the no-trade relative price of cars at Home?

3. Suppose that each worker in the Foreign country can produce two cars or three TVs. Assume that Foreign also has four workers.

   a. Graph the production possibilities frontier for the Foreign country.
   b. What is the no-trade relative price of cars in Foreign?
   c. Using the information provided in Problem 2 regarding Home, in which good does Foreign have a comparative advantage, and why?

4. Suppose that in the absence of trade, Home consumes nine cars and two TVs, while Foreign consumes two cars and nine TVs. Add the indifference curve for each country to the figures in Problems 2 and 3. Label the production possibilities frontier (PPF), indifference curve (U_1), and the no-trade equilibrium consumption and production for each country.

5. Now suppose the world relative price of cars is $P_C/P_{TV} = 1$.

   a. In what good will each country specialize? Briefly explain why.
   b. Graph the new world price line for each country in the figures in Problem 4, and add a new indifference curve (U_2) for each country in the trade equilibrium.
   c. Label the exports and imports for each country. How does the amount of Home exports compare with Foreign imports?
   d. Does each country gain from trade? Briefly explain why or why not.

6. Answer the following questions using the information given by the accompanying table:

	Home Country	Foreign Country	Absolute Advantage
Number of bicycles produced per hour	4	2	?
Number of snowboards produced per hour	6	8	?
Comparative advantage	?	?	

   a. Complete the table for this problem in the same manner as Table 2-2.

b. Which country has an absolute advantage in the production of bicycles? Which country has an absolute advantage in the production of snowboards?
c. What is the opportunity cost of bicycles in terms of snowboards at Home? What is the opportunity cost of bicycles in terms of snowboards in Foreign?
d. Which product will Home export, and which product does Foreign export? Briefly explain why.

7. Assume that Home and Foreign produce two goods, TVs and cars, and use the information below to answer the following questions:

In the No-Trade Equilibrium

Home Country		Foreign Country	
$Wage_{TV} = 12$	$Wage_C = ?$	$Wage^*_{TV} = ?$	$Wage^*_C = 6$
$MPL_{TV} = 2$	$MPL_C = ?$	$MPL^*_{TV} = ?$	$MPL^*_C = 1$
$P_{TV} = ?$	$P_C = 4$	$P^*_{TV} = 3$	$P^*_C = ?$

a. What is the marginal product of labor for TVs and cars in the Home country? What is the no-trade relative price of TVs at Home?
b. What is the marginal product of labor for TVs and cars in the Foreign country? What is the no-trade relative price of TVs in Foreign?
c. Suppose the world relative price of TVs in the trade equilibrium is $P_{TV}/P_C = 1$. Which good will each country export? Briefly explain why.
d. In the trade equilibrium, what is the real wage at Home in terms of cars and in terms of TVs? How do these values compare with the real wage in terms of either good in the no-trade equilibrium?
e. In the trade equilibrium, what is the real wage in Foreign in terms of TVs and in terms of cars? How do these values compare with the real wage in terms of either good in the no-trade equilibrium?
f. In the trade equilibrium, do Foreign workers earn more or less than those at Home, measured in terms of their ability to purchase goods? Explain why.

8. Why do some low-wage countries, such as China, pose a threat to manufacturers in industrial countries, such as the United States, whereas other low-wage countries, such as Haiti, do not?

Answer Problems 9 to 11 using the chapter information for Home and Foreign.

9. a. Suppose that the number of workers doubles in Home. What happens to the Home PPF and what happens to the no-trade relative price of wheat?
b. Suppose that there is technological progress in the wheat industry such that Home can produce more wheat with the same amount of labor. What happens to the Home PPF, and what happens to the relative price of wheat? Describe what would happen if a similar change occurred in the cloth industry.

10. a. Using Figure 2-5, show that an increase in the relative price of wheat from its world relative price of $\frac{2}{3}$ will raise Home's utility.
b. Using Figure 2-6, show that an increase in the relative price of wheat from its world relative price of $\frac{2}{3}$ will lower Foreign's utility. What is Foreign's utility when the world relative price reaches 1, and what happens in Foreign when the world relative price of wheat rises above that level?

11. *(This is a harder question.)* Suppose that the Home country is much larger than the Foreign country. For example, suppose we double the number of workers at Home from 25 to 50. Then Home is willing to export up to 100 bushels of wheat at its no-trade price of $P_W/P_C = \frac{1}{2}$ rather than 50 bushels of wheat as shown in Figure 2-11. In the following, we draw a new version of Figure 2-11, with the larger Home country.

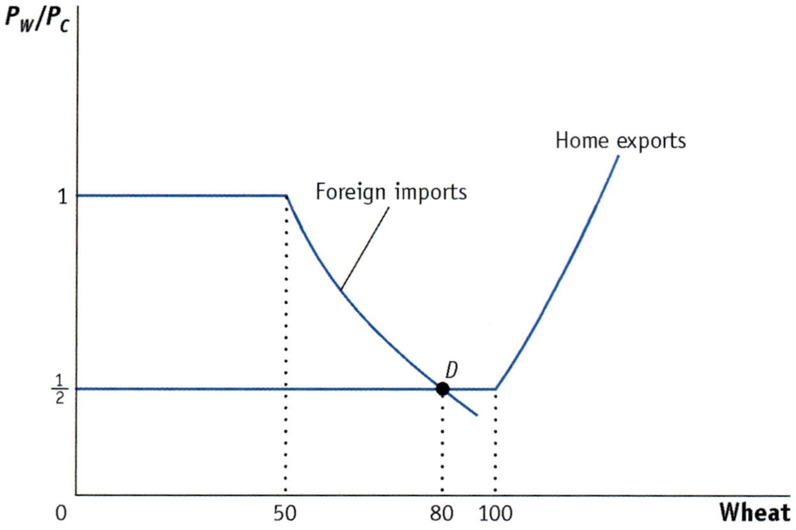

a. From this figure, what is the new world relative price of wheat (at point D)?

b. Using this new world equilibrium price, draw a new version of the trade equilibrium in Home and in Foreign, and show the production point and consumption point in each country.

c. Are there gains from trade in both countries? Explain why or why not.

12. Using the results from Problem 11, explain why the Ricardian model predicts that Mexico would gain more than the United States when the two countries signed the North American Free Trade Agreement, establishing free trade between them.

3

Gains and Losses from Trade in the Specific-Factors Model

The time has come, the awaited day, a historic day in which Bolivia retakes absolute control of our natural resources.

Evo Morales, President of Bolivia, 2006[1]

If we do not take action, those who have the most reason to be dissatisfied with our present rate of growth will be tempted to seek shortsighted and narrow solutions—to resist automation, to reduce the work week to 35 hours or even lower, to shut out imports, or to raise prices in a vain effort to obtain full capacity profits on under-capacity operations. But these are all self-defeating expedients which can only restrict the economy, not expand it.

President John F. Kennedy, New York Economic Club, 1962

Over the span of three years, 2003 to 2005, Bolivia had three presidents. This rapid succession at the highest level of government was largely a result of public dissatisfaction with the distribution of gains that had come from exporting natural gas. Many people, including the indigenous Aymara Indians, believed that most of these gains had gone to multinational oil corporations, with little distributed to the citizens of the country in which the gas deposits and refineries are located.

Violent protests in September 2003 led to the resignation of President Gonzalo Sánchez de Lozada, who was replaced by Carlos Mesa, a writer and television journalist. He promised to respect the views of the indigenous people of Bolivia and in July 2004 held a referendum on whether the country should export natural gas. The referendum included provisions to ensure that more of the profits from natural gas exports would go to the Bolivian government rather than to foreign companies. With these assurances, the referendum passed, and in May 2005 taxes on foreign oil companies were sharply

[1] Speech from the San Alberto field operated by Petrobras, "Bolivia Nationalizes Natural Gas Industry," *USA Today*, May 1, 2006.

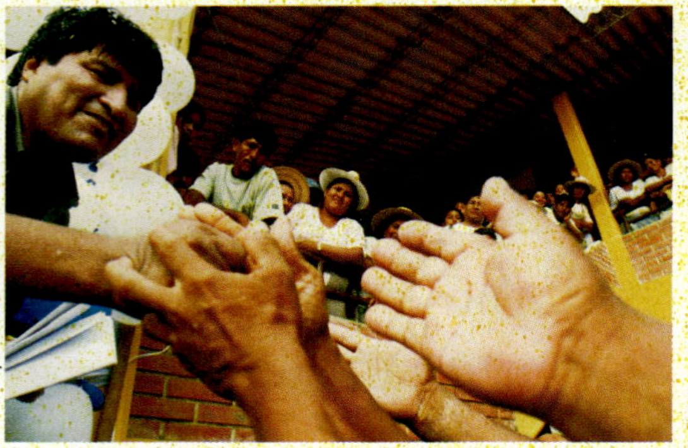
AP Photos/Dado Galdieri

Evo Morales and his supporters.

increased. But many protestors wanted more and forced President Mesa to resign within the year. Elections were held again in December 2005, and Evo Morales scored a decisive victory, becoming the first Aymara Indian elected to president in Bolivia's 180-year history. In May 2006 he nationalized the gas industry, which meant that all natural gas resources were placed under the control of the state-owned energy company. With this policy change, foreign investors lost their majority ownership claims to gas fields, pipelines, and refineries that they had built and lost a significant portion of the profits from the sales of Bolivian natural gas. This drastic step, which was criticized heavily by foreign governments, followed a trend in some other Latin American countries toward taking control of oil and gas resources.

The Bolivian experience illustrates the difficulty of ensuring that all people within a country share in the gains from trade. Exports of Bolivia's natural gas are expected to generate earnings of some $500 million per year, which are the gains from exporting. But the difficulty of sharing these gains among Bolivia's citizenry makes the export of gas a contentious issue. Although the export of natural gas clearly generated gains for the foreign-owned and state-owned companies that sold the resources, the indigenous peoples have only begun to share in those gains.

The new constitution in 2009 gives indigenous peoples control over natural resources in their territories. In addition to oil and gas, those resources include lithium, a key ingredient to make batteries for electric cars, which is found in abundance in Bolivia. Companies from Japan and Europe are trying to make deals to extract this resource, but the government of Evo Morales is proceeding cautiously. And the indigenous peoples are working to ensure that they also gain from this valuable resource.[2]

A key lesson from this chapter is that in most cases, opening a country to trade generates winners *and* losers. In general, the gains of those who benefit from trade exceed the losses of those who are harmed, and in this sense there are "overall" gains from trade. That was a lesson from the Ricardian model in the last chapter. But our argument in the last chapter that trade generates gains for *all* workers was too simple because, in the Ricardian model, labor was the only factor of production. Once we make the more realistic assumption that capital and land are also factors of production, then trade will generate gains for some factors and losses for others. Our goal in this chapter is to determine who gains and who loses from trade and under what circumstances.

The model we use to analyze the role of international trade in determining the earnings of labor, land, and capital assumes that one industry (agriculture) uses labor and land and the other industry (manufacturing) uses labor and capital. This model is sometimes called the **specific-factors model** because land is *specific* to the agriculture sector and capital is *specific* to the manufacturing sector; labor is used in both sectors, so it is not specific to either one. The idea that land is specific to agriculture and that capital is specific to manufacturing might be true in the short run but does not really hold in the long run. In later chapters, we develop a long-run model, in which capital and other resources can be shifted from use in one industry to use in another. For now we focus on the short-run specific-factors model, which will offer many new insights about the gains from trade beyond those obtained from the Ricardian model.

[2] You can read more about this case in Simon Romero, "In Bolivia, Untapped Bounty Meets Nationalism," *New York Times*, February 3, 2009, from which this paragraph is drawn.

1 Specific-Factors Model

We address the following question in the specific-factors model: How does trade affect the earnings of labor, land, and capital? We have already seen from our study of the Ricardian model that when a country is opened to free trade, the relative price of exports rises and the relative price of imports falls. Thus, the question of how trade affects factor earnings is really a question of how changes in *relative prices* affect the earnings of labor, land, and capital. The idea we develop in this section is that the earnings of *specific* or *fixed factors* (such as capital and land) will go up or down the most due to changes in relative prices (i.e., they are the most sensitive to relative price changes) because in the short run they are "stuck" in a sector and cannot be employed elsewhere. In contrast, mobile factors (such as labor) can offset their losses somewhat by seeking employment in other industries.

As in our study of international trade in Chapter 2, we will have two countries, called Home and Foreign. We first discuss the Home country.

The Home Country

Let us call the two industries in the specific-factors model "manufacturing" and "agriculture." Manufacturing uses labor and capital, whereas agriculture uses labor and land. In each industry, increases in the amount of labor used are subject to **diminishing returns;** that is, the marginal product of labor declines as the amount of labor used in the industry increases. Figure 3-1, panel (a), plots output against the amount of labor used in production, and shows diminishing returns for the manufacturing industry. As more labor is used, the output of manufacturing goes up, but it does so at

FIGURE 3-1

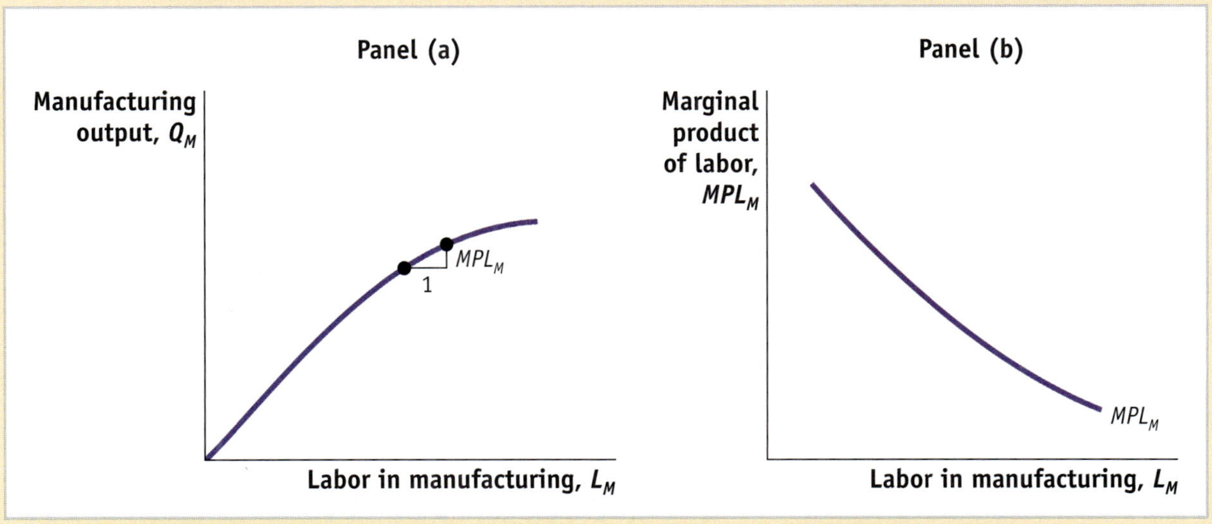

Panel (a) Manufacturing Output As more labor is used, manufacturing input increases, but it does so at a diminishing rate. The slope of the curve measures the marginal product of labor, which declines as the quantity of labor used in manufacturing increases.

Panel (b) Diminishing Marginal Product of Labor An increase in the amount of labor used in manufacturing lowers the marginal product of labor.

a diminishing rate. The slope of the curve in Figure 3-1 measures the marginal product of labor, which declines as labor increases.

Figure 3-1, panel (b), graphs MPL_M, the marginal product of labor in manufacturing, against the labor used in manufacturing L_M. This curve slopes downward due to diminishing returns. Likewise, in the agriculture sector (not drawn), the marginal product of labor MPL_A also diminishes as the amount of labor used in agriculture L_A increases.

Production Possibilities Frontier Combining the output for the two industries, manufacturing and agriculture, we obtain the production possibilities frontier (PPF) for the economy (Figure 3-2). Because of the diminishing returns to labor in both sectors, the PPF is *bowed out* or concave with respect to the graph's origin. (You may recognize this familiar shape from your introductory economics class.)

By using the marginal products of labor in each sector, we can determine the slope of the PPF. Starting at point *A* in Figure 3-2, suppose that one unit of labor leaves agriculture and enters manufacturing so that the economy's new output is at point *B*. The drop in agricultural output is MPL_A, and the increase in manufacturing output is MPL_M. The slope of the PPF between points *A* and *B* is the negative of the ratio of marginal products, or $-MPL_A/MPL_M$. This ratio can be interpreted as the opportunity cost of producing one unit of manufacturing, the cost of one unit of manufacturing in terms of the amount of food (the agricultural good) that would need to be given up to produce it.

Opportunity Cost and Prices As in the Ricardian model, the slope of the PPF, which is the opportunity cost of manufacturing, also equals the relative price of manufacturing. To understand why this is so, recall that in competitive markets, firms hire labor up to the point at which the cost of one more hour of labor (the wage) equals the value of one more hour of labor in terms of output. In turn, the value of one more hour of labor equals the amount of goods produced in that hour (the marginal product of labor) times the price of the good. In manufacturing, labor will be hired to the

FIGURE 3-2

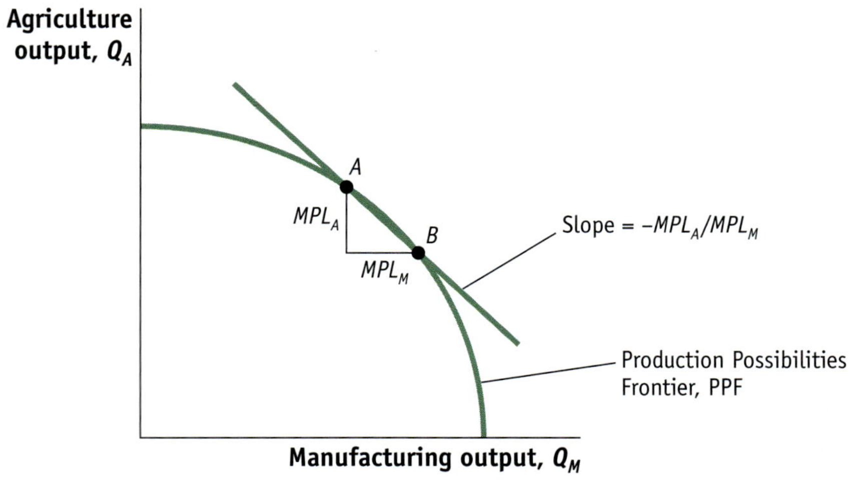

Production Possibilities Frontier The production possibilities frontier shows the amount of agricultural and manufacturing outputs that can be produced in the economy with labor. Its slope equals $-MPL_A/MPL_M$, the ratio of the marginal products of labor in the two industries. The slope of the PPF can be interpreted as the opportunity cost of the manufacturing output—it is the amount of the agricultural good that would need to be given up to obtain one more unit of output in the manufacturing sector.

point at which the wage W equals the price of manufacturing P_M times the marginal product of labor in manufacturing MPL_M:

$$W = P_M \cdot MPL_M$$

Similarly, in agriculture, labor will be hired to the point at which the wage W equals the price of manufacturing P_A times the marginal product of labor in manufacturing MPL_A:

$$W = P_A \cdot MPL_A$$

Because we are assuming that labor is free to move between sectors, the wages in these two equations must be equal. If the wage were not the same in both sectors, labor would move to the sector with the higher wage. This movement would continue until the increase in the amount of labor in the high-wage sector drove down the wage, and the decrease in amount of labor in the low-wage sector drove up the wage, until the wages were equal. By setting the two wage equations equal, we obtain $P_M \cdot MPL_M = P_A \cdot MPL_A$, and by rearranging terms, we get

$$(P_M / P_A) = (MPL_A / MPL_M)$$

This equation shows that the relative price of manufacturing (P_M / P_A) equals the opportunity cost of manufacturing (MPL_A / MPL_M), the slope of the production possibilities frontier. These relative prices also reflect the value that Home consumers put on manufacturing versus food. In the absence of international trade, the equilibrium for the Home economy is at point *A* in Figure 3-3, where the relative price of manufacturing (P_M / P_A) equals the slope of the PPF as well as the slope of the indifference curve for a representative consumer with utility of U_1. The intuition for the no-trade equilibrium is exactly the same as for the Ricardian model in Chapter 2: equilibrium occurs at the tangency of the PPF and the consumer's indifference curve. This point on the PPF corresponds to the highest possible level of utility for the consumer.

FIGURE 3-3

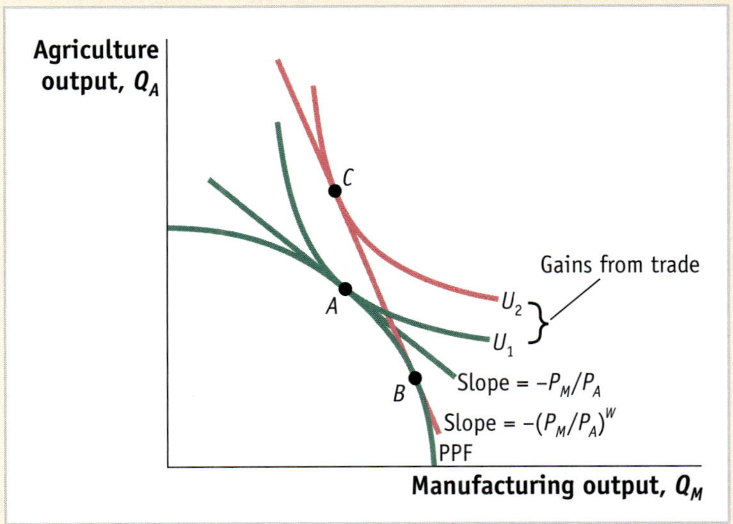

Increase in the Relative Price of Manufactures In the absence of international trade, the economy produces and consumes at point *A*. The relative price of manufactures, P_M/P_A, is the slope of the line tangent to the PPF and indifference curve, U_1, at point *A*. With international trade, the economy is able to produce at point *B* and consume at point *C*. The world relative price of manufactures, $(P_M/P_A)^W$, is the slope of the line *BC*. The rise in utility from U_1 to U_2 is a measure of the gains from trade for the economy.

The Foreign Country

In this chapter, we do not discuss the Foreign country in any detail. Instead, we simply assume that the no-trade relative price of manufacturing in Foreign (P^*_M/P^*_A) differs from the no-trade price (P_M/P_A) at Home. There are several reasons why these prices can differ. In the previous chapter, we showed how differences in productivities across countries cause the no-trade relative prices to differ across countries. That is the key assumption, or starting point, of the Ricardian model. Another reason for relative prices to differ, which we have not yet investigated, is that the amounts of labor, capital, or land found in the two countries are different. (That will be the key assumption of the Heckscher–Ohlin model, which we discuss in the next chapter.)

For now, we will not explain why the no-trade relative prices differ across countries but will take it for granted that this is not unusual. For the sake of focusing on one case, let us assume that the Home no-trade relative price of manufacturing is *lower* than the Foreign relative price, $(P_M/P_A) < (P^*_M/P^*_A)$. This assumption means that Home can produce manufactured goods relatively cheaper than Foreign, or, equivalently, that Home has a comparative advantage in manufacturing.

Overall Gains from Trade

Starting at the no-trade equilibrium point *A* in Figure 3-3, suppose that the Home country opens up to international trade with Foreign. Once trade is opened, we expect that the world equilibrium relative price; that is, the relative price in *all* countries $(P_M/P_A)^W$, will lie between the no-trade relative prices in the two countries, so

$$(P_M/P_A) < (P_M/P_A)^W < (P^*_M/P^*_A)$$

This equation shows us that when Home opens to trade, the relative price of manufacturing will *rise*, from (P_M/P_A) to $(P_M/P_A)^W$; conversely, for Foreign, the relative price of manufacturing will *fall*, from (P^*_M/P^*_A) to $(P_M/P_A)^W$. With trade, the world relative price $(P_M/P_A)^W$ is represented by a line with that slope that is tangent to Home's PPF, line *BC* in Figure 3-3. The increase in the Home relative price of manufactured goods is shown by the steeper slope of the world relative price line as compared with the Home no-trade price line (through point *A*).

What is the effect of this increase in (P_M/P_A) at Home? The higher relative price of the manufactured good at Home attracts more workers into that sector, which now produces at point *B* rather than *A*. As before, production takes place at the point along the Home PPF tangent to the relative price line, where equality of wages across industries is attained. The country can then export manufactures and import agricultural products along the international price line *BC*, and it reaches its highest level of utility, U_2, at point *C*. The difference in utility between U_2 and U_1 is a measure of the country's overall gains from trade. (These overall gains would be zero if the relative prices with trade were equal to the no-trade relative prices, but they can never be negative—a country can never be made worse off by opening to trade.)

Notice that the good whose relative price goes up (manufacturing, for Home) is exported and the good whose relative price goes down (agriculture, for Home) is imported. By exporting manufactured goods at a higher price and importing food at a lower price, Home is better off than it was in the absence of trade. To measure the gains from trade, economists rely on the price increases for exports and the price decreases for imports to determine how much extra consumption a country can afford. The following application considers the magnitude of the overall gains from trade in historical cases in which the gains have been measured.

APPLICATION

How Large Are the Gains from Trade?

How large are the overall gains from trade? There are a few historical examples of countries that have moved from **autarky** (i.e., no trade) to free trade, or vice versa, quickly enough that we can use the years before and after this shift to estimate the gains from trade.

One such episode in the United States occurred between December 1807 and March 1809, when the U.S. Congress imposed a nearly complete halt to international trade at the request of President Thomas Jefferson. A complete stop to all trade is called an **embargo.** The United States imposed its embargo because Britain was at war with Napoleon, and Britain wanted to prevent ships from arriving in France that might be carrying supplies or munitions. As a result, Britain patrolled the eastern coast of the United States and seized U.S. ships that were bound across the Atlantic. To safeguard its own ships and possibly inflict economic losses on Britain, the United States declared a trade embargo for 14 months from 1807 to 1809. The embargo was not complete, however; the United States still traded with some countries, such as Canada and Mexico, that didn't have to be reached by ship.

As you might expect, U.S. trade fell dramatically during this period. Exports (such as cotton, flour, tobacco, and rice) fell from about $49 million in 1807 to $9 million in 1809. The drop in the value of exports reflects both a drop in the quantity exported and a drop in the price of exports. Recall that in Chapter 2 we defined the terms of trade of a country as the price of its export goods divided by the price of its import goods, so a drop in the price of U.S. exports is a fall in its terms of trade, which is a loss for the United States. According to one study, the cost of the trade embargo to the United States was about 5% of gross domestic product (GDP). That is, U.S. GDP was 5% lower than it would have been without the trade embargo. The cost of the embargo was offset somewhat because trade was not completely eliminated and because some U.S. producers were able to shift their efforts to producing goods (such as cloth and glass) that had previously been imported. Thus, we can take 5% of GDP as a lower estimate of what the gains from trade for the United States would have been relative to a situation with no trade.

Is 5% of GDP a large or small number? It is large when we think that a recession that reduced GDP by 5% in one year would be regarded as a very deep downturn.[3] To get another perspective, instead of comparing the costs of the embargo with overall GDP, we can instead compare them with the size of U.S. exports, which were 13% of GDP before the embargo. Taking the ratio of these numbers, we conclude that the cost of the embargo was more than one-third of the value of exports.

Another historical case was Japan's rapid opening to the world economy in 1854, after 200 years of self-imposed autarky. In this case, military action by Commodore Matthew Perry of the United States forced Japan to open up its borders so that the

[3] The most severe downturn ever in the United States was the Great Depression of the 1930s. U.S. real GDP fell each year between 1929 and 1933 by an average of 9% per year and then began to recover. It was not until 1939 that the United States regained the same level of real GDP that it had in 1929.

United States could establish commercial ties. When trade was opened, the prices of Japanese exports to the United States (such as silk and tea) rose, and the prices of U.S. imports (such as woolens) fell. These price movements were a terms-of-trade gain for Japan, very much like the movement from the no-trade point A in Figure 3-3 to a trade equilibrium at points B and C. According to one estimate, Japan's gains from trade after its opening were 4 to 5% of GDP.[4] The gains were not one-sided, however; Japan's trading partners—such as the United States—also gained from being able to trade in the newly opened markets. ■

2 Earnings of Labor

Because there are overall gains from trade, at least *someone* in the economy must be better off, but it does not mean that *everyone* is better off. The goal of this chapter is to explore how a change in relative prices, such as that shown in Figure 3-3, feeds back onto the earnings of workers, landowners, and capital owners. We begin our study of the specific-factors model by looking at what happens to the wages earned by labor when there is an increase in the relative price of manufactures.

Determination of Wages

To determine wages, it is convenient to take the marginal product of labor in manufacturing (MPL_M), which was shown in Figure 3-2, and the marginal product of labor in agriculture (MPL_A), and put them in one diagram.

First, we add the amount of labor used in manufacturing L_M and the amount used in agriculture L_A to give us the total amount of labor in the economy $\overline{L}$:

$$L_M + L_A = \overline{L}$$

Figure 3-4 shows the total amount of labor $\overline{L}$ on the horizontal axis. The amount of labor used in manufacturing L_M is measured from left (0_M) to right, while the amount of labor used in agriculture L_A is measured from right (0_A) to left. Each point on the horizontal axis indicates how much labor is used in manufacturing (measured from left to right) and how much labor is used in agriculture (measured from right to left). For example, point L indicates that 0_ML units of labor are used in manufacturing and 0_AL units of labor are used in agriculture, which adds up to $\overline{L}$ units of labor in total.

The second step in determining wages is to multiply the marginal product of labor in each sector by the price of the good in that sector (P_M or P_A). As we discussed earlier, in competitive markets, firms will hire labor up to the point at which the cost of one more hour of labor (the wage) equals the value of one more hour in production, which is the marginal product of labor times the price of the good. In each industry, then, labor will be hired until

$$W = P_M \cdot MPL_M \text{ in manufacturing}$$

$$W = P_A \cdot MPL_A \text{ in agriculture}$$

In Figure 3-4, we draw the graph of $P_M \cdot MPL_M$ as downward-sloping. This curve is basically the same as the marginal product of labor MPL_M curve in Figure 3-2,

[4] Daniel M. Bernhofen and John C. Brown, March 2005, "Estimating the Comparative Advantage Gains from Trade," *American Economic Review*, 95(1), 208–225.

FIGURE 3-4

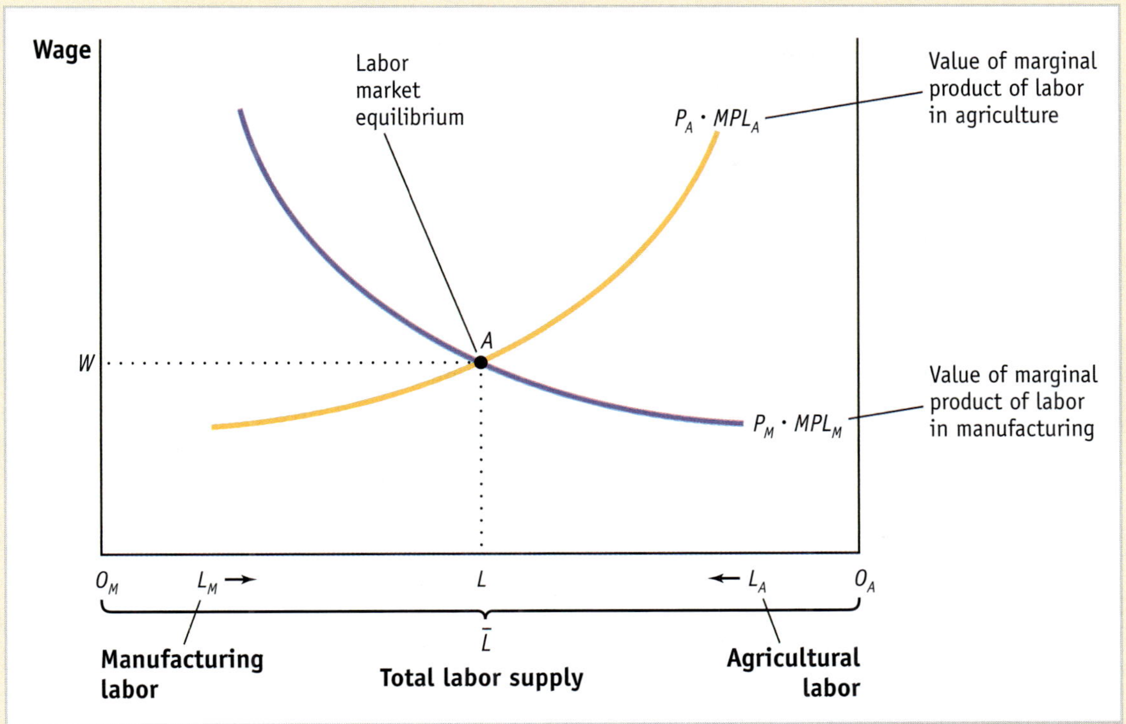

Allocation of Labor between Manufacturing and Agriculture The amount of labor used in manufacturing is measured from left to right along the horizontal axis, and the amount of labor used in agriculture is measured from right to left. Labor market equilibrium is at point *A*. At the equilibrium wage of *W*, manufacturing uses 0_ML units of labor and agriculture uses 0_AL units.

except that it is now multiplied by the price of the manufactured good. When we draw the graph of $P_A \cdot MPL_A$ for agriculture, however, it slopes upward. This is because we are measuring the labor used in agriculture L_A from *right to left* in the diagram: the marginal product of labor in agriculture falls as the amount of labor increases (moving from right to left).

Equilibrium Wage The equilibrium wage is found at point *A*, the intersection of the curves $P_M \cdot MPL_M$ and $P_A \cdot MPL_A$ in Figure 3-4. At this point, 0_ML units of labor are used in manufacturing, and firms in that industry are willing to pay the wage $W = P_M \cdot MPL_M$. In addition, 0_AL units of labor are used in agriculture, and farmers are willing to pay the wage $W = P_A \cdot MPL_A$. Because wages are equal in the two sectors, there is no reason for labor to move, and the labor market is in equilibrium.

Change in Relative Price of Manufactures

Now that we have shown how the wage is determined in the specific-factors model, we want to ask how the wage *changes* in response to an increase in the relative price of manufactures. That is, as the relative price of manufactures rises (shown in Figure 3-3), and the economy shifts from its no-trade equilibrium at point *A* to its trade equilibrium with production and consumption at points B and C, what is the effect on the earnings of each factor of production? In particular, what are the changes in the wage, and in the earnings of capital owners in manufacturing and landowners in agriculture?

Effect on the Wage An increase in the relative price of manufacturing P_M/P_A can occur due to either an increase in P_M or a decrease in P_A. Both these price movements will have the same effect on the **real wage;** that is, on the amount of manufactures and food that a worker can afford to buy. For convenience, let us suppose that the price of manufacturing P_M rises, while the price of agriculture P_A does not change.

When P_M rises, the curve $P_M \cdot MPL_M$ shifts up to $P'_M \cdot MPL_M$, as shown in Figure 3-5. The vertical rise in this curve is exactly $\Delta P_M \cdot MPL_M$, as illustrated in the diagram. (We use the symbol Δ, delta, to stand for the *change* in a variable.) The new intersection of the two curves occurs at point B, where the wage is W' and the allocation of labor between the two sectors is identified by point L'. The equilibrium wage has risen from W to W', the amount of labor used in the manufacturing sector has increased from $0_M L$ to $0_M L'$, and the amount of labor used in agriculture has fallen from $0_A L$ to $0_A L'$.

Effect on Real Wages The fact that the wage has risen does not really tell us whether workers are better off or worse off in terms of the amount of food and manufactured goods they can buy. To answer this question, we have to take into account any change in the prices of these goods. For instance, the amount of food that a worker can afford to buy with his or her hourly wage is W/P_A.[5] Because W has increased from W to W' and we have assumed that P_A has not changed, workers can afford to buy more food. In other words, the real wage has increased in terms of food.

The amount of the manufactured good that a worker can buy is measured by W/P_M. While W has increased, P_M has also increased, so at first glance we do not know whether W/P_M has increased or decreased. However, Figure 3-5 can help us figure this out. Notice that as we've drawn Figure 3-5, the increase in the wage from W to W' is less than the vertical increase $\Delta P_M \cdot MPL_M$ that occurred in the $P_M \cdot MPL_M$ curve. We can write this condition as

$$\Delta W < \Delta P_M \cdot MPL_M$$

To see how W/P_M has changed, divide both sides of this equation by the initial wage W (which equals $P_M \cdot MPL_M$) to obtain

$$\frac{\Delta W}{W} < \frac{\Delta P_M \cdot MPL_M}{P_M \cdot MPL_M} = \frac{\Delta P_M}{P_M}$$

where the final ratio is obtained because we canceled out MPL_M in the numerator and denominator of the middle ratio. The term $\Delta W/W$ in this equation is the *percentage change in wages.* For example, suppose the initial wage is \$8 per hour and it rises to \$10 per hour. Then $\Delta W/W = \$2/\$8 = 0.25$, which is a 25% increase in the wage. Similarly, the term $\Delta P_M/P_M$ is the *percentage change in the price of manufactured goods.* When $\Delta W/W < \Delta P_M/P_M$, then the percentage increase in the wage is *less than* the percentage increase in the price of the manufactured good. This inequality means that the

[5] For example, suppose that you earn \$8 per hour, and your favorite snack costs \$2. Then you could afford to buy \$8/\$2 = 4 of these snacks after working for one hour.

FIGURE 3-5

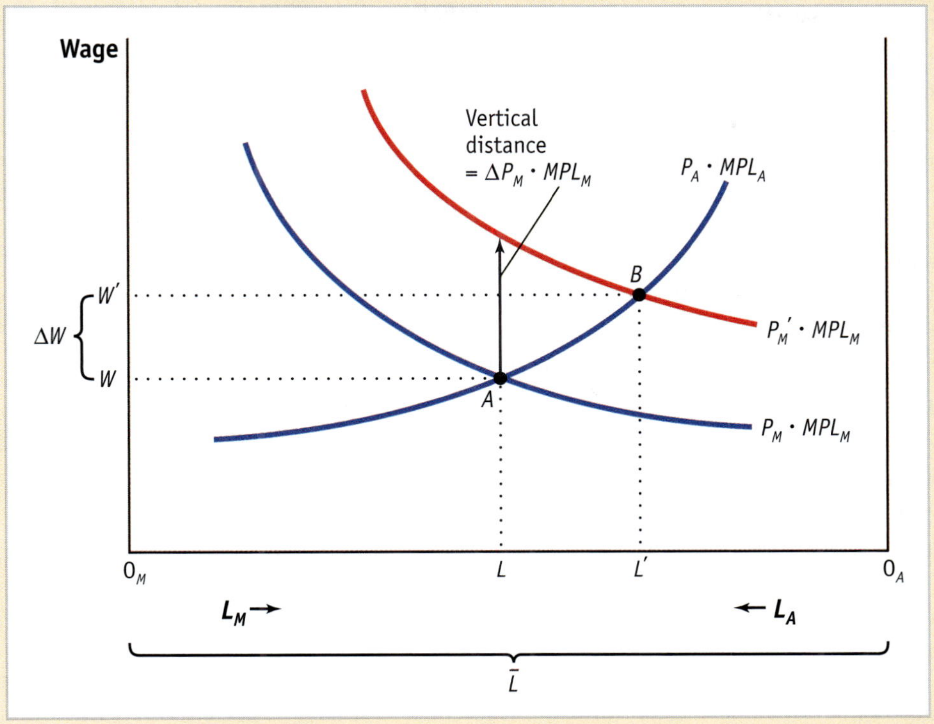

Increase in the Price of Manufactured Goods With an increase in the price of the manufactured good, the curve $P_M \cdot MPL_M$ shifts up to $P'_M \cdot MPL_M$ and the equilibrium shifts from point *A* to point *B*. The amount of labor used in manufacturing rises from 0_ML to $0_ML'$, and the amount of labor used in agriculture falls from 0_AL to $0_AL'$. The wage increases from *W* to *W'*, but this increase is less than the upward shift $\Delta P_M \cdot MPL_M$.

amount of the manufactured good that can be purchased with the wage has fallen, so the *real wage in terms of the manufactured good* W/P_M has decreased.[6]

Overall Impact on Labor We have now determined that as a result of our assumption of an increase in the relative price of manufactured goods, the *real wage in terms of food has increased and the real wage in terms of the manufactured good has decreased.* In this case, we assumed that the increase in relative price was caused by an increase in the price of manufactures with a constant price of agriculture. Notice, though, that if we had assumed a constant price of manufactures and a decrease in the price of agriculture (taken together, an increase in the relative price of manufactures), then we would have arrived at the same effects on the real wage in terms of both products.

Is labor better off or worse off after the price increase? We cannot tell. A person who spends most of his or her income on manufactured goods is worse off because fewer manufactured goods can be bought, but a person who spends most of his or her income on food is better off because more food is affordable. The bottom line is that in the specific-factors model, the increase in the price of the manufactured good has an ambiguous effect on the real wage and therefore an *ambiguous* effect on the well-being of workers.

[6] For example, suppose that the manufactured good is compact discs (CDs), which initially cost \$16 and then rise in price to \$24. The increase in the price of CDs is \$8, and so the percentage increase in the price of CDs is $\Delta P_M/P_M = \$8/\$16 = 0.50 = 50\%$. Suppose also that the wage has increased from \$8 to \$10 per hour, or 25%. Using the initial prices, by working one hour, you could afford to buy $W/P_M = \$8/\$16 = 0.5$, or one-half of a CD. Using the new prices, by working one hour, you can afford to buy $W/P_M = \$10/\$24 = 0.42$, or about four-tenths of a CD. So, your real wage measured in terms of CDs has gone down.

The conclusion that we cannot tell whether workers are better off or worse off from the opening of trade in the specific-factors model might seem wishy-washy to you, but it is important for several reasons. First, this result is different from what we found in the Ricardian model of Chapter 2, in which the real wage increases with the opening of trade so that workers are always unambiguously better off than in the absence of trade.[7] In the specific-factors model, that is no longer the case; the opening of trade and the shift in relative prices raise the real wage in terms of one good but lower it in terms of the other good. Second, our results for the specific-factors model serve as a warning against making unqualified statements about the effect of trade on workers, such as "Trade is bad for workers" or "Trade is good for workers." Even in the specific-factors model, which is simplified by considering only two industries and not allowing capital or land to move between them, we have found that the effects of opening trade on the real wage are complicated. In reality, the effect of trade on real wages is often more complex still.

Unemployment in the Specific-Factors Model We have ignored one significant, realistic feature in the specific-factors model: unemployment. You may often see online news stories about workers who are laid off because of import competition and who face a period of unemployment. Despite this outcome, most economists do not believe that trade necessarily harms workers overall. It is true that we have ignored unemployment in the specific-factors model: the labor employed in manufacturing L_M plus the labor employed in agriculture L_A always sums to the total labor supply $\bar{L}$, which means that there is no unemployment. One of the reasons we ignore unemployment in this model is that it is usually treated as a macroeconomic phenomenon, caused by business cycles, and it is hard to combine business cycle models with international trade models to isolate the effects of trade on workers. But the other, simpler reason is that even when people are laid off because of import competition, many of them do find new jobs within a reasonable period of time, and sometimes they find jobs with *higher* wages, as shown in the next application. Therefore, even if we take into account spells of unemployment, once we recognize that workers can find new jobs—possibly in export industries that are expanding—then we still cannot conclude that trade is necessarily good or bad for workers.

In the two applications that follow, we look at some evidence from the United States on the amount of time it takes to find new jobs and on the wages earned, and at attempts by governments to compensate workers who lose their jobs because of import competition. This type of compensation is called **Trade Adjustment Assistance (TAA)** in the United States.

APPLICATION

Manufacturing and Services in the United States: Employment and Wages across Sectors

Although the specific-factors model emphasizes manufacturing and agriculture, the amount of labor devoted to agriculture in most industrialized countries is small. A larger sector in industrialized countries is that of **services,** which includes wholesale

[7] The only situation in which workers do not gain from trade in the Ricardian model is if the Home country is very large, as discussed in Problem 11 of Chapter 2, such that the international relative price equals the no-trade relative price. In that case, Home workers are no better off from international trade but also no worse off.

and retail trade, finance, law, education, information technology, software engineering, consulting, and medical and government services. In the United States and most industrial countries, the service sector is larger than the manufacturing sector and much larger than the agriculture sector.

In Figure 3-6, we show employment in the manufacturing sector of the United States, both in terms of the number of workers employed in it and as a percentage of total employment in the economy. Using either measure, employment in manufacturing has been falling over time; given zero or negative growth in the agriculture sector, this indicates that the service sector has been growing. In Figure 3-7, we show the real wages earned by production—or blue-collar—workers in manufacturing, in all private services, and in information services (a subset of private services).[8] While wages were slightly higher in manufacturing than in private services from 1974 through 2007, all private service wages have been higher since 2008. This change is due in part to the effect of wages in the *information service* industry, which are substantially higher than those in manufacturing. For example, average hourly earnings in all private services were $18.40 per hour in 2009 and slightly lower—$18.30 per hour—in manufacturing overall. But in information services, average wages were much higher—$25.60 per hour.

FIGURE 3-6

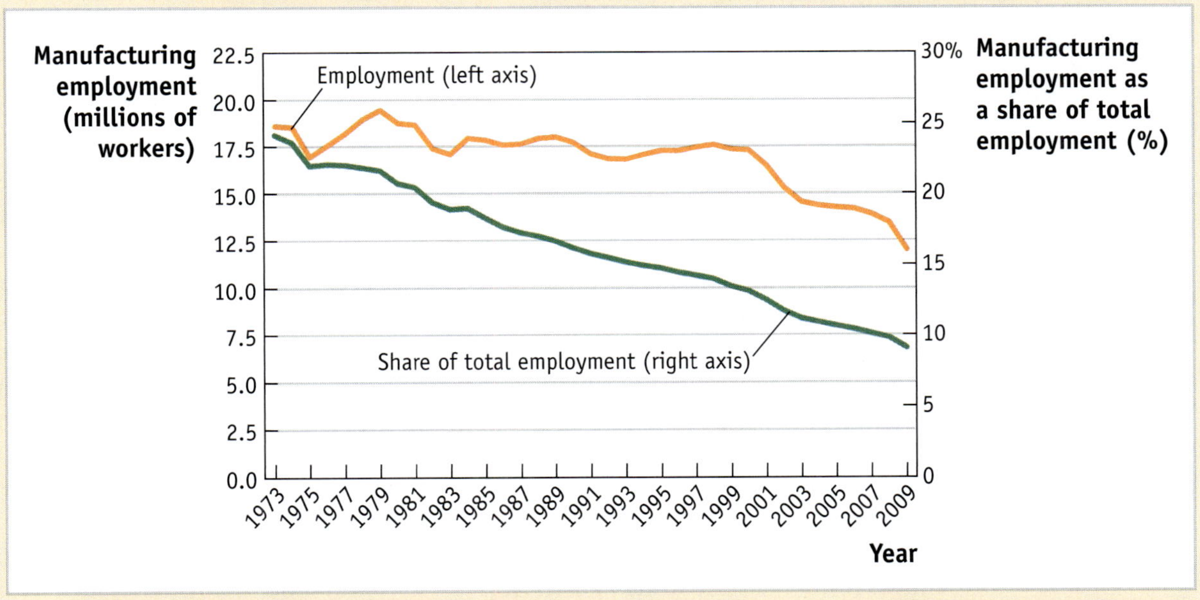

U.S. Manufacturing Sector Employment, 1973–2009 Employment in the U.S. manufacturing sector is shown on the left axis, and the share of manufacturing employment in total U.S. employment is shown on the right axis. Both manufacturing employment and its share in total employment have been falling over time, indicating that the service sector has been growing.

Source: Economic Report of the President, 2010, Table B46.

[8] The real wages shown in Figure 3-7 are measured relative to consumer prices in 2008 and represent the average hourly earnings for *production* workers, those workers involved in the assembly of services or products. Production workers are sometimes called "blue-collar" workers and typically earn hourly wages. The other category of workers, *nonproduction* workers, includes managers and all those who work at a desk. They are sometimes called "white-collar" workers and typically earn annual salaries instead of hourly wages.

FIGURE 3-7

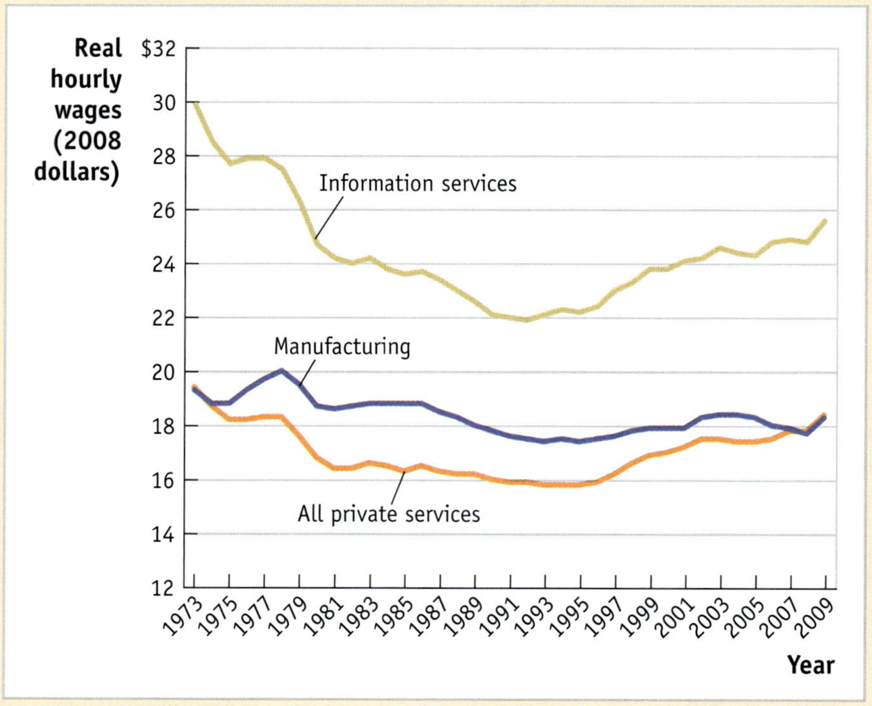

Real Hourly Earnings of Production Workers This chart shows the real wages (in constant 2008 dollars) earned by production workers in U.S. manufacturing, in all private services, and in information services (a subset of all private services). While wages were slightly higher in manufacturing than in all private services from 1974 through 2007, all private service wages have been higher since 2008. This change is due in part to the effect of wages in the information service industry, which are substantially higher than those in manufacturing. Real wages for production workers fell in most years between 1979 and 1995 but have been rising since then.

Source: http://www.bls.gov, Historical Data for the "B" Tables of the Employment Situation Release.

In both manufacturing and services, many workers are *displaced* or laid off each year and need to look for other jobs. In the three years from January 2005 to December 2007, for example, about 0.9 million workers were displaced in manufacturing and 2.3 million in all service industries, as shown in Table 3-1.[9] Of those laid off in manufacturing, 64% were reemployed by January 2008, and about half of these (49%) earned less in their new jobs. For services, however, 68% were reemployed by January 2008, and slightly more than half of these (56%) earned the same *or more* in their new jobs. The recession that began in 2008 clearly increased the number of displaced workers. From January 2008 to December 2009 the total number of displaced workers increased to 5.1 million, of which 2.1 million had been employed in manufacturing.

There are four lessons that we can take away from this comparison of employment and wages in manufacturing and services. First, wages differ across different sectors in the economy, so our theoretical assumption that wages are the same in agriculture and manufacturing is a simplification. Second, many workers are displaced each year and must find jobs elsewhere. Some of these workers may be laid off due to competition from imports, but there are other reasons, too—for instance, products that used to be purchased go out of fashion, firms reorganize as computers and other

[9] There were a smaller number of workers displaced in mining and construction (293,000), totaling 3.6 million overall. These were all displaced "long-tenured" people who had worked for at least three years with their former employer. There were another 4.6 million displaced people who had worked for less than three years with their former employer.

TABLE 3-1

Job Losses in Manufacturing and Service Industries, 2005–2009 This table shows the number of displaced (or laid-off) workers in manufacturing and service industries from 2005 to 2009. Between 64 and 68% of the workers displaced from 2005 to 2007 were reemployed by January 2008, with about one-half earning less in their new jobs and one-half earning the same or more, with slightly more workers reemployed in service industries earning more at their new job. However, the recession that began in 2008 clearly increased the number of displaced workers. From January 2008 to December 2009 the total number of displaced workers increased to 5.1 million, of which 2.1 million had been employed in manufacturing.

		PERCENTAGES			
Industry	Total Displaced Workers (thousands) January 2005–December 2007	Workers Reemployed by January 2008	Of the Workers Reemployed:		Total Displaced Workers (thousands) January 2008–December 2009
			Earn Less in New Job	Earn Same or More in New Job	
Total	3,641	67%	44%	55%	5,087
Manufacturing industries	876	64%	49%	51%	2,117
Service industries	2,312	68%	44%	56%	n.a.

n.a. = not available.

Source: U.S. Bureau of Labor Statistics.

technological advances become available, and firms change locations. Third, the majority of displaced workers find a new job within two or three years but not necessarily at the same wage. Typically, older workers (age 45 to 64) experience earnings losses when shifting between jobs, whereas younger workers (age 25 to 44) are often able to find a new job with the same or higher wages. Finally, when we measure wages in real terms by adjusting for inflation in the price of consumer goods, we see that real wages for all production workers fell in most years between 1979 and 1995 (we examine the reasons for that fall in later chapters) but have been rising slightly since then. ■

APPLICATION

Trade Adjustment Assistance Programs: Financing the Adjustment Costs of Trade

Should the government step in to compensate workers who are looking for jobs or who do not find them in a reasonable period of time? The unemployment insurance program in the United States provides some compensation, regardless of the reason for the layoff. In addition, the *Trade Adjustment Assistance (TAA)* program offers additional unemployment insurance payments and health insurance to workers who are laid off because of import competition and who are enrolled in a retraining program. The quotation from President Kennedy at the beginning of the chapter comes from a speech he made introducing the TAA program in 1962. He believed that this program was needed to compensate those Americans who lost their jobs due to international trade. Since 1993 there has also been a special TAA program under the North

American Free Trade Agreement (NAFTA) for workers who are laid off as a result of import competition from Mexico or Canada.[10] Recently, as part of the jobs stimulus bill signed by President Obama on February 17, 2009, workers in the service sector (as well as farmers) who lose their jobs due to trade can now also apply for TAA benefits. This extension is described in **Headlines: Services Workers Are Now Eligible for Trade Adjustment Assistance.**

Other countries also have programs like TAA to compensate those harmed by trade. A particularly interesting example occurred with the unification of East and West Germany on June 30, 1990. On that date, all barriers to trade between the countries were removed as well as all barriers to the movement of labor and capital between the two regions. The pressure from labor unions to achieve wage parity (equality) between the East and West meant that companies in former East Germany were faced with wages that were far above what they could afford to pay. According to one estimate, only 8% of former East German companies would be profitable at the higher wages paid in the West. In the absence of government intervention, it could be expected that severe bankruptcy and unemployment would result, leading to massive migration of East German workers to the former West Germany.

Economists studying this situation proposed that deep wage subsidies, or "flexible employment bonuses," should be given in former East Germany, thereby allowing factories to employ their workers while paying only a fraction of their wages. Furthermore, they argued that the wage subsidies would essentially pay for themselves because without them the government would have to provide unemployment insurance on a massive scale to the people left without jobs.[11] As it turns out, wage subsidies of this type were not used, and unemployment in the East and migration to the West continue to be challenging policy issues for the united Germany. ■

3 Earnings of Capital and Land

Let us now return to the specific-factors model. We have found that with the opening of trade and an increase in the relative price of manufactures, there are overall gains for the country, but labor does not necessarily gain. What about the gains to the other factors of production, either the capital used in manufacturing or the land used in agriculture? Capital and land are the two specific factors of production that cannot shift between the two industries; let us now look at the effect of the increase in the relative price of manufactures on the earnings of these specific factors.

Determining the Payments to Capital and Land

In each industry, capital and land earn what is left over from sales revenue after paying labor. Labor (L_M and L_A) earns the wage W, so total payments to labor in manufacturing are $W \cdot L_M$ and in agriculture are $W \cdot L_A$. By subtracting the payments to labor from the sales revenue earned in each industry, we end up with the payments

[10] We discuss the North American Free Trade Agreement in a later chapter and provide more details there on how many workers applied for benefits under the NAFTA-TAA program.
[11] George Akerlof, Andrew Rose, Janet Yellen, and Helga Hessenius, 1991, "East Germany in from the Cold: The Economic Aftermath of Currency Union," *Brookings Papers on Economic Activity*, Vol.1, 1–87.

HEADLINES

Services Workers Are Now Eligible for Trade Adjustment Assistance

President Kennedy first introduced Trade Adjustment Assistance (TAA) in the United States in 1962, for workers in manufacturing. This article described how it was recently extended to include service workers.

In today's era of global supply chains, high-speed Internet connection, and container shipping, Kennedy's concerns remain relevant: technology and trade mean growth, innovation and better living standards, but also change and instability. (Research early in this decade typically found that international competition accounted for about 2 percent of layoffs.) But while concerns may be permanent, specific programs and policies fade unless they adapt to changing times. And despite its periodic update, until this week TAA remained designed for an older world. Most notably, it barred support for services workers facing Internet-based competition . . . .

In this context, yesterday's stimulus bill signing contained the first fundamental change to the TAA program in a half-century. An accord three years in the making, overseen by Senators Max Baucus (D-MT) and Charles Grassley (R-IA), reshapes TAA for the 21st century. The new program, set out in 184 pages of legal text, has three basic changes:

- More workers are eligible: Service-industry employees will be fully eligible for TAA services, making the program relevant to the high-tech economy. So will workers whose businesses move abroad, regardless of the destination. The reform also eases eligibility for farmers and fishermen.
- They get more help: The reform raises training support from $220 million to $575 million, hikes support for health insurance from 65 percent to 80 percent of premiums, gives states $86 million a year to pay for TAA caseworkers, creates a $230 million program to support communities dealing with plant closure, and triples support for businesses managing sudden trade competition.
- They are more likely to know their rights: The bill also creates a special Labor Department TAA office to ensure that eligible workers know their options.

Kennedy's innovation is thus adapted to the 21st-century economy, guaranteeing today's workers the support their grandparents enjoyed. A bit of good news, in a year when it is all too rare.

Source: Excerpted from Progressive Policy Institute trade fact of the week, "Services Workers are Now Eligible for Trade Adjustment Assistance," February 18, 2009.

to capital and to land. If Q_M is the output in manufacturing and Q_A is the output in agriculture, the revenue earned in each industry is $P_M \cdot Q_M$ and $P_A \cdot Q_A$, and the payments to capital and to land are

$$\text{Payments to capital} = P_M \cdot Q_M - W \cdot L_M$$

$$\text{Payments to land} = P_A \cdot Q_A - W \cdot L_A$$

It will be useful to take these payments one step further and break them down into the earnings of each unit of capital and land. To do so, we need to know the quantity of capital and land. We denote the quantity of land used in agriculture as T acres and the quantity of capital (number of machines) used in manufacturing as K. Thus, the earnings of one unit of capital (a machine, for instance), which we call R_K, and the earnings of an acre of land, which we call R_T, are calculated as

$$R_K = \frac{\text{Payments to capital}}{K} = \frac{P_M \cdot Q_M - W \cdot L_M}{K}$$

$$R_T = \frac{\text{Payments to land}}{T} = \frac{P_A \cdot Q_A - W \cdot L_A}{T}$$

Economists call R_K the **rental on capital** and R_T the **rental on land.** The use of the term "rental" does not mean that the factory owners or farmers rent their machines or land from someone else, although they could. Instead, the rental on machines and land reflects what these factors of production earn during a period when they are used in manufacturing and agriculture. Alternatively, the rental is the amount these factors *could* earn if they were rented to someone else over that same time.

There is a second way to calculate the rentals, which will look similar to the formula we have used for wages. In each industry, wages reflect the marginal product of labor times the price of the good, $W = P_M \cdot MPL_M = P_A \cdot MPL_A$. Similarly, capital and land rentals can be calculated as

$$R_K = P_M \cdot MPK_M \text{ and } R_T = P_A \cdot MPT_A$$

where MPK_M is the marginal product of capital in manufacturing, and MPT_A is the marginal product of land in agriculture. These marginal product formulas give the same values for the rentals as first calculating the payments to capital and land, as we just did, and then dividing by the quantity of capital and land. We will use both approaches to obtain rental values, depending on which is easiest.

Change in the Real Rental on Capital Now that we understand how the rentals on capital and land are determined, we can look at what happens to them when the price of the manufactured good P_M rises, holding constant the price in agriculture P_A. From Figure 3-5, we know that the wage rises throughout the economy and that labor shifts from agriculture into manufacturing. As more labor is used in manufacturing, the marginal product of capital will rise because each machine has more labor to work it. In addition, as labor leaves agriculture, the marginal product of land will fall because each acre of land has fewer laborers to work it. The general conclusion is that *an increase in the quantity of labor used in an industry will raise the marginal product of the factor specific to that industry, and a decrease in labor will lower the marginal product of the specific factor.* This outcome does not contradict the law of diminishing returns, which states that an increase in labor will lower the marginal product *of labor* because now we are talking about how a change in labor affects the marginal product of *another factor*.

Using the preceding formulas for the rentals, we can summarize the results so far with

$$P_M \uparrow \Rightarrow \begin{Bmatrix} L_M \uparrow, \text{ so that } MPK_M = R_K/P_M \uparrow \\ \\ L_A \downarrow, \text{ so that } MPT_A = R_T/P_A \downarrow \end{Bmatrix}$$

That is, the increase in the marginal product of capital in manufacturing means that R_K/P_M also increases. Because R_K is the rental for capital, R_K/P_M is the amount of the manufactured good that can be purchased with this rent. Thus, the fact that R_K/P_M increases means that the real rental on capital in terms of the manufactured good has gone up. For the increase in the real rental on capital to occur even though the price of the manufactured good has gone up, too, the percentage increase in R_K must be greater than the percentage increase in P_M.[12]

The amount of food that can be purchased by capital owners is R_K/P_A. Because R_K has increased, and P_A is fixed, R_K/P_A must also increase; in other words, the real rental

[12] For example, if the price of manufactured goods rises by 6% and the rental on capital rises by 10%, then owners of capital can afford to buy 4% more of the manufactured good.

on capital in terms of food has also gone up. Because capital owners can afford to buy more of both goods, they are clearly better off when the price of the manufactured good rises. Unlike labor, whose real wage increased in terms of one good but fell in terms of the other, capital owners clearly gain from the rise in the relative price of manufactured goods.

Change in the Real Rental on Land Let us now consider what happens to the landowners. With labor leaving agriculture, the marginal product of each acre falls, so R_T/P_A also falls. Because R_T is the rental on land, R_T/P_A is the amount of food that can be purchased with this rent. The fact that R_T/P_A falls means that the real rental on land in terms of food has gone down, so landowners cannot afford to buy as much food. Because the price of food is unchanged while the price of the manufactured good has gone up, landowners will not be able to afford to buy as much of the manufactured good either. Thus, landowners are clearly worse off from the rise in the price of the manufactured good because they can afford to buy less of both goods.

Summary The real earnings of capital owners and landowners move in opposite directions, an outcome that illustrates a general conclusion: *an increase in the relative price of an industry's output will increase the real rental earned by the factor specific to that industry but will decrease the real rental of factors specific to other industries.* This conclusion means that the specific factors used in export industries will generally gain as trade is opened and the relative price of exports rises, but the specific factors used in import industries will generally lose as trade is opened and the relative price of imports falls.

Numerical Example

We have come a long way in our study of the specific-factors model and conclude by presenting a numerical example of how an increase in the relative price of manufactures affects the earnings of labor, capital, and land. This example reviews the results we have obtained so far using actual numbers. Suppose that the manufacturing industry has the following payments to labor and capital:

Manufacturing: Sales revenue $= P_M \cdot Q_M = \$100$

Payments to labor $= W \cdot L_M = \$60$

Payments to capital $= R_K \cdot K = \$40$

Notice that 60% of sales revenue in manufacturing goes to labor, and 40% goes to capital.

In agriculture, suppose that the payments to labor and land are as follows:

Agriculture: Sales revenue $= P_A \cdot Q_A = \$100$

Payments to labor $= W \cdot L_A = \$50$

Payments to land $= R_T \cdot T = \$50$

In the agriculture industry, we assume that land and labor each earn 50% of the sales revenue.

An increase in the relative price of manufactures P_M/P_A can be caused by an increase in P_M or a decrease in P_A. To be specific, suppose that the price of manufactures P_M rises by 10%, whereas the price of agriculture P_A does not change at all. We have found in our earlier discussion that $\Delta W/W$, the percentage change in the wage, will be between the percentage change in these two industry prices. So let us suppose that $\Delta W/W$, is 5%. We summarize these output and factor price changes as follows:

Manufacturing: Percentage increase in price = $\Delta P_M/P_M = 10\%$

Agriculture: Percentage increase in price = $\Delta P_A/P_A = 0\%$

Both industries: Percentage increase in the wage = $\Delta W/W = 5\%$

Notice that the increase in the wage applies in both industries because wages are always equalized across sectors.

Change in the Rental on Capital Our goal is to use the preceding data for manufacturing and agriculture to compute the change in the rental on capital and the change in the rental on land. Let's start with the equation for the rental on capital, which was computed by subtracting wage payments from sales revenue and then dividing by the amount of capital:

$$R_K = \frac{\text{Payments to capital}}{K} = \frac{P_M \cdot Q_M - W \cdot L_M}{K}$$

If the price of manufactured goods rises by $\Delta P_M > 0$, holding constant the price in agriculture, then the change in the rental is

$$\Delta R_K = \frac{\Delta P_M \cdot Q_M - \Delta W \cdot L_M}{K}$$

We want to rewrite this equation using percentage changes, like $\Delta P_M/P_M$, $\Delta W/W$, and $\Delta R_K/R_K$. To achieve this, divide both sides by R_K and rewrite the equation as

$$\frac{\Delta R_K}{R_K} = \frac{(\Delta P_M/P_M) \cdot P_M \cdot Q_M - (\Delta W/W) \cdot W \cdot L_M}{R_K \cdot K}$$

You can cancel terms in this equation to check that it is the same as before.

The term $\Delta P_M/P_M$ in this equation is the percentage change in the price of manufacturing, whereas $\Delta W/W$ is the percentage change in the wage. Given this information, along with the preceding data on the payments to labor, capital, and sales revenue, we can compute the percentage change in the rental on capital:

$$\frac{\Delta R_K}{R_K} = \frac{(10\% \cdot 100 - 5\% \cdot 60)}{40} = 17.5\%$$

We see that the percentage increase in the rental on capital, 17.5%, *exceeds* the percentage increase in the relative price of manufacturing, 10% (so $\Delta R_K/R_K > \Delta P_M/P_M > 0$). This outcome holds no matter what numbers are used in the preceding formula, provided that the percentage increase in the wage is less than the percentage increase in the price of the manufactured good (as proved in Figure 3-5).

Change in the Rental on Land We can use the same approach to examine the change in the rental on land. Continuing to assume that the price of the manufactured good rises, while the price in agriculture stays the same ($\Delta P_A = 0$), the change in the land rental is

$$\Delta R_T = \frac{0 \cdot Q_A - \Delta W \cdot L_A}{T}$$

Because the wage is increasing, $\Delta W > 0$, it follows immediately that the *rental on land is falling*, $\Delta R_T < 0$. The percentage amount by which it falls can be calculated by rewriting the above equation as

$$\frac{\Delta R_T}{R_T} = -\frac{\Delta W}{W}\left(\frac{W \cdot L_A}{R_T \cdot T}\right)$$

Using these earlier data for agriculture in this formula, we get

$$\frac{\Delta R_T}{R_T} = -5\%\left(\frac{50}{50}\right) = -5\%$$

In this case, the land rent falls by the same percentage amount that the wage increases. This equality occurs because we assumed that labor and land receive the same share of sales revenue in agriculture (50% each). If labor receives a higher share of revenue than land, then the rent on land will fall even more; if it receives a lower share, then the rent on land won't fall as much.

General Equation for the Change in Factor Prices By summarizing our results in a single equation, we can see how all the changes in factor and industry prices are related. Under the assumption that the price of the manufactured good increased but the price of the agricultural good did not change, we have shown the following:

$$\underbrace{\Delta R_T/R_T < 0}_{\text{Real rental on land falls}} < \underbrace{\Delta W/W < \Delta P_M/P_M}_{\text{Change in the real wage is ambiguous}} < \underbrace{\Delta R_K/R_K}_{\text{Real rental on capital rises}}, \text{ for an increase in } P_M$$

In other words, wages rise but not as much as the percentage increase in the price of the manufactured good; the rental on capital (which is specific to the manufacturing sector) rises by more than the manufacturing price, so capital owners are better off; and the rental on land (which is the specific factor in the other sector) falls, so landowners are worse off.

What happens if the price of the manufactured good falls? Then the inequalities are reversed, and the equation becomes

$$\underbrace{\Delta R_K/R_K < \Delta P_M/P_M}_{\text{Real rental on capital falls}} < \underbrace{\Delta W/W < 0}_{\text{Change in the real wage is ambiguous}} < \underbrace{\Delta R_T/R_T}_{\text{Real rental on land rises}}, \text{ for a decrease in } P_M$$

In this case, wages fall but by less than the percentage decrease in the manufactured good; the rental on capital (which is specific to the manufacturing sector) falls by more than the manufacturing price, so capital owners are worse off; and the rental on land (which is the specific factor in the other sector) rises, so landowners are better off.

What happens if the *price of the agricultural good rises*? You can probably guess based on the previous example that this change will benefit land and harm capital. The equation summarizing the changes in all three factor earnings becomes

$$\underbrace{\Delta R_K/R_K < 0}_{\text{Real rental on capital falls}} < \underbrace{\Delta W/W < \Delta P_A/P_A}_{\text{Change in the real wage is ambiguous}} < \underbrace{\Delta R_T/R_T}_{\text{Real rental on land rises}}, \text{ for an increase in } P_A$$

Note that it is the specific factor in the agricultural sector that gains and the specific factor in manufacturing that loses. The general result of these summary equations is that *the specific factor in the sector whose relative price has increased gains, the specific factor in the other sector loses, and labor is "caught in the middle," with its real wage increasing in terms of one good but falling in terms of the other*. These equations summarize the response of all three factor prices in the short run, when capital and land are specific to each sector but labor is mobile.

What It All Means

Our results from the specific-factors model show that the earnings of *specific factors* change the most from changes in relative prices due to international trade. Regardless of which good's price changes, the earnings of capital and land show the most extreme changes in their rentals, whereas the changes in the wages paid to labor are in the middle. Intuitively, these extreme changes in factor prices occur because the specific factors are not able to leave their sectors and find employment elsewhere. Labor benefits by its opportunity to move between sectors and earn the same wage in each, but the interests of capital and land are opposed to each other: one gains and the other loses. This suggests that we ought to be able to find real-world examples in which a change in international prices leads to losses for either capitalists or landowners. There are many such examples, and we discuss one in the next application.

APPLICATION

Prices in Agriculture

At the end of the previous chapter, we discussed the Prebisch–Singer hypothesis, which states that the prices of primary commodities tend to fall over time. Although we argued that this hypothesis does not hold for all primary commodities, it does hold for some agricultural goods: the relative prices of cotton, palm oil, rice, sugar, rubber, wheat, and wool declined for more than half the years between 1900 and 1998. Generally, agricultural prices fall as countries become more efficient at growing crops and begin exporting them. From our study of the specific-factors model, it will be landowners (i.e., farmers) who lose in real terms from this decline in the relative price of agricultural products. On the other hand, capital owners gain in real terms, and changes in the real wage are ambiguous. Faced with declining real earnings in the agriculture sector, governments and other groups often take actions to prevent the incomes of farmers from falling.

Coffee Prices An example of an agricultural commodity with particularly volatile prices is coffee. The price of coffee on world markets fluctuates a great deal from year to year because of weather and also because of the entry of new suppliers in Brazil and new supplying countries such as Vietnam. The movements in the real wholesale price of coffee (measured in 2008 dollars) are shown in Figure 3-8. Wholesale prices were at a high of $3.00 per pound in 1986, then fell to a low of 83¢ per pound in 1993, rose to $1.77 in 1995, and then fell to 50¢ per pound in 2001. Since 2001 there has been a sustained increase in both price and quantity, implying a shift in import demand. By 2008 prices had risen to $1.24 per pound. These dramatic fluctuations in prices create equally large movements in the real incomes of farmers, making it difficult for them to sustain a living. The very low prices in 2001 created a crisis in the coffee-growing regions of Central America, requiring humanitarian aid for farmers and their families. The governments of coffee-growing regions in Central America and Asia cannot afford to protect their coffee farmers by propping up prices, as do the industrial countries.

FIGURE 3-8

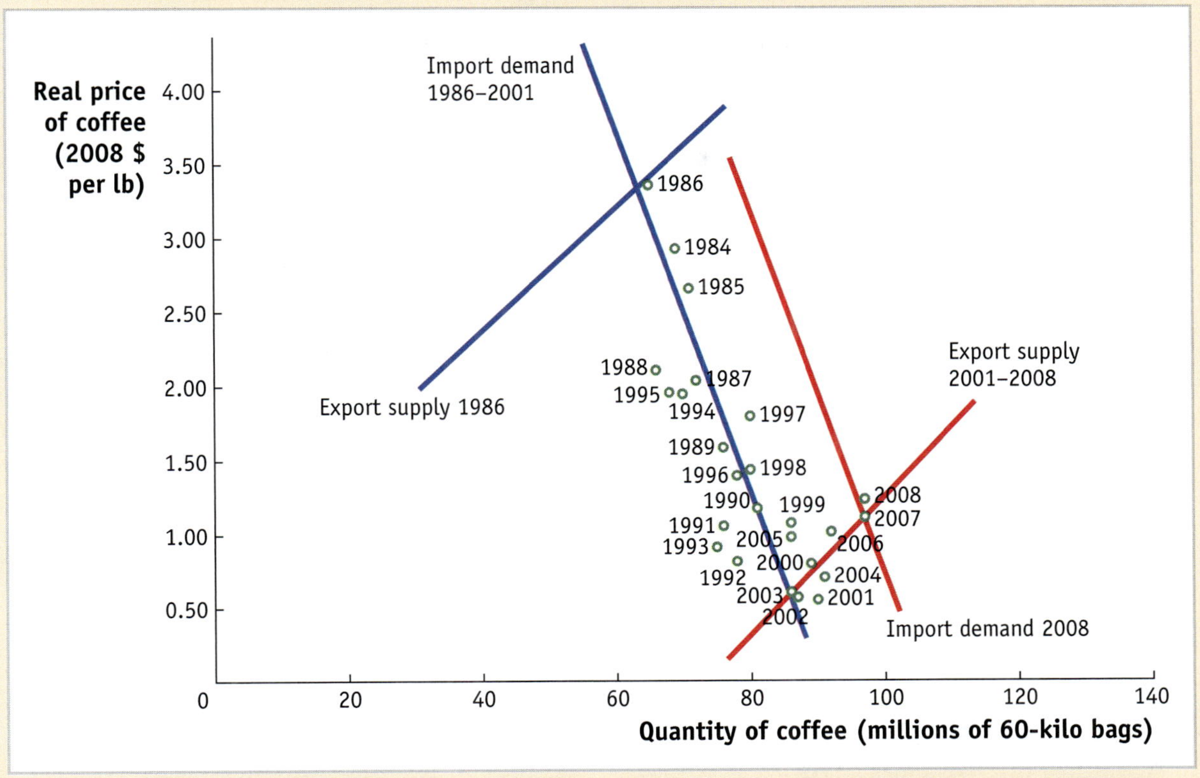

World Coffee Market Real wholesale prices for coffee have fluctuated greatly on world markets. Using 2008 dollars, prices were at a high of about $3.00 per pound in 1986, fell to 83¢ per pound in 1993, rose to $1.77 in 1995, and then fell to 50¢ per pound in 2001. Since 2001 there has been a sustained increase in both price and quantity, implying a shift in import demand. By 2008 prices had risen to $1.24 per pound. Corresponding to these price fluctuations, the quantity of world coffee exports was at a low in 1986 (65 million bags) and at a high in 2008 (97 million bags), as supplies from Brazil and Vietnam increased.

Source: International Coffee Organization, http://www.ico.org.

According to the specific-factors model, big fluctuations in coffee prices are extremely disruptive to the real earnings of landowners in coffee-exporting developing countries, many of whom are small farmers and their families. Can anything be done to avoid the kind of boom-and-bust cycle that occurs regularly in coffee markets?

Photo Courtesy TransFair USA © 2007

Groups like TransFair USA ensure coffee farmers like Santiago Rivera, pictured here, a more stable source of income over time.

Fair-Trade Coffee One idea that is gaining appeal is to sell coffee from developing countries directly to consumers in industrial countries, thereby avoiding the middlemen (such as local buyers, millers, exporters, shippers, and importers) and ensuring a minimum price for the farmers. You may have seen "fair-trade" coffee at your favorite coffeehouse. This coffee first appeared in the United States in 1999, imported by a group called TransFair USA that is committed to passing more of the profits back to the growers. TransFair USA is an example of a nongovernmental organization that is trying to help farmers by raising prices, and the consumer gets the choice of whether to purchase this higher-priced product. In addition to coffee, TransFair USA has been applying its Fair Trade label to imports of cocoa, tea, rice, sugar, bananas, mangoes, pineapples, and grapes.

World coffee prices recovered in 2005, which meant that groups like TransFair USA faced a dilemma: the fair-trade prices that they had guaranteed to farmers were actually less than the world price of coffee. The accompanying article **Headlines: Rise in Coffee Prices—Great for Farmers, Tough on Co-ops** describes how some farmers were tempted to break their contracts with local co-ops (at fixed, fair-trade prices) to deliver coffee to local middlemen at prevailing world prices. TransFair USA and similar organizations purchase coffee at higher than the market price when the market is low (as in 2001), but in other years (like 2005) the fair-trade price is below the market price. Essentially, TransFair USA is offering farmers a form of *insurance* whereby the fair-trade price of coffee will not fluctuate too much, ensuring them a more stable source of income over time. By protecting farmers against the boom-and-bust cycle of fluctuating prices, they are able to enjoy greater gains from trade by exporting their coffee. So when you consider buying a cup of fair-trade coffee at your favorite coffeehouse, you are supporting coffee farmers who rely on the efforts of groups like TransFair USA to raise their incomes, and applying the logic of the specific-factors model, all at the same time! ■

HEADLINES

Rise in Coffee Prices—Great for Farmers, Tough on Co-ops

TransFair USA guarantees a minimum purchase price for coffee farmers, acting as insurance against a falling market price. But during periods when the market price is rising, it is challenging to ensure that farmers deliver their coffee.

During winter and spring of the 2005 harvest, a dilemma surfaced in rural areas of Central America and Mexico. Fair-trade cooperative managers found it increasingly difficult to get members to deliver coffee to their own organization at fair-trade prices. The co-op managers were holding contracts that were set months before at fixed fair-trade prices of $1.26 per pound, but now the world coffee price was higher. Growers were seeing some of the highest prices paid in five years, and the temptation was great to sell their coffee to the highest local bidder, instead of delivering it as promised to their own co-ops.

In most cases, the co-ops' leaders were able to convince farmers to deliver coffee, but often based on arguments of loyalty, as the fair-trade fixed price was now lower than the premium prices being offered by the local middleman. It was not the model that the founders of fair-trade coffee pricing had envisioned when they created the program.

"It's worth noting that we were pleased to see prices rise in late 2004," says Christopher Himes, TransFair USA's Director of Certification and Finance. "This price rise, in conjunction with the impact fair trade was already having, increased the income and living standards of coffee farmers around the world. The most challenging thing during this time for TransFair USA was the speed with which the local differentials [between the fair-trade price and the world price] rose in Indonesia. They quickly skyrocketed to 80 cents [per pound] or higher, making the market value of farmers' coffee higher than that of some of the . . . fair-trade contracts."

Source: David Griswold, http://www.FreshCup.com, June 2005.

4 Conclusions

In the Ricardian model of Chapter 2, we showed that free trade could never make a country worse off, and in most cases free trade would make it better off. This result remains true when we add land and capital as factors of production, in addition to labor. Provided that the relative price with international trade differs from the no-trade relative price, then a country gains from international trade. This conclusion does not mean, however, that each and every factor of production gains. On the contrary, we have shown in this chapter that the change in relative prices due to the opening of trade creates winners and losers. Some factors of production gain in real terms and other factors of production lose. To demonstrate this result, we have used a short-run model, in which labor is mobile between sectors and land and capital are each specific to their sectors.

Classical economists believed that, in the short run, factors of production that could not move between industries would lose the most from trade. We have found that this is true for the factor that is specific to the import-competing industry. That industry suffers a drop in its relative price because of international trade, which leads to a fall in the real rental on the specific factor in that industry. On the other hand, the specific factor in the export industry—whose relative price rises with the opening of trade—enjoys an increase in its real rental. Labor is mobile between the two industries, which allows it to avoid such extreme changes in its wage—real wages rise in terms of one good but fall in terms of the other good, so we cannot tell whether workers are better off or worse off after a country opens to trade.

Economists have carefully proved that, in theory, the gains of individuals due to opening trade exceed the losses. This result means that, in principle, the government should be able to tax the winners and compensate the losers so that everyone is better off because of trade. In practice, it is very difficult to design programs to achieve that level of compensation. In this chapter, we looked at one compensation program—Trade Adjustment Assistance—that is used in the United States and other countries to compensate people who are laid off because of import competition. There are many other policies (such as import tariffs and quotas) that are intended to protect individuals from the effect of price changes resulting from international trade, and we examine these policies later in the book.

KEY POINTS

1. Opening a country to international trade leads to overall gains, but in a model with several factors of production, some factors of production will lose.
2. The fact that some people are harmed because of trade sometimes creates social tensions that may be strong enough to topple governments. A recent example is Bolivia, where the citizens in the early 2000s could not agree on how to share the gains from exporting natural gas.
3. In the specific-factors model, factors of production that cannot move between industries will gain or lose the most from opening a country to trade. The factor of production that is specific to the import industry will lose in real terms, as the relative price of the import good falls. The factor of production that is specific to the export industry will gain in real terms, as the relative price of the export good rises.

4. In the specific-factors model, labor can move between the industries and earns the same wage in each. When the relative price of either good changes, then the real wage rises when measured in terms of one good but falls when measured in terms of the other good. Without knowing how much of each good workers prefer to consume, we cannot say whether workers are better off or worse off because of trade.
5. Economists do not normally count the costs of unemployment as a loss from trade because people are often able to find new jobs. In the United States, for example, about two-thirds of people laid off from manufacturing or services companies find new jobs within two or three years, although sometimes at lower wages.
6. Trade Adjustment Assistance policies are intended to compensate those who are harmed due to trade by providing additional income during the period of unemployment. Recently, the Trade Adjustment Assistance program in the United States was expanded to include workers laid off due to trade in service industries.
7. Even when many people are employed in export activities, such as those involved in coffee export from certain developing countries, fluctuations in the world market price can lead to large changes in income for growers and workers.

KEY TERMS

specific-factors model, p. 60
diminishing returns, p. 61
autarky, p. 65
embargo, p. 65
real wage, p. 68
Trade Adjustment Assistance (TAA), p. 70
services, p. 70
rental on capital, p. 76
rental on land, p. 76

PROBLEMS

1. Why is the specific-factors model referred to as a short-run model?
2. Figure 3-7 presents wages in the manufacturing and services sectors for the period 1973 to 2009. Is the difference in wages across sectors consistent with either the Ricardian model studied in Chapter 2 or the specific-factors model? Explain why or why not.
3. In the gains from trade diagram in Figure 3-3, suppose that instead of having a rise in the relative price of manufactures, there is instead a fall in that relative price.
   a. Starting at the no-trade point *A* in Figure 3-3, show what would happen to production and consumption.
   b. Which good is exported and which is imported?
   c. Explain why the overall gains from trade are still positive.
4. Starting from equilibrium in the specific-factors model, suppose the price of manufactured goods falls so that wages fall from W' to W in Figure 3-5.
   a. Show that the percentage fall in the wage is less than the percentage fall in the price of manufacturing so that the real wage of labor in terms of manufactured goods goes up.
   b. What happens to the real wage of labor in terms of agriculture?
   c. Are workers better off, worse off, or is the outcome ambiguous?
5. Use the information given here to answer the following questions:

   Manufacturing:

   Sales revenue = $P_M \cdot Q_M = 150$
   Payments to labor = $W \cdot L_M = 100$
   Payments to capital = $R_K \cdot K = 50$

Agriculture:

Sales revenue = $P_A \cdot Q_A = 150$
Payments to labor = $W \cdot L_A = 50$
Payments to land = $R_T \cdot T = 100$

Holding the price of manufacturing constant, suppose the increase in the price of agriculture is 10% and the increase in the wage is 5%.

a. Determine the impact of the increase in the price of agriculture on the rental on land and the rental on capital.
b. Explain what has happened to the real rental on land and the real rental on capital.

6. If instead of the situation given in Problem 5, the price of manufacturing were to fall by 10%, would landowners or capital owners be better off? Explain. How would the decrease in the price of manufacturing affect labor? Explain.

7. Read the article by Lori G. Kletzer and Robert E. Litan, "A Prescription to Relieve Worker Anxiety," Policy Brief 01-2 (Washington, D.C.: Peterson Institute for International Economics), available online at http://www.iie.com/publications/pb/PP1-2.htm, which refers to the U.S. recession of 2000 and 2001. Then answer the following:

a. Under the version of Trade Adjustment Assistance (TAA) in the United States that they refer to, how many extra weeks of unemployment insurance are workers eligible for? What two criteria must workers meet to qualify for this extra unemployment insurance?
b. Consider the proposal for "wage insurance" that Kletzer and Litan make in their article. What criteria would workers need to qualify for this insurance? What amount of extra income would they receive from the insurance?
c. If Kletzer and Litan's new plan for "wage insurance" had been adopted by the United States, what would have been the budgetary cost in 1999, when unemployment was 4.2%? How does this compare with the amount that is now spent on unemployment insurance?

8. In the specific-factors model, assume that the price of agricultural goods decreases while the price of manufactured goods is unchanged ($\Delta P_A/P_A < 0$ and $\Delta P_M/P_M = 0$). Arrange the following terms in ascending order:

$\Delta R_T/R_T$ $\Delta R_K/R_K$ $\Delta P_A/P_A$ $\Delta P_M/P_M$ $\Delta W/W$

Hint: Try starting with a diagram like Figure 3-5, but change the price of agricultural goods instead.

9. Suppose two countries, Canada and Mexico, produce two goods: timber and televisions. Assume that land is specific to timber, capital is specific to televisions, and labor is free to move between the two industries. When Canada and Mexico engage in free trade, the relative price of televisions falls in Canada and the relative price of timber falls in Mexico.

a. In a graph similar to Figure 3-5, show how the wage changes in Canada due to a fall in the price of televisions, holding constant the price of timber. Can we predict that change in the real wage?
b. What is the impact of opening trade on the rentals on capital and land in Canada? Can we predict that change in the real rentals on capital and land?
c. What is the impact of opening trade on the rentals on capital and land in Mexico? Can we predict that change in the real rentals on capital and land?
d. In each country, has the specific factor in the export industry gained or lost and has the specific factor in the import industry gained or lost?

10. Home produces two goods, computers and wheat, for which capital is specific to computers, land is specific to wheat, and labor is mobile between the two industries. Home has 100 workers and 100 units of capital but only 10 units of land.

a. Draw a graph similar to Figure 3-1 with the output of wheat on the horizontal axis and the labor in wheat on the vertical axis. What is the relationship between the output of wheat and the marginal product of labor in the wheat industry as more labor is used?

b. Draw the production possibilities frontier for Home with wheat on the horizontal axis and computers on the vertical axis.

c. Explain how the price of wheat relative to computers is determined in the absence of trade.

d. Reproduce Figure 3-4 with the amount of labor used in wheat measuring from left to right along the horizontal axis and the amount of labor used in computers moving in the reverse direction.

e. Assume that due to international trade, the price of wheat rises. Analyze the effect of the increase in the price of wheat on the allocation of labor between the two sectors.

11. Similar to Home in Problem 10, Foreign also produces computers and wheat using capital, which is specific to computers; land, which is specific to wheat; and labor, which is mobile between the two sectors. Foreign has 100 workers and 100 units of land but only 10 units of capital. It has the same production functions as Home.

 a. Will the no-trade relative price of wheat be higher in Home or in Foreign? Explain why you expect this outcome.

 b. When trade is opened, what happens to the relative price of wheat in Foreign and to the relative price of wheat in Home?

 c. Based on your answer to (b), predict the effect of opening trade on the rental on land in each country, which is specific to wheat. What about the rental on capital, which is specific to computers?

12. In the text, we learned that workers displaced by import competition are eligible for compensation through the Trade Adjustment Assistance program. Firms are also eligible for support through Trade Adjustment Assistance for Firms, a federal program that provides financial assistance to manufacturers affected by import competition. Go to http://www.taacenters.org to read about this program, and answer the following:

 a. What criteria does a firm have to satisfy to quality for benefits?

 b. What amount of money is provided to firms, and for what purpose?

 c. Provide an argument for and an argument against the continued funding of this federal program.

NET WORK

The Bureau of Labor Statistics regularly releases information on the changes in employment, wages, and displacement of workers at http://www.bls.gov. Find one recent announcement and summarize that information. How does the information in that announcement compare with the trends in the application just discussed on employment and wages in manufacturing and services?

4

Trade and Resources: The Heckscher-Ohlin Model

God did not bestow all products upon all parts of the earth, but distributed His gifts over different regions, to the end that men might cultivate a social relationship because one would have need of the help of another. And so He called commerce into being, that all men might be able to have common enjoyment of the fruits of the earth, no matter where produced.

Libanius (AD 314–393), *Orations* (III)

Nature, by giving a diversity of geniuses, climates, and soils, to different nations, has secured their mutual intercourse and commerce. . . . The industry of the nations, from whom they import, receives encouragement: Their own is also [i]ncreased, by the sale of the commodities which they give in exchange.

David Hume, *Essays, Moral, Political, and Literary*, 1752, Part II, Essay VI, "On the Jealousy of Trade"

In Chapter 2, we examined U.S. imports of snowboards. We argued there that the resources found in a country would influence its pattern of international trade. Canada's export of snowboards to the United States reflects its mountains and cold climate, as do the exports of snowboards to the United States from Austria, Spain, France, Bulgaria, and Switzerland. Because each country's resources are different and because resources are spread unevenly around the world, countries have a reason to trade the goods made with these resources. This is an old idea, as shown by the quotations at the beginning of this chapter; the first is from the fourth-century Greek scholar Libanius, and the second is from the eighteenth-century philosopher David Hume.

In this chapter, we outline the **Heckscher-Ohlin model,** a model that assumes that trade occurs because countries have different resources. This model contrasts with the Ricardian model, which assumed that trade occurs because countries use their technological comparative advantage to specialize in the production of different goods. The model is named after the Swedish economists Eli Heckscher, who wrote about his views of international trade in a 1919 article, and his student Bertil Ohlin, who further developed these ideas in his 1924 dissertation.

The Heckscher-Ohlin model was developed at the end of a "golden age" of international trade (as described in Chapter 1) that lasted from about 1890 until 1914, when World War I started. Those years saw dramatic improvements in transportation: the steamship and the railroad allowed for a great increase in the amount of international trade. For these reasons, there was a considerable increase in the ratio of trade to GDP between 1890 and 1914. It is not surprising, then, that Heckscher and Ohlin would want to explain the large increase in trade that they had witnessed in their own lifetimes. The ability to transport machines across borders meant that they did not look to differences in technologies across countries as the reason for trade, as Ricardo had done. Instead, they assumed that technologies were the same across countries, and they used the uneven distribution of resources across countries to explain trade patterns.

Even today, there are many examples of international trade driven by the land, labor, and capital resources found in each country. Canada, for example, has a large amount of land and therefore exports agricultural and forestry products, as well as pertroleum; the United States, Western Europe, and Japan have many highly skilled workers and much capital and export sophisticated services and manufactured goods; China and other Asian countries have a large number of workers and moderate but growing amounts of capital and export less sophisticated manufactured goods; and so on. We study these and other examples of international trade in this chapter.

Our first goal is to describe the Heckscher-Ohlin model of trade. The specific-factors model that we studied in the previous chapter was a short-run model because capital and land could not move between the industries. In contrast, the Heckscher-Ohlin model is a long-run model because all factors of production can move between the industries. It is difficult to deal with three factors of production (labor, capital, and land) in both industries, so, instead, we assume that there are just two factors (labor and capital).

After predicting the long-run pattern of trade between countries using the Heckscher-Ohlin model, our second goal is to examine the empirical evidence on the Heckscher-Ohlin model. Although you might think it is obvious that a country's exports will be based on the resources the country has in abundance, it turns out that this prediction does not always hold true in practice. To obtain better predictions from the Heckscher-Ohlin model, we extend the model in several directions, first by allowing for more than two factors of production and second by allowing countries to differ in their technologies, as in the Ricardian model. Both extensions make the predictions from the Heckscher-Ohlin model match more closely the trade patterns in the world economy today.

The third goal of the chapter is to investigate how the opening of trade between the two countries affects the payments to labor and to capital in each of them. We use the Heckscher-Ohlin model to predict which factor(s) gain when international trade begins and which factor(s) lose.

1 Heckscher-Ohlin Model

In building the Heckscher-Ohlin (HO) model, we suppose there are two countries, Home and Foreign, each of which produces two goods, computers and shoes, using two factors of production, labor and capital. Using symbols for capital (K) and labor (L), we can add up the resources used in each industry to get the total for the economy. For example, the amount of capital Home uses in shoes K_S, plus the amount of capital used in computers K_C, adds up to the total capital available in the economy $\overline{K}$, so that $K_C + K_S = \overline{K}$. The same applies for Foreign: $K_C^* + K_S^* = \overline{K}^*$. Similarly, the amount of labor Home uses in shoes L_S, and the amount of labor used in computers L_C, add up to the total labor in the economy $\overline{L}$, so that $L_C + L_S = \overline{L}$. The same applies for Foreign: $L_C^* + L_S^* = \overline{L}^*$.

Assumptions of the Heckscher-Ohlin Model

Because the Heckscher-Ohlin (HO) model describes the economy in the long run, the assumptions used differ from those in the short-run specific-factors model of Chapter 3:

Assumption 1: Both factors can move freely between the industries.

This assumption implies that if both industries are actually producing, then capital must earn the same rental R in each of them. The reason for this result is that if capital earned a higher rental in one industry than the other, then all capital would move to the industry with the higher rental and the other industry would shut down. This result differs from the specific-factors model in which capital in manufacturing and land in agriculture earned different rentals in their respective industries. But like the specific-factor model, if both industries are producing, then all labor earns the same wage W in each of them.

Our second assumption concerns how the factors are combined to make shoes and computers:

Assumption 2: Shoe production is labor-intensive; that is, it requires more labor per unit of capital to produce shoes than computers, so that $L_S/K_S > L_C/K_C$

Another way to state this assumption is to say that computer production is capital-intensive; that is, more capital per worker is used to produce computers than to produce shoes, so that $K_C/L_C > K_S/L_S$. The idea that shoes use more labor per unit of capital, and computers use more capital per worker, matches how most of us think about the technologies used in these two industries.

In Figure 4-1, the demands for labor relative to capital in each industry (L_C/K_C and L_S/K_S) are graphed against the wage relative to the rental on capital, W/R (or the wage-rental ratio). These two curves slope down just like regular demand curves: as W/R rises, the quantity of labor demanded relative to the quantity of capital demanded falls. As we work through the HO model, remember that these are *relative* demand curves for labor; the "quantity" on the horizontal axis is the ratio of labor to capital used in production, and the "price" is the ratio of the labor wage to the capital rental. Assumption 2 says that the relative demand curve in shoes, L_S/K_S in Figure 4-1, lies to the right of the relative demand curve in computers L_C/K_C, because shoe production is more labor-intensive.

Whereas the preceding assumptions have focused on the production process within each country, the HO model requires assumptions that apply across countries as well. Our next assumption is that the amounts of labor and capital found in Home and Foreign are different:

FIGURE 4-1

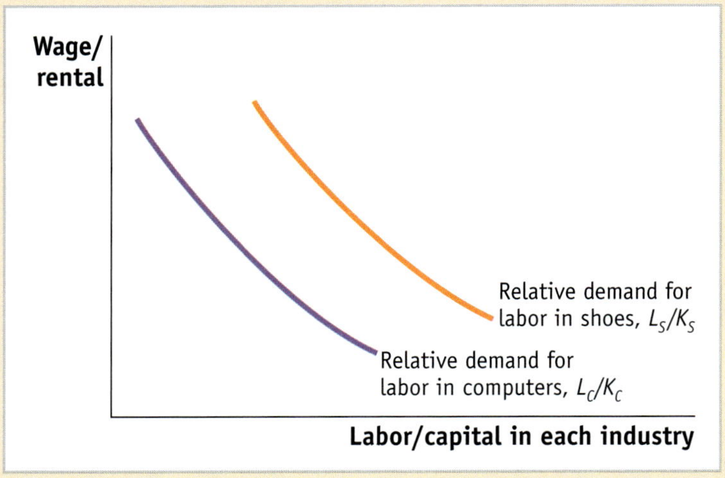

Labor Intensity of Each Industry The demand for labor relative to capital is assumed to be higher in shoes than in computers, $L_S/K_S > L_C/K_C$. These two curves slope down just like regular demand curves, but in this case, they are *relative* demand curves for labor (i.e., demand for labor divided by demand for capital).

Assumption 3: Foreign is labor-abundant, by which we mean that the labor–capital ratio in Foreign exceeds that in Home, $\overline{L}^*/\overline{K}^* > \overline{L}/\overline{K}$. Equivalently, Home is capital-abundant, so that $\overline{K}/\overline{L} > \overline{K}^*/\overline{L}^*$.

There are many reasons for labor, capital, and other resources to differ across countries: countries differ in their geographic size and populations, previous waves of immigration or emigration may have changed a country's population, countries are at different stages of development and so have differing amounts of capital, and so on. If we were considering land in the HO model, Home and Foreign would have different amounts of usable land due to the shape of their borders and to differences in topography and climate. In building the HO model, we do not consider why the amounts of labor, capital, or land differ across countries but simply accept these differences as important determinants of why countries engage in international trade.

Assumption 3 focuses on a particular case, in which Foreign is labor-abundant and Home is capital-abundant. This assumption is true, for example, if Foreign has a larger workforce than Home ($\overline{L}^* > \overline{L}$) and Foreign and Home have equal amounts of capital, $\overline{K}^* = \overline{K}$. Under these circumstances, $\overline{L}^*/\overline{K}^* > \overline{L}/\overline{K}$, so Foreign is labor-abundant. Conversely, the capital–labor ratio in Home exceeds that in Foreign, $\overline{K}/\overline{L} > \overline{K}^*/\overline{L}^*$, so the Home country is capital-abundant.

Assumption 4: The final outputs, shoes and computers, can be traded freely (i.e., without any restrictions) between nations, but labor and capital do not move between countries.

In this chapter, we do not allow labor or capital to move between countries. We relax this assumption in the next chapter, in which we investigate the movement of labor between countries through immigration as well as the movement of capital between countries through foreign direct investment.

Our final two assumptions involve the technologies of firms and tastes of consumers across countries:

Assumption 5: The technologies used to produce the two goods are identical across the countries.

This assumption is the opposite of that made in the Ricardian model (Chapter 2), which assumes that technological differences across countries are the reason for trade. It is not realistic to assume that technologies are the same across countries because often the technologies used in rich versus poor countries are quite different (as described in the following application). Although assumption 5 is not very realistic, it allows us to focus on a single reason for trade: the different amounts of labor and capital found in each country. Later in this chapter, we use data to test the validity of the HO model and find that the model performs better when assumption 5 is not used.

Our final assumption is as follows:

Assumption 6: Consumer tastes are the same across countries, and preferences for computers and shoes do not vary with a country's level of income.

That is, we suppose that a poorer country will buy fewer shoes and computers, but will buy them in the same ratio as a wealthier country facing the same prices. Again, this assumption is not very realistic: consumers in poor countries do spend more of their income on shoes, clothing, and other basic goods than on computers, whereas in rich countries a higher share of income can be spent on computers and other electronic goods than on footwear and clothing. Assumption 6 is another simplifying assumption that again allows us to focus attention on the differences in resources as the sole reason for trade.

APPLICATION

Are Factor Intensities the Same across Countries?

One of our assumptions for the HO model is that the same good (shoes) is labor-intensive in both countries. Specifically, we assume that in both countries, shoe production has a higher labor–capital ratio than does computer production. Although it might seem obvious that this assumption holds for shoes and computers, it is not so obvious when comparing other products, say, shoes and call centers.

In principle, all countries have access to the same technologies for making footwear. In practice, however, the machines used in the United States are different from those used in Asia and elsewhere. While much of the footwear in the world is produced in developing nations, the United States retains a small number of shoe factories. New Balance, which manufactures sneakers, has five plants in the New England states, and 25% of the shoes it sells in North America are produced in the United States. One of their plants is in Norridgewock, Maine, where employees operate computerized equipment that allows one person to do the work of six.[1] This is a far cry from the plants in Asia that produce shoes for Nike, Reebok, and other U.S. producers. Because Asian plants use old

AP Photo/Robert F. Bukaty

Despite its ninteenth-century exterior, this New Balance factory in Maine houses advanced shoe-manufacturing technology.

[1] This description of the New Balance plant is drawn from Aaron Bernstein, "Low-Skilled Jobs: Do They Have to Move?" *BusinessWeek*, February 26, 2001, 94–95.

technology (such as individual sewing machines), they use more workers to operate less productive machines.

In call centers, on the other hand, technologies (and, therefore, factor intensities) are similar across countries. Each employee works with a telephone and a personal computer, so call centers in the United States and India are similar in terms of the amount of capital per worker that they require. The telephone and personal computer, costing several thousand dollars, are much less expensive than the automated manufacturing machines in the New Balance plant in the United States, which cost tens or hundreds of thousands of dollars. So the manufacture of footwear in the New Balance plant is capital-intensive as compared with a U.S. call center. In India, by contrast, the sewing machine used to produce footwear is cheaper than the computer used in the call center. So footwear production in India is labor-intensive as compared with the call center, which is the opposite of what holds in the United States. This example illustrates a **reversal of factor intensities** between the two countries.

The same reversal of factor intensities is seen when we compare the agricultural sector across countries. In the United States, agriculture is capital-intensive. Each farmer works with tens of thousands of dollars in mechanized, computerized equipment, allowing a farm to be maintained by only a handful of workers. In many developing countries, however, agriculture is labor-intensive. Farms are worked by many laborers with little or no mechanized equipment. The reason that this labor-intensive technology is used in agriculture in developing nations is that capital equipment is expensive relative to the wages earned.

In assumption 2 and Figure 4-1, we assume that the labor–capital ratio (L/K) of one industry exceeds that of the other industry *regardless of the wage-rental ratio* (W/R). That is, whether labor is cheap (as in a developing country) or expensive (as in the United States), we are assuming that the same industry (shoes, in our example) is labor-intensive in both countries. This assumption may not be true for footwear or for agriculture, as we have just seen. In our treatment of the HO model, we will ignore the possibility of factor intensity reversals. The reason for ignoring these is to get a definite prediction from the model about the pattern of trade between countries so that we can see what happens to the price of goods and the earnings of factors when countries trade with each other. ■

No-Trade Equilibrium

In assumption 3, we outlined the difference in the amount of labor and capital found at Home and in Foreign. Our goal is to use these differences in resources to predict the pattern of trade. To do this, we begin by studying the equilibrium in each country in the absence of trade.

Production Possibilities Frontiers To determine the no-trade equilibria in Home and Foreign, we start by drawing the production possibilities frontiers (PPFs) in each country as shown in Figure 4-2. Under our assumptions that Home is capital-abundant and that computer production is capital-intensive, Home is capable of producing more computers than shoes. The Home PPF drawn in panel (a) is skewed in the direction of computers to reflect Home's greater capability to produce computers. Similarly, because Foreign is labor-abundant and shoe production is labor-intensive, the Foreign PPF shown in panel (b) is skewed in the direction of shoes, reflecting Foreign's greater capability to produce shoes. These particular shapes for the PPFs are reasonable given the assumptions we have made. When we continue our study of the Heckscher-Ohlin (HO) model in

FIGURE 4-2

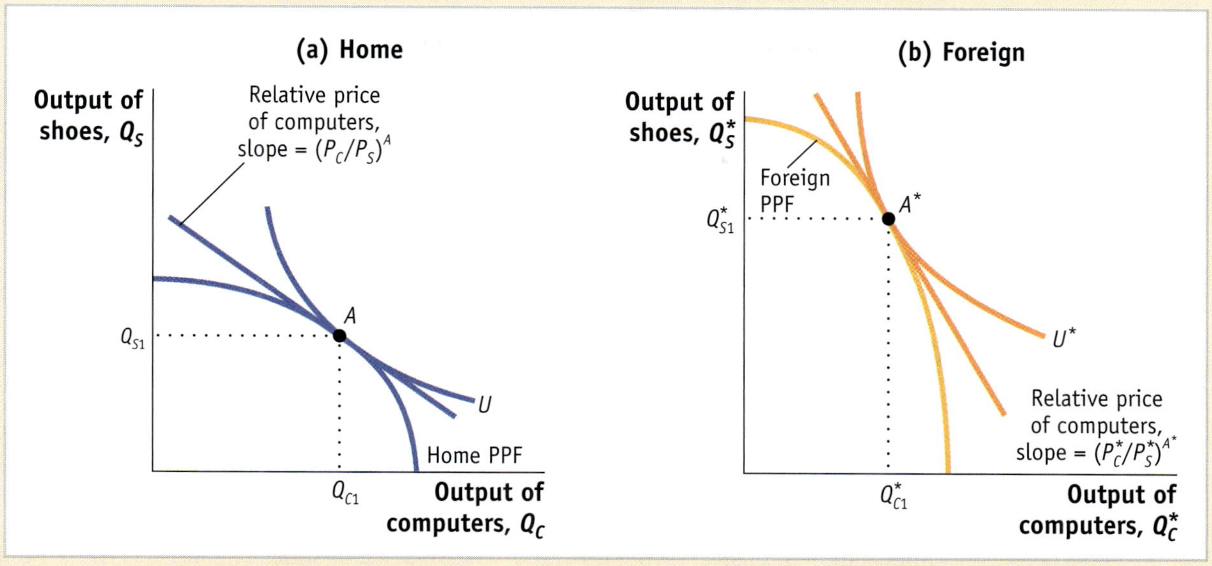

No-Trade Equilibria in Home and Foreign The Home production possibilities frontier (PPF) is shown in panel (a), and the Foreign PPF is shown in panel (b). Because Home is capital-abundant and computers are capital-intensive, the Home PPF is skewed toward computers. Home preferences are summarized by the indifference curve, U, and the Home no-trade (or autarky) equilibrium is at point A, with a low relative price of computers, as indicated by the flat slope of $(P_C/P_S)^A$. Foreign is labor-abundant and shoes are labor-intensive, so the Foreign PPF is skewed toward shoes. Foreign preferences are summarized by the indifference curve, U^*, and the Foreign no-trade equilibrium is at point A^*, with a higher relative price of computers, as indicated by the steeper slope of $(P_C^*/P_S^*)^{A^*}$.

Chapter 5, we prove that the PPFs must take this shape.[2] For now, we accept these shapes of the PPF and use them as the starting point for our study of the HO model.

Indifference Curves Another assumption of the Heckscher-Ohlin model (assumption 6) is that consumer tastes are the same across countries. As we did in the Ricardian model, we graph consumer tastes using indifference curves. Two of these curves are shown in Figure 4-2 (U and U^* for Home and Foreign, respectively); one is tangent to Home's PPF, and the other is tangent to Foreign's PPF. Notice that these indifference curves are the same shape in both countries, as required by assumption 6. They are tangent to the PPFs at different points because of the distinct shapes of the PPFs just described.

The slope of an indifference curve equals the amount that consumers are willing to pay for computers measured in terms of shoes rather than dollars. The slope of the PPF equals the opportunity cost of producing one more computer in terms of shoes given up. When the slope of an indifference curve equals the slope of a PPF, the relative price that consumers are willing to pay for computers equals the opportunity cost of producing them, so this point is the no-trade equilibrium.[3] The common slope of the indifference curve and PPF at their tangency equals the relative price of computers

[2] See Problem 7 in Chapter 5.

[3] Remember that the slope of an indifference curve or PPF reflects the relative price of the good on the *horizontal* axis, which is computers in Figure 4-2.

P_C/P_S. A steeply sloped price line implies a high relative price of computers, whereas a flat price line implies a low relative price for computers.

No-Trade Equilibrium Price Given the differently shaped PPFs, the indifference curves of each country will be tangent to the PPFs at different production points, corresponding to different relative price lines across the two countries. In Home the no-trade or autarky equilibrium is shown by point A, at which Home produces Q_{C1} of computers and Q_{S1} of shoes at the relative price of $(P_C/P_S)^A$. Because the Home PPF is skewed toward computers, the slope of the Home price line $(P_C/P_S)^A$ is quite flat, indicating a low relative price of computers. In Foreign, the no-trade or autarky equilibrium is shown by point A^* at which Foreign produces Q^*_{C1} of computers and Q^*_{S1} of shoes at the relative price of $(P^*_C/P^*_S)^{A^*}$. Because the Foreign PPF is skewed toward shoes, the slope of the Foreign price line $(P^*_C/P^*_S)^{A^*}$ is quite steep, indicating a high relative price of computers. Therefore, the result from comparing the no-trade equilibria in Figure 4-2 is that the *no-trade relative price of computers at Home is lower than in Foreign*. (Equivalently, we can say that the no-trade relative price of shoes at Home is higher than in Foreign.)

These comparisons of the no-trade prices reflect the differing amounts of labor found in the two countries: the Foreign country has abundant labor, and shoe production is labor-intensive, so the no-trade relative price of shoes is lower in Foreign than in Home. That Foreigners are willing to give up more shoes for one computer reflects the fact that Foreign resources are suited to making more shoes. The same logic applies to Home, which is relatively abundant in capital. Because computer production is capital-intensive, Home has a lower no-trade relative price of computers than Foreign. Thus, Home residents need to give up fewer shoes to obtain one computer, reflecting the fact that their resources are suited to making more computers.

Free-Trade Equilibrium

We are now in a position to determine the pattern of trade between the countries. To do so, we proceed in several steps. First, we consider what happens when the world relative price of computers is *above* the no-trade relative price of computers at Home, and trace out the Home export supply of computers. Second, we consider what happens when the world relative price is *below* the no-trade relative price of computers in Foreign, and trace out the Foreign import demand for computers. Finally, we put together the Home export supply and Foreign import demand to determine the equilibrium relative price of computers with international trade.

Home Equilibrium with Free Trade The first step is displayed in Figure 4-3. We have already seen in Figure 4-2 that the no-trade relative price of computers is lower in Home than in Foreign. Under free trade, we expect the equilibrium relative price of computers to lie between the no-trade relative prices in each country (as we already found in the Ricardian model of Chapter 2). Because the no-trade relative price of computers is lower at Home, the free-trade equilibrium price will be above the no-trade price at Home. Therefore, panel (a) of Figure 4-3 shows the Home PPF with a free-trade or world relative price of computers, $(P_C/P_S)^W$, higher than the no-trade Home relative price, $(P_C/P_S)^A$, shown in panel (a) of Figure 4-2.

The no-trade equilibrium at Home, point A, has the quantities (Q_{C1}, Q_{S1}) for computers and shoes, shown in Figure 4-2. At the higher world relative price of computers, Home production moves from point A, (Q_{C1}, Q_{S1}), to point B in Figure 4-3, (Q_{C2}, Q_{S2}),

FIGURE 4-3

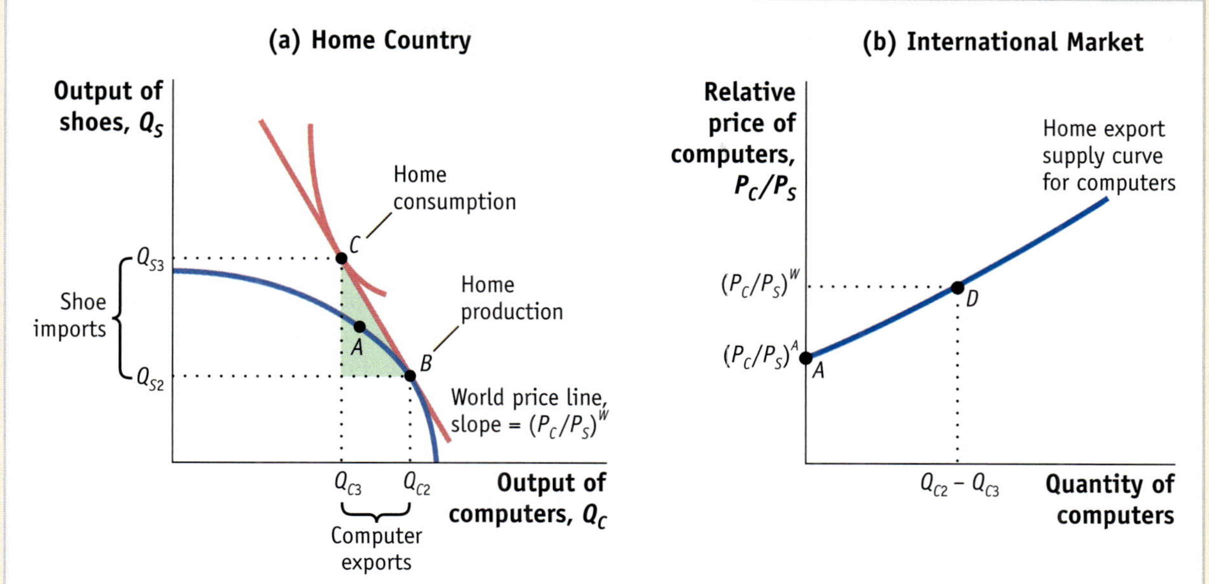

International Free-Trade Equilibrium at Home At the free-trade world relative price of computers, $(P_C/P_S)^W$, Home produces at point *B* in panel (a) and consumes at point *C*, exporting computers and importing shoes. (Point *A* is the no-trade equilibrium.) The "trade triangle" has a base equal to the Home exports of computers (the difference between the amount produced and the amount consumed with trade, $Q_{C2} - Q_{C3}$). The height of this triangle is the Home imports of shoes (the difference between the amount consumed of shoes and the amount produced with trade, $Q_{S3} - Q_{S2}$). In panel (b), we show Home exports of computers equal to zero at the no-trade relative price, $(P_C/P_S)^A$, and equal to $(Q_{C2} - Q_{C3})$ at the free-trade relative price, $(P_C/P_S)^W$.

with more computers and fewer shoes. Thus, with free trade, Home produces fewer shoes and specializes further in computers to take advantage of higher world relative prices of computers. Because Home can now engage in trade at the world relative price, Home's consumption can now lie on any point along the world price line through *B* with slope $(P_C/P_S)^W$. The highest Home utility is obtained at point *C*, which is tangent to the world price line $(P_C/P_S)^W$ and has the quantities consumed (Q_{C3}, Q_{S3}).

We can now define the Home "trade triangle," which is the triangle connecting points *B* and *C*, shown in panel (a) of Figure 4-3. Point *B* is where Home is producing and point *C* is where it is consuming, and the line connecting the two points represents the amount of trade at the world relative price. The base of this triangle is the Home exports of computers (the difference between the amount produced and the amount consumed with trade, or $Q_{C2} - Q_{C3}$). The height of this triangle is the Home imports of shoes (the difference between the amount consumed of shoes and the amount produced with trade, or $Q_{S3} - Q_{S2}$).

In panel (b) of Figure 4-3, we graph the Home exports of computers against their relative price. In the no-trade equilibrium, the Home relative price of computers was $(P_C/P_S)^A$, and exports of computers were zero. This no-trade equilibrium is shown by point *A* in panel (b). Under free trade, the relative price of computers is $(P_C/P_S)^W$, and exports of computers are the difference between the amount produced and amount consumed with trade, or $(Q_{C2} - Q_{C3})$. This free-trade equilibrium is shown by point *D* in panel (b). Joining up points A and D, we obtain the Home export supply curve of computers. It is upward-sloping because at higher relative prices as compared with the no-trade price, Home is willing to specialize further in computers to export more of them.

Foreign Equilibrium with Free Trade We proceed in a similar fashion for the Foreign country. In panel (a) of Figure 4-4, the Foreign no-trade equilibrium is at point A^*, with the high equilibrium relative price of computers $(P_C^*/P_S^*)^{A*}$. Because the Foreign no-trade relative price was higher than at Home, and we expect the free-trade relative price to lie between, it follows that the free-trade or world equilibrium price of computers $(P_C/P_S)^W$ is lower than the no-trade Foreign price $(P_C^*/P_S^*)^{A*}$.

At the world relative price, Foreign production moves from point A^*, (Q_{C1}^*, Q_{S1}^*), to point B^*, (Q_{C2}^*, Q_{S2}^*), with more shoes and fewer computers. Thus, with free trade, Foreign specializes further in shoes and produces fewer computers. Because Foreign can now engage in trade at the world relative price, Foreign's consumption can now lie on any point along the world price line through B^* with slope $(P_C/P_S)^W$. The highest Foreign utility is obtained at point C^*, which is tangent to the world price line $(P_C/P_S)^W$ and has the quantities consumed (Q_{C3}^*, Q_{S3}^*). Once again, we can connect points B^* and C^* to form a "trade triangle." The base of this triangle is Foreign imports of computers

FIGURE 4-4

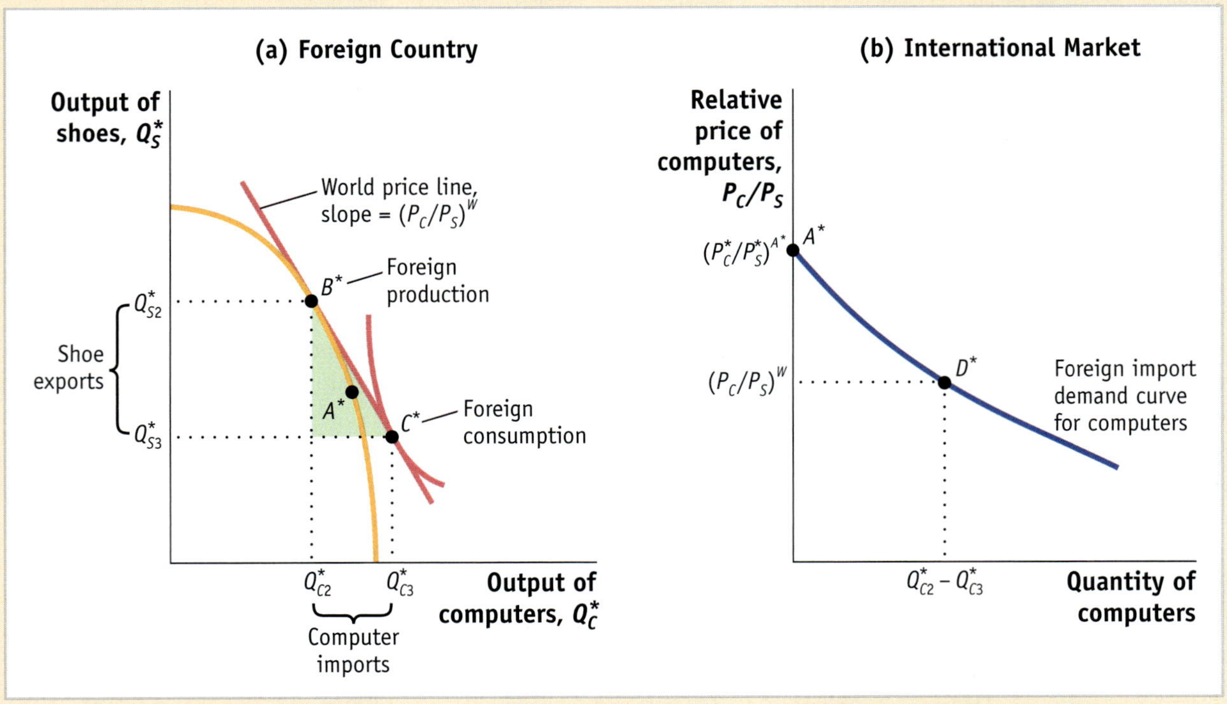

International Free-Trade Equilibrium in Foreign At the free-trade world relative price of computers, $(P_C/P_S)^W$, Foreign produces at point B^* in panel (a) and consumes at point C^*, importing computers and exporting shoes. (Point A^* is the no-trade equilibrium.) The "trade triangle" has a base equal to Foreign imports of computers (the difference between the consumption of computers and the amount produced with trade, $Q_{C3}^* - Q_{C2}^*$). The height of this triangle is Foreign exports of shoes (the difference between the production of shoes and the amount consumed with trade, $Q_{S2}^* - Q_{S3}^*$). In panel (b), we show Foreign imports of computers equal to zero at the no-trade relative price, $(P_C^*/P_S^*)^{A*}$, and equal to $(Q_{C3}^* - Q_{C2}^*)$ at the free-trade relative price, $(P_C/P_S)^W$.

(the difference between consumption of computers and production with trade, or $Q^*_{C3} - Q^*_{C2}$), and the height is Foreign exports of shoes (the difference between production and consumption with trade, or $Q^*_{S2} - Q^*_{S3}$).

In panel (b) of Figure 4-4, we graph Foreign's imports of computers against its relative price. In the no-trade equilibrium, the Foreign relative price of computers was $(P^*_C/P^*_S)^{A*}$, and imports of computers were zero. This no-trade equilibrium is shown by the point A^* in panel (b). Under free trade, the relative price of computers is $(P_C/P_S)^W$, and imports of computers are the difference between the amount produced and amount consumed with trade, or $(Q^*_{C3} - Q^*_{C2})$. This free-trade equilibrium is shown by the point D^* in panel (b). Joining up points A^* and D^*, we obtain the Foreign import demand curve for computers. It is downward-sloping because at lower relative prices as compared with no-trade, Foreign specializes more in shoes and exports these in exchange for computers.

Equilibrium Price with Free Trade As we see in Figure 4-5, the equilibrium relative price of computers with free trade is determined by the intersection of the Home export supply and Foreign import demand curves, at point D (the same as point D in Figure 4-3 or D^* in Figure 4-4). At that relative price, the quantity of computers that the Home country wants to export equals the quantity of computers that Foreign wants to import; that is, $(Q_{C2} - Q_{C3}) = (Q^*_{C3} - Q^*_{C2})$. Because exports equal imports, there is no reason for the relative price to change and so this is a **free-trade equilibrium.** Another way to see the equilibrium graphically is to notice that in panel (a) of Figures 4-3 and 4-4, the trade triangles of the two countries are identical in size—what one country wants to sell is the same as what the other country wants to buy.

Pattern of Trade Using the free-trade equilibrium, we have determined the pattern of trade between the two countries. Home exports computers, the good that uses intensively the factor of production (capital) found in abundance at Home. Foreign exports shoes, the good that uses intensively the factor of production (labor) found in abundance there. This important result is called the **Heckscher-Ohlin theorem.**

FIGURE 4-5

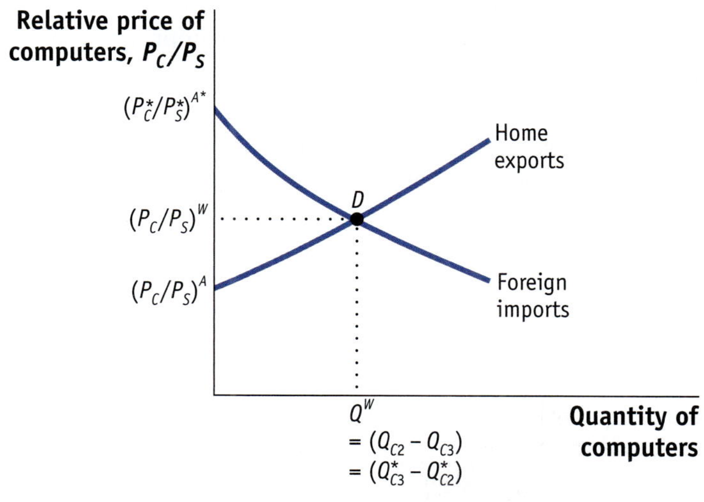

Determination of the Free-Trade World Equilibrium Price The world relative price of computers in the free-trade equilibrium is determined at the intersection of the Home export supply and Foreign import demand, at point *D*. At this relative price, the quantity of computers that Home wants to export, $(Q_{C2} - Q_{C3})$, just equals the quantity of computers that Foreign wants to import, $(Q^*_{C3} - Q^*_{C2})$.

Heckscher-Ohlin Theorem: With two goods and two factors, each country will export the good that uses intensively the factor of production it has in abundance and will import the other good.

It is useful to review the assumptions we made at the beginning of the chapter to see how they lead to the Heckscher-Ohlin theorem.

Assumption 1: Labor and capital flow freely between the industries.
Assumption 2: The production of shoes is labor-intensive as compared with computer production, which is capital-intensive.
Assumption 3: The amounts of labor and capital found in the two countries differ, with Foreign abundant in labor and Home abundant in capital.
Assumption 4: There is free international trade in goods.
Assumption 5: The technologies for producing shoes and computers are the same across countries.
Assumption 6: Tastes are the same across countries.

Assumptions 1 to 3 allowed us to draw the PPFs of the two countries as illustrated in Figure 4-2, and in conjunction with assumptions 5 and 6, they allowed us to determine that the no-trade relative price of computers in Home was lower than the no-trade relative price of computers in Foreign; that is, $(P_C/P_S)^A$ was less than $(P^*_C/P^*_S)^{A*}$. This key result enabled us to determine the starting points for the Home export supply curve for computers (point A) and the Foreign import demand curve for computers (point A^*) in panel (b) of Figures 4-3 and 4-4. Using those starting points, we put together the upward-sloping Home export supply curve and downward-sloping Foreign import demand curve. We see from Figure 4-5 that the relative price of computers in the free-trade equilibrium lies between the no-trade relative prices (which confirms the expectation we had when drawing Figures 4-3 and 4-4).

Therefore, when Home opens to trade, its relative price of computers rises from the no-trade equilibrium relative price $(P_C/P_S)^A$, to the free-trade equilibrium price $(P_C/P_S)^W$, giving Home firms an incentive to export computers. That is, higher prices give Home an incentive to produce more computers than it wants to consume, and export the difference. Similarly, when Foreign opens to trade, its relative price of computers falls from the no-trade equilibrium price $(P^*_C/P^*_S)^{A*}$, to the trade equilibrium price $(P_C/P_S)^W$, encouraging Foreign consumers to import computers from Home. That is, lower prices give Foreign an incentive to consume more computers than it wants to produce, importing the difference.

You might think that the Heckscher-Ohlin theorem is somewhat obvious. It makes sense that countries will export goods that are produced easily because the factors of production are found in abundance. It turns out, however, that this prediction does not always work in practice, as we discuss in the next section.

2 Testing the Heckscher-Ohlin Model

The first test of the Heckscher-Ohlin theorem was performed by economist Wassily Leontief in 1953, using data for the United States from 1947. We will describe his test below and show that he reached a surprising conclusion, which is called **Leontief's paradox.** After that, we will discuss more recent data for many countries that can be used to test the Heckscher-Ohlin model.

Leontief's Paradox

To test the Heckscher-Ohlin theorem, Leontief measured the amounts of labor and capital used in all industries needed to produce $1 million of U.S. exports and to produce $1 million of imports into the United States. His results are shown in Table 4-1.

TABLE 4-1

Leontief's Test Leontief used the numbers in this table to test the Heckscher-Ohlin theorem. Each column shows the amount of capital or labor needed to produce $1 million worth of exports from, or imports into, the United States in 1947. As shown in the last row, the capital–labor ratio for exports was less than the capital–labor ratio for imports, which is a paradoxical finding.

	Exports	Imports
Capital ($ millions)	2.55	3.1
Labor (person-years)	182	170
Capital/labor ($/person)	14,000	18,200

Source: Wassily Leontief, 1953, "Domestic Production and Foreign Trade: The American Capital Position Re-examined," Proceedings of the American Philosophical Society, *97,September, 332–349. Reprinted in Richard Caves and Harry G. Johnson, eds., 1968,* Readings in International Economics *(Homewood, IL: Irwin).*

Leontief first measured the amount of capital and labor required in the production of $1 million worth of U.S. exports. To arrive at these figures, Leontief measured the labor and capital used *directly* in the production of final good exports in each industry. He also measured the labor and capital used *indirectly* in the industries that produced the intermediate inputs used in making the exports. From the first row of Table 4-1, we see that $2.55 million worth of capital was used to produce $1 million of exports. This amount of capital seems much too high, until we recognize that what is being measured is the total stock, which exceeds that part of the capital stock that was actually used to produce exports that year: the capital used that year would be measured by the depreciation on this stock. For labor, 182 person-years were used to produce the exports. Taking the ratio of these, we find that each person employed (directly or indirectly) in producing exports was working with $14,000 worth of capital.

Turning to the import side of the calculation, Leontief immediately ran into a problem—he could not measure the amount of labor and capital used to produce imports because he didn't have data on foreign technologies. To get around this difficulty, Leontief did what many researchers have done since—he simply used the data on U.S. technology to calculate estimated amounts of labor and capital used in imports from abroad. Does this approach invalidate Leontief's test of the Heckscher-Ohlin model? Not really, because the Heckscher-Ohlin model assumes that technologies are the same across countries, so Leontief is building this assumption into the calculations needed to test the theorem.

Using U.S. technology to measure the labor and capital used directly and indirectly in producing imports, Leontief arrived at the estimates in the last column of Table 4-1: $3.1 million of capital and 170 person-years were used in the production of $1 million worth of U.S. imports, so the capital–labor ratio for imports was $18,200 per worker. Notice that this amount *exceeds* the capital–labor ratio for exports of $14,000 per worker.

Leontief supposed correctly that in 1947 the United States was abundant in capital relative to the rest of the world. Thus, from the Heckscher-Ohlin theorem, Leontief expected that the United States would export capital-intensive goods and import labor-intensive goods. What Leontief actually found, however, was just the opposite: the capital–labor ratio for U.S. imports was *higher* than the capital–labor ratio found for U.S. exports! This finding contradicted the Heckscher-Ohlin theorem and came to be called Leontief's paradox.

Explanations A wide range of explanations has been offered for Leontief's paradox, including the following:

- U.S. and foreign technologies are not the same, in contrast to what the Heckscher-Ohlin theorem and Leontief assumed.

- By focusing only on labor and capital, Leontief ignored land abundance in the United States.
- Leontief should have distinguished between skilled and unskilled labor (because it would not be surprising to find that U.S. exports are intensive in skilled labor).
- The data for 1947 may be unusual because World War II had ended just two years earlier.
- The United States was not engaged in completely free trade, as the Heckscher-Ohlin theorem assumes.

Several of the additional possible explanations for the Leontief paradox depend on having more than two factors of production. The United States is abundant in land, for example, and that might explain why in 1947 it was exporting labor-intensive products: these might have been agricultural products, which use land intensively and, in 1947, might also have used labor intensively. By ignoring land, Leontief was therefore not performing an accurate test of the Heckscher-Ohlin theorem. Alternatively, it might be that the United States was mainly exporting goods that used skilled labor. This is certainly true today, with the United States being a leading exporter of high-technology products, and was probably also true in 1947. By not distinguishing between skilled versus unskilled labor, Leontief was again giving an inaccurate picture of the factors of production used in U.S. trade.

Research in later years aimed to redo the test that Leontief performed, while taking into account land, skilled versus unskilled labor, checking whether the Heckscher-Ohlin theorem holds in other years, and so on. We now discuss the data that can be used to test the Heckscher-Ohlin theorem in a more recent year—2000.

Factor Endowments in the New Millenium

In Figure 4-6, we show the country shares of six factors of production and world GDP in 2000, broken down by select countries (the United States, China, Japan, India, Germany, the United Kingdom, France, and Canada) and then the rest of the world. To determine whether a country is abundant in a certain factor, we compare the country's share of that factor with its share of world GDP. If its share of a factor exceeds its share of world GDP, then we conclude that the country is **abundant in that factor,** and if its share in a certain factor is less than its share of world GDP, then we conclude that the country is **scarce in that factor.** This definition allows us to calculate factor abundance in a setting with as many factors and countries as we want.

Capital Abundance For example, in the first bar graph of Figure 4-6, we see that in 2000, 24% of the world's physical capital was located in the United States, with 8.7% located in China, 13.3% in Japan, 3.6% in India, 7.5% in Germany, and so on. When we compare these numbers with the final bar in the graph, which shows each country's percentage of world GDP, we see that in 2000 the United States had 21.6% of world GDP, China had 11.2%, Japan 7.5%, India 5.5%, Germany 4.7%, and so on. Because the United States had 24% of the world's capital and 21.6% of world GDP, we can conclude that the United States was abundant in physical capital in 2000. Japan had 13.3% of the world's capital and 7.5% of world GDP, so it was also abundant in capital, as was Germany (with 7.5% of the world's capital and 4.7% of world GDP). The opposite holds for China, India, and the group of countries included in the rest of the world: their shares of world capital were less than their shares of GDP, so they were scarce in capital.

FIGURE 4-6

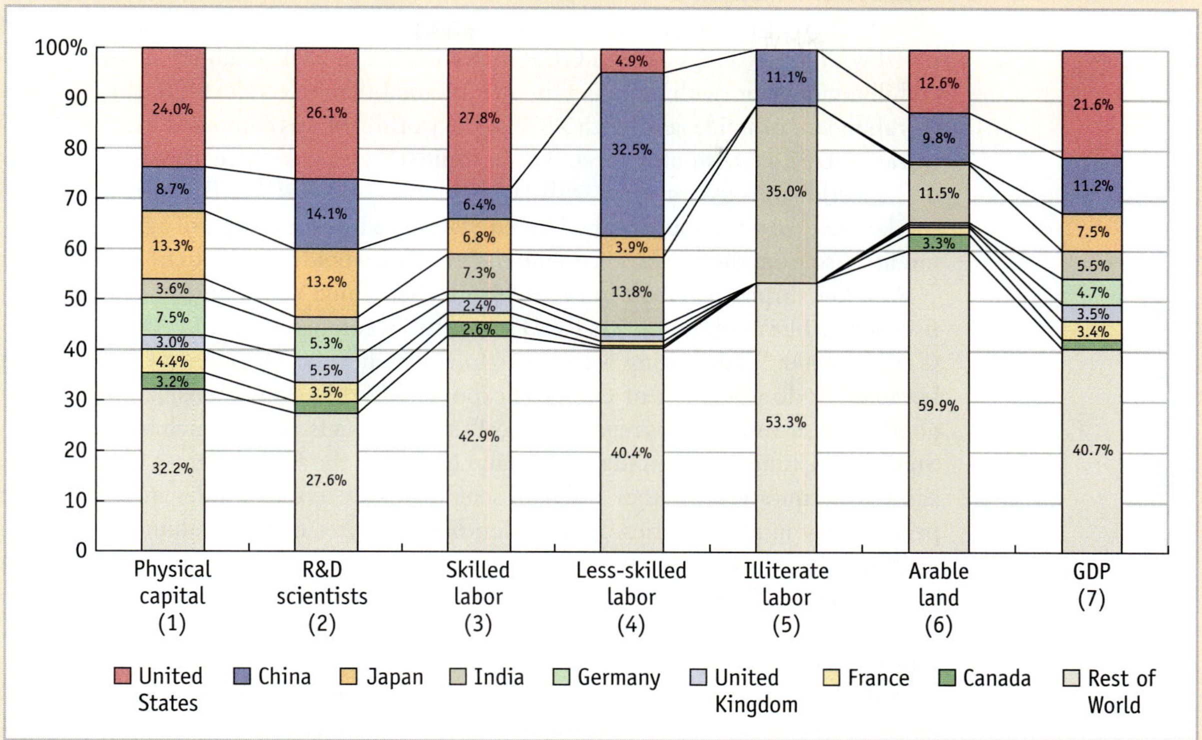

Country Factor Endowments, 2000 Shown here are country shares of six factors of production in the year 2000, for eight selected countries and the rest of the world. In the first bar graph, we see that 24% of the world's physical capital in 2000 was located in the United States, with 9% located in China, 13% located in Japan, and so on. In the final bar graph, we see that in 2000 the United States had 22% of world GDP, China had 11%, Japan had 8%, and so on. When a country's factor share is larger than its share of GDP, then the country is abundant in that factor, and when a country's factor share is less than its share of GDP, then the country is scarce in that factor.

Notes:

(1) The product of 1990 capital per worker (Penn World Table) and 2000 total labor force (World Bank, World Development Indicators). China figure based on Gregory Chow and Kui-Wai Li, 2002, "China's Economic Growth: 1952–2010," *Economic Development and Cultural Change,* 51, 247–256. There are 63 countries included.

(2) The product of R&D researcher intensity and total population (World Bank, World Development Indicators). There are 55 countries included.

(3) Labor force with tertiary education (World Bank, World Development Indicators); when unavailable, population 25 and over with postsecondary education was used (R. J. Barro and J. W. Lee, 2000, "International Data on Educational Attainment: Updates and Implications," Center for International Development at Harvard University, Working Paper No. 42). There are 123 countries included.

(4) Labor force with primary and/or secondary education (World Bank, World Development Indicators); when unavailable, population 25 and over with primary and/or secondary education was used (R. J. Barro and J. W. Lee, 2000, "International Data on Educational Attainment: Updates and Implications," Center for International Development at Harvard University, Working Paper No. 42). There are 123 countries included.

(5) The product of one minus the adult literacy rate and the adult population in 2004 (World Bank, World Development Indicators). There are 136 countries included.

(6) Hectares of arable land (World Bank, World Development Indicators). There are 196 countries included.

(7) Gross domestic product converted to 2000 international dollars using purchasing power parity rates (World Bank, World Development Indicators). There are 169 countries included.

Labor and Land Abundance We can use a similar comparison to determine whether each country is abundant in R&D scientists, in types of labor distinguished by skill, in arable land, or any other factor of production. For example, the United States was abundant in R&D scientists in 2000 (with 26.1% of the world's total as compared with 21.6%

of the world's GDP) and also skilled labor (workers with more than a high school education) but was scarce in less-skilled labor (workers with a high school education or less) and illiterate labor. India was scarce in R&D scientists (with 2.5% of the world's total as compared with 5.5% of the world's GDP) but abundant in skilled labor, semiskilled labor, and illiterate labor (with shares of the world's total that exceed its GDP share). Canada was abundant in arable land (with 3.3% of the world's total as compared with 1.9% of the world's GDP), as we would expect. But the United States was scarce in arable land (12.6% of the world's total as compared with 21.6% of the world's GDP). That is a surprising result because we often think of the United States as a major exporter of agricultural commodities, so from the Heckscher-Ohlin theorem, we would expect it to be land-abundant.

Another surprising result in Figure 4-6 is that China was abundant in R&D scientists: it had 14.1% of the world's R&D scientists, as compared with 11.2% of the world's GDP in 2000. This finding also seems to contradict the Heckscher-Ohlin theorem, because we do not think of China as exporting highly skill-intensive manufactured goods. These observations regarding R&D scientists (a factor in which both the United States and China were abundant) and land (in which the United States was scarce) can cause us to question whether an R&D scientist or an acre of arable land has the same productivity in all countries. If not, then our measures of factor abundance are misleading: if an R&D scientist in the United States is more productive than his or her counterpart in China, then it does not make sense to just compare each country's share of these with each country's share of GDP; and likewise, if an acre of arable land is more productive in the United States than in other countries, then we should not compare the share of land in each country with each country's share of GDP. Instead, we need to make some adjustment for the differing productivities of R&D scientists and land across countries. In other words, we need to abandon the original Heckscher-Ohlin assumption of identical technologies across countries.

Differing Productivities across Countries

Leontief himself suggested that we should abandon the assumption that technologies are the same across countries and instead allow for differing productivities, as in the Ricardian model. Remember that in the original formulation of the paradox, Leontief had found that the United States was exporting labor-intensive products even though it was capital-abundant at that time. One explanation for this outcome would be that labor is highly productive in the United States and less productive in the rest of the world. If that is the case, then the **effective labor force** in the United States, the labor force times its productivity (which measures how much output the labor force can produce), is much larger than it appears to be when we just count people. If this is true, perhaps the United States is abundant in *skilled* labor after all (like R&D scientists), and it should be no surprise that it is exporting labor-intensive products.

We now explore how differing productivities can be introduced into the Heckscher-Ohlin model. In addition to allowing labor to have a differing productivity across countries, we can also allow capital, land, and other factors of production to have differing productivity across countries.

Measuring Factor Abundance Once Again

To allow factors of production to differ in their productivities across countries, we define the **effective factor endowment** as the actual amount of a factor found in a country times its productivity:

$$\text{Effective factor endowment} = \text{Actual factor endowment} \cdot \text{Factor productivity}$$

The amount of an effective factor found in the world is obtained by adding up the effective factor endowments across all countries. Then to determine whether a country is abundant in a certain factor, we compare the country's share of that *effective* factor with its share of world GDP. If its share of an effective factor exceeds its share of world GDP, then we conclude that the country is **abundant in that effective factor;** if its share of an effective factor is less than its share of world GDP, then we conclude that the country is **scarce in that effective factor.** We can illustrate this approach to measuring effective factor endowments using two examples: R&D scientists and arable land.

Effective R&D Scientists The productivity of an R&D scientist depends on the laboratory equipment, computers, and other types of material with which he or she has to work. R&D scientists working in different countries will not necessarily have the same productivities because the equipment they have available to them differs. A simple way to measure the equipment they have available is to use a country's *R&D spending per scientist*. If a country has more R&D spending per scientist, then its productivity will be higher, but if there is less R&D spending per scientist, then its productivity will be lower. To measure the effective number of R&D scientists in each country, we take the total number of scientists and multiply that by the R&D spending per scientist:

Effective R&D scientists = Actual R&D scientists • R&D spending per scientist

Using the R&D spending per scientist in this way to obtain effective R&D scientists is one method to correct for differences in the productivity of scientists across countries. It is not the only way to make such a correction because there are other measures that could be used for the productivity of scientists (e.g., we could use scientific publications available in a country, or the number of research universities). The advantage of using R&D spending per scientist is that this information is collected annually for many countries, so using this method to obtain a measure of effective R&D scientists means that we can easily compare the share of each country with the world total.[4] Those shares are shown in Figure 4-7.

In the first bar graph of Figure 4-7, we repeat from Figure 4-6 each country's share of world R&D scientists, not corrected for productivity differences. In the second bar graph, we show each country's share of effective scientists, using the R&D spending per scientist to correct for productivity. The United States had 26.1% of the world's total R&D scientists in 2000 (in the first bar) but 37.1% of the world's effective scientists (in the second bar). So the United States was more abundant in effective R&D scientists in 2000 than it was in the number of scientists. Likewise, Japan and India both had more shares of effective R&D scientists as compared with their number of scientists, with a 13.2% and 2.5% share of scientists for each country compared with 14% and 2.9% in the share of effective scientists, respectively. But China's share of R&D scientists fell by half when correcting for productivity, from a 14.1% share in the number of R&D scientists to a 7% share in effective R&D scientists. Since China's share of world GDP was 11.1% in 2000, it became scarce in effective R&D scientists once we made this productivity correction.

China has increased its spending on R&D in recent years and, according to news reports, exceeded the level of R&D spending in Japan for 2006 and later years. Even

[4] Notice that by correcting the number of R&D scientists by the R&D spending per scientist, we end up with the total R&D spending in each country: Effective R&D scientists = Actual R&D scientists • R&D spending per scientist = Total R&D spending. So a country's share of effective R&D scientists equals its share of world R&D spending.

FIGURE 4-7

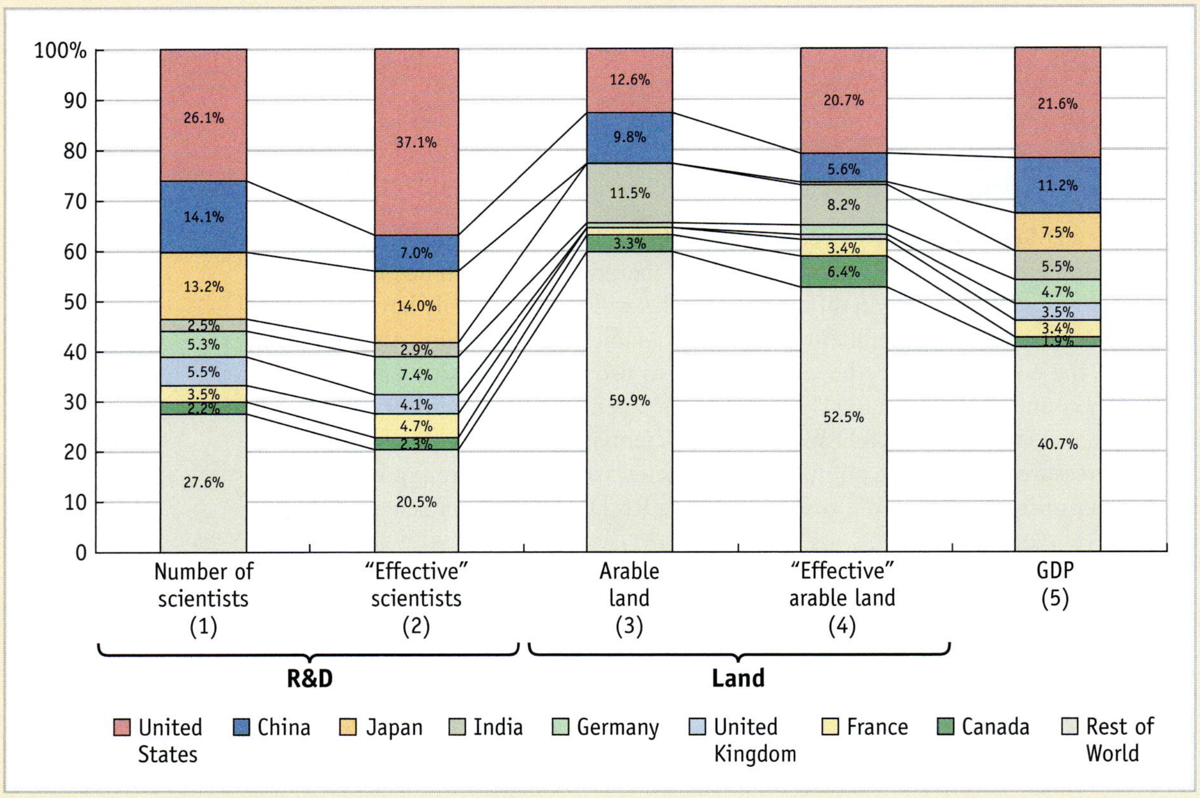

"Effective" Factor Endowments, 2000 Shown here are country shares of R&D scientists and land in 2000, using first the information from Figure 4.6, and then making an adjustment for the productivity of each factor across countries to obtain the "effective" shares. China was abundant in R&D scientists in 2000 (since it had 14% of the world's R&D scientists as compared with 11% of the world's GDP) but scarce in effective R&D scientists (because it had 7% of the world's effective R&D scientists as compared with 11% of the world's GDP). The United States was scarce in arable land when using the number of acres (since it had 13% of the world's land as compared with 22% of the world's GDP) but neither scarce nor abundant in effective land (since it had 21% of the world's effective land, which nearly equaled its share of the world's GDP).

Notes:
(1) The product of R&D researcher intensity and total population (World Bank, World Development Indicators). There are 55 countries included.
(2) R&D expenditure in units of purchasing power parity (World Bank, World Development Indicators). There are 74 countries included.
(3) Hectares of arable land (World Bank, World Development Indicators). There are 196 countries included.
(4) Productivity adjustment based on agriculture TFP estimation (based on data from the Food and Agriculture Organization of the United Nations). There are 152 countries included.
(5) Gross domestic product converted to 2000 international dollars using purchasing power parity rates (World Bank, World Development Indicators). There are 169 countries included.

when compared with the United States, China is taking the lead in some areas of R&D. An example is in research on "green" technologies, such as wind and solar power. As described in **Headlines: China Drawing High-Tech Research from U.S.,** American companies are now being attracted to China by a combination of inexpensive land and skilled labor. According to this article, we would expect China's share of effective R&D scientists to have grown significantly in recent years.

Effective Arable Land As we did for R&D scientists, we also need to correct arable land for its differing productivity across countries. To make this correction, we use a

HEADLINES

China Drawing High-Tech Research from U.S.

Applied Materials, a well-known firm in Silicon Valley, recently announced plans to establish a large laboratory in Xi'an, China, as described in this article.

XI'AN, China—For years, many of China's best and brightest left for the United States, where high-tech industry was more cutting-edge. But Mark R. Pinto is moving in the opposite direction. Mr. Pinto is the first chief technology officer of a major American tech company to move to China. The company, Applied Materials, is one of Silicon Valley's most prominent firms. It supplied equipment used to perfect the first computer chips. Today, it is the world's biggest supplier of the equipment used to make semiconductors, solar panels and flat-panel displays.

In addition to moving Mr. Pinto and his family to Beijing in January, Applied Materials, whose headquarters are in Santa Clara, Calif., has just built its newest and largest research labs here. Last week, it even held its annual shareholders' meeting in Xi'an. It is hardly alone. Companies—and their engineers—are being drawn here more and more as China develops a high-tech economy that increasingly competes directly with the United States. . . .

Not just drawn by China's markets, Western companies are also attracted to China's huge reservoirs of cheap, highly skilled engineers—and the subsidies offered by many Chinese cities and regions, particularly for green energy companies. Now, Mr. Pinto said, researchers from the United States and Europe have to be ready to move to China if they want to do cutting-edge work on solar manufacturing because the new Applied Materials complex here is the only research center that can fit an entire solar panel assembly line. "If you really want to have an impact on this field, this is just such a tremendous laboratory," he said. . . .

Locally, the Xi'an city government sold a 75-year land lease to Applied Materials at a deep discount and is reimbursing the company for roughly a quarter of the lab complex's operating costs for five years, said Gang Zou, the site's general manager. The two labs, the first of their kind anywhere in the world, are each bigger than two American football fields. Applied Materials continues to develop the electronic guts of its complex machines at laboratories in the United States and Europe. But putting all the machines together and figuring out processes to make them work in unison will be done in Xi'an. The two labs, one on top of the other, will become operational once they are fully outfitted late this year. . . .

Source: Keith Bradsher, "China Drawing High-Tech Research from U.S.," The New York Times, *March 17, 2010.*

measure of agricultural productivity in each country. Then the effective amount of arable land found in a country is

$$\text{Effective arable land} = \text{Actual arable land} \cdot \text{Productivity in agriculture}$$

We will not discuss here the exact method for measuring productivity in agriculture, except to say that it compares the output in each country with the inputs of labor, capital, and land: countries with higher output as compared with inputs are the more productive, and countries with lower output as compared with inputs are the less productive. The United States has very high productivity in agriculture, whereas China has lower productivity.

In the third bar graph of Figure 4-7, we repeat from Figure 4-6 each country's share of arable land, not corrected for productivity differences. In the fourth bar graph, we show each country's share of effective arable land in 2000, corrected for productivity differences. The United States had 12.6% of the world's total arable land (in the third bar), as compared with 21.6% of the world's GDP (in the final bar), so it was scarce in land in 2000 without making any productivity correction. But when measured by effective arable land, the United States had 20.7% of the world's total (in the fourth bar), as compared with 21.6% of the world's GDP (in the final bar). These two numbers are so close that we should conclude *the United States was neither abundant nor scarce in effective arable land*: its share of the world's total approximately equaled its share of the world's GDP.

TABLE 4-2

U.S. Food Trade and Total Agricultural Trade, 2000–2009 This table shows that U.S. food trade has fluctuated between positive and negative net exports since 2000, which is consistent with our finding that the United States is neither abundant nor scarce in land. Total agriculture trade (including nonfood items like cotton) has positive net exports, however.

	2000	2001	2002	2003	2004	2005	2006	2007	2008	2009
U.S. food trade, 2000–2009 (billions of U.S. dollars)										
Exports	41.4	42.5	43.2	48.3	50.0	51.7	57.8	75.4	97.4	82.8
Imports	41.4	42.0	44.7	50.1	55.7	61.6	68.9	74.0	81.3	73.8
Net exports	0.0	0.5	−1.5	−1.8	−5.7	−9.9	−11.1	1.4	16.1	9.0
U.S. agricultural trade, 2000–2009 (billions of U.S. dollars)										
Exports	51.3	53.7	53.1	59.4	61.4	63.2	70.9	90.0	115.3	98.6
Imports	39.2	39.5	42.0	47.5	54.2	59.5	65.5	72.1	80.7	71.9
Net exports	12.1	14.1	11.1	11.9	7.2	3.7	5.5	17.9	34.6	26.7

Source: Total agricultural trade compiled by USDA using data from Census Bureau, U.S. Department of Commerce. U.S. food trade data provided by the USDA, Foreign Agricultural Service.

How does this conclusion compare with U.S. trade in agriculture? We often think of the United States as a major exporter of agricultural goods, but this pattern is changing. In Table 4-2, we show the U.S. exports and imports of food products and total agricultural trade. This table shows that U.S. food trade has fluctuated between positive and negative net exports since 2000, which is consistent with our finding that the United States is neither abundant nor scarce in land. Total agriculture trade (including nonfood items like cotton) continues to have positive net exports, however.

Leontief's Paradox Once Again

Our discussion of factor endowments in 2000 shows that it is possible for countries to be abundant in more that one factor of production: the United States and Japan are both abundant in physical capital and R&D scientists, and the United States is also abundant in skilled labor (see Figure 4-6). We have also found that it is sometimes important to correct that actual amount of a factor of production for its productivity, obtaining the effective factor endowment. Now we can apply these ideas to the United States in 1947 to reexamine the Leontief paradox.

Using a sample of 30 countries for which GDP information is available in 1947, the U.S. share of those countries' GDP was 37%. That estimate of the U.S. share of "world" GDP is shown in the last bar graph of Figure 4-8. To determine whether the United States was abundant in physical capital or labor, we need to estimate its share of the world endowments of these factors.

Capital Abundance It is hard to estimate the U.S. share of the world capital stock in the postwar years. But given the devastation of the capital stock in Europe and Japan due to World War II, we can presume that the U.S. share of world capital was more than 37%. That estimate (or really a "guesstimate") means that the U.S. share of world

FIGURE 4-8

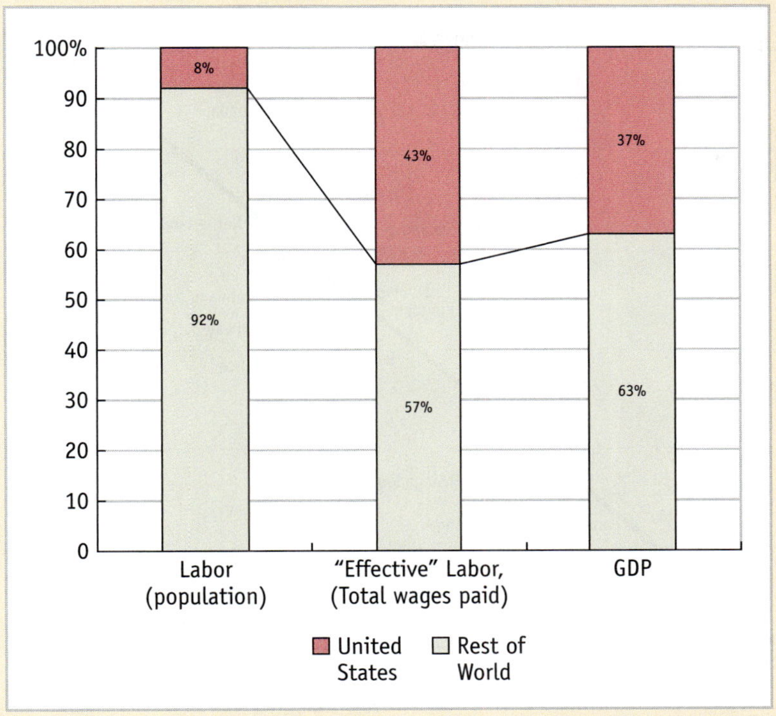

Labor Endowment and GDP for the United States and Rest of World, 1947 Shown here are the share of labor, "effective" labor, and GDP of the United States and the rest of the world (measured by 30 countries for which data are available) in 1947. The United States had only 8% of the world's population, as compared with 37% of the world's GDP, so it was very scarce in labor. But when we measure effective labor by the total wages paid in each country, then the United States had 43% of the world's effective labor as compared with 37% of GDP, so it was abundant in effective labor.

Source: Author's own calculations.

capital exceeds the U.S. share of world GDP, so that the United States was abundant in capital in 1947.

Labor Abundance What about the abundance of labor for the United States? If we do not correct labor for productivity difference across countries, then the population of each country is a rough measure of its labor force. The U.S. share of population for the sample of 35 countries in 1947 was very small, about 8%, which is shown in the first bar graph of Figure 4-8. This estimate of labor abundance is much less than the U.S. share of GDP, 37%. According to that comparison, the United States was scarce in labor (its share of that factor was less than its share of GDP).

Labor Productivity Using the U.S. share of population is not the right way to measure the U.S. labor endowment, however, because it does not correct for differences in the productivity of labor across countries. A good way to make that correction is to use wages paid to workers as a measure of their productivity. To illustrate why this is a good approach, in Figure 4-9 we plot the wages of workers in various countries and the estimated productivity of workers in 1990. The vertical axis in Figure 4-9 measures wages earned across a sample of 33 countries, measured relative to (i.e., as a percentage of) the United States. Only one country—Canada—has wages higher than those in the United States (probably reflecting greater union pressure in that country). All other countries have lower wages, ranging from Austria and Switzerland with wages that are about 95% of the U.S. wage, to Ireland, France, and Finland, with wages at about 50% of the U.S. level, to Bangladesh and Sri Lanka, with wages at about 5% of the U.S. level.

FIGURE 4-9

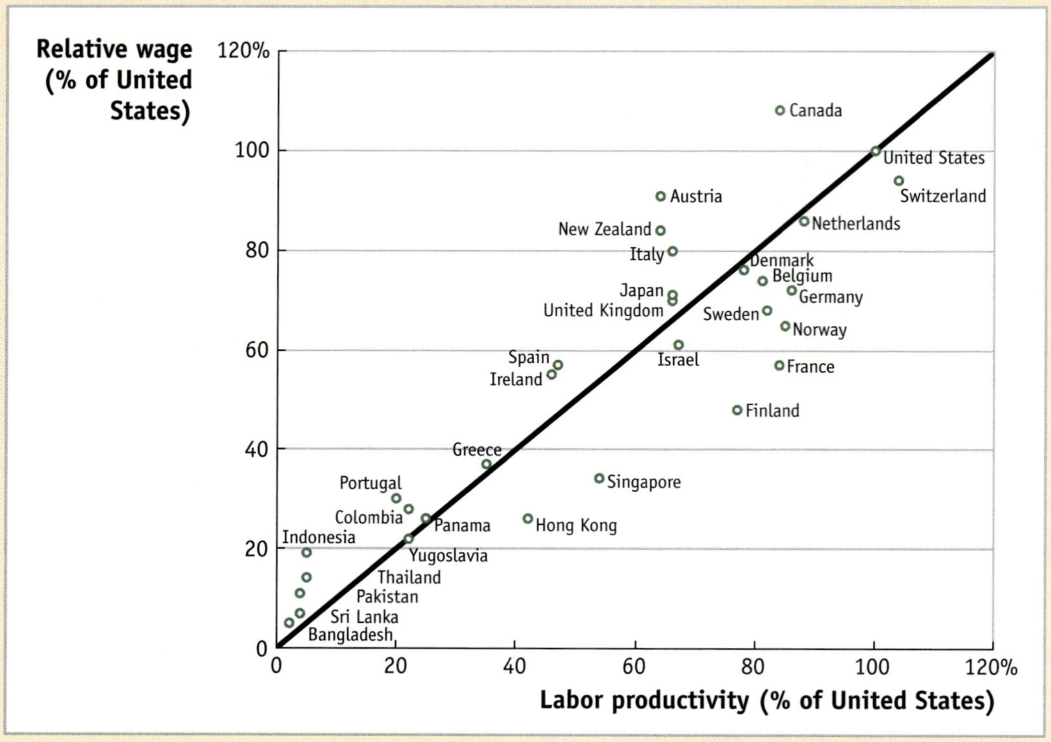

Labor Productivity and Wages Shown here are estimated labor productivities across countries, and their wages, relative to the United States in 1990. Notice that the labor and wages were highly correlated across countries: the points roughly line up along the 45-degree line. While this close connection between wages and labor productivity holds for the data in 1990, we expect that it also held in 1947, so that we can use wages to adjust for labor productivity in explaining the Leontief paradox.

Source: Daniel Trefler, 1993, "International Factor Price Differences: Leontief was Right!" Journal of Political Economy, *101(6), December, 961–987.*

The horizontal axis in Figure 4-9 measures labor productivity in various countries relative to that in the United States. For example, labor productivity in Canada is 80% of that in the United States; labor productivity in Austria and New Zealand is about 60% of that in the United States; and labor productivity in Indonesia, Thailand, Pakistan, Sri Lanka, and Bangladesh is about 5% of that in the United States. Notice that the labor productivities (on the horizontal axis) and wages (on the vertical axis) are highly correlated across countries: the points in Figure 4-9 line up approximately along the 45-degree line. This close connection between wages and labor productivity holds for the data in 1990, we expect that it also held in 1947, so that we can use wages to adjust for labor productivity in explaining the Leontief Paradox.

Effective Labor Abundance As suggested by Figure 4-9, wages across countries are strongly correlated with the productivity of labor. Going back to the data for 1947, which Leontief used, we use the wages earned by labor to measure the productivity of labor in each country. Then the *effective* amount of labor found in each country equals the actual amount of labor times the wage. Multiplying the amount of labor in each country by average wages, we obtain total wages paid to labor. That information is available for 30 countries in 1947, and we have already found that the United States accounted for 37% of the GDP of these countries, as shown in the final bar in Figure 4-8. Adding up total wages paid to labor across the 30 countries and comparing it with the United States, we find that the United States accounted for 43% of wages paid to labor in these 30 countries, as shown in the bar labeled "effective" labor. By comparing this estimate with the United States share of world GDP of 37% in 1947, we see that the United States was abundant in effective labor, taking into account the differing productivity of labor across countries. So not only was the United States abundant in capital, it was also abundant in effective—or skilled—labor in 1947, just as we have also found for the year 2000!

Summary In Leontief's test of the Heckscher-Ohlin theorem, he found that the capital–labor ratio for exports from the United States in 1947 was less than the capital–labor ratio for imports. That finding seemed to contradict the Heckscher-Ohlin theorem if we think of the United States as being capital-abundant: in that case, it should be exporting capital-intensive goods (with a high capital–labor ratio). But now we have found that the United States was abundant in *both* capital *and* labor in 1947, once we correct for the productivity of labor by using its wage. Basically, the relatively low population and number of workers in the United States are boosted upward by high U.S. wages, making the effective labor force seem much larger—large enough so that the U.S. share of wordwide wages even exceeds its share of GDP.

Such a finding means the United States was *also* abundant in effective—or skilled—labor in 1947, just as it is today. Armed with this finding, it is not surprising that Leontief found exports from the United States in 1947 used relatively less capital and more labor than did imports: that pattern simply reflects the high productivity of labor in the United States and its abundance of this effective factor. As Leontief himself proposed, once we take into account differences in the productivity of factors across countries, there is no "paradox" after all, at least in the data for 1947. For more recent years, too, taking account of factor productivity differences across countries is important when testing the Heckscher-Ohlin theorem.[5]

3 Effects of Trade on Factor Prices

In the Heckscher-Ohlin model developed in the previous sections, Home exported computers and Foreign exported shoes. Furthermore, we found in our model that the relative price of computers *rose* at Home from the no-trade equilibrium to the trade equilibrium (this higher relative price with trade is why computers are exported). Conversely, the relative price of computers *fell* in Foreign from the no-trade equilibrium to the trade equilibrium (this lower relative price with trade is why computers are imported abroad). The question we ask now is how the changes in the relative prices of goods affect the wage paid to labor in each country and the rental earned by capital. We begin by showing how the wage and rental are determined, focusing on Home.

[5] Readers who want to learn more about testing the HO model can consult the appendix to this chapter, which further discusses the Leontief Paradox and summarizes factor endowment and trade data in a recent year.

Effect of Trade on the Wage and Rental of Home

To determine the wage and rental, we go back to Figure 4-1, which showed that the quantity of labor demanded relative to the quantity of capital demanded in each industry at Home depends on the relative wage at Home W/R. We can use these relative demands for labor in each industry to derive an economy-wide relative demand for labor, which can then be compared with the economy-wide relative supply of labor $\overline{L}/\overline{K}$. By comparing the economy-wide relative demand and supply, just as we do in any supply and demand context, we can determine Home's relative wage. Moreover, we can evaluate what happens to the relative wage when the Home relative price of computers rises after Home starts trading.

Economy-Wide Relative Demand for Labor To derive an economy-wide relative demand for labor, we use the conditions that the quantities of labor and capital used in each industry add up to the total available labor and capital: $L_C + L_S = \overline{L}$ and $K_C + K_S = \overline{K}$. We can divide total labor by total capital to get

$$\underbrace{\frac{\overline{L}}{\overline{K}}}_{\text{Relative supply}} = \frac{L_C + L_S}{\overline{K}} = \underbrace{\frac{L_C}{K_C}\cdot\left(\frac{K_C}{\overline{K}}\right) + \frac{L_S}{K_S}\cdot\left(\frac{K_S}{\overline{K}}\right)}_{\text{Relative demand}}$$

The left-hand side of this equation is the economy-wide supply of labor relative to capital, or relative supply. The right-hand side is the economy-wide demand for labor relative to capital, or relative demand. The relative demand is a weighted average of the labor–capital ratio in each industry. This weighted average is obtained by multiplying the labor–capital ratio for each industry, L_C/K_C and L_S/K_S, by the terms $K_C/\overline{K}$ and $K_S/\overline{K}$, the shares of total capital employed in each industry. These two terms must add up to 1, $(K_C/\overline{K}) + (K_S/\overline{K}) = 1$, because capital must be employed in one industry or the other.

The determination of Home's equilibrium relative wage is shown in Figure 4-10 as the intersection of the relative supply and relative demand curves. The supply of labor relative to the supply of capital, the relative supply $(\overline{L}/\overline{K})$, is shown as a vertical line

FIGURE 4-10

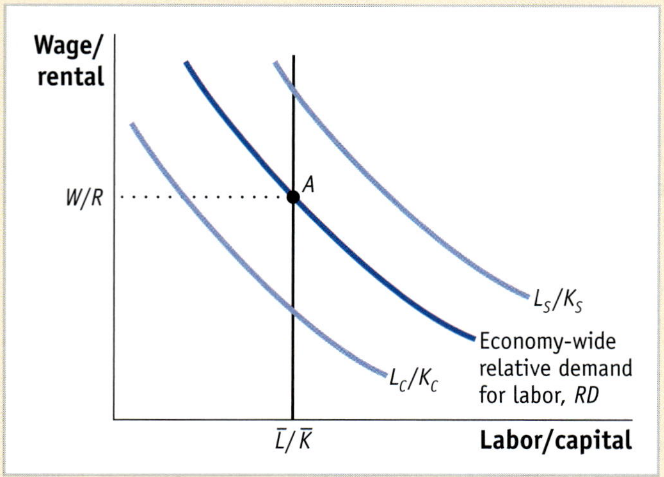

Determination of Home Wage/Rental The economy-wide relative demand for labor, *RD*, is an average of the L_C/K_C and L_S/K_S curves and lies between these curves. The relative supply, $\overline{L}/\overline{K}$, is shown by a vertical line because the total amount of resources in Home is fixed. The equilibrium point *A*, at which relative demand *RD* intersects relative supply $\overline{L}/\overline{K}$, determines the wage relative to the rental, *W/R*.

because the total amounts of labor and capital do not depend on the relative wage; they are fixed by the total amount of factor resources in each country. Because the relative demand (the *RD* curve in the graph) is an average of the L_C/K_C and L_S/K_S curves from Figure 4-1, it therefore lies *between* these two curves. The point at which relative demand intersects relative supply, point *A*, tells us that the wage relative to the rental is *W/R* (from the vertical axis). Point *A* describes an equilibrium in the labor and capital markets and combines these two markets into a single diagram by showing relative supply equal to relative demand.

Increase in the Relative Price of Computers When Home opens itself to trade, it faces a higher relative price of computers; that is, P_C/P_S increases at Home. We illustrate this higher relative price using Home's production possibilities frontier in Figure 4-11. At the no-trade or autarky equilibrium, point *A*, the relative price of computers is $(P_C/P_S)^A$ and the computer industry produces Q_{C1}, while the shoe industry produces Q_{S1}. With a rise in the relative price of computers to $(P_C/P_S)^W$, the computer industry increases its output to Q_{C2}, and the shoe industry decreases its output to Q_{S2}. With this shift in production, labor and capital both move from shoe production to computer production. What is the effect of these resource movements on the relative supply and relative demand for labor?

The effects are shown in Figure 4-12. Relative supply $\overline{L}/\overline{K}$ is the same as before because the total amounts of labor and capital available in Home have not changed. The relative demand for labor changes, however, because capital has shifted to the computer industry. This shift affects the terms used in the weighted average: $(K_C/\overline{K})$ rises and $(K_S/\overline{K})$ falls. The relative demand for labor in the economy is now more weighted toward computers and less weighted toward the shoe industry. In Figure 4-12, the change in the weights shifts the relative demand curve from RD_1 to RD_2. The curve shifts in the direction of the relative demand curve for computers, and the equilibrium moves from point *A* to *B*.

FIGURE 4-11

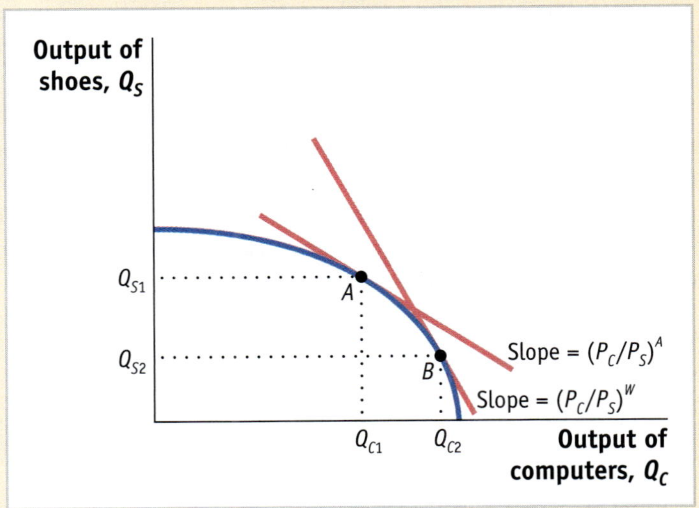

Increase in the Price of Computers Initially, Home is at a no-trade equilibrium at point *A* with a relative price of computers of $(P_C/P_S)^A$. An increase in the relative price of computers to the world price, as illustrated by the steeper world price line, $(P_C/P_S)^W$, shifts production from point *A* to *B*. At point *B*, there is a higher output of computers and a lower output of shoes, $Q_{C2} > Q_{C1}$ and $Q_{S2} < Q_{S1}$.

FIGURE 4-12

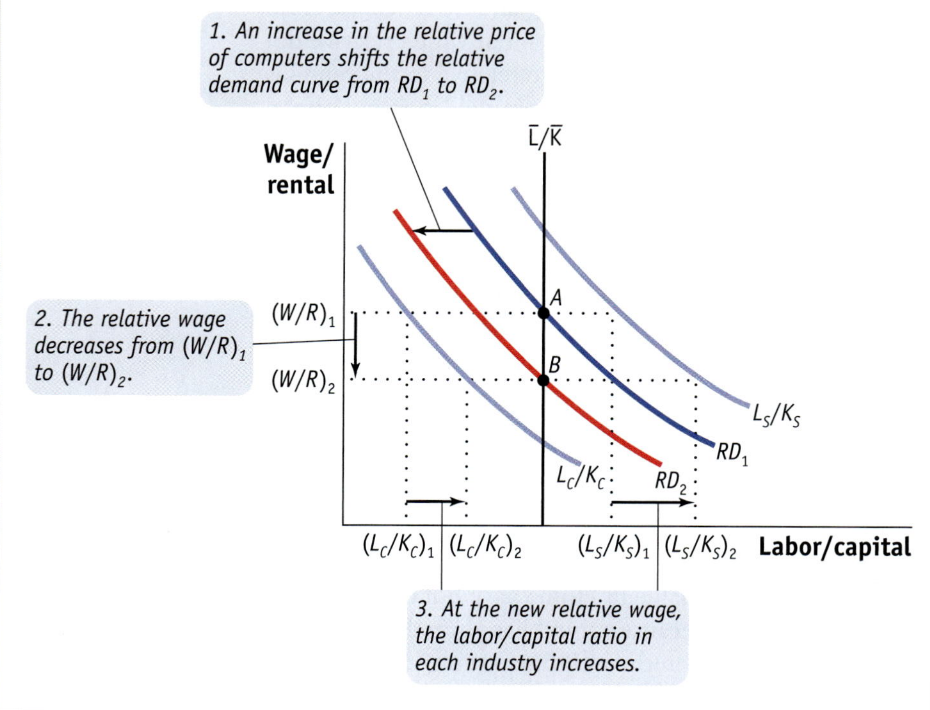

Effect of a Higher Relative Price of Computers on Wage/Rental An increase in the relative price of computers shifts the economy-wide relative demand for labor, RD_1, toward the relative demand for labor in the computer industry, L_C/K_C. The new relative demand curve, RD_2, intersects the relative supply curve for labor at a lower relative wage, $(W/R)_2$. As a result, the wage relative to the rental falls from $(W/R)_1$ to $(W/R)_2$. The lower relative wage causes both industries to increase their labor–capital ratios, as illustrated by the increase in both L_C/K_C and L_S/K_S at the new relative wage.

The impacts on all the variables are as follows. First, the relative wage W/R falls from $(W/R)_1$ to $(W/R)_2$, reflecting the fall in the relative demand for labor as both factors move into computer production from shoe production. Second, the lower relative wage induces *both* industries to hire more workers per unit of capital (a move down along their relative demand curves). In the shoe industry, for instance, the new, lower relative wage $(W/R)_2$ intersects the relative demand curve for labor L_S/K_S at a point corresponding to a higher L/K level than the initial relative wage $(W/R)_1$. That is, $(L_S/K_S)_2 > (L_S/K_S)_1$, and the same argument holds for the computer industry. As a result, the labor–capital ratio rises in both shoes and computers.

How is it possible for the labor–capital ratio to rise in *both* industries when the amount of labor and capital available in total is fixed? The answer is that more labor per unit of capital is released from shoes than is needed to operate that capital in computers (because computers require fewer workers per machine). As the relative price of computers rises, computer output rises while shoe output falls, and labor is "freed up" to be used more in both industries. In terms of our earlier equation for relative supply and relative demand, the changes in response to the increase in the relative price of computers P_C/P_S are

$$\underbrace{\frac{\overline{L}}{\overline{K}}}_{\substack{\text{Relative supply}\\ \text{No change}}} = \underbrace{\underset{\uparrow}{\frac{L_C}{K_C}}\cdot\underset{\uparrow}{\left(\frac{K_C}{\overline{K}}\right)} + \underset{\uparrow}{\frac{L_S}{K_S}}\cdot\underset{\downarrow}{\left(\frac{K_S}{\overline{K}}\right)}}_{\substack{\text{Relative demand}\\ \text{No change in total}}}$$

The relative supply of labor has not changed, so relative demand for labor cannot change overall. Since some of the individual components of relative demand have increased, other components must decrease to keep the overall relative demand the same. After the rise in the price of computers, even more capital will be used in the computer industry ($K_C/\overline{K}$ rises while $K_S/\overline{K}$ falls) because the output of computers rises and the output of shoes falls. This shift in weights on the right-hand side pulls down the overall relative demand for labor (this is necessarily true since $L_C/K_C < L_S/K_S$ by assumption). But because the relative supply on the left-hand side doesn't change, another feature must increase the relative demand for labor: this feature is the increased labor–capital ratios in *both* industries. In this way, relative demand continues to equal relative supply at point B, and at the same time, the labor–capital ratios have risen in both industries.

Determination of the Real Wage and Real Rental

To summarize, we have found that an increase in the relative price of computers—which are capital-intensive—leads to a fall in the relative wage (W/R). In turn, the decrease in the relative wage leads to an increase in the labor–capital ratio used in each industry (L_C/K_C and L_S/K_S). Our goal in this section is to determine who gains and who loses from these changes. For this purpose, it is not enough to know how the *relative* wage changes; instead, we want to determine the change in the *real wage* and *real rental;* that is, the change in the quantity of shoes and computers that each factor of production can purchase. With the results we have already obtained, it will be fairly easy to determine the change in the real wage and real rental.

Change in the Real Rental Because the labor–capital ratio increases in both industries, the marginal product of capital also increases in both industries. This is because there are more people to work with each piece of capital. This result follows from our earlier argument that when a machine has more labor to work it, it will be more productive, and the marginal product of capital will go up. In both industries, the rental on capital is determined by its marginal product and by the prices of the goods:

$$R = P_C \cdot MPK_C \text{ and } R = P_S \cdot MPK_S$$

Because capital can move freely between industries in the long run, the rental on capital is equalized across them. By using the result that both marginal products of capital increase and by rearranging the previous equations, we see that

$$MPK_C = R/P_C \uparrow \text{ and } MPK_S = R/P_S \uparrow$$

Remember that R/P_C measures that quantity of computers that can be purchased with the rental, whereas R/P_S measures the quantity of shoes that can be bought with the rental. When both of these go up, the real rental on capital (in terms of either good) *increases*. Therefore, capital owners are clearly better off when the relative price of computers increases. Notice that computers is the capital-intensive industry, so the more general result is that *an increase in the relative price of a good will benefit the factor of production used intensively in producing that good.*

Change in the Real Wage To understand what happens to the real wage when the relative price of computers rises, we again use the result that the labor–capital ratio increases in *both* industries. The law of diminishing returns tells us that the marginal product of labor must fall in both industries (since there are more workers on each machine). In both industries, the wage is determined by the marginal product of labor and the prices of the goods:

$$W = P_C \cdot MPL_C \text{ and } W = P_S \cdot MPL_S$$

Using the result that the marginal product of labor falls in both industries, we see that

$$MPL_C = W/P_C \downarrow \text{ and } MPL_S = W/P_S \downarrow$$

Therefore, the quantity of computers that can be purchased with the wage (W/P_C) and the quantity of shoes that can be purchased with the wage (W/P_S) both fall. These decreases mean that the real wage (in terms of either good) is *reduced*, and labor is clearly worse off due to the increase in the relative price of computers.

We can summarize our results with the following theorem, first derived by economists Wolfgang Stolper and Paul Samuelson.

Stolper-Samuelson Theorem: In the long run, when all factors are mobile, an increase in the relative price of a good will increase the real earnings of the factor used intensively in the production of that good and decrease the real earnings of the other factor.

For our example, the **Stolper-Samuelson theorem** predicts that when Home opens to trade and faces a higher relative price of computers, the real rental on capital in Home rises and the real wage in Home falls. In Foreign, the changes in real factor prices are just the reverse. When Foreign opens to trade and faces a lower relative price of computers, the real rental falls and the real wage rises. Remember that Foreign is abundant in labor, so our finding that labor is better off there, but worse off at Home, means that workers in the labor-abundant country gain from trade but workers in the capital-abundant country lose. In addition, capital in the capital-abundant country (Home) gains, and capital in the labor-abundant country loses. These results are sometimes summarized by saying that in the Heckscher-Ohlin model, *the abundant factor gains from trade, and the scarce factor loses from trade.*[6]

Changes in the Real Wage and Rental: A Numerical Example

To illustrate the Stolper-Samuelson theorem, we use a numerical example to show how much the real wage and rental can change in response to a change in price. Suppose that the computer and shoe industries have the following data:

Computers:

Sales revenue $= P_C \cdot Q_C = 100$

Earnings of labor $= W \cdot L_C = 50$

Earnings of capital $= R \cdot K_C = 50$

Shoes:

Sales revenue $= P_S \cdot Q_S = 100$

Earnings of labor $= W \cdot L_S = 60$

Earnings of capital $= R \cdot K_S = 40$

[6] This result follows logically from combining the Heckscher-Ohlin theorem with the Stolper-Samuelson theorem.

Notice that shoes are more labor-intensive than computers: the share of total revenue paid to labor in shoes (60/100 = 60%) is more than that share in computers (50/100 = 50%).

When Home and Foreign undertake trade, the relative price of computers rises. For simplicity we assume that this occurs because the price of computers P_C rises, while the price of shoes P_S does not change:

Computers: Percentage increase in price $= \Delta P_C/P_C = 10\%$

Shoes: Percentage increase in price $= \Delta P_S/P_S = 0\%$

Our goal is to see how the increase in the relative price of computers translates into long-run changes in the wage W paid to labor and the rental on capital R. Remember that the rental on capital can be calculated by taking total sales revenue in each industry, subtracting the payments to labor, and dividing by the amount of capital. This calculation gives us the following formulas for the rental in each industry:[7]

$$R = \frac{P_C \cdot Q_C - W \cdot L_C}{K_C}, \text{ for computers}$$

$$R = \frac{P_S \cdot Q_S - W \cdot L_S}{K_S}, \text{ for shoes}$$

The price of computers has risen, so $\Delta P_C > 0$, holding fixed the price of shoes, $\Delta P_S = 0$. We can trace through how this affects the rental by changing P_C and W in the previous two equations:

$$\Delta R = \frac{\Delta P_C \cdot Q_C - \Delta W \cdot L_C}{K_C}, \text{ for computers}$$

$$\Delta R = \frac{0 \cdot Q_C - \Delta W \cdot L_S}{K_S}, \text{ for shoes}$$

It is convenient to work with percentage changes in the variables. For computers, $\Delta P_C/P_C$ is the percentage change in price. Similarly, $\Delta W/W$ is the percentage change in the wage, and $\Delta R/R$ is the percentage change in the rental of capital. We can introduce these terms into the preceding formulas by rewriting them as

$$\frac{\Delta R}{R} = \left(\frac{\Delta P_C}{P_C}\right)\left(\frac{P_C \cdot Q_C}{R \cdot K_C}\right) - \left(\frac{\Delta W}{W}\right)\left(\frac{W \cdot L_C}{R \cdot K_C}\right), \text{ for computers}$$

$$\frac{\Delta R}{R} = -\left(\frac{\Delta W}{W}\right)\left(\frac{W \cdot L_S}{R \cdot K_S}\right), \text{ for shoes}$$

(You should cancel terms in these equations to check that they are the same as before.)

Now we'll plug the above data for shoes and computers into these formulas:

$$\frac{\Delta R}{R} = 10\% \cdot \left(\frac{100}{50}\right) - \left(\frac{\Delta W}{W}\right)\left(\frac{50}{50}\right), \text{ for computers}$$

$$\frac{\Delta R}{R} = -\left(\frac{\Delta W}{W}\right)\left(\frac{60}{40}\right), \text{ for shoes}$$

[7] Remember that due to factor mobility, the rental is the same in each industry, but it is helpful here to derive two separate equations for the percentage change in rental by industry.

Our goal is to find out by how much rental and wage change given changes in the relative price of the final goods, so we are trying to solve for two unknowns ($\Delta R/R$ and $\Delta W/W$) from the two equations given here. A good way to do this is to reduce the two equations with two unknowns into a single equation with one unknown. This can be done by subtracting one equation from the other, as follows:

$$\frac{\Delta R}{R} = 10\% \cdot \left(\frac{100}{50}\right) - \left(\frac{\Delta W}{W}\right)\left(\frac{50}{50}\right), \text{ for computers}$$

$$\text{Minus:} \quad \frac{\Delta R}{R} = 0 - \left(\frac{\Delta W}{W}\right)\left(\frac{60}{40}\right), \text{ for shoes}$$

$$\text{Equals:} \quad 0 = 10\% \cdot \left(\frac{100}{50}\right) + \left(\frac{\Delta W}{W}\right)\left(\frac{20}{40}\right)$$

Simplifying the last line, we get $0 = 20\% + \left(\frac{\Delta W}{W}\right)\left(\frac{1}{2}\right)$, so that

$$\left(\frac{\Delta W}{W}\right) = \frac{-20\%}{\left(\frac{1}{2}\right)} = -40\%, \text{ is the change in wages}$$

So when the price of computers increases by 10%, the wage falls by 40%. With the wage falling, labor can no longer afford to buy as many computers (W/P_C has fallen since W is falling and P_C has increased) or as many pairs of shoes (W/P_S has fallen since W is falling and P_S has not changed). In other words, the *real wage* measured in terms of either good has *fallen*, so labor is clearly worse off.

To find the change in the rental paid to capital (R/R), we can take our solution for $W/W = -40\%$,[8] and plug it into the equation for the change in the rental in the shoes sector:

$$\frac{\Delta R}{R} = -\left(\frac{\Delta W}{W}\right)\left(\frac{60}{40}\right) = 40\% \cdot \left(\frac{60}{40}\right) = 60\%, \text{ change in rental}$$

The rental on capital increases by 60% when the price of computers rises by 10%, so the rental increases even more (in percentage terms) than the price. Because the rental increases by more than the price of computers in percentage terms, it follows that (R/P_C) rises: owners of capital can afford to buy more computers, even though their price has gone up. In addition, they can afford to buy more shoes (R/P_S also rises, since R rises and P_S is constant). Thus, the real rental measured in terms of either good has *gone up*, and capital owners are clearly better off.

General Equation for the Long-Run Change in Factor Prices The long-run results of a change in factor prices can be summarized in the following equation:

$$\underbrace{\Delta W/W < 0}_{\text{Real wage falls}} < \underbrace{\Delta P_C/P_C < \Delta R/R}_{\text{Real rental increases}}, \text{ for an increase in } P_C$$

---

[8] You should check that you get the same answer if instead you plug the change in the wage into the formula for the change in the rental in the computer sector.

That is, the increase in the price of computers (10%) leads to an even larger increase in the rental on capital (60%) and a decrease in the wage (-40%). If, instead, the price of computers falls, then these inequalities are reversed, and we get

$$\underbrace{\Delta R/R < \Delta P_C/P_C}_{\text{Real rental falls}} \underbrace{< 0 < \Delta W/W}_{\text{Real wage increases}}, \text{ for an decrease in } P_C$$

What happens if the relative price of shoes increases? From the Stolper-Samuelson theorem, we know that this change will benefit labor, which is used intensively in shoe production, and will harm capital. The equation summarizing the changes in factor earnings when the price of shoes increases is

$$\underbrace{\Delta R/R < 0}_{\text{Real rental falls}} \underbrace{< \Delta P_S/P_S < \Delta W/W}_{\text{Real wage increases}}, \text{ for an increase in } P_S$$

These equations relating the changes in product prices to changes in factor prices are sometimes called the "magnification effect" because they show how changes in the prices of goods have *magnified effects* on the earnings of factors: even a modest fluctuation in the relative prices of goods on world markets can lead to exaggerated changes in the long-run earnings of both factors. This result tells us that some groups—those employed intensively in export industries—can be expected to support opening an economy to trade because an increase in export prices increases their real earnings. But other groups—those employed intensively in import industries—can be expected to oppose free trade because the decrease in import prices decreases their real earnings. The following application examines the opinions that different factors of production have taken toward free trade.

APPLICATION

Opinions toward Free Trade

Countries sometimes conduct surveys about their citizens' attitudes toward free trade. A survey conducted in the United States by the National Elections Studies (NES) in 1992 included the following question:

> Some people have suggested placing new limits on foreign imports in order to protect American jobs. Others say that such limits would raise consumer prices and hurt American exports. Do you favor or oppose placing limits on imports, or haven't you thought much about this?

Respondents to the survey could either answer that they "favor" placing limits on imports, meaning that they do not support free trade, or that they "oppose" limits on imports, meaning that they support free trade. How do these answers compare with characteristics of the respondents, such as their wages, skills, or the industries in which they work?

According to the specific-factors model, in the short run we do not know whether labor will gain or lose from free trade, but we do know that the specific factor in the export sector gains, and the specific factor in the import sector loses. Think about an extension of this model, in which, in addition to their wage, labor also earns some part of the rental on the specific factor in their industry. This assumption is true for farmers, for example, who work in agriculture and may own their land; it can also be true for workers in manufacturing if their salary includes a bonus that is based on the profits earned by capital. In those situations, we would expect that workers in export industries will support free trade (since the specific factor in that industry gains), but workers in import-competing industries will be against free trade (since the specific factor in that industry loses). In the short run, then, the *industry of employment* of workers will affect their attitudes toward free trade.

In the long-run Heckscher-Ohlin model, however, the industry of employment should not matter. According to the Stolper-Samuelson theorem, an increase in the relative price of exports will benefit the factor of production used intensively in exports and harm the other factor, regardless of the industry in which these factors of production actually work (remember that each factor of production earns the same wage or rental across industries in the long run). In the United States, export industries tend to use skilled labor intensively for research and development and other scientific work. An increase in the relative price of exports will benefit skilled labor in the long run, regardless of whether these workers are employed in export-oriented industries or import-competing industries. Conversely, an increase in the relative price of exports will harm unskilled labor, regardless of where these workers are employed. In the long run, then, the *skill level* of workers should determine their attitudes toward free trade.

In the 1992 NES survey, the industry of employment was somewhat important in explaining the respondents' attitudes toward free trade, but their skill level was much more important.[9] That is, workers in export-oriented industries are somewhat more likely to favor free trade, with those in import-competing industries favoring import restrictions, but this statistical relationship is not strong. A much more important determinant of the attitudes toward free trade is the skill level of workers, as measured by their wages or their years of education. Workers with lower wages or fewer years of education are more likely to favor import restrictions, whereas those with higher wages and more years of education favor free trade. This finding suggests that the respondents to the survey are basing their answer on their *long-run* earnings, as predicted by the Heckscher-Ohlin model and Stolper-Samuelson theorem, rather than on their short-run industry of employment, as predicted by the specific-factors model.

There is an interesting extension to these findings, however. The survey also asked respondents whether they owned a home. It turns out that people who own homes in communities in which the local industries face a lot of import competition are much more likely to oppose free trade. Examples of this are towns in the northeastern states where people have been employed by textiles mills, or in the midwestern states where people have been employed by automobile, steel, and other heavy industries. But people who own homes in communities in which the industries benefit from export opportunities, such as the high-tech areas in Boston or in Silicon Valley, California, are much more likely to support free trade. We can think of a house as a specific factor, since it cannot move locations. So the attitudes in this part of the NES survey conform to the short-run specific-factors model: people are very concerned about the asset value of their homes, just as the owners of specific factors in our model are concerned about the rental earned by the factor of production they own. ■

[9] See Kenneth F. Scheve and Matthew J. Slaughter, 2001, "What Determines Individual Trade-Policy Preferences?" *Journal of International Economics*, 54, 267–292.

4 Conclusions

The Heckscher-Ohlin framework is one of the most widely used models in explaining trade patterns. It isolates the effect of different factor endowments across countries and determines the impact of these differences on trade patterns, relative prices, and factor returns. This approach is a major departure from the view that technology differences determine trade patterns as we saw in the Ricardian model and is also a departure from the short-run specific-factors model that we studied in Chapter 3.

In this chapter, we have investigated some empirical tests of the Heckscher-Ohlin theorem; that is, tests to determine whether countries actually export the goods that use their abundant factor intensively. The body of literature testing the theorem originates in Leontief's puzzling finding that U.S. exports just after World War II were relatively labor-intensive. Although the original formulation of his test did not seem to support the HO theorem, later research has reformulated the test to measure the effective endowments of labor, capital, and other factors found in each country. Using this approach, we found that the United States was abundant in effective labor, and we also presume that it was abundant in capital. The United States had a positive factor content of net exports for both labor and capital in 1947, which is consistent with the finding of Leontief, so there was really no "paradox" after all.

By focusing on the factor intensities among goods (i.e., the relative amount of labor and capital used in production), the Heckscher-Ohlin model also provides clear guidance as to who gains and who loses from the opening of trade. In the specific-factors model, an increase in the relative price of a good leads to real gains for the specific factor used in that industry, losses for the other specific factor, and an ambiguous change in the real wage for labor. In contrast, the HO model predicts real gains for the factor used intensively in the export good, whose relative price goes up with the opening of trade, and real losses for the other factor. Having just two factors, both of which are fully mobile between the industries, leads to a very clear prediction about who gains and who loses from trade in the long run.

KEY POINTS

1. In the Heckscher-Ohlin model, we assume that the technologies are the same across countries and that countries trade because the available resources (labor, capital, and land) differ across countries.
2. The Heckscher-Ohlin model is a long-run framework, so labor, capital, and other resources can move freely between the industries.
3. With two goods, two factors, and two countries, the Heckscher-Ohlin model predicts that a country will export the good that uses its abundant factor intensively and import the other good.
4. The first test of the Heckscher-Ohlin model was made by Leontief using U.S. data for 1947. He found that U.S. exports were less capital-intensive and more labor-intensive than U.S. imports. This was a paradoxical finding because the United States was abundant in capital.
5. The assumption of identical technologies used in the Heckscher-Ohlin model does not hold in practice. Current research has extended the empirical tests of the Heckscher-Ohlin model to allow for many factors and countries, along with differing productivities of factors across countries. When we allow for different productivities

of labor in 1947, we find that the United States is abundant in effective—or skilled—labor, which explains the Leontief paradox.

6. According to the Stolper-Samuelson theorem, an increase in the relative price of a good will cause the real earnings of labor and capital to move in opposite directions: the factor used intensively in the industry whose relative price goes up will find its earnings increased, and the real earnings of the other factor will fall.
7. Putting together the Heckscher-Ohlin theorem and the Stolper-Samuelson theorem, we conclude that a country's abundant factor gains from the opening of trade (because the relative price of exports goes up), and its scarce factor loses from the opening of trade.

KEY TERMS

Heckscher-Ohlin model, p. 87
reversal of factor intensities, p. 92
free-trade equilibrium, p. 97
Heckscher-Ohlin theorem, p. 97
Leontief's paradox, p. 98
abundant in that factor, p. 100
scarce in that factor, p. 100
effective labor force, p. 102
effective factor endowment, p. 102
abundant in that effective factor, p. 103
scarce in that effective factor, p. 103
Stolper-Samuelson theorem, p. 114

PROBLEMS

1. This problem uses the Heckscher-Ohlin model to predict the direction of trade. Consider the production of handmade rugs and assembly line robots in Canada and India.
   a. Which country would you expect to be relatively labor-abundant, and which is capital-abundant? Why?
   b. Which industry would you expect to be relatively labor-intensive, and which is capital-intensive? Why?
   c. Given your answers to (a) and (b), draw production possibilities frontiers for each country. Assuming that consumer preferences are the same in both countries, add indifference curves and relative price lines (without trade) to your PPF graphs. What do the slopes of the price lines tell you about the direction of trade?
   d. Allowing for trade between countries, redraw the graphs and include a "trade triangle" for each country. Identify and label the vertical and horizontal sides of the triangles as either imports or exports.
2. Leontief's paradox is an example of testing a trade model using actual data observations. If Leontief had observed that the amount of labor needed per $1 million of U.S. exports was 100 person-years instead of 182, would he have reached the same conclusion? Explain.

3. Suppose there are drastic technological improvements in shoe production at Home such that shoe factories can operate almost completely with computer-aided machines. Consider the following data for the Home country:

Computers: Sales revenue = $P_C Q_C = 100$

Payments to labor = $WL_C = 50$

Payments to capital = $RK_C = 50$

Percentage increase in the price = $\Delta P_C / P_C = 0\%$

Shoes: Sales revenue = $P_S Q_S = 100$

Payments to labor = $WL_S = 5$

Payments to capital = $RK_S = 95$

Percentage increase in the price = $\Delta P_S / P_S = 50\%$

a. Which industry is capital-intensive? Is this a reasonable question, given that some industries are capital-intensive in some countries and labor-intensive in others?
b. Given the percentage changes in output prices in the data provided, calculate the percentage change in the rental on capital.
c. How does the magnitude of this change compare with that of labor?
d. Which factor gains in real terms, and which factor loses? Are these results consistent with the Stolper-Samuelson theorem?

4. Using the information in the chapter, suppose Home doubles in size, while Foreign remains the same. Show that an equal proportional increase in capital and labor at Home will change the relative price of computers, wage, rental on capital, and the amount traded but not the pattern of trade.

5. Using a diagram similar to Figure 4-12, show the effect of a decrease in the relative price of computers in Foreign. What happens to the wage relative to the rental? Is there an increase in the labor–capital ratio in each industry? Explain.

6. Suppose when Russia opens to trade, it imports automobiles, a capital-intensive good.
a. According to the Heckscher-Ohlin theorem, is Russia capital-abundant or labor-abundant? Briefly explain.
b. What is the impact of opening trade on the real wage in Russia?
c. What is the impact of opening trade on the real rental on capital?
d. Which group (capital owner or labor) would support policies to limit free trade? Briefly explain.

7. In Figure 4-3, we show how the movement from the no-trade equilibrium point A to a trade equilibrium at a higher relative price of computers leads to an upward-sloping export supply, from points A to D in panel (b).
a. Suppose that the relative price of computers continues to rise in panel (a), and label the production and consumption points at several higher prices.
b. In panel (b), extend the export supply curve to show the quantity of exports at the higher relative prices of computers.
c. What happens to the export supply curve when the price of computers is high enough? Can you explain why this happens? *Hint:* An increase in the relative price of a country's export good means that the country is richer because its terms of trade have improved. Explain how that can lead to fewer exports as their price rises.

8. In 2008 the Ukraine successfully negotiated terms to become a member of the World Trade Organization. Consequently, countries such as those in western Europe are shifting toward free trade with the Ukraine. What does the Stolper-Samuelson theorem predict about the impact of the shift on the real wage of unskilled labor in western Europe? In the Ukraine?

9. The following are data on U.S. exports and imports in 2007 at the two-digit Harmonized Schedule (HS) level. Which products do you think support the Heckscher-Ohlin theorem? Which products are inconsistent?

HS Code	Product	Export ($ billions)	Import ($ billions)
22	Beverages	3.6	14.7
30	Pharmaceutical products	40.7	55.6
52	Cotton	4.9	0.8
61	Apparel	1.9	33.3
64	Footwear	1.0	17.6
72	Iron and steel	15.4	12.4
74	Copper	5.0	6.4
85	Electric machinery	124.9	212.1
87	Vehicles	73.6	131.9
88	Aircraft	83.0	18.4
94	Furniture	7.0	30.1
95	Toys	7.0	27.6

Source: International Trade Administration, U.S. Department of Commerce.

10. Following are data for soybean yield, production, and trade for 2007:

Suppose that the countries listed in the table are engaged in free trade and that soybean production is land-intensive. Answer the following:

a. In which countries does land benefit from free trade in soybeans? Explain.
b. In which countries does land lose from free trade in soybeans? Explain.
c. In which countries does the move to free trade in soybeans have little or no effect on the land rental? Explain.

	Yield (metric ton/hectare)	Production (100,000 metric ton)	Export (100,000 metric ton)	Imports (100,000 metric ton)
Australia	2.44	3.2	0.3	1.0
Brazil	2.81	5,785.7	2,373.4	9.8
Canada	2.30	269.6	186.8	21.3
China	1.45	1,272.5	45.7	3,315.0
France	2.60	8.5	1.7	49.4
Ireland	3.13	40.8	2.0	8.4
Japan	1.64	22.7	0.1	416.1
Mexico	1.41	8.8	0.0	361.1
Russian Federation	0.92	65.0	1.7	12.5
United States	2.81	7,286.0	2,984.0	27.6

Source: Food and Agriculture Organization.

11. According to the Heckscher-Ohlin model, two countries can equalize wage differences by either engaging in international trade in goods or allowing skilled and unskilled labor to freely move between the two countries. Discuss whether this is true or false, and explain why.

12. According to the standard Heckscher-Ohlin model with two factors (capital and labor) and two goods, movement of Turkish migrants to Germany would decrease the amount of capital-intensive products produced in Germany. Discuss whether this is true or false, and explain why.

NET WORK

See the New Balance plant in Skowhegan, Maine, at http://www.youtube.com/watch?v=ittvWwCS5QI. What shoes are produced there, and what is the "Super Team 33"?

APPENDIX TO CHAPTER 4

The Sign Test in the Heckscher-Ohlin Model

Modern research on the Heckscher-Ohlin (HO) model allows for many goods, factors, and countries as well as differing technologies across countries. In this appendix, we discuss a method called the "sign test" that can be used to test the HO model. In addition to allowing for many goods, factors, and countries, the sign test can also be extended to allow for differing technologies across countries.

Measuring the Factor Content of Trade

The first question is, How do we measure the factor intensity of exports and imports when there are thousands of products traded between countries? How can we summarize all that information into categories that allow us to test the Heckscher-Ohlin model?

It turns out that Leontief's test gives us a good way to answer this question. Recall that Leontief measured the amount of labor and capital used to produce $1 million worth of U.S. exports and $1 million worth of U.S. imports. His numbers are shown in the second and fourth columns of Table 4A-1. If we multiply his numbers shown in Table 4A-1 by the actual value of U.S. exports, which were $16,700 million in 1947, and U.S. imports, which were $6,200 million, we obtain the values for "total exports" and "total imports" shown in Table 4A-1. These values are called the "factor content of exports" and "factor content of imports," respectively, and they measure the amounts of labor and capital used to produce exports and imports.

TABLE 4A-1

Factor Content of Trade for the United States, 1947 This table extends Leontief's test of the Heckscher-Ohlin model to measure the factor content of net exports. The first column for exports and for imports shows the amount of capital or labor needed per $1 million worth of exports from or imports into the United States, for 1947. The second column for each shows the amount of capital or labor needed for the total exports from or imports into the United States. The final column is the difference between the totals for exports and imports.

	EXPORTS, *X*		IMPORTS, *M*		NET EXPORTS (*X* – *M*)
	For $1 Million Exports	For Total Exports	For $1 Million Imports	For Total Imports	
Capital ($ millions)	2.55	42,600	3.1	19,200	23,400
Labor (person-years)	182	3.04 million	170	1.05 million	2 million
Capital/labor ($/person)	14,000	14,000	18,200	18,200	16,700

Source: Edward E. Leamer, 1980, "The Leontief Paradox, Reconsidered," Journal of Political Economy, *88(3), 495–503. Reprinted in Edward E. Leamer, ed., 2001,* International Economics *(New York: Worth), pp. 142–149.*

By taking the difference between the factor content of exports and the factor content of imports, we obtain the *factor content of net exports*, shown in the final column of Table 4A-1. In 1947 the net exports of the United States required $23.4 billion worth of capital and 2 million person-years. The fact that both these factor contents are positive indicates that the United States was running a trade surplus (with the value of exports greater than the value of imports) that year. This finding is not surprising. The United States exported large amounts of goods to help the countries of Europe rebuild after the devastation of World War II (which had just ended in 1945).

The Sign Test

We make use of the factor content of trade in developing a test for the Heckscher-Ohlin model, called the sign test. This test states that if a country is abundant in an effective factor, then that factor's content in net exports should be positive, but if a country is scarce in an effective factor, then that factor's content in net exports should be negative. To measure whether a factor is abundant or scarce in a country, we compare the amount of the effective factor found there with that country's share of world GDP, as we did in Figures 4-7 and 4-8. So the form of the sign test is as follows:

Sign of (country's % share of effective factor – % share of world GDP)

= Sign of country's factor content of net exports

For example, the finding in Table 4A-1 that the United States was a net exporter of capital in 1947, as measured by its factor content of net exports, means that according to the sign test, it should also be abundant in capital. That prediction from the sign test is confirmed in our discussion on pages 106–107, where we argued that the U.S. share of the world capital stock in 1947 exceeds its share of world GDP. Likewise, the finding in Table 4A-1 that the United States was a net exporter of labor in 1947 means that according to the sign test, it should also be abundant in effective labor. That prediction is also confirmed in Figure 4-8, where we show that the U.S. share of the world effective labor in 1947 (43%) exceeds its share of world GDP (37%).

The Sign Test in a Recent Year

We now turn to the sign test in a recent year—1990—using 9 factors of production and 33 countries. The factors of production are capital; seven kinds of labor (professional, technical, clerical, sales, service, agricultural, and production workers); and two kinds of arable land (cropland and pasture). We allow capital, seven types of labor, and two types of land to differ in their productivities across countries.

The countries include poor nations, middle-income nations, and countries with per capita incomes nearly equal to those in the United States. Like Leontief, we use the technology of the United States to construct the factor contents of net exports. With 33 countries and 9 factors, there are $33 \cdot 9 = 297$ sign tests that can be made. Rather than show the results for every country, we instead group the nations by their GDP per capita, from lowest to highest. The results of the sign test are shown in Table 4A-2.

For the countries with low GDP per capita (less than one-third of the U.S. level), the first row of Table 4A-2 shows that, on average, nearly 6 out of 9 effective factors pass the sign test. When we consider the middle-income countries (with GDP per capita between one-third and two-thirds of the U.S. level), the sign test passes for 5.7 out of

TABLE 4A-2

The Sign Test for 33 Countries with Differing Technologies, 1990 This table shows the sign test for the Heckscher-Ohlin model for 1990, allowing for different technologies across countries. There are 33 countries included in the study and 9 factors of production. All countries have more factors passing the sign test than failing it, especially the low- and medium-income countries. These results show that the sign test holds true when we allow productivities to differ across countries.

Country Group	GDP per Capita (% of U.S. GDP)	Number of Factors Passing Sign Test	Number of Factors Failing Sign Test
Lowest GDP per capita	4–33	5.9	3.1
Middle GDP per capita	33–66	5.7	3.3
Highest GDP per capita	66–100	5.3	3.7
All countries	4–100	5.6	3.4

Note: The countries with low GDP per capita are Bangladesh, Pakistan, Indonesia, Sri Lanka, Thailand, Colombia, Panama, Yugoslavia, Portugal, and Uruguay. The countries with middle GDP per capita are Greece, Ireland, Spain, Israel, Hong Kong, New Zealand, and Austria. The countries with high GDP per capita are Singapore, Italy, the United Kingdom, Japan, Belgium, Trinidad, the Netherlands, Finland, Denmark, former West Germany, France, Sweden, Norway, Switzerland, Canada, and the United States.

Source: Computed from Daniel Trefler, 1995, "The Case of Missing Trade and Other Mysteries," American Economic Review, *85(5), December, 1029–1046. Reprinted in Edward E. Leamer, ed., 2001,* International Economics *(New York: Worth), pp. 151–175.*

9 factors, on average, which is again close to 6 out of 9. In contrast, for the richest countries, the sign test using effective factors of production does not perform as well, passing for 5.3 factors out of 9, while failing for 3.7 factors. Combining all the countries, the sign test is successful in more than one-half of the cases (passing for 5.6 factors out of 9, on average). These results show that the predictions of the Heckscher-Ohlin model hold true, especially for low- and medium-income countries, when they are tested on a global dataset for a recent year.

5

Movement of Labor and Capital between Countries

After World War I, laws were passed severely limiting immigration. Only a trickle of immigrants has been admitted since then. . . . By keeping labor supply down, immigration policy tends to keep wages high.

Paul Samuelson, *Economics*, 1964

Amidst growing dissent, housing and job shortages as well as a plummeting economy, Cuban Premier Fidel Castro withdrew his guards from the Peruvian embassy in Havana on April 4, 1980. . . . Less than 48 hours after the guards were removed, throngs of Cubans crowded into the lushly landscaped gardens at the embassy, requesting asylum. . . . By mid-April, Carter issued a Presidential Memorandum allowing up to 3,500 refugees sanctuary in the U.S. . . . But the Carter Administration was taken by surprise when on April 21, refugees started arriving on Florida's shores—their numbers would eventually reach 125,000.

"Memories of Mariel, 20 Years Later"[1]

From May to September 1980, boatloads of refugees from Cuba arrived in Miami, Florida. For political reasons, Fidel Castro had allowed them to leave freely from the port of Mariel, Cuba, during that brief period of time. Known as "the Mariel boat lift," this influx of about 125,000 refugees to Miami increased the city's Cuban population by 20% and its overall population by about 7%. The widespread unemployment of many of the refugees during the summer of 1980 led many people to expect that the wages of other workers in Miami would be held down by the Mariel immigrants.

Not surprisingly, the refugees were less skilled than the other workers in Miami, as is confirmed by looking at their wages: the immigrants initially earned about one-third less than other Cubans in Miami. What is surprising, however, is that this influx

[1] Judy L. Silverstein, "Memories of Mariel, 20 Years Later," *U.S. Coast Guard Reservist*, 47(3), April/May 2000, electronic edition.

of low-skilled immigrants does not appear to have pulled down the wages of other less skilled workers in Miami.[2] The wages for low-skilled workers in Miami essentially followed national trends over this period, despite the large inflow of workers from Cuba. This finding seems to contradict the prediction of basic supply and demand theory—that a higher supply of workers should bid down their wage and that restricting immigration will raise the wages for local workers. This is the principle stated by Paul Samuelson in the quote at the beginning of this chapter. The fact that wages in Miami did not respond to the inflow of Mariel refugees calls for an explanation, which is one goal of this chapter.

A similar outcome occurred in a more recent case of sudden migration, the emigration of Russian Jews to Israel after 1989, when the Soviet Union relaxed its restrictions on such departures. From late 1989 to 1996, some 670,000 Russian Jews emigrated to Israel, which increased the population in Israel by 11% and its workforce by 14%. This wave of immigration was especially notable because the Russian immigrants were more highly skilled than the existing Israeli population. But despite this large influx of immigrants, the relative wages of high-skilled workers in Israel actually *rose* during the 1990s. Careful studies of this episode can find little or no negative impact of the Russian immigrants on the wages of other high-skilled workers.[3]

These emigrations were of different types of workers—the Cuban workers were low-skilled and the Russian emigrants high-skilled—but they share the finding that large inflows of workers need not depress wages in the areas where they settle. In other cases of large-scale migration—such as occurred from Europe to America during the 1800s and 1900s—wages did indeed fall due to the inflow of immigrants. So the Mariel boat lift and Russian emigration to Israel should be seen as special: they are cases in which the economic principles of supply and demand do not at first glance work as we would expect them to.

In this chapter, we begin our study of the movement of labor across countries by explaining the case in which immigration leads to a fall in wages, as we normally expect. The model we use is the **specific-factors model,** the short-run model introduced in Chapter 3. That model allows labor to move between industries but keeps capital and land specific to each industry. To study migration, we allow labor to move between countries as well as industries, while still keeping capital and land specific to each industry.

Next, we use the long-run Heckscher-Ohlin model, from Chapter 4, in which capital and land can also move between industries. In the long run, an increase in labor *will not* lower the wage, as illustrated by the Mariel boat lift to Miami and the Russian emigration to Israel. This outcome occurs because industries have more time to respond to the inflow of workers by adjusting their outputs. It turns out that by adjusting industry output enough, the economy can absorb the new workers without changing the wage for existing workers. The explanation for this surprising outcome relies on the assumption that industries are able to sell their outputs on international markets.

To give a brief idea of how this long-run explanation will work, think about the highly skilled scientists and engineers emigrating from Russia to Israel. The only

---

[2] See David Card, January 1990, "The Impact of the Mariel Boatlift on the Miami Labor Market," *Industrial Labor Relations Review*, 43(2), 245–257.

[3] See Neil Gandal, Gordon Hanson, and Matthew Slaughter, 2004, "Technology, Trade and Adjustment to Immigration in Israel," *European Economic Review*, 48(2), 403–428.

way to employ the large number of these workers at the going wages would be to increase the number of scientific and engineering projects in which Israeli companies are engaged. Where does the demand for these new projects come from? It is unlikely this demand would be generated in Israel alone, and more likely that it would come from Israeli *exports* to the rest of the world. We see then that the ability of Israel to export products making use of the highly skilled immigrants is essential to our explanation: with international demand, it is possible for the Russian immigrants to be fully employed in export activities without lowering wages in Israel. Likewise, with the influx of low-skilled Cuban immigrants to Miami, many of whom could work in the textile and apparel industry or in agriculture, it is the ability of Florida to export those products that allows the workers to be employed at the going wages.

After studying what happens in the short run and long run when labor moves across countries, we study the effects of foreign direct investment (FDI), the movement of capital across countries. FDI occurs when a company from one country owns a company in another country. We conclude the chapter by discussing the gains to the host and destination countries, and to the world, from the movement of labor or capital between countries.

1 Movement of Labor between Countries: Migration

We begin with the examples of labor migration described by the Mariel boat lift and the Russian migration to Israel. We can think of each migration as a movement of labor from the Foreign country to the Home country. What is the impact of this movement of labor on wages paid at Home? To answer this question, we make use of our work in Chapter 3, in which we studied how the wages paid to labor and the rentals paid to capital and land are determined by the prices of the goods produced. The prices of goods themselves are determined by supply and demand in world markets. In the analysis that follows, we treat the prices of goods as fixed and ask how the Home wage and the rentals paid to capital and land change as labor moves between countries.

Effects of Immigration in the Short Run: Specific-Factors Model

We begin our study of the effect of factor movements between countries by using the specific-factors model we learned in Chapter 3 to analyze the short run, when labor is mobile among Home industries, but land and capital are fixed. After that, we consider the long run, when all factors are mobile among industries at Home.

Determining the Wage Figure 5-1 shows a diagram that we used in Chapter 3 to determine the equilibrium wage paid to labor. The horizontal axis measures the total amount of labor in the economy $\overline{L}$, which consists of the labor used in manufacturing L_M and the amount used in agriculture L_A:

$$L_M + L_A = \overline{L}$$

In Figure 5-1, the amount of labor used in manufacturing L_M is measured from left (0_M) to right, and the amount of labor used in agriculture L_A is measured from right (0_A) to left.

FIGURE 5-1

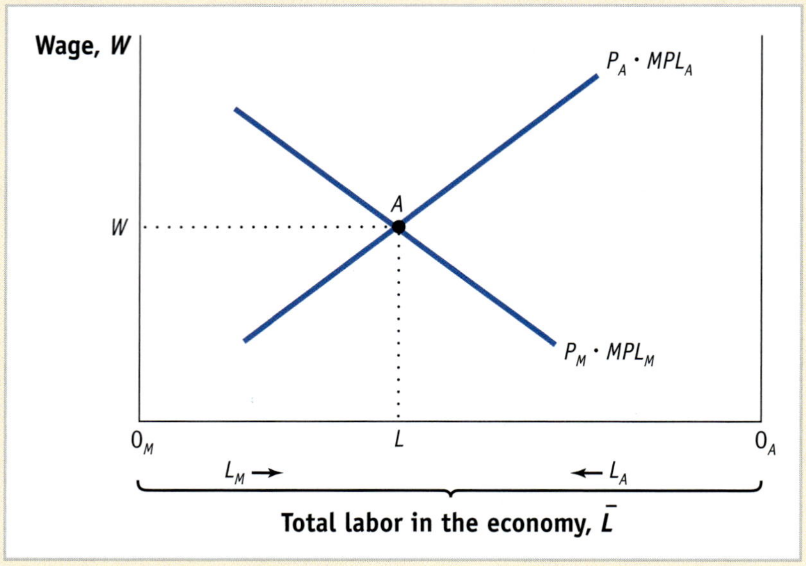

Home Labor Market The Home wage is determined at point A, the intersection of the marginal product of labor curves $P_M \cdot MPL_M$ and $P_A \cdot MPL_A$ in manufacturing and agriculture, respectively. The amount of labor used in manufacturing is measured from left to right, starting at the origin 0_M, and the amount of labor used in agriculture is measured from right to left, starting at the origin 0_A. At point A, 0_ML units of labor are used in manufacturing and 0_AL units of labor are used in agriculture.

The two curves in Figure 5-1 take the marginal product of labor in each sector and multiply it by the price (P_M or P_A) in that sector. The graph of $P_M \cdot MPL_M$ is downward-sloping because as more labor is used in manufacturing, the marginal product of labor in that industry declines, and wages fall. The graph of $P_A \cdot MPL_A$ for agriculture is upward-sloping because we are measuring the labor used in agriculture L_A from *right to left* in the diagram: as more labor is used in agriculture (moving from right to left), the marginal product of labor in agriculture falls, and wages fall.

The equilibrium wage is at point A, the intersection of the marginal product curves $P_M \cdot MPL_M$ and $P_A \cdot MPL_A$ in Figure 5-1. At this point, 0_ML units of labor are used in manufacturing, and firms in that industry are willing to pay the wage $W = P_M \cdot MPL_M$. In addition, 0_AL units of labor are used in agriculture, and farmers are willing to pay the wage $W = P_A \cdot MPL_A$. Because wages are equal in the two sectors, there is no reason for labor to move between them, and the Home labor market is in equilibrium.

In the Foreign country, a similar diagram applies. We do not draw this but assume that the equilibrium wage abroad W^* is less than W in Home. This assumption would apply to the Cuban refugees, for example, who moved to Miami and to the Russian emigrants who moved to Israel to earn higher wages as well as enjoy more freedom. As a result of this difference in wages, workers from Foreign would want to immigrate to Home and the Home workforce would increase by an amount ΔL, reflecting the number of immigrants.

Effect of Immigration on the Wage in Home The effects of immigration are shown in Figure 5-2. Because the number of workers at Home has grown by ΔL, we expand the size of the horizontal axis from $\bar{L}$ to $\bar{L}' = \bar{L} + \Delta L$. The right-most point on the horizontal axis, which is the origin 0_A for the agriculture industry, shifts to the right by the amount ΔL. As this origin moves rightward, it carries along with it the

FIGURE 5-2

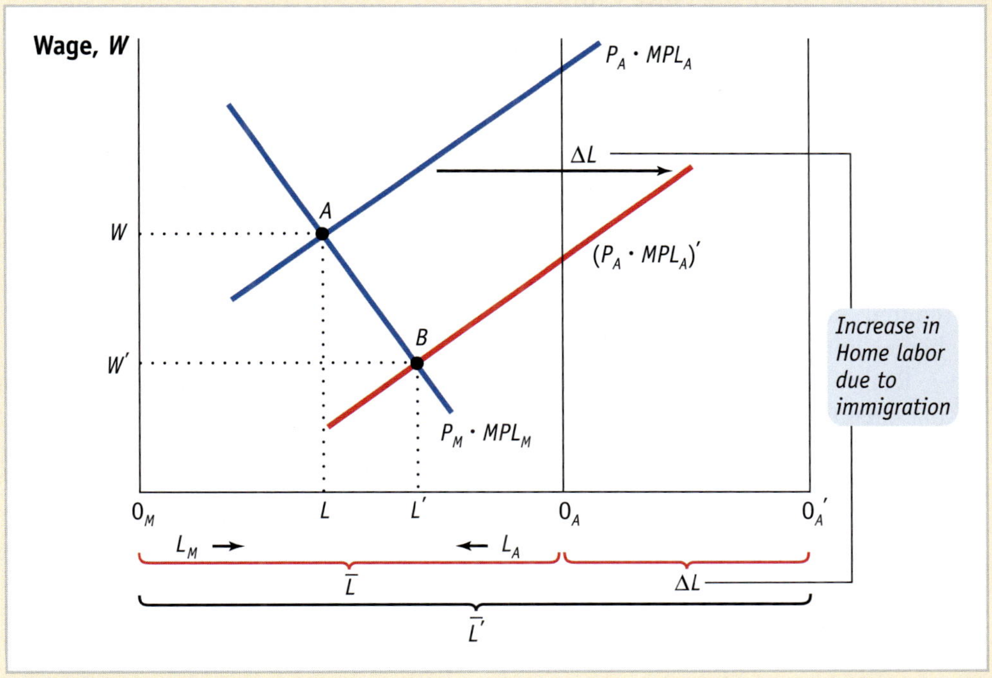

Increase in Home Labor When the amount of labor at Home increases by the amount ΔL, the origin for agriculture shifts to the right by that amount, from 0_A to $0'_A$. The marginal product of labor curve in agriculture also shifts right by the amount ΔL. Equilibrium in the Home labor market is now at point *B*: wages have fallen to *W′* and the amount of labor has increased in manufacturing (to $0_ML'$) and in agriculture (to $0'_AL'$).

marginal product curve $P_A \cdot MPL_A$ for the agriculture industry (because the marginal product of labor curve is graphed relative to its origin). That curve shifts to the right by exactly the amount ΔL, the increase in the Home workforce. There is no shift in the marginal product curve $P_M \cdot MPL_M$ for the manufacturing industry because the origin 0_M for manufacturing has not changed.[4]

The new equilibrium Home wage is at point *B*, the intersection of the marginal product curves. At the new equilibrium, the wage is lower. Notice that the extra workers ΔL arriving at Home are shared between the agriculture and manufacturing industries: the number of workers employed in manufacturing is now $0_ML'$, which is higher than 0_ML, and the number of workers employed in agriculture is $0'_AL'$, which is also higher than 0_AL.[5] Because both industries have more workers but fixed amounts of capital and land, the wage in both industries declines due to the diminishing marginal product of labor.

We see, then, that the specific-factors model predicts that an inflow of labor will lower wages in the country in which the workers are arriving. This prediction has been confirmed in numerous episodes of large-scale immigration, as described in the applications that follow.

[4] If, instead, we had added labor to the left-hand side of the graph, the origin and marginal product curve for manufacturing would have shifted and those of agriculture would have remained the same, yielding the same final results as in Figure 5-2—the wage falls and both industries use more labor.

[5] We know that the number of workers employed in agriculture rises because the increase in workers in manufacturing, from 0_ML to $0_ML'$, is less than the total increase in labor ΔL.

APPLICATION

Immigration to the New World

Between 1870 and 1913, some 30 million Europeans left their homes in the "Old World" to emigrate to the "New World" of North and South America and Australia. The population of Argentina rose by 60% due to immigration, and Australia and Canada gained 30% more people. The population of the United States increased by 17% as a result of immigration (and it absorbed the largest number of people, more than 15 million). The migrants left the Old World for the opportunities present in the New and, most important, for the higher real wages. In Figure 5-3, we show an index of average real wages in European countries and in the New World (an average of the United States, Canada, and Australia).[6] In 1870 real wages were nearly three times higher in the New World than in Europe—120 as compared with 40.

Real wages in both locations grew over time as capital accumulated and raised the marginal product of labor. But due to the large-scale immigration to the New World, wages grew more slowly there. By 1913, just before the onset of World War I, the wage index in the New World was at 160, so real wages had grown by (160 – 120)/120 = 33% over 43 years. In Europe, however, the wage index reached 75 by 1913, an increase of (75 – 40)/40 = 88% over 43 years. In 1870 real wages in the New World were three times as high as those in Europe, but by 1913 this wage gap was substantially reduced, and

FIGURE 5-3

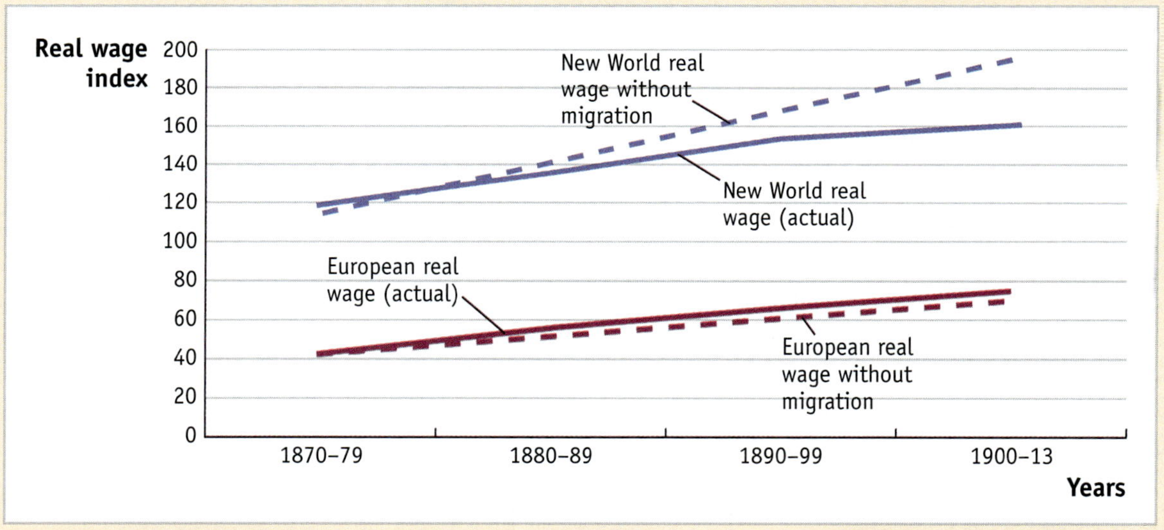

Wages in Europe and the New World Large-scale migration from Europe to the New World in America and Australia closed the wage gap between the two locations. In 1870 wages in the New World were almost three times as high as wages in Europe, whereas in 1910 they were about twice as high. Migration also slowed the growth of wages in the New World relative to what they would have been without migration and allowed for slightly faster growth of wages in Europe.

Source: Alan M. Taylor and Jeffrey G. Williamson, 1997, "Convergence in the Age of Mass Migration," European Review of Economic History, *1, April, 27–63.*

[6] From Alan M. Taylor and Jeffrey G. Williamson, 1997, "Convergence in the Age of Mass Migration," *European Review of Economic History*, 1, April, 27–63.

wages in the New World were only about twice as high as those in Europe. Large-scale migration therefore contributed to a "convergence" of real wages across the continents.

In Figure 5-3, we also show estimates of what real wages would have been if migration had not occurred. Those estimates are obtained by calculating how the marginal product of labor would have grown with capital accumulation but without the immigration. Comparing the actual real wages with the no-migration estimates, we see that the growth of wages in the New World was slowed due to immigration (workers arriving), while wages in Europe grew slightly faster due to emigration (workers leaving). ■

APPLICATION

Immigration to the United States and Europe Today

The largest amount of migration is no longer from Europe to the "New World." Instead, workers from developing countries immigrate to wealthier countries in the European Union and North America, when they can. In many cases, the immigration includes a mix of low-skilled workers and high-skilled workers. During the 1960s and 1970s, some European countries actively recruited guest workers, called *gastarbeiters* in West Germany, to fill labor shortages in unskilled jobs. Many of these foreign workers have remained in Germany for years, some for generations, so they are no longer "guests" but long-term residents. At the end of 1994, about 2.1 million foreigners were employed in western Germany, with citizens of Turkey, the former Yugoslavia, Greece, and Italy representing the largest groups.

Today, the European Union has expanded to include many of the countries in Eastern Europe, and in principle there is free migration within the European Union.[7] In practice, it can still be difficult for countries to absorb all the workers who want to enter, whether they come from within or outside the Union. That especially has been the case during the recent downturn in the global economy, as described in **Headlines: Europe Sours on Labor Migration.**

In the United States, immigration policy is debated in Congress nearly every year. Indeed, after jobs and health care, immigration ranks among the top issues in surveys of voters. On the same day as the historic vote on health care in the House of Representatives, March 21, 2009, there was a large rally in Washington, D.C., for immigration reform, including a procedure by which illegal immigrants can become legal. It is estimated that there are about 12 million illegal immigrants in the United States, many of them from Mexico. Gaining control over U.S. borders is one goal of immigration policy, but focusing on that goal alone obscures the fact that the majority of immigrants are legal. For example, agricultural workers have been allowed to enter the United States under special visa programs, thereby providing inexpensive labor to harvest crops. More recently, there has been a special program for engineers, scientists, and other skilled workers needed in high-technology industries, who are

[7] Prior to 2004, the European Union consisted of 15 countries: Belgium, France, Germany, Italy, Luxembourg, and the Netherlands (founding members in 1952); Denmark, Ireland, and the United Kingdom (added in 1973); Greece (added in 1981); Portugal and Spain (added in 1986); and Austria, Finland, and Sweden (added in 1995). On May 1, 2004, 10 more countries were added: Cyprus, the Czech Republic, Estonia, Hungary, Lithuania, Latvia, Malta, Poland, Slovakia, and Slovenia. Citizens from these countries were then permitted to work anywhere in the European Economic Area (EEA), which consists of the countries of the EU plus Iceland, Liechtenstein, and Norway. However, member countries of the EEA can adopt a seven-year moratorium on allowing labor mobility if they wish.

HEADLINES

Europe Sours on Labor Migration

With unemployment soaring, many EU countries want the migrant workers they once courted to return home as soon as possible.

Chultem Choijusuren was watching television in Ulan Bator when he decided to climb aboard the globalization bandwagon. According to an ad he had seen, companies in the Czech Republic were paying young mechanics "€1,000 a month." Most people in the Mongolian steppes were already familiar with the small Eastern European country. After all, many young people from here had studied in Prague during the two countries' Socialist pasts. . . .

Choijusuren is part of the army of migrants that has moved westward from developing countries in recent years, with one in three choosing Europe as their destination. After the European Union's eastward expansion in 2004, tens of thousands of Asians found jobs in Polish, Czech and Slovak factories, where they were welcomed with open arms to fill the jobs that one million Poles and hundreds of thousands of Czechs, Balts, Slovaks and Hungarians had left behind when they in turn migrated to the wealthier EU countries. Ireland, Great Britain and Sweden, unlike Germany and Austria, had immediately opened their borders to citizens of the new member states, and Spain followed suit two years later.

Construction companies and restaurants in these countries were only too pleased to employ the cheap labor from the East. More and more families hired Polish women to clean their houses or nannies with Slavic accents to put their children to bed. The migrants' wages were modest, and yet in some cases three times as high as they were at home. The newcomers sent as much of their earnings home as possible, injecting capital that helped their hometowns gain unprecedented prosperity.

Once the global economic crisis erupted those days were over. Unemployment has risen twice as fast in Great Britain and Spain as elsewhere in Europe. Now the citizens of Western European countries need the jobs themselves, and their governments are resorting to all kinds of tricks and incentives to get rid of the willing hands they once needed so badly.

Globalization has turned 200 million people into migrant workers in the last few decades. One fifth of them are Europeans, less than one tenth are Africans and 3 percent are from Latin America. Now the trend is reversing itself, a shift that generally affects those who came from Europe's poorest regions and from emerging and developing nations. Officials at the United Nations International Labour Organization (ILO) fear that 30 million people around the globe could lose their livelihoods by the end of the year. . . .

Source: Excerpted from Renate Flottau, Thomas Hüetlin, Jan Puhl, and Helene Zuber, "Europe Sours on Labor Migration," Business Week, *March 19, 2009.*

AP Photo/Gene Blythe

Agricultural migrant workers in the United States.

awarded H-1B visas. This program was established under the Clinton administration and continues today.

The combination of legal and illegal immigrants in the United States creates a "U-shaped" pattern between the number of immigrants and their educational level, as shown in Figure 5-4, for 2008. Among those workers in the United States with only 0 to 8 years of education, more than 70% were foreign-born, and for those with 8 to 11 years of education, more than 20% were foreign-born. These two categories of high school dropouts include many illegal immigrants and attract much attention in the U.S. debate over immigration, even though they make up only 10% of U.S. workers. At the other end of the spectrum, 10% of U.S. workers have master's degrees or Ph.D.'s, and in these categories, the foreign-born make up 16% and nearly 30%, respectively, of the U.S. workforce. In the middle educational levels, consisting of high school and

FIGURE 5-4

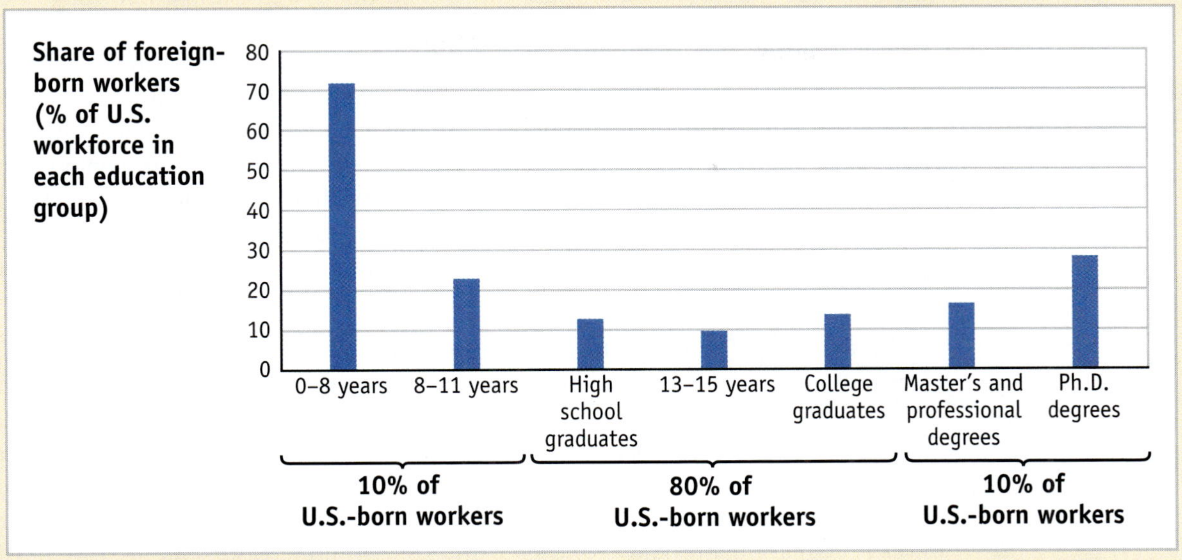

Share of Foreign-Born Workers in U.S. Workforce, 2008 This figure shows the share of foreign-born workers in the U.S. workforce, categorized by educational level. For example, among workers with only 0 to 8 years of education, more than 70% were foreign-born; for those with 9 to 11 years of education, more than 20% were foreign-born. At the other end of the spectrum, the foreign-born make up 16% of workers with master's and professional degrees and almost 30% of those with Ph.D.'s. In the middle educational levels (high school and college graduates), there are much smaller shares of foreign-born workers, ranging from 10 to 15%. In contrast, only about 10% of U.S.-born workers are categorized in each of the low-education and high-education groups; most U.S.-born workers are either high school graduates or college graduates.

Source: 2008 American Community Survey, U.S. Census Bureau.

college graduates and comprising 80% of the U.S. labor force, foreign-born workers have much smaller shares (10–15%). Figure 5-4 shows that immigrants into the United States compete primarily with workers at the lowest and highest ends of the educational levels and much less with the majority of U.S.-born workers with mid-levels of education.

The lesson that we should take from Figure 5-4 is that illegal immigrants into the United States compete primarily with the lowest-educated workers and that legal immigrants compete with workers at the highest educational levels. If we extend the specific-factors model to allow for several types of labor distinguished by educational level but continue to treat capital and land as fixed, then the greatest negative impact of immigration on wages would be for the lowest- and highest-educated U.S. workers. That prediction is supported by estimates of the effect of immigration on U.S. wages: from 1990 to 2004, immigration led to a fall in wages of 9% for high school dropouts and 5% for college graduates. But the impact of immigration on the wages of the majority of U.S. workers (those with mid-levels of education) is much less: wages of high school graduates decreased by 2.4% from 1990 to 2004, and wages of individuals with less than four years of college decreased by less than 1%. The negative impact of immigration on wages is thus fairly modest for most workers and is offset when capital moves between industries, as discussed later in the chapter. ■

Other Effects of Immigration in the Short Run

The previous application shows that the United States and Europe have both welcomed foreign workers into specific industries, such as agriculture and the high-tech industry, even though these workers compete with domestic workers in those industries. This observation suggests that there must be benefits to the industries involved. We can measure the potential benefits by the payments to capital and land, which we refer to as "rentals." We saw in Chapter 3 that there are two ways to compute the rentals: either as the earnings left over in the industry after paying labor or as the marginal product of capital or land times the price of the good produced in each industry. Under either method, the owners of capital and land benefit from the reduction in wages due to immigration.

Rentals on Capital and Land Under the first method for computing the rentals, we take the revenue earned in either manufacturing or agriculture and subtract the payments to labor. If wages fall, then there is more left over as earnings of capital and land, so these rentals are higher. Under the second method for computing rentals, capital and land earn their marginal product in each industry times the price of the industry's good. As more labor is hired in each industry (because wages are lower), the marginal products of capital and land both increase. The increase in the marginal product occurs because each machine or acre of land has more workers available to it, and that machine or acre of land is therefore more productive. So under the second method, too, the marginal products of capital and land rise and so do their rentals.

From this line of reasoning, we should not be surprised that owners of capital and land often support more open borders, which provides them with foreign workers who can be employed in their industries. The restriction on immigration in a country should therefore be seen as a compromise between entrepreneurs and landowners who might welcome the foreign labor; local unions and workers who view migrants as a potential source of competition leading to lower wages; and the immigrant groups themselves, who if they are large enough (such as the Cuban population in Miami) might also have the ability to influence the political outcome on immigration policy.

Effect of Immigration on Industry Output One final effect of labor immigration is its effect on the output of the industries. In Figure 5-2, the increase in the labor force due to immigration led to more workers being employed in each of the industries: employment increased from $0_M L$ to $0_M L'$ in manufacturing and from $0_A L$ to $0'_A L'$ in agriculture. With more workers and the same amount of capital or land, the output of both industries rises. This outcome is shown in Figure 5-5—immigration leads to an outward shift in the production possibilities frontier (PPF). With constant prices of goods (as we assumed earlier, because prices are determined by world supply and demand), the output of the industries rises from point A to point B.

Although it may seem obvious that having more labor in an economy will increase the output of both industries, it turns out that this result depends on the short-run nature of the specific-factors model, when capital and land in each industry are fixed. If instead these resources can move between the industries, as would occur in the long run, then the output of one industry will increase but that of the other industry will decline, as we explain in the next section.

FIGURE 5-5

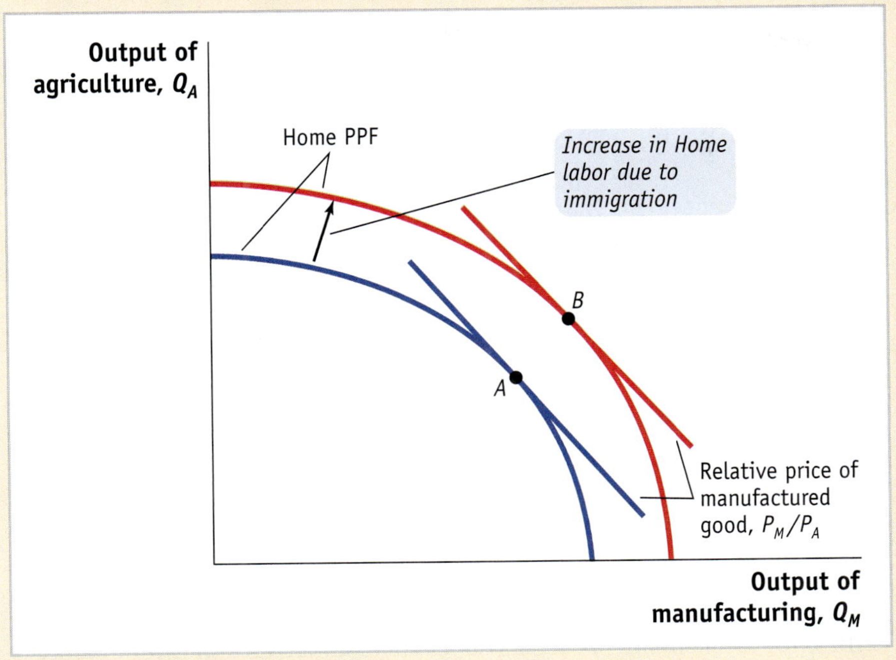

Shift in Home Production Possibilities Curve With the increase in labor at Home from immigration, the production possibilities frontier shifts outward and the output of both industries increases, from point *A* to point *B*. Output in both industries increases because of the short-run nature of the specific-factors model; in the short run, land and capital do not move between the industries, and the extra labor in the economy is shared between both industries.

Effects of Immigration in the Long Run

We turn now to the long run, in which all factors are free to move between industries. Because it is complicated to analyze a model with three factors of production—capital, land, and labor—all of which are fully mobile between industries, we will ignore land and assume that only labor and capital are used to produce two goods: computers and shoes. The long-run model is just like the Heckscher-Ohlin model studied in the previous chapter except that we will now allow labor to move between countries. (Later in the chapter, we will allow capital to move between the countries.)

The amount of capital used in computers is K_C, and the amount of capital used in shoe production is K_S. These quantities add up to the total capital available in the economy: $K_C + K_S = \bar{K}$. Because capital is fully mobile between the two sectors in the long run, it must earn the same rental R in each. The amount of labor used to manufacture computers is L_C, and the labor used in shoe production is L_S. These amounts add up to the total labor in the economy, $L_C + L_S = \bar{L}$, and all labor earns the same wage of W in both sectors.

In our analysis, we make the realistic assumption that more labor per machine is used in shoe production than in computer production. That assumption means that shoe production is labor-intensive compared with computer production, so the labor–capital ratio in shoes is higher than it is in computers: $L_S/K_S > L_C/K_C$. Computer production, then, is capital-intensive compared with shoes, and the capital–labor ratio is higher in computers: $K_C/L_C > K_S/L_S$.

"You seem familiar, yet somehow strange—are you by any chance Canadian?"

FIGURE 5-6

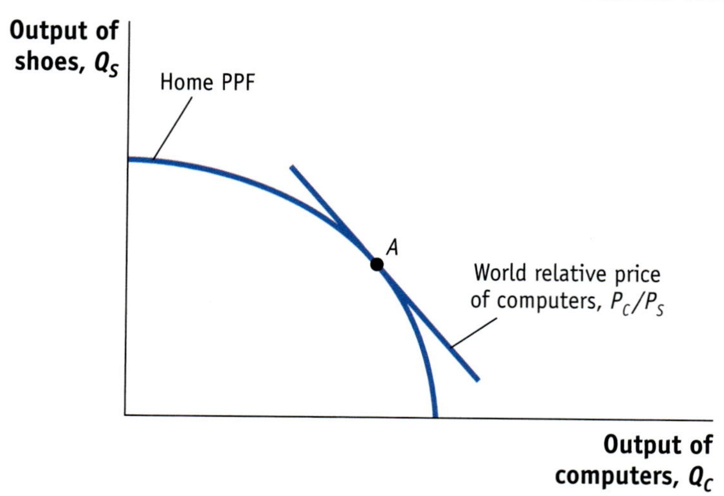

Production Possibilities Frontier Shown here is the production possibilities frontier (PPF) between two manufactured goods, computers and shoes, with initial equilibrium at point *A*. Domestic production takes place at point *A*, which is the point of tangency between the world price line and the PPF.

The PPF for an economy producing shoes and computers is shown in Figure 5-6. Given the prices of both goods (determined by supply and demand in world markets), the equilibrium outputs are shown at point *A*, at the tangency of the PPF and world relative price line. Our goal in this section is to see how the equilibrium is affected by having an inflow of labor into Home as a result of immigration.

Box Diagram To analyze the effect of immigration, it is useful to develop a new diagram to keep track of the amount of labor and capital used in each industry. Shown as a "box diagram" in Figure 5-7, the length of the top and bottom horizontal axes is the total amount of labor $\bar{L}$ at Home, and the length of the right and left vertical axes is the total amount of capital $\bar{K}$ at Home. A point like point *A* in the diagram indicates that 0_SL units of labor and 0_SK units of capital are used in shoes, while 0_CL units of labor and 0_CK units of capital are used in computers. Another way to express this is that the line 0_SA shows the amount of labor and capital used in shoes and the line 0_CA shows the amount of labor and capital used in computers.

Notice that the line 0_SA for shoes is flatter than the line 0_CA for computers. We can calculate the slopes of these lines by dividing the vertical distance by the horizontal distance (the rise over the run). The slope of 0_SA is $0_SK/0_SL$, the capital–labor ratio used in the shoe industry. Likewise, the slope of 0_CA is $0_CK/0_CL$, the capital–labor ratio for computers. The line 0_SA is flatter than 0_CA, so the capital–labor ratio in the shoe industry is less than that in computers; that is, there are fewer units of capital per worker in the shoe industry. This is precisely the assumption that we made earlier. It is a realistic assumption given that the manufacture of computer components such as semiconductors requires highly precise and expensive equipment, which is operated by a small number of workers. Shoe production, on the other hand, requires more workers and a smaller amount of capital.

Determination of the Real Wage and Real Rental In addition to determining the amount of labor and capital used in each industry in the long run, we also need

FIGURE 5-7

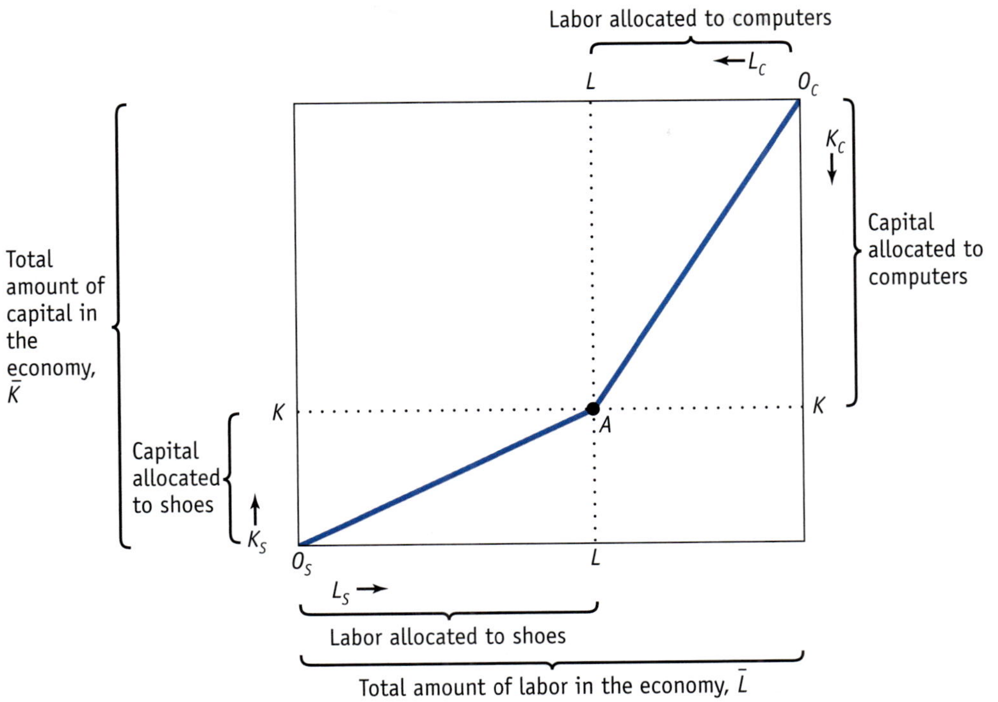

Allocation of Labor and Capital in a Box Diagram The top and bottom axes of the box diagram measure the amount of labor, $\bar{L}$, in the economy, and the side axes measure the amount of capital, $\bar{K}$. At point A, 0_SL units of labor and 0_SK units of capital are used in shoe production, and 0_CL units of labor and 0_CK units of capital are used in computers. The K/L ratios in the two industries are measured by the slopes of 0_SA and 0_CA, respectively.

to determine the wage and rental in the economy. To do so, we use the logic introduced in Chapter 3: the wage and rental are determined by the marginal products of labor and capital, which are in turn determined by the capital–labor ratio in either industry. If there is a higher capital–labor ratio (i.e., if there are more machines per worker), then by the law of diminishing returns, the marginal product of capital and the real rental must be lower. Having more machines per worker means that the marginal product of labor (and hence the real wage) is higher because each worker is more productive. On the other hand, if there is a higher labor–capital ratio (more workers per machine), then the marginal product of labor must be lower because of diminishing returns, and hence the real wage is lower, too. In addition, having more workers per machine means that the marginal product of capital and the real rental are both higher.

The important point to remember is that each amount of labor and capital used in Figure 5-7 along line 0_SA corresponds to a particular capital–labor ratio for shoe manufacture and therefore a particular real wage and real rental. We now consider how the labor and capital used in each industry will change due to immigration at Home. Although the total amount of labor and capital used in each industry changes, we will show that the capital–labor ratios are unaffected by immigration, which means that the immigrants can be absorbed with no change at all in the real wage and real rental.

Increase in the Amount of Home Labor Suppose that because of immigration, the amount of labor at Home increases from $\overline{L}$ to $\overline{L}' = \overline{L} + \Delta L$. This increase expands the labor axes in the box diagram, as shown in Figure 5-8. Rather than allocating $\overline{L}$ labor and $\overline{K}$ capital between the two industries, we must now allocate $\overline{L}'$ labor and $\overline{K}$ capital. The question is how much labor and capital will be used in each industry so that the total amount of both factors is fully employed?

You might think that the only way to employ the extra labor is to allocate more of it to both industries (as occurred in the short-run specific-factors model). This outcome would tend to lower the marginal product of labor in both industries and therefore lower the wage. But it turns out that such an outcome will not occur in the long-run model because when capital is also able to move between the industries, industry outputs will adjust to keep the capital–labor ratios in each industry constant. Instead of allocating the extra labor to both industries, all the extra labor (ΔL) will be allocated to shoes, the *labor*-intensive industry. Moreover, along with that extra labor,

FIGURE 5-8

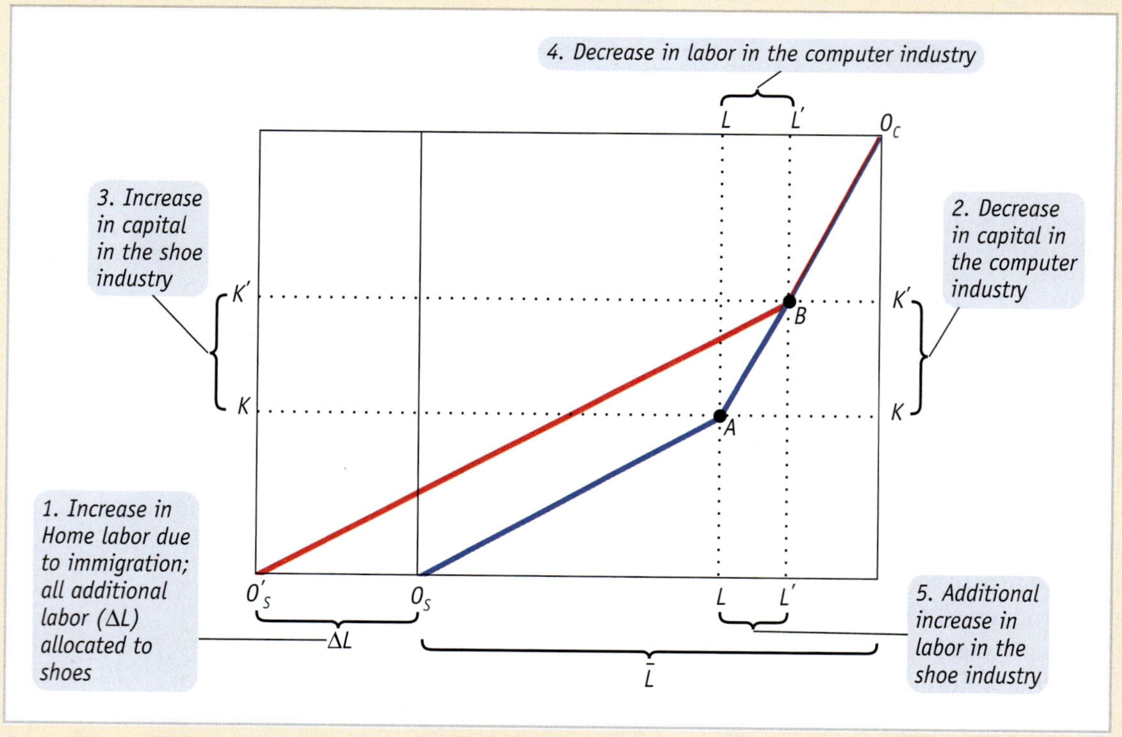

Increase in Home Labor With an increase in Home labor from $\overline{L}$ to $\overline{L} + \Delta L$, the origin for the shoe industry shifts from O_S to O'_S. At point B, O'_SL' units of labor and O'_SK' units of capital are used in shoes, whereas O_CL' units of labor and O_CK' units of capital are used in computers. In the long run, industry outputs adjust so that the capital–labor ratios in each industry at point B (the slopes of O'_SB and O_CB) are unchanged from the initial equilibrium at point A (the slopes of O_SA and O_CA). To achieve this outcome, all new labor resulting from immigration is allocated to the shoe industry, and capital and *additional* labor are transferred from computers to shoes, keeping the capital–labor ratio in both industries unchanged.

some capital is withdrawn from computers and allocated to shoes. To maintain the capital–labor ratio in the computer industry, some labor will also leave the computer industry, along with the capital, and go to the shoe industry. Because all the new workers in the shoe industry (immigrants plus former computer workers) have the same amount of capital to work with as the shoe workers prior to immigration, the capital–labor ratio in the shoe industry stays the same. *In this way, the capital–labor ratio in each industry is unchanged and the additional labor in the economy is fully employed.*

This outcome is illustrated in Figure 5-8, where the initial equilibrium is at point A. With the inflow of labor due to immigration, the labor axis expands from $\overline{L}$ to $\overline{L} + \Delta L$, and the origin for the shoe industry shifts from 0_S to $0'_S$. Consider point B as a possible new equilibrium. At this point, $0'_SL'$ units of labor and $0'_SK'$ units of capital are used in shoes, while $0_CL'$ units of labor and $0_CK'$ units of capital are used in computers. Notice that the lines 0_SA and $0'_SB$ are parallel and have the same slope, and similarly, the lines 0_CA and 0_CB have the same slope. The extra labor has been employed by *expanding* the amount of labor and capital used in shoes (the line $0'_SB$ is longer than 0_SA) and *contracting* the amount of labor and capital used in computers (the line 0_CB is smaller than 0_CA). That the lines have the same slope means that the capital–labor ratio used in each industry is exactly the same before and after the inflow of labor.

What has happened to the wage and rentals in the economy? Because the capital–labor ratios are unchanged in both industries, the marginal products of labor and capital are also unchanged. Therefore, the wage and rental do not change at all due to the immigration of labor! This result is very different from what happens in the short-run specific-factors model, which showed that immigration depressed the wage and raised the rental on capital and land. In the long-run model, when capital can move between industries, an inflow of labor has no impact on the wage and rental. Instead, the extra labor is employed in shoes, by combining it with capital and additional labor that has shifted out of computers. In that way, the capital–labor ratios in both industries are unchanged, as are the wage and rental.

Effect of Immigration on Industry Outputs What is the effect of immigration on the output of each industry? We have already seen from Figure 5-8 that more labor and capital are used in the labor-intensive industry (shoes), whereas less labor and capital are used in the capital-intensive industry (computers). Because the factors of production both increase or both decrease, it follows that the output of shoes expands and the output of computers contracts.

This outcome is shown in Figure 5-9, which shows the outward shift of the PPF due to the increase in the labor endowment at Home. Given the prices of computers and shoes, the initial equilibrium was at point A. At this point, the slope of the PPF equals the relative price of computers, as shown by the slope of the line tangent to the PPF. With unchanged prices for the goods, and more labor in the economy, the equilibrium moves to point B, with greater output of shoes but reduced output of computers. Notice that the slope of the PPFs at points A and B is identical because the relative price of computers is unchanged. As suggested by the diagram, the expansion in the amount of labor leads to an uneven outward shift of the PPF—it shifts out more in the direction of shoes (the labor-intensive industry) than in the direction of computers. This asymmetric shift illustrates that the new labor is employed in shoes and that this additional labor pulls capital and additional labor out of computers in the long run, to establish the new equilibrium at point B. *The finding that an increase in labor will expand one industry but contract the other holds only in the long run; in the short run, as we*

FIGURE 5-9

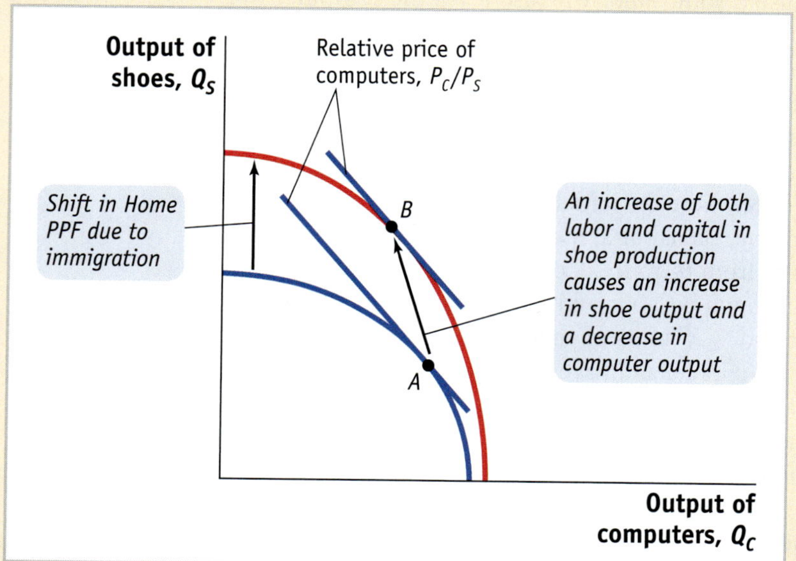

The Long-Run Effect on Industry Outputs of an Increase in Home Labor With an increase in the amount of labor at Home, the PPF shifts outward. The output of shoes increases, while the output of computers declines as the equilibrium moves from point *A* to *B*. The prices of goods have not changed, so the slopes of the PPFs at points *A* and *B* (i.e., the relative price of computers) are equal.

saw in Figure 5-5, both industries will expand. This finding shows how much the long-run model differs from the short-run model. The long-run result is named after the economist T. N. Rybczynski, who first discovered it.

Rybczynski Theorem

In the Heckscher-Ohlin model with two goods and two factors, an increase in the amount of a factor found in an economy will increase the output of the industry using that factor intensively and decrease the output of the other industry.

We have proved the Rybczynski theorem for the case of immigration, where labor in the economy grows. As we argue later in the chapter, the same theorem holds when capital in the economy grows: in this case, the industry using capital intensively expands and the other industry contracts.[8]

Effect of Immigration on Factor Prices The **Rybczynski theorem,** which applies to the long-run Heckscher-Ohlin model with two goods and two factors of production, states that an increase in labor will expand output in one industry but contract output in the other industry. Notice that the change in outputs in the Rybczynski theorem goes hand in hand with the previous finding that the wage and rental will not change due to an increase in labor (or capital). The reason that factor prices do not need to change is that the economy can absorb the extra amount of a factor by increasing the output of the industry using that factor intensively and reducing the output of the other industry. The finding that factor prices do not change is sometimes called the **factor price insensitivity** result.

[8] Furthermore, the Rybczynski theorem can be used to compare the output of the same industry across two countries, where the two countries have identical technologies but differing factor endowments as in the Heckscher-Ohlin model. See Problem 7 at the end of the chapter.

Factor Price Insensitivity

In the Heckscher-Ohlin model with two goods and two factors, an increase in the amount of a factor found in an economy can be absorbed by changing the outputs of the industries, without any change in the factor prices.

The applications that follow offer evidence of changes in output that absorb new additions to the labor force, as predicted by the Rybczynski theorem, without requiring large changes in factor prices, as predicted by the factor price insensitivity result.

APPLICATION

The Effects of the Mariel Boat Lift on Industry Output in Miami

Now that we have a better understanding of long-run adjustments due to changes in factor endowments, let us return to the case of the Mariel boat lift to Miami in 1980. We know that the Cuban refugees were less skilled than the average labor force in Miami. According to the Rybczynski theorem, then, we expect some unskilled-labor–intensive industry, such as footwear or apparel, to expand. In addition, we expect that some skill-intensive industry, such as the high-tech industry, will contract. Figure 5-10 shows how this prediction lines up with the evidence from Miami and some comparison cities.[9]

Panel (a) of Figure 5-10 shows real value-added in the apparel industry for Miami and for an average of comparison cities. **Real value-added** measures the payments to labor and capital in an industry corrected for inflation. Thus, real value-added is a way to measure the output of the industry. We divide output by the population of the city to obtain real value-added per capita, which measures the output of the industry adjusted for the city size.

Panel (a) shows that the apparel industry was declining in Miami and the comparison cities before 1980. After the boat lift, the industry continued to decline but at a slower rate in Miami; the trend of output per capita for Miami has a smaller slope (and hence a smaller rate of decline in output) than that of the trend for comparison cities from 1980 onward. Notice that there is an increase in industry output in Miami from 1983 to 1984 (which may be due to new data collected that year), but even when averaging this out as the trend lines do, the industry decline in Miami is slightly slower than in the comparison cities after 1980. This graph provides some evidence of the Rybczynski theorem at work: the reduction in the apparel industry in Miami was slower than it would have been without the inflow of immigrants.

What about the second prediction of the Rybczynski theorem: Did the output of any other industry in Miami fall because of the immigration? Panel (b) of Figure 5-10 shows that the output of a group of skill-intensive industries (including motor vehicles, electronic equipment, and aircraft) fell more rapidly in Miami after 1980. These data may also provide some evidence in favor of the Rybczynski theorem. However, it also happened that with the influx of refugees, there was a flight of homeowners away from Miami, and some of these were probably high-skilled workers. So the decline in the group of skill-intensive industries, shown in panel (b), could instead be due to this population decline.

The change in industry outputs in Miami provides some evidence in favor of the Rybczynski theorem. Do these changes in industry outputs in Miami also provide an

[9] Figure 5-10 and the material in this application are drawn from Ethan Lewis, 2004, "How Did the Miami Labor Market Absorb the Mariel Immigrants?" Federal Reserve Bank of Philadelphia Working Paper No. 04-3.

FIGURE 5-10

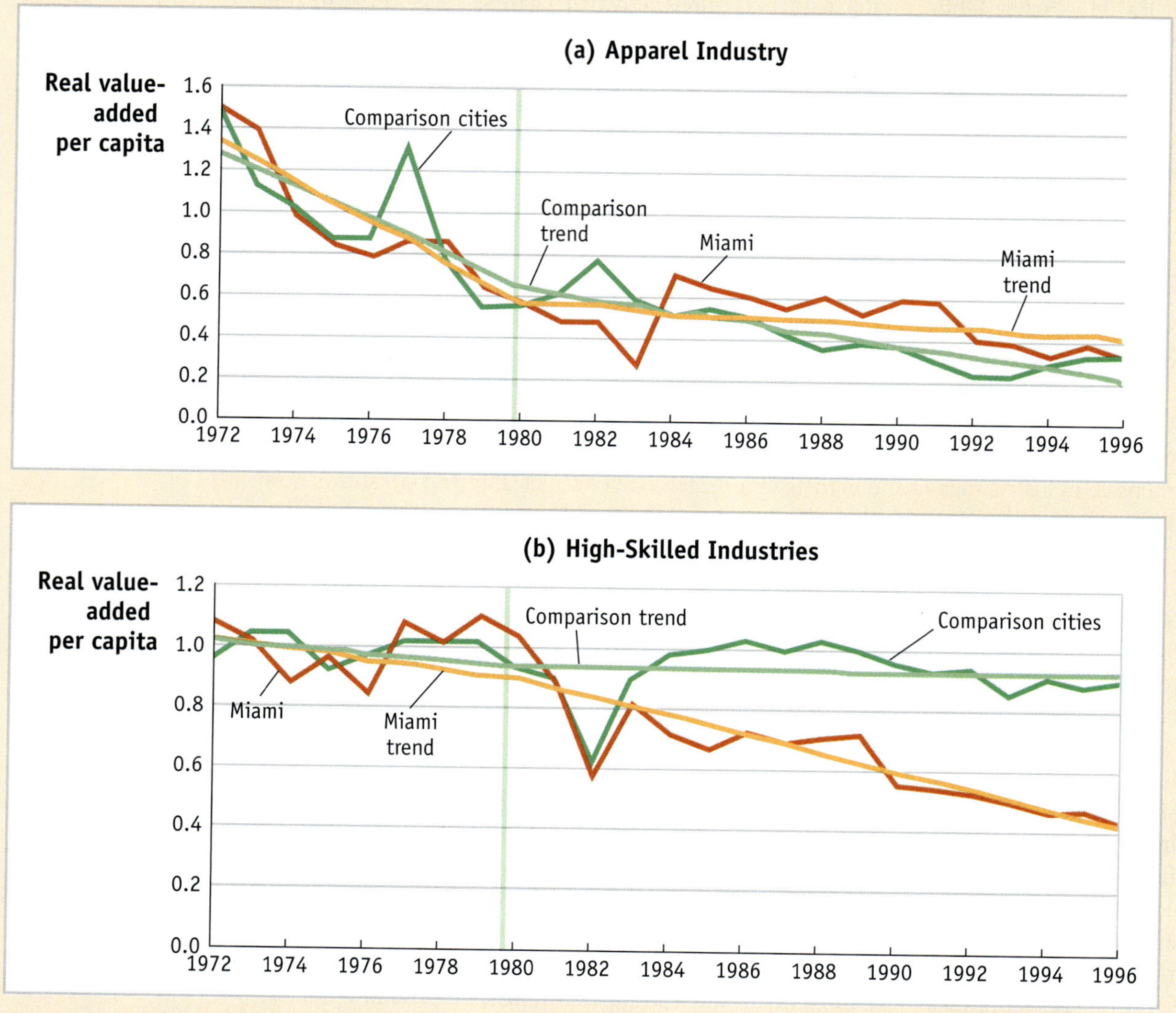

Industry Value-Added in Miami Shown here are real value-added in the apparel industry and in high-skilled industries (measured relative to the city population), for Miami and an average of comparison cities. In panel (a), with the inflow of refugees from Cuba in 1980, real value-added in the apparel industry in Miami rose from 1983 to 1984, and the trend decline of this industry in Miami was slower (i.e., value-added did not fall as fast) after 1980 than in the comparison cities. In panel (b), real value-added in Miami in high-skilled industries fell faster after 1980 than in the comparison cities. Both these findings are consistent with the Rybczynksi theorem.

Source: Ethan Lewis, 2004, "How Did the Miami Labor Market Absorb the Mariel Immigrants?" Federal Reserve Bank of Philadelphia Working Paper No. 04-3.

adequate explanation for why wages of unskilled workers did not decline, or is there some other explanation? An alternative explanation for the finding that wages did not change comes from comparing the use of computers in Miami with national trends. Beginning in the early 1980s, computers became increasingly used in the workplace. The adoption of computers is called a "skill-biased technological change." That is, computers led to an increase in the demand for high-skilled workers and reduced the hiring of low-skilled workers. This trend occurred across the United States and in other countries.

In Miami, however, computers were adopted somewhat more slowly than in cities with similar industry mix and ethnic populations. One explanation for this finding is that firms in many industries, not just apparel, employed the Mariel refugees and other low-skilled workers rather than switching to computer technologies. Evidence to support this finding is that the Mariel refugees were, in fact, employed in many industries. Only about 20% worked in manufacturing (5% in apparel), and the remainder worked in service industries. The idea that the firms may have slowed the adoption of new technologies to employ the Mariel emigrants is hard to prove conclusively, however. We suggest it here as an alternative to the Rybczynski theorem to explain how the refugees could be absorbed across many industries rather than just in the industries using unskilled labor, such as apparel. ■

APPLICATION

Immigration and U.S. Wages, 1990–2004

In 1980, the year of the Mariel boat lift, the percentage of foreign-born people in the U.S. population was 6.2%. The percentage grew to 12.9% in 2005, so there was slightly more than a doubling of foreign-born people in 25 years.[10] How has this wave of recent immigration affected U.S. wages?

Part A of Table 5-1 reports the estimated impact of the immigration from 1990 to 2004 on the wages of various workers, distinguished by their educational level. The first row in part A summarizes the estimates from the specific-factors model, when capital and land are kept fixed within all industries. As we discussed in an earlier application,

TABLE 5-1

Immigration and Wages in the United States This table shows the estimated effect of immigration on the wages of workers, depending on their educational level. Immigration has the greatest impact on workers with very low or high levels of education and only a small impact on those workers with middle levels of education (12–15 years). The impact is even smaller in the long run, when capital adjusts to keep the real return to capital fixed in each industry.

	PERCENTAGE CHANGE IN THE WAGE OF WORKERS WITH EDUCATIONAL LEVEL				
	Less Than 12 Years	12 Years	13–15 Years	16 Years or More	Overall Average
Part A: Effect of Total Immigration, 1990–2004					
Method:					
Capital and land fixed	−9.0	−2.4	−0.8	−5.0	−3.2
Real return to capital fixed	−4.4	1.0	2.2	−0.2	0.3
Part B: Effect of Illegal Immigration, 1990–2004					
Method:					
Real return to capital fixed	−7.9	0.8	0.8	0.8	0.1

Source: Gianmarco I.P. Ottaviano and Giovanni Peri, 2005 "Rethinking Gains from Immigration: Theory and Evidence from the U.S." National Bureau of Economic Research working paper no. 11672.

[10] This information on foreign-born people is available from the United Nations, at http://www.esa.un.org/migration.

the greatest negative impact of immigration is on workers with less than 12 years of education, followed by college graduates (those with greater than 16 years), and then followed by high school graduates and those with some college. Overall, the average impact of immigration on U.S. wages over this period is –3.2%, so there is a fall in wages, consistent with the specific-factors model.

A different story emerges, however, if instead of keeping capital fixed, we hold constant the real rental on capital. Under this approach, we allow capital to grow in each industry to accommodate the inflow of immigrants, so that there is no change in the real rental. This approach is similar to the long-run model we have discussed, except that there are several types of labor, distinguished by their education levels, and the prices of goods and labor are not constant over the period examined. In the second row of part A, we see that total U.S. immigration has a negative impact on workers with the lowest and highest levels of education and a *positive* impact on the other workers (due to the growth in capital). The average U.S. wage now rises by 0.3% due to immigration (combined with capital growth), rather than falling.

In part B of Table 5-1, we focus on the illegal immigration to the United States from 1990 to 2004, rather than total immigration, keeping the real return to capital fixed. In this case, the wages of only the lowest-educated people are negatively affected. All other workers gain from illegal immigration, once we take into account the growth in capital that is expected to occur. ■

2 Movement of Capital between Countries: Foreign Direct Investment

To continue our examination of what happens to wages and rentals when factors can move across borders, we turn now to look at how capital can move from one country to another through **foreign direct investment (FDI),** which occurs when a firm from one country owns a company in another country. How much does the company have to own for foreign direct investment to occur? Definitions vary, but the Department of Commerce in the United States uses 10%: if a foreign company acquires 10% or more of a U.S. firm, then that is counted as an FDI inflow to the United States, and if a U.S. company acquires 10% or more of a foreign firm, then that is counted as an FDI outflow from the United States.

When a company builds a plant in a foreign country, it is sometimes called "greenfield FDI" (because we imagine the site for the plant starting with grass on it). When a firm buys an existing foreign plant, it is called "acquisition FDI" (or sometimes "brownfield FDI"). Having capital move from high-wage to low-wage countries to earn a higher rental is the traditional view of FDI, and the viewpoint we take in this chapter.[11]

Greenfield Investment

Our focus in this section will be on greenfield investment; that is, the building of new plants abroad. We model FDI as a movement of capital between countries, just as we modeled the movement of labor between countries. The key question we ask is: How

[11] As discussed in Chapter 1, there are many instances of FDI that do not fit with this traditional view.

does the movement of capital into a country affect the earnings of labor and capital there? This question is similar to the one we asked for immigration, so the earlier graphs that we developed can be modified to address FDI.

FDI in the Short Run: Specific-Factors Model

We begin by modeling FDI in the short run, using the specific-factors model. In that model, the manufacturing industry uses capital and labor and the agriculture industry uses land and labor, so as capital flows into the economy, it will be used in manufacturing. The additional capital will raise the marginal product of labor in manufacturing because workers there have more machines with which to work. Therefore, as capital flows into the economy, it will shift out the curve $P_M \cdot MPL_M$ for the manufacturing industry as shown in panel (a) of Figure 5-11.

Effect of FDI on the Wage As a result of this shift, the equilibrium wage increases, from W to W'. More workers are drawn into the manufacturing industry, and the labor used there increases from $0_M L$ to $0_M L'$. Because these workers are pulled out of agriculture, the labor used there shrinks from $0_A L$ to $0_A L'$ (measuring from right to left).

Effect of FDI on the Industry Outputs It is easy to determine the effect of an inflow of FDI on industry outputs. Because workers are pulled out of agriculture, and there is no change in the amount of land used there, output of the agriculture industry must fall. With an increase in the number of workers used in manufacturing and an increase in capital used there, the output of the manufacturing industry must rise.

FIGURE 5-11

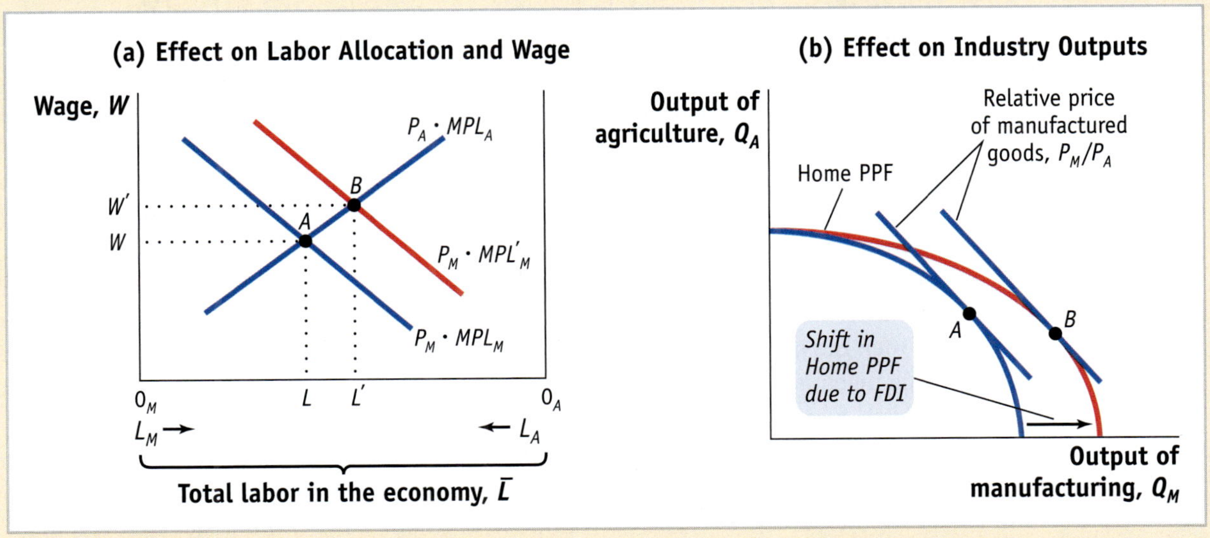

Increase in the Capital Stock in the Short Run In panel (a), an inflow of capital into the manufacturing sector shifts out the marginal product of labor curve in that sector. The equilibrium in the labor market moves from point *A* to *B*, and the wage increases from W to W'. Labor used in the manufacturing industry increases from $0_M L$ to $0_M L'$. These workers are pulled out of agriculture, so the labor used there shrinks from $0_A L$ to $0_A L'$. In panel (b), with the inflow of capital into manufacturing, and the extra labor used in that sector, the output of manufacturing increases. Because labor has been drawn out of agriculture, the output of that sector falls. These changes in outputs are shown by the outward shift of the PPF (due to the increase in capital) and the movement from point *A* to point *B*.

These changes in output are shown in panel (b) of Figure 5-11 by the outward shift of the production possibilities frontier. At constant prices for goods (i.e., the relative price lines have the same slope before and after the increase in capital), the equilibrium outputs shift from point *A* to point *B*, with more manufacturing output and less agricultural output.

Effect of FDI on the Rentals Finally, we can determine the impact of the inflow of capital on the rental earned by capital and the rental earned by land. It is easiest to start with the agriculture industry. Because fewer workers are employed there, each acre of land cannot be cultivated as intensively as before, and the marginal product of land must fall. One way to measure the rental on land *T* is by the value of its marginal product, $R_T = P_A \cdot MPT_A$. With the fall in the marginal product of land (MPT_A), and no change in the price of agricultural goods, the rental on land falls.

Now let us consider manufacturing, which uses more capital and more labor than before. One way to measure the rental on capital is by the value of the marginal product of capital, or $R_K = P_M \cdot MPK_M$. Using this method, however, it is difficult to determine how the rental on capital changes. As capital flows into manufacturing, the marginal product of capital falls because of diminishing returns. That effect reduces the rental on capital. But as labor is drawn into manufacturing, the marginal product of capital tends to rise. So we do not know at first glance how the rental on capital changes overall.

Fortunately, we can resolve this difficulty by using another method to measure the rental on capital. We take the revenue earned in manufacturing and subtract the payments to labor. If wages are higher, and everything else is the same, then there must be a reduced amount of funds left over as earnings of capital, so the rental is lower.

Let us apply this line of reasoning more carefully to see how the inflow of FDI affects the rental on capital. In Figure 5-12, we begin at point *A* and then assume the capital stock expands due to FDI. Suppose we hold the wage constant, and let the labor used in manufacturing expand up to point *C*. Because the wage is the same at points *A* and *C*, the marginal product of labor in manufacturing must also be the same (since the wage is $W = P_M \cdot MPL_M$). The only way that the marginal product of labor can remain constant is for each worker to have the same amount of capital to work with as he or she had before the capital inflow. In other words, the capital–labor ratio in manufacturing L_M/K_M must be the same at points *A* and *C*: the expansion of capital in manufacturing is just matched by a proportional expansion of labor into manufacturing. But if the capital–labor ratio in manufacturing is identical at points *A* and *C*, then the marginal product of capital must also be equal at these two points (because each machine has the same number of people working on it). Therefore, the rental on capital, $R_K = P_M \cdot MPK_M$, is also equal at points *A* and *C*.

Now let's see what happens as the manufacturing wage increases while holding constant the amount of capital used in that sector. The increase in the wage will move us up the curve $P_M \cdot MPL'_M$ from point *C* to point *B*. As the wage rises, less labor is used in manufacturing. With less labor used on each machine in manufacturing, the marginal product of capital and the rental on capital must fall. This result confirms our earlier reasoning: when wages are higher and the amount of capital used in manufacturing is the same, then the earnings of capital (i.e., its rental) must be lower. Because the rental on capital is the same at points *A* and *C* but is lower at point *B* than *C*, the overall effect of the FDI inflow is to reduce the rental on capital. We learned previously that the FDI inflow also reduces the rental on land, so both rentals fall.

FIGURE 5-12

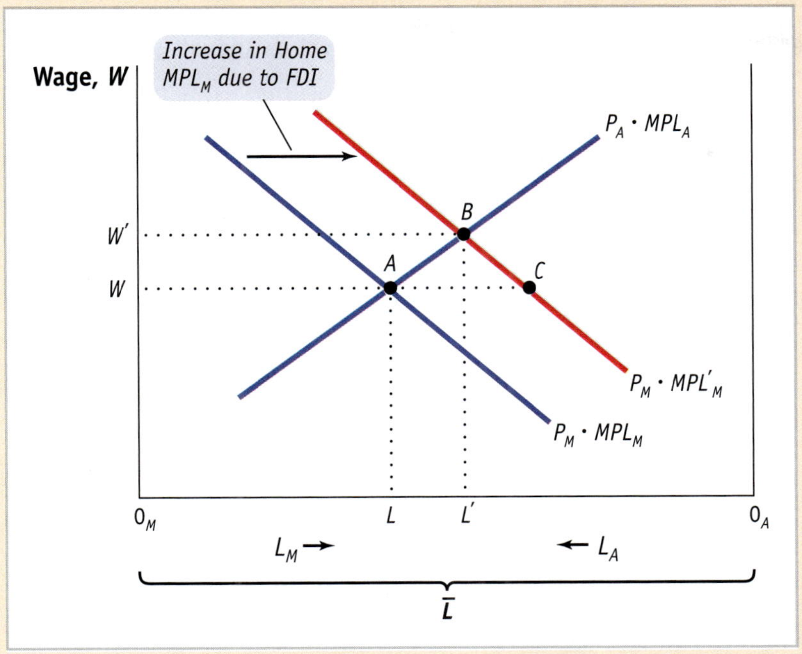

The Effect of an Increase in Capital Stock on the Rental on Capital By carefully tracing through how the capital-labor ratio in manufacturing is affected by the movement from *A* to *C* (where wages and hence the capital-labor ratio do not change), and then the movement from *C* to *B* (where wages and the capital-labor ratio both increase), we conclude that the rental on capital is lower at point *B* than at point *A*. Therefore, the rental on capital declines when the capital stock increases through FDI.

FDI in the Long Run

The results of FDI in the long run, when capital and labor can move between industries, differ from those we saw in the short-run specific-factors model. To model FDI in the long run, we assume again that there are two industries—computers and shoes—both of which use two factors of production: labor and capital. Computers are capital-intensive as compared with shoes, meaning that K_C/L_C exceeds K_S/L_S.

In panel (a) of Figure 5-13, we show the initial allocation of labor and capital between the two industries at point *A*. The labor and capital used in the shoe industry are 0_SL and 0_SK, so this combination is measured by the line 0_SA. The labor and capital used in computers are 0_CL and 0_CK, so this combination is measured by the line 0_CA. That amount of labor and capital used in each industry produces the output of shoes and computers shown by point *A* on the PPF in panel (b).

Effect of FDI on Outputs and Factor Prices An inflow of FDI causes the amount of capital in the economy to increase. That increase expands the right and left sides of the box in panel (a) of Figure 5-13 and shifts the origin up to $0'_C$. The new allocation of factors between the industries is shown at point *B*. Now the labor and capital used in the shoe industry are measured by 0_SB, which is shorter than the line 0_SA. Therefore, less labor and less capital are used in the production of footwear, and shoe output falls. The labor and capital used in computers are measured by $0'_CB$, which is longer than the line 0_CA. Therefore, more labor and more capital are used in computers, and the output of that industry rises.

The change in outputs of shoes and computers is shown by the shift from point *A* to point *B* in panel (b) of Figure 5-13. In accordance with the Rybczynski theorem, the increase in capital through FDI has increased the output of the capital-intensive industry

FIGURE 5-13

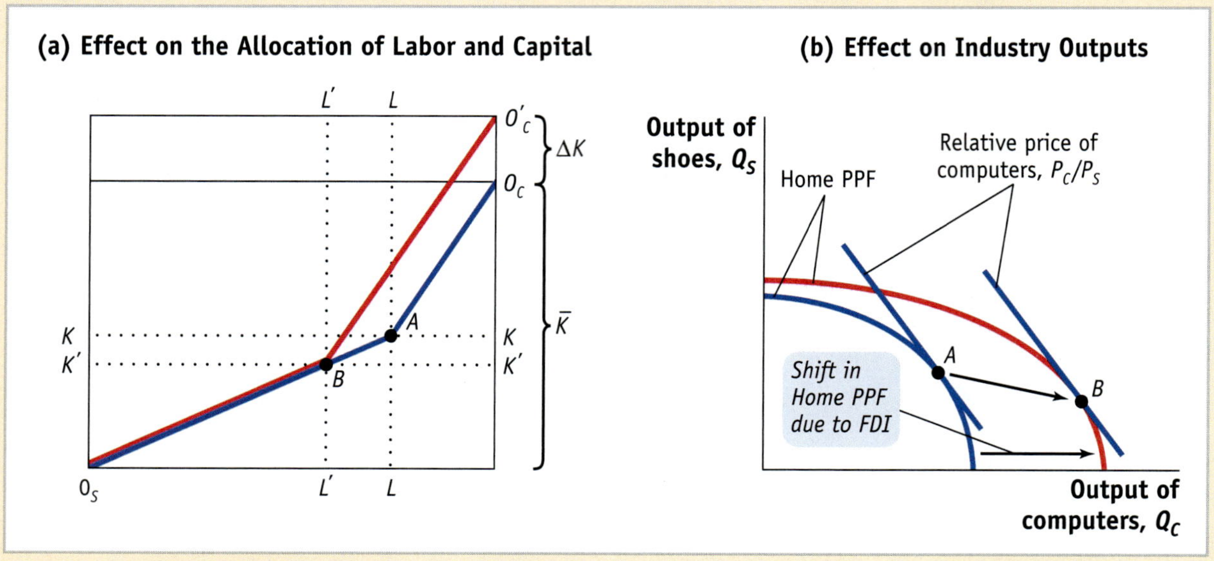

Increase in the Capital Stock in the Long Run In panel (a), the top and bottom axes of the box diagram measure the amount of labor in the economy, and the right and left axes measure the amount of capital. The initial equilibrium is at point *A*. When there is an inflow of capital, the equilibrium moves to point *B*. Similar to the box diagram for immigration (Figure 5-8), the *K*/*L* ratios remain unchanged by allocating the new capital, as well as additional capital and labor from shoes, to computers. In panel (b), with the increase in the amount of capital at Home from increased FDI, the PPF shifts outward. The output of computers increases while the output of shoes declines as the equilibrium moves from point *A* to *B*. Because the prices of goods have not changed, the slopes of the PPFs at points *A* and *B* are equal.

(computers) and reduced the output of the labor-intensive industry (shoes). Furthermore, this change in outputs is achieved *with no change* in the capital–labor ratios in either industry: the lines $0'_CB$ and 0_SB have the same slopes as 0_CA and 0_SA, respectively.

Because the capital–labor ratios are unchanged in the two industries, the wage and the rental on capital are also unchanged. Each person has the same amount of capital to work with in his or her industry, and each machine has the same number of workers. The marginal products of labor and capital are unchanged in the two industries, as are the factor prices. This outcome is basically the same as that for immigration in the long run: in the long-run model, an inflow of *either* factor of production will leave factor prices unchanged.

When discussing immigration, we found cases in which wages were reduced (the short-run prediction) and other cases in which wages have been constant (the long-run prediction). What about for foreign direct investment? Does it tend to lower rentals or leave them unchanged? There are fewer studies of this question, but we next consider an important application for Singapore.

APPLICATION

The Effect of FDI on Rentals and Wages in Singapore

For many years, Singapore has encouraged foreign firms to establish subsidiaries within its borders, especially in the electronics industry. For example, hard disk drives are assembled in Singapore by Seagate (an American company), Samsung (a Korean company), and Fujitsu (a Japanese company). Singapore has the fourth largest amount of FDI in the world (measured by stock of foreign capital found there), following China, Mexico, and Brazil, even though it is much smaller than those economies.[12] As capital in Singapore has grown, what has happened to the rental and to the wage?

One way to answer this question is to estimate the marginal product of capital in Singapore, using a production function that applies to the entire economy. The overall capital–labor ratio in Singapore has grown by about 5% per year from 1970 to 1990. Because of diminishing returns, it follows that the marginal product of capital (equal to the real rental) has fallen, by an average of 3.4% per year as shown in part A of Table 5-2. At the same time, each worker has more capital to work with, so the marginal product of labor (equal to the real wage) has grown by an average of 1.6% per year, as also shown in part A. These estimates of the falling rental and rising wage are consistent with the short-run specific-factors model.

But there is a second way to calculate a rental on capital besides using the marginal product. Under this second approach, we start with the price P_K of some capital equipment. If that equipment was rented rather than purchased, what would its rental

TABLE 5-2

Real Rental and Wages in Singapore This table shows the growth rate in the real rental and real wages in Singapore, depending on the method used to construct these factor prices. In part A, a production function approach is used to construct the factor prices, and the real rental falls over time because of the growth in capital. As a result, implied productivity growth is negative. In part B, the rental and wages are constructed from data on payments to capital and labor in Singapore, and real wages grow over time, while the real rental either grows or falls slightly. As a result, implied productivity growth is positive.

	ANNUAL GROWTH RATE (%)		
	Real Rental	**Real Wages**	**Implied Productivity**
Part A: Using Production Function and Marginal Products			
Time Period:			
1970–1980	-5.0	2.6	-1.5
1980–1990	-1.9	0.5	-0.7
1970–1990	-3.4	1.6	-1.1
Part B: Using Calculated Rental and Actual Wages			
Interest Rate Used and Time Period:			
Bank lending rate (1968–1990)	1.6	2.7	2.2
Return on equity (1971–1990)	-0.2	3.2	1.5
Earnings-price ratio (1973–1990)	-0.5	3.6	1.6

Sources: Part A from Alwyn Young, 1995, "The Tyranny of Numbers: Confronting the Statistical Realities of the East Asian Growth Experience," Quarterly Journal of Economics, *110(3), August, 641–680.*

Part B from Chang-Tai Hsieh, 2002, "What Explains the Industrial Revolution in East Asia? Evidence from the Factor Markets," American Economic Review, *92(3), 502–526.*

[12] In 2005 China had $318 billion in foreign capital, with another $533 billion in Hong Kong; Mexico had $210 billion; Brazil $202 billion; and Singapore $189 billion, which was 7% of the total foreign capital in developing countries.

be? Let us suppose that the rental agency needs to make the same rate of return on renting the capital equipment that it would make if it invested its money in some financial asset, such as a savings account in a bank or the stock market. If it invested P_K and the asset had the interest rate of i, then it could expect to earn $P_K \cdot i$ from that asset. On the other hand, if it rents out the equipment, then that machinery also suffers wear and tear, and the rental agency needs to recover that cost, too. If d is the rate of depreciation of the capital equipment (the fraction of it that is used up each year), then to earn the same return on a financial asset as from renting out the equipment, the rental agency must receive $P_K \cdot (i + d)$. This formula is an estimate of R, the rental on capital. Dividing by an overall price index P, the real rental is

$$\frac{R}{P} = \frac{P_K}{P} \cdot (i + d)$$

In part B of Table 5-2, we show the growth rate in the real rental, computed from this formula, which depends on the interest rate used. In the first row, we use the bank lending rate for i, and the computed real rental grows by 1.6% per year. In the next rows, we use two interest rates from the stock market: the return on equity (what you would earn from investing in stocks) and the earnings–price ratio (the profits that each firm earns divided by the value of its outstanding stocks). In both these latter cases, the calculated real rental falls slightly over time, by 0.2% and 0.5% per year, much less than the fall in the real rental in part A. According to the calculated real rentals in part B, there is little evidence of a downward fall in the rentals over time.

In part B, we also show the real wage, computed from actual wages paid in Singapore. Real wages grow substantially over time—between 2.7 and 3.6% per year, depending on the exact interest rate and time period used. This is not what we predicted from our long-run model, in which factor prices would be unchanged by an inflow of capital, because the capital–labor ratios are constant (so the marginal product of labor would not change). That real wages are growing in Singapore, with little change in the real rental, is an indication that there is *productivity growth* in the economy, which leads to an increase in the marginal product of labor *and* in the real wage.

We will not discuss how productivity growth is actually measured[13] but just report the findings from the studies in Table 5-2: in part B, productivity growth is between 1.5 and 2.2% per year, depending on the time period, but in part A, productivity growth is negative! The reason that productivity growth is so much higher in part B is because the average of the growth in the real wage and real rental is rising, which indicates that productivity growth has occurred. In contrast, in part A the average of the growth in the real wage and real rental is zero or negative, indicating that no productivity growth has occurred.

The idea that Singapore might have zero productivity growth contradicts what many people believe about its economy and the economies of other fast-growing Asian countries, which were thought to exhibit "miraculous" growth during this period of time. If productivity growth is zero or negative, then all growth is due only to capital accumulation, and FDI has no spillover benefits to the local economy. Positive productivity growth, as shown in part B, indicates that the free-market policies pursued by Singapore stimulated innovations in the manufacture of goods that have

[13] The calculation of productivity growth is discussed in Problem 10.

resulted in higher productivity and lower costs. This is what many economists and policy makers believe happened in Singapore, but this belief is challenged by the productivity calculations in part A. Which scenario is correct—zero or positive productivity growth for Singapore—is a source of ongoing debate in economics. Read the item **Headlines: The Myth of Asia's Miracle** for one interpretation of the growth in Singapore and elsewhere in Asia. ■

3 Gains from Labor and Capital Flows

Foreign investment and immigration are both controversial policy issues. Most countries impose limits on FDI at some time in their development but later become open to foreign investment. Nearly all countries impose limits on the inflow of people. In the United States, controls on immigration were first established by the Quota Law

HEADLINES

The Myth of Asia's Miracle

A CAUTIONARY FABLE: Once upon a time, Western opinion leaders found themselves both impressed and frightened by the extraordinary growth rates achieved by a set of Eastern economies. Although those economies were still substantially poorer and smaller than those of the West, the speed with which they had transformed themselves from peasant societies into industrial powerhouses, their continuing ability to achieve growth rates several times higher than the advanced nations, and their increasing ability to challenge or even surpass American and European technology in certain areas seemed to call into question the dominance not only of Western power but of Western ideology. The leaders of those nations did not share our faith in free markets or unlimited civil liberties. They asserted with increasing self-confidence that their system was superior: societies that accepted strong, even authoritarian governments and were willing to limit individual liberties in the interest of the common good, take charge of their economics, and sacrifice short-run consumer interests for the sake of long-run growth would eventually outperform the increasingly chaotic societies of the West. And a growing minority of Western intellectuals agreed.

The gap between Western and Eastern economic performance eventually became a political issue. The Democrats recaptured the White House under the leadership of a young, energetic new president who pledged to "get the country moving again"—a pledge that, to him and his closest advisers, meant accelerating America's economic growth to meet the Eastern challenge.

The time, of course, was the early 1960s. The dynamic young president was John F. Kennedy. The technological feats that so alarmed the West were the launch of Sputnik and the early Soviet lead in space. And the rapidly growing Eastern economies were those of the Soviet Union and its satellite nations.

Were you tricked by this fable? Did you think that the "Eastern economies" that the author, Paul Krugman, referred to in the beginning were the Asian economies? Krugman is using this rhetorical trick to suggest that the high growth of the Asian economies is not too different from the growth of the Soviet Union in the 1950s and 1960s, which was due to capital accumulation but without much productivity growth. Other economists disagree and believe that Asian growth is due in significant part to improved productivity, in addition to capital accumulation.

Source: Excerpted from Paul Krugman, 1994, "The Myth of Asia's Miracle," Foreign Affairs, *November/December, 63–79.*

of 1921, which limited the number of people arriving annually from each country of origin. The Immigration and Nationality Act Amendments of 1965 revised the country-specific limits and allowed immigration on a first-come, first-served basis, up to an annual limit, with special allowances for family members and people in certain occupations. Subsequent revisions to the immigration laws in the United States have established penalties for employers who knowingly hire illegal immigrants, have allowed some illegal immigrants to gain citizenship, or have tightened border controls and deported other illegal immigrants.

Why is immigration so controversial? A glance at articles in the newspaper or on the Internet will show that some groups oppose the spending of public funds on immigrants, such as for schooling, medical care, or welfare. Other groups fear the competition for jobs created by the inflow of foreign workers. We have already seen that immigration creates gains and losses for different groups, often lowering the wage for workers in similar jobs but providing benefits to firms hiring these workers.

This finding raises the important question: Does immigration provide an overall gain to the host country, not including the gains to the immigrants themselves? We presume that the immigrants are better off from higher wages in the country to which they move.[14] But what about the other workers and owners of capital and land in the host country? In the short run, we learned that workers in the host country face competition from the immigrants and receive lower wages, while owners of capital and land benefit from immigration. When we add up these various gains and losses, are there "overall gains" to the destination country, in the same way as we have found overall gains from trade? Fortunately, this outcome turns out to be true.

Immigration benefits the host country in the specific-factors model, not including the income of the immigrants themselves. If we include the immigrant earnings with Foreign income, then we find that emigration benefits the Foreign country, too. The same argument can be made for FDI. An inflow of capital benefits the host country, not including the extra earnings of foreign capital. By counting those extra earnings in Foreign income, then FDI also benefits the source country of the capital. After showing these theoretical results, we discuss how large the overall gains from immigration or FDI flows might be in practice.

Gains from Immigration

To measure the gains from immigration, we will use the specific-factors model. In Figure 5-14, we measure the *world* amount of labor on the horizontal axis, which equals $\bar{L} + \bar{L}^*$. The number of workers in the Home country $\bar{L}$ is measured from left (the origin 0) to right. The number of workers in Foreign $\bar{L}^*$ is measured from right (0^*) to left. Each point on the horizontal axis indicates how many workers are located in the two countries. For example, point L indicates that $0L$ workers are located in Home, and 0^*L workers are located in the Foreign country.

Wages at Home and Abroad We already know from our discussion earlier in the chapter that as immigrants enter the Home country, the wage is reduced. In Figure 5-14, we graph this relationship as a downward-sloping line labeled "Home wage." With Home workers of $0L$ before immigration, the wage is W at point A. If

[14] This ignores cases in which the immigrants regret the decision to move because of hardship in making the passage or discrimination once they arrive.

FIGURE 5-14

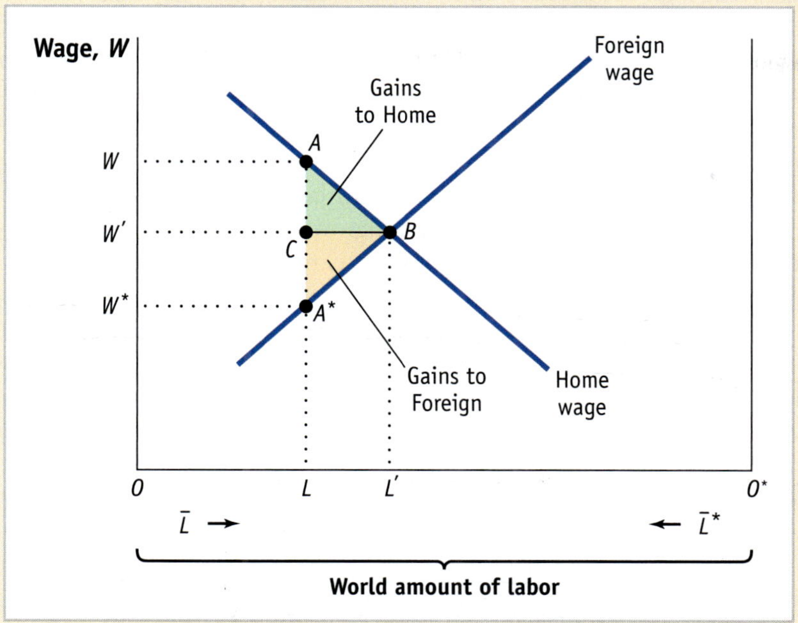

World Labor Market Initially, Home has OL workers and Foreign has 0^*L workers. The Home wage is W, as determined at point A, which is higher than the Foreign wage W^* at A^*. Workers will move from Foreign to Home to receive higher wages. The equilibrium with full migration is at point B, where wages are equalized at W'. The gain to Home from migration is measured by triangle ABC, and triangle A^*BC represents the gains to Foreign.

Foreign workers enter and the Home labor force grows to $0L'$, then the Home wage is reduced to W' at point B. The downward-sloping "Home wage" line illustrates the inverse relationship between the number of Home workers and their wage. You can think of this line as a labor demand curve, not for a single industry, but for the economy as a whole.

Similarly, in the Foreign country, there is an inverse relationship between the numbers of workers and their wage. Before any emigration, the labor force in Foreign is 0^*L, and we show the wage at W^* at point A^*. That is lower than the Home wage of W, so some workers will want to migrate from Foreign to Home. Remembering that we measure the Foreign workers from right (0^*) to left, when the labor force abroad shrinks from 0^*L to $0^*L'$, the Foreign wages rise from W^* to W' at point B. We see that as Foreign workers leave, it benefits those left behind by raising their wages.

We will refer to point B as the **equilibrium with full migration.** At this point, the wages earned at Home and abroad are equalized at W'. It would certainly take a long time for migration to lead to complete wage equality across countries. In our discussion of emigration from the Old World to the New, we saw in Figure 5-3 that real wages in the New World were still twice as high as wages in Europe even after 40 years of large-scale migration. So the equilibrium with full migration is reached only in the very long run. The question we want to answer is whether this migration has benefited the workers (not including the immigrants), labor, and capital in the Home country. In addition, we want to know whether migration has benefited the Foreign country, including the migrants.

Gains for the Home Country To determine whether there are overall gains for Home, we need to measure the contribution of each Foreign worker to the output of one good or the other in that country. This measurement is easy to do. The marginal product of labor in either industry (multiplied by the price of shoes or computers) equals the Home wage. So the first Foreign worker to migrate has a marginal product equal to the Home wage, which is W at point A. As more Foreign workers migrate, the marginal product of labor in both Home industries falls due to diminishing returns. We can measure the immigrants' marginal product by the wage that is paid at Home, which falls from W to W' as we move down the Home wage curve from point A to B.

At the equilibrium with full migration, point B, *all* Foreign immigrants are paid the Home wage of W'. But all Foreign workers except the last one to enter had a marginal product of labor that is above W': the first Foreign worker had a marginal product of W, and the later Foreign immigrants have lower marginal products, ranging from W to W'. Therefore, their contribution to the output of goods in the Home economy *exceeds* the wage that they are paid. The first Foreign immigrant had a marginal product of W but receives the wage W', so the gain to the Home economy from having that worker is $(W - W')$. Likewise, each immigrant to come later has a marginal product between W and W' but is still paid the wage W', so the difference between their marginal products and wages is a gain for the Home economy.

Adding the gains to the Home economy from the Foreign workers, we end up with the triangle ABC, which represents the Home gains as a result of full immigration. The reason for these gains is the law of diminishing returns: as more Foreign immigrants enter the Home workforce, their marginal products fall, and because the wage equals the marginal product of the last worker, it must be less than the marginal products of the earlier immigrants. This economic logic guarantees gains to the Home country from migration.

Gains for the Foreign Country Now consider the Foreign country. To assess the overall gains from emigration, we include the wages received by the migrants who left in calculating Foreign income. These wages are often returned to their families (see **Side Bar: Immigrants and Their Remittances**), but even if they are not, we still incorporate the wages earned by the immigrants in our measure of Foreign income because that is from where the migrants originally came.

In the absence of any emigration, the Foreign wage is W^*, the marginal product of labor in either industry abroad (multiplied by the price of that product in Foreign). As Foreign workers emigrate, the marginal product of labor remaining in Foreign rises, and the Foreign wage rises from W^* to W' (or from points A^* to B in Figure 5-14). Each of these higher marginal products or wages—between W^* and W'—equals the drop in Foreign output (of either good) from having workers leave.

Under full migration, all Foreign migrants earn the wage W' in the Home country. Notice that this wage is *higher* than their Foreign marginal products of labor, which are between W^* and W'. The difference between the wage earned by the migrants and their Foreign marginal products equals the gain to Foreign. Adding up the gains over all Foreign emigrants, we obtain the triangle A^*BC. This gain represents the earnings of the emigrants over and above the drop in output that occurs when they leave Foreign.

World Gains from Migration Combining the gains to the Home and Foreign countries, we obtain the triangular region ABA^*, the world gains from immigration. This magnitude is not too difficult to measure in practice. Turning the triangle on its side, its base equals $(W - W^*)$, the difference in the Home and Foreign wage in the absence of any migration. The height of the triangle is $(L' - L)$, the number of foreign

SIDE BAR

Immigrants and Their Remittances

Immigrants often send a substantial portion of their earnings back home, which we refer to as "remittances." According to estimates from the World Bank, remittances to developing countries were $336 billion in 2008, up from $289 billion in 2007. Economists at the World Bank had believed that the global recession and resulting high global unemployment would limit the ability of migrants to send money to their home countries. However, it appears that in 2008 many migrants reduced their own consumption rather than decreasing their remittances to those they have left behind. A sharp decline in private capital flows in 2008 made remittances an even more important source of external financing throughout the developing world. The strength of remittances in the face of the recession was driven largely by strong growth in flows to South Asia, home to the two largest recipients of remittances: India and China. Remittances declined by 6% in 2009 to $316 billion. Moderate growth in South Asian remittances prevented this slide from being larger.

Especially in times of economic turmoil, remittances are an important supplement to official foreign aid. In Table 5-3, we show the remittances received by some developing countries in 2007, as compared with their net foreign aid. For all countries except Sudan, the income sent home by emigrants is a larger source of income than official aid.

The fact that emigrants return some of their income back home may not be enough to compensate their home countries for the loss of their labor. To calculate any gain to the home countries from the emigration of their workers, we need to include *all the earnings* of the emigrants in their home countries' income. In reality, however, emigrants do not send all their income home, so the countries they leave can lose from their outflow. Consider, for example, the case of highly educated migrants. In 2000 there were 1 million Indian-born people with college educations living in the 30 wealthy countries of the Organization for Economic Co-operation and Development (OECD). That amounts to 4.3% of India's large number of college graduates. In 2008 53% of Indian-born migrants living in the OECD had a post-secondary education. For Asia as a whole, 38% of migrants living in the OECD had a post-secondary education. But for smaller countries, the outflow is much larger. Almost 47% of Ghana's college-educated labor force lives in OECD countries, and for Guyana, the percentage is 89%.[15] Unless these migrants return most of their earnings back home, those countries lose from the outflow of these highly educated workers.

To address this concern, Jagdish Bhagwati (an Indian-born economist now at Columbia University in New York) has proposed that countries impose a "brain drain" tax on the outflow of educated workers. The idea is to tax the earnings of people living outside the countries in which they were born and, through an organization such as the United Nations, return the proceeds from the tax to the countries that lose the most workers. In that way, countries with an outflow of educated workers would be compensated, at least in part, for the outflow. A "brain drain" tax has been widely debated but so far has not actually been used in practice.

TABLE 5-3

Workers' Remittances and Net Foreign Aid, 2007

Shown here are the remittances received by various countries from their citizens working abroad. In many cases, these remittances are larger than the official aid received by the countries. An exception was Sudan, which was experiencing a humanitarian crisis in 2007 so that aid was high.

Country	Remittances Received ($ millions)	Net Aid Received ($ millions)
Albania	1,468	305
Bangladesh	6,562	1,502
Brazil	4,382	297
Colombia	4,523	731
Croatia	1,394	164
Dominican Republic	3,414	128
India	38,666	1,298
Mexico	27,136	121
Morocco	6,730	1,090
Sudan	1,769	2,104
Vietnam	5,500	2,497

Source: World Development Indicators, The World Bank.

[15] These percentages are obtained from "Fruit That Falls Far from the Tree," *The Economist*, November 3, 2005, which draws on a World Bank study, and from the 2008 OECD Migration Outlook.

workers that would emigrate in the equilibrium with full migration. So the area of the triangle is $\frac{1}{2}(W - W^*) \cdot (L' - L)$. To solve for the area, we need to know the difference in wages before any migration and the number of people who would emigrate.

One way to think about the world gains from migration is that they equal the *increase in world GDP due to immigration*. To understand why this is so, think about the first person to migrate from Foreign to Home. That person earns the wage W^* in Foreign, which equals his or her marginal product times the price in the industry in which he or she works. When this individual leaves Foreign, GDP in that country falls by W^*. Once he or she moves to Home, he or she earns W, which again reflects the marginal product times the industry price. So W equals the increase in Home GDP when the immigrant begins working. The difference between the Home and Foreign wages therefore equals the net increase in world GDP due to migration. By adding up this amount across all migrants, we obtain the triangular region ABA^*, the increase in world GDP and the world gains due to migration.

In practice, however, there are other costs that immigrants bear that would make the gains from immigration less than the increase in world GDP. Immigrants often face sizable moving costs, including the psychological costs of missing their families and home countries as well as monetary payments to traffickers of illegal immigrants. These costs should be subtracted from the increase in GDP to obtain the net gains. Because all the moving costs are hard to quantify, however, in the next application we measure the net gains from immigration by the increase in Home or world GDP.

APPLICATION

Gains from Migration

How large are the gains from immigration? For the United States, a study by the economist George Borjas puts the net gain from immigration at about 0.1% of GDP (one-tenth of 1% of GDP). That value is obtained by using a stock of immigrants equal to 10% of the workforce in the United States and assuming that the immigrants compete for the same jobs as U.S. workers. If instead we assume the immigrants are lower-skilled on average than the U.S. population, then the low-skilled immigrants can complement the higher-skilled U.S. population, and the gains from immigration in the United States are somewhat higher, up to 0.4% of GDP. These estimates are shown in the first row of Table 5-4. The net gains to the United States in this case equal the increase in U.S. GDP.

Borjas's estimates for the U.S. gains from immigration may seem small, but lying behind these numbers is a larger shift in income from labor to capital and landowners. Labor loses from immigration, while capital and landowners gain, and the net effect of all these changes in real income is the gain in GDP that Borjas estimates. For the net gain of 0.1% of U.S. GDP due to immigration, Borjas estimates that capital would gain 2% and domestic labor would lose 1.9% of GDP. These figures lead him to conclude, "The relatively small size of the immigration surplus [that is, the gain in GDP]—particularly when compared to the very large wealth transfers caused by immigration [that is, the shift in income from labor to capital]—probably explains why the debate over immigration policy has usually focused on the potentially harmful labor market impacts rather than the overall increase in native income."

Other calculations suggest that the overall gains from immigration could be somewhat larger than Borjas's estimates. In the second row of Table 5-4, we report figures

TABLE 5-4

Gains from Immigration The results from several studies of immigration are shown in this table. The second column shows the amount of immigration (as a percentage of the Home labor force), and the third column shows the increase in Home GDP or the increase in GDP of the region.

	AMOUNT OF IMMIGRATION	
	(% of Home labor)	Increase in GDP (%)
Part A: Calculation of Home Gains		
Study used:		
Borjas (1995, 1999), U.S. gains	10	0.1–0.4
Kremer and Watt (2006), Household workers	7	1.2–1.4
Part B: Calculation of Regional Gains		
Study used:		
Walmsley and Winters (2005),		
From developed to developing countries	3	0.6
Klein and Ventura (2006),		
Enlargement of the European Union		
After 10 years	0.8–1.8	0.2–0.7
After 25 years	2.5–5.0	0.6–1.8
After 50 years	4.8–8.8	1.7–4.5
Very long run	na	8
Common Labor Market in NAFTA		
After 10 years	1.0–2.4	0.1–0.4
After 25 years	2.8–5.5	0.4–1.0
After 50 years	4.4–9.1	1.3–3.0
Very long run	na	10.5

na: Not available from the study.

Sources: George Borjas, 1995, "The Economic Benefits from Immigration," Journal of Economic Perspectives, *9(2), 3–22.*

George Borjas, 1999, "The Economic Analysis of Immigration." In Orley Ashenfelter and David Card, eds., Handbook of Labor Economics, *Vol. 3A (Amsterdam: North Holland), pp. 1697–1760.*

Paul Klein and Gustavo Ventura, 2006, "Productivity Differences and the Dynamic Effects of Labour Movements," University of Western Ontario and Pennsylvania State University.

Michael Kremer and Stanley Watt, 2006, "The Globalization of Household Production," Harvard University.

Terrie Louise Walmsley and L. Alan Winters, 2005, "Relaxing the Restrictions on the Temporary Movement of Natural Persons: A Simulation Analysis," Journal of Economic Integration, *20(4), December, 688–726.*

from a study by Kremer and Watt that focuses on just one type of immigrant: household workers. Foreign household workers, who are primarily female, make up 10% or more of the labor force in Bahrain, Kuwait, and Saudi Arabia and about 7% of the labor force in Hong Kong and Singapore. The presence of these household workers often allows another member of that household—typically, a highly educated woman—to seek employment in her Home country. Thus, the immigration of low-skilled household workers allows for an increase in the high-skilled supply of individuals at Home, generating higher Home GDP as a result. It is estimated that this type of immigration, if it accounts for 7% of the workforce as in some countries, would increase Home GDP by about 1.2 to 1.4%.

In part B of Table 5-4, we report results from estimates of gains due to migration for several regions of the world. The first study, by Walmsley and Winters, found that an increase in labor supply to developed countries of 3%, as a result of immigration from the developing countries, would create world gains of 0.6% of world GDP. This calculation is similar to the triangle of gains ABA^* shown in Figure 5-14. The next study, by Klein and Ventura, obtains larger estimates of the world gains by modeling the differences in technology across countries. Under this approach, wealthier regions have higher productivity, so an immigrant moving there will be more productive than at home. This productivity increase is offset somewhat by a skill loss for the immigrant (since the immigrant may not find the job for which he or she is best suited, at least initially). Nevertheless, the assumed skill loss is less than the productivity difference between countries, so immigrants are always more productive in the country to which they move.

In their study, Klein and Ventura consider the recent enlargement of the European Union (EU) from 15 countries to 25. Workers from the newly added Eastern European countries are, in principle, permitted to work anywhere in the EU, though in practice this will create some new policy issues for the EU.[16] Klein and Ventura assume that the original 15 EU countries are twice as productive as the newly added countries. During the first 10 years, they find that the population of those 15 EU countries increases by 0.8 to 1.8%, and the combined GDP in the EU increases by 0.2 to 0.7%. The range of these estimates comes from different assumptions on the skill losses of immigrants when they move, and also the psychological costs of their moving, which slow down the extent of migration. As time passes, however, more people flow from Eastern to Western Europe, and GDP continues to rise. In 25 years, they estimate that the combined GDP of the EU will increase by 0.6 to 1.8%, and over 50 years, the increase in GDP will be 1.7 to 4.5%. In the very long run (more than 100 years), much of the population of the eastern EU will have shifted to the west, and GDP will have risen by 8%.

Next, Klein and Ventura consider a common labor market within the North American Free Trade Area (NAFTA), established in 1994, which consists of Canada, Mexico, and the United States. Although NAFTA allows for free international trade between these countries, labor mobility is not free. So the experiment that Klein and Ventura consider is to allow workers from Mexico to migrate freely to the United States and Canada, which are assumed to have workers who are 1.7 times as productive as those from Mexico. During the first 10 years, they predict that the population of the United States and Canada increases by 1.0 to 2.4% due to the immigration from Mexico, and the combined GDP in the NAFTA region increases by 0.1 to 0.4%. After 25 years, they estimate that the combined GDP of the region increases by 0.4 to 1.0%, and over 50 years, the increase in GDP is 1.3 to 3.0%. In the very long run, much of the population of Mexico will have moved to the United States or Canada, and the combined GDP of the NAFTA region will have risen by 10.5%. ■

Gains from Foreign Direct Investment

A diagram very similar to Figure 5-14 can be used to measure the gains from FDI. In Figure 5-15, we show the world amount of capital on the horizontal axis, which equals $\bar{K} + \bar{K}^*$. The rental earned in each country is on the vertical axis. With OK units of

[16] See note 7.

FIGURE 5-15

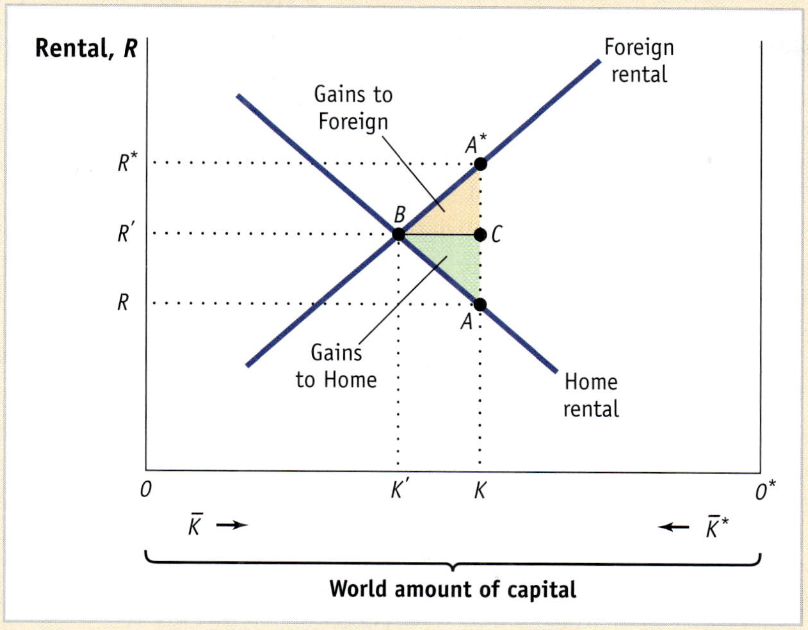

World Capital Market With OK units of capital at Home, the Home rental is R at point A. The remaining capital O^*K is in Foreign, and the Foreign rental is R^* at point A^*. Capital will move from Home to Foreign to receive a higher rental. The equilibrium with full capital flows is at point B, where rentals are equalized at R'. Triangle ABC measures the gains to Home from the capital outflow, and triangle A^*BC measures the gains to Foreign.

capital employed at Home (measured from left to right), the Home rental is R, determined at point A. The remaining capital O^*K (measured from right to left) is in Foreign, and the Foreign rental is R^*, determined at point A^*.

Because the Foreign rental is higher than that at Home, capital will flow from Home to Foreign. As it enters Foreign, the additional capital will reduce the marginal product of capital and bid down the rental. Likewise, as capital leaves Home, the marginal product of capital will increase, and the Home rental will be bid up. The equilibrium with full capital flows is at point B, where rentals are equalized at R'. Similar to what we found in the case of immigration, the gains to Home from the capital outflow is the triangle ABC, while the gains to Foreign is the triangle A^*BC, and the world gains are A^*BA.

4 Conclusions

Immigration, the movement of workers between countries, potentially affects the wages in the host country in which the workers arrive. In the short-run specific-factor model, a larger supply of workers due to immigration will lower wages. Most immigrants into the United States have either the lowest or the highest amounts of education. As a result, after an inflow of labor from other countries, the wages of these two groups of workers fall in the short run. The majority of U.S. workers, those with mid-levels of education, are not affected that much by immigration. Moreover, the arrival of immigrants is beneficial to owners of capital and land in the specific-factors model. As wages are reduced in the short run, the rentals on capital and land will rise. This result helps to explain why landowners lobby for programs to allow agricultural workers to immigrate at least temporarily, and why other industries support increased immigration, such as H1-B visas for workers in the high-technology and other professional industries.

In a long-run framework, when capital can move between industries, the fall in wages will not occur. Instead, the industries that use labor intensively can expand and other industries contract, so that the immigrants become employed without any fall in wages. This change in industry outputs is the main finding of the Rybczynski theorem. The evidence from the Mariel boat lift in 1980 suggests that a readjustment of industry outputs along these lines occurred in Miami after the arrival of immigrants from Cuba: the output of the apparel industry fell by less than predicted from other cities, whereas the output of some skill-intensive industries fell by more than predicted.

The movement of capital between countries is referred to as foreign direct investment (FDI) and has effects analogous to immigration. In the short run, the entry of foreign capital into a country will lower the rental on capital, raise wages, and lower the rental on land. But in the long run, when capital and land can move between industries, these changes in the wage and rentals need not occur. Instead, industry outputs can adjust according to the Rybczynski theorem so that the extra capital is fully employed without any change in the wage or rentals. Evidence from Singapore suggests that foreign capital can be absorbed without a large decline in the rental or the marginal product of capital, though this is an area of ongoing debate in economics.

Both immigration and FDI create world gains as labor and capital move from countries with low marginal products to countries with high marginal products. Gains for the host country are created because the inflow of labor and capital is paid an amount that is less than its full contribution to GDP in the host country. At the same time, there are also gains to the labor and capital in the country they leave, provided that the income earned by the emigrants or capital is included in that country's welfare.

KEY POINTS

1. Holding the amount of capital and land fixed in both industries, as in the specific-factors model, immigration leads to a fall in wages. This was the case, for example, with the mass migration to the New World in the nineteenth century.
2. As wages fall due to immigration, the marginal products of the specific factors (capital and land) rise, and therefore their rentals also increase.
3. Fixing the amount of capital and land in a country is a reasonable assumption in the short run, but in the longer run, firms will move capital between industries, which will change the effect of immigration on wages and rentals.
4. In a long-run model with two goods and two factors, both of which are perfectly mobile between the industries, additional labor from immigration will be absorbed entirely by the labor-intensive industry. Furthermore, the labor-intensive industry will also absorb additional capital and labor from the capital-intensive industry, so its capital–labor ratio does not change in the long run. Because the capital–labor ratio in each industry does not change, the wage and rentals remain the same as well. This results in what is known as factor price insensitivity.
5. According to the Rybczynski theorem, immigration will lead to an increase in output in the labor-intensive industry and a decrease in the

output of the capital-intensive industry. This result is different from that of the short-run specific-factors model, in which immigration leads to increased output in both industries.

6. Besides trade in goods and the movement of labor, another way that countries interact with one another is through investment. When a company owns property, plant, or equipment in another country, it is called foreign direct investment, or FDI.

7. In the short run, FDI lowers the rentals on capital and land and raises wages. In the long run, the extra capital can be absorbed in the capital-intensive industry without any change in the wage or rental.

8. According to the Rybczynski theorem, FDI will lead to an increase in the output of the capital-intensive industry and a decrease in the output of the labor-intensive industry.

9. The movement of capital and labor generates overall gains for both the source and host countries, provided that the income of the emigrants is included in the source country's welfare. Hence, there are global gains from immigration and FDI.

KEY TERMS

specific-factors model, p. 128
Rybczynski theorem, p. 142
factor price insensitivity, p. 142
real value-added, p. 143
foreign direct investment (FDI), p. 146
equilibrium with full migration, p. 155

PROBLEMS

1. In the short-run specific-factors model, examine the impact on a small country following a natural disaster that decreases it population. Assume that land is specific to agriculture and capital is specific to manufacturing, whereas labor is free to move between the two sectors.
   a. In a diagram similar to Figure 5-2, determine the impact of the decrease in the workforce on the output of each industry and the equilibrium wage.
   b. What happens to the rentals on capital and land?

2. How would your answer to Problem 1 change if instead we use the long-run model, with shoes and computers produced using labor and capital?

3. Consider an increase in the supply of labor due to immigration, and use the long-run model. Figure 5-8 shows the box diagram and the leftward shift of the origin for the shoe industry. Redraw this diagram but instead shift to the right the origin for computers. That is, expand the labor axis by the amount ΔL but shift it to the right rather than to the left. With the new diagram, show how the amount of labor and capital in shoes and computers is determined, without any change in factor prices. Carefully explain what has happened to the amount of labor and capital used in each industry and to the output of each industry.

4. In the short-run specific-factors model, consider a decrease in the stock of land. For example, suppose a natural disaster decreases the quantity of arable land used for planting crops.
   a. Redraw panel (a) of Figure 5-11 starting from the initial equilibrium at point A.
   b. What is the effect of this change in land on the quantity of labor in each industry and on the equilibrium wage?

c. What is the effect on the rental on land and the rental on capital?

d. Now suppose that the international community wants to help the country struck by the natural disaster and decides to do so by increasing its level of FDI. So the rest of the world increases its investment in physical capital in the stricken country. Illustrate the effect of this policy on the equilibrium wage and rentals.

5. According to part A of Table 5-1, what education level loses most (i.e., has the greatest decrease in wage) from immigration to the United States? Does this result depend on keeping the rental on capital constant? Explain why or why not.

6. Suppose that computers use 2 units of capital for each worker, so that $K_C = 2 \cdot L_C$, whereas shoes use 0.5 units of capital for each worker, so that $K_S = 0.5 \cdot L_S$. There are 100 workers and 100 units of capital in the economy.

   a. Solve for the amount of labor and capital used in each industry.

   Hint: The box diagram shown in Figure 5-7 means that the amount of labor and capital used in each industry must add up to the total for the economy, so that

   $$K_C + K_S = 100 \text{ and } L_C + L_S = 100$$

   Use the facts that $K_C = 2 \cdot L_C$ and $K_S = 0.5 \cdot L_S$ to rewrite these equations as

   $$2 \cdot L_C + 0.5 \cdot L_S = 100 \text{ and } L_C + L_S = 100$$

   Use these two equations to solve for L_C and L_S, and then calculate the amount of capital used in each industry using $K_C = 2 \cdot L_C$ and $K_S = 0.5 \cdot L_S$.

   b. Suppose that the number of workers increases to 125 due to immigration, keeping total capital fixed at 100. Again, solve for the amount of labor and capital used in each industry. *Hint:* Redo the calculations from part (a), but using $L_C + L_S = 125$.

   c. Suppose instead that the amount of capital increases to 125 due to FDI, keeping the total number of workers fixed at 100. Again solve for the amount of labor and capital used in each industry. *Hint:* Redo the calculations from part (a), using $K_C + K_S = 125$.

   d. Explain how your results in parts (b) and (c) are related to the Rybczynski theorem.

The questions 7 and 8 explore the implications of the Rybczynski theorem and the factor price insensitivity result for the Heckscher-Ohlin model from Chapter 4.

7. In this question, we use the Rybczynski theorem to review the derivation of the Heckscher-Ohlin theorem.

   a. Start at the no-trade equilibrium point A on the Home PPF in Figure 4-2, panel (a). Suppose that through immigration, the amount of labor in Home grows. Draw the new PPF, and label the point B where production would occur with the same prices for goods. *Hint:* You can refer to Figure 5-9 to see the effect of immigration on the PPF.

   b. Suppose that the only difference between Foreign and Home is that Foreign has more labor. Otherwise, the technologies used to produce each good are the same across countries. Then how does the Foreign PPF compare with the new Home PPF (including immigration) that you drew in part (a)? Is point B the no-trade equilibrium in Foreign? Explain why or why not.

   c. Illustrate a new point A^* that is the no-trade equilibrium in Foreign. How do the relative no-trade prices of computers compare in Home and Foreign? Therefore, what will be the pattern of trade between the countries, and why?

8. Continuing from Problem 7, we now use the factor price insensitivity result to compare factor prices across countries in the Heckscher-Ohlin model.

a. Illustrate the international trade equilibrium on the Home and Foreign production possibilities frontiers. *Hint:* You can refer to Figure 4-3 to see the international trade equilibrium.
b. Suppose that the only difference between Foreign and Home is that Foreign has more labor. Otherwise, the technologies used to produce each good are the same across countries. Then, according to the factor price insensitivity result, how will the wage and rental compare in the two countries?
c. Call the result in part (b) "factor price equalization." Is this a realistic result? *Hint:* You can refer to Figure 4-9 to see wages across countries.
d. Based on our extension of the Heckscher-Ohlin model at the end of Chapter 4, what is one reason why the factor price equalization result does not hold in reality?

9. Recall the formula from the application "The Effect of FDI on Rentals and Wages in Singapore." Give an intuitive explanation for this formula for the rental rate. *Hint:* Describe one side of the equation as a marginal benefit and the other as a marginal cost.

10. In Table 5-2, we show the growth in the real rental and real wages in Singapore, along with the implied productivity growth. One way to calculate the productivity growth is to take the average of the growth in the real rental and real wage. The idea is that firms can afford to pay more to labor and capital if there is productivity growth, so in that case real factor prices should be growing. But if there is no productivity growth, then the average of the growth in the real rental and real wage should be close to zero.

    To calculate the average of the growth in the real factor prices, we use the shares of GDP going to capital and labor. Specifically, we multiply the growth in the real rental by the capital share of GDP and add the growth in the real wage multiplied by the labor share of GDP. Then answer the following:

    a. For a capital-rich country like Singapore, the share of capital in GDP is about one-half and the share of labor is also one-half. Using these shares, calculate the average of the growth in the real rental and real wage shown in each row of Table 5-2. How do your answers compare with the productivity growth shown in the last column of Table 5-2?
    b. For an industrialized country like the United States, the share of capital in GDP is about one-third and the share of labor in GDP is about two-thirds. Using these shares, calculate the average of the growth in the real rental and real wage shown in each row of Table 5-2. How do your answers now compare with the productivity growth shown in the last column?

11. Figure 5-14 is a supply and demand diagram for the world labor market. Starting at points A and A^*, consider a situation in which some Foreign workers migrate to Home but not enough to reach the equilibrium with full migration (point B). As a result of the migration, the Home wage decreases from W to $W'' > W'$, and the Foreign wage increases from W^* to $W^{**} < W'$.
    a. Are there gains that accrue to the Home country? If so, redraw the graph and identify the magnitude of the gains for each country. If not, say why not.
    b. Are there gains that accrue to the Foreign country? If so, again show the magnitude of these gains in the diagram and also show the world gains.

12. A housekeeper from the Philippines is contemplating immigrating to Singapore in search of higher wages. Suppose the housekeeper earns approximately \$2,000 annually and expects to find a job in Singapore worth approximately \$5,000 annually for a period of three years. Furthermore, assume that the cost of living in Singapore is \$500 more per year than at home.

a. What can we say about the productivity of housekeepers in Singapore versus the Philippines? Explain.
b. What is the total gain to the housekeeper from migrating?
c. Is there a corresponding gain for the employer in Singapore? Explain.

NET WORK

Immigration is frequently debated in the United States and other countries. Find the most recent news report dealing with immigration policy in the United States, and briefly summarize the issues discussed.

6

Increasing Returns to Scale and Monopolistic Competition

Foreign trade, then, . . . [is] highly beneficial to a country, as it increases the amount and variety of the objects on which revenue may be expended.

David Ricardo, *On the Principles of Political Economy and Taxation*, Chapter 7

The idea that a simple government policy [free trade between Canada and the United States] could raise productivity so dramatically is to me truly remarkable.

Professor Daniel Trefler, University of Toronto, 2005

In Chapter 2, we looked at data for U.S. snowboard imports and considered the reasons why the United States imports this product from so many different countries. Now we look at another sporting good that the United States imports *and exports* in large quantities to illustrate how a country can both buy a product and sell it to other countries. In 2009 the United States imported golf clubs from 25 countries and exported them to 83 countries. In Table 6-1, we list the 12 countries that sell the most golf clubs to the United States and the 12 countries to which the United States sells the most golf clubs. The table also lists the amounts bought or sold and their average wholesale prices.

In panel (a), we see that China sells the most clubs to the United States, providing $254 million worth of golf clubs at an average price of $18 each. Next is Thailand, selling $14 million of clubs at an average wholesale price of $102 each. Vietnam comes next, exporting $7 million of clubs at an average price of $14, followed by Japan, selling $6 million of clubs with an average price of $125. The higher average prices of Thai and Japanese clubs compared with Chinese and Vietnamese clubs most likely indicate that the clubs Thailand and Japan sell are of much higher quality. The clubs from most of the other top-selling countries (except Malaysia) have wholesale prices below $55. There are a few other countries (not among the top 12) that export one or two custom-made clubs to the United States, with prices of $2,000 or more![1] In total, the United States imported $284 million of golf clubs in 2009.

[1] There was one golf club imported from Ireland in 2009 at a price of $2,096, and one club imported from the Netherlands at a price of $4,000.

TABLE 6-1

U.S. Imports and Exports of Golf Clubs, 2009 This table shows the value, quantity, and average price for golf clubs imported into and exported from the United States. Many of the same countries both sell golf clubs to and buy golf clubs from the United States, illustrating what we call intra-industry trade.

(a) IMPORTS

Rank	Country	Value of Imports (millions)	Quantity of Golf Clubs (thousands)	Average Price ($/club)
1	China	$254.2	14,482	18
2	Thailand	13.5	132	102
3	Vietnam	7.2	504	14
4	Japan	5.8	47	125
5	Taiwan	1.1	69	16
6	Malaysia	1.1	12	89
7	Mexico	0.3	40	8
8	Hong Kong	0.3	16	18
9	Macao	0.2	5	43
10	United Kingdom	0.1	12	10
11	Canada	0.1	3	25
12	Korea	0.1	1	54
13-25	Various countries	0.1	11	8
	All 25 countries	284.2	15,335	19

(b) EXPORTS

Rank	Country	Value of Imports (millions)	Quantity of Golf Clubs (thousands)	Average Price ($/club)
1	Canada	$64.9	837	77
2	Japan	41.7	430	97
3	United Kingdom	35.8	446	80
4	Korea	33.9	419	81
5	Australia	14.1	189	75
6	Singapore	6.8	65	104
7	Hong Kong	6.7	72	92
8	Argentina	2.7	35	77
9	Malaysia	2.5	31	83
10	South Africa	2.3	25	93
11	Netherlands	1.8	18	102
12	Thailand	1.7	22	77
13-83	Various countries	11.3	136	83
	All 83 countries	226.2	2,725	83

Source: U.S. International Trade Commission Interactive Tariff and Trade DataWeb at http://dataweb.usitc.gov/.

On the export side, shown in panel (b), the top destination for U.S. clubs is Canada, followed by Japan and the UnitedKingdom (with its world-famous golf courses in Scotland). Notice that these three countries are also among the top 12 countries selling golf clubs to the United States. The average price for U.S. exports varies between $75 and $104 per club, higher than the price of all the imported clubs except those from Thailand, Japan, and Malaysia, which suggests that the United States is exporting high-quality clubs.

Many of the countries that sell to the United States also buy from the United States: 7 of the top 12 selling countries were also among the top 12 countries buying U.S. golf clubs in 2009. Of the top 25 selling countries, 24 also bought U.S. golf clubs. In fact, the value of U.S. imports ($284 million) and the value of U.S. exports ($226 million) are similar. Why does the United States export and import golf clubs to and from the same countries? The answer to this question is one of the "new" explanations for trade that we study in this chapter and the next. The Ricardian model (Chapter 2) and the Heckscher-Ohlin model (Chapter 4) explained why nations would either import or export a good, but those models do not predict the simultaneous import and export of a product, as we observe for golf clubs and many other goods.

To explain why countries import and export the same product , we need to change some assumptions made in the Ricardian and Heckscher-Ohlin models. In those models, we assumed that markets were perfectly competitive, which means there are many small producers, each producing a homogeneous (identical) product, so none of them can influence the market price for the product. As we know just from walking down the aisles in a grocery or department store, most goods are **differentiated goods;** that is, they are not identical. Based on price differences in Table 6-1, we can see that the traded golf clubs are of different types and quality. So in this chapter, we drop the assumption that the goods are homogeneous, as in perfect competition, and instead will assume that goods are differentiated and allow for **imperfect competition,** in which case firms can influence the price that they charge.

The new explanation for trade explored in this chapter involves a type of imperfect competition called **monopolistic competition,** which has two key features. The first feature, just mentioned, is that the goods produced by different firms are differentiated. By offering different products, firms are able to exert some control over the price they can charge for their particular product. Because the market in which the firms operate is not a perfectly competitive one, they do not have to accept the market price, and by increasing their price, they do not lose all their business to competitors. On the other hand, because these firms are not monopolists (i.e., they are not the only firm that produces this type of product), they cannot charge prices as high as a monopolist would. When firms produce differentiated products, they retain some ability to set the price for their product, but not as much as a monopolist would have.

The second feature of monopolistic competition is **increasing returns to scale,** by which we mean that the average costs for a firm fall as more output is produced. For this reason, firms tend to specialize in the product lines that are most successful—by selling more of those products, the average cost for the production of the successful products falls. Firms can lower their average costs by selling more in their home markets but can possibly attain even lower costs from selling more in foreign markets through exporting. So increasing returns to scale create a reason for trade to occur even when the trading countries are similar in their technologies and factor endowments. Increasing returns to scale set the monopolistic competition trade model apart from the logic of the Ricardian and Heckscher-Ohlin models.

In this chapter, we describe a model of trade under monopolistic competition that incorporates these features of product differentiation and increasing returns to scale. After describing the monopolistic competition model, the next goal of the chapter is to discuss how this model helps us to explain trade patterns that we observe today. In our golf club example, countries specialize in different varieties of the same type of product and trade them; this type of trade is called **intra-industry trade** because it deals with imports and exports in the same industry. The monopolistic competition model explains this trade pattern and also predicts that larger countries will trade more with one another. Just as the force of gravity is strongest between two large objects, the monopolistic competition model implies that large countries (as measured by their GDP) should trade the most.[2] There is a good deal of empirical evidence to support this prediction, which is called the **gravity equation.**

The monopolistic competition model also helps us to understand the effects of **free-trade agreements,** in which free trade occurs among a group of countries. In this chapter, we use the North American Free Trade Agreement (NAFTA) to illustrate the predictions of the monopolistic competition model. The policy implications of free-trade agreements are discussed later in a later chapter.

1 Basics of Imperfect Competition

Monopolistic competition incorporates some aspects of a monopoly (firms have control over the prices they charge) and some aspects of perfect competition (many firms are selling). Before presenting the monopolistic competition model, it is useful to review the case of monopoly, which is a single firm selling a product. The monopoly firm faces the industry demand curve. After that, we briefly discuss the case of **duopoly,** when there are two firms selling a product. Our focus will be on the demand facing each of the two firms. Understanding what happens to demand in a duopoly will help us understand how demand is determined when there are many firms selling differentiated products, as occurs in monopolistic competition.

Monopoly Equilibrium

In Figure 6-1, the industry demand curve is shown by *D*. For the monopolist to sell more, the price must fall, and so the demand curve slopes downward. This fall in price means that the extra revenue earned by the monopolist from selling another unit is less than the price of that unit—the extra revenue earned equals the price charged for that unit *minus* the fall in price times the quantity sold of all earlier units. The extra revenue earned from selling one more unit is called the **marginal revenue** and is shown by the curve *MR* in Figure 6-1. The marginal revenue curve lies below the demand curve *D* because the extra revenue earned from selling another unit is less than the price.

To maximize its profits, the monopolist sells up to the point at which the marginal revenue *MR* earned from selling one more unit equals the **marginal cost** *MC* of producing one more unit. In Figure 6-1, the marginal cost curve is shown by

[2] If you have read Chapter 1, you will know that large countries do indeed trade the most, as seen in the map of world trade.

FIGURE 6-1

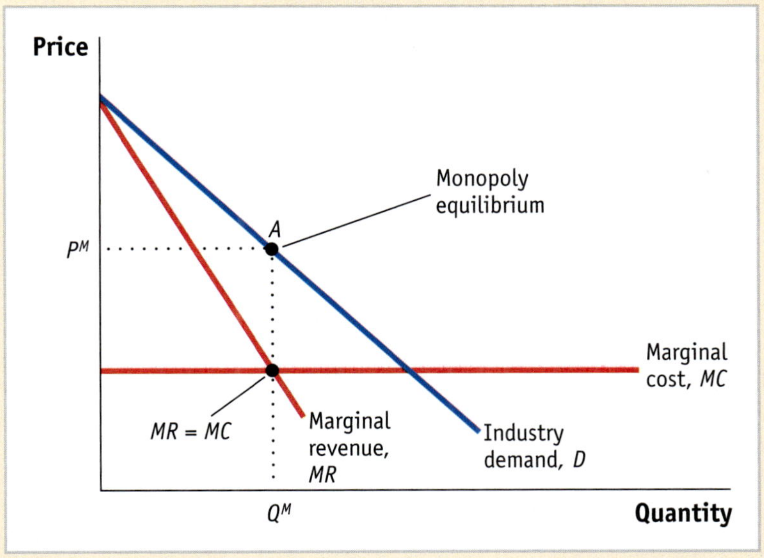

Monopoly Equilibrium The monopolist chooses the profit-maximizing quantity, Q^M, at which marginal revenue equals marginal cost. From that quantity, we trace up to the demand curve and over to the price axis to see that the monopolist charges the price P^M. The monopoly equilibrium is at point *A*.

MC. Because we have assumed, for simplicity, that marginal costs are constant, the *MC* curve is flat, although this does not need to be the case. To have marginal revenue equal marginal costs, the monopolist sells the quantity Q^M. To find the profit-maximizing price the monopolist charges, we trace up from quantity Q^M to point *A* on the demand curve and then over to the price axis. The price charged by the monopolist P^M is the price that allows the monopolist to earn the highest level of profits and is therefore the monopoly equilibrium.

Demand with Duopoly

Let us compare a monopoly with a duopoly, a market structure in which two firms are selling a product. We will not solve for the duopoly equilibrium but will just study how the introduction of a second firm affects the demand facing each of the firms. Knowing how demand is affected by the introduction of a second firm will help us understand how demand is determined when there are many firms, as there are in monopolistic competition.

In Figure 6-2, the industry faces the demand curve *D*. If there are two firms in the industry and they charge the same price, then the demand curve facing each firm is *D*/2. For example, if both firms charged the price P_1, then the industry demand is at point *A*, and each firm's demand is at point *B* on curve *D*/2. The two firms share the market equally, each selling exactly one-half of the total market demand, $Q_2 = Q_1/2$.

If one firm charges a price different from the other firm, however, the demand facing both firms changes. Suppose that one firm charges a lower price P_2, while the other firm keeps its price at P_1. If the firms are selling the same homogeneous product, then the firm charging the lower price would get all the demand (shown by point *C*), which is Q_3 at the price P_2. Now suppose that the products are not homogeneous but instead are differentiated. In that case, the firm with the lower price P_2 will

FIGURE 6-2

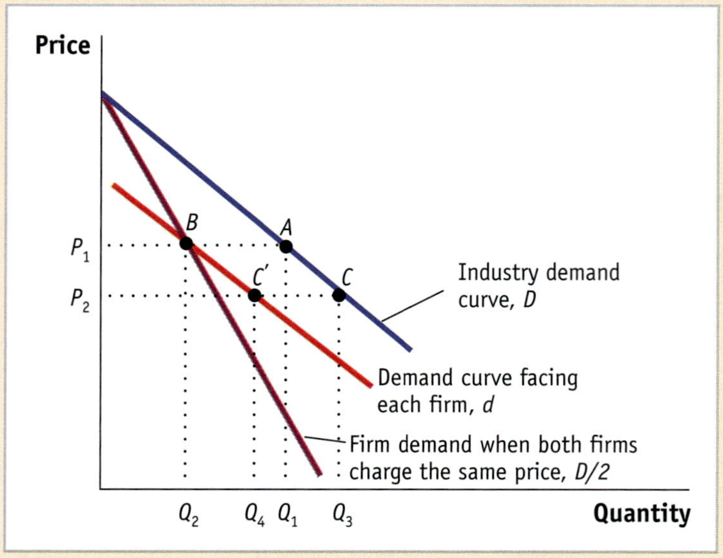

Demand Curves with Duopoly When there are two firms in the market and they both charge the same price, each firm faces the demand curve $D/2$. At the price P_1, the industry produces Q_1 at point A and each firm produces $Q_2 = Q_1/2$ at point B. If both firms produce identical products and one firm lowers its price to P_2, all consumers will buy from that firm only; the firm that lowers its price will face the demand curve, D, and sell Q_3 at point C. Alternatively, if the products are differentiated, the firm that lowers its price will take some, but not all, sales from the other firm; it will face the demand curve, d, and at P_2 it will sell Q_4 at point C'.

capture more of the market than the firm with the higher price P_1, but will not capture the entire market. Because the products are not precisely the same (for instance, in our golf club example the higher-priced club is of better quality than the less expensive club), some consumers will still want to buy the other firm's product even though its price is higher. The firm selling at the lower price P_2 now sells the quantity Q_4, for example, at point C'.

The demand curve d is the demand curve for the firm that lowered its price from P_1 to P_2, even though the other firm held its price at P_1. As we have illustrated, the demand curve d is *flatter* than the demand curve $D/2$. This means that each firm faces a more elastic demand curve than $D/2$: when only one firm lowers its price, it increases its quantity sold by more than when all firms lower their prices. Not only is the quantity demanded in the industry increasing, but in addition, the firm lowering its price is taking away some of the quantity demanded from the other firm. In summary, the demand curve d facing each firm producing in a duopoly is more elastic than the demand curve $D/2$ it faces when the firms charge the same price.

2 Trade under Monopolistic Competition

We begin our study of monopolistic competition by carefully stating the assumptions of the model, which are as follows:

Assumption 1: Each firm produces a good that is similar to but differentiated from the goods that other firms in the industry produce.

Because each firm's product is somewhat different from the goods of the other firms, a firm can raise its prices without losing all its customers to other firms. Thus, each firm faces a downward-sloping demand curve for its product and has some control over the price it charges. This is different from perfect competition, in which all firms produce exactly the same product and therefore must sell at exactly the same market-determined price.

Assumption 2: There are many firms in the industry.

The discussion of duopoly demand in the previous section helps us to think about the demand curve facing a firm under monopolistic competition, when there are many firms in the industry. If the number of firms is *N*, then *D*/*N* is the share of demand that each firm faces when the firms are all charging the same price. When only one firm lowers its price, however, it will face a flatter demand curve *d*. We will begin describing the model by focusing on the demand curve *d* and later bring back the demand curve *D*/*N*.

The first two assumptions are about the demand facing each firm; the third assumption is about each firm's cost structure:

Assumption 3: Firms produce using a technology with increasing returns to scale.

The assumptions underlying monopolistic competition differ from our usual assumptions on firm costs by allowing for increasing returns to scale, a production technology in which the average costs of production fall as the quantity produced increases. This relationship is shown in Figure 6-3, in which average costs are labeled AC. The assumption that average costs fall as quantity increases means that marginal costs, labeled *MC*, must be *below* average costs. Why? Think about whether a new student coming into your class will raise or lower the class average grade. If the new student's average is below the existing class average, then when he or she enters, the class average will fall. In the same way, when *MC* is less than *AC*, then *AC* must be falling.[3]

FIGURE 6-3

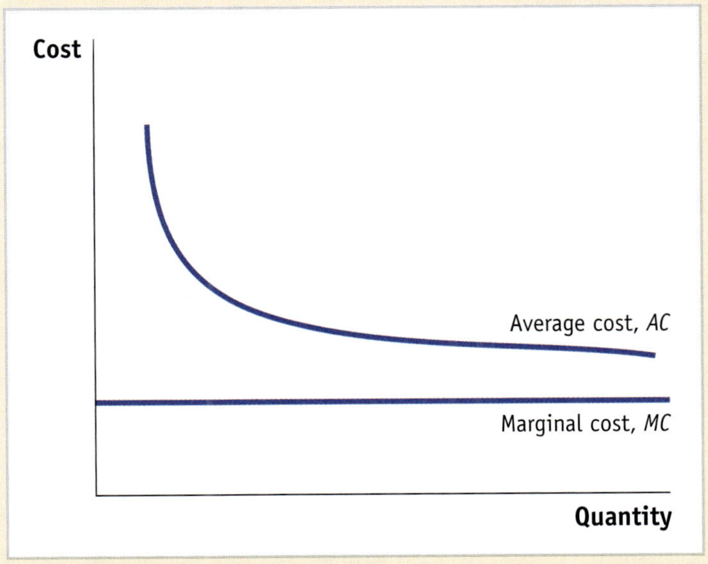

Increasing Returns to Scale This diagram shows the average cost, *AC*, and marginal cost, *MC*, of a firm. Increasing returns to scale cause average costs to fall as the quantity produced increases. Marginal cost is below average cost and is drawn as constant for simplicity.

[3] For simplicity, we assume that marginal costs are constant, but this need not be the case.

Numerical Example As an example of the cost curves in Figure 6-3, suppose that the firm has the following cost data:

Fixed costs = $100

Marginal costs = $10 per unit

Given these costs, the average costs for this firm for various quantities are as shown in Table 6-2.

Notice that as the quantity produced rises, average costs fall and eventually become close to the marginal costs of $10 per unit, as shown in Figure 6-3.

Assumption 3 means that average cost is above marginal cost. Assumption 1 means that firms have some control over the price they charge and these firms charge a price that is also above marginal cost (we learn why in a later section).

Whenever the price charged is above average costs, then a firm earns **monopoly profits.** Our final assumption describes what happens to profits in a monopolistically competitive industry in the long run:

Assumption 4: Because firms can enter and exit the industry freely, monopoly profits are zero in the long run.

Recall that under perfect competition, we assume there are many firms in the industry and that in a long-run equilibrium each firm's profits must be zero. In monopolistic competition, there is the same requirement for a long-run equilibrium. We assume that firms can enter and exit the industry freely; this means that firms will enter as long as it is possible to make monopoly profits, and as more firms enter, the profits per firm fall. We will see that this condition leads to a long-run equilibrium in which profits for each firm are zero, just as in perfect competition!

Equilibrium without Trade

Short-Run Equilibrium The short-run equilibrium for a firm under monopolistic competition, shown in Figure 6-4, is similar to a monopoly equilibrium. The demand

TABLE 6-2

Cost Information for the Firm This table illustrates increasing returns to scale, in which average costs fall as quantity rises.

Quantity Q	Variable Costs = $Q \cdot MC$ (MC = $10)	Total Costs = Variable Costs + Fixed Costs (FC = $100)	Average Costs = Total Costs/Quantity
10	$100	$200	$20
20	200	300	15
30	300	400	13.3
40	400	500	12.5
50	500	600	12
100	1,000	1,100	11
Large Q	10 • Q	10 • Q + 100	Close to 10

FIGURE 6-4

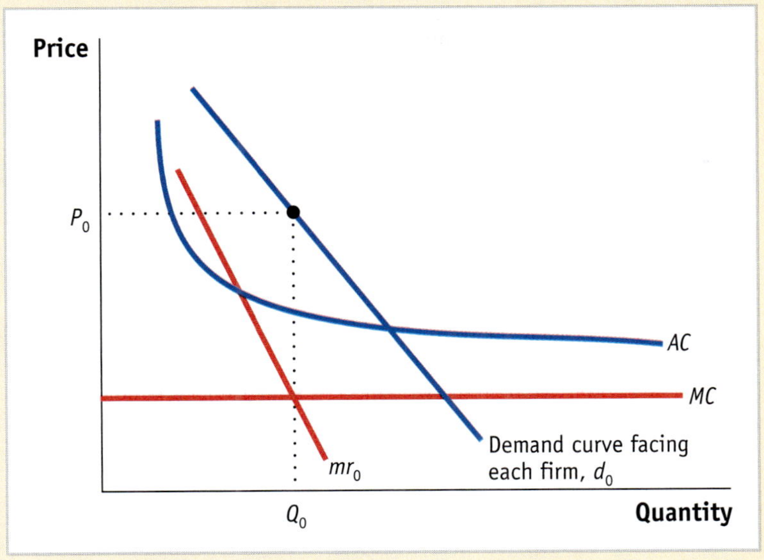

Short-Run Monopolistic Competition Equilibrium without Trade The short-run equilibrium under monopolistic competition is the same as a monopoly equilibrium. The firm chooses to produce the quantity Q_0 at which the firm's marginal revenue, mr_0, equals its marginal cost, *MC*. The price charged is P_0. Because price exceeds average cost, the firm makes monopoly profits.

curve faced by each firm is labeled d_0, the marginal revenue curve is labeled mr_0, and the marginal cost curve of each firm is shown by MC. Each firm maximizes profits by producing Q_0, the quantity at which marginal revenue equals marginal cost. Tracing up from this quantity to the demand curve shows that the price charged by the firms is P_0. Because the price exceeds average costs at the quantity Q_0, the firm earns monopoly profits.

Long-Run Equilibrium In a monopolistically competitive market, new firms continue to enter the industry as long as monopoly profits are earned. In the long run, the entry of new firms draws demand away from existing firms, causing demand curve d_0 to shift to the left until no firm in the industry earns positive monopoly profits (Figure 6-5). Moreover, when new firms enter and there are more product varieties available to consumers, the d_0 curve faced by each firm becomes more elastic, or flatter. We expect the d_0 curve to become more elastic as more firms enter because each product is similar to the other existing products; therefore, as the number of close substitutes increases, consumers become more price-sensitive.

New firms continue to enter the industry until the price charged by each firm is on the average cost curve and monopoly profits are zero. At this point, the industry is in a long-run equilibrium, with no reason for any further entry or exit. The long-run equilibrium without trade is shown in Figure 6-5. Again, the demand curve for the firm is labeled d, with the short-run demand curve denoted d_0 and the long-run demand curve denoted d_1 (with corresponding marginal revenue curve mr_1). Marginal revenue equals marginal cost at quantity Q_1. At this quantity, all firms in the industry charge price P^A. The price P^A equals average cost at point A, where the demand curve d_1 is tangent to the average cost curve. Because the price equals average costs, the firm is earning zero monopoly profits and there is no incentive for firms to enter or exit the industry. Thus, point A is the firm's (and the industry's) long-run equilibrium without trade. Notice that the long-run equilibrium curve d_1 is to the left of and more elastic (flatter) than the short-run curve d_0.

FIGURE 6-5

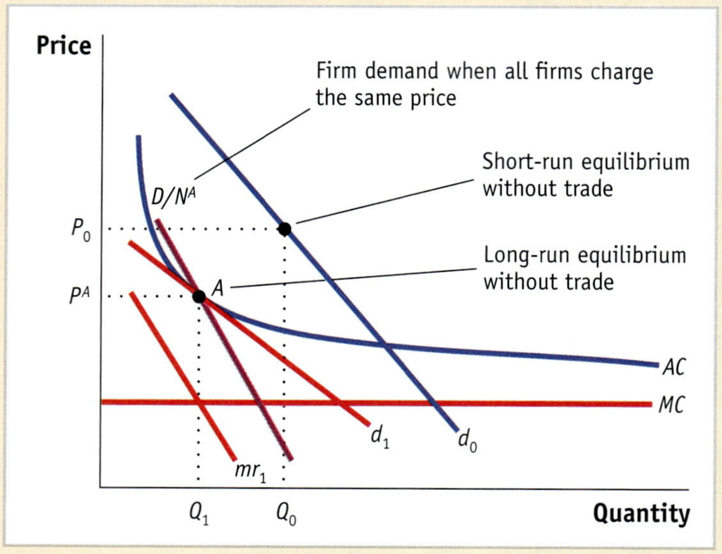

Long-Run Monopolistic Competition Equilibrium without Trade Drawn by the possibility of making profits in the short-run equilibrium, new firms enter the industry and the firm's demand curve, d_0, shifts to the left and becomes more elastic (i.e., flatter), shown by d_1. The long-run equilibrium under monopolistic competition occurs at the quantity Q_1 where the marginal revenue curve, mr_1 (associated with demand curve d_1), equals marginal cost. At that quantity, the no-trade price, P^A, equals average costs at point A. In the long-run equilibrium, firms earn zero monopoly profits and there is no entry or exit. The quantity produced by each firm is less than in short-run equilibrium (Figure 6-4). Q_1 is less than Q_0 because new firms have entered the industry. With a greater number of firms and hence more varieties available to consumers, the demand for each variety d_1 is less then d_0. The demand curve D/N^A shows the no-trade demand when all firms charge the same price.

Before we allow for international trade, we need to introduce another curve into Figure 6-5. The firm's demand curve d_1 shows the quantity demanded depending on the price charged by that firm, holding the price charged by all other firms fixed. In contrast, there is another demand curve that shows the quantity demanded from each firm when all firms in the industry charge the *same price*. This other demand curve is the total market demand D divided by the number of firms in the absence of trade N^A. In Figure 6-5, we label the second demand curve as D/N^A. We omit drawing total industry demand D itself so we do not clutter the diagram.

The demand curve d_1 is flatter, or more elastic, than the demand curve D/N^A. We discussed why that is the case under duopoly (see Figure 6-2) and can review the reason again now. Starting at point A, consider a drop in the price by just one firm, which increases the quantity demanded along the d_1 curve for that firm. The demand curve d_1 is quite elastic, meaning that the drop in price leads to a large increase in the quantity purchased because customers are attracted away from other firms. If instead all firms drop their price by the same amount, along the curve D/N^A, then each firm will not attract as many customers away from other firms. When all firms drop their prices equally, then the increase in quantity demanded from each firm along industry curve D/N^A is less than the increase along the firm's curve d_1. Thus, demand is less elastic along the demand curve D/N^A, which is why it is steeper than the d_1 curve. As we proceed with our analysis of opening trade under monopolistic competition, it will be helpful to keep track of both of these demand curves.

Equilibrium with Free Trade

Let us now allow for free trade between Home and Foreign in this industry. For simplicity, we assume that Home and Foreign countries are exactly the same, with the same number of consumers, the same factor endowments, the same technology and cost curves, and the same number of firms in the no-trade equilibrium. If there were no increasing returns to scale, there would be no reason at all for international trade to occur. Under the Ricardian model, for example, countries with identical technologies would not trade because their no-trade relative prices would be equal. Likewise, under the Heckscher-Ohlin model, countries with identical factor endowments would not trade because their no-trade relative prices would be the same. Under monopolistic competition, however, two identical countries will still engage in international trade because increasing returns to scale exist.

Short-Run Equilibrium with Trade We will take as given the number of firms in the no-trade equilibrium in each country N^A and use this number of firms to determine the short-run equilibrium with trade. Our starting point is the long-run equilibrium without trade, as shown by point A in Figure 6-5 and reproduced in Figure 6-6. When we allow free trade between Home and Foreign, the number of consumers available to each firm doubles (because there is an equal number of consumers in each country) as does the number of firms (because there is an equal number of firms in each country). Because there are not only twice as many consumers but also twice as many firms, the demand curve D/N^A is the same as it was before, $2D/2N^A = D/N^A$. In other words, point A is still on the demand curve D/N^A, as shown in Figure 6-6.

Free trade doubles the number of firms, which also doubles the product varieties available to consumers. With a greater number of product varieties available to consumers, their demand for each individual variety will be *more elastic*. That is, if one firm drops its price below the no-trade price P^A, then it can expect to attract an even greater number of customers away from other firms. Before trade the firm would attract additional Home customers only, but after trade it will attract additional Home and Foreign consumers. In Figure 6-6, this consumer response is shown by the firm's new demand curve d_2, which is more elastic than its no-trade demand curve d_1. As a result, the demand curve d_2 is no longer tangent to the average cost curve at point A

FIGURE 6-6

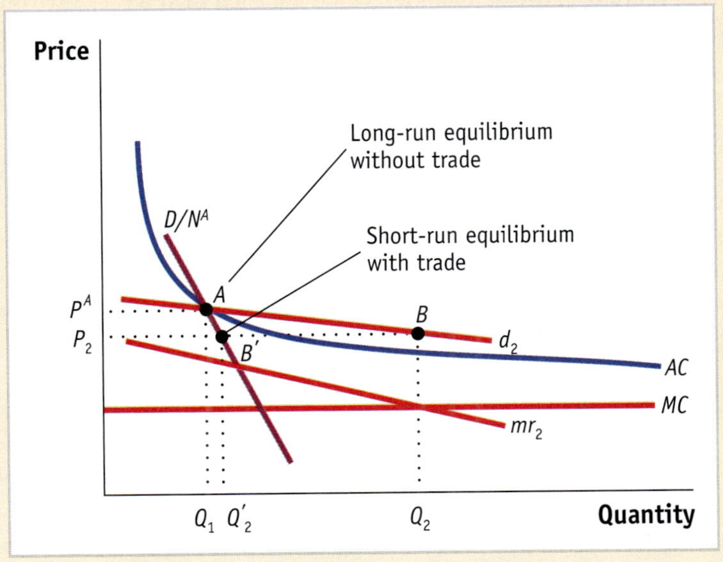

Short-Run Monopolistic Competition Equilibrium with Trade When trade is opened, the larger market makes the firm's demand curve more elastic, as shown by d_2 (with corresponding marginal revenue curve, mr_2). The firm chooses to produce the quantity Q_2 at which marginal revenue equals marginal costs; this quantity corresponds to a price of P_2. With sales of Q_2 at price P_2, the firm will make monopoly profits because price is greater than AC. When *all* firms lower their prices to P_2, however, the relevant demand curve is D/N^A, which indicates that they can sell only Q'_2 at price P_2. At this short-run equilibrium (point B'), price is less than average cost and all firms incur losses. As a result, some firms are forced to exit the industry.

but is *above* average costs for prices below P^A. The new demand curve d_2 has a corresponding marginal revenue curve mr_2, as shown in Figure 6-6.

With the new demand curve d_2 and new marginal revenue curve mr_2, the firm again needs to choose its profit-maximizing level of production. As usual, that level will be where marginal revenue equals marginal cost at Q_2. When we trace from Q_2 up to point B on the firm's demand curve d_2, then over to the price axis, we see that the firm will charge P_2. Because P_2 is above average costs at point B, the firm will make positive monopoly profits. We can see clearly the firm's incentive to lower its price: at point A it earns zero monopoly profits and at point B it earns positive profits. Producing Q_2 and selling it at P_2 is the firm's profit-maximizing position.

This happy scenario for the firm is not the end of the story, however. *Every* firm in the industry (in both Home and Foreign) has the same incentive to lower its price in the hope of attracting customers away from all the other firms and earning monopoly profits. When all firms lower their prices at the same time, however, the quantity demanded from each firm increases along the demand curve D/N^A, not along d_2. Remember that the D/N^A curve shows the demand faced by each firm when all firms in the industry charge the same price. With the prices of all firms lowered to P_2, they will each sell the quantity Q'_2 at point B' rather than their expected sales of Q_2 at point B. At point B', the price charged is *less than* average costs, so every firm is incurring a loss. In the short-run equilibrium with trade, firms lower their prices, expecting to make profits at point B, but end up making losses at point B'.

Point B' is not the long-run equilibrium because the losses will bankrupt some firms and cause them to exit from the industry. This exit will increase demand (both d and D/N^A) for the remaining firms and decrease the number of product varieties available to consumers. To understand where the new long-run equilibrium occurs, we turn to a new diagram.

Long-Run Equilibrium with Trade Due to the exit of firms, the number of firms remaining in each country after trade is less than it was before trade. Let us call the number of firms in each country after trade is opened N^T, where $N^T < N^A$. This reduction in the number of firms increases the share of demand facing each one, so that $D/N^T > D/N^A$. In Figure 6-7, the demand D/N^T facing each firm lies to the right of the demand D/N^A in the earlier figures. We show the long-run equilibrium with trade at point C. At point C, the demand curve d_3 facing an individual firm is tangent to the average cost curve AC. In addition, the marginal revenue curve mr_3 intersects the marginal cost curve MC.

How does this long-run equilibrium compare to that without trade? First of all, despite the exit of some firms in each country, we still expect that the world number of products, which is $2N^T$ (the number produced in each country N^T times two countries), exceeds the number of products N^A available in each country before trade, $2N^T > N^A$. It follows that the demand curve d_3 facing each firm must be more elastic than demand d_1 in the absence of trade: the availability of imported products makes consumers more price-sensitive than they were before trade, so the demand curve d_3 is more elastic than demand d_1 in Figure 6-5. At free-trade equilibrium (point C), each firm still in operation charges a lower price than it did with no trade, $P^W < P^A$, and produces a higher quantity, $Q_3 > Q_1$. The drop in prices and increase in quantity for each firm go hand in hand: as the quantity produced by each surviving firm increases, average costs fall due to increasing returns to scale, and so do the prices charged by firms.

FIGURE 6-7

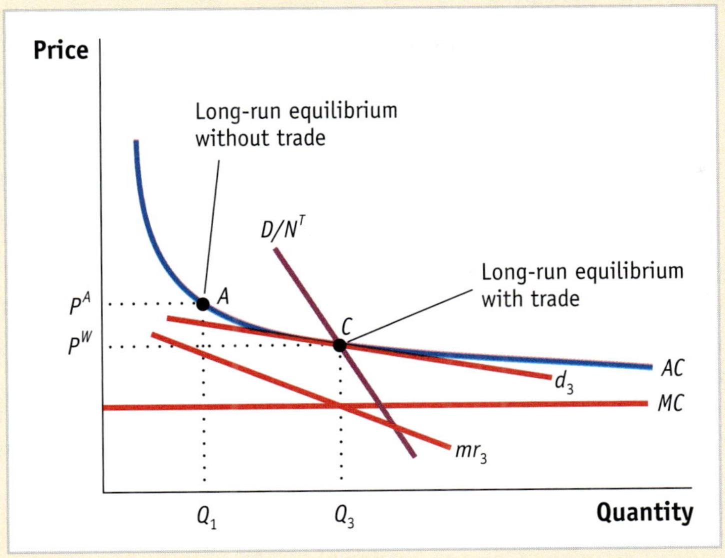

Long-Run Monopolistic Competition Equilibrium with Trade The long-run equilibrium with trade occurs at point C. At this point, profits are maximized for each firm producing Q_3 (which satisfies $mr_3 = MC$) and charging price P^W (which equals AC). Since monopoly profits are zero when price equals average cost, no firms enter or exit the industry. Compared with the long-run equilibrium without trade (Figure 6-5), d_3 (along with mr_3) has shifted out as domestic firms exited the industry and has become more elastic due to the greater total number of varieties with trade, $2N^T > N^A$. Compared with the long-run equilibrium without trade at point A, the trade equilibrium at point C has a lower price and higher sales by all surviving firms.

Gains from Trade The long-run equilibrium at point C has two sources of gains from trade for consumers. First, the price has fallen as compared with point A, so consumers benefit for that reason. A good way to think about this drop in the price is that it reflects increasing returns to scale, with average costs falling as the output of firms rises. The drop in average costs is a rise in productivity for these surviving firms because output can be produced more cheaply. So consumers gain from the drop in price, which is the result of the rise in productivity.

There is a second source of gains from trade to consumers. We assume that consumers obtain higher surplus when there are more product varieties available to buy, and hence the increase in variety is a source of gain for consumers. Within each country, some firms exit the market after trade begins, so fewer product varieties are produced by the remaining domestic firms. However, because consumers can buy products from both Home and Foreign firms, the *total* number of varieties available with trade is greater than the number of varieties available in any one country before trade, $2N^T > N^A$. Thus, in addition to the drop in prices, there is an added consumer gain from the availability of additional product varieties.

Adjustment Costs from Trade Against these long-run gains from trade, there are short-run adjustment costs as some firms in each country shut down and exit the industry. The workers in those firms will experience a spell of unemployment as they look for new jobs. Over the long run, however, we expect these workers to find new positions, so we view these costs as temporary. We do not build these adjustment costs into the model because they are short-term, but we are still interested in how large these costs might be in practice. To compare the short-run adjustment costs with the long-run gains from trade, we next look at the evidence from Canada, Mexico, and the United States under the North American Free Trade Agreement. We will see that the predictions of the monopolistic competition model hold reasonably well in each case.

3 The North American Free Trade Agreement

The idea that free trade will expand the range of products available to consumers is not new—it is even mentioned by David Ricardo in the quote at the beginning of this chapter. But the ability to carefully model the effects of trade under monopolistic competition *is* new and was developed in research during the 1980s by Professors Elhanan Helpman, Paul Krugman, and the late Kelvin Lancaster. That research was not just theoretical but was used to shed light on free-trade agreements, which guarantee free trade among a group of countries. In 1989, for example, Canada and the United States entered into a free-trade agreement, and in 1994 they were joined by Mexico in the North American Free Trade Agreement (NAFTA). The potential for Canadian firms to expand their output (and enjoy lower average costs) by selling in the United States and Mexico was a key factor in Canada's decision to enter into these free-trade agreements. The quote from the Canadian economist Daniel Trefler at the beginning of the chapter shows that there was indeed a rise in productivity in Canada because of the free-trade agreements. We use NAFTA to illustrate the gains and costs predicted by the monopolistic competition model.

Gains and Adjustment Costs for Canada under NAFTA

Studies in Canada dating back to the 1960s predicted substantial gains from free trade with the United States because Canadian firms would expand their scale of operations to serve the larger market and lower their costs. A set of simulations based on the monopolistic competition model performed by the Canadian economist Richard Harris in the mid-1980s influenced Canadian policy makers to proceed with the free-trade agreement with the United States in 1989. Enough time has passed since then to look back and see how Canada has fared under the trade agreements with the United States and Mexico.

Headlines: What Happened When Two Countries Liberalized Trade? Pain, then Gain describes what happened in Canada. Using data from 1988 to 1996, Professor Daniel Trefler of the University of Toronto found short-run adjustment costs of 100,000 lost jobs, or 5% of manufacturing employment. Some industries that faced particularly large tariff cuts saw their employment fall by as much as 12%. These are very large declines in employment. Over time, however, these job losses were more than made up for by the creation of new jobs elsewhere in manufacturing, so there were no long-run job losses as a result of the free-trade agreement.

What about long-run gains? Trefler found a large positive effect on the productivity of firms, with productivity rising as much as 15% over eight years in the industries most affected by tariff cuts, or a compound growth rate of 1.9% per year. For manufacturing overall, productivity rose by 6%, for a compound growth rate of 0.7% per year. The difference between these two numbers, which is 1.9 – 0.7 = 1.2% per year, is an estimate of how free trade with the United States affected the Canadian industries most affected by the tariff cuts over and above the impact on other industries. The productivity growth in Canada allowed for a modest rise in real earnings of 3% over the eight-year period. We conclude that the prediction of the monopolistic competition model that surviving firms increase their productivity is confirmed for Canadian manufacturing. Those productivity gains led to a fall in prices for consumers and a rise in real earnings for workers, which demonstrates the first source of the gains from trade. The second source of gains from trade—increased product variety for Canadian consumers—was not measured in the study by Professor Trefler but has been estimated for the United States, as discussed later in this chapter.

HEADLINES

What Happened When Two Countries Liberalized Trade? Pain, Then Gain

The following article is based on an interview with Professor Daniel Trefler, University of Toronto, who studied the impact of the Canada-U.S. Free Trade Agreement on Canadian manufacturing industries.[4]

Economists argue for free trade. They have two centuries of theory and experience to back them up. And they have recent empirical studies of how the liberalization of trade has increased productivity in less-developed countries like Chile and India. Lowering trade barriers, they maintain, not only cuts costs for consumers but aids economic growth and makes the general public better off.

Even so, free trade is a tough sell. . . . "We talk a lot about the benefits of free trade agreements, but when it comes to academics studying it, we know next to nothing in terms of hard-core facts about what happens when two rich countries liberalize trade," Professor Trefler, of the Rotman School of Management at the University of Toronto, said in an interview. His article, "The Long and Short of the Canada-U.S. Free Trade Agreement," uses detailed data on both Canadian industries and individual companies to address these gaps. . . .

Not surprisingly, the Canadian industries that had relied on tariffs to protect them "were hammered" when those barriers disappeared, Professor Trefler said. "They saw their employment fall by 12 percent," he said, meaning one in eight workers lost their jobs. In manufacturing as a whole, the trade agreement reduced employment by 5 percent.

"Employment losses of 5 percent translate into 100,000 lost jobs and strike me as large," he wrote, "not least because only a relatively small number of industries experienced deep tariff concessions." No wonder free trade agreements touch off so much opposition. As painful as those layoffs were, however, the job losses were a short-term effect. Over the long run, employment in Canada did not drop, and manufacturing employment remains more robust than in other industrialized countries.

"Within 10 years, the lost employment was made up by employment gains in other parts of manufacturing," Professor Trefler found. Although low-productivity plants shut down, high-productivity Canadian manufacturers not only expanded into the United States but further improved their operations. Along the way, they hired enough new workers to make up for losses elsewhere. "The average effect of the U.S. tariff cuts on Canadian employment was thus a wash: the employment losses by less-productive firms offset the employment gains by more productive firms," Professor Trefler wrote in an e-mail message, citing further research. . . .

In addition, he said, "there is absolutely no evidence" that the trade agreement worsened income inequality. The big story is that lowering tariffs set off a productivity boom. Formerly sheltered Canadian companies began to compete with and compare themselves with more efficient American businesses. Some went under, but others significantly improved operations. The productivity gains were huge. In the formerly sheltered industries most affected by the tariff cuts, labor productivity jumped 15 percent, at least half from closing inefficient plants. "This translates into an enormous compound annual growth rate of 1.9 percent," he wrote.

But closing plants is not the whole story, or even half of it. Among export-oriented industries, which expanded after the agreement, data from individual plants show an increase in labor productivity of 14 percent. Manufacturing productivity as a whole jumped 6 percent. "The idea that a simple government policy could raise productivity so dramatically is to me truly remarkable," Professor Trefler said.

[4] Daniel Trefler, 2004, "The Long and Short of the Canada-U.S. Free Trade Agreement," *American Economic Review*, 94(4), September, 870–895.

Source: Excerpted from Virginia Postrel, "Economic Scene," New York Times, *January 27, 2005, p. C2.*

Gains and Adjustment Costs for Mexico under NAFTA

In the mid-1980s Mexican President Miguel de la Madrid embarked on a program of economic liberalization that included land reform and greater openness to foreign investment. Tariffs with the United States were as high as 100% on some goods, and there were many restrictions on the operations of foreign firms. De la Madrid believed that the economic reforms were needed to boost growth and incomes in

Photo by David McNew/Getty Images

Mexico is waiting for its trucks to be allowed to cross the border for long-haul trips into the United States.

Mexico. Joining NAFTA with the United States and Canada in 1994 was a way to ensure the permanence of the reforms already under way. Under NAFTA, Mexican tariffs on U.S. goods declined from an average of 14% in 1990 to 1% in 2001.[5] In addition, U.S. tariffs on Mexican imports fell as well, though from levels that were much lower to begin with in most industries.

How did the fall in tariffs under NAFTA affect the Mexican economy? We will review the evidence on productivity and wages below, but first, you should read **Headlines: NAFTA Turns 15, Bravo!** This editorial was written in 2009, the fifteenth anniversary of the beginning of NAFTA. There were many editorials written that year from differing viewpoints, critiquing various aspects of NAFTA. This article appeared in a U.S.-based pro-business publication focusing on Latin-American businesses. It makes a number of arguments in favor of NAFTA that we have also discussed, including increasing returns to scale and product variety for consumers. But it also points out some defects of NAFTA, including the tardiness of the United States to allow an open border for trucks from Mexico,[6] and the environmental and labor side agreements (discussed in a later chapter).

Productivity in Mexico As we did for Canada, let us investigate the impact of NAFTA on productivity in Mexico. In panel (a) of Figure 6-8, we show the growth in labor productivity for two types of manufacturing firms: the maquiladora plants, which are close to the border and produce almost exclusively for export to the United States, and all other non-maquiladora manufacturing plants in Mexico.[7] The maquiladora plants should be most affected by NAFTA. In panel (b), we also show what happened to real wages and real incomes.

For the maquiladora plants in panel (a), productivity rose 45% from 1994 (when Mexico joined NAFTA) to 2003, a compound growth rate of 4.1% per year over nine years. For the non-maquiladora plants, productivity rose overall by 25% from 1994 to 2003, 2.5% per year. The difference between these two numbers, which is 1.6% per year, is an estimate of the impact of NAFTA on the productivity of the maquiladora plants over and above the increase in productivity that occurred in the rest of Mexico.

Real Wages and Incomes Real wages in the maquiladora and non-maquiladora plants are shown in panel (b) of Figure 6-8. From 1994 to 1997, there was a fall of more than 20% in real wages in both sectors, despite a rise in productivity in the non-maquiladora sector. This fall in real wages is not what we expect from the monopolistic competition model, so why did it occur?

---

[5] Trade was not completely free in 2001 because the tariff reductions under NAFTA were phased in for periods as long as 15 years. Tariff cuts in the agriculture sector in Mexico had the longest phase-in period.

[6] The U.S. spending bill signed by President Obama in 2009 eliminated a pilot program that would have allowed Mexican long-haul trucks to transport cargo throughout the United States. In retaliation, Mexico imposed tariffs on $2.4 billion worth of American goods. See Elisabeth Malkin, "Nafta's Promise, Unfulfilled," *The New York Times*, March 24, 2009, electronic edition.

[7] Labor productivity for the *maquiladoras* is real value-added per worker and for non-*maquiladoras* is real output per worker. Both are taken from Gary C. Hufbauer and Jeffrey J. Schott, 2005, *NAFTA Revisited: Achievements and Challenges* (Washington, D.C.: Peterson Institute for International Economics), Table 1-9, p. 45.

FIGURE 6-8

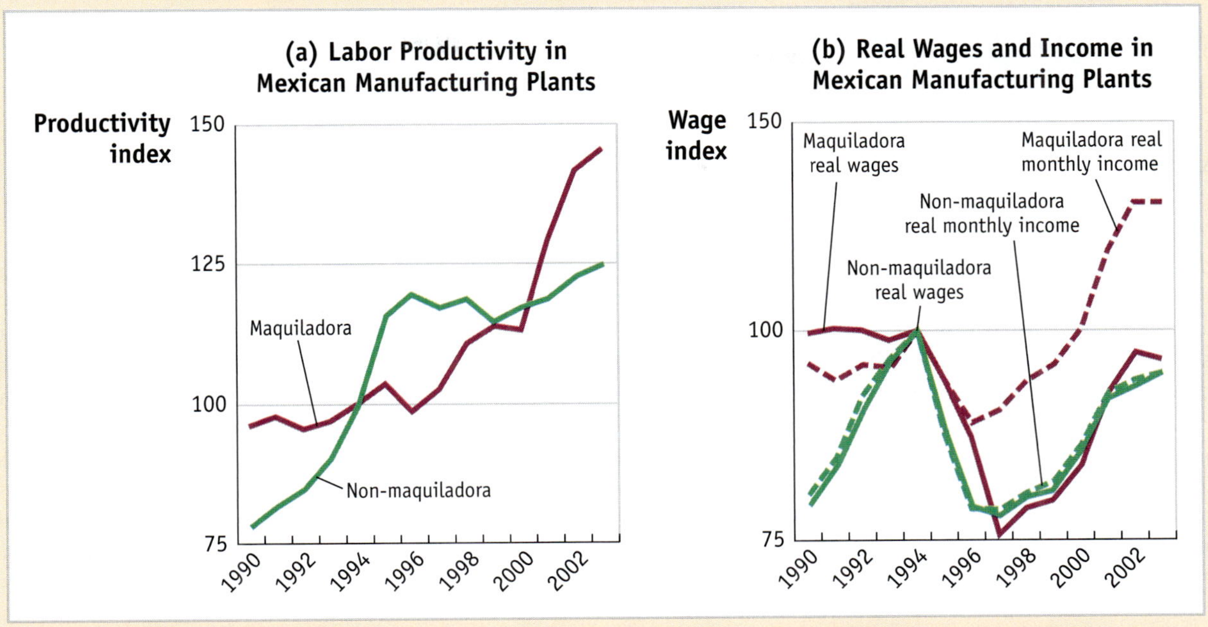

Labor Productivity and Wages in Mexico Panel (a) shows labor productivity for workers in the maquiladora Mexican manufacturing plants and for workers in non-maquiladora plants in the rest of Mexico. Panel (b) shows wages and monthly income for workers in maquiladora and non-maquiladora plants. Productivity and real monthly income grew faster in the maquiladora plants because of increased trade with the United States.

Source: Gary C. Hufbauer and Jeffrey J. Schott, 2005, NAFTA Revisited: Achievements and Challenges *(Washington, D.C.: Peterson Institute for International Economics), p. 45.*

Shortly after Mexico joined NAFTA, it suffered a financial crisis that led to a large devaluation of the peso. It would be incorrect to attribute the peso crisis to Mexico's joining NAFTA, even though both events occurred the same year. Prior to 1994 Mexico followed a fixed exchange-rate policy, but in late 1994 it switched to a flexible exchange-rate regime instead, and the peso devalued to much less than its former fixed value. Details about exchange-rate regimes and the reasons for switching from a fixed to flexible exchange rate are covered in international macroeconomics. For now, the key idea is that when the peso's value falls, it becomes more expensive for Mexico to import goods from the United States because the peso price of imports goes up. The Mexican consumer price index also goes up, and as a result, real wages for Mexican workers fall.

The maquiladora sector, located beside the U.S. border, was more susceptible to the exchange-rate change and did not experience much of a gain in productivity over that period because of the increased cost of inputs imported from the United States. Workers in both the maquiladora and non-maquiladora sectors had to pay higher prices for imported goods, which is reflected in higher Mexican consumer prices. So the decline in real wages for workers in both sectors is similar. This decline was short-lived, however, and real wages in both sectors began to rise again in 1998. By 2003 real wages in both sectors had risen to nearly equal their value in 1994. This means that workers in Mexico did not gain or lose due to NAFTA on average: the productivity gains were not shared with workers, which is a disappointing finding, but real wages at least recovered from the effects of the peso crisis.

HEADLINES

NAFTA Turns 15, Bravo!

This editorial discussed the impact of NAFTA on the U.S. and Mexican economies. It appeared in a U.S.-based pro-business publication focusing on Latin-American businesses.

As Americans and Mexicans celebrated the start of a new year yesterday, they had reason to celebrate another milestone as well: The North American Free Trade Agreement (NAFTA) turned 15. Despite the slowdown in both the U.S. and Mexican economies, trade between the two nations was expected to set a new record last year. In the first half of 2008, U.S.-Mexico trade grew by 9.6 percent to $183.7 billion. That follows a record $347 billion in trade in 2007. Compare that to the $81.5 billion in total two-way trade in 1993, the last year before NAFTA was implemented.

NAFTA has without a doubt been the primary reason for that success. It dramatically opened up Mexico's economy to U.S. goods and investments, helping boost revenues for many U.S. companies. At the same time, Mexican companies were able to get duty-free access to the world's largest market, resulting in more sales and more jobs there. The trade growth has meant benefits for both consumers and companies on each side of the border.

While China clearly dominates many of the products we buy in U.S. stores these days, Mexico also plays an important role. Mexico ranks third behind Canada and China among the top exporters to the U.S. market. But Mexico beats China when it comes to buying U.S. goods. During the first ten months last year [2008], Mexico imported U.S. products worth $129.4 billion—or more than twice the $61.0 billion China (with a much larger economy) bought from us. . . .

NAFTA has benefited consumers in the U.S. through greater choice of products, in terms of selection, quality, and price, including many that are less expensive than pre-NAFTA. . . . NAFTA has allowed U.S. manufacturing giants from General Motors to General Electric to use economies of scale for their production lines. Prior to NAFTA, GM's assembly plants in Mexico assembled small volumes of many products, which resulted in high costs and somewhat inferior quality, says Mustafa Mohatarem, GM's chief economist. Now its plants in Mexico specialize in few high-volume products, resulting in low cost and high quality, he points out. The result benefits both U.S. and Mexican consumers. . . .

To be sure, NAFTA is not perfect. For one, it didn't even touch on Mexico's sensitive oil sector, which should have been part of a comprehensive free trade agreement. Neither did it offer any teeth when it came to violations. For example, the shameful U.S. disregard for the NAFTA regulations on allowing Mexican trucks to enter the United States. Only in September last year [2008], as part of a pilot program by the Bush Administration, did the first Mexican trucks enter the United States—after a delay of eight years . . . thanks to opposition from U.S. unions and lawmakers. . . . Many economists also are critical of NAFTA's labor and environmental side agreements, which President Bill Clinton negotiated in order to support the treaty.

However, all in all NAFTA has been of major benefit for both the United States and Mexico. Any renegotiation of NAFTA, as president-elect Barack Obama pledged during last year's campaign, would negatively harm both economies just as they now suffer from economic recession. It would also harm our relations with Mexico, our top trading partner in Latin America. Hopefully, pragmatism will win the day in Washington, D.C. this year, as our new president aims to find a way to get the U.S. economy back on track. Leaving NAFTA alone would be a good start.

In the meantime, we congratulate NAFTA on its 15 years. *Feliz Cumpleaños.*

Source: Editors, Latin Business Chronicle, *January 2, 2009, electronic edition.*

The picture is somewhat better if instead of real wages, we look at real monthly income, which includes higher-income employees who earn salaries rather than wages.[8] In panel (b), for the non-maquiladora sector, the data on real wages and real monthly income move together closely. But in the maquiladora sector, real monthly

[8] Wage data refer to production workers who are involved in assembly-line and similar activities. Income data refer to all employees, including production and nonproduction workers.

incomes were indeed higher in 2003 than in 1994, indicating some gains for workers in the manufacturing plants most affected by NAFTA. This conclusion is reinforced by other evidence from Mexico, which shows that higher-income workers fared better than unskilled workers in the maquiladora sector and better than workers in the rest of Mexico.[9] From this evidence, the higher-income workers in the maquiladora sector gained most from NAFTA in the long run.

Adjustment Costs in Mexico When Mexico joined NAFTA, it was expected that the short-run adjustment costs would fall especially hard on the agricultural sector in Mexico, such as the corn industry, because it would face strong import competition from the United States. For that reason, the tariff reductions in agriculture were phased in over 15 years. The evidence to date suggests that the farmers growing corn in Mexico did not suffer as much as was feared.[10] There were several reasons for this outcome. First, the poorest farmers do not sell the corn they grow but consume it themselves and buy any extra corn they need. These farmers benefited from cheaper import prices for corn from the United States. Second, the Mexican government was able to use subsidies to offset the reduction in income for other corn farmers. Surprisingly, the total production of corn in Mexico rose following NAFTA instead of falling.

Turning to the manufacturing sector, we should again distinguish the maquiladora and non-maquiladora plants. For the maquiladora plants, employment grew rapidly following NAFTA, from 584,000 workers in 1994 to a peak of 1.29 million workers in 2000. After that, however, the maquiladora sector entered a downturn, due to several factors: the United States entered a recession, reducing demand for Mexican exports; China was competing for U.S. sales by exporting products similar to those sold by Mexico; and the Mexican peso became overvalued, making it difficult to export abroad. For all these reasons, employment in the maquiladora sector fell after 2000, to 1.1 million workers in 2003. It is not clear whether we should count this decline in employment as a short-run adjustment cost due to NAFTA, nor is it clear how long it will take the maquiladora sector to recover. What is apparent is that the maquiladora sector faces increasing international competition (not all due to NAFTA), which can be expected to raise the volatility of its output and employment, and that volatility can be counted as a cost of international trade for workers who are displaced.

Gains and Adjustment Costs for the United States under NAFTA

Studies on the effects of NAFTA on the United States have not estimated its effects on the productivity of American firms, perhaps because Canada and Mexico are only two of many export markets for the United States, and it would be hard to identify the impact of their tariff reductions. Instead, to measure the long-run gains from NAFTA and other trade agreements, researchers have estimated the second source of gains from trade: the expansion of import varieties available to consumers. For the United States, we will compare the long-run gains to consumers from expanded product varieties with the short-run adjustment costs from exiting firms and unemployment.

---

[9] Gordon H. Hanson, 2007, "Globalization, Labor Income and Poverty in Mexico." In Ann Harrison, ed., *Globalization and Poverty* (Chicago: University of Chicago Press; Washington, D.C.: National Bureau of Economic Research [NBER]), pp. 417–452.

[10] See Margaret McMillan, Alix Peterson Zwane, and Nava Ashraf, 2007, "My Policies or Yours: Does OECD Support for Agriculture Increase Poverty in Developing Countries?" In Ann Harrison, ed., *Globalization and Poverty* (Chicago: University of Chicago Press; Washington, D.C.: NBER), pp. 183–232.

Expansion of Variety to the United States To understand how NAFTA affected the range of products available to American consumers, Table 6-3 shows the variety of goods Mexico exported to the United States in 1990 and 2001. To interpret these numbers, start with the 1990 export variety in agriculture of 42%. That figure means that 42% of all the agricultural products the United States imported in 1990, from any country, also came from Mexico. For instance, avocados, bananas, cucumbers, and tomatoes imported from various Central or South American countries were also imported to the United States from Mexico. Measuring the variety of products Mexico exported to the United States does not take into account the *amount* that Mexico sells of each product; rather, it counts the *number* of different types of products Mexico sells to the United States as compared with the total number of products the United States imports from all countries.

From 1990 to 2001, the range of agricultural products that Mexico exported to the United States expanded from 42 to 51%. That compound growth rate of 1.9% per year is close to the average annual growth rate for export variety in all industries shown in the last column of Table 6-3, which is 2.2% per year. Export variety grew at a faster rate in the wood and paper industry (with a compound growth rate of 2.6% per year), petroleum and plastics (2.5% growth), and electronics (4.6% growth). The industries in which there has traditionally been a lot of trade between the United States and Mexico—such as machinery and transport (including autos) and textiles and garments—have slower growth in export variety because Mexico was exporting a wide range of products in these industries to the United States even before joining NAFTA.

The increase in the variety of products exported from Mexico to the United States under NAFTA is a source of gains from trade for American consumers. The United States has also imported more product varieties over time from many other countries, too, especially developing countries. According to one estimate, the total number of product varieties imported into the United States from 1972 to 2001 has increased by four times. Furthermore, that expansion in import variety has had the same beneficial impact on consumers as a reduction in import prices of 1.2% per year.[11] That

TABLE 6-3

Mexico's Export Variety to the United States, 1990–2001 This table shows the extent of variety in Mexican exports to the United States, by industry. From 1990 to 2001, export variety grew in every industry, as U.S. tariffs were reduced due to NAFTA. All figures are percentages.

	Agriculture	Textiles and Garments	Wood and Paper	Petroleum and Plastics	Mining and Metals	Machinery and Transport	Electronics	Average
1990	42%	71%	47%	55%	47%	66%	40%	52%
2001	51	83	63	73	56	76	66	67
Annual growth	1.9	1.4	2.6	2.5	1.7	1.3	4.6	2.2

Source: Robert Feenstra and Hiau Looi Kee, 2007, "Trade Liberalization and Export Variety: A Comparison of Mexico and China," The World Economy, *30(1), 5–21.*

[11] Christian Broda and David E. Weinstein, 2006, "Globalization and the Gains from Variety," *Quarterly Journal of Economics*, 121(2), May, 541–585.

equivalent price reduction is a measure of the gains from trade due to the expansion of varieties exported to the United States from all countries.

Unfortunately, we do not have a separate estimate of the gains from the growth of export varieties from Mexico alone, which averages 2.2% per year from Table 6-3. Suppose we use the same 1.2% price reduction estimate for Mexico that has been found for all countries. That is, we assume that the growth in export variety from Mexico leads to the same beneficial impact on U.S. consumers as a reduction in Mexican import prices of 1.2% per year, or about one-half as much as the growth in export variety itself. In 1994, the first year of NAFTA, Mexico exported $50 billion in merchandise goods to the United States and by 2001 this sum had grown to $131 billion. Using $90 billion as an average of these two values, a 1.2% reduction in the prices for Mexican imports would save U.S. consumers $90 billion • 1.2% = $1.1 billion per year. We will assume that all these savings are due to NAFTA, though even without NAFTA, there would likely have been some growth in export variety from Mexico.

It is crucial to realize that these consumer savings are *permanent* and that they *increase over time* as export varieties from Mexico continue to grow. Thus, in the first year of NAFTA, we estimate a gain to U.S. consumers of $1.1 billion; in the second year a gain of $2.2 billion, equivalent to a total fall in prices of 2.4%; in the third year a gain of $3.3 billion; and so on. Adding these up over the first nine years of NAFTA, the total benefit to consumers was $49.5 billion, or an average of $5.5 billion per year. In 2003, the tenth year of NAFTA, consumers would gain by $11 billion as compared with 1994. This gain will continue to grow as Mexico further increases the range of varieties exported to the United States.

Adjustment Costs in the United States Adjustment costs in the United States come as firms exit the market because of import competition and the workers employed by those firms are temporarily unemployed. One way to measure that temporary unemployment is to look at the claims under the U.S. **Trade Adjustment Assistance (TAA)** provisions. The TAA program offers assistance to workers in manufacturing who lose their jobs because of import competition. As we discussed in Chapter 3, the North American Free Trade Agreement included a special extension of TAA to workers laid off due to import competition because of NAFTA.

By looking at claims under that program, we can get an idea of the unemployment caused by NAFTA, one of the short-run costs of the agreement. From 1994 to 2002, some 525,000 workers, or about 58,000 per year, lost their jobs and were certified as adversely affected by trade or investment with Canada or Mexico under the NAFTA-TAA program.[12] As a result, these workers were entitled to additional unemployment benefits. This number is probably the most accurate estimate we have of the temporary unemployment caused by NAFTA.

How large is the displacement of 58,000 workers per year due to NAFTA? We can compare this number with overall job displacement in the United States. Over the three years from January 1999 to December 2001, 4 million workers were displaced, about one-third of whom were in manufacturing. So the annual number of workers displaced in manufacturing was 4 million • $(\frac{1}{3}) \cdot (\frac{1}{3})$ = 444,000 workers per year. Thus,

[12] The information in this paragraph is drawn from Gary Clyde Hufbauer and Jeffrey J. Schott, 2006, *NAFTA Revisited: Achievements and Challenges* (Washington, D.C.: Peterson Institute for International Economics), pp. 38–42.

the NAFTA layoffs of 58,000 workers were about 13% of the total displacement in manufacturing, which is a substantial amount.

Rather than compare the displacement caused by NAFTA with the total displacement in manufacturing, however, we can instead evaluate the wages lost by displaced workers and compare this amount with the consumer gains. In Chapter 3 (see **Application: Manufacturing and Services**), we learned that about two-thirds of workers laid off in manufacturing are reemployed within three years. Some workers are reemployed in less than three years; for some, it takes longer. To simplify the problem, suppose that the *average* length of unemployment for laid-off workers is three years.[13] Average yearly earnings for production workers in manufacturing were $31,000 in 2000, so each displaced worker lost $93,000 in wages (three times the workers' average annual income).[14] Total lost wages caused by displacement would be 58,000 workers displaced per year times $93,000, or $5.4 billion per year during the first nine years of NAFTA.

These private costs of $5.4 billion are nearly equal to the average welfare gains of $5.5 billion per year due to the expansion of import varieties from Mexico from 1994 to 2002, as computed previously. But the gains from increased product variety *continue and grow over time* as new imported products become available to American consumers. Recall from the previous calculation that the gains from the ongoing expansion of product varieties from Mexico were $11 billion in 2003, the tenth year of NAFTA, or twice as high as the $5.4 billion costs of adjustment. As the consumer gains continue to grow, adjustment costs due to job losses fall. Thus, the consumer gains from increased variety, when summed over years, considerably exceed the private losses from displacement. This outcome is guaranteed to occur because the gains from expanded import varieties occur *every year* that the imports are available, whereas labor displacement is a temporary phenomenon.

The calculation we have made shows that the gains to U.S. consumers from greater import variety from Mexico, when summed over time, are more than the private costs of adjustment. In practice, the actual compensation received by workers is much less than their costs of adjustment. In 2002 the NAFTA–TAA program was consolidated with the general TAA program in the United States, so there is no further record of layoffs as a result of NAFTA. Under the Trade Act of 2002, the funding for TAA was increased from $400 million to $1.2 billion per year and some other improvements to the program were made, such as providing a health-care subsidy for laid-off workers. In addition, as part of the jobs stimulus bill signed by President Obama on February 17, 2009, workers in the service sector (as well as farmers) who lose their jobs due to trade can now also apply for TAA benefits, as was discussed in Chapter 3. It would be desirable to continue to expand the TAA program to include more workers who face layoffs due to increased global competition.

Summary of NAFTA In this section, we have been able to measure, at least in part, the long-run gains and short-run costs from NAFTA for Canada, Mexico, and the United States. The monopolistic competition model indicates two sources of gains from trade: the rise in productivity due to expanded output by surviving firms, which leads to lower prices, and the expansion in the overall number of varieties of products

[13] We show in Problem 8 at the end of the chapter that this assumption is accurate.

[14] We are not considering the additional losses if the new job has lower wages than earned previously.

available to consumers with trade, despite the exit of some firms in each country. For Mexico and Canada, we measured the long-run gains by the improvement in productivity for exporters as compared with other manufacturing firms. For the United States, we measured the long-run gains using the expansion of varieties from Mexico, and the equivalent drop in price faced by U.S. consumers. It is clear that for Canada and the United States, the long-run gains considerably exceed the short-run costs. The picture is less optimistic for Mexico because the gains have not been reflected in the growth of real wages for production workers (due in part to the peso crisis). The real earnings of higher-income workers in the maquiladora sector have risen, however, so they have been the principal beneficiaries of NAFTA so far.

4 Intra-Industry Trade and the Gravity Equation

In the monopolistic competition model, countries both import and export different varieties of differentiated goods. This result differs from the Ricardian and Heckscher-Ohlin models that we studied in Chapters 2 and 4: in those models, countries either export or import a good but do not export and import the same good simultaneously. Under monopolistic competition, countries will specialize in producing different varieties of a differentiated good and will trade those varieties back and forth. As we saw from the example of golf clubs at the beginning of the chapter, this is a common trade pattern that we call intra-industry trade.

Index of Intra-Industry Trade

To develop the idea of intra-industry trade, let us go back to the golf club example at the beginning of the chapter. In 2009 the United States imported \$284.2 million in golf clubs and exported \$226.2 million. When the amounts of imports and exports are similar for a good, as they are here, it is an indication that nearly all the trade in that good is intra-industry trade. The **index of intra-industry** trade tells us what proportion of trade in each product involves both imports and exports: a high index (up to 100%) indicates that an equal amount of the good is imported and exported, whereas a low index (0%) indicates that the good is either imported or exported but not both.

The formula for the index of intra-industry trade is

$$(\text{Index of intra-industry trade}) = \frac{\text{Minimum of imports and exports}}{\frac{1}{2}(\text{Imports} + \text{exports})}$$

For golf clubs, shown in Table 6-1, the minimum of imports and exports is \$226.2 million, and the average of imports and exports is $\frac{1}{2}(226.2 + 284.2) = \$255.2$ million. So $\frac{226.2}{255.2} = 89\%$ of the U.S. trade in golf clubs is intra-industry trade; that is, it involves both exporting and importing of golf clubs.

In Table 6-4, we show some other examples of intra-industry trade in other products for the United States. Products such as vaccines, small cars, and whiskey have a high index of intra-industry trade. These are all examples of highly differentiated products: for small cars and whiskey, each exporting country sells products that are different from those of other exporting countries, including the United States. So it is not surprising that we both export and import these products. On the other hand, products such as men's shorts, telephones, natural gas, sunglasses, and apples have a low index of intra-industry trade. Some of these goods are homogeneous, such as

TABLE 6-4

Index of Intra-Industry Trade for the United States, 2009 Shown here are value of imports, value of exports, and the index of intra-industry trade for a number of products. When the value of imports is close to the value of exports, such as for golf clubs, then the index of intra-industry trade is highest, and when a product is mainly imported or exported (but not both), then the index of intra-industry trade is lowest.

Product	Value of Imports ($ millions)	Value of Export ($ millions)	Index of Intra-Industry Trade (%)
Golf clubs	284	226	89
Vaccines	2,027	2,763	85
Whiskey	1,166	752	78
Mattresses	133	48	53
Golf carts	29	86	50
Small cars	40,527	11,778	45
Natural gas	12,391	2,790	37
Sunglasses	848	184	36
Frozen orange juice	3	17	33
Apples	139	752	31
Large-passenger aircraft	4,955	31,322	27
Telephones	761	71	17
Men's shorts	542	9	3

Source: U.S. International Trade Commission, Interactive Tariff and Trade DataWeb, at http://dataweb.usitc.gov/.

apples and natural gas. These goods are closer to fitting the assumptions of the Ricardian or Heckscher-Ohlin model of perfect competition with homogeneous goods, which are either imported or exported. Other goods such as fax machines and sunglasses are differentiated but are mostly imported into the United States simply because they can be produced at lower costs abroad. To obtain a high index of intra-industry trade, it is necessary for the good to be differentiated *and* for costs to be similar in the Home and Foreign countries, leading to both imports and exports.

The Gravity Equation

The index of intra-industry trade measures the degree of intra-industry trade for a product but does not tell us anything about the total amount of trade. To explain the value of trade, we need a different equation, called the "gravity equation." This equation was given its name by a Dutch economist and Nobel laureate, Jan Tinbergen. Tinbergen was trained in physics, so he thought about the trade between countries as similar to the force of gravity between objects: Newton's universal law of gravitation states that objects with larger mass, or that are closer to each other, have a greater gravitational pull between them. Tinbergen's gravity equation for trade states that countries with larger GDPs, or that are closer to each other, have more trade between them. Both these equations can be explained simply—even if you have never studied physics, you will be able to grasp their meanings. The point is that just as the force of gravity is strongest between two large objects, the monopolistic competition model predicts that large countries (as measured by their GDP) should trade the most with each other. There is much empirical evidence to support this prediction, as we will show.

Newton's Universal Law of Gravitation Suppose that two objects each have mass M_1 and M_2 and are located distance d apart. According to Newton's universal law of gravitation, the force of gravity F_g between these two objects is

$$F_g = G \cdot \frac{M_1 \cdot M_2}{d^2}$$

where G is a constant that tells us the magnitude of this relationship. The larger each object is, or the closer they are to each other, the greater is the force of gravity between them.

The Gravity Equation in Trade The equation proposed by Tinbergen to explain trade between countries is similar to Newton's law of gravity, except that instead of the mass of two objects, we use the GDP of two countries, and instead of predicting the force of gravity, we are predicting the amount of trade between them. The gravity equation in trade is

$$\text{Trade} = B \cdot \frac{GDP_1 \cdot GDP_2}{dist^n}$$

where Trade is the amount of trade (measured by imports, exports, or their average) between two countries, GDP_1 and GDP_2 are their gross domestic products, and $dist$ is the distance between them. Notice that we use the exponent n on distance, $dist^n$, rather than $dist^2$ as in Newton's law of gravity, because we are not sure of the precise relationship between distance and trade. The term B in front of the gravity equation is a constant that indicates the relationship between the "gravity term" (i.e., $GDP_1 \cdot GDP_2/dist^n$) and Trade. It can also be interpreted as summarizing the effects of all factors (other than size and distance) that influence the amount of trade between two countries; such factors include tariffs (which would lower the amount of trade and reduce B), sharing a common border (which would increase trade and raise B), and so on.

According to the gravity equation, the larger the countries are (as measured by their GDP), or the closer they are to each other, the greater is the amount of trade between them. This connection among economic size, distance, and trade is an implication of the monopolistic competition model that we have studied in this chapter. The monopolistic competition model implies that larger countries trade the most for two reasons: larger countries export more because they produce more product varieties, and they import more because their demand is higher. Therefore, larger countries trade more in both exports and imports.

Deriving the Gravity Equation To explain more carefully why the gravity equation holds in the monopolistic competition model, we can work through some algebra using the GDPs of the various countries. Start with the GDP of Country 1, GDP_1. Each of the goods produced in Country 1 is a differentiated product, so they are different from the varieties produced in other countries. Every other country will demand the goods of Country 1 (because they are different from their home-produced goods), and the amount of their demand will depend on two factors: (1) the relative size of the importing country (larger countries demand more) and (2) the distance between the two countries (being farther away leads to higher transportation costs and less trade).

To measure the relative size of each importing country, we use its share of world GDP. Specifically, we define Country 2's share of world GDP as $Share_2 = GDP_2/GDP_W$. To measure the transportation costs involved in trade, we use distance raised to a power, or $dist^n$. Using these definitions, exports from Country 1 to Country 2 will equal the goods available in Country 1 (GDP_1), times the relative size of Country 2 ($Share_2$), divided by the transportation costs between them ($dist^n$), so that

$$\text{Trade} = B \cdot \frac{GDP_1 \cdot Share_2}{dist^n} = \left(\frac{1}{GDP_W}\right)\frac{GDP_1 \cdot GDP_2}{dist^n}$$

This equation for the trade between Countries 1 and 2 looks similar to the gravity equation, especially if we think of the term $(1/GDP_W)$ as the constant term B. We see from this equation that the trade between two countries will be proportional to their relative sizes, measured by the product of their GDPs (the greater the size of the countries, the larger is trade), and inversely proportional to the distance between them (the smaller the distance, the larger is trade). The following application explores how well the gravity equation works in practice.

APPLICATION

The Gravity Equation for Canada and the United States

We can apply the gravity equation to trade between any pair of countries, or even to trade between the provinces or states of one country and another. Panel (a) of Figure 6-9 shows data collected on the value of trade between Canadian provinces and U.S. states in 1993. On the horizontal axis, we show the gravity term:

$$\text{Gravity term} = \frac{GDP_1 \cdot GDP_2}{dist^{1.25}}$$

where GDP_1 is the gross domestic product of a U.S. state (in billions of U.S. dollars), GDP_2 is the gross domestic product of a Canadian province (in billions of U.S. dollars), and *dist* is the distance between them (in miles). We use the exponent 1.25 on the distance term because it has been shown in other research studies to describe the relationship between distance and trade value quite well. The horizontal axis is plotted as a logarithmic scale, with values from 0.001 to 100. A higher value along the horizontal axis indicates either a large GDP for the trading province and state or a smaller distance between them.

The vertical axis in Figure 6-9 shows the 1993 value of exports (in millions of U.S. dollars) between a Canadian province and U.S. state or between a U.S. state and Canadian province; this is the value of trade for the province–state pair. That axis is also plotted as a logarithmic scale, with values from \$0.001 million (or \$1,000) to \$100,000 million (or \$100 billion) in trade. There are 30 states and 10 provinces included in the study, so there are a total of 600 possible trade flows between them (though some of those flows are zero, indicating that no exporting takes place). Each of the points in panel (a) represents the trade flow and gravity term between one state and one province.

We can see from the set of points in panel (a) that states and provinces with a higher gravity term between them (measured on the horizontal axis) also tend to have more trade (measured on the vertical axis). That strong, positive relationship shown by the set of points in panel (a) demonstrates that the gravity equation holds well empirically. Panel (a) also shows the "best fit" straight line through the set of points, which has the following equation:

FIGURE 6-9

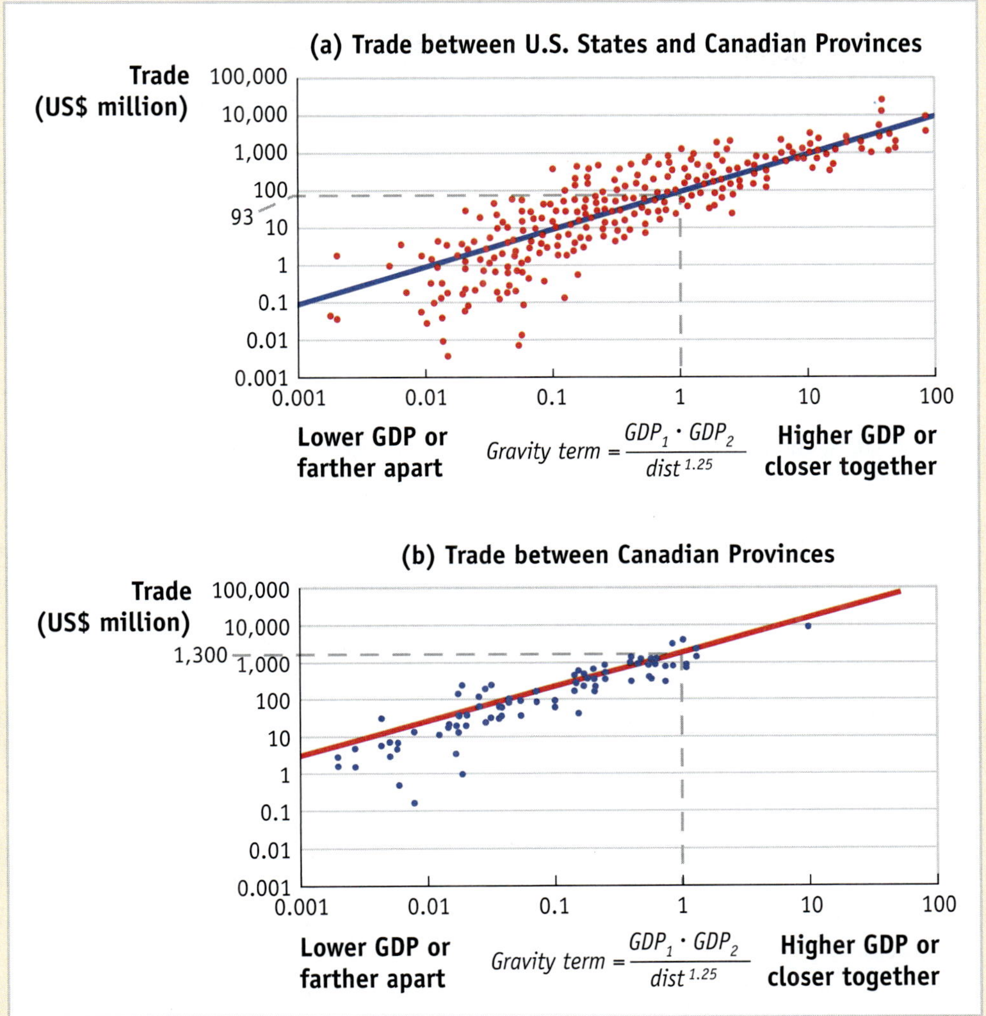

Gravity Equation for the United States and Canada, 1993 Plotted in these figures are the dollar value of exports in 1993 and the gravity term (plotted in log scale). Panel (a) shows these variables for trade between 10 Canadian provinces and 30 U.S. states. When the gravity term is 1, for example, the amount of trade between a province and state is $93 million. Panel (b) shows these variables for trade between 10 Canadian provinces. When the gravity term is 1, the amount of trade between the provinces is $1.3 billion, 14 times larger than between a province and a state. These graphs illustrate two important points: there is a positive relationship between country size (as measured by GDP) and trade volume, and there is much more trade within Canada than between Canada and the United States.

Source: Author's calculations using data from James A. Anderson and Eric van Wincoop, 2003, "Gravity with Gravitas: A Solution to the Border Puzzle," American Economic Review, *170–192.*

$$\text{Trade} = 93\,\frac{GDP_1 \cdot GDP_2}{dist^{1.25}}$$

The constant term $B = 93$ gives the best fit to this gravity equation for Canadian provinces and U.S. states. When the gravity term equals 1, as illustrated in panel (a), then the predicted amount of trade between that state and province is $93 million. The closest example to this point is Alberta and New Jersey. In 1993 there were $94 million in exports from Alberta to New Jersey and they had a gravity term of approximately 1.

Trade within Canada Because the gravity equation works well at predicting international trade between provinces and states in different countries, it should also work well at predicting trade *within* a country, or *intra-national* trade. To explore this idea, panel (b) of Figure 6-9 graphs the value of exports (in millions of U.S. dollars) between any two Canadian provinces, along with the gravity term for those provinces. The scale of the axes in panel (b) is the same as in panel (a). From panel (b), we again see that there is a strong, positive relationship between the gravity term between two provinces (measured on the horizontal axis) and their trade (measured on the vertical axis). The "best fit" straight line through the set of points has the following equation:

$$\text{Trade} = 1{,}300 \cdot \frac{GDP_1 \cdot GDP_2}{dist^{1.25}}$$

That is, the constant term $B = 1{,}300$ gives the best fit to this gravity equation for Canadian provinces. When the gravity term equals 1, as illustrated in panel (b), then the predicted amount of trade between two provinces is $1,300 million, or $1.3 billion. The closest example to this combination is between British Columbia and Alberta: in 1993 their gravity term was approximately 1.3 and British Columbia exported $1.4 billion of goods to Alberta.

Comparing the gravity equation for international trade between Canada and the United States with the gravity equation for intra-national trade in Canada, the constant term for Canadian trade is much bigger—1,300 as compared with 93. Taking the ratio of these two constant terms (1,300/93 = 14), we find that on average there is 14 times more trade *within* Canada than occurs across the border! That number is even higher if we consider an earlier year, 1988, just before Canada and the United States signed the Canada-U.S. Free Trade Agreement in 1989. In 1988 intra-national trade within Canada was 22 times higher than international trade between Canada and the United States.[15] Even though that ratio fell from 1988 to 1993 due to the free-trade agreement between Canada and the United States, it is still remarkable that there is so much more trade *within* Canada than across the border, or more generally, so much more intra-national than international trade.

The finding that trade across borders is less than trade within countries reflects all the barriers to trade that occur between countries. Factors that make it easier or more difficult to trade goods between countries are often called **border effects,** and they include the following:

- Taxes imposed when imported goods enter into a country, **tariffs**
- Limits on the number of items allowed to cross the border, **quotas**
- Other administrative rules and regulations affecting trade, including the time required for goods to clear customs
- Geographic factors such as whether the countries share a border
- Cultural factors such as whether the countries have a common language that might make trade easier

[15] That conclusion comes from John McCallum, 1995, "National Borders Matter," *American Economic Review*, 615–623. The 1993 data used in Figure 6-9 derive from James A. Anderson and Eric van Wincoop, 2003, "Gravity with Gravitas: A Solution to the Border Puzzle," *American Economic Review*, 170–192.

In the gravity equation, all the factors that influence the amount of trade are reflected in the constant B. As we have seen, the value of this constant differs for trade within a country versus trade between countries. In later chapters, we explore in detail the consequences of tariffs, quotas, and other barriers to trade. The lesson from the gravity equation is that such barriers to trade can potentially have a large impact on the amount of international trade as compared with intra-national trade. ■

5 Conclusions

When firms have differentiated products and increasing returns to scale, the potential exists for gains from trade above and beyond those that we studied in earlier chapters under perfect competition. We have demonstrated these additional gains using a model of monopolistic competition. In this model, trade will occur even between countries that are identical because the potential to sell in a larger market will induce firms to lower their prices below those charged in the absence of trade. When all firms lower their prices, however, some firms are no longer profitable and exit the market. The remaining firms expand their output, lowering their average costs through increasing returns to scale. The reduction in average costs lowers the prices charged by firms, creating gains for consumers in the importing country. In addition, because each firm produces a differentiated product, trade between countries allows for the importing of product varieties that are different from those produced domestically, creating a second source of gains for consumers.

When some firms have to exit the market, short-run adjustment costs arise within this model because of worker displacement. Using examples from Canada, Mexico, and the United States, we have argued that the short-run adjustment costs are less than the long-run gains. Regional trade agreements like the North American Free Trade Agreement (NAFTA) are a good application of the monopolistic competition model. Another application is the "gravity equation," which states that countries that are larger or closer to each other will trade more. That prediction is supported by looking at data on trade between countries. Research has also shown that trade within countries is even larger than trade between countries.

KEY POINTS

1. The monopolistic competition model assumes differentiated products, many firms, and increasing returns to scale. Firms enter whenever there are profits to be earned, so profits are zero in the long-run equilibrium.

2. When trade opens between two countries, the demand curve faced by each firm becomes more elastic, as consumers have more choices and become more price-sensitive. Firms then lower their prices in an attempt to capture consumers from their competitors and obtain profits. When all firms do so, however, some firms incur losses and are forced to leave the market.

3. Introducing international trade under monopolistic competition leads to additional gains from trade for two reasons: (i) lower prices as firms expand their output and lower their average costs and (ii) additional imported product varieties available to consumers. There are also short-run adjustment costs, such as unemployment, as some firms exit the market.

4. The assumption of differentiated goods helps us to understand why countries often import and export varieties of the same type of good. That outcome occurs with the model of monopolistic competition.

5. The gravity equation states that countries with higher GDP, or that are close, will trade more. In addition, research has shown that there is more trade within countries than between countries.

KEY TERMS

differentiated goods, p. 169
imperfect competition, p. 169
monopolistic competition, p. 169
increasing returns to scale, p. 169
intra-industry trade, p. 170
gravity equation, p. 170
free-trade agreements, p. 170
duopoly, p. 170
marginal revenue, p. 170
marginal cost, p. 170
monopoly profits, p. 174
Trade Adjustment Assistance (TAA), p. 187
index of intra-industry trade, p. 189
border effects, p. 194
tariffs, p. 194
quotas, p. 194

PROBLEMS

1. Explain how increasing returns to scale in production can be a basis for trade.

2. Why is trade within a country greater than trade between countries?

3. Starting from the long-run equilibrium without trade in the monopolistic competition model, as illustrated in Figure 6-5, consider what happens when the Home country begins trading with two other identical countries. Because the countries are all the same, the number of consumers in the world is three times larger than in a single country, and the number of firms in the world is three times larger than in a single country.
   a. Compared with the no-trade equilibrium, how much does industry demand *D* increase? How much does the number of firms (or product varieties) increase? Does the demand curve D/N^A still apply after the opening of trade? Explain why or why not.
   b. Does the d_1 curve shift or pivot due to the opening of trade? Explain why or why not.
   c. Compare your answer to (b) with the case in which Home trades with only one other identical country. Specifically, compare the elasticity of the demand curve d_1 in the two cases.
   d. Illustrate the long-run equilibrium with trade, and compare it with the long-run equilibrium when Home trades with only one other identical country.

4. Starting from the long-run trade equilibrium in the monopolistic competition model, as illustrated in Figure 6-7, consider what happens when industry demand *D* increases. For instance, suppose that this is the market for cars, and lower gasoline prices generate higher demand *D*.
   a. Redraw Figure 6-7 for the Home market and show the shift in the D/N^T curve and the new short-run equilibrium.
   b. From the new short-run equilibrium, is there exit or entry of firms, and why?
   c. Describe where the new long-run equilibrium occurs, and explain what has happened to the number of firms and the prices they charge.

5. Our derivation of the gravity equation from the monopolistic competition model used the following logic:
   (i) Each country produces many products.
   (ii) Each country demands all of the products that every other country produces.
   (iii) Thus, large countries demand more imports from other countries.

   The gravity equation relationship does not hold in the Heckscher-Ohlin model. Explain how the logic of the gravity equation breaks down in the Heckscher-Ohlin model; that is, which of the statements just listed is no longer true in the Heckscher-Ohlin model?

6. The United States, France, and Italy are among the world's largest producers. To answer the following questions, assume that their markets are monopolistically competitive, and use the gravity equation with $B = 93$ and $n = 1.25$.

	GDP in 2009 ($ billions)	Distance from the United States (miles)
France	2,635	5,544
Italy	2,090	6,229
United States	14,270	—

a. Using the gravity equation, compare the expected level of trade between the United States and France and between the United States and Italy.
b. The distance between Paris and Rome is 694 miles. Would you expect more French trade with Italy or with the United States? Explain what variable (i.e., country size or distance) drives your result.

7. What evidence is there that Canada is better off under the free-trade agreement with the United States?

8. In the section "Gains and Adjustment Costs for the United States under NAFTA," we calculated the lost wages of workers displaced because of NAFTA. Prior experience in the manufacturing sector shows that about two-thirds of these workers obtain new jobs within three years. One way to think about that reemployment process is that one-third of workers find jobs in the first year, and another one-third of remaining unemployed workers find a job each subsequent year. Using this approach, in the table that follows, we show that one-third of workers get a job in the first year (column 2), leaving two-thirds of workers unemployed (column 4). In the second year, another $(\frac{1}{3}) \cdot (\frac{2}{3}) = \frac{2}{9}$ of workers get a job (column 2), so that $\frac{1}{3} + \frac{2}{9} = \frac{5}{9}$ of the workers are employed (column 3). That leaves $\frac{4}{9}$ of the workers unemployed (column 4) at the end of the second year.

Year	Fraction Finding Job	Total Fraction Employed	Total Fraction Unemployed
1	$\frac{1}{3}$	$\frac{1}{3}$	$1 - \frac{1}{3} = \frac{2}{3}$
2	$\frac{1}{3} \cdot \frac{2}{3} = \frac{2}{9}$	$\frac{1}{3} + \frac{2}{9} = \frac{5}{9}$	$1 - \frac{5}{9} = \frac{4}{9}$
3	$\frac{1}{3} \cdot \frac{4}{9} = \frac{4}{27}$		
4			
5			
6	$\frac{1}{3} \cdot \left(\frac{2}{3}\right)^{Year-1}$		

a. Fill in two more rows of the table using the same approach as for the first two rows.
b. Notice that the fraction of workers finding a job each year (column 2) has the formula

$$\text{Fraction finding job} = \tfrac{1}{3} \cdot \left(\tfrac{2}{3}\right)^{Year-1}$$

Using this formula, fill in six more values for the fraction of workers finding a job (column 2), up to year 10.

c. To calculate the average spell of unemployment, we take the fraction of workers finding jobs (column 2), multiply it by the years of unemployment (column 1), and add up the result over all the rows. By adding up over 10 rows, calculate what the average spell of unemployment is. What do you expect to get when adding up over 20 rows?

d. Compare your answer to (c) with the average three-year spell of unemployment on page 188. Was that number accurate?

9. a. Of two products, rice and paintings, which product do you expect to have a higher index of intra-industry trade? Why?

b. Access the U.S. TradeStats Express website at http://tse.export.gov/. Click on "National Trade Data" and then "Global Patterns of U.S. Merchandise Trade." Under the "Product" section, change the item to rice (HS 1006) and obtain the export and import values. Do the same for paintings (HS 9701); then calculate the intra-industry trade index for rice and paintings in 2009. Do your calculations confirm your expectation from part (a)? If your answers did not confirm your expectation, explain.

NETWORK

In this chapter, we included the editorial **Headlines: NAFTA Turns 15, Bravo!** There were many other editorials written in 2009, for the fifteenth anniversary of NAFTA. Find another editorial on the Web, and summarize the pro and con arguments that it makes for NAFTA.

7

Offshoring of Goods and Services

One facet of increased services trade is the increased use of offshore outsourcing in which a company relocates labor-intensive service-industry functions to another country. . . . When a good or service is produced more cheaply abroad, it makes more sense to import it than to make or provide it domestically.

Economic Report of the President, 2004, p. 229

Increasing numbers of Americans . . . perceive offshoring . . . as an actual or potential threat to their jobs or to their wages even if they hold onto their jobs.

Jagdish Bhagwati and Alan S. Blinder, 2007, *Offshoring of American Jobs*

We should . . . encourage . . . businesses to stay within our borders, it's time to finally slash the tax breaks for companies that ship our jobs overseas.

President Barack Obama, State of the Union address, January 27, 2010

If you take the battery out of your cell phone to see where the phone was produced, you will likely see several countries listed inside. Motorola, for example, is a U.S. company that produces some of its cell phones in Singapore using batteries and a battery charger made in China. Nokia is a Finnish company that produces some of its American-sold cell phones in the United States using batteries made in Japan and software that was written in India. Apple produces its iPhone in facilities found in China, Taiwan, Thailand, Malaysia, Singapore, South Korea, the Czech Republic, Philippines, and the United States. A vast array of products, including simple toys like the Barbie doll and sophisticated items like airplanes and personal computers, consist of materials, parts, components, and services that are produced in numerous countries. The following excerpt from a *New York Times* article illustrates this observation:[1]

[1] Louis Uchitelle, "Why Hasn't a Weak Dollar Slowed Imports?" *New York Times*, April 8, 2005, online edition.

> General Electric in the United States and Snechma of France . . . jointly manufacture the jet engine for Boeing's 737 and Airbus's 320. G.E. makes the "hot section" at its plant in Cincinnati, while Snechma manufactures the giant fans in France. They ship these components to each other and each partner does the final assembly of the engines for its customers. In addition, G.E. makes smaller jet engines for the commuter planes that Bombardier makes in Canada and Embraer makes in Brazil. The engines are exported to those countries, but 24 percent of the value of the engines comes from components imported from Japan.

The provision of a service or the production of various parts of a good in different countries that are then used or assembled into a final good in another location is called **foreign outsourcing** or, more simply, **offshoring.** We will not worry about the distinction between these two terms (see **Side Bar: "Foreign Outsourcing" versus "Offshoring"**), but will use "offshoring" because it has become most commonly used by economists.[2]

Offshoring is a type of international trade that differs from the type of trade analyzed in the Ricardian and Heckscher-Ohlin models; the goods traded in those models were final goods. Offshoring is trade in *intermediate inputs*, which can sometimes cross borders several times before being incorporated into a final good that can be sold domestically or abroad. Offshoring is a relatively new phenomenon in world trade.[3] The amount of world trade relative to the GDPs of countries was high even in the late nineteenth and early twentieth centuries. But it is unlikely that a good would have crossed borders multiple times at several stages of production because the costs of transportation and communication were too high. Today, however, these costs have fallen so much that it is now economical to combine the labor and capital resources of several countries to produce a good or service. Indeed, if you have ever called for help with your laptop, chances are that you have spoken with someone at a call center in India, which shows just how low the costs of communication have become!

Is offshoring different from the type of trade examined in the Ricardian and Heckscher-Ohlin models? From one point of view, the answer is no. Offshoring allows a company to purchase inexpensive goods or services abroad, just as consumers can purchase lower-priced goods from abroad in the Ricardian and Heckscher-Ohlin models. This is what the quote from the *Economic Report of the President* at the beginning of the chapter suggests: with offshoring we import those goods and services that are cheaper to produce abroad. From another point of view, however, offshoring is different. Companies now have the opportunity to send *a portion* of their activities to other countries. The jobs associated with those activities leave the United States, and by paying lower wages abroad, U.S. firms lower their costs and pass on these savings to consumers. Offshoring results in lower prices but changes the mix of jobs located in the United States. Higher-skilled workers in the United States, engaged in activities such as marketing and research, will be combined with less skilled workers abroad, engaged in assembling products. In a sense, offshoring is similar to immigration in that U.S. firms are able to employ foreign workers, even though those workers do not have to leave their home countries.

[2] Both "foreign outsourcing" and "offshoring" have been coined recently to describe this new type of international trade. The earliest known use of the word "outsourcing" is a quotation from an American auto executive in the *Journal of the Royal Society of Arts*, 1979, who said, "We are so short of professional engineers in the motor industry that we are having to outsource design work to Germany" (William Safire, "On Language," *New York Times Magazine*, March 21, 2004, p. 30).

[3] There is also the concept of *domestic outsourcing*, which occurs when a company decides to shift some of its production activities from one location to another within the same country. In this text, outsourcing always means *foreign outsourcing*.

SIDE BAR

"Foreign Outsourcing" versus "Offshoring"

In discussions of foreign outsourcing, we often hear the term "offshoring." The quote from the *Economic Report of the President* at the beginning of the chapter combined these terms as "offshore outsourcing." Is there a difference between "foreign outsourcing" and "offshoring"?

The term "offshoring" is sometimes used to refer to a company moving some of its operations overseas but retaining ownership of those operations. In other words, the company moves some operations offshore but does not move production outside of its own firm. Intel, for example, produces microchips in China and Costa Rica using subsidiaries that it owns. Intel has engaged in foreign direct investment (FDI) to establish these offshore subsidiaries.

Mattel, on the other hand, arranges for the production of the Barbie doll in several different countries. Unlike Intel, however, Mattel does not actually own the firms in those countries. Furthermore, Mattel lets these firms purchase their inputs (like the hair and cloth for the dolls) from whichever sources are most economical. Mattel is engaging in foreign outsourcing as it contracts with these firms abroad but has not done any FDI.

Dell is an intermediate case. Dell assembles its computers overseas in firms it does not own, so it is outsourcing rather than offshoring the assembly. However, Dell exercises careful control over the inputs (such as computer parts) that these overseas firms use. Dell outsources the assembly but monitors the overseas firms closely to ensure the high quality of the computers being assembled.

In this chapter, we will not worry about the distinction between "offshoring" and "foreign outsourcing" and will use the term "offshoring" whenever the components of a good or service are produced in several countries, regardless of who owns the plants that provide the components or services.

The first goal of this chapter is to examine in detail the phenomenon of offshoring and describe in what ways it differs from trade in final products. We discuss how offshoring affects the demand for high-skilled and low-skilled labor and the wages paid to those workers. Since the early 1980s, there has been a significant change in the pattern of wage payments in the United States and other countries—the wages of skilled workers have been rising relative to those of less skilled workers. We will examine whether this change in relative wages is the result of offshoring or whether there are other explanations for it.

A second goal of the chapter is to discuss the gains from offshoring. We argue that offshoring creates gains from trade, similar to those seen from the trade of final goods in the Ricardian or Heckscher-Ohlin models. But having overall gains from trade for a country does not necessarily mean that every person in the country gains. As the second quote at the beginning of the chapter shows, many workers are fearful that their jobs and wages are threatened by offshoring. We focus attention on how offshoring affects high-skilled versus low-skilled workers.

A third goal of the chapter is to examine the response to offshoring in the United States. The final quotation at the beginning of the chapter, from the 2010 State of the Union address by President Obama, indicates that he proposes to limit tax breaks to companies engaged in offshoring. Many economists would disagree with this proposal, and argue instead that offshoring has overall benefits. We examine these arguments and also discuss the newest trend of "inshoring" activities back into the United States.

1 A Model of Offshoring

To develop a model of offshoring, we need to identify all the activities involved in producing and marketing a good or service. These activities are illustrated in Figure 7-1. Panel (a) describes the activities in the order in which they are performed (starting with

FIGURE 7-1

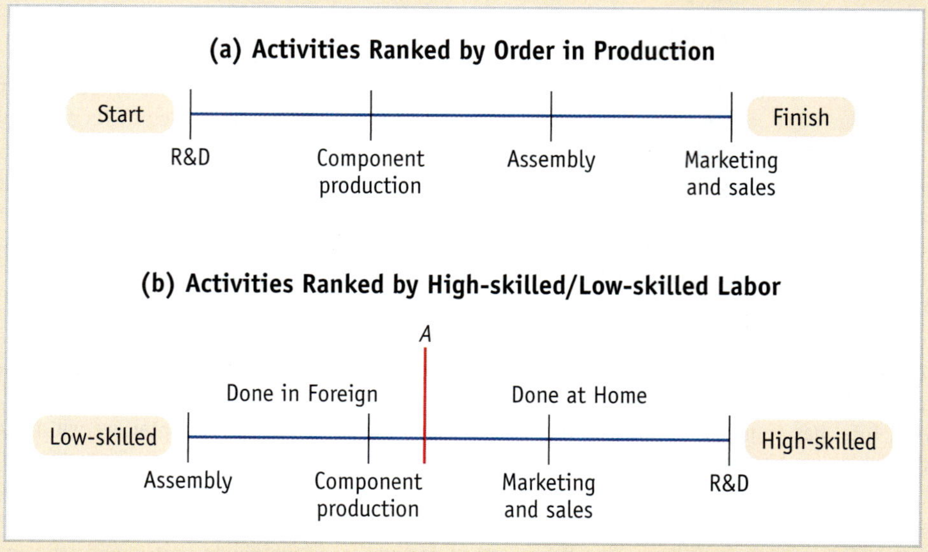

The Value Chain of a Product Any product has many different activities involved in its manufacture. Panel (a) lists some of these activities for a given product in the order in which they occur. The value chain in (b) lists these same activities in order of the amount of high-skilled/low-skilled labor used in each. In panel (b), the assembly activity, on the left, uses the least skilled labor, and R&D, on the right, uses the most skilled labor. Because we assume that the relative wage of skilled labor is higher at Home and that trade and capital costs are uniform across activities, there is a point on the value chain, shown by line A, below which all activities are offshored to Foreign and above which all activities are performed at Home.

research and development [R&D] and ending with marketing and after-sales service). For instance, in producing a television, the design and engineering are developed first; components such as wiring, casing, and screens are manufactured next; and finally the television is assembled into its final version and sold to consumers.

For the purpose of building a model of offshoring, however, it is more useful to line up the activities according to the ratio of high-skilled/low-skilled labor used, as in panel (b). We start with the less skilled activities, such as the manufacture and assembly of simple components (like the case or the electric cord for the television), then move to more complex components (like the screen). Next are the supporting service activities such as accounting, order processing, and product service (sometimes called "back-office" activities because the customer does not see them). Finally, we come to activities that use more skilled labor, such as marketing and sales ("front-office" activities), and those that use the most skilled labor such as R&D.

Value Chain of Activities

The whole set of activities that we have illustrated in Figures 7-1(a) and 7-1(b) is sometimes called the **value chain** for the product, with each activity adding more value to the combined product. All these activities do not need to be done in one country—a firm can transfer some of these activities abroad by offshoring them when it is more economical to do so. By lining up the activities in terms of the relative amount of skilled labor they require, we can predict which activities are likely to be transferred abroad. This prediction depends on several assumptions, which follow.

Relative Wage of Skilled Workers Let W_L be the wage of low-skilled labor in Home and W_H the wage of high-skilled labor. Similarly, let W^*_L and W^*_H be the wages of low-skilled and high-skilled workers in Foreign. Our first assumption is that Foreign wages are less than those at Home, $W^*_L < W_L$ and $W^*_H < W_H$, and that the *relative wage* of low-skilled labor is lower in Foreign than at Home, so $W^*_L/W^*_H < W_L/W_H$. This assumption is realistic because low-skilled labor in developing countries receives especially low wages.

Costs of Capital and Trade As the firm considers sending some activities abroad, it knows that it will lower its labor costs because wages in Foreign are lower. However, the firm must also take into account the extra costs of doing business in Foreign. In many cases, the firm pays more to capital through (1) higher prices to build a factory or higher prices for utilities such as electricity and fuel; (2) extra costs involved in transportation and communication, which will be especially high if Foreign is still developing roads, ports, and telephone capabilities; and (3) the extra costs from tariffs if Foreign imposes taxes on goods (such as component parts) when they come into the country. We lump together costs 2 and 3 into what we call "trade costs."

Higher capital and trade costs in Foreign can prevent a Home firm from offshoring all its activities abroad. In making the decision of what to offshore, the Home firm will balance the savings from lower wages against the extra costs of capital and trade.

Our second assumption is that these extra costs apply *uniformly* across all the activities in the value chain; that is, these extra costs add, say, 10% to each and every component of operation in Foreign as compared with Home. Unlike our assumption about relative wages in Home and Foreign, this assumption is a bit unrealistic. For instance, the extra costs of transportation versus those of communication are quite different in countries such as China and India; good roads for transport have developed slowly, while communications technology has developed rapidly. As a result, technology in telephones is advanced in those countries, so cell phones are often cheaper there than in the United States and Europe. In this case, the higher infrastructure costs will affect the activities that rely on transportation more than activities that rely on communication.

Slicing the Value Chain Now suppose that the Home firm with the value chain in Figure 7-1(b) considers transferring some of these activities from Home to Foreign. Which activities will be transferred? Based on our assumptions that $W^*_L/W^*_H < W_L/W_H$ and that the extra costs of capital and trade apply uniformly, it makes sense for the firm to send abroad the activities that are the least skilled and labor-intensive and keep at Home the activities that are the most skilled and labor-intensive. Looking at Figure 7-1, all activities to the left of the vertical line A might be done in Foreign, for example, whereas those activities to the right of the vertical line will be done in Home. We can refer to this transfer of activities as "slicing the value chain."[4]

[4] This term is drawn from Paul Krugman, 1995, "Growing World Trade: Causes and Consequences," *Brookings Papers on Economic Activity*, 1.

Activities to the left of line A are sent abroad because the cost savings from paying lower wages in Foreign are greatest for activities that require less skilled labor. Because the extra costs of capital and trade are uniform across activities, the cost savings on wages are most important in determining which activities to transfer and which to keep at Home.

Relative Demand for Skilled Labor Now that we know the division of activities between Home and Foreign, we can graph the demand for labor in each country, as illustrated in Figure 7-2. For Home, we add up the demand for high-skilled labor H and low-skilled labor L for all the activities to the right of line A in Figure 7-1(b). Taking the ratio of these, in panel (a) we graph the relative demand for skilled labor at Home H/L against the relative wage W_H/W_L. This relative demand curve slopes downward because a higher relative wage for skilled labor would cause Home firms to substitute less skilled labor in some activities. For example, if the relative wage of skilled labor increased, Home firms might hire high school rather than college graduates to serve on a sales force and then train them on the job.

In Foreign, we add up the demand for high-skilled labor H^* and for low-skilled labor L^* for all the activities to the left of line A^*. Panel (b) graphs the relative demand for skilled labor in Foreign H^*/L^* against the relative wage W^*_H/W^*_L. Again, this curve slopes downward because a higher relative wage for skilled labor would cause Foreign firms to substitute less skilled labor in some activities. In each country, we can add a relative supply curve to the diagram, which is upward-sloping because a higher relative wage for skilled labor causes more skilled individuals to enter this industry. For instance, if the high-skilled wage increases relative to the low-skilled wage in either country, then individuals will invest more in schooling to equip themselves with the skills necessary to earn the higher relative wage.

FIGURE 7-2

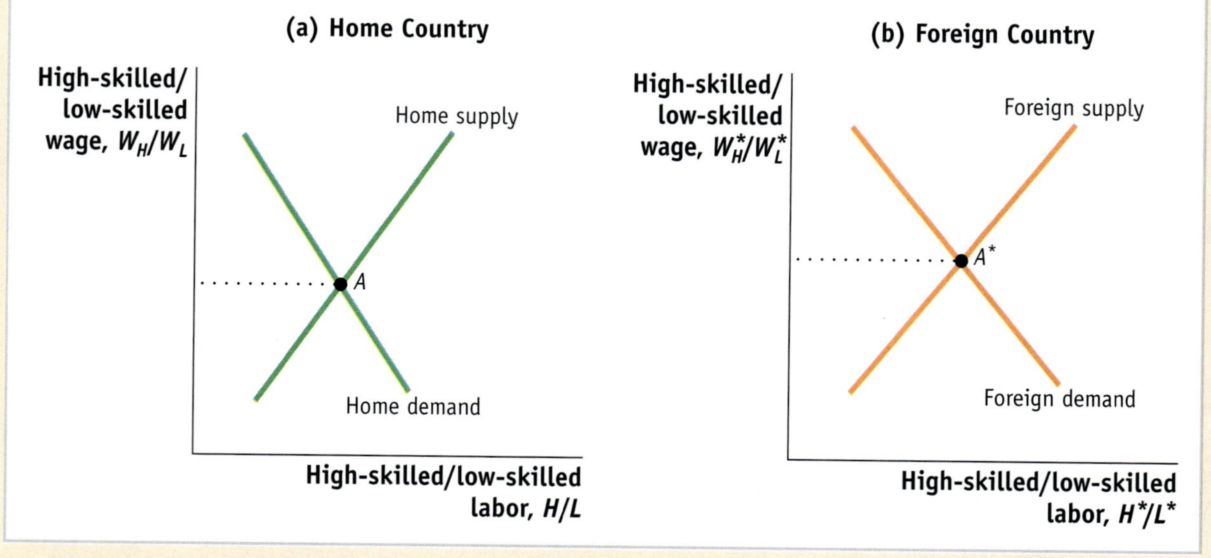

Relative Demand and Supply for High-Skilled/Low-Skilled Labor In panel (a), we show the relative demand and supply for skilled labor at Home, H/L, depending on the relative wage, W_H/W_L. The equilibrium relative wage at Home is determined at A. In panel (b), we show the relative demand and supply for skilled labor in Foreign, H^*/L^*, depending on the relative wage, W^*_H/W^*_L. The Foreign equilibrium is at point A^*.

The intersection of the relative demand and relative supply curves, at points A and A^*, gives the equilibrium relative wage in this industry in each country and the equilibrium relative employment of high-skilled/low-skilled workers. Starting at these points, next we study how the equilibrium changes as Home offshores more activities to Foreign.

Changing the Costs of Trade

Suppose now that the costs of capital or trade in Foreign fall. For example, the North American Free Trade Agreement (NAFTA) lowered tariffs charged on goods crossing the U.S.-Mexico border. This fall in trade costs made it easier for U.S. firms to offshore to Mexico. And even before NAFTA, Mexico had liberalized the rules concerning foreign ownership of capital there, thereby lowering the cost of capital for U.S. firms. Another example is India, which in 1991 eliminated many regulations that had been hindering businesses, communications, and foreign investment. Before 1991 it was difficult for a new business to start, or even to secure a phone or fax line in India; after 1991 the regulations on domestic and foreign-owned business were simplified, and communication technology improved dramatically with cell phones and fiber-optic cables. These policy changes made India more attractive to foreign investors and firms interested in offshoring.

Change in Home Labor Demand and Relative Wage When the costs of capital or trade decline in Foreign, it becomes desirable to shift more activities in the value chain from Home to Foreign. Figure 7-3 illustrates this change with the shift of the dividing line from A to B. The activities between A and B, which used to be done at Home, are now done in Foreign. As an example, consider the transfer of television production from the United States to Mexico. As U.S. firms first shifted manufacturing to Mexico, the chassis of the televisions were constructed there. Later on, electronic circuits were constructed in Mexico, and later still the picture tubes were manufactured there.[5]

FIGURE 7-3

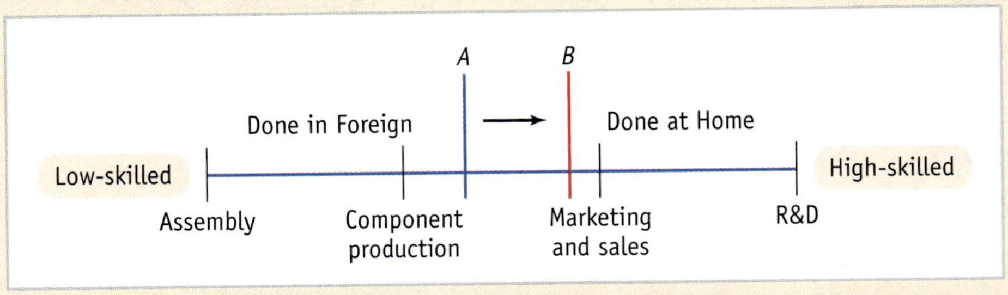

Offshoring on the Value Chain As the costs of capital or trade fall in the Foreign country, a Home firm will find it profitable to offshore more activities. Offshoring shifts the dividing line between Home and Foreign production from A to B. The activities between A and B, which formerly were done at Home, are now done in Foreign. Notice that these activities are more skill-intensive than the activities formerly done in Foreign (to the left of A) but less skill-intensive than the activities now done at Home (to the right of B).

[5] Martin Kenney and Richard Florida, 1994, "Japanese Maquiladoras: Production Organization and Global Commodity Chains," *World Development*, 22(1), 27–44.

How does this increase in offshoring affect the relative demand for skilled labor in each country? First consider the Home country. Notice that the activities no longer performed at Home (i.e., those between *A* and *B*) are *less* skill-intensive than the activities still done there (those to the right of *B*). This means that the activities now done at Home are more skilled and labor-intensive, on average, than the activities formerly done at Home. For this reason, the relative demand for skilled labor at Home will increase, and the Home demand curve will shift to the right, as shown in Figure 7-4, panel (a). Note that this diagram does not show the *absolute* quantity of labor demanded, which we expect would fall for both high-skilled and low-skilled labor when there is more offshoring; instead, we are graphing the *relative* demand for high-skilled/low-skilled labor, which increases because the activities still done at Home are more skill-intensive than before the decrease in trade and capital costs. With the increase in the relative demand for skilled labor, the equilibrium will shift from point *A* to point *B* at Home; that is, the relative wage of skilled labor will increase because of offshoring.

Change in Foreign Labor Demand and Relative Wage Now let's look at what happens in Foreign when Home offshores more of its production activities to Foreign. How will offshoring affect the relative demand for labor and relative wage in Foreign? As we saw in Figure 7-3, the activities that are newly offshored to Foreign (those between *A* and *B*) are *more* skill-intensive than the activities that were initially offshored

FIGURE 7-4

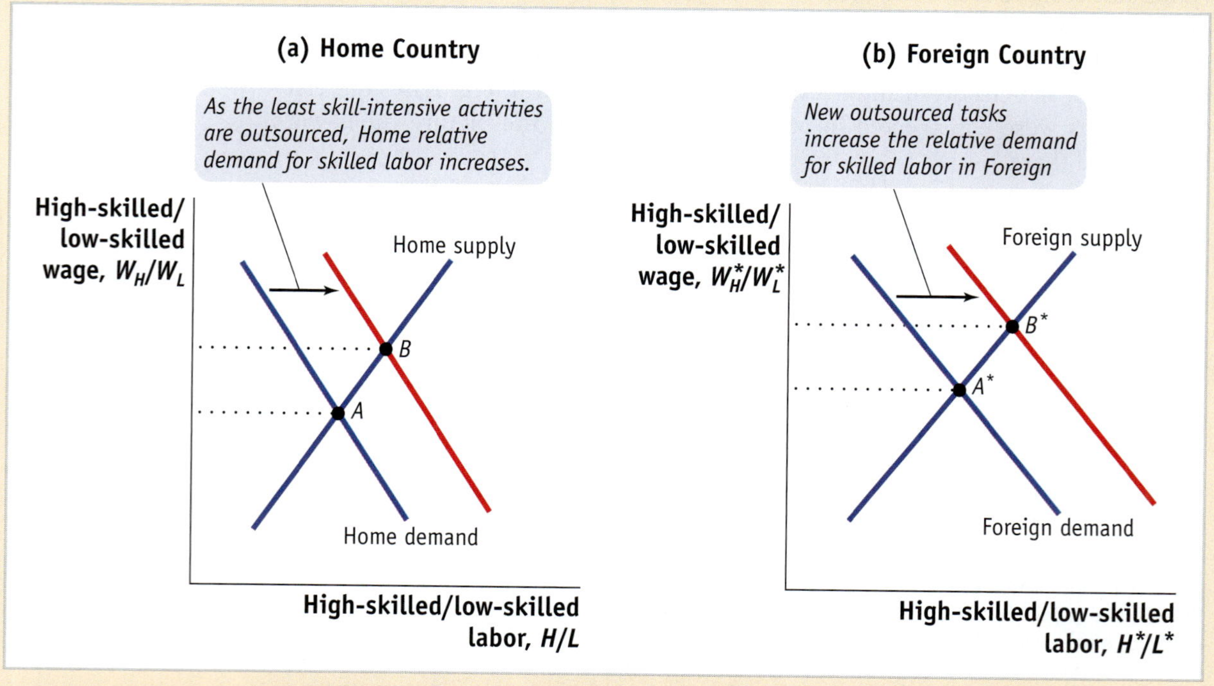

Change in the Relative Demand for High-Skilled/Low-Skilled Labor With greater offshoring from Home to Foreign, some of the activities requiring less skill that were formerly done at Home are now done abroad. It follows that the relative demand for skilled labor at Home increases, and the relative wage rises from point *A* to point *B*. The relative demand for skilled labor in Foreign also increases because the activities shifted to Foreign are more skill-intensive than those formerly done there. It follows that the relative wage for skilled labor in Foreign also rises, from point A^* to point B^*.

to Foreign (those to the left of A). This means that the range of activities now done in Foreign is more skilled and labor-intensive, on average, than the set of activities formerly done there. For this reason, the relative demand for skilled labor in Foreign also increases, and the Foreign demand curve shifts to the right, as shown in panel (b) of Figure 7-4. With this increase in the relative demand for skilled labor, the equilibrium shifts from point A^* to point B^*. As a result of Home's increased offshoring to Foreign, then, the relative wage of skilled labor increases in Foreign. The conclusion from our model is that *both* countries experience an increase in the relative wage of skilled labor because of increased offshoring.

It might seem surprising that a shift of activities from one country to the other can increase the relative demand for skilled labor in *both* countries. An example drawn from your classroom experience might help you to understand how this can happen. Suppose you have a friend who is majoring in physics but is finding it difficult: he is scoring below average in a class he is taking. So you invite him to join you in an economics class, and it turns out that your friend has a knack for economics: he scores above average in that class. How does your friend's transfer from physics to economics affect the class averages? Because your friend was performing below average in the physics class, when he leaves the class, his departure raises the class average (computed now using the students still there, not including him). Because he performs better than average in the economics class, his arrival raises the class average there, too (computed using everyone, including him). Thus, this student's move from one class to another raises the average in both classes.

This result is just like the logic of the offshoring model: as activities in the middle of the value chain are shifted from Home to Foreign, they raise the relative demand for skilled labor in both countries because these activities are the *least* skill-intensive of those formerly done at Home but the *most* skill-intensive of tasks done in Foreign. That is why the relative demand for skilled labor increases in both countries, along with the relative wage of skilled labor. This result is one of the most important predictions from our offshoring model and it would not occur in our earlier models of trade, such as the Heckscher-Ohlin model.[6] We now turn to evidence from the United States and Mexico to see whether this prediction is borne out.

APPLICATION

Change in Relative Wages across Countries

Since the early 1980s, the wages of high-skilled workers have risen relative to those of low-skilled workers in many countries. The relative wage of skilled workers in industrial countries (such as the United States, Australia, Canada, Japan, Sweden, and the United Kingdom) and in developing countries (such as Hong Kong, Chile, and Mexico) has increased. Our offshoring model predicts that the relative wage of skilled workers will rise in *both* the country doing the offshoring and the country receiving the new activities. At first glance, that prediction seems to be consistent with the change in wages that has actually occurred. Let us dig more deeply, however, using evidence from the United States and Mexico, to see what the change in wages has been and whether it is due to offshoring.

[6] The Heckscher-Ohlin model tells us that the factor prices in the two countries will move toward equality when they open trade. So the wage relative to the capital rental will move in different directions in the two countries due to the opening of trade, not in the same direction.

Change in Relative Wages in the United States

To measure the wages of skilled and low-skilled workers, we can use data from the manufacturing sector on "production" and "nonproduction" workers. As their name suggests, production workers are involved in the manufacture and assembly of goods, whereas nonproduction workers are involved in supporting service activities. Firms are required to report wages for both types of workers. We could also call these two types of workers "blue collar" and "white collar." Generally, nonproduction workers require more education, and so we will treat these workers as "high-skilled," whereas the production workers are treated here as "low-skilled" workers.[7]

Relative Wage of Nonproduction Workers Figure 7-5 shows the average annual earnings of nonproduction workers relative to production workers (analogous to the ratio of high-skilled to low-skilled wages, or W_H/W_L) in U.S. manufacturing from 1958 to 2006. We see that relative earnings moved erratically from 1958 to 1967, and that from 1968 to about 1983, relative wages were on a downward trend. It is generally accepted that the relative wage fell during this period because of an increase in the supply of college graduates, skilled workers who moved into nonproduction jobs (the increase in supply would bring down the nonproduction wage, so the relative wage

FIGURE 7-5

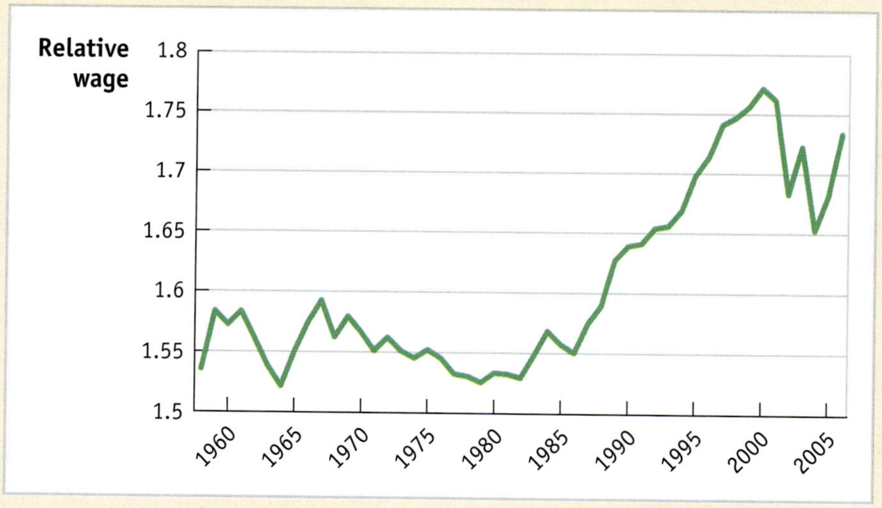

Relative Wage of Nonproduction/Production Workers, U.S. Manufacturing This diagram shows the average wage of nonproduction workers divided by the average wage of production workers in U.S. manufacturing. This ratio of wages moved erratically during the 1960s and 1970s, although showing some downward trend. This trend reversed itself during the 1980s and 1990s, when the relative wage of nonproduction workers increased until 2000. This trend means that the relative wage of production, or low-skilled, workers fell during the 1980s and 1990s. In more recent years the relative wage has become quite volatile, falling substantially in 2002 and 2004, then rising in 2005 and 2006.

Source: Annual Survey of Manufacturers *and National Bureau of Economic Research (NBER) productivity database, updated from U.S. Bureau of the Census.*

[7] This distinction is far from perfect, however. Nonproduction workers include clerical and custodial staff, for example, who may be less skilled than some production workers.

would also fall). Starting in 1983, however, this trend reversed itself and the relative wage of nonproduction workers increased steadily to 2000. Since that time the relative wage has become quite volatile.

"SORRY, THE BOARD IS *OUTSOURCING* YOUR JOB TO A GUY IN INDIA WHO'LL BE *CEO* FOR A *TENTH* OF YOUR SALARY."

David Horsey. Represented by Tribune Media Services (http://www.Comicspage.com).

Relative Employment of Nonproduction Workers

In Figure 7-6, we see that there was a steady increase in the ratio of nonproduction to production workers employed in U.S. manufacturing until the early 1990s. Such a trend indicates that firms were hiring fewer production, or low-skilled workers, relative to nonproduction workers. Then during the 1990s the ratio of nonproduction to production workers fell. Most recently, the ratio has increased slightly.

The increase in the relative supply of college graduates from 1968 to early 1983 is consistent with the reduction in the relative wage of nonproduction workers, as shown in Figure 7-5, and with the increase in their relative employment, as shown in Figure 7-6. But after 1983 the story changes. We would normally think that the rising relative wage of nonproduction workers should have led to a shift in employment *away* from nonproduction workers, but it did not; as shown in Figure 7-6, the relative employment of nonproduction workers continued to rise from 1980 to about 1990, then fell until 1997. How can there be both

FIGURE 7-6

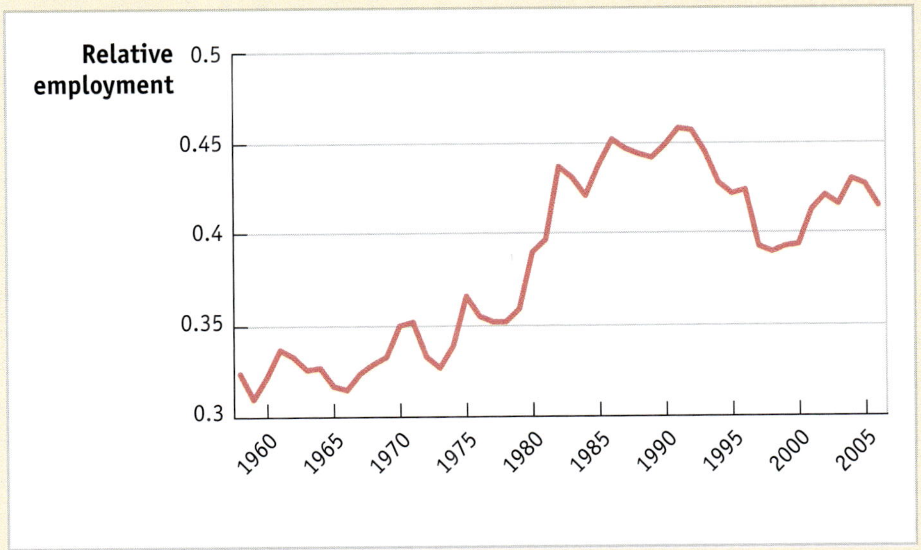

Relative Employment of Nonproduction/Production Workers, U.S. Manufacturing This diagram shows the employment of nonproduction workers in U.S. manufacturing divided by the employment of production workers. There was a steady increase in the ratio of nonproduction to production workers employed in U.S. manufacturing until the early 1990s. That trend indicates firms were hiring fewer production workers relative to nonproduction workers. During the 1990s there was a fall in the ratio of nonproduction to production workers, and then a rise again after 2000.

Source: Annual Survey of Manufacturers *and NBER productivity database, updated from U.S. Bureau of the Census.*

an increase in the relative wage and an increase in the relative employment of nonproduction workers? The only explanation consistent with these facts is that during the 1980s there was an *outward shift* in the relative demand for nonproduction (skilled) workers, which led to a simultaneous increase in their relative employment *and* in their wages.

This conclusion is illustrated in Figure 7-7, in which we plot the relative wage of nonproduction workers and their relative employment from 1979 to 1990. As we have already noted, both the relative wage and relative employment of nonproduction workers rose during the 1980s. The only way this pattern can be consistent with a supply and demand diagram is if the relative demand curve for skilled labor increases, as illustrated. This increased demand would lead to an increase in the relative wage for skilled labor and an increase in its relative employment, the pattern seen in the data for the United States.

Explanations What factors can lead to an increase in the relative demand for skilled labor? One explanation is offshoring. An increase in demand for high-skilled workers, at the expense of low-skilled workers, can arise from offshoring, as shown by the rightward shift in the relative demand for skilled labor in Figure 7-4(a). The evidence from the manufacturing sector in the United States is strongly consistent with our model of offshoring.

There is, however, a second possible explanation for the increase in the relative demand for skilled workers in the United States. In the 1980s personal computers began to appear in the workplace. The addition of computers in the workplace can increase the demand for skilled workers to operate them. The shift in relative demand toward

FIGURE 7-7

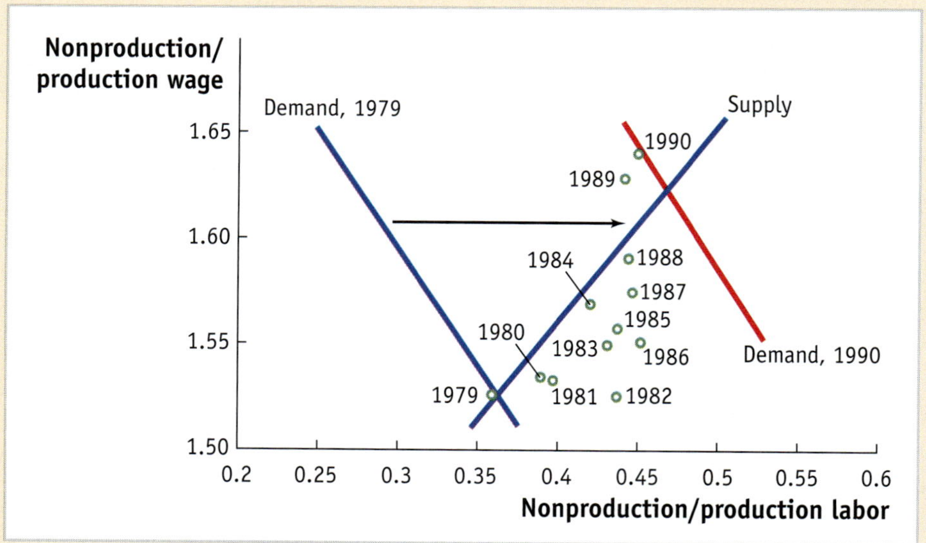

Supply and Demand for Nonproduction/Production Workers in the 1980s This diagram shows the average wage of nonproduction workers divided by the average wage of production workers on the vertical axis, and on the horizontal axis the employment of nonproduction workers divided by the employment of production workers. Both the relative wage and the relative employment of nonproduction, or skilled, workers rose in U.S. manufacturing during the 1980s, indicating that the relative demand curve must have shifted to the right.

Source: NBER productivity database.

skilled workers because of the use of computers and other high-tech equipment is called **skill-biased technological change.** Given these two potential explanations for the same observation, how can we determine which of these factors was most responsible for the actual change in wages?

Answering this question has been the topic of many research studies in economics. The approach that most authors take is to measure skill-biased technological change and offshoring in terms of some underlying variables. For skill-biased technological change, for example, we might use the amount of computers and other high-technology equipment used in manufacturing industries. For offshoring, we could use the imports of intermediate inputs into manufacturing industries. By studying how the use of high-tech equipment and the imports of intermediate inputs have grown and comparing this to the wage movements in industries, we can determine the contribution of each factor toward explaining the wage movements.

The results from one study of this type are shown in Table 7-1. The goal of this study was to explain two observations. First, it sought to explain the increase in the share of **total wage payments** going to nonproduction (high-skilled) labor in U.S. manufacturing industries from 1979 to 1990 (part A). Because wage payments equal the wage times the number of workers hired, this statistic captures both the rising relative wage and the rising relative employment of skilled workers. Second, the study analyzed the increase in the *relative wage* of nonproduction labor in particular over the same period (part B).[8]

The study considered two possible explanations for the two observations: offshoring and the use of high-tech equipment such as computers. Offshoring was measured as the intermediate inputs imported by each industry. For example, the U.S. auto industry builds seats, dashboards, and other car parts in Mexico and then imports these for assembly in the United States. In addition, high-technology equipment can be measured in two ways: either as a fraction of the total capital equipment installed in each industry or as a fraction of new investment in capital that is devoted to computers and other high-tech devices. In the first method, high-tech equipment is measured as a fraction of the capital *stock*, and in the second method, high-tech equipment is measured as a fraction of the annual *flow* of new investment. In the early 1980s a large portion of the flow of new investment in some industries was devoted to computers and other high-tech devices, but a much smaller fraction of the capital stock consisted of that equipment. In Table 7-1, we report results from both measures because the results differ depending on which measure is used.

Using the first measure of high-tech equipment (as a fraction of the capital stock), the results in the first row of part A show that between 20 and 23% of the increase in the share of wage payments going to the nonproduction workers can be explained by offshoring, and between 8 and 12% of that increase can be explained by the growing use of high-tech capital. The remainder is unexplained by these two factors. Thus, using the first measure of high-tech equipment, it appears that offshoring was more important than high-tech capital in explaining the change in relative demand for skilled workers.

[8] To illustrate the distinction between parts A and B, consider the following example. If nonproduction workers earn \$25 per hour and 5 are hired, and production workers earn \$10 per hour and 20 are hired, then the total wage payments are \$25 • 5 + \$10 • 20 = \$325, and the relative wage of nonproduction labor is \$25/\$10 = 2.5. In contrast, the share of total wage payments going to nonproduction workers is then \$125/\$325 = 38%, which equals the actual, average share of wages going to nonproduction workers in U.S. manufacturing from 1979 to 1990.

TABLE 7-1

Increase in the Relative Wage of Nonproduction Labor in U.S. Manufacturing, 1979–1990 This table shows the estimated effects of offshoring and the use of high-technology equipment on the wages earned by nonproduction (or skilled) workers. Part A focuses on how these two variables affect the share of wage payments going to nonproduction workers. Part B shows how these two variables affect the relative wage of nonproduction workers.

	PERCENT OF TOTAL INCREASE EXPLAINED BY EACH FACTOR	
	Offshoring	**High-Technology Equipment**
Part A: Share of Wage Payments Going to Nonproduction Workers		
Measurement of high-tech equipment:		
As a share of the capital stock	20–23	8–12
As a share of capital flow (i.e., new investment)	13	37
Part B: Relative Wage of Nonproduction/Production Workers		
Measurement of high-tech equipment:		
As a share of the capital stock	21–27	29–32
As a share of capital flow (i.e., new investment)	12	99

Source: Robert C. Feenstra and Gordon H. Hanson, August 1999, "The Impact of Outsourcing and High-Technology Capital on Wages: Estimates for the United States, 1979–1990," Quarterly Journal of Economics, *114(3), 907–940.*

The story is different, however, if we instead use offshoring and the second measure of high-tech equipment (a fraction of new investment), as shown in the second row of part A. In that case, offshoring explains only 13% of the increase in the nonproduction share of wages, whereas high-tech investment explains 37% of that increase. So we see from these results that both offshoring and high-tech equipment are important explanations for the increase in the relative wage of skilled labor in the United States, but which one is *most* important depends on how we measure the high-tech equipment.

In part B, we repeat the results but now try to explain the increase in the relative wage of nonproduction workers. Using the first measure of high-tech equipment (a fraction of the capital stock), the results in the first row of part B show that between 21 and 27% of the increase in the relative wage of nonproduction workers can be explained by offshoring, and between 29 and 32% of that increase can be explained by the growing use of high-tech capital. In the second row of part B, we use the other measure of high-tech equipment (a fraction of new investment). In that case, the large spending on high-tech equipment in new investment can explain *nearly all* (99%) of the increased relative wage for nonproduction workers, leaving little room for offshoring to play much of a role (it explains only 12% of the increase in the relative wage). These results are lopsided enough that we might be skeptical of using new investment to measure high-tech equipment and therefore prefer the results in the first rows of parts A and B, using the capital stocks.

Summing up, we conclude that both offshoring and high-tech equipment are important explanations for the increase in the relative wage of nonproduction/production labor in U.S. manufacturing, but it is difficult to judge which is more important because the results depend on how we measure the high-tech equipment.

Change in Relative Wages in Mexico

Our model of offshoring predicts that the relative wage of skilled labor will rise in *both* countries. We have already seen (in Figure 7-1) that the relative wage of nonproduction (skilled) labor rises in the United States. But what about for Mexico?

In Figure 7-8, we show the relative wage of nonproduction/production labor in Mexico from 1964 to 1994. The data used in Figure 7-8 come from the census of industries in Mexico, which occurs infrequently, so there are only a few turning points in the graph. We can see that the relative wage of nonproduction workers fell from 1964 to 1985, then rose until 1994. The fall in the relative wage from 1964 to 1985 is similar to the pattern in the United States and probably occurred because of an increased supply of skilled labor in the workforce. More important, the rise in the relative wage of nonproduction workers from 1985 to 1994 is also similar to what happened in the United States and illustrates the prediction of our model of offshoring: that relative wages move in the *same* direction in both countries.

After 1994 the change in the relative wage of nonproduction workers in Mexico depends on whether we look at the maquiladora sector, which are the industrial plants near Mexico's border with the United States engaged in offshoring, or the non-maquiladora plants. For the maquiladora sector, the evidence in Figure 6-8(b) in Chapter 6 showed that real monthly income (including production workers and nonproduction workers) rises faster than real wages (for production workers). That evidence means there is a continuing rise in the relative wage of nonproduction (skilled) workers, at least in the

FIGURE 7-8

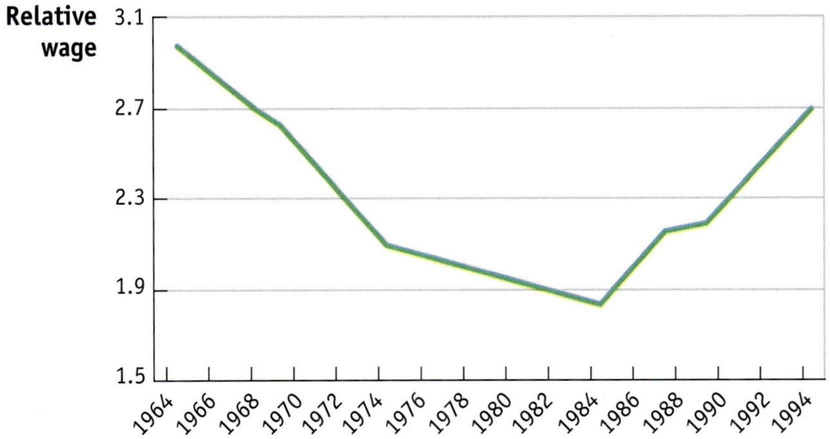

Relative Wage of Nonproduction/Production Workers, Mexico Manufacturing This diagram shows the wage of nonproduction workers in the manufacturing sector of Mexico divided by the wage of production workers. After declining during the 1960s and 1970s, this relative wage began to move upward in the mid-1980s, at the same time that the relative wage of nonproduction workers was increasing in the United States (see Figure 7-5). The relative wage in Mexico continued to rise until 1994, when NAFTA began.

Sources: Robert C. Feenstra and Gordon H. Hanson, May 1997, "Foreign Direct Investment and Relative Wages: Evidence from Mexico's Maquiladoras," Journal of International Economics, *4, 371–393; and Raymond Robertson, December 2004, "Relative Prices and Wage Inequality: Evidence from Mexico,"* Journal of International Economics, *64, 387–409.*

maquiladora sector. For the non-maquiladora plants in the rest of Mexico, however, the evidence is that the relative wage of nonproduction workers fell after 1994.

The year 1994 is special because that is when the North American Free Trade Agreement (NAFTA) was formed, establishing free trade between the United States, Canada, and Mexico. Tariffs between the United States and Mexico were reduced starting in 1994: the tariffs in some products were eliminated that year, and other tariff reductions were phased in over five or ten years. According to one research study, the tariff reductions in Mexico tended to favor the import of skill-intensive goods from the United States.[9] So after 1994 the prices of those goods fell in Mexico, which might explain why the relative wage of nonproduction labor also fell in the non-maquiladora plants.

Summing up, the changes in relative prices in the United States and Mexico match each other during the period from 1964 to 1985 (with relative wages falling) and during the period from 1985 to 1994 (with relative wages rising in both countries). Offshoring from the United States to Mexico rose from 1985 to 1994, so the rise in relative wages matches our prediction from the model of offshoring. After 1994 the relative wages move in opposite directions in the maquiladora and non-maquiladora plants in Mexico, which appears to be due to the start of NAFTA. ■

2 The Gains from Offshoring

We have shown that offshoring can shift the relative demand for labor and therefore raise the relative wage for skilled workers. Because the relative wage for low-skilled workers is the reciprocal of the high-skilled relative wage, it falls in both countries. High-skilled labor gains and low-skilled labor loses in relative terms. On the other hand, the ability of firms to relocate some production activities abroad means that their costs are reduced. In a competitive market, lower costs mean lower prices, so offshoring benefits consumers. Our goal in this section is to try to balance the potential losses faced by some groups (low-skilled labor) with the gains enjoyed by others (high-skilled labor and consumers). Our argument in previous chapters on the Ricardian and Heckscher-Ohlin models has been that international trade generates more gains than losses. Now we have to ask whether the same is true for offshoring.

One answer to this question comes from a surprising source. The Nobel laureate Paul Samuelson has been among the foremost proponents of global free trade, but in 2004 he had the following to say about the gains from foreign outsourcing:[10]

> Most noneconomists are fearful when an emerging China or India, helped by their still low real wages, outsourcing and miracle export-led developments, cause layoffs from good American jobs. This is a hot issue now, and in the coming decade, it will not go away. Prominent and competent mainstream economists enter in the debate to educate and correct warm-hearted protestors who are against globalization. Here is a fair paraphrase of the argumentation that has been used. . . .
>
> Yes, good jobs may be lost here in the short run. But still total U.S. net national product *must, by the economic laws of comparative advantage, be raised in the long run (and in China, too)*. The gains of the winners from free trade, properly measured,

---

[9] Raymond Robertson, 2004, "Relative Prices and Wage Inequality: Evidence from Mexico," *Journal of International Economics*, 64, 387–409. Notice that this pattern of tariff cuts violates the assumption that we made in the model of offshoring, that the costs of trade (or changes in these costs) are uniform across all activities.
[10] Paul Samuelson, Summer 2004, "Where Ricardo and Mill Rebut and Confirm Arguments of Mainstream Economists Supporting Globalization," *Journal of Economic Perspectives*, 18(3), 135–146.

> work out to exceed the losses of the losers. . . . Correct economic law recognizes that some American groups can be hurt by dynamic free trade. But correct economic law vindicates the word "creative" destruction by its proof that the gains of the American winners are big enough to more than compensate the losers.

Does this paraphrase by Samuelson sound familiar? You can find passages much like it in this chapter and earlier ones, saying that the gains from trade exceed the losses. But listen to what Samuelson says next:

> The last paragraph can be only an innuendo. For it is dead wrong about [the] *necessary* surplus of winnings over losings.

So Samuelson seems to be saying that the winnings for those who gain from trade *do not necessarily* exceed the losses for those who lose. How can this be? His last statement seems to contradict much of what we have learned in this book. Or does it?

Simplified Offshoring Model

To understand Samuelson's comments, we can use a simplified version of the offshoring model we have developed in this chapter. Instead of having many activities involved in the production of a good, suppose that there are only *two* activities: components production and research and development (R&D). Each of these activities uses high-skilled and low-skilled labor, but we assume that components production uses low-skilled labor intensively and that R&D uses skilled labor intensively. As in our earlier model, we assume that the costs of capital are equal in the two activities and do not discuss this factor. Our goal will be to compare a no-trade situation with an equilibrium with trade through offshoring, to determine whether there are overall gains from trade.

Suppose that the firm has a certain amount of high-skilled (H) and low-skilled (L) labor to devote to components and R&D. It is free to move these workers between the two activities. For example, scientists could be used in the research lab or could instead be used to determine the best method to produce components; similarly, workers who are assembling components can instead assist with the construction of full-scale models in the research lab. Given the amount of high-skilled and low-skilled labor used in total, we can graph a production possibilities frontier (PPF) for the firm between components and R&D activities, as shown in Figure 7-9. This PPF looks just like the production possibilities frontier for a country, except that now we apply it to a single firm. Points on the PPF, such as *A*, correspond to differing amounts of high-skilled and low-skilled labor used in the components and R&D activities. Moving left from point *A* to another point on the PPF, for example, would involve shifting some high-skilled and low-skilled labor from the production of components into the research lab.

Production in the Absence of Offshoring

Now that we have the PPF for the firm, we can analyze an equilibrium for the firm, just as we have previously done for an entire economy. Suppose initially that the firm cannot engage in offshoring of its activities. This assumption means that the component production and R&D done at Home are used to manufacture a final product at Home: it cannot assemble any components in Foreign, and likewise, it cannot send any of its R&D results abroad to be used in a Foreign plant.

The two production activities are used to produce a final good. To determine how much of the final good is produced, we can use **isoquants.** An isoquant is similar to a consumer's indifference curve, except that instead of utility, it illustrates the production

FIGURE 7-9

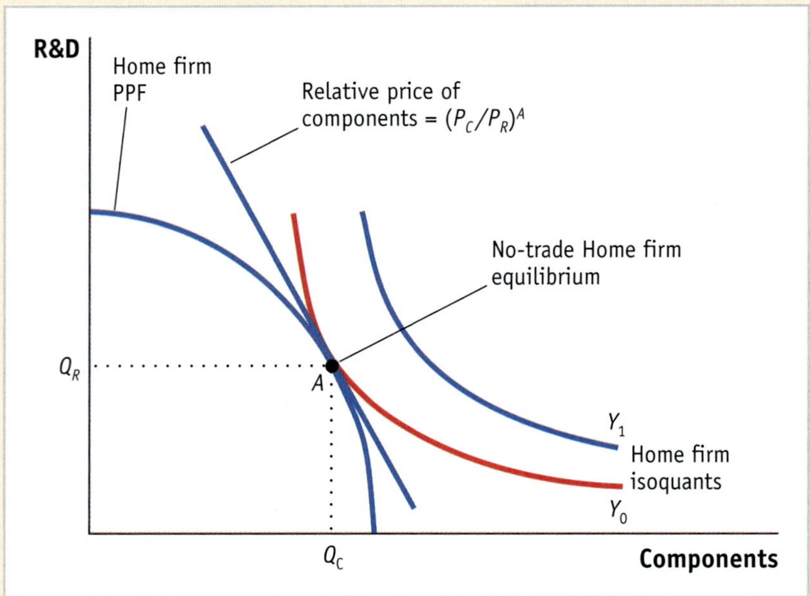

No-Trade Equilibrium for the Home Firm The PPF shows the combinations of components and R&D that can be undertaken by a firm with a given amount of labor and capital. In the absence of offshoring, the firm produces at *A*, using quantities Q_C of components and Q_R of R&D to produce amount Y_0 of the final good. The line tangent to the isoquant through point *A* measures the value that the firm puts on components relative to R&D, or their relative price, $(P_C/P_R)^A$. Amount Y_1 of the final good cannot be produced in the absence of offshoring because it lies outside the PPF for the firm.

of the firm; it is a curve along which the output of the firm is constant despite changing combinations of inputs. Two of these isoquants are labeled as Y_0 and Y_1 in Figure 7-9. The quantity of the final good Y_0 can be produced using the quantity Q_C of components and the quantity Q_R of R&D, shown at point *A* in the figure. Notice that the isoquant Y_0 is tangent to the PPF at point *A*, which indicates that this isoquant is the highest amount of the final good that can be produced using any combination of components and R&D on the PPF. The quantity of the final good Y_1 cannot be produced in the absence of offshoring because it lies outside the PPF. Thus, point *A* is the amount of components and R&D that the firm chooses in the absence of offshoring or what we will call the "no-trade" or "autarky" equilibrium for short.

Through the no-trade equilibrium *A* in Figure 7-9, we draw a line with the slope of the isoquant at point *A*. The slope of the isoquant measures the value, or price, that the firm puts on components relative to R&D. We can think of these prices as internal to the firm, reflecting the marginal costs of production of the two activities. An automobile company, for example, would be able to compute the extra labor and other inputs needed to produce some components of a car and that would be its internal price of components P_C. Similarly, it could compute the marginal cost of developing one more prototype of a new vehicle, which is the internal price of R&D or P_R. The slope of the price line through point *A* is the price of components relative to the price of R&D, $(P_C/P_R)^A$, in the absence of offshoring.[11]

Equilibrium with Offshoring Now suppose that the firm can import and export its production activities through offshoring. For example, some of the components could be done in a Foreign plant and then imported by the Home firm. Alternatively,

[11] Recall that the slope of a price line is the relative price of the good on the horizontal axis, which is Components in Figure 7-9.

some R&D done at Home can be exported to a Foreign plant and used there. In either case, the quantity of the final good is no longer constrained by the Home PPF. Just as in the Ricardian and Heckscher-Ohlin models, in which a higher level of utility (indifference curve) can be obtained if countries specialize and trade with each other, here a higher level of production (isoquant) is possible by trading intermediate activities.

We refer to the relative price of the two activities that the Home firm has available through offshoring as the world relative price or $(P_C/P_R)^{W1}$. Let us assume that the world relative price of components is cheaper than Home's no-trade relative price, $(P_C/P_R)^{W1} < (P_C/P_R)^A$. That assumption means the Home firm can import components at a lower relative price than it can produce them itself. The assumption that $(P_C/P_R)^{W1} < (P_C/P_R)^A$ is similar to the assumption we made in the previous section, that the relative wage of low-skilled labor is lower in Foreign, $W_L^*/W_H^* < W_L/W_H$. With a lower relative wage of low-skilled labor in Foreign, the components assembly will also be cheaper in Foreign. It follows that Home will want to offshore components, which are cheaper abroad, while the Home firm will be exporting R&D (i.e., offshoring it to Foreign firms), which is cheaper at Home.

The Home equilibrium with offshoring is illustrated in Figure 7-10. The world relative price of components is tangent to the PPF at point *B*. Notice that the world relative price line is *flatter* than the no-trade relative price line at Home. The flattening

FIGURE 7-10

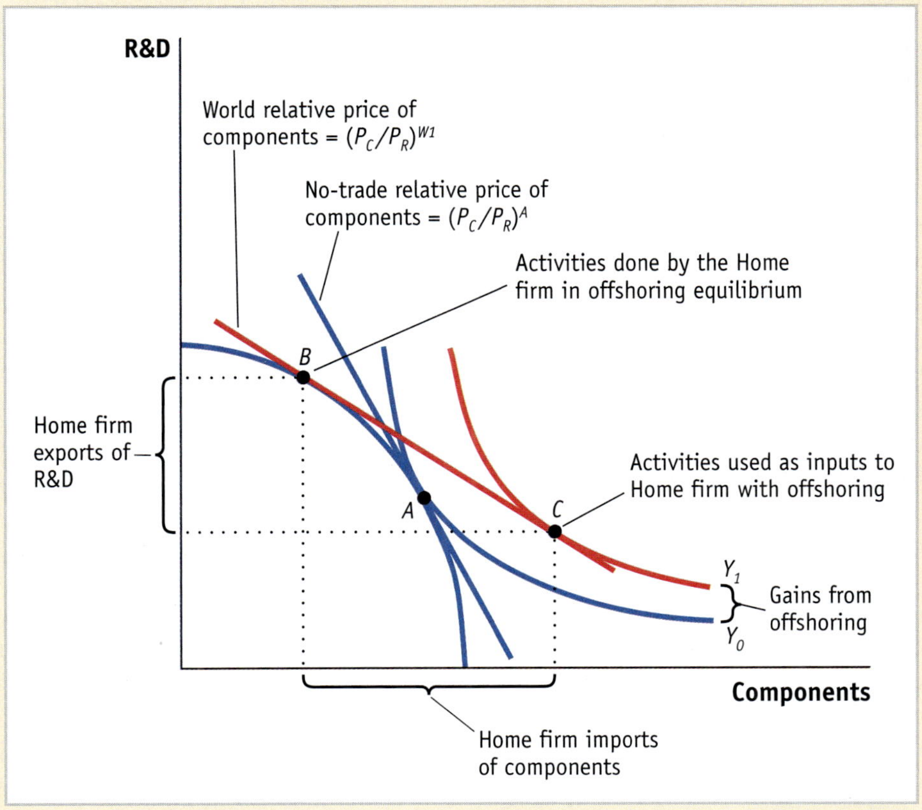

Offshoring Equilibrium for the Home Firm In the presence of offshoring, the Home firm will do more R&D and less component production, at point *B*. The Home firm then exports R&D activities and imports components at the world relative price of components, which allows it to produce the amount Y_1 of the final good. The difference between Y_0 and Y_1 represents the gains to the Home firm from offshoring.

of the price line reflects the lower world relative price of components as compared with the no-trade relative price at Home. As a result of this fall in the relative price of components, the Home firm undertakes more R&D and less component production, moving from point A to point B on its PPF.

Starting at point B on its PPF, the Home firm now exports R&D and imports components, moving along the relative price line to point C. Therefore, through offshoring the firm is able to move off of its PPF to point C. At that point, the isoquant labeled Y_1 is tangent to the world price line, indicating that the maximum amount of the final good Y_1 is being produced. Notice that this production of the final good exceeds the amount Y_0 that the Home produced in the absence of offshoring.

Gains from Offshoring within the Firm The increase in the amount of the final good produced—from Y_0 to Y_1—is a measure of the gains from trade to the Home firm through offshoring. Using the same total amount of high-skilled and low-skilled labor at Home as before, the company is able to produce more of the final good through its ability to offshore components and R&D. Because more of the final good is produced with the same overall amount of high-skilled and low-skilled labor available in Home, the Home company is more productive. Its costs of production fall, and we expect that the price of its final product also falls. The gains for this company are therefore spread to consumers, too.

For these reasons, we agree with the quote about offshoring at the beginning of the chapter: "When a good or service is produced more cheaply abroad, it makes more sense to import it than to make or provide it domestically." In our example, component production is cheaper in Foreign than in Home, so Home imports components from Foreign. There are overall gains from offshoring. That is our first conclusion: *when comparing a no-trade situation to the equilibrium with offshoring, and assuming that the world relative price differs from that at Home, there are always gains from offshoring.*

To see how this conclusion is related to the earlier quotation from Samuelson, we need to introduce one more feature into our discussion. Rather than just comparing the no-trade situation with the offshoring equilibrium, we need to also consider the impact of offshoring on a country's *terms of trade*.

Terms of Trade

As explained in Chapters 2 and 3, the terms of trade equal the price of a country's exports divided by the price of its imports. In the example we are discussing, the Home terms of trade are $(P_R/P_C)^{W1}$, because Home is exporting R&D and importing components. A rise in the terms of trade indicates that a country is obtaining a higher price for its exports, or paying a lower price for its imports, both of which benefit the country. Conversely, a fall in the terms of trade harms a country because it is paying more for its imports or selling its exports for less.

In his paper, Samuelson contrasts two cases. In the first, the Foreign country improves its productivity in the good that it exports (components), thereby lowering the price of components; in the second, the Foreign country improves its productivity in the good that Home exports (R&D services), thereby lowering *that* price. These two cases lead to very different implications for the terms of trade and Home gains, so we consider each in turn.

Fall in the Price of Components Turning to Figure 7-11, let the Home country start at the equilibrium with offshoring shown by points *B* and *C*. From that situation, suppose there is a *fall* in the relative price of component production. That price might fall, for instance, if the Foreign country improves its productivity in components, thereby lowering the price paid by Home for this service. Because components are being imported by Home, a fall in their price is a *rise* in the Home terms of trade, to $(P_R/P_C)^{W2}$. Let us trace how this change in the terms of trade will affect the Home equilibrium.

Because of the fall in the relative price of components, the world price line shown in Figure 7-11 becomes *flatter*. Production will shift to point *B′*, and by exporting R&D and importing components along the world price line, the firm ends up at point *C′*. Production of the final good at point *C′* is Y_2, which exceeds the production Y_1 in the initial equilibrium with offshoring.[12] Thus, the Home firm enjoys *greater* gains from offshoring when the price of components falls. This is the first case considered by Samuelson, and it reinforces our conclusions that offshoring leads to overall gains.

FIGURE 7-11

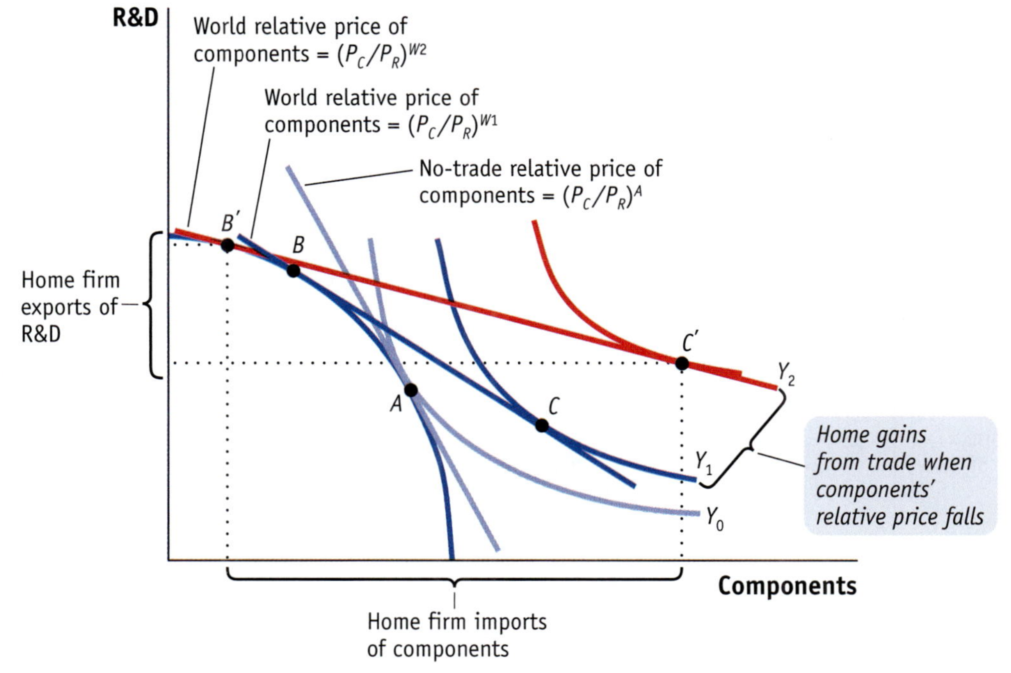

Fall in the Price of Component If the relative price of components falls from $(P_C/P_R)^{W1}$ to $(P_C/P_R)^{W2}$, then the Home firm will do even more R&D and less components production, at point *B′* rather than *B*. The increase in the terms of trade allows the Home firm to produce output Y_2 at point *C′*, and the gains from trade are higher than in the initial offshoring equilibrium (points *B* and *C*).

[12] Notice that the fall in the relative price of components leads to an increase in the amount of components imported but that the amount of R&D exported from Home does not necessarily increase. You are asked to explore this case further in Problem 10 at the end of the chapter.

Fall in the Price of R&D We also need to consider the second case identified by Samuelson, and that is when there is a fall in the price of R&D services rather than components. This is what Samuelson has in mind when he argues that offshoring might allow developing countries, such as India, to gain a comparative advantage in those activities in which the United States formerly had comparative advantage. As Indian companies like Wipro (an information technology services company headquartered in Bangalore) engage in more R&D activities, they are directly competing with American companies exporting the same services. So this competition can lower the world price of R&D services.

In Figure 7-12, we reproduce Figure 7-10, including the Home no-trade equilibrium at point *A* and the Home production point *B* with offshoring. Starting at point *B*, a fall in the world relative price of R&D will lead to a *steeper* price line (because the slope of the price line is the world relative price of components, which increases when P_R *falls*). At the new price $(P_C/P_R)^{W3}$, Home shifts production to point *B″* and, by exporting R&D and importing components, moves to point *C″*. Notice that final output has *fallen* from Y_1 to Y_3. Therefore, the fall in the price of R&D services leads to losses for the Home firm.

To explain where the losses are coming from, notice that Home is exporting R&D and importing components in the initial offshoring equilibrium (points *B* and *C*), so its

FIGURE 7-12

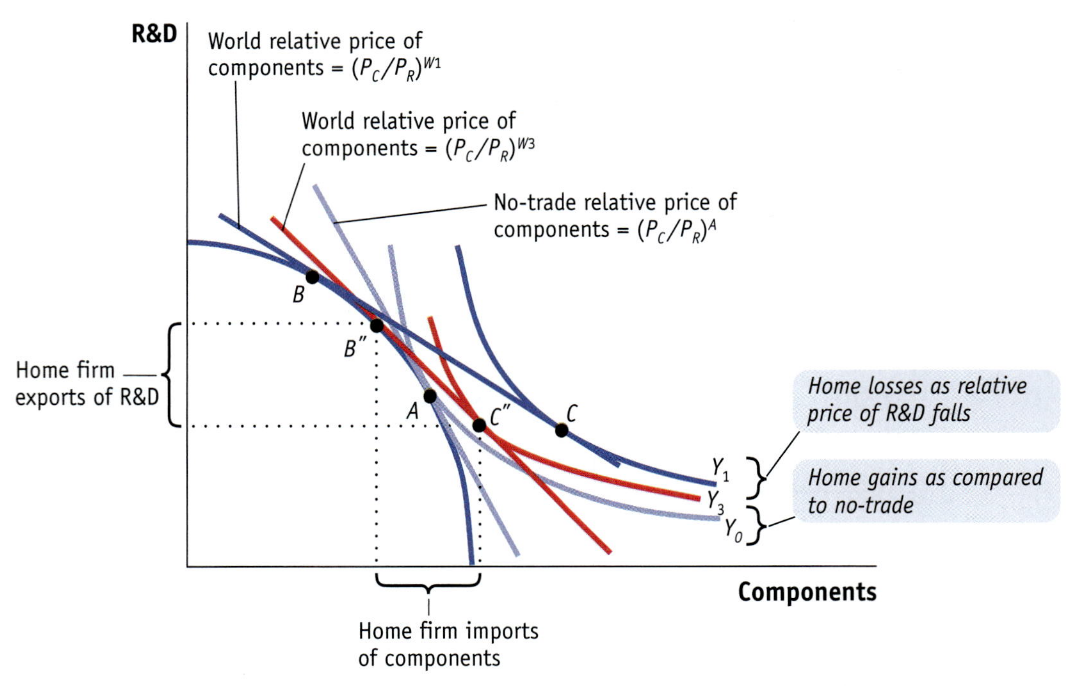

A Fall in the Price of R&D A fall in the relative price of R&D makes the world price line steeper, $(P_C/P_R)^{W3}$. As a result, the Home firm reduces its R&D activities and increases its components activities, moving from *B* to *B″* along the PPF. At the new world relative price, the Home firm faces a terms-of-trade loss and can no longer export each unit of R&D for as many components as it could in the initial offshoring equilibrium. The final good output is reduced from Y_1 to Y_3 at point *C″*. Notice that the final good output, Y_3, is still higher than output without trade, Y_0. After the fall in the relative price of R&D, there are still gains from trade relative to no-trade (point *A*) but losses relative to the initial offshoring equilibrium (points *B* and *C*).

terms of trade are the price of R&D divided by the price of components (P_R/P_C). With the fall in the price of R&D, the Home terms of trade have *worsened*, and Home is worse off compared with its initial offshoring equilibrium. Samuelson's point is that the United States *could* be worse off if China or India becomes more competitive in, and lowers the prices of, the products that the United States itself is exporting, such as R&D services. This is theoretically correct. Although it may be surprising to think of the United States being in this position, the idea that a country will suffer when its terms of trade fall is familiar to us from developing-country examples (such as the Prebisch-Singer hypothesis) in earlier chapters.

Furthermore, notice that final output of Y_3 is still higher than Y_0, the no-offshoring output. *Therefore, there are still Home gains from offshoring at C'' as compared with the no-trade equilibrium at A.* It follows that Home can never be worse off with trade as compared with no trade. Samuelson's point is that a country is worse off when its terms of trade fall, even though it is still better off than in the absence of trade. With the fall in the terms of trade, some factors of production will lose and others will gain, but in this case the gains of the winners are not enough to compensate the losses of the losers. Our simple model of offshoring illustrates Samuelson's point.

The offshoring that occurred from the United States in the 1980s and the 1990s often concerned manufacturing activities. But today, the focus is frequently one of the newer forms of offshoring, the offshoring of **business services** to foreign countries. Business services are activities such as accounting, auditing, human resources, order processing, telemarketing, and after-sales service, like getting help with your computer (see **Side Bar: Offshoring Microsoft Windows**). Firms in the United States are increasingly

SIDE BAR

Offshoring Microsoft Windows

Have you ever been frustrated in your attempt to install a new version of Microsoft Windows on your computer? Well, you are not alone. It just so happens that Microsoft Corporation, located in Seattle, Washington, also avoids loading upgrades of the Windows software onto its own computers. Who loads these upgrades? It turns out that Wipro, an Indian high-tech firm, manages Microsoft's computers in the nighttime hours in Seattle, which is during the daytime hours in Bangalore, India.

Called "infrastructure outsourcing," the remote management of computer resources is just one example of service outsourcing. Wipro performs infrastructure outsourcing for Microsoft and also for Royal Dutch Shell, which is one of the largest oil companies in the world. During the nonoperating hours in those companies, Wipro remotely accesses their computers, performs routine maintenance, troubleshoots for viruses, repairs corrupt files, and checks for other problems that can arise. As the sun rises in Seattle, the computers at Microsoft are better than when the employees left the night before, which makes those employees more productive in their own computer work. In the future, perhaps universities in the United States will also use infrastructure outsourcing to maintain their computer systems so that the computers in your dormitory, too, will be maintained during the nighttime hours by programmers in India!

AP Photo/Gautam Singh

They could be talking to you.

transferring these activities to India, where the wages of educated workers are much lower than in the United States. This is the sort of competition that Samuelson had in mind when he spoke of China and India improving their productivity and comparative advantage in activities that the United States already exports. The next application discusses the magnitude of service exports and also the changes in their prices.

APPLICATION

U.S. Terms of Trade and Service Exports

Because Samuelson's argument is a theoretical one, the next step is to examine the evidence for the United States. If the United States has been facing competition in R&D and the other skill-intensive activities that we export, then we would expect the terms of trade to fall. Conversely, if the United States has been offshoring in manufacturing, then the opportunity to import lower-priced intermediate inputs should lead to a rise in the terms of trade.

Merchandise Prices To evaluate these ideas, we make use of data on the terms of trade for the United States. In Figure 7-13, we first show the terms of trade for the United States for merchandise goods (excluding petroleum), which is the gold line.[13]

FIGURE 7-13

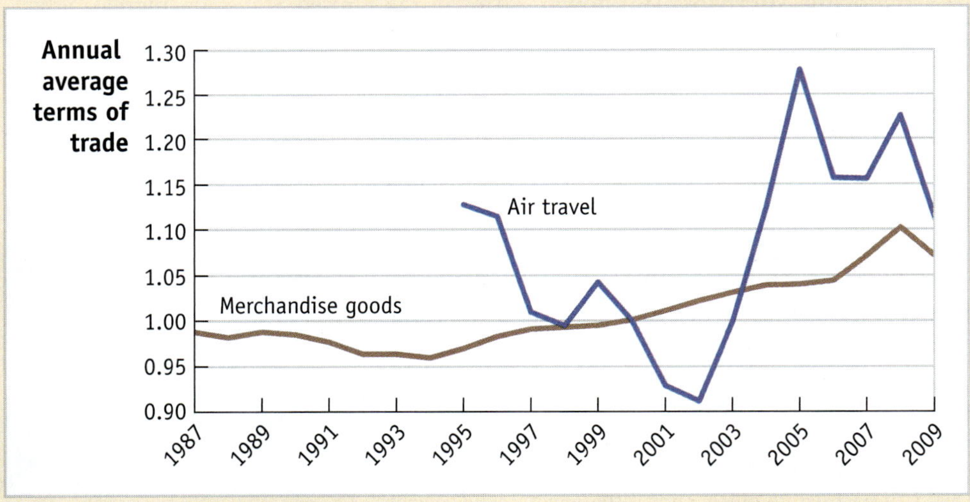

Terms of Trade for the United States, 1987–2009 Shown here are the U.S. terms of trade for merchandise goods (excluding petroleum) and for air travel services. The terms of trade for merchandise goods fell from 1987 to 1994 and then rose to 2008, with a slight dip in 2009. The terms of trade for air travel services are more volatile, falling from 1995 to 2002, rising until 2005 and falling erratically until 2009. In sum, we do not see a pattern of declining terms of trade in either of these sectors.

Source: Bureau of Labor Statistics.

[13] Merchandise goods include agriculture, mining, and manufacturing. We have excluded petroleum because its world price is determined by conditions such as shortages and wars and behaves quite differently from the prices of other merchandise goods.

The terms of trade for goods fell from 1987 to 1994 but have been rising since then, with a slight dip in 2009. The improvement in the merchandise terms of trade shows that we are able to import intermediate inputs (and also import final goods) at lower prices over time. This rise in the terms of trade means that there are increasing gains from trade in merchandise goods for the United States.

Service Prices For trade in services, such as finance, insurance, and R&D, it is very difficult to measure their prices in international trade. These services are tailored to the buyer and, as a result, there are not standardized prices. For this reason, we do not have an overall measure of the terms of trade in services. There is one type of service, however, for which it is relatively easy to collect international prices: air travel. The terms of trade in air travel equal the price that foreigners pay for travel on U.S. airlines (a service export) divided by the price that Americans pay on foreign airlines (a service import). In Figure 7-13, we also show the U.S. terms of trade in air travel that are available since 1995. The terms of trade in air travel are quite volatile, falling from 1995 to 2002, then rising to 2005, and falling erratically again afterward. For this one category of services, the terms of trade improvement from 2002 to 2005 indicates growing gains from trade for the United States, the same result we found for merchandise goods. Summing up, there is no evidence to date that the falling terms of trade that Samuelson is concerned about have occurred for the United States.

Service Trade What about other traded services? Although standard prices are not available, data on the *amount* of service exports and imports for the United States are collected annually. These data are shown in Table 7-2 for 2008. The United States runs a substantial surplus in services trade, with exports of $525 billion and imports of $364 billion. Categories of service exports that exceed imports include several types of business, professional, and technical services (but in computer and information services, the United States now runs a deficit); education (which is exported when a foreign student studies in the United States); financial services; travel; and royalties and license fees (which are collected from foreign firms when they use U.S. patents and trademarks or are paid abroad when we use foreign patents). The fact that exports exceed imports in many categories in Table 7-2 means that the United States has a comparative advantage in traded services. Indeed, the U.S. surplus in business, professional, and technical services is among the highest in the world, similar to that of the United Kingdom and higher than that of Hong Kong and India. London is a world financial center and competes with New York and other U.S. cities, which explains the high trade surplus of the United Kingdom, whereas Hong Kong is a regional hub for transportation and offshoring to China. The

TABLE 7-2

U.S. Trade in Services, 2008 ($ millions) This table shows U.S. exports and imports in the major categories of services trade for 2008.

	Exports	Imports
Computer and information services	12,599	16,139
Management and consulting services	26,942	21,565
R&D and testing services	17,139	14,885
Operational leasing	7,942	958
Other business, professional, and technical services	48,901	22,736
Total business, professional, and technical services	$113,525	$76,284
Education	17,796	5,204
Financial services	60,190	19,143
Insurance services	10,756	42,939
Telecommunications	9,163	7,193
Total other private services	$233,529	$153,267
Travel	110,090	79,743
Passenger fares	31,623	32,597
Other transporation	58,945	72,143
Royalties and license fees	91,599	26,616
Other services	22,099	2,505
Total private services	$525,786	$364,366

Source: U.S. Bureau of Economic Analysis.

FIGURE 7-14

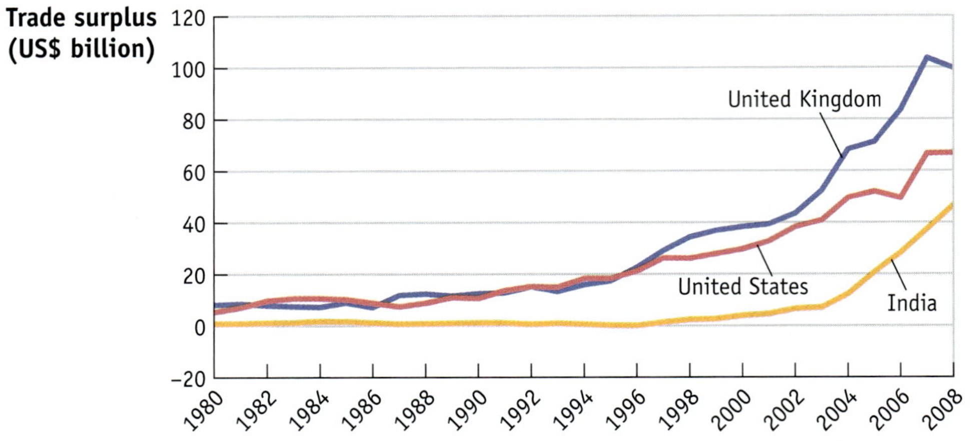

Trade Surplus in Business Services This figure shows the combined trade surplus in computer and information services, other business services, and financial services for the United States, the United Kingdom, and India from 1980 to 2008. The U.S. surplus in these categories of services has been growing steadily since about 1985 and up until 1995 shows a very similar pattern to the trade surplus from the United Kingdom, its chief competitor. Since 1995 the surplus of the United Kingdom has grown faster, mainly due to its exports of financial services. India's surplus began growing around 1995 and derives entirely from its exports of computer and information services.

Source: International Monetary Fund.

combined trade balance in computer and information services, other business services, and financial services for the United States, the United Kingdom, and India since 1980 are graphed in Figure 7-14.

The U.S. surplus in these categories of services has been growing steadily since about 1985 and up until 1995 shows a very similar pattern to the trade surplus from the United Kingdom, its chief competitor. Since 1995 the surplus of the United Kingdom has grown faster, mainly due to its exports of financial services. India's surplus began growing around 1995 and derives entirely from its exports of computer and information services. In 2008 the combined U.S. surplus in computers, other business services, and financial services ($66 billion) was 50% greater than that in India ($46 billion), but 50% smaller than in the United Kingdom ($99 billion).

What will these surpluses look like a decade or two from now? It is difficult to project, but notice that as the Indian surplus began growing in Figure 7-14, the rise in the U.S. surplus slowed down. Indian net exports of computer and information services have grown by $46 billion since 1997, while U.S. net exports in this category have fallen by $7.5 billion. Although it is too soon to tell whether such trends will continue, it is at least possible that in a decade or two, India's overall surplus in service exports could overtake that of the United States. Only time will tell whether the United States will eventually face the same type of competition from India in its service exports that it has already faced for many years from the United Kingdom. ■

3 The Politics and Future of Offshoring

Offshoring is controversial and is often the topic of political debate. In February 2004 the first quote at the beginning of this chapter appeared in the *Economic Report of the President*. The writer of that sentence, Harvard economist N. Gregory Mankiw, who was chairman of the Council of Economic Advisors, also said that "outsourcing is just a new way of doing international trade. More things are tradable than were tradable in the past, and that's a good thing." Those comments were widely criticized by the Democrats and Republicans alike, and Professor Mankiw later apologized in a letter to the House of Representatives, writing, "My lack of clarity left the wrong impression that I praised the loss of U.S. jobs."

In the Democratic primary elections of 2007 and in the presidential campaign of 2008, this topic came up again. Senators Barack Obama and Hillary Clinton both promised that, if elected, they would end tax breaks for companies earning profits overseas:[14]

> **Obama, Nov. 3, 2007:** When I am president, I will end the tax giveaways to companies that ship our jobs overseas, and I will put the money in the pockets of working Americans, and seniors, and homeowners who deserve a break.

> **Clinton, Nov. 19, 2007:** And we are going to finally close the tax loopholes and stop giving tax breaks to companies that ship jobs overseas. Enough with outsourcing American jobs using taxpayer dollars.

To what tax breaks were Mr. Obama and Ms. Clinton referring? The United States taxes corporate profits at 35%, a high rate when compared with the corporate tax rates in other countries. Profit earned by overseas subsidiaries of U.S. companies, however, goes untaxed by the U.S. government provided that such a subsidiary stays overseas and does not appear on the books of the parent company in the United States. That tax provision gives U.S. multinational companies an incentive to use these funds overseas for further investment in the subsidiary, but it does not necessarily lead them to move jobs overseas in the first place. Eventually, when these profits are moved back to the parent company in the United States, they are taxed at the normal rate.

President Obama recently announced that he would follow through on his campaign pledge to end the tax break on overseas profits of multinational firms, as indicated by the quotation at the beginning of this chapter: "We should . . . encourage . . . businesses to stay within our borders, it's time to finally slash the tax breaks for companies that ship our jobs overseas." That change in policy does not have much support from economists. One strongly worded response comes from Matthew Slaughter, Professor at Dartmouth College, in **Headlines: How to Destroy American Jobs.** He cites evidence that U.S. multinationals have added roughly as many jobs in the United States as they have added abroad, and argues that these jobs in the United States depend on the ability of the multinationals to offshore other jobs.

In addition to the employment statistics, Professor Slaughter also cites evidence that U.S. multinational firms conducted nearly 90% of all private-sector R&D in the United States, and that these firms account for the majority of U.S. productivity gains.

---

[14] These quotations and some material that follows are taken from http://www.factcheck.org/askfactcheck/what_kind_of_tax_breaks_does_the.html.

HEADLINES

How to Destroy American Jobs

This article argues that offshoring by multinational companies supports an increase in jobs at home, and that these jobs would be lost by policies to restrict offshoring.

Deep in the president's budget released Monday [February 1, 2010] appear a set of proposals headed "Reform U.S. International Tax System." If these proposals are enacted, U.S.-based multinational firms will face $122.2 billion in tax increases over the next decade. This is a natural follow-up to President Obama's sweeping plan announced last May [2009] entitled "Leveling the Playing Field: Curbing Tax Havens and Removing Tax Incentives for Shifting Jobs Overseas."

The fundamental assumption behind these proposals is that U.S. multinationals expand abroad only to "export" jobs out of the country. Thus, taxing their foreign operations more would boost tax revenues here and create desperately needed U.S. jobs. This is simply wrong. These tax increases would not create American jobs, they would destroy them.

Academic research, including most recently that done by Harvard's Mihir Desai and Fritz Foley and University of Michigan's James Hines, has consistently found that expansion abroad by U.S. multinationals tends to support jobs based in the U.S. More investment and employment abroad are strongly associated with more investment and employment in American parent companies.

When parent firms based in the U.S. hire workers in their foreign affiliates, the skills and occupations of these workers are often complementary; they aren't substitutes. More hiring abroad stimulates more U.S. hiring. For example, as Wal-Mart has opened stores abroad, it has created hundreds of U.S. jobs for workers to coordinate the distribution of goods worldwide. The expansion of these foreign affiliates—whether to serve foreign customers, or to save costs—also expands the overall scale of multinationals.

Expanding abroad also allows firms to refine their scope of activities. For example, exporting routine production means that employees in the U.S. can focus on higher value-added tasks such as R&D, marketing and general management. The total impact of this process is much richer than an overly simplistic story of exporting jobs. But the ultimate proof lies in the empirical evidence.

Consider total employment spanning 1988 through 2007 (the most recent year of data available from the U.S. Bureau of Economic Analysis). Over that time, employment in affiliates rose by 5.3 million—to 11.7 million from 6.4 million. Over that same period, employment in U.S. parent companies increased by nearly as much—4.3 million—to 22 million from 17.7 million. Indeed, research repeatedly shows that foreign-affiliate expansion tends to expand U.S. parent activity. . . .

The major policy challenge facing the U.S. today is not just to create jobs, but to create high-paying private-sector jobs linked to investment and trade. Which firms can create these jobs? U.S.-based multinationals. They—along with similarly performing U.S. affiliates of foreign-based multinationals—have long been among the strongest companies in the U.S. economy.

These two groups of firms accounted for the majority of the post-1995 acceleration in U.S. productivity growth, the foundation of rising standards of living for everyone. They tend to create high-paying jobs—27.5 million in 2007. . . . And these firms also conducted $240.2 billion in research and development, a remarkable 89.2% of all U.S. private-sector R&D.

To climb out of the recession, we need to create millions of the kinds of jobs that U.S. multinationals tend to create. Economic policy on all fronts should be encouraging job growth by these firms. The proposed international-tax reforms do precisely the opposite.

Source: Matthew J. Slaughter, "How to Destroy American Jobs," Wall Street Journal, *February 3, 2010, p. A17.*

Direct evidence on the positive impact of offshoring on productivity comes from another source, a 2005 study of the offshoring of material inputs and services by U.S. manufacturing firms in the 1990s.[15] Over the eight years from 1992 to 2000, that study found that service offshoring can explain between 11 and 13% of the total

[15] Mary Amiti and Shang-Jin Wei, 2005, "Service Offshoring, Productivity, and Employment: Evidence from the United States," International Monetary Fund, IMF Working Paper 05/238; and 2006, "Service Offshoring and Productivity: Evidence from the United States," National Bureau of Economic Research (NBER) Working Paper No. 11926.

increase in productivity within the U.S. manufacturing sector. In addition, the offshoring of material inputs explains between 3 and 6% of the increase in manufacturing productivity. Combining these effects, offshoring explains between 15 and 20% of overall productivity growth in the manufacturing sector. Evidence of this type makes economists reluctant to impose additional taxes on U.S. companies that engage in offshoring, because of the possible adverse effects on productivity here in the United States.

On the other hand, changes in economic conditions that lead firms to *voluntarily* bring some activities back home would be viewed favorably by most economists. There is some evidence that economic conditions have changed in that direction, as described in **Headlines: Caterpillar Joins "Onshoring" Trend.** A combination of stimulus spending in the United States, lower wages, and a weak U.S. dollar (which makes it more expensive to operate overseas) has led some companies to "onshore" their activities back to the United States. This trend has also occurred because companies are finding that communication with overseas suppliers can be slow and costly.

The Future of U.S. Comparative Advantage

Just as in our model of this chapter, the recent "onshoring" trend shows that companies usually avoid offshoring *all* activities from the United States: the extra communication and trade costs involved need to be balanced against the lower foreign wages to find the right amount of offshoring. Most often companies find it

HEADLINES

Caterpillar Joins "Onshoring" Trend

Some American companies have found it advantageous to take activities they had previously shifted overseas and move them back home, in what is called "onshoring."

Caterpillar, Inc. is considering relocating some heavy-equipment overseas production to a new U.S. plant, part of a growing movement among manufacturers to bring more operations back home—a shift that will likely spark fierce competition among states for new manufacturing jobs. The trend, known as onshoring or reshoring, is gaining momentum as a weak U.S. dollar makes it costlier to import products from overseas. Manufacturers are also counting on White House jobs incentives, as well as their ability to negotiate lower prices from U.S. suppliers who were hurt by the downturn and willing to bargain.

After a decade of rapid globalization, economists say companies are seeing disadvantages of offshore production, including shipping costs, complicated logistics, and quality issues. Political unrest and theft of intellectual property pose additional risks. "If you want to keep your supply chain tight, it's hard to do that with a 16-hour plane ride from Shanghai to Ohio," said Cliff Waldman, an economist with the Manufacturers Alliance/MAPI, a public policy and economics research group in Arlington, Virginia.

General Electric Co. said last June it would move production of some water heaters from China to its facility in Louisville, Kentucky, starting in 2011. A GE spokeswoman said a 2005 labor agreement under which new employees would be paid $13 an hour, [instead of the] nearly $20 an hour [they once made], "enabled us to be more competitive." . . .

Source: Kris Maher and Bob Tita, "Caterpillar Joins 'Onshoring' Trend," Wall Street Journal, *March 11, 2010, p. A17.*

advantageous to keep some activities in the United States (such as those using more highly skilled labor or relying on close communication with customers) and move other activities abroad (using less skilled labor and involving more routine activities). The fear sometimes expressed in the popular press that offshoring threatens the elimination of most manufacturing and service jobs in the United States is overstated. The ability to offshore a portion of the production process allows other activities to remain in the United States.

A good example to illustrate this point is the offshoring of medical services. The transcription of doctors' notes from spoken to written form was one of the first service activities offshore to India. Since then, other types of medical services have also been offshored, and a *New York Times* article in 2003 identified the reading of X-rays—or radiology—as the next area that could shift overseas: "It turns out that even American radiologists, with their years of training and annual salaries of $250,000 or more, worry about their jobs moving to countries with lower wages, in much the same way that garment knitters, blast-furnace operators and data-entry clerks do. . . . Radiology may just be the start of patient care performed overseas."[16]

It turns out, however, that the types of radiology jobs that can potentially be transferred overseas are very limited.[17] Radiology is a high-paying profession precisely because the reading of X-rays is difficult and takes years of training and practice to perfect. X-rays are normally analyzed in the same hospital where the patient is being treated. In a few cases of specific diseases, such as the reading of mammograms for breast cancer, it is possible that the work can be outsourced (i.e., performed outside the hospital), either domestically or offshore. Firms known as "nighthawks" already provide some outsourcing services to hospitals, principally during nighttime hours. Nighthawk firms are headquartered in the United States but have radiologists at offshore sites, including Australia, Israel, Spain, and India. These nighttime services allow smaller hospitals that cannot afford a full-time night radiologist to obtain readings during evening hours, and allow the nighthawk firms to keep their radiologists fully employed by combining the demand from multiple hospitals.

The outsoucing to nighthawk firms is a natural response to the round-the-clock demand for hospital services but less-than-full-time demand for radiologists on-site. Often these nighttime services are used only for preliminary reads, leading to immediate treatment of patients; the X-ray image is then read again by the staff radiologist in the United States the next day. That is, in many cases, the services being outsourced are not directly competing for the daytime jobs but, instead, are complements to these U.S. jobs.

Radiology is under no imminent threat from outsourcing because the profession involves decisions that cannot be codified in written rules. Much of the radiologist's knowledge is gained from reading countless X-rays with complex images and shadows, and the ability to recognize patterns cannot easily be passed on to another person or

[16] Andrew Pollack, "Who's Reading Your X-Ray: Jobs in Medical Care, Too, Can Be Outsourced Overseas," *New York Times*, November 16, 2003, section 3, pp. 1, 9.

[17] The material in the following paragraphs is drawn from Frank Levy and Ari Goelman, "Offshoring and Radiology," presented at the Brookings Institute Trade Forum May 12–13, 2005.

firm. It follows that the work cannot be outsourced except for the nighttime activities of nighthawk firms, which actually work in conjunction with the daytime activities in major hospitals.

In every profession there will always be jobs that cannot be performed by someone who is not on-site. For many of the service activities listed in Table 7-2, the United States will continue to have comparative advantage even while facing foreign competition. In many manufacturing industries, the United States will continue to maintain some activities at home, such as R&D and marketing, even while shifting a portion of the production process abroad. Finally, we should recognize that the ability to offshore to Mexico or India ultimately makes the U.S. companies involved more profitable and therefore better able to withstand foreign competition.

4 Conclusions

In this chapter, we have studied a type of trade that is becoming increasingly important: offshoring, by which we mean the shifting of some production activities to another country, while other production activities are kept at Home. Rather than trading final goods, like wheat for cloth as in the Ricardian model of Chapter 2, or computers for shoes as in the Heckscher-Ohlin model of Chapter 4, with offshoring each good can be produced in stages in several countries and then assembled in a final location.

In the model of offshoring we presented, because low-skilled labor is relatively cheap abroad, it makes sense for Home to offshore to the Foreign country those activities that are less skill-intensive, while keeping at Home those activities that are more skill-intensive. "Slicing" the value chain in this way is consistent with the idea of comparative advantage, because each country is engaged in the activities for which its labor is relatively cheaper. From *both* the Home and Foreign point of view, the ratio of high-skilled/low-skilled labor in value chain activities goes up. A major finding of this chapter, then, is that an increase in offshoring will raise the relative demand (and hence relative wage) for skilled labor in *both* countries.

In a simplified model in which there are only two activities, we found that a fall in the world price of the low-skilled and labor-intensive input will lead to gains to the Home firm from offshoring. But in contrast, a fall in the price of the skilled labor-intensive input would lead to losses to the Home firm, as compared with the prior trade equilibrium. Such a price change is a terms-of-trade loss for Home, leading to losses from the lower relative price of exports. So even though Home gains overall from offshoring (producing at least as much as it would in a no-offshoring equilibrium), it is still the case that competition in the input being exported by Home will make it worse off.

Dan Wasserman. Represented by Tribune Media Services (http://www.Comicspage.com).

We concluded the chapter by exploring offshoring in service activities, a topic that has received much attention in the media recently. Offshoring from the United States to Mexico consists mainly of low-skilled jobs; offshoring from the United States to India consists of higher-skilled jobs performed by college-educated Indians. This new type of offshoring has been made possible by information and communication technologies (such as the Internet and fiber-optic cables) and has allowed cities like Bangalore, India, to establish service centers for U.S. companies. These facilities not only answer questions from customers in the United States and worldwide, they are also engaged in accounting and finance, writing software, R&D, and many other skilled business services.

The fact that it is not only *possible* to shift these activities to India but *economical* to do so shows how new technologies make possible patterns of international trade that would have been unimaginable a decade ago. Such changes show "globalization" at work. Does the offshoring of service activities pose any threat to white-collar workers in the United States? There is no simple answer. On the one hand, we presented evidence that service offshoring provides productivity gains, and therefore gains from trade, to the United States. But as always, having gains from trade does not mean that everyone gains: there can be winners and losers. For service offshoring, it is possible that skilled workers will see a potential reduction in their wages, just as low-skilled labor bore the brunt of the impact from offshoring in the 1980s. Nevertheless, it is still the case that the United States, like the United Kingdom and other European countries, continues to have a comparative advantage in exporting various types of business services. Although India is making rapid progress in the area of computer and information services, there are still many types of service activities that need be done locally and cannot be outsourced. One likely prediction is that the activities in the United States that cannot be codified in written rules and procedures, and that benefit from face-to-face contact as well as proximity to other highly skilled individuals in related industries, will continue to have comparative advantage.

KEY POINTS

1. The provision of a service or the production of various parts of a good in different countries for assembly into a final good in another location is called foreign outsourcing or offshoring.
2. We can apply the same ideas that we developed for trade in final goods among countries to the trade of intermediate offshored activities. For instance, if low-skilled labor is relatively inexpensive in the Foreign country, then the activities that are least skill-intensive will be offshored there, and Home will engage in the activities that are more skill-intensive.
3. We can also predict what happens to relative wages of skilled labor when there is a change in trading costs and more offshoring. Our model predicts that the relative demand for skilled labor *increases in both countries*. This result helps to

explain the observation that relative wages have been increasing in the United States and in other countries at the same time.

4. In an overall sense, there are gains from offshoring, because the specialization of countries in different production activities allows firms in both countries to produce a higher level of final goods. That increase in output represents a productivity gain, and the gains from trade.

5. With service offshoring, it is possible that a country like India will have rising productivity in activities in which the United States has comparative advantage, such as R&D. Rising productivity in India would lead to a fall in the price of R&D, which is a terms-of-trade loss for the United States. For that reason, the United States could lose due to service offshoring, though it still gains as compared with a situation of no offshoring at all.

KEY TERMS

foreign outsourcing, p. 200
offshoring, p. 200
value chain, p. 202
skill-biased technological change, p. 211
total wage payments, p. 211
isoquants, p. 215
business services, p. 221

PROBLEMS

1. Consider an offshoring model in which the hours of labor used in four activities in the United States and Mexico are as follows:

   Note that labor hours in Mexico are twice those in the United States, reflecting Mexico's lower productivity. Also note that the ratio of high-skilled to low-skilled labor used in each activity increases as we move to the right, from 1/5 in assembly, to 10/1 in R&D.

   Suppose that the wage of U.S. low-skilled workers is $10 per hour and that of high-skilled workers is $25 per hour, and that the wage of Mexican low-skilled workers is $1 per hour and that of high-skilled workers is $5 per hour (these values are made up to be convenient, not realistic). Also suppose that the trade costs are 25%, 30%, or 50%, which means that an additional 25%, 30%, or 50% is added to the costs of offshoring to Mexico.

Hours of Labor Used in Each Activity (per unit of output):

	Assembly	Component Production	Office Services	R&D
Low-skilled labor	Mexico: 20	Mexico: 12	Mexico: 8	Mexico: 4
	U.S.: 5	U.S.: 3	U.S.: 2	U.S.: 1
High-skilled labor	Mexico: 4	Mexico: 4	Mexico: 8	Mexico: 40
	U.S.: 1	U.S.: 1	U.S.: 2	U.S.: 10
High-skilled/low-skilled ratio	1/5	1/3	1/1	10/1

a. Fill in the blank cells in the following table by computing the costs of production of each activity in each country (two cells are filled in for you):

	Assembly	Component Production	Office Services	R&D
Mexico	$40			
United States				
Imported by United States from Mexico, Trade Costs = 25%				
Imported by United States from Mexico, Trade Costs = 30%	$52			
Imported by United States from Mexico, Trade Costs = 50%				

b. With trade costs of 50%, where is the value chain sliced? That is, which activities are cheaper to import from Mexico and which are cheaper to produce in the United States?

c. With trade costs of 30%, and then 25%, where is the value chain sliced?

2. Consider an offshoring model in which Home's skilled labor has a higher relative wage than Foreign's skilled labor and in which the costs of capital and trade are uniform across production activities.

   a. Will Home's offshored production activities be high or low on the value chain for a given product? That is, will Home offshore production activities that are skilled and labor-intensive, or low-skilled and labor-intensive? Explain.

   b. Suppose that Home uniformly increases its tariff level, effectively increasing the cost of importing all goods and services from abroad. How does this affect the slicing of the value chain?

   c. Draw relative labor supply and demand diagrams for Home and Foreign showing the effect of this change. What happens to the relative wage in each country?

3. Consider a U.S. firm's production of automobiles, including research and development and component production.

   a. Starting from a no-trade equilibrium in a PPF diagram, illustrate the gains from offshoring if the United States has a comparative advantage in component production.

   b. Now suppose that advances in engineering abroad decrease the relative price of research and development. Illustrate this change on your diagram and state the implications for production in the United States.

   c. Does the U.S. firm gain from advances in research and development abroad? Explain why or why not.

4. Consider the model of a firm that produces final goods using R&D and components as inputs, with cost data as follows:

Components: Total costs of production = $P_C \cdot Q_C = 100$

Earnings of high-skilled labor = $W_H \cdot H_C = 10$

Earnings of low-skilled labor = $W_L \cdot L_C = 40$

Earnings of capital = $R \cdot K_C = 50$

Share of total costs paid to high-skilled labor = 10/100 = 10%

Share of total costs paid to low-skilled labor = 40/100 = 40%

R&D: Total costs of R&D = $P_R \cdot Q_R = 100$

Earnings of high-skilled labor = $W_H \cdot H_R = 40$

Earnings of low-skilled labor = $W_L \cdot L_R = 10$

Earnings of capital = $R \cdot K_R = 50$

Share of total costs paid to high-skilled labor = 40/100 = 40%

Share of total costs paid to low-skilled labor = 10/100 = 10%

a. In which factor(s) is components intensive? In which factor(s) is R&D intensive?

b. Suppose that due to the opening of trade, the price of components fall by $\Delta P_C/P_C = -10\%$, while the price of R&D remains unchanged, $\Delta P_R/P_R = 0$. Using the hint below, calculate the change in the wage of skilled and low-skilled labor.

Hint: We follow a procedure similar to that used in Chapter 4 when calculating the change in factor prices in the Heckscher-Ohlin model. First, write the total costs in each activity as consisting of the payments to labor and capital:

$$P_C \cdot Q_C = R \cdot K_C + W_H \cdot H_C + W_L \cdot L_C,$$
for components

$$P_R \cdot Q_R = R \cdot K_R + W_H \cdot H_R + W_L \cdot L_R,$$
for R&D

Because we assume that 50% of costs in either components or R&D is always paid to capital, then $R \cdot K_C = 0.5(P_C \cdot Q_C)$ and $R \cdot K_R = 0.5(P_R \cdot Q_R)$, so we can rewrite the above two equations as

$$0.5(P_C \cdot Q_C) = W_H \cdot H_C + W_L \cdot L_C,$$
for components

$$0.5(P_R \cdot Q_R) = W_H \cdot H_R + W_L \cdot L_R,$$
for R&D

Taking the change in these equations:

$$0.5(\Delta P_C \cdot Q_C) = \Delta W_H \cdot H_C + \Delta W_L \cdot L_C,$$
for components

$$0.5(\Delta P_R \cdot Q_R) = \Delta W_H \cdot H_R + \Delta W_L \cdot L_R,$$
for R&D

Dividing the equations by $(\Delta P_C \cdot Q_C)$ and $(\Delta P_R \cdot Q_R)$, respectively, we can rewrite the equations as

$$0.5\left(\frac{\Delta P_C}{P_C}\right) = \left(\frac{\Delta W_H}{W_H}\right)\left(\frac{W_H \cdot H_C}{P_C \cdot Q_C}\right) + \left(\frac{\Delta W_L}{W_L}\right)\left(\frac{W_L \cdot L_C}{P_C \cdot Q_C}\right),$$
for components

$$0.5\left(\frac{\Delta P_R}{P_R}\right) = \left(\frac{\Delta W_H}{W_H}\right)\left(\frac{W_H \cdot H_R}{P_R \cdot Q_R}\right) + \left(\frac{\Delta W_L}{W_L}\right)\left(\frac{W_L \cdot L_R}{P_R \cdot Q_R}\right),$$
for R&D

Use the cost shares and price change data in these formulas to get

$$-5\% = \left(\frac{\Delta W_H}{W_H}\right)\left(\frac{10}{100}\right) + \left(\frac{\Delta W_L}{W_L}\right)\left(\frac{40}{100}\right),$$
for components

$$0 = \left(\frac{\Delta W_H}{W_H}\right)\left(\frac{40}{100}\right) + \left(\frac{\Delta W_L}{W_L}\right)\left(\frac{10}{100}\right),$$
for R&D

Now solve these two equations for the change in the high-skilled wage ($\Delta W_H/W_H$), and the change in the low-skilled wage ($\Delta W_L/W_L$).

c. What has happened to the *relative wage* of high-skilled/low-skilled labor? Does this match the predictions of the offshoring model in this chapter?

5. Consider the model of a firm that produces final goods using R&D and components as inputs, with cost data as follows:

Components: Total costs of production = $P_C \cdot Q_C = 100$

Earnings of high-skilled labor = $W_H \cdot H_C = 25$

Earnings of low-skilled labor = $W_L \cdot L_C = 25$

Earnings of capital = $R \cdot K_C = 50$

Share of total costs paid to high-skilled labor = 25/100 = 25%

Share of total costs paid to low-skilled labor = 25/100 = 25%

R&D: Total costs of R&D = $P_R \cdot Q_R = 100$

Earnings of high-skilled labor = $W_H \cdot H_R = 30$

Earnings of low-skilled labor = $W_L \cdot L_R = 20$

Earnings of capital = $R \cdot K_R = 50$

Share of total costs paid to high-skilled labor = 30/100 = 30%

Share of total costs paid to low-skilled labor = 20/100 = 20%

a. In which factor(s) is components intensive? In which factor(s) is research intensive?

b. Suppose that due to the opening of trade, the relative price of R&D increases, $\Delta P_R/P_R = 10\%$, whereas the price of components stays unchanged, $\Delta P_C/P_C = 0$. Calculate the change in the relative wage of high-skilled and low-skilled labor.

c. What has happened to the *relative wage* of high-skilled/low-skilled labor? How does this result compare to Problem 4, and explain why it is similar or different.

6. The following diagram shows what happened to the relative wage and relative demand for skilled labor in the U.S. manufacturing sector during the 1990s. These points are plotted using the data from Figures 7-5 and 7-6.

a. What must have happened to the supply and demand curves to explain this change in relative wage and relative employment?

b. Why do you think the supply and demand curves shifted this way? *Hint:* Think about where the workers who leave manufacturing might be going.

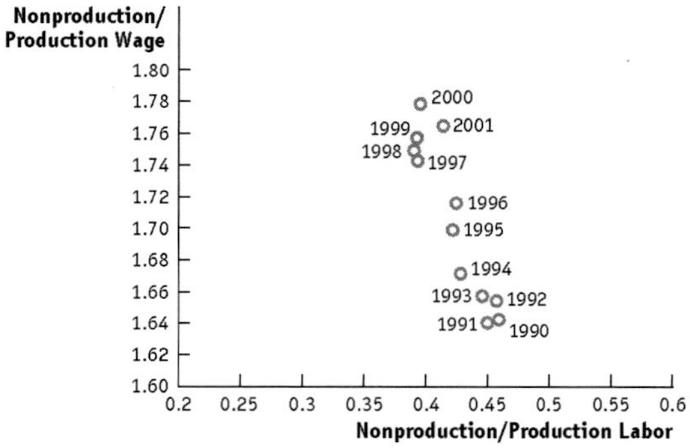

7. Read the following excerpt, and using what you have learned in this chapter, discuss how offshoring creates opportunities for the countries involved.

Sudhakar Shenoy, chief executive of Information Management Consultants (IMC) in Reston, makes an effective pitch for offshoring.

Several years ago IMC saw a market developing for software that would allow biotech companies to make better and faster use of the new human genome research.

Doing it here, Shenoy calculated, would cost several million dollars, which he figured would have priced the product too high for most customers. But by having a small group of engineers at IMC's Indian subsidiary do much of the coding work, he was able to bring the project in at $500,000. The result: IMC now has a thriving line of business in bioinformatics, with major clients and a growing payroll of six-figure PhDs here. And there are more engineers than ever—six here for every one in India.

But that's only part of the good-news story. In Pune, where IMC's Indian operations are located, an airport under construction will require lots of U.S. engineering, design and electronics. At the same time, IMC's Indian engineers, who earned annual salaries of $3,500 a decade ago, now command up to $12,000—enough to buy all manner of imported consumer goods.

Source: Excerpted from Steven Pearlstein, "Still Short of the Offshoring Ideal," *Washington Post*, March 12, 2004.

8. The quote from the 2004 *Economic Report of the President* at the beginning of the chapter generated a lot of controversy that year, as discussed at the beginning of section 3 here. The chairman of the Council, N. Gregory Mankiw, made the following additional comments in a speech while presenting the report: "Outsourcing is just a new way of doing international trade. More things are tradable than were tradable in the past, and that's a good thing."

   Those statements quickly led to reactions from both Democratic and Republican members of Congress. Tom Daschle, then the Democratic Senate minority leader, said, "If this is the administration's position, they owe an apology to every worker in America." Dennis Hastert, then Republican Speaker of the House, said, "Outsourcing can be a problem for American workers and the American economy." John Kerry, the 2004 Democratic presidential candidate, referred to businesses that offshored as "Benedict Arnold corporations." In response, Mankiw clarified his earlier comments: "My lack of clarity left the wrong impression that I praised the loss of U.S. jobs."

   Although you might feel that these statements just represented a squabble between politicians trying to score points during a presidential campaign, it is still worth trying to sort out who gains and who loses from offshoring.

   a. Why does Mankiw say that "outsourcing is a good thing" Who is it good for in the United States? Are there overall gains for the United States? Explain with a diagram.
   b. Later in this chapter, Paul Samuelson is quoted as saying that there is no "necessary surplus of winnings over losings" due to offshoring. Use Figure 7-12 to carefully explain why Samuelson says this.

9. In Figure 7-11, we saw that a fall in the relative price of components leads to an increase in the amount of components imported but that the amount of R&D exported from Home does not necessarily increase. To explore this further, complete the following:

   a. Let the relative price of components continue to fall in Figure 7-11, and show in a graph what happens to the equilibrium point on the isoquant for the final good.
   b. Now draw another graph that has the relative price of components on the vertical axis and the imports of components on the horizontal axis. Start at the no-trade relative price of components, where imports are zero. Then label the various world relative prices of components on the vertical axis, and graph the quantity of imports at each price. Can we be sure that the import demand curve slopes downward?
   c. Now draw a new graph that has the relative price of R&D on the vertical axis and the exports of R&D on the horizontal axis. Start at

the no-trade relative price of R&D, where exports are zero. Then label the various world relative prices of R&D on the vertical axis, and graph the quantity of exports at each price. When the relative price of R&D is high enough, what do you notice about the export supply curve?

10. Why might it be relatively easier for a developing country like India to export service activities through offshoring than to participate in the global economy by producing manufacturing components?

11. It is widely noted that even though China is the favored destination for manufacturing offshoring, it is far behind India in the business of offshored services. What differences between these two countries might account for this observation?

8

Import Tariffs and Quotas under Perfect Competition

I take this action to give our domestic steel industry an opportunity to adjust to surges in foreign imports, recognizing the harm from 50 years of foreign government intervention in the global steel market, which has resulted in bankruptcies, serious dislocation, and job loss.

President George W. Bush, in press statement announcing new "safeguard" tariffs on imported steel, March 5, 2002

The president decided to remedy the clear disruption to the U.S. tire industry based on the facts and the law in this case.

President Barack Obama's spokesman, Robert Gibbs, announcing new "safeguard" tariffs on tires imported from China, September 11, 2009

On September 11, 2009, President Barack Obama announced a tariff of 35% on imports of tires made in China, meaning that these products would be taxed as they crossed the U.S. border. This tariff was requested by the United Steelworkers of America, the union that represents American tire workers. After strong lobbying pressure from the union, the tariff was enacted. By approving this tariff, it is believed that President Obama won additional support from the labor movement for the health-care bill that would be considered later that year.

The tariff on Chinese-made tires announced by President Obama was not the first instance of a U.S. president—of either party—approved an import tariff soon after being elected. During the 2000 presidential campaign, George W. Bush promised that he would consider implementing a tariff on imports of steel. That promise was made for political purposes: It helped Bush secure votes in Pennsylvania, West Virginia, and Ohio, states that produce large amounts of steel. After he was elected, the U.S. tariffs on steel were increased in

March 2002, though they were removed less than two years later, as we discuss later in this chapter.

The steel and tire tariffs are examples of **trade policy**, a government action meant to influence the amount of international trade. In earlier chapters, we learned that the opening of trade normally creates both winners and losers. Because the gains from trade are unevenly spread, it follows that firms, industries, and labor unions often feel that the government should do something to help limit their losses (or maximize their gains) from international trade. That "something" is trade policy, which includes the use of **import tariffs** (taxes on imports), **import quotas** (quantity limits on imports), and subsidies for exports. In this chapter, we begin our investigation of trade policies by focusing on the effects of tariffs and quotas in a perfectly competitive industry. In the next chapter, we continue by discussing the use of import tariffs and quotas when the industry is imperfectly competitive.

President Obama and President Bush could not just put tariffs on imports of tires made in China and foreign steel. Rather, they had to follow the rules governing the use of tariffs that the United States and many other countries have agreed to follow. Under these rules, countries can temporarily increase tariffs to safeguard an industry against import competition. This "safeguard" rationale was used to increase the U.S. tariffs on steel and tires. The international body that governs these rules is called the World Trade Organization (WTO); its precursor was the General Agreement on Tariffs and Trade (GATT). This chapter first looks briefly at the history and development of the WTO and GATT.

Once the international context for setting trade policy has been established, the chapter examines in detail the most commonly used trade policy, the tariff. We explain the reasons why countries apply tariffs and the consequences of these tariffs on the producers and consumers in the importing and exporting countries. We show that import tariffs typically lead to welfare losses for "small" importing countries, by which we mean countries that are too small to affect world prices. Following that, we examine the situation for a "large" importing country, meaning a country that is a large enough buyer for its tariff to affect world prices. In that case, we find that the importing country can possibly gain by applying a tariff, but only at the expense of the exporting countries.

A third purpose of the chapter is to examine the use of an import quota, which is a limit on the quantity of a good that can be imported from a foreign country. Past examples of import quotas in the United States include limits on the imports of agricultural goods, automobiles, and steel. More recently, the United States and Europe imposed temporary quotas on the import of textile and apparel products from China. We note that, like a tariff, an import quota often imposes a cost on the importing country. Furthermore, we argue that the cost of quotas can sometimes be even greater than the cost of tariffs. For that reason, the use of quotas has been greatly reduced under the WTO, though they are still used in some cases.

Throughout this chapter, we assume that firms are perfectly competitive. That is, each firm produces a homogeneous good and is small compared with the market, which comprises many firms. Under perfect competition, each firm is a price taker in its market. In the next chapter, we learn that tariffs and quotas have different effects in imperfectly competitive markets.

1 A Brief History of the World Trade Organization

As we discussed in Chapter 1, during the period between the First and Second World Wars, unusually high tariffs between countries reduced the volume of world trade. When peace was reestablished following World War II, representatives of the Allied countries met on several occasions to discuss the rebuilding of Europe and issues such as high trade barriers and unstable exchange rates. One of these conferences, held in Bretton Woods, New Hampshire, in July 1944, established the International Monetary Fund (IMF) and the International Bank for Reconstruction and Development, later known as the World Bank. A second conference held at the Palais des Nations, in Geneva, Switzerland, in 1947 established the General Agreement on Tariffs and Trade (GATT), the purpose of which was to reduce barriers to international trade between nations.[1]

Under the GATT, countries met periodically for negotiations, called "rounds," to lower trade restrictions between countries. Each round is named for the country in which the meeting took place. The Uruguay Round of negotiations, which lasted from 1986 to 1994, established the World Trade Organization (WTO) on January 1, 1995. The WTO is a greatly expanded version of the GATT. It keeps most of the GATT's earlier provisions but adds rules that govern an expanded set of global interactions (including trade in services and intellectual property protection) through binding agreements. The most recent round of WTO negotiations, the Doha Round, began in Doha, Qatar, in November 2001.

Although the goal of the WTO is to keep tariffs low, it allows countries to charge a higher tariff on a specific import under some conditions. In **Side Bar: Key Provisions of the GATT,** we show some of the articles of the GATT that still govern trade in the WTO. Some of the main provisions are as follows:

1. A nation must extend the same tariffs to all trading partners that are WTO members. Article I of the GATT, the "most favored nation" clause, states that every country belonging to the WTO must be treated the same: if a country imposes low tariffs on one trading partner, then those low tariffs must be extended to every other trading partner belonging to the WTO.[2]

2. Tariffs may be imposed in response to unfair trade practices such as **dumping.** As we discuss in a later chapter, "dumping" is defined as the sale of export goods in another country at a price less than that charged at home, or alternatively, at a price less than costs of production and shipping. Article VI of the GATT states that an importing country may impose a tariff on goods being dumped into its country by a foreign exporter.

3. Countries should not limit the quantity of goods and services that they import. Article XI states that countries should not maintain quotas against imports. We discuss exceptions to this rule later in this chapter.

4. Countries should declare **export subsidies** provided to particular firms, sectors, or industries. Article XVI deals with export subsidies, benefits such as tax

[1] A history of the GATT is provided in Douglas A. Irwin, Petros C. Mavroidis, and Alan O. Sykes, 2008, *The Genesis of the GATT* (New York: Cambridge University Press).

[2] In the United States, the granting of most favored nation trade status to a country is now called "normal trade relations" because most countries now belong to the WTO and enjoy that status.

breaks or other incentives for firms that produce goods specifically for export. The article states that countries should notify each other of the extent of subsidies and discuss the possibility of eliminating them. During the Doha Round of WTO negotiations, the elimination of agricultural subsidies has recently been discussed.

5. Countries can temporarily raise tariffs for certain products. Article XIX, called the **safeguard provision** or the **escape clause,** is our focus in this chapter. Article XIX lists the conditions under which a country can temporarily raise tariffs on particular products. It states that a country can apply a tariff when it imports "any product . . . in such increased quantities and under such conditions as to cause or threaten serious injury to domestic producers." In other words, the importing country can temporarily raise the tariff when domestic producers are suffering due to import competition.

   The steel tariff of March 2002 is an example of a tariff that was applied by the United States under Article XIX of the GATT. European governments strenuously objected to the steel tariffs, however, and filed a complaint against the United States with the WTO. A panel at the WTO ruled in favor of the European countries. This ruling entitled them to retaliate against the United States by putting tariffs of their own on some $2.2 billion worth of U.S. exports. This pressure from Europe, along with pressure from companies in the United States that had been purchasing the cheaper imported steel, led President Bush to remove the steel tariffs in December 2003. Later in the chapter, we discuss the steel tariff in more detail, and see how Article XIX of the GATT is reflected in U.S. trade laws.

6. **Regional trade agreements** are permitted under Article XXIV of the GATT. The GATT recognizes the ability of blocs of countries to form two types of regional trade agreements: (i) **free-trade areas,** in which a group of countries voluntarily agrees to remove trade barriers between themselves, and (ii) **customs unions,** which are free-trade areas in which the countries also adopt identical tariffs between themselves and the rest of the world. We discuss regional trade agreements in a later chapter.

2 The Gains from Trade

In earlier chapters, we demonstrated the gains from trade using a production possibilities frontier and indifference curves. We now instead demonstrate the gains from trade using Home demand and supply curves, together with the concepts of **consumer surplus** and **producer surplus.** You may already be familiar with these concepts from an earlier economics course, but we provide a brief review here.

Consumer and Producer Surplus

Suppose that Home consumers have the demand curve D in panel (a) of Figure 8-1 and face the price of P_1. Then total demand is D_1 units. For the last unit purchased, the consumer buying it values that unit at close to its purchase price of P_1, so he or

SIDE BAR

Key Provisions of the GATT

ARTICLE I

General Most-Favoured-Nation Treatment

1. With respect to customs duties . . . and with respect to all rules and formalities in connection with importation and exportation . . . any advantage, favour, privilege or immunity granted by any contracting party to any product originating in or destined for any other country shall be accorded immediately and unconditionally to the like product originating in or destined for the territories of all other contracting parties. . . .

ARTICLE VI

Anti-Dumping and Countervailing Duties

1. The contracting parties recognize that dumping, by which products of one country are introduced into the commerce of another country at less than the normal value of the products, is to be condemned if it causes or threatens material injury to an established industry. . . . [A]product is to be considered . . . less than its normal value, if the price of the product exported from one country to another
   a. is less than the comparable price . . . for the like product when destined for consumption in the exporting country, or,
   b. in the absence of such domestic price, is less than either
      i) the highest comparable price for the like product for export to any third country in the ordinary course of trade, or
      ii) the cost of production of the product in the country of origin plus a reasonable addition for selling cost and profit. . . .

ARTICLE XI

General Elimination of Quantitative Restrictions

1. No prohibitions or restrictions other than duties, taxes or other charges, whether made effective through quotas, import or export licenses or other measures, shall be instituted or maintained by any contracting party on the importation of any product of the territory of any other contracting party or on the exportation or sale for export of any product destined for the territory of any other contracting party. . . .

ARTICLE XVI

Subsidies

1. If any contracting party grants or maintains any subsidy, including any form of income or price support, which operates directly or indirectly to increase exports of any product from, or to reduce imports of any product into, its territory, it shall notify the contracting parties in writing of the extent and nature of the subsidization. In any case in which it is determined that serious prejudice to the interests of any other contracting party is caused or threatened by any such subsidization, the contracting party granting the subsidy shall, upon request, discuss with the other contracting party . . . the possibility of limiting the subsidization.

ARTICLE XIX

Emergency Action on Imports of Particular Products

1.
   a. If, as a result of unforeseen developments and of the effect of the obligations incurred by a contracting party under this Agreement, including tariff concessions, any product is being imported into the territory of that contracting party in such increased quantities and under such conditions as to cause or threaten serious injury to domestic producers in that territory of like or directly competitive products, the contracting party shall be free, in respect of such product, and to the extent and for such time as may be necessary to prevent or remedy such injury, to suspend the obligation in whole or in part or to withdraw or modify the concession. . . .

ARTICLE XXIV

Territorial Application—Frontier Traffic—Customs Unions and Free-Trade Areas

4. The contracting parties recognize the desirability of increasing freedom of trade by the development, through voluntary agreements, of closer integration between the economies of the countries party to such agreements. They also recognize that the purpose of a customs union or of a free-trade area should be to facilitate trade between the constituent territories and not to raise barriers to the trade of other contracting parties with such territories.
5. Accordingly, the provisions of this Agreement shall not prevent [the formation of customs unions and free-trade areas, provided that:]
   a. . . . the duties [with outside parties] shall not on the whole be higher or more restrictive than the general incidence of the duties . . . prior to the formation. . . .

Source: http://www.wto.org/english/docs_e/legal_e/gatt47_01_e.htm#articleI.

she obtains little or no surplus over the purchase price. But for all the earlier units purchased (from 0 to D_1 units), the consumers valued the product at *higher than* its purchase price: the consumers' willingness to pay for the product equals the height of the demand curve. For example, the person buying unit D_2 would have been willing to pay the price of P_2, which is the height of the demand curve at that quantity. Therefore, that individual obtains the surplus of $(P_2 - P_1)$ from being able to purchase the good at the price P_1.

For each unit purchased before D_1, the value that the consumer places on the product exceeds the purchase price of P_1. Adding up the surplus obtained on each unit purchased, from 0 to D_1, we can measure consumer surplus (*CS*) as the shaded region below the demand curve and above the price P_1. This region measures the satisfaction that consumers receive from the purchased quantity D_1, over and above the amount $P_1 \cdot D_1$ that they have paid.

Panel (b) of Figure 8-1 illustrates producer surplus. This panel shows the supply curve of an industry; the height of the curve represents the firm's marginal cost at each level of production. At the price of P_1, the industry will supply S_1. For the last unit supplied, the price P_1 equals the marginal cost of production for the firm supplying that unit. But for all earlier units supplied (from 0 to S_1 units), the firms were able to produce those units at a marginal cost *less than* the price P_1. For example, the firm supplying unit S_0 could produce it with a marginal cost of P_0, which is the height of the supply curve at that quantity. Therefore, that firm obtains the producer surplus of $(P_1 - P_0)$ from being able to sell the good at the price P_1.

FIGURE 8-1

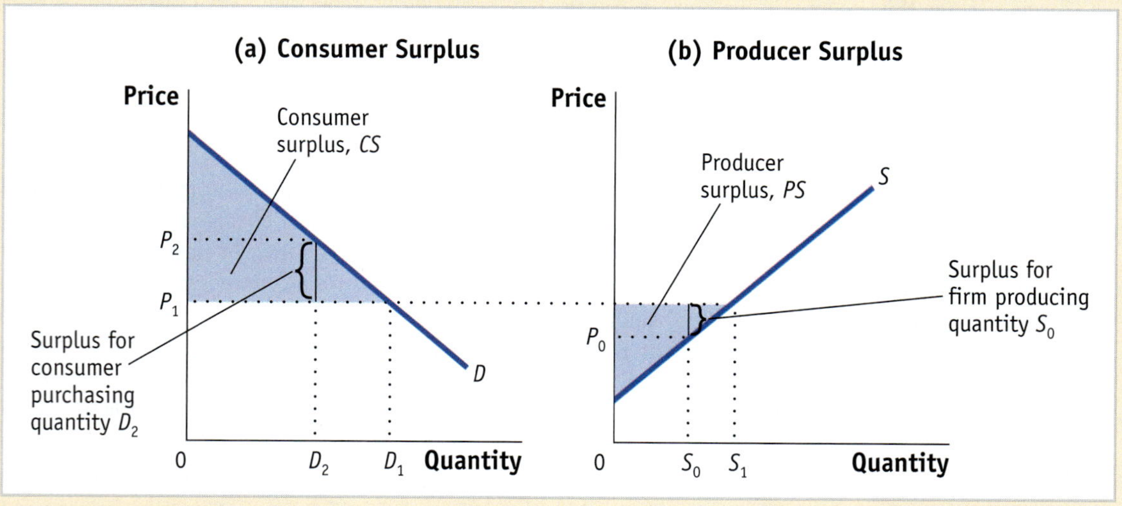

Consumer and Producer Surplus In panel (a), the consumer surplus from purchasing quantity D_1 at price P_1 is the area below the demand curve and above that price. The consumer who purchases D_2 is willing to pay price P_2 but has to pay only P_1. The difference is the consumer surplus and represents the satisfaction of consumers over and above the amount paid. In panel (b), the producer surplus from supplying the quantity S_1 at the price P_1 is the area above the supply curve and below that price. The supplier who supplies unit S_0 has marginal costs of P_0 but sells it for P_1. The difference is the producer surplus and represents the return to fixed factors of production in the industry.

For each unit sold before S_1, the marginal cost to the firm is less than the sale price of P_1. Adding up the producer surplus obtained for each unit sold, from 0 to S_1, we obtain producer surplus (*PS*) as the shaded region in panel (b) above the supply curve and below the price of P_1. It is tempting to think of producer surplus as the profits of firms, since for all units before S_1, the marginal cost of production is less than the sale price of P_1. But a more accurate definition of producer surplus is that it equals the *return to fixed factors of production in the industry*. That is, producer surplus is the difference between the sales revenue $P_1 \cdot S_1$ and the total variable costs of production (i.e., wages paid to labor and the costs of intermediate inputs). If there are fixed factors such as capital or land in the industry, as in the specific-factors model we studied in Chapter 3, then producer surplus equals the returns to these fixed factors of production. We might still loosely refer to this return as the "profit" earned in the industry, but it is important to understand that producer surplus is not *monopoly profits*, because we are assuming perfect competition (i.e., zero monopoly profits) throughout this chapter.[3]

Home Welfare

To examine the effects of trade on a country's welfare, we consider once again a world composed of two countries, Home and Foreign, with each country consisting of producers and consumers. Total Home welfare can be measured by adding up consumer and producer surplus. As you would expect, the greater the total amount of Home welfare, the better off are the consumers and producers overall in the economy. To measure the gains from trade, we will compare Home welfare in no-trade and free-trade situations.

No Trade In panel (a) of Figure 8-2, we combine the Home demand and supply curves in a single diagram. The no-trade equilibrium occurs at the autarky price of P^A, where the quantity demanded equals the quantity supplied, of Q_0. Consumer surplus is the region above the price of P^A and below the demand curve, which is labeled as *CS* in panel (a) and also shown as area a in panel (b). Producer surplus is the area below the price of P^A and above the supply curve, which is labeled as *PS* in panel (a) and also shown as area $(b + c)$ in panel (b). So the sum of consumer surplus and producer surplus is the area between the demand and supply curves, or $CS + PS$ = area $(a + b + c)$. That area equals Home welfare in the market for this good in the absence of international trade.

Free Trade for a Small Country Now suppose that Home can engage in international trade for this good. As we have discussed in earlier chapters, the world price P^W is determined by the intersection of supply and demand in the world market. Generally, there will be many countries buying and selling on the world market. We will suppose that the Home country is a **small country,** by which we mean that it is small in comparison with all the other countries buying and selling this product. For that reason, Home will be a *price taker* in the world market: it faces the fixed world price of P^W, and its own level of demand and supply for this product has no influence on the world price.

In panel (b) of Figure 8-2, we assume that the world price P^W is *below* the Home no-trade price of P^A. At the lower price, Home demand will increase from Q_0 under

[3] Recall from Chapter 6 that under imperfect competition, firms can influence the price of their goods and hence earn positive monopoly profits.

FIGURE 8-2

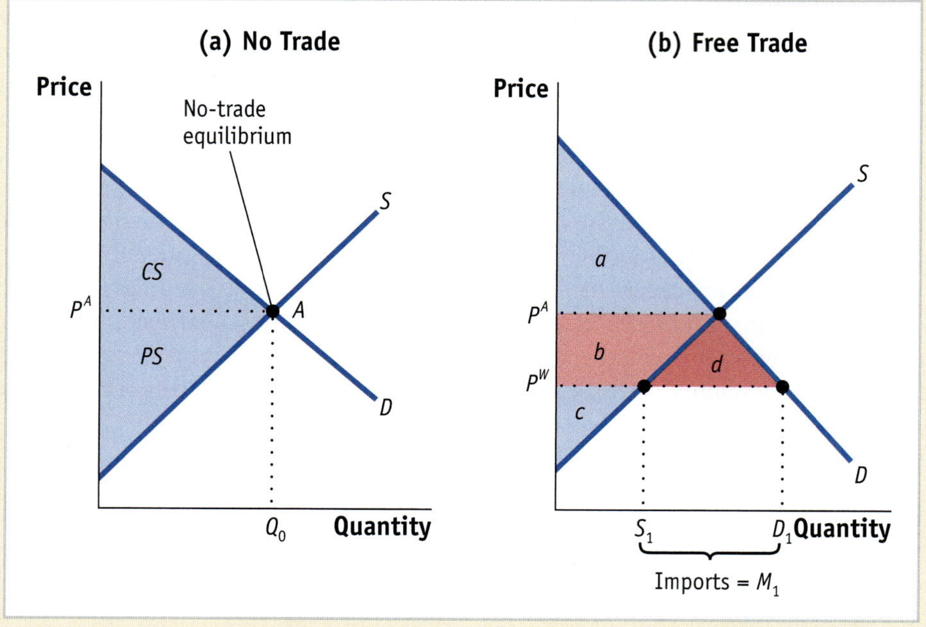

The Gains from Free Trade at Home With Home demand of D and supply of S, the no-trade equilibrium is at point A, at the price P^A producing Q_0. With free trade, the world price is P^W, so quantity demanded increases to D_1 and quantity supplied falls to S_1. Since quantity demanded exceeds quantity supplied, Home imports $D_1 - S_1$. Consumer surplus increases by the area $(b + d)$, and producer surplus falls by area b. The gains from trade are measured by area d.

no trade to D_1, and Home supply will decrease from Q_0 under no trade to S_1. The difference between D_1 and S_1 is *imports* of the good, or $M_1 = D_1 - S_1$. Because the world price P^W is below the no-trade price of P^A, the Home country is an importer of the product at the world price. If, instead, P^W were above P^A, then Home would be an exporter of the product at the world price.

Gains from Trade Now that we have established the free-trade equilibrium at price P^W, it is easy to measure Home welfare as the sum of consumer and producer surplus with trade, and compare it with the no-trade situation. In panel (b) of Figure 8-2, Home consumer surplus at the price P^W equals the area $(a + b + d)$, which is the area below the demand curve and above the price P^W. In the absence of trade, consumer surplus was the area a, so the drop in price from P^A to P^W has increased consumer surplus by the amount $(b + d)$. Home consumers clearly gain from the drop in price.

Home firms, on the other hand, suffer a decrease in producer surplus from the drop in price. In panel (b), Home producer surplus at the price P^W equals the area c, which is the area above the supply curve and below the price P^W. In the absence of trade, producer surplus was the area $(b + c)$, so the drop in price from P^A to P^W has decreased producer surplus by the amount b. Home firms clearly lose from the drop in price.

Comparing the gains of consumers, $(b + d)$, with the losses of producers, area b, we see that consumers gain more than the producers lose, which indicates that total

Home welfare (the sum of consumer surplus and producer surplus) has gone up. We can calculate the total change in Home welfare due to the opening of trade by adding the *changes* in consumer surplus and producer surplus:

Rise in consumer surplus:	$+ (b + d)$
Fall in producer surplus:	$- b$
Net effect on Home welfare:	$+d$

The area d is a measure of the *gains from trade* for the importing country due to free trade in this good. It is similar to the gains from trade that we have identified in earlier chapters using the production possibilities frontier and indifference curves, but it is easier to measure: the triangle d has a base equal to free-trade imports $M_1 = D_1 - S_1$, and a height that is the drop in price, $P^A - P^W$, so the gains from trade equal the area of the triangle, $\frac{1}{2} \cdot (P^A - P^W) \cdot M_1$. Of course, with many goods being imported, we would need to add up the areas of the triangles for each good and take into account the net gains on the export side to determine the overall gains from trade for a country. Since gains are positive for each individual good, after summing all imported and exported goods, the gains from trade are still positive.

Home Import Demand Curve

Before introducing a tariff, we use Figure 8-3 to derive the **import demand curve,** which shows the relationship between the world price of a good and the quantity of imports demanded by Home consumers. We first derived this curve in Chapter 2, for

FIGURE 8-3

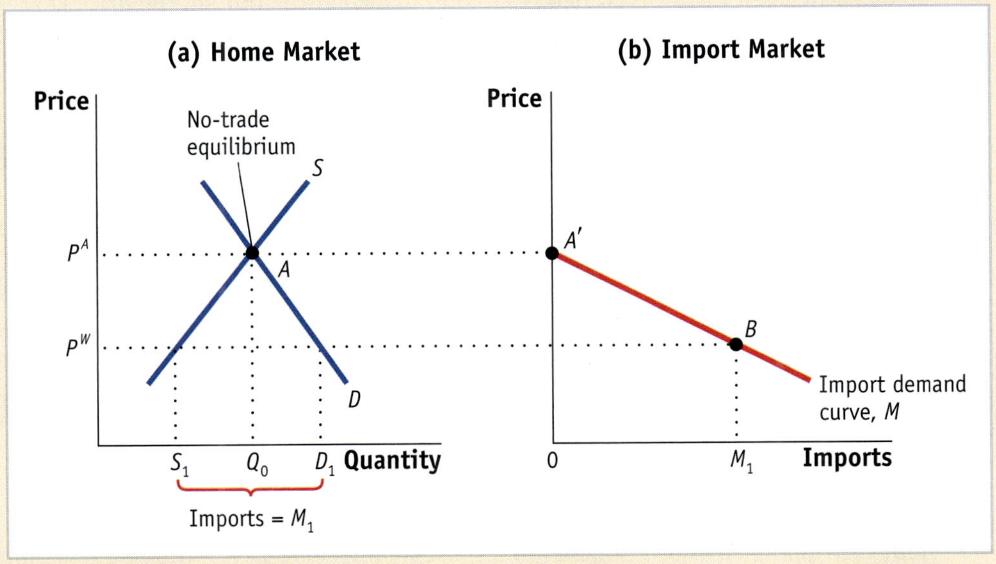

Home Import Demand With Home demand of D and supply of S, the no-trade equilibrium is at point A, with the price P^A and import quantity Q_0. Import demand at this price is zero, as shown by the point A' in panel (b). At a lower world price of P^W, import demand is $M_1 = D_1 - S_1$, as shown by point B. Joining up all points between A' and B, we obtain the import demand curve, M.

the Ricardian model. We now briefly review the derivation of the import demand curve before analyzing the effect of an import tariff on prices and welfare.

In panel (a) of Figure 8-3, we again show the downward-sloping Home demand curve (*D*) and the upward-sloping Home supply curve (*S*). The no-trade equilibrium is at point *A*, which determines Home's no-trade equilibrium price P^A, and its no-trade equilibrium quantity of Q_0. Because quantity demanded equals quantity supplied, there are zero imports of this product. Zero imports is shown as point *A′* in panel (b).

Now suppose the world price is at P^W, below the no-trade price of P^A. At the price of P^W, the quantity demanded in Home is D_1, but the quantity supplied by Home suppliers is only S_1. Therefore, the quantity imported is $M_1 = D_1 - S_1$, as shown by the point *B* in panel (b). Joining points *A′* and *B*, we obtain the downward-sloping import demand curve *M*.

Notice that the import demand curve applies for all prices *below* the no-trade price of P^A in Figure 8-3. Having lower prices leads to greater Home demand and less Home supply and, therefore, positive imports. What happens if the world price is *above* the no-trade price? In that case, the higher price would lead to greater Home supply and less Home demand, so Home would become an exporter of the product.

3 Import Tariffs for a Small Country

We can now use this supply and demand framework to show what happens when a small country imposes a tariff. As we have already explained, an importing country is "small" if its tariff does not have any effect on the world price of the good on which the tariff is applied. As we will see, the Home price of the good will increase due to the tariff. Because the tariff (which is a tax) is applied at the border, the price charged to Home consumers will increase by the amount of the tariff.

Free Trade for a Small Country

In Figure 8-4, we again show the free-trade equilibrium for the Home country. In panel (b), the Foreign export supply curve X^* is horizontal at the world price P^W. The horizontal export supply curve means that Home can import any amount at the price P^W without having an impact on that price. The free-trade equilibrium is determined by the intersection of the Foreign export supply and the Home import demand curves, which is point *B* in panel (b), at the world price P^W. At that price, Home demand is D_1 and Home supply is S_1, shown in panel (a). Imports at the world price P^W are then just the difference between demand and supply, or $M_1 = D_1 - S_1$.

Effect of the Tariff

With the import tariff of *t* dollars, the export supply curve facing the Home country shifts up by exactly that amount, reflecting the higher price that must be paid to import the good. The shift in the Foreign export supply curve is analogous to the shift in domestic supply caused by a sales tax, as you may have seen in earlier economics courses; it reflects an effective increase in the costs of the firm. In panel (b) of Figure 8-4,

FIGURE 8-4

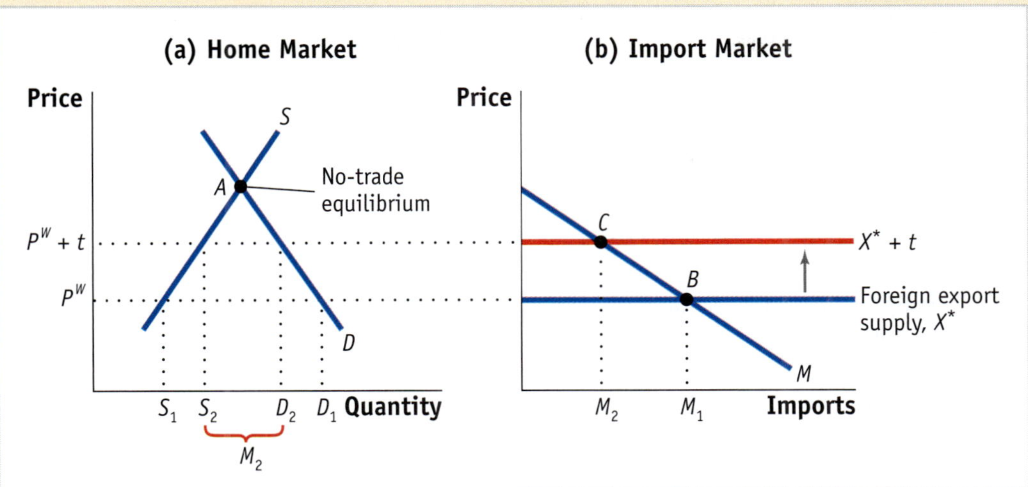

Tariff for a Small Country Applying a tariff of t dollars will increase the import price from P^W to $P^W + t$. The domestic price of that good also rises to $P^W + t$. This price rise leads to an increase in Home supply from S_1 to S_2, and a decrease in Home demand from D_1 to D_2, in panel (a). Imports fall due to the tariff, from M_1 to M_2 in panel (b). As a result, the equilibrium shifts from point B to C.

the export supply curve shifts up to $X^* + t$. The intersection of the post-tariff export supply curve and the import demand curve now occurs at the price of $P^W + t$ and the import quantity of M_2. The import tariff has reduced the amount imported, from M_1 under free trade to M_2 under the tariff, due to its higher price.

We assume that the imported product is identical to the domestic alternative that is available. For example, if the imported product is a women's cruiser bicycle, then the Home demand curve D in panel (a) is the demand for women's cruisers, and the Home supply curve is the supply of women's cruisers. When the import price rises to $P^W + t$, then we expect that the Home price for locally produced bicycles will rise by the same amount. This is because at the higher import price of $P^W + t$, the quantity of cruisers demanded at Home falls from its free-trade quantity of D_1 to D_2. At the same time, the higher price will encourage Home firms to increase the quantity of cruisers they supply from the free-trade quantity of S_1 to S_2. As firms increase the quantity they produce, however, the marginal costs of production rise. The Home supply curve (S) reflects these marginal costs, so the Home price will rise along the supply curve until Home firms are supplying the quantity S_2, at a marginal cost just equal to the import price of $P^W + t$. Since marginal costs equal $P^W + t$, the price charged by Home firms will also equal $P^W + t$, and the domestic price will equal the import price.

Summing up, Home demand at the new price is D_2, Home supply is S_2, and the difference between these are Home imports of $M_2 = D_2 - S_2$. Foreign exporters still receive the "net-of-tariff" price (i.e., the Home price minus the tariff) of P^W, but Home consumers pay the higher price $P^W + t$. We now investigate how the rise in the Home price from P^W to $P^W + t$ affects consumer surplus, producer surplus, and overall Home welfare.

Effect of the Tariff on Consumer Surplus In Figure 8-5, we again show the effect of the tariff of t dollars, which is to increase the price of the imported and domestic good from P^W to $P^W + t$. Under free trade, consumer surplus in panel (a) was the area under the demand curve and above P^W. With the tariff, consumers now pay the higher price, $P^W + t$, and their surplus is the area under the demand curve and above the price $P^W + t$. The fall in consumer surplus due to the tariff is the area between the two prices and to the left of Home demand, which is $(a + b + c + d)$ in panel (a) of Figure 8-5. This area is the amount that consumers lose due to the higher price caused by the tariff.

Effect of the Tariff on Producer Surplus We can also trace the impact of the tariff on producer surplus. Under free trade, producer surplus was the area above the supply curve in panel (a) and below the price of P^W. With the tariff, producer surplus is the area above the supply curve and below the price $P^W + t$: since the tariff increases the Home price, firms are able to sell more goods at a higher price, thus increasing their surplus. We can illustrate this rise in producer surplus as the amount between the two prices and to the left of Home supply, which is labeled as a in panel (a). This area is the amount that Home firms gain due to the higher price caused by the tariff.

As we have just explained, the rise in producer surplus should be thought of as an increase in the return to fixed factors (capital or land) in the industry. Sometimes we even think of labor as a partially fixed factor because the skills learned in one industry cannot necessarily be transferred to other industries. In that case, it is reasonable to think that the increase in Home producer surplus can also benefit Home workers in the import-competing industry, along with capital and land, but this benefit comes at the expense of consumer surplus.

Effect of the Tariff on Government Revenue In addition to affecting consumers and producers, the tariff also affects government revenue. The amount of revenue collected is the tariff t times the quantity of imports $(D_2 - S_2)$. In Figure 8-5, panel (a), this revenue is shown by the area c. The collection of revenue is a gain for the government in the importing country.

Overall Effect of the Tariff on Welfare We are now in a position to summarize the impact of the tariff on the welfare of the Home importing country, which is the sum of producer surplus, consumer surplus, and government revenues. Thus, our approach is to *add up* these impacts to obtain a net effect. In adding up the loss of consumers and the gains of producers, one dollar of consumer surplus is the same as one dollar of producer surplus or government revenue. In other words, we do not care whether the consumers facing higher prices are poor or rich, and do not care whether the specific factors in the industry (capital, land, and possibly labor) earn a lot or a little. Under this approach, transferring one dollar from consumer to producer surplus will have no impact on overall welfare: the decrease in consumer surplus will cancel out the increase in producer surplus.

You may object to this method of evaluating overall welfare, and feel that a dollar taken away from a poor consumer and given to a rich producer represents a net loss of overall welfare, rather than zero effect, as in our approach. We should be careful in evaluating the impact of tariffs on different income groups in the society, especially for poor countries or countries with a high degree of inequality among income groups. But for now we ignore this concern and simply add up consumer surplus, producer surplus, and government revenue. Keep in mind that under this approach we are just evaluating the *efficiency* of tariffs and not their effect on equity (i.e., how fair the tariff is to one group versus another).

FIGURE 8-5

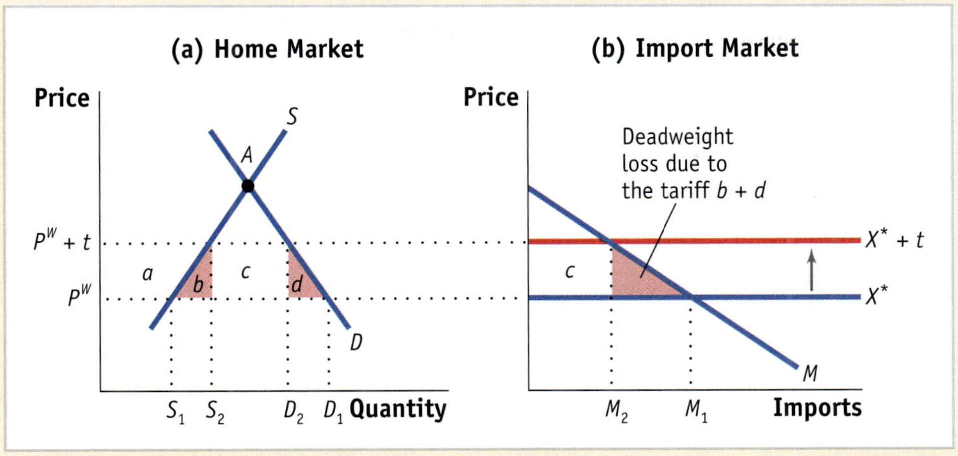

Effect of Tariff on Welfare The tariff increases the price from P^W to $P^W + t$. As a result, consumer surplus falls by $(a + b + c + d)$. Producer surplus rises by area a, and government revenue increases by the area c. Therefore, the net loss in welfare, the deadweight loss to Home, is $(b + d)$, which is measured by the two triangles b and d in panel (a) or the single (combined) triangle $b + d$ in panel (b).

The overall impact of the tariff in the small country can be summarized as follows:

Fall in consumer surplus:	$-(a + b + c + d)$
Rise in producer surplus:	$+a$
Rise in government revenue:	+ c
Net effect on Home welfare:	$\mathbf{-(b + d)}$

In Figure 8-5(b), the triangle $(b + d)$ is the *net welfare loss* in a small importing country due to the tariff. We sometimes refer to this area as a **deadweight loss,** meaning that it is not offset by a gain elsewhere in the economy. Notice that in panel (a) the area a, which is a gain for producers, just cancels out that portion of the consumer surplus loss; the area a is effectively a transfer from consumers to producers via the higher domestic prices induced by the tariff. Likewise, area c, the gain in government revenue, also cancels out that portion of the consumer surplus loss; this is a transfer from consumers to the government. Thus, the area $(b + d)$ is the remaining loss for consumers that is not offset by a gain elsewhere. This deadweight loss is measured by the two triangles, b and d, in panel (a), or by the combined triangle $(b + d)$ in panel (b). The two triangles b and d of deadweight loss can each be given a precise interpretation, as follows.

Production Loss Notice that the base of triangle b is the net increase in Home supply due to the tariff, from S_1 to S_2. The height of this triangle is the increase in marginal costs due to the increase in supply. The unit S_1 was produced at a marginal cost equal to P^W, which is the free-trade price, but every unit above that amount is produced with higher marginal costs. The fact that marginal costs exceed the world price means that this country is producing the good inefficiently: it would be cheaper to import it rather than produce the extra quantity at home. The area of triangle b equals the increase in marginal costs for the extra units produced and can be interpreted as the **production loss** (or the *efficiency loss*) for the economy due to producing at marginal costs above the world price. Notice that the production loss is only a portion of the overall deadweight loss, which is $(b + d)$ in Figure 8-5.

Consumption Loss The triangle d in panel (a) (the other part of the deadweight loss) can also be given a precise interpretation. Because of the tariff and the price increase from P^W to $P^W + t$, the quantity consumed at Home is reduced from D_1 to D_2. The area of the triangle d can be interpreted as the drop in consumer surplus for those individuals who are no longer able to consume the units between D_1 and D_2 because of the higher price. We refer to this drop in consumer surplus as the **consumption loss** for the economy.

Why and How Are Tariffs Applied?

Our finding that a tariff always leads to deadweight losses for a small importing country explains why most economists oppose the use of tariffs. If a small country suffers a loss when it imposes a tariff, why do so many have tariffs as part of their trade policies? One answer is that a developing country does not have any other source of government revenue. Import tariffs are "easy to collect" because every country has customs agents at major ports checking the goods that cross the border. It is easy to tax imports, even though the deadweight loss from using a tariff is typically higher than the deadweight loss from using "hard-to-collect" taxes, such as income taxes or value-added taxes. These taxes are hard to collect because they require individuals and firms to honestly report earnings, and the government cannot check every report (as they can check imports at the border). Still, to the extent that developing countries recognize that tariffs have a higher deadweight loss, we would expect that over time they would shift away from such easy-to-collect taxes. That is exactly what has occurred, according to one research study.[4] The fraction of total tax revenue collected from "easy to collect" taxes such as tariffs fell during the 1980s and 1990s, especially in developing countries, whereas the fraction of revenue raised from "hard to collect" taxes rose over this same period.

A second reason why tariffs are used even though they have a deadweight loss is politics. The tariff benefits the Home producers, as we have seen, so if the government cares more about producer surplus than consumer surplus, it might decide to use the tariff despite the deadweight loss it incurs. Indeed, the benefits to producers (and their workers) are typically more concentrated on specific firms and states than the costs to consumers, which are spread nationwide. This is our interpretation of the tariff that President George W. Bush granted to the steel industry in 2002: its benefits were concentrated in the steel-producing states of Pennsylvania, West Virginia, and Ohio, and its costs to consumers—in this case, steel-using industries—were spread more widely.[5] For the tariff on tires imported from China, approved by President Barack Obama in 2009, the argument is a bit different. This tariff was requested by

---

[4] Joshua Aizenman and Yothin Jinjarak, January 2006, "Globalization and Developing Countries—A Shrinking Tax Base?" National Bureau of Economic Research (NBER) Working Paper No. 11933.

[5] Although the steel tariff was used to obtain votes from the steel-producing states, it also served another political purpose. In 2002 President George W. Bush faced a vote on whether the president should be granted "fast-track authority" to negotiate trade agreements with other countries. Fast-track authority allows the president to present a new trade agreement to the Congress for an up-or-down vote within 90 days, without having the terms of the trade agreement revised by the Congress. This authority expires every five years. In 2002 the steel tariff prompted some members of Congress to vote in favor of fast-track authority, which passed in Congress by only two votes. More recently, fast-track authority, also called "trade promotion authority," was not renewed by Congress and was allowed to lapse on July 1, 2007.

the United Steelworkers of America, the union who represents workers in the U.S. tire industry, and it is expected to benefit those workers. But U.S. tire producers did not support the tariff because many of them already manufacture tires in other countries—especially China—and this tariff will make it more costly for them to do so.

In both the steel and tire cases, the president was not free to impose just any tariff, but had to follow the rules of the GATT discussed earlier in this chapter. Recall that Article XIX of the GATT, known as the "safeguard" or "escape clause," allows a temporary tariff to be used under certain circumstances. GATT Article XIX is mirrored in U.S. trade law. In **Side Bar: Safeguard Tariffs,** we list the key passages for two sections of the Trade Act of 1974, as amended, both of which deal with safeguard tariffs.

First, Section 201 states that a tariff can be requested by the president, by the House of Representatives, by the Senate, or by any other party such as a firm or union that files a petition with the U.S. International Trade Commission (ITC). That commission determines whether rising imports have been a "a substantial cause of serious injury, or threat thereof, to the U.S. industry. . . ." The commission then makes a recommendation to the president who has the final authority to approve or veto the tariff. Section 201 goes further in defining a "substantial cause" as a "cause that is important and not less than any other cause." Although this kind of legal language sounds quite obscure, it basically means that rising imports have to be *the most important* cause of injury to justify import protection. The steel tariff used by President Bush met this criterion, but as we shall see in later chapters, many other requests for tariffs do not meet this criterion and are not approved.

SIDE BAR

Safeguard Tariffs

The U.S. Trade Act of 1974, as amended, describes conditions under which tariffs can be applied in the United States, and it mirrors the provisions of the GATT and WTO. Two sections of the Trade Act of 1974 deal with the use of "safeguard" tariffs:

Section 201

Upon the filing of a petition. . . , the request of the President or the Trade Representative, the resolution of either the Committee on Ways and Means of the House of Representatives or the Committee on Finance of the Senate, or on its own motion, the [International Trade] Commission shall promptly make an investigation to determine whether an article is being imported into the United States in such increased quantities as to be a *substantial cause of serious injury, or the threat thereof, to the domestic industry* producing an article like or directly competitive with the imported article.

. . . For purposes of this section, the term "substantial cause" means a cause which is *important and not less than any other cause.*

Section 421

Upon the filing of a petition . . . the United States International Trade Commission . . . shall promptly make an investigation to determine whether products of the People's Republic of China are being imported into the United States in such increased quantities or under such conditions as to *cause or threaten to cause market disruption to the domestic producers* of like or directly competitive products.

. . . (1) For purposes of this section, *market disruption* exists whenever imports of an article like or directly competitive with an article produced by a domestic industry are increasing rapidly, either absolutely or relatively, so as to be a *significant cause of material injury, or threat of material injury, to the domestic industry.*

(2) For purposes of paragraph (1), the term "significant cause" refers to a cause which contributes significantly to the material injury of the domestic industry, *but need not be equal to or greater than any other cause.* [Italics added]

Source: http://www4.law.cornell.edu/uscode/19/usc_sec_19_00002252——000-.html and http://www4.law.cornell.edu/uscode/19/usc_sec_19_00002451——000-.html.

A second, more recent amendment to the Trade Act of 1974 is Section 421 that applies only to China. This provision was added by the United States as a condition to China's joining the WTO in 2001.[6] Because the United States was worried about exceptional surges in imports from China, it drafted this legislation so that tariffs could be applied in such a case. Under Section 421, various groups can file a petition with the U.S. International Trade Commission, which makes a recommendation to the president. The commission must determine whether rising imports from China cause "market disruption" in a U.S. industry, which means "a significant cause of material injury, or threat of material injury, to the domestic industry." Furthermore, the term "significant cause" refers to "a cause which contributes significantly to the material injury of the domestic industry, but need not be equal to or greater than any other cause." Again, the legal language can be hard to follow, but it indicates that tariffs can be applied even when rising imports from China *are not the most important* cause of injury to the domestic industry. Section 421 can therefore be applied under weaker conditions than Section 201, and it was used by President Obama to justify the tariff on tires imported from China.

APPLICATION

U.S. Tariffs on Steel and Tires

The U.S. steel and tire tariffs highlight the political motivation for applying tariffs despite the deadweight losses associated with them. We can use our small-country model introduced previously to calculate a rough estimate of how costly these tariffs were in terms of welfare. Although the United States may not be a small country when it comes to its influence on import and export prices, it is a good starting point for our analysis, and we will examine the large-country case in the next section. For now, we stay with our small-country model and illustrate the deadweight loss due to a tariff with the U.S. steel tariff in place from March 2002 to December 2003. After that calculation, we compare the steel tariff with the more recent tariff on tires.

Oliphant Universal Press Syndicate

To fulfill his campaign promise to protect the steel industry, President George W. Bush requested that the ITC initiate a Section 201 investigation into the steel industry. This was one of the few times that a president had initiated a Section 201 action; usually, firms or unions in an industry apply to the ITC for import protection. After investigating, the ITC determined that the conditions of Section 201 and Article XIX were met and recommended that tariffs be put in place to protect the U.S. steel industry. The tariffs recommended by the ITC varied across products, ranging from 10 to 20% for the first year, as shown in Table 8-1, and then falling over time so as to be eliminated after three years.

[6] Section 421 was added to U.S. trade law for 12 years, and is due to expire in 2013.

TABLE 8-1

U.S. ITC Recommended and Actual Tariffs for Steel Shown here are the tariffs recommended by the U.S. International Trade Commission for steel imports, and the actual tariffs that were applied in the first year.

Product Category	U.S. ITC Recommendation (First Year, %)	Actual U.S. Tariff (First Year, %)
Carbon and Alloy Flat Products		
Slab	20	30
Flat products	20	30
Tin mill products	U*	30
Carbon and Alloy Long Products		
Hot-rolled bar	20	30
Cold-finished bar	20	30
Rebar	10	15
Carbon and Alloy Tubular Products		
Tubular products	?**	15
Alloy fittings and flanges	13	13
Stainless and Tool Steel Products		
Stainless steel bar	15	15
Stainless steel rod	?**	15
Stainless steel wire	U*	8

* U: Uncertain—the ITC was divided on whether a tariff should be used or not.

** ?: A specific recommendation was not made by the U.S. ITC.

Source: Robert Read, 2005, "The Political Economy of Trade Protection: The Determinants and Welfare Impact of the 2002 U.S. Emergency Steel Safeguard Measures," The World Economy, *1119–1137.*

The ITC decision was based on several factors.[7] First, imports had been rising and prices were falling in the steel industry from 1998 to early 2001, leading to substantial losses for U.S. firms. Those losses, along with falling investment and employment, met the condition of "serious injury." An explanation given by the ITC for the falling import prices was that the U.S. dollar appreciated substantially prior to 2001: as the dollar rises in value, foreign currencies become cheaper and so do imported products such as steel, as occurred during this period. To meet the criterion of Section 201 and Article XIX, rising imports need to be a "substantial cause" of serious injury, which is defined as "a cause which is important and not less than any other cause." Sometimes another cause of injury to U.S. firms can be a domestic recession, but that was not the case in the years preceding 2001, when demand for steel products was rising.[8]

President Bush accepted the recommendation of the ITC but applied even higher tariffs, ranging from 8 to 30%, as shown in Table 8-1, with 30% tariffs applied to the

[7] We focus here on the ITC conclusions for flat-rolled carbon steel, from U.S. International Trade Commission, 2001, Steel: Investigation No. TA-201-73, Volume I, Publication 3479, Washington, D.C.

[8] A short recession began in the United States in March 2001 and ended eight months later, in November 2001.

most commonly used steel products (such as flat-rolled steel sheets and steel slab). Initially, the tariffs were meant to be in place for three years and to decline over time. Knowing that U.S. trading partners would be upset by this action, President Bush exempted some countries from the tariffs on steel. The countries exempted included Canada, Mexico, Jordan, and Israel, all of which have free-trade agreements with the United States, and 100 small developing countries that were exporting only a very small amount of steel to the United States.

Deadweight Loss Due to the Steel Tariff To measure the deadweight loss due to the tariffs levied on steel, we need to estimate the area of the triangle $b + d$ in Figure 8-5(b). The base of this triangle is the change in imports due to the tariffs, or $\Delta M = M_1 - M_2$. The height of the triangle is the increase in the domestic price due to the tariff, or $\Delta P = t$. So the deadweight loss equals

$$DWL = \frac{1}{2} \cdot t \cdot \Delta M$$

It is convenient to measure the deadweight loss relative to the value of imports, which is $P^W \cdot M$. We will also use the percentage tariff, which is t/P^W, and the percentage change in the quantity of imports, which is $\%\Delta M = \Delta M/M$. The deadweight loss relative to the value of imports can then be rewritten as

$$\frac{DWL}{P^W \cdot M} = \frac{1}{2} \cdot \frac{t \cdot \Delta M}{P^W \cdot M} = \frac{1}{2} \cdot \left(\frac{t}{P^W}\right) \cdot \%\Delta M$$

For the tariffs on steel, the most commonly used products had a tariff of 30%, so that is the percentage increase in the price: $t/P^W = 0.3$. It turns out that the quantity of steel imports also fell by 30% the first year after the tariff was imposed, so that $\%\Delta M = 0.3$. Therefore, the deadweight loss is

$$\frac{DWL}{P^W \cdot M} = \frac{1}{2}(0.3 \cdot 0.3) = 0.045, \text{ or } 4.5\% \text{ of the import value}$$

The value of steel imports that were affected by the tariff was about \$4.7 billion in the year prior to March 2002 and \$3.5 billion in the year after March 2002, so average imports over the two years were $\frac{1}{2}(4.7 + 3.5) = \$4.1$ billion (these values do not include the tariffs).[9]

If we apply the deadweight loss of 4.5% to the average import value of \$4.1 billion, then the dollar magnitude of deadweight loss is $0.045 \cdot 4.1$ billion = \$185 million. As we discussed earlier, this deadweight loss reflects the net annual loss to the United States from applying the tariff. If you are a steelworker, then you might think that the price of \$185 million is money well spent to protect your job, at least temporarily. On the other hand, if you are a consumer of steel, then you will probably object to the higher prices and deadweight loss. In fact, many of the U.S. firms that purchase steel—such as firms producing automobiles—objected to the tariffs and encouraged President Bush to end them early. But the biggest objections to the tariffs came from exporting countries whose firms were affected by the tariffs, especially the European countries.

[9] The drop in imports of 30% corresponds to a fall in import value of \$1.2 billion (since $1.2/4.1 \approx 0.30$, or 30%).

Response of the European Countries The tariffs on steel most heavily affected Europe, Japan, and South Korea, along with some developing countries (Brazil, India, Turkey, Moldova, Romania, Thailand, and Venezuela) that were exporting a significant amount of steel to the United States. These countries objected to the restriction on their ability to sell steel to the United States.

The countries in the European Union (EU) therefore took action by bringing the case to the WTO. They were joined by Brazil, China, Japan, South Korea, New Zealand, Norway, and Switzerland. The WTO has a formal **dispute settlement procedure** under which countries that believe that the WTO rules have not been followed can bring their complaint and have it evaluated. The WTO evaluated this case and, in early November 2003, ruled that the United States had failed to sufficiently prove that its steel industry had been harmed by a sudden increase in imports and therefore did not have the right to impose "safeguard" tariffs.

The WTO ruling was made on legal grounds: that the United States had essentially failed to prove its case (i.e., its eligibility for Article XIX protection).[10] But there are also economic grounds for doubting the wisdom of the safeguard tariffs in the first place. Even if we accept that there might be an argument on equity or fairness grounds for temporarily protecting an industry facing import competition, it is hard to argue that such protection should occur because of a change in exchange rates. The U.S. dollar appreciated for much of the 1990s, including the period before 2001 on which the ITC focused, leading to much lower prices for imported steel. But the appreciation of the dollar also lowered the prices for *all other* import products, so many other industries in the United States faced import competition, too. On fairness grounds, there is no special reason to single out the steel industry for protection.

The WTO ruling entitled the European Union and other countries to retaliate against the United States by imposing tariffs of their own against U.S. exports. The European countries quickly began to draw up a list of products—totaling some $2.2 billion in U.S. exports—against which they would apply tariffs. The European countries naturally picked products that would have the greatest negative impact on the United States, such as oranges from Florida, where Jeb Bush, the president's brother, was governor.

The threat of tariffs being imposed on these products led President Bush to reconsider the U.S. tariffs on steel. On December 5, 2003, he announced that they would be suspended after being in place for only 19 months rather than the three years as initially planned. This chain of events illustrates how the use of tariffs by an importer can easily lead to a response by exporters and a **tariff war.** The elimination of the steel tariffs by President Bush avoided such a retaliatory tariff war.

Tariff on Tires The tariff on tires imported from China, announced on September 11, 2009, was applied so recently that the information needed to make a deadweight loss calculation is not available. Instead, we will discuss the similarities and differences with the steel tariff.

[10] One of the legal reasons for the WTO ruling was that imports of flat-rolled steel into the United States had fallen from 1998 to 2001, so this product did not meet the requirement that imports had to be increasing to receive Article XIX protection. Even though imports of other steel products were rising, flat-rolled steel was considered one of the most important imported products.

One key difference between these tariffs has already been pointed out: the tire tariff was applied to imports from a single country—China—under Section 421 of U.S. trade law, whereas the steel tariff was applied against many countries under Section 201. The tire tariff is the first time that Section 421, which was added to U.S. trade law when China joined the WTO in 2001, has been used.

A second difference between these cases is that steel producers in the United States supported that tariff, but no U.S. tire producers joined in the request for the tariff on tires. Rather, the petition for a tariff on tires imported from China was brought to the International Trade Commission by the United Steelworkers of America, the union that represents workers in the tire industry. There are ten producers of tires in the United States, and seven of them—including well-known firms like Goodyear, Michelin, Cooper, and Bridgestone—also produce tires in China and other countries. These firms naturally did not want the tariff put in place because it would harm rather than help them. In terms of the model we developed in this chapter, the producer surplus of these U.S. firms would fall rather than increase due to the tariff, which suggests that the deadweight loss from the tariff on tires could be larger than for the steel tariff (where U.S. firms gained producer surplus).

There are also a number of similarities in the two cases. As it did for the steel tariff, the International Trade Commission recommended three years of protection for tires, with tariffs on a declining schedule: 55% in the first year, then 45%, and then 35%, on top of the 4% existing tariff. President Obama instead imposed additional tariffs of 35% in the first year, then 30%, and then 25% in the third year.

Also similar to what occurred in the steel case, the tariff on tires led to retaliation. China responded with actual or potential tariffs on products such as chicken feet (a local delicacy), auto parts, certain nylon products, and even passenger cars. For its part, the United States went on to apply new tariffs on steel pipe imported from China, and also investigated several other products. Although these actions by both countries may not represent a full-fledged trade war, they are at least a skirmish, and they run the risk of not only worsening relations between the countries but also imposing costs on consumers of all these products.

The final, and perhaps most important, similarity with the steel case is that China has made an official complaint to the WTO under its dispute settlement procedure, just as the European countries did in the steel case. On January 11, 2010, the WTO announced that it would review the U.S. tariff on tires to determine whether it was applied in accord with the relevant trade laws. It is too early to know the outcome of this WTO review. As in the steel case, the WTO might find that the United States did not prove the case for the tariff on tires, and therefore allow China to retaliate if the tariff is not removed. Alternatively, because Section 421 allows a tariff to be imposed under weaker conditions than Section 201, the WTO might rule in favor of the United States. In either case, this tariff should not last longer than three years, and it could be removed earlier to avoid retaliation, as occurred in the steel case. ■

4 Import Tariffs for a Large Country

Under the small-country assumption that we have used so far, we know for sure that the deadweight loss is positive; that is, the importing country is always harmed by the tariff. The small-country assumption means that the world price P^W is unchanged by the tariff applied by the importing country. If we consider a large enough importing country or a **large country**, however, then we might expect that its tariff will change the world price. In that case, the welfare for a large importing country can be improved by a tariff, as we now show.

Foreign Export Supply

If the Home country is large, then we can no longer assume that it faces a Foreign export supply curve X^* that is horizontal at the given world price P^W. Instead, we need to derive the Foreign export supply curve using the Foreign market demand and supply curves. In panel (a) of Figure 8-6, we show the Foreign demand curve D^* and supply curve S^*. These intersect at the point A^*, with a no-trade equilibrium price of P^{A^*}. Because Foreign demand equals supply at that price, Foreign exports are zero, which we show by point $A^{*\prime}$ in panel (b), where we graph Foreign exports against their price.

Now suppose the world price P^W is above the Foreign no-trade price of P^{A^*}. At the price of P^W, the Foreign quantity demanded is lower, at D_1^* in panel (a), but the quantity supplied by Foreign firms is larger, at S_1^*. Because Foreign supply exceeds demand, Foreign will export the amount $X_1^* = S_1^* - D_1^*$ at the price of P^W, as shown by the

FIGURE 8-6

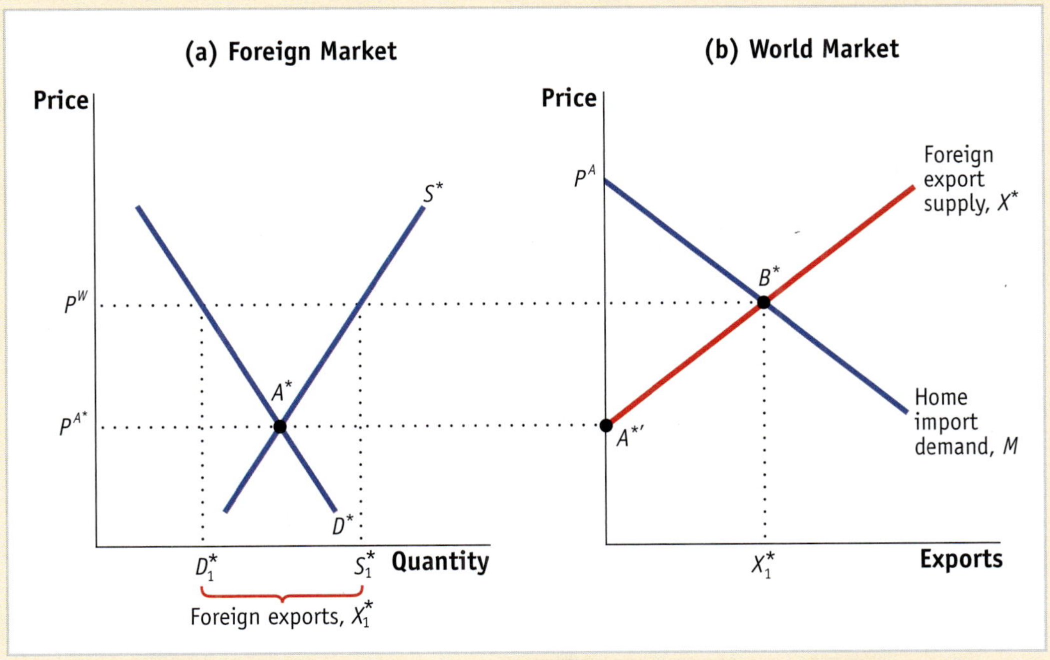

Foreign Export Supply In panel (a), with Foreign demand of D^* and Foreign supply of S^*, the no-trade equilibrium in Foreign is at point A^*, with the price of P^{A^*}. At this price, the Foreign market is in equilibrium and Foreign exports are zero—point A^* in panel (a) and point $A^{*\prime}$ in panel (b), respectively. When the world price P^W is higher than Foreign's no-trade price, the quantity supplied by Foreign, S_1^*, exceeds the quantity demanded by Foreign, D_1^*, and Foreign exports $X_1^* = S_1^* - D_1^*$. In panel (b), joining up points $A^{*\prime}$ *and* B^*, we obtain the upward-sloping export supply curve X^*. With the Home import demand of M, the world equilibrium is at point B^*, with the price P^W.

point B^* in panel (b). Drawing a line through points $A^{*\prime}$ and B^*, we obtain the upward-sloping Foreign export supply curve X^*.

We can then combine the Foreign export supply curve X^* and Home import demand curve M, which is also shown in panel (b). They intersect at the price P^W, the world equilibrium price. Notice that the Home import demand curve starts at the no-trade price P^A on the price axis, whereas the Foreign export supply curve starts at the price P^{A*}. As we have drawn them, the Foreign no-trade price is lower, $P^{A*} < P^A$. In Chapters 2 to 5 of this book, a country with comparative advantage in a good would have a lower no-trade relative price and would become an exporter when trade was opened. Likewise, in panel (b), Foreign exports the good since its no-trade price P^{A*} is lower than the world price, and Home imports the good since its no-trade price P^A is higher that the world price. So the world equilibrium illustrated in panel (b) is similar to that in some of the trade models presented in earlier chapters.

Effect of the Tariff

In panel (b) of Figure 8-7, we repeat the Home import demand curve M and Foreign export supply curve X^*, with the world equilibrium at B^*. When Home applies a tariff of t dollars, the cost to Foreign producers of supplying the Home market is t more than it was before. Because of this increase in costs, the Foreign export supply curve shifts up by exactly the amount of the tariff, as shown in panel (b) with the shift from X^* to $X^* + t$. The $X^* + t$ curve intersects import demand M at point C, which establishes the Home price (including the tariff) paid by consumers. On the other hand, the Foreign exporters receive the net-of-tariff price, which is directly below the point C

FIGURE 8-7

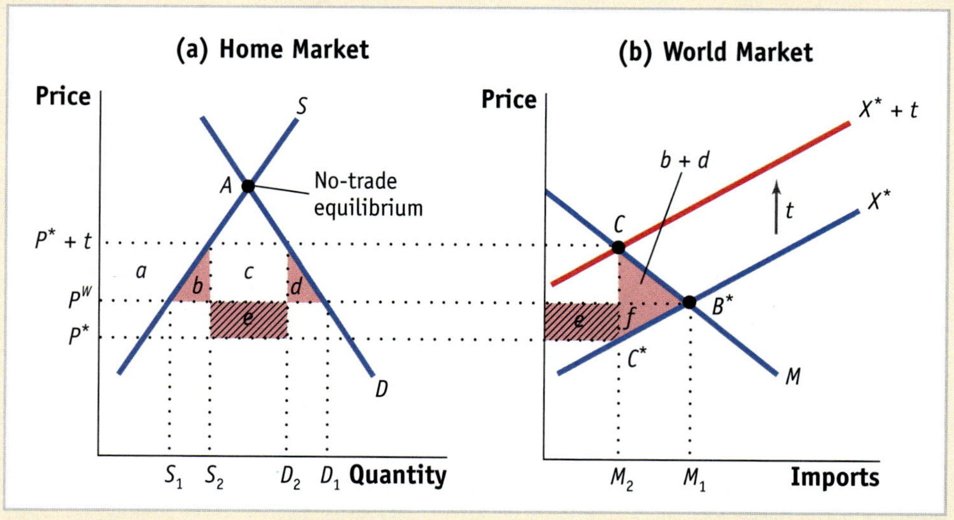

Tariff for a Large Country The tariff shifts up the export supply curve from X^* to $X^* + t$. As a result, the Home price increases from P^W to $P^* + t$, and the Foreign price falls from P^W to P^*. The deadweight loss at Home is the area of the triangle $(b + d)$, and Home also has a terms-of-trade gain of area e. Foreign loses the area $(e + f)$, so the net loss in world welfare is the triangle $(b + d + f)$.

by exactly the amount t, at point C^*. Let us call the price received by Foreign exporters P^*, at point C^*, which is the new world price.

The important feature of the new equilibrium is that the price Home pays for its imports, $P^* + t$, rises by *less than* the amount of the tariff t as compared with the initial world price P^W. The reason that the Home price rises by less than the full amount of the tariff is that the price received by Foreign exporters, P^*, has fallen as compared with the initial world price P^W. So Foreign producers are essentially "absorbing" a part of the tariff, by lowering their price from P^W (in the initial free-trade equilibrium) to P^* (after the tariff).

In sum, we can interpret the tariff as driving a wedge between what Home consumers pay and what Foreign producers receive, with the difference (of t) going to the Home government. As is the case with many taxes, the amount of the tariff (t) is shared by both consumers and producers.

Terms of Trade In Chapter 2, we defined the **terms of trade** for a country as the ratio of export prices to import prices. Generally, an improvement in the terms of trade indicates a gain for a country because it is either receiving more for its exports or paying less for its imports. To measure the Home terms of trade, we want to use the net-of-tariff import price P^* (received by Foreign firms) since that is the total amount transferred from Home to Foreign for each import. Because this price has fallen (from its initial world price of P^W), it follows that the Home terms of trade have increased. We might expect, therefore, that the Home country gains from the tariff in terms of Home welfare. To determine whether that is the case, we need to analyze the impact on the welfare of Home consumers, producers, and government revenue, which we do in Figure 8-7.

Home Welfare In panel (a), the Home consumer price increases from P^W to $P^* + t$, which makes consumers worse off. The drop in consumer surplus is represented by the area between these two prices and to the left of the demand curve D, which is shown by $(a + b + c + d)$. At the same time, the price received by Home firms rises from P^W to $P^* + t$, making Home firms better off. The increase in producer surplus equals the area between these two prices, and to the left of the supply curve S, which is the amount a. Finally, we also need to keep track of the changes in government revenue. Revenue collected from the tariff equals the amount of the tariff (t) times the new amount of imports, which is $M_2 = D_2 - S_2$. Therefore, government revenue equals the area $(c + e)$ in panel (a).

By summing the change in consumer surplus, producer surplus, and government revenue, we obtain the overall impact of the tariff in the large country, as follows:

Fall in consumer surplus:	$-(a + b + c + d)$
Rise in producer surplus:	$+a$
Rise in government revenue:	$+(c + e)$
Net effect on Home welfare:	$\boldsymbol{+e - (b + d)}$

The triangle $(b + d)$ is the deadweight loss due to the tariff (just as it is for a small country). But for the large country, there is also a source of gain—the area e—that offsets this deadweight loss. If e exceeds $(b + d)$, then Home is better off due to the tariff; if e is less than $(b + d)$, then Home is worse off.

Notice that the area e is a rectangle whose height is the fall in the price that Foreign exporters receive, the difference between P^W and P^*. The base of this rectangle equals the quantity of imports, M_2. Multiplying the drop in the import price by the quantity of imports to obtain the area e, we obtain a precise measure of the **terms-of-trade gain** for the importer. If this terms-of-trade gain exceeds the deadweight loss of the tariff, which is $(b + d)$, then Home gains from the tariff.

Thus, we see that a large importer might gain by the application of a tariff. We can add this to our list of reasons why countries use tariffs, in addition to their being a source of government revenue or a tool for political purposes. However, for the large country, any net gain from the tariff comes at the expense of the Foreign exporters, as we show next.

Foreign and World Welfare While Home might gain from the tariff, Foreign, the exporting country, definitely loses. In panel (b) of Figure 8-7, the Foreign loss is measured by the area $(e + f)$. We should think of $(e + f)$ as the loss in Foreign producer surplus from selling fewer goods to Home at a lower price. Notice that the area e is the terms-of-trade gain for Home but an equivalent terms of trade *loss* for Foreign; Home's gain comes at the expense of Foreign. In addition, the large-country tariff incurs an extra deadweight loss of f in Foreign, so the combined total outweighs the benefits to Home. For this reason, we sometimes call a tariff imposed by a large country a "beggar thy neighbor" tariff.

Adding together the change in Home welfare and Foreign welfare, the area e cancels out and we are left with a *net loss* in world welfare of $(b + d + f)$, the triangle in panel (b). This area is a deadweight loss for the world. The terms-of-trade gain that Home has extracted from the Foreign country by using a tariff comes at the expense of the Foreign exporters, and in addition, there is an added world deadweight loss. The fact that the large-country tariff leads to a world deadweight loss is another reason that most economists oppose the use of tariffs.

Optimal Tariff for a Large Importing Country We have found that a large importer might gain by the application of tariffs, but have yet to determine what *level* of tariff a country should apply in order to maximize welfare. It turns out there is a shortcut method we can use to evaluate the effect of the tariff on the welfare of a large importing country. The shortcut method uses the concept of the **optimal tariff.**

The optimal tariff is defined as the tariff that leads to the maximum increase in welfare for the importing country. For a large importing country, a small tariff initially increases welfare because the terms-of-trade gain exceeds the deadweight loss. That is, the area of the rectangle e in panel (a) of Figure 8-7 exceeds the area of the triangle $(b + d)$ in panel (b) when the tariff is small enough. The reason for this is that both the height and base of the triangle $(b + d)$ shrink to zero when the tariff is very small, so the area of the triangle is very small indeed; but for the rectangle e, only the height shrinks to zero when the tariff is small, so the area of the rectangle exceeds that of the triangle. By this mathematical reasoning, the Home gains are positive—$e > (b + d)$—when the Home tariff is sufficiently small.

In Figure 8-8, we graph Home welfare against the level of the tariff. Free trade is at point B, where the tariff is zero. A small increase in the tariff, as we have just noted, leads to an *increase* in Home welfare (because the terms-of-trade gain exceeds the deadweight loss). Therefore, starting at point B, the graph of Home welfare must be upward-sloping. But what if the tariff is very large? If the tariff is too large, then welfare will fall *below* the free-trade level of welfare. For example, with a prohibitive tariff so high that no imports are purchased at all, then the importer's welfare will be at the no-trade level, shown by point A. So while the graph of welfare must be increasing for a small tariff from point B, as the tariff increases, welfare eventually falls past the free-trade level at point B' to the no-trade welfare at point A.

FIGURE 8-8

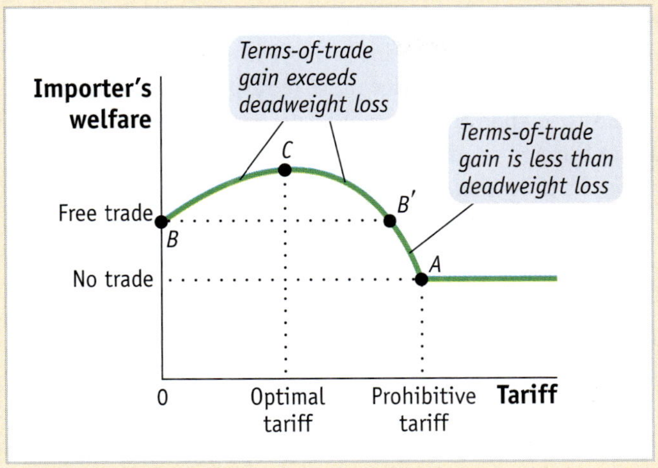

Tariffs and Welfare for a Large Country For a large importing country, a tariff initially increases the importer's welfare because the terms-of-trade gain exceeds the deadweight loss. So the importer's welfare rises from point *B*. Welfare continues to rise until the tariff is at its optimal level (point *C*). After that, welfare falls. If the tariff is too large (greater than at *B*′), then welfare will fall below the free-trade level. For a prohibitive tariff, with no imports at all, the importer's welfare will be at the no-trade level, at point *A*.

Given that points *B* and *A* are both on the graph of the importer's welfare (for free trade and no trade, respectively) and that welfare must be rising after point *B*, it follows that there must be a highest point of welfare, shown by point *C*. At this point, the importer's welfare is highest because the difference between the terms-of-trade gain and deadweight loss is maximized. We will call the tariff at that point the "optimal tariff." For increases in the tariff beyond its optimal level (i.e., between points *C* and *A*), the importer's welfare falls because the deadweight loss due to the tariff overwhelms the terms-of-trade gain. But whenever the tariff is below its optimal level, between points *B* and *C*, then welfare is higher than its free-trade level because the terms-of-trade gain exceeds the deadweight loss.

Optimal Tariff Formula It turns out that there is a simple formula for the optimal tariff. The formula depends on the elasticity of Foreign export supply, which we call E^*_X. Recall that the elasticity of any supply curve is the percentage increase in supply caused by a percentage increase in price. Likewise, the elasticity of the Foreign export supply curve is the percentage change in the quantity exported in response to a percent change in the world price of the export. If the export supply curve is very steep, then there is little response of the quantity supplied, and so the elasticity E^*_X is low. Conversely, if the export supply curve is very flat, there is a large response of the quantity supplied due to a change in the world price, and so E^*_X is high. Recall also that a small importing country faces a perfectly horizontal, or perfectly elastic, Foreign export supply curve, which means that the elasticity of Foreign export supply is infinite.

Using the elasticity of Foreign export supply, the optimal tariff equals

$$\text{optimal tariff} = \frac{1}{E^*_X}$$

That is, the optimal tariff (measured as a percentage) equals the inverse of the elasticity of Foreign export supply. For a small importing country, the elasticity of Foreign export supply is infinite, and so the optimal tariff is zero. That result makes sense, since any tariff higher than zero leads to a deadweight loss for the importer (and no terms-of-trade gain), so the best tariff to choose is zero, or free trade.

For a large importing country however, the Foreign export supply is less than infinite, and we can use this formula to compute the optimal tariff. As the elasticity of Foreign export supply decreases (which means that the Foreign export supply curve is steeper), the optimal tariff is higher. The reason for this result is that with a steep Foreign export supply curve, Foreign exporters will lower their price more in response to the tariff.[11] For instance, if E^*_X decreases from 3 to 2, then the optimal tariff increases from $\frac{1}{3} = 33\%$ to $\frac{1}{2} = 50\%$, reflecting the fact that Foreign producers are willing to lower their prices more, taking on a larger share of the tariff burden. In that case, the Home country obtains a larger terms-of-trade increase and hence the optimal level of the tariff is higher.

APPLICATION

U.S. Tariffs on Steel Once Again

Let us return to the U.S. tariff on steel, and reevaluate the effect on U.S. welfare in the large-country case. The calculation of the deadweight loss that we did earlier in the application assumed that the United States was a small country, facing fixed world prices for steel. In that case, the 30% tariff on steel was fully reflected in U.S. prices, which rose by 30%. But what if the import prices for steel in the United States did not rise by the full amount of the tariff? If the United States is a large enough importer of steel, then the Foreign export price will fall and the U.S. import price will rise by less than the tariff. It is then possible that the United States gained from the tariff.

To determine whether the United States gained from the tariff on steel products, we can compute the deadweight loss (area $b + d$) and the terms-of-trade gain (area e) for each imported steel product using the optimum tariff formula.

Optimal Tariffs for Steel Let us apply this formula to the U.S. steel tariffs to see how the tariffs applied compare with the theoretical optimal tariff. In Table 8-2, we show various steel products along with their respective elasticities of export supply to the United States. By taking the inverse of each export supply elasticity, we obtain the optimal tariff. For example, alloy steel flat-rolled products (the first item) have a low export supply elasticity, 0.27, so they have a very high optimal tariff of $1/0.27 = 3.7 = 370\%$. In contrast, iron and nonalloy steel flat-rolled products (the last item) have a very high export supply elasticity of 750, so the optimal tariff is $1/750 \approx 0\%$. Products between these have optimal tariffs ranging from 1 to 125%.

In the final column of Table 8-2, we show the actual tariffs that were applied to these products. For alloy steel flat-rolled products (the first item), the actual tariff was 30%, which is far below the optimal tariff. That means the terms-of-trade gain for that product was higher than the deadweight loss: the tariff is on the portion of the welfare graph between B and C in Figure 8-8, and U.S. welfare is above its free-trade level. The same holds for iron and steel bars, rods, angles, and shapes, for which the tariffs of 15 to 30% are again less than their optimal level, so the United States obtains a terms-of-trade gain that exceeds the deadweight loss. However, for iron and steel tubes, pipes, and fittings, the U.S. tariffs were 13 to 15%, but the optimal tariff for that product was only 1%. Because of the very high elasticity of export supply, the United States has practically no effect on the world price, so the deadweight loss for that product exceeds the terms-of-trade gain.

[11] See Problem 3 at the end of the chapter, where you will show that steeper export supply leads Foreign to absorb more of the tariff.

TABLE 8-2

Optimal Tariffs for Steel Products This table shows optimal tariffs for steel products, calculated with the elasticity formula.

Product Category	Elasticity of Export Supply	Optimal Tariff (%)	Actual Tariff (%)
Alloy steel flat-rolled products	0.27	370	30
Iron and steel rails and railway track	0.80	125	0
Iron and steel bars, rods, angles, shapes	0.80	125	15–30
Ferrous waste and scrap	17	6	0
Iron and steel tubes, pipes, and fittings	90	1	13–15
Iron and nonalloy steel flat-rolled products	750	0	0

Source: Elasticities of export supply provided by Christian Broda and David Weinstein, May 2006, "Globalization and the Gains from Variety," Quarterly Journal of Economics, *121(2), 541–585.*

To summarize, for the three product categories in Table 8-2 where the United States applied tariffs, in two products the terms-of-trade gain exceeded the deadweight loss, so U.S. welfare rose due to the tariff, but in a third case the deadweight loss was larger, so U.S. welfare fell due to the tariff. The first two products illustrate the large-country case for tariffs, in which the welfare of the importer can rise due to a tariff, whereas the third product illustrates the small-country case, in which the importer loses from the tariff.

From the information given in Table 8-2, we do not know whether the United States gained or lost overall from the steel tariffs: that calculation would require adding up the gains and losses due to the tariff over all imported steel products, which we have not done. But in the end, we should keep in mind that any rise in U.S. welfare comes at the expense of exporting countries. Even if there was an overall terms-of-trade gain for the United States when adding up across all steel products, that gain would be at the expense of the European countries and other steel exporters. As we have already discussed, the steel exporters objected to the U.S. tariffs at the WTO and were entitled to apply *retaliatory* tariffs of their own against U.S. products. If these tariffs had been applied, they would have eliminated and reversed any U.S. gain. By removing the tariffs in less than two years, the United States avoided a costly tariff war. Indeed, that is one of the main goals of the WTO: by allowing exporting countries to retaliate with tariffs, the WTO prevents importers from using optimal tariffs to their own advantage. In a later chapter, we show more carefully how such a tariff war will end up being costly to all countries involved. ■

5 Import Quotas

On January 1, 2005, China was poised to become the world's largest exporter of textiles and apparel. On that date, a system of worldwide import quotas known as the **Multifibre Arrangement (MFA)** was abolished. Import quotas are a restriction on the amount of a particular good that one country can purchase from another country. Under the Multifibre Arrangement, begun in 1974, import quotas restricted the amount of nearly every textile and apparel product that was imported to Canada, the European countries, and the United States. These countries limited their textile imports to protect their own domestic firms producing those products. With the end of the MFA, China was ready to enjoy greatly increased exports—but this did not occur. The threat of import competition from China led the United States and Europe to negotiate *new* temporary import quotas with China, as we discuss in this section.

Besides the MFA, there are many other examples of import quotas. For example, since 1993 Europe had a quota on the imports of bananas that allowed for a greater number of bananas to enter from its former colonies in Africa than from Latin America. In 2005 that quota was simplified and converted into a tariff, even though that tariff still discriminated among countries based on their colonial past. Then in 2009 Europe agreed to reduce the tariff on Latin American bananas, effectively bringing to an end this "banana war" that had lasted for more than 15 years (see **Headlines: Banana Wars**). Another example is the quota on U.S. imports of sugar, which is still

HEADLINES

Banana Wars

This article discusses a well-known example of a quota that applied to European imports of bananas. The quota and discriminatory tariff on bananas from Latin America finally ended in late 2009.

I can hardly believe the banana wars are over. The dispute started back in 1993 when the European Union set quotas favoring banana imports from Ivory Coast, the Windward Islands and other former colonies at the expense of imports from Latin America. American banana companies and the Latin American countries where they grow their bananas sued the E.U., accusing it of rigging an unfair trade deal, first under the GATT and then under the W.T.O.

The suit dragged on for years, and at several points threatened to spark an all-out trade war between Washington and Europe. In 1999, after a meeting on Kosovo was hijacked by the banana crisis, the secretary of state then, Madeleine Albright, declared in exasperation: "I never in my life thought I would spend so much time on bananas."

It finally ended this month when the E.U. said it would continue to grant tariff-free access to its former colonies but would reduce tariffs on Latin American bananas by 35 percent over seven years. The United States and Latin American producers agreed to drop their case. After all the roiling, what strikes me now is how little people seem to care. That says a lot about how attitudes toward trade have changed.

When this started, trade was trumpeted as the single most important tool for development. Europe insisted that its special treatment of its former colonies was central to its post-imperial responsibilities. The United States and Latin American countries vowed to hold the line for free trade—over bananas at least—to make it a tool of development for all.

Today nobody talks about bananas. Stalled global trade talks (remember Doha?) barely get mentioned. There are a lot of problems out there, including the collapse of world trade in the wake of the global recession and the looming threat of protectionism. Yet there has also been a rethinking about trade's supposed silver bullet role in economic development.

China's growth stands as a beacon for the power of trade. But others that have hitched their economic strategy to trade, like Mexico, have found prosperity elusive. Despite growing banana exports, both the Latin American banana exporters and Europe's impoverished former colonies remain poor.

One thing we have learned over the past 15 years is that trade is necessary but not sufficient for development. Countries also need investment in infrastructure, technology and human capital. They need credit. They need legitimate institutions—like clean courts to battle monopolies—and help building them. Putting up a few barriers against banana imports, or tearing a few of them down, can't do it all.

Source: Eduardo Porter, The New York Times, *December 29, 2009, p. A30.*

HEADLINES

Sweet Opportunity

This article discusses another well-known example of a quota that applies to imports of sugar into the United States. It argues that in 2006 there was an opportunity to remove the quota (since world prices had risen to equal U.S. domestic prices), but that removal did not occur.

It isn't often that circumstances hand the government a chance to remove trade barriers without harming a coddled U.S. industry. But the current surge in world sugar prices is serving up precisely that opportunity to President Bush. The U.S. sugar program is a Rauschenberg painting of farm loans and price supports that guarantees American sugar producers a set price for their crops. If producers cannot sell their sugar at a break-even price after accounting for their loans, they are entitled to sell the excess to the U.S. Department of Agriculture.

To keep U.S. prices high enough to ensure that a mountain of sugar doesn't get dumped on Uncle Sam, the U.S. in turn keeps supplies down by imposing import quotas on its trading partners. But with the world price for raw cane sugar, including delivery, hovering around 18 cents per pound, the farm loan-rate at 18 cents for cane sugar (and 23 cents for beet sugar) and the U.S. economy experiencing sugar shortages, the U.S. market could be opened without incurring huge costs at the USDA. . . .

The U.S. price of sugar has been two to three times higher than the world price for the past 25 years. The longer that imbalance has persisted, the more inefficient U.S. sugar producers have become. And, paradoxically, the more powerful they have become as a special interest blocking U.S. trade expansion. Now that a spike in world prices has put the U.S. on par with foreign producers, there is a window of opportunity to do away with a sugar program that costs American jobs and has become a source of trade friction around the world.

Source: Excerpted from a Wall Street Journal *editorial, February 6, 2006, p. A14.*

in place despite calls for its removal (see **Headlines: Sweet Opportunity**). In this section, we explain how quotas affect the importing and exporting countries and examine the differences between quotas and tariffs. Like a tariff, an import quota often imposes a welfare cost on the importing country. But we will find that quotas can often lead to higher welfare losses for the importer than tariffs.

Import Quota in a Small Country

Applying an import quota for a small country is similar to applying a tariff, so we can use the graphs developed earlier in the chapter to analyze quotas, too.

Free-Trade Equilibrium In panel (a) of Figure 8-9, we show the Home demand curve D and the Home supply curve S. At the free-trade world price of P^W, Home quantity demanded is D_1 and quantity supplied is S_1, so imports are $M_1 = D_1 - S_1$. The import demand curve $M = D - S$ is shown in panel (b). The assumption that the Home country is small means that the fixed world price P^W is not affected by the import quota, so under free trade, the Foreign export supply curve X^* is a horizontal line at the world price P^W. The Home import demand curve M and Foreign export supply curve X^* intersect at point B, resulting in the free-trade level of imports, M_1.

Effect of the Quota Now suppose that an import quota of $M_2 < M_1$ is imposed, meaning that the quantity imported cannot exceed this amount. This quota effectively establishes a vertical export supply curve labeled as $\overline{X}$ in panel (b), which fixes the

FIGURE 8-9

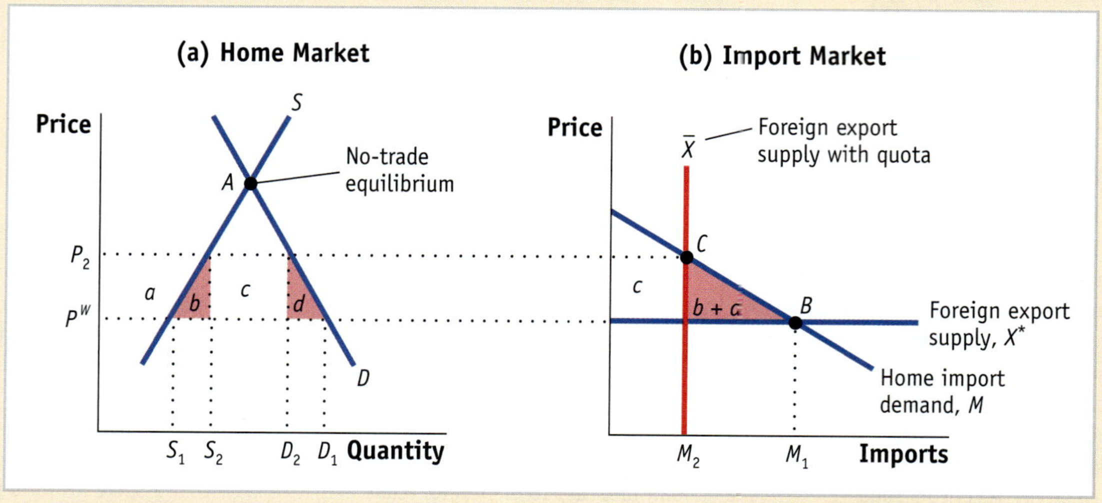

Quota for a Small Country Under free trade, the Foreign export supply curve is horizontal at the world price, P^W, and the free-trade equilibrium is at point B with imports of M_1. Applying an import quota of $M_2 < M_1$ leads to the vertical export supply curve $\bar{X}$ with the equilibrium at point C. The quota increases the import price from P^W to P_2. There would be the same impact on price and quantities if instead of the quota, a tariff of $t = P_2 - P^W$ had been used.

import quantity at M_2. The vertical export supply curve now intersects import demand at point C, which establishes the Home price of P_2. In panel (a), the price of P_2 leads firms to increase the quantity supplied to S_2 and consumers to decrease their quantity demanded to D_2.

The import quota therefore leads to an increase in the Home price and a reduction in Home imports, just like a tariff. Furthermore, notice that there would be an equivalent effect on the import price and quantity if instead of the quota, the government had imposed an import tariff of $t = P_2 - P^W$. That is, the tariff of $t = P_2 - P^W$ would raise the Home price to P_2 and reduce imports o the level M_2. We conclude that for every level of the import quota, there is an **equivalent import tariff** that would lead to the same Home price and quantity of imports.[12]

Effect on Welfare As we have shown, the quota leads to an increase in the Home price. The rise in the price for consumers leads to a fall in consumer surplus. That fall is measured by the area between the prices P_2 and P^W and to the left of the demand curve, which is the area $(a + b + c + d)$ in panel (a) of Figure 8-9. On the other hand, the increase in the price facing Home producers leads to a gain in producer surplus. That gain is measured by the area between the prices P_2 and P^W and to the left of the supply curve, which is the area a in Figure 8-9(a). These two welfare effects are the same as would occur under a tariff.

[12] As we show in the next chapter, this conclusion depends on our assumption of perfect competition and does not hold without that assumption.

The quota and tariff differ, however, in terms of area *c*, which would be collected as government revenue under a tariff. Under the quota, this area equals the difference between the domestic price P_2 and the world price P^W, times the quantity of imports M_2. Therefore, whoever is actually importing the good will be able to earn the difference between the world price P^W and the higher Home price P_2 by selling the imports in the Home market. We call the difference between these two prices the *rent* associated with the quota, and hence the area *c* represents the total **quota rents.** There are four possible ways that these quota rents can be allocated:

1. Giving the Quota to Home Firms First, **quota licenses** (i.e., permits to import the quantity allowed under the quota system) can be given to Home firms, which are then able to import at the world price P^W and sell locally at P_2, earning the difference between these as rents. An example of this is the dairy industry in the United States, in which U.S. producers of cheese receive licenses to import from abroad. With home firms earning the rents *c*, the net effect of the quota on Home welfare is

Fall in consumer surplus:	$-(a + b + c + d)$
Rise in producer surplus:	$+a$
Quota rents earned at Home	+ c
Net effect on Home welfare:	$-(b + d)$

We see from this calculation that the net effect on Home welfare is a loss of amount $(b + d)$. That loss is the same as what we found in Section 3 of this chapter for the loss of a tariff in a small country. As in that section, we still refer to $(b + d)$ as a deadweight loss.

2. Rent Seeking One complication of simply giving valuable quota licenses to Home firms is that these firms may engage in some kind of inefficient activities to obtain them. For example, suppose that Home firms are producing batteries and import the chemical needed as an input. If licenses for the imported chemicals are allocated in proportion to each firm's production of batteries in the previous years, then the Home firms will likely produce more batteries than they can sell (and at lower quality) *just to obtain the import licenses for the following year.* Alternatively, firms might engage in bribery or other lobbying activities to obtain the licenses. These kinds of inefficient activities done to obtain quota licenses are called **rent seeking.** It has been suggested that the waste of resources devoted to rent-seeking activities could be as large as the value of rents themselves so that the area c would be wasted rather than accrue to Home firms. If rent seeking occurs, the welfare loss due to the quota would be

Fall in consumer surplus:	$-(a + b + c + d)$
Rise in producer surplus:	$+a$
Net effect on Home welfare:	$-(b + c + d)$

The waste of resources due to rent seeking leads to a fall in Home welfare of $(b + c + d)$, which is larger than that for a tariff. It is often thought that rent seeking is more severe in some developing countries where rules are not well enforced and officials are willing to take bribes in exchange for the licenses.

3. Auctioning the Quota A third possibility for allocating the rents that come from the quota is for the government of the importing country to auction off the quota licenses. This occurred in Australia and New Zealand during the 1980s. In Australia, the auctions covered imports of textiles, apparel, footwear, and motor vehicles. The quota auctions used for imports of textiles and apparel in Australia were an alternative to the Multifibre Arrangement (MFA). Auctions of import quotas have also been proposed in the United States but have never actually occurred.[13] In a well-organized, competitive auction, the revenue collected should exactly equal the value of the rents, so that area *c* would be earned by the Home government. Using the auction method to allocate quota rents, the net loss in domestic welfare due to the quota becomes

Fall in consumer surplus:	$-(a + b + c + d)$
Rise in producer surplus:	$+a$
Auction revenue earned at Home	$+c$
Net effect on Home welfare:	$-(b + d)$

The net effect on Home welfare in this case is the deadweight loss of $(b + d)$, which is once again the same loss as incurred from a tariff.

4. "Voluntary" Export Restraint The final possibility for allocating quota rents is for the government of the importing country to give authority for implementing the quota to the government of the *exporting* country. Because the exporting country allocates the quota among its own producers, this is sometimes called a **"voluntary" export restraint (VER),** or a **"voluntary" restraint agreement (VRA).** In the 1980s the United States used this type of arrangement to restrict Japanese automobile imports. In that case, Japan's Ministry of International Trade and Industry (MITI), a government agency that implements Japan's trade policies, told each Japanese auto manufacturer how much it could export to the United States. In this case, the quota rents are earned by foreign producers, so the loss in Home welfare equals

Fall in consumer surplus:	$-(a + b + c + d)$
Rise in producer surplus:	$+a$
Net effect on Home welfare:	$-(b + c + d)$

The VER gives a higher net loss $(b + c + d)$ for the importer than does a tariff because the quota rents are earned by foreign exporters. This result raises the question of why VERs are used at all. One answer is that by giving the quota rents to firms in the exporting country, that country is much less likely to retaliate by adopting import tariffs or quotas of its own. In other words, the transfer of quota rents to the exporter becomes a way to avoid a tariff or quota war.

[13] The proposals to auction import quotas in the United States were made during the 1980s; see C. Fred Bergsten, 1987, *Auction Quotas and United States Trade Policy* (Washington, D.C.: Peterson Institute for International Economics). Government auctions have occurred in the United States for bandwidth in radio frequencies and also for off-shore oil drilling.

Costs of Import Quotas in the United States

Table 8-3 presents some estimates of the home deadweight losses, along with the quota rents, for major U.S. quotas in the years around 1985. In all cases except dairy, the rents were earned by foreign exporters. We discuss the case of automobiles in the next chapter, for which the quota rents earned by foreigners range from $2 billion to $8 billion. Textiles and apparel also had very large quota rents and U.S. deadweight losses (about $5 billion each) under the MFA. In addition, the MFA imposed large losses on the Foreign exporting countries, due to rent-seeking activities by exporters to obtain the quota permits. Adding up the costs shown in Table 8-3, the total U.S. deadweight loss from these quotas was in the range of $8 billion to $12 billion annually in the mid-1980s, whereas the quota rents transferred to foreigners were another $7 billion to $17 billion annually.

TABLE 8-3

Annual Cost of U.S. Import Protection ($ billions)
Shown here are estimates of the dead weight losses and quota rents due to U.S. import quotas in the 1980s, for the years around 1985. Many of these quotas are no longer in place today.

	U.S. Deadweight Loss ($) (area *b* + *d*)	Quota Rents ($) (area *c*)
Automobiles	0.2–1.2	2.2–7.9
Dairy	1.4	0.25*
Steel	0.1–0.3	0.7–2.0
Sugar	0.1	0.4–1.3
Textiles and apparel	4.9–5.9	4.0–6.1
Import tariffs	1.2–3.4	0
Total	7.9–12.3	7.3–17.3

* In dairy the quota rents are earned by U.S. importers and so are not included in the total.

Source: Robert Feenstra, Summer 1992, "How Costly Is Protectionism?" Journal of *Economic Perspectives, 159–178.*

Some, but not all, of these costs for the United States are no longer relevant today. The quota in automobiles ceased being applied after 1987 because Japanese producers built plants in the United States and therefore reduced their imports. The quotas in the steel industry were replaced by the "safeguard" tariffs that President Bush temporarily imposed from 2002 to 2003. But the quotas used in sugar remain, and while the MFA expired on January 1, 2005, it has been replaced by a new set of quotas with China. There is the prospect of continuing losses for the United States due to quotas in these industries, as we discuss in the next application to textiles and apparel.

APPLICATION

China and the Multifibre Arrangement

One of the founding principles of GATT was that countries should not use quotas to restrict imports (see Article XI of **Side Bar: Key Provisions of the GATT**). The Multifibre Arrangement (MFA), organized under the auspices of the GATT in 1974, was a major exception to that principle and allowed the industrial countries to restrict imports of textile and apparel products from the developing countries. Importing countries could join the MFA and arrange quotas bilaterally (i.e., after negotiating with exporters) or unilaterally (on their own). In practice, the import quotas established under the MFA were very detailed and specified the amount of each textile and apparel product that each developing country could sell to countries including Canada, Europe, and the United States.

Although the amount of the quotas was occasionally revised upward, it did not keep up with the increasing ability of new supplying countries to sell. Under the Uruguay Round of WTO negotiations held from 1986 to 1994, developing countries were able to negotiate an end to this system of import quotas. The MFA expired on January 1, 2005. The biggest potential supplier of textile and apparel products was China, so the expiration of the MFA meant that China could export as much as it wanted to other countries—or so it thought. The potential for a huge increase in exports from China posed a problem for many other countries. Some developing countries expected that rising exports from China would compete with their own export of apparel items, on which many workers depended for their livelihood. The large producers in importing countries were also concerned with the potential rise in Chinese exports because it could lead to the loss of jobs for their own workers in textiles and apparel.

Growth in Exports from China Immediately after January 1, 2005, exports of textiles and apparel from China grew rapidly. For example, exports of Chinese tights and pantyhose to the European Union increased by 2,000% in January and February, as compared with a year earlier; imports of pullovers and jerseys from China jumped nearly 1,000%; and imports of trousers more than tripled. Overall in 2005, China's textile and apparel imports to the United States rose by more than 40% as compared with the year before, as shown in Figure 8-10, where we include the top 20 exporters to the U.S. market.[14] In panel (a), we show the change in the value of textile and apparel imports from each country. The surge of imports from China came at the expense of some higher-cost exporters, such as South Korea, Hong Kong, and Taiwan, whose exports to the United States declined by 10 to 20%.

In panel (b) of Figure 8-10, we show the percentage change in the prices of textiles and apparel products from each country, depending on whether the products were "constrained goods," subject to the MFA quota before January 1, 2005. China has the largest drop in prices from 2004 to 2005, 38% in the "constrained goods" categories. Many other countries also experienced a substantial fall in their prices due to the end of the MFA quota: 18% for Pakistan; 16% for Cambodia; and 8 to 9% for the Philippines, Bangladesh, India, Indonesia, and Sri Lanka. A drop in price due to the removal of the import quota is exactly what we predict from the theory, as we move from the price P_2 in Figure 8-9 to the free-trade price P^W. Surprisingly, a few countries in Figure 8-10 show increases in their prices, such as Mexico. However, less than 1% of Mexico's sales of textiles and apparel to the United States was constrained by the quota, so that price increase does not appear to be due to the removal of the MFA.

Welfare Cost of MFA Given the drop in prices in 2005 from countries selling to the United States, it is possible to estimate the welfare loss due to the MFA. The United States did not auction the quota licenses for textiles and apparel so the quota rents were earned by foreign exporting firms. That means the welfare loss for the United States due to the MFA is the area $(b + c + d)$ in Figure 8-9. Using the price drops from 2004 to 2005, that area is estimated to be in the range of \$6.5 billion to \$16.2 billion in 2005.[15] The simple average of these estimates is \$11.4 billion as the total cost to the United States. To put that welfare loss in perspective, there were 111 million households in the United States in 2005, and the typical household spent

---

[14] Figure 8-10 and the welfare estimates in the following paragraphs are from James Harrigan and Geoffrey Barrows, 2009, "Testing the Theory of Trade Policy: Evidence from the Abrupt End of the Multifibre Arrangement," *The Review of Economics and Statistics*, vol. 91(2), pp. 282–294.

[15] Notice that this range of estimates for 2005 is comparable with (but wider than) the range of estimates for the welfare costs of textiles and apparel in Table 8-3, which is \$8.9 billion to \$12 billion for 1985, obtained by adding up the deadweight loss and the quota rents.

FIGURE 8-10

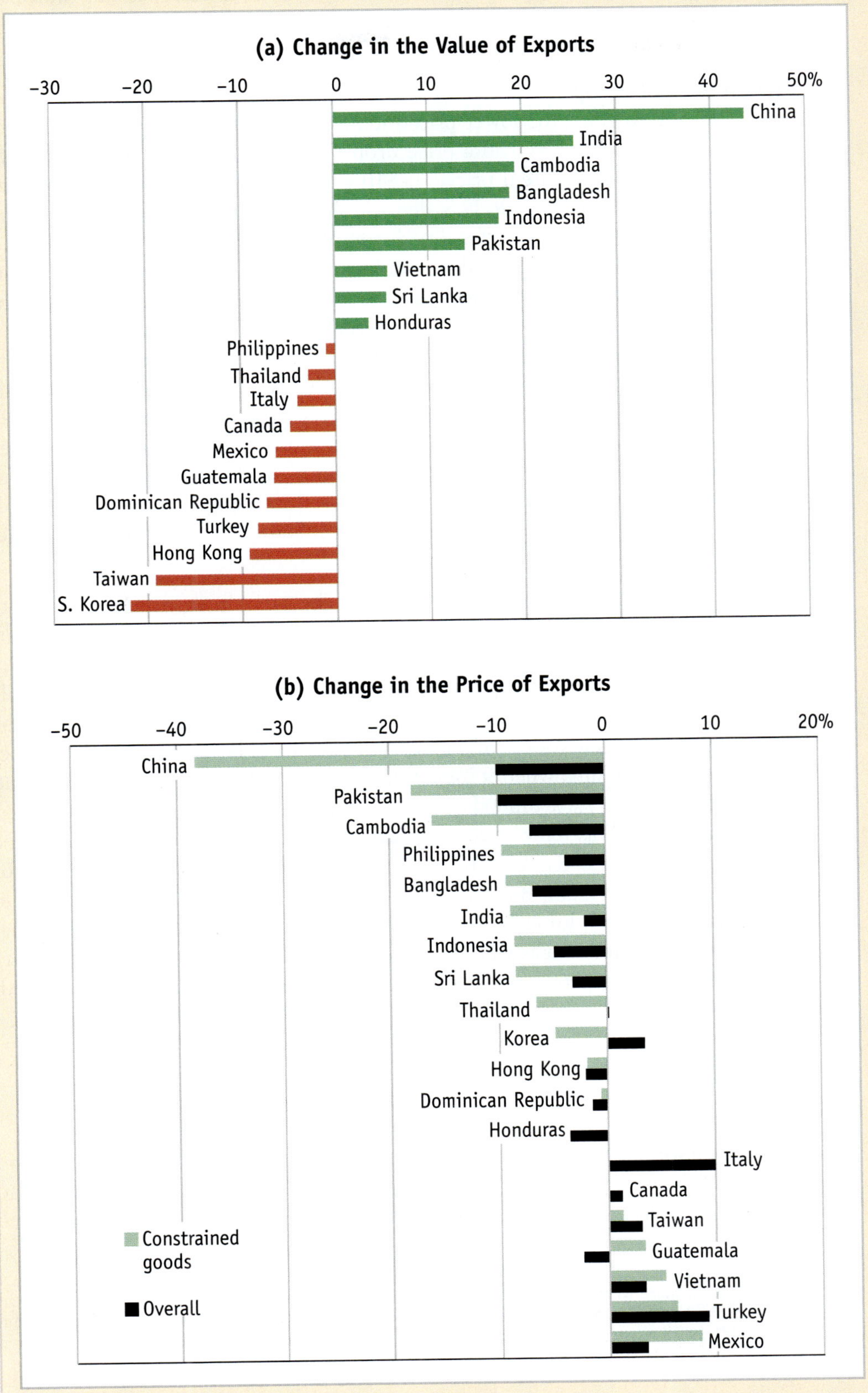

Changes in Clothing and Textile Exports to the United States after the MFA, 2004–2005 After the expiration of the Multifibre Arrangement (MFA), the value of clothing and textile exports from China rose dramatically, as shown in panel (a). This reflects the surge in the quantity of exports that were formerly constrained under the MFA as well as a shift to Chinese exports from other, higher-cost producers such as Hong Kong, Taiwan, and South Korea. In panel (b), we see that the prices of goods constrained by the MFA typically fell by more than the average change in export prices after the MFA's expiry. This is exactly what our theory of quotas predicts: The removal of quotas lowers import prices for consumers.

Source: James Harrigan and Geoffrey Barrows, 2009, "Testing the Theory of Trade Policy: Evidence from the Abrupt End of the Multifibre Arrangement," The Review of Economics and Statistics, *vol. 91(2), pp. 282–294.*

about $1,400 on apparel. Dividing the loss of $11.4 billion by the 111 million households, we obtain about $100 per household, or 7% of their annual spending on apparel as the welfare cost of the MFA.[16]

Import Quality Besides the overall decline in prices, there was also an interesting pattern to the price drops: the prices of textile and apparel products dropped the most (in percentage terms) for the lower-priced items. So, an inexpensive T-shirt coming from China and priced at $1 had a price drop of more than 38% (more than 38¢), whereas a more expensive item priced at $10 experienced a price drop of less than 38% (less than $3.80). As a result, U.S. demand shifted toward the lower-priced items imported from China: there was "quality downgrading" in the exports from China.

To understand why this quality downgrading occurred, it is easiest to think about the problem in reverse: when a quota like the MFA is applied, what is the effect on quality? The MFA, like most other quotas, was applied to the *quantity* of the import sent to each country: it was applied to yards of cloth, or number of shirts, or dozens of pairs of socks, and so on. Faced with a quota of that type, the exporting firm would have an incentive to *upgrade* the type of cloth, shirts, or socks that it sells, since selling a higher value for the same quantity will still meet the quota limitation. So when the MFA starts, we expect to see "quality upgrading" in the exports for each country. By the same logic, when the MFA was removed, there was "quality downgrading" in the exports from China to the United States and exports from other countries, too.

Reaction of the United States and Europe The surge in exports from China to the United States and Europe was short-lived, however. The European Union threatened to impose new quotas on Chinese exports, and in response, China agreed on June 11, 2005, to "voluntary" export restraints that would limit its growth of textile exports to about 10% per year through the end of 2008. For the United States, the ability to negotiate a new system of quotas with China had been guaranteed by a special agreement with China when it joined the WTO in 2001. Under this agreement, China was limited to a 7.5% annual growth in its textile exports to the United States, from 2005 to 2008. This temporary quota expired at the end of 2008, at which time we might have expected the U.S. textile and apparel industry to renew its call for quota protection once again. But due to the worldwide recession, Chinese exports in this industry were much lower in 2009 than they had been in earlier years. For that reason, China indicated that it would not accept any further limitation on its ability to export textile and apparel products to the United States and to Europe, and both these quotas expired. ■

6 Conclusions

A tariff on imports is the most commonly used trade policy tool. In this chapter, we have studied the effect of tariffs on consumers and producers in both importing and exporting countries. We have looked at several different cases. First, we assumed

[16] In comparison, there were 737,000 U.S. workers in the textile and apparel industries in 2004, with an average annual salary of $31,500. If we divide the total loss of $11.4 billion by all these workers, we obtain about $15,500 per job protected in the U.S.industry, or about one-half of the annual salary of each worker.

that the importing country is so small that it does not affect the world price of the imported good. In that case, the price faced by consumers and producers in the importing country will rise by the full amount of the tariff. With a rise in the consumer price, there is a drop in consumer surplus; and with a rise in the producer price, there is a gain in producer surplus. In addition, the government collects revenue from the tariff. When we add together all these effects—the drop in consumer surplus, gain in producer surplus, and government revenue collected—we still get a *net loss* for the importing country. We have referred to that loss as the deadweight loss resulting from the tariff.

The fact that a small importing country always has a net loss from a tariff explains why most economists oppose the use of tariffs. Still, this result leaves open the question of why tariffs are used. One reason that tariffs are used, despite their deadweight loss, is that they are an easy way for governments to raise revenue, especially in developing countries. A second reason is politics: the government might care more about protecting firms than avoiding losses for consumers. A third reason is that the small-country assumption may not hold in practice: countries may be large enough importers of a product so that a tariff will affect its world price. In this large-country case, the decrease in imports demanded due to the tariff causes foreign exporters to lower their prices. Of course, consumer and producer prices in the importing country still go up, since these prices include the tariff, but they rise by less than the full amount of the tariff. We have shown that if we add up the drop in consumer surplus, gain in producer surplus, and government revenue collected, it is possible for a small tariff to generate welfare gains for the importing country.

Still, any gain for the importer in this large-country case comes at the expense of the foreign exporters. For that reason, the use of a tariff in the large-country case is sometimes called a "beggar thy neighbor" policy. We have found that the drop in the exporter's welfare due to the tariff is greater than the gain in the importer's welfare. Therefore, the world loses overall because of the tariff. This is another reason that most economists oppose their use.

In addition to an import tariff, we have also studied import quotas, which restrict the quantity of imports into a country. The WTO has tried to limit the use of import quotas and has been somewhat successful. For example, the Multifibre Arrangement (MFA) was a complex system of quotas intended to restrict the import of textiles and apparel into many industrialized countries. It was supposed to end on January 1, 2005, but both the United States and the European Union then established new quotas against imports of textiles and apparel from China, which expired at the end of 2008. The United States continues to have a quota on imports of sugar, and up until very recently, the European Union had a quota and then a discriminatory tariff on imports of bananas (that "banana war" has now ended). These are some of the best-known import quotas, and there are other examples, too.

Under perfect competition, the effect of applying an import quota is similar to the effect of applying an import tariff: they both lead to an increase in the domestic price in the importing country, with a loss for consumers and a gain for producers. One difference, however, is that under a tariff the government in the importing country collects revenue, whereas under a quota, whoever is able to bring in the import earns the difference between the domestic and world prices, called "quota rents." For example, if firms in the importing country have the licenses to bring in imports, then they earn the quota rents. Alternatively, if resources are wasted by firms trying to capture these rents, then there is an additional deadweight loss. It is more common, however, for the foreign exporters to earn the quota rents, as occurs under a "voluntary" export restraint, administered by the foreign government. A fourth possibility is that the government in the importing country auctions the quota licenses, in which case it earns the equivalent of the quota rents as auction revenue; this case is identical to the tariff in its welfare outcome.

KEY POINTS

1. The government of a country can use laws and regulations, called "trade policies," to affect international trade flows. An import tariff, which is a tax at the border, is the most commonly used trade policy.
2. The rules governing trade policies in most countries are outlined by the General Agreement on Tariffs and Trade (GATT), an international legal convention adopted after World War II to promote increased international trade. Since 1995 the new name for the GATT is the World Trade Organization (WTO).
3. In a small country, the quantity of imports demanded is assumed to be very small compared with the total world market. For this reason, the importer faces a fixed world price. In that case, the price faced by consumers and producers in the importing country will rise by the full amount of the tariff.
4. The use of a tariff by a small importing country always leads to a net loss in welfare. We call that loss the "deadweight loss."
5. In a large country, the decrease in imports demanded due to the tariff causes foreign exporters to lower their prices. Consumer and producer prices in the importing country still go up, since these prices include the tariff, but they rise by less than the full amount of the tariff (since the exporter price falls).
6. The use of a tariff for a large country can lead to a net gain in welfare because the price charged by the exporter has fallen; this is a terms-of-trade gain for the importer.
7. The "optimal tariff" is the tariff amount that maximizes welfare for the importer. For a small country, the optimal tariff is zero since any tariff leads to a net loss. For a large country, however, the optimal tariff is positive.
8. The formula for the optimal tariff states that it depends inversely on the foreign export supply elasticity. If the foreign export supply elasticity is high, then the optimal tariff is low, but if the foreign export supply elasticity is low, then the optimal tariff is high.
9. "Import quotas" restrict the quantity of a particular import, thereby increasing the domestic price, increasing domestic production, and creating a benefit for those who are allowed to import the quantity allotted. These benefits are called "quota rents."
10. Assuming perfectly competitive markets for goods, quotas are similar to tariffs since the restriction in the amount imported leads to a higher domestic price. However, the welfare implications of quotas are different from those of tariffs depending on who earns the quota rents. These rents might be earned by firms in the importing country (if they have the licenses to import the good), or by firms in the exporting country (if the foreign government administers the quota), or by the government in the importing country (if it auctions off the quota licenses). The last case is most similar to a tariff, since the importing government earns the revenue.

KEY TERMS

trade policy, p. 238
import tariff, p. 238
import quota, p. 238
dumping, p. 239
export subsidies, p. 239
safeguard provision, p. 240
escape clause, p. 240
regional trade agreements, p. 240
free-trade areas, p. 240
customs unions, p. 240
consumer surplus, p. 240
producer surplus, p. 240
small country, p. 243
import demand curve, p. 245
deadweight loss, p. 249
production loss, p. 249
consumption loss, p. 250
dispute settlement procedure, p. 255
tariff war, p. 255
large country, p. 257
terms of trade, p. 259
terms-of-trade gain, p. 260
optimal tariff, p. 260
Multifibre Arrangement (MFA), p. 263
equivalent import tariff, p. 266
quota rents, p. 267
quota licenses, p. 267
rent seeking, p. 267
"voluntary" export restraint (VER), p. 268
"voluntary" restraint agreement (VRA), p. 268

PROBLEMS

1. The following questions refer to **Side Bar: Key Provisions of the GATT.**
   a. If the United States applies a tariff to a particular product (e.g., steel) imported from one country, what is the implication for its steel tariffs applied to all other countries according to the "most favored nation" principle?
   b. Is Article XXIV an exception to most favored nation treatment? Explain why or why not.
   c. Under the GATT articles, instead of a tariff, can a country impose a quota (quantitative restriction) on the number of goods imported? What has been one exception to this rule in practice?
2. Consider a small country applying a tariff t to imports of a good like that represented in Figure 8-5.
   a. Suppose that the country decides to *reduce* its tariff to t'. Redraw the graphs for the Home and import markets and illustrate this change. What happens to the quantity and price of goods produced at Home? What happens to the quantity of imports?
   b. Are there gains or losses to domestic consumer surplus due to the reduction in tariff? Are there gains or losses to domestic producer surplus due to the reduction in tariff? How is government revenue affected by the policy change? Illustrate these on your graphs.
   c. What is the overall gain or loss in welfare due to the policy change?
3. Consider a large country applying a tariff t to imports of a good like that represented in Figure 8-7.
   a. How does the export supply curve in panel (b) compare with that in the small-country case? Explain why these are different.
   b. Explain how the tariff affects the price paid by consumers in the *importing* country and the price received by producers in the *exporting* country. Use graphs to illustrate how the prices are affected if (i) the export supply curve is very elastic (flat) or (ii) the export supply curve is inelastic (steep).
4. Consider a large country applying a tariff t to imports of a good like that represented in Figure 8-7. How does the size of the terms-of-trade gain compare with the size of the deadweight loss when (i) the tariff is very small and (ii) the tariff is very large? Use graphs to illustrate your answer.

5. a. If the foreign export supply is perfectly elastic, what is the optimal tariff Home should apply to increase welfare? Explain.
   b. If the foreign export supply is less than perfectly elastic, what is the formula for the optimal tariff Home should apply to increase welfare?
   c. What happens to Home welfare if it applies a tariff higher than the optimal tariff?

6. Rank the following in ascending order of Home welfare and justify your answers. If two items are equivalent, indicate this accordingly.
   a. Tariff of t in a small country corresponding to the quantity of imports M
   b. Tariff of t in a large country corresponding to the same quantity of imports M
   c. Tariff of t' in a large country corresponding to the quantity of imports $M' > M$

7. Rank the following in ascending order of Home welfare and justify your answers. If two items are equivalent, indicate this accordingly.
   a. Tariff of t in a small country corresponding to the quantity of imports M
   b. Quota with the same imports M in a small country, with quota licenses distributed to Home firms and no rent seeking
   c. Quota of M in a small country with quota licenses auctioned to Home firms
   d. Quota of M in a small country with the quota given to the exporting firms
   e. Quota of M in a small country with quota licenses distributed to rent-seeking Home firms

8. Why did President George W. Bush suspend the U.S. tariffs on steel 17 months ahead of schedule?

9. What provision of U.S. trade law was used by President Barack Obama to apply a tariff on tires imported from China? Does this provision make it easier or harder to apply a tariff than Section 201?

10. No U.S. tire producers joined in the request for the tariff on tires in 2009. Rather, the petition for a tariff on tires imported from China was brought by the United Steelworkers of American, the union who represents workers in the tire industry. Why did major tire manufactures operating in the United States, such as Goodyear, Michelin, Cooper, and Bridgestone, not support the tariff?

11. Suppose Home is a small country. Use the graphs below to answer the questions.

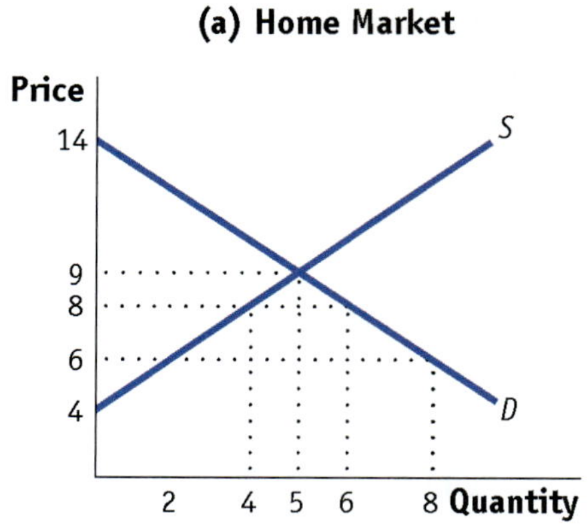

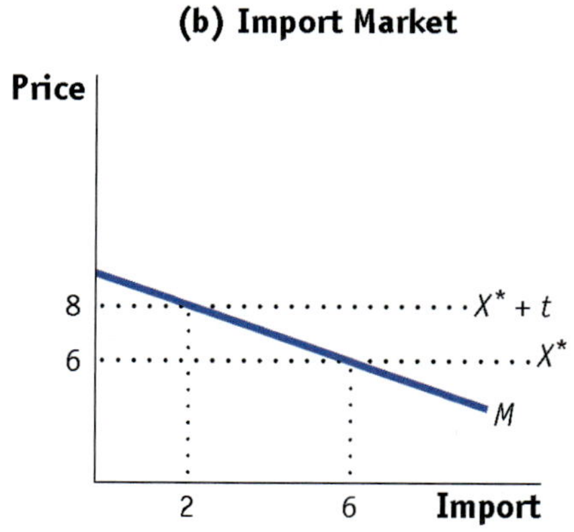

   a. Calculate Home consumer surplus and producer surplus in the absence of trade.
   b. Now suppose that Home engages in trade and faces the world price, $P^* = \$6$. Determine the consumer and producer surplus under free trade. Does Home benefit from trade? Explain.

c. Concerned about the welfare of the local producers, the Home government imposes a tariff in the amount of \$2 (i.e., t = \$2). Determine the net effect of the tariff on the Home economy.

12. Refer to the graphs in Problem 11. Suppose that instead of a tariff, Home applies an import quota limiting the amount Foreign can sell to 2 units.

    a. Determine the net effect of the import quota on the Home economy if the quota licenses are allocated to local producers.
    b. Calculate the net effect of the import quota on Home welfare if the quota rents are earned by Foreign exporters.
    c. How do your answers to parts (a) and (b) compare with part (c) of Problem 11?

13. Consider a small country applying a tariff t as in Figure 8-5. Instead of a tariff on *all* units imported, however, we will suppose that the tariff applies only to imports *in excess* of some quota amount M' (which is less than the total imports). This is called a "tariff-rate quota" (TRQ) and is commonly used on agricultural goods.

    a. Redraw Figure 8-5, introducing the quota amount M'. Remember that the tariff applies only to imports *in excess* of this amount. With this in mind, what is the rectangle of tariff revenue collected? What is the rectangle of quota rents? Explain briefly what quota rents mean in this scenario.
    b. How does the use of a TRQ rather than a tariff at the same rate affect Home welfare? How does the TRQ, as compared with a tariff at the same rate, affect Foreign welfare? Does it depend on who gets the quota rents?
    c. Based on your answer to (b), why do you think TRQs are used quite often?

14. Consider the following hypothetical information pertaining to a country's imports, consumption, and production of T-shirts following the removal of the MFA quota:

	With MFA	Without MFA (Free Trade)
World price (\$/shirt)	2.00	2.00
Domestic price (\$/shirt)	2.50	2.00
Domestic consumption (million shirts/year)	100	125
Domestic production (million shirts/year)	75	50
Imports (million shirts/year)	25	75

    a. Graph the effects of the quota removal on domestic consumption and production.
    b. Determine the gain in consumer surplus from the removal of the quota.
    c. Determine the loss in producer surplus from the removal of the quota.
    d. Calculate the quota rents that were earned under the quota.
    e. Determine how much the country has gained from removal of the quota.

15. Suppose that a producer in China is constrained by the MFA to sell a certain number of shirts, regardless of the type of shirt. For a T-shirt selling for \$2.00 under free trade, the MFA quota leads to an increase in price to \$2.50. For a dress shirt selling for \$10.00, the MFA will also lead to an increase in price.

	With MFA	Without MFA (Free Trade)
Domestic price of T-shirt (\$/shirt)	2.50	2.00
Domestic price of dress shirt (\$/shirt)	?	10.00

    a. Suppose that the MFA leads to an increase in the price of dress shirts from \$10 to \$11. Will the producer be willing to export both T-shirts and dress shirts? (Remember that only a fixed number of shirts can be exported, but of any type.) Explain why or why not.
    b. For the producer to be willing to sell *both* T-shirts and dress shirts, what must be the price of dress shirts under the MFA?

c. Based on your answer to part (b), calculate the price of dress shirts *relative* to T-shirts before and after the MFA. What has happened to the relative price due to the MFA?

d. Based on your answer to part (c), what will happen to the relative demand in the United States for dress shirts versus T-shirts from this producer due to the MFA?

e. Thinking now of the total export bundle of this producer, does the MFA lead to quality upgrading or downgrading? How about the removal of the MFA?

NET WORK

Go to http://www.wto.org/, and find out how many countries belong to the WTO. Which countries joined most recently?

Go to http://www.usitc.gov/trade_remedy/about_global_safeguard_inv.htm, and read about Section 201 and Section 421 of U.S. Trade Act of 1974. What are the differences between these sections? What are some recent cases?

9

Import Tariffs and Quotas under Imperfect Competition

If there were an Economist's Creed, it would surely contain the affirmations "I understand the Principle of Comparative Advantage" and "I advocate Free Trade." . . . Yet the case for free trade is currently more at doubt than at any time since since the 1817 publication of Ricardo's Principles of Political Economy.

Paul Krugman, "Is Free Trade Passé?' *Journal of Economic Perspectives*, 1(2), Fall 1987, p. 131

The case for free trade, as brought up-to-date from 1817 to 1987, is therefore alive and well. This is not to say that we have not learned its strengths and weaknesses, its nuances and subtleties, with greater understanding in light of the new developments.

Jagdish Bhagwati, "Is Free Trade Passé After All?" *Weltwirtschaftliches Archiv/Review of World Economics*, 125(1), March 1989, p. 43

If the case of heavyweight motorcycles is to be considered the only successful escape-clause [tariff], it is because it caused little harm and it helped Harley-Davidson get a bank loan so it could diversify.

John Suomela, chief economist, U.S. International Trade Commission, 1993[1]

In a recent survey of economists, 87% agreed with the statement "tariffs and import quotas usually reduce general economic welfare."[2] It is no exaggeration to say that this belief has been a guiding principle of the international institutions established to govern the world economy since World War II, especially the World Trade Organization. That belief is the message from the previous chapter, which showed that the application of tariffs and quotas will reduce welfare for a small country. We also found that

[1] Cited in Douglas A. Irwin, 2002, *Free Trade under Fire* (Princeton, NJ: Princeton University Press), pp. 136–137.
[2] Robert Whaples and Jac C. Heckelman, 2005, "Public Choice Economics: Where Is There Consensus?" *American Economist*, 49(1), pp. 66-78.

although a large country might gain from the application of a tariff, that gain would come at the expense of its trading partners, so the *world* as a whole would still lose. So there is really no good economic argument for the use of tariffs or quotas.

Still, you might wonder if that is really the whole story. We gave several recent examples of tariffs and quotas in the previous chapter, and there are many more examples if we look to countries at earlier stages in their development. For example, during the 1800s the United States had average tariff rates that fluctuated between 10 and 50%. These tariff rates were at times even higher than the Smoot–Hawley tariff that was applied during the Great Depression and peaked at 25%. Likewise, countries that industrialized after World War II, like Japan, South Korea, and Taiwan, started with high tariffs and quotas that were eliminated only slowly and incompletely. More recently, China had very high tariffs before it joined the World Trade Organization in 2001, and it still enjoys tariffs in some industries that are well above those in the United States or Europe.

These observations can lead us to wonder if there are some arguments in favor of tariffs that are missing from our treatment in the previous chapter, which dealt with perfect competition. Do the effects of trade policies differ when markets are imperfectly competitive? We explore the answer to this question in this chapter and the next.

This question received a good deal of attention from trade economists in the 1980s, in a body of research that became known as **strategic trade policy.** The idea of strategic trade policy was that government trade policies could give a strategic advantage to Home firms in imperfectly competitive markets that would enable them to compete more effectively with Foreign firms. Initially, the economists writing in this area thought that their research would challenge the idea that free trade is best for a country, an idea expressed in Paul Krugman's quote at the beginning of the chapter. As more research was done, however, supporters of strategic trade policy theory realized that the new arguments were limited in their scope: in some cases, the use of tariffs or quotas would backfire and harm the Home country, and in other cases, their use would give results similar to the large country case we analyzed in the previous chapter. We will give examples of both outcomes. Taken together, these example of strategic trade policy lead to the conclusion expressed in the opening quotation from Jagdish Bhagwati, that the case for free trade is "alive and well," but that we have "learned its strengths and weaknesses, its nuances and subtleties."

To explore strategic trade policy, we need to abandon the assumption that markets are perfectly competitive, an assumption that was central to the treatment of the tariff and quota in the previous chapter. Instead, we need to allow for imperfect competition which we defined in Chapter 6 as the market conditions that exist when firms have influence over the price that they charge, and can charge a price above marginal costs for their goods. Recall that imperfect competition can arise when there is a small number of producers, as in a monopoly or oligopoly, or if products are differentiated from one another, as we assumed in our model of monopolistic competition in Chapter 6. In this chapter, we use the extreme case of a single producer—a Home or Foreign monopoly—to see how tariffs and quotas affect prices, trade, and welfare. In practice, imperfectly competitive industries often have more than one firm, but focusing on the monopoly case will give us the clearest sense of how the effects of these policy tools differ from those under perfect competition.

In this chapter, we begin by analyzing the effects of tariffs and quotas under the assumption of a Home monopoly. In the perfectly competitive framework of the previous chapter, quotas and tariffs have an equivalent impact on Home prices. In imperfectly competitive markets, however, these two trade policy instruments have *different* effects on Home prices, so the choice of which, if any, trade policy to implement must take these different effects into account.

The second case we analyze is a Foreign monopoly that exports to the Home market. We analyze the effect of an import tariff applied by the Home country and find that the tariff has effects similar to those in the large-country case under perfect competition (described in the previous chapter) in which the Home country can potentially gain from the tariff. A specific example of a Foreign monopolist is the Foreign **discriminating monopoly,** which charges a lower price to Home than to firms in its own local market and is therefore **dumping** its product into the Home market. A tariff applied against the Foreign discriminating monopoly is called an **antidumping duty.** Because of the special way in which antidumping duties are applied, they are unlikely to result in gains for the Home country and instead result in losses.

The final case we analyze is an **infant industry** at Home, by which we mean an industry that is too young to have achieved its lowest costs. Often these industries comprise a small number of firms. In our analysis, we assume there is only one firm, so it is again a case of Home monopoly. The special feature of this Home firm is that it cannot compete effectively under free trade, because the world price is below its minimum cost of production today, so the firm makes a loss. But by increasing its output today, the firm will learn how to produce its output more efficiently, and therefore have lower costs in the future, so that it can compete profitably at the world price. One way to achieve this end is for the government to step in and offer assistance, such as with a tariff, that will help the firm to survive long enough to achieve lower, world-competitive costs. This policy is called an "infant industry tariff."

Although we include the infant industry tariff argument in this chapter on strategic trade policy, it is actually a much older argument, dating back to the writings of John Stuart Mill (1806–1873). We will give several examples of infant industries, including the automobile industry in China, which imposed very high tariffs and quotas on foreign cars before it joined the WTO in 2001. We also use this argument to analyze the tariff used in the 1980s to protect Harley-Davidson motorcycles in the United States. The key policy question for an infant industry is whether a government should impose a temporary tariff today, to protect infant industry from competition, thereby keeping it in business long enough for it to learn how to achieve lower costs (and thus competitive prices) in the future.

1 Tariffs and Quotas with Home Monopoly

To illustrate the effect of tariffs and quotas under imperfect competition, we will start with the example of a Home monopolist—a single firm selling a homogeneous good. In this case, free trade introduces many more firms selling the same good into the Home market, which eliminates the monopolist's ability to charge a price higher than its marginal cost (the free-trade equilibrium results in a perfectly competitive Home market). As we will show, tariffs and quotas affect this trade equilibrium differently because of their impact on the Home monopoly's **market power,** the extent to which a firm can choose its price. With a tariff, the Home monopolist still competes against a large number of importers and so its market power is limited.

With an import quota, on the other hand, once the quota limit is reached, the monopolist is the only producer able to sell in the Home market; hence, the Home monopolist can exercise its market power once again. This section describes the Home equilibrium with and without trade and explains this difference between tariffs and quotas.

No-Trade Equilibrium

We begin by showing in Figure 9-1 the no-trade equilibrium with a Home monopoly. The Home demand curve is shown by *D*, and because it is downward-sloping, as the monopolist sells more, the price will fall. This fall in price means that the extra revenue earned by the monopolist from selling one more unit is less than the price: the extra revenue earned equals the price charged for that unit *minus* the fall in price times the quantity sold of all earlier units. The extra revenue earned from selling one more unit, the **marginal revenue,** is shown by curve *MR* in Figure 9-1.

To maximize its profits, the monopolist produces at the point where the marginal revenue *MR* earned from selling one more unit equals the marginal cost *MC* of producing one more unit. As shown in Figure 9-1, the monopolist produces quantity Q^M. Tracing up from Q^M to point A on the demand curve and then over to the price axis, the price charged by the monopolist is P^M. This price enables the monopolist to earn the highest profits and is the monopoly equilibrium in the absence of international trade.

Comparison with Perfect Competition We can contrast the monopoly equilibrium with the perfect competition equilibrium in the absence of trade. Instead of a single firm, suppose there are many firms in the industry. We assume that all these firms combined have the same cost conditions as the monopolist, so the industry marginal cost is identical to the monopolist's marginal cost curve of *MC*. Because a perfectly competitive industry will produce where price equals marginal cost, the *MC* curve is also the industry supply curve. The no-trade equilibrium under perfect competition

FIGURE 9-1

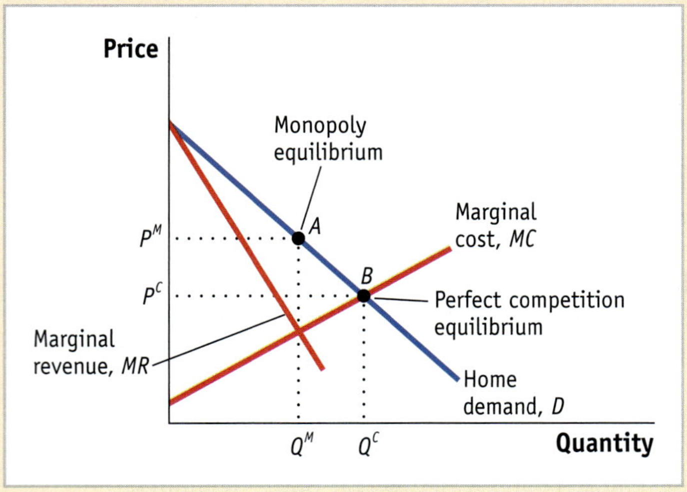

No-Trade Equilibrium In the absence of international trade, the monopoly equilibrium at Home occurs at the quantity Q^M, where marginal revenue equals marginal cost. From that quantity, we trace up to the demand curve at point *A*, and the price charged is P^M. Under perfect competition, the industry supply curve is *MC*, so the no-trade equilibrium would occur where demand equals supply (point *B*), at the quantity Q^C and the price P^C.

occurs where supply equals demand (the quantity Q^C and the price P^C). The competitive price P^C is less than the monopoly price P^M, and the competitive quantity Q^C *is* higher than the monopoly quantity Q^M. This comparison shows that in the absence of trade, the monopolist restricts its quantity sold to increase the market price. Under free trade, however, the monopolist cannot limit quantity and raise price, as we investigate next.

Free-Trade Equilibrium

Suppose now that Home engages in international trade. We will treat Home as a "small country," which means that it faces the fixed world price of P^W. In Figure 9-2, we draw a horizontal line at that price and label it as X^*, the Foreign export supply curve. At that price, Foreign will supply any quantity of imports (because Home is a small country, the Foreign export supply is perfectly elastic). Likewise, the Home monopolist can sell as much as it desires at the price of P^W (because it is able to export at the world price) but cannot charge any more than that price at Home. If it charged a higher price, Home consumers would import the product instead. Therefore, the Foreign supply curve of X^* is *also* the new demand curve facing the Home monopolist: the original no-trade Home demand of D no longer applies.

Because this new demand curve facing the Home monopolist is horizontal, the Home firm's new marginal revenue curve is the same as the demand curve, so $X^* = MR^*$. To understand why this is so, remember that marginal revenue equals the price earned from selling one more unit *minus* the fall in price times the quantity sold of all earlier units. For a horizontal demand curve, there is no fall in price from selling more because additional units sell for P^W, the same price for which the earlier units sell. Thus, marginal revenue is the price earned from selling another unit, P^W. Therefore, the demand curve X^* facing the Home monopolist is identical to the marginal revenue curve; the no-trade marginal revenue of MR no longer applies.

FIGURE 9-2

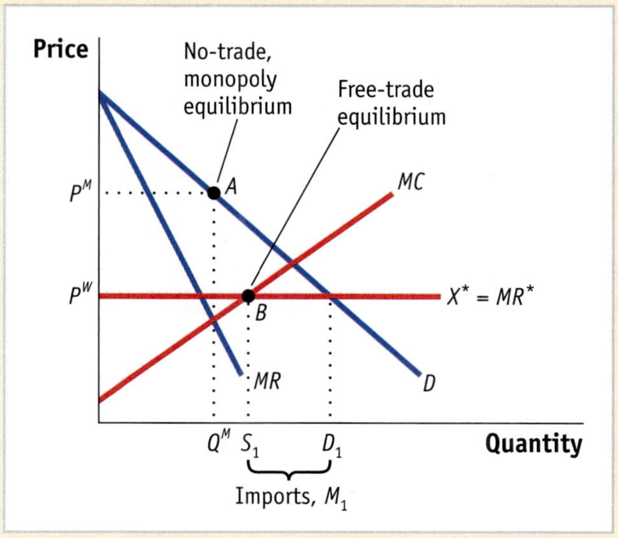

Home Monopoly's Free-Trade Equilibrium Under free trade at the fixed world price P^W, Home faces Foreign export supply of X^* at that price. Because the Home firm cannot raise its price above P^W without losing all its customers to imports, X^* is now also the demand curve faced by the Home monopolist. Because the price is fixed, the marginal revenue MR^* is the same as the demand curve. Profits are maximized at point B, where marginal revenue equals marginal costs. The Home firm supplies S_1, and Home consumers demand D_1. The difference between these is imports, $M_1 = D_1 - S_1$. Because the Home monopoly now sets its price at marginal cost, the same free-trade equilibrium holds under perfect competition.

To maximize profits under the new free-trade market conditions, the monopolist will set marginal revenue equal to marginal cost (point B in Figure 9-2) and will supply S_1 at the price P^W. At the price P^W, Home consumers demand D_1, which is more than the Home supply of S_1. The difference between demand and supply is Home imports under free trade, or $M_1 = D_1 - S_1$.

Comparison with Perfect Competition Let us once again compare this monopoly equilibrium to the perfect competition equilibrium, now with free trade. As before, we assume that the cost conditions facing the competitive firms are the same as those facing the monopolist, so the industry supply curve under perfect competition is equal to the monopolist's marginal cost curve of MC. With free trade and perfect competition, the industry will supply the quantity S_1, where the price P^W equals marginal cost, and consumers will demand the quantity D_1 at the price P^W. Under free trade for a small country, then, a Home monopolist produces the same quantity and charges the same price as a perfectly competitive industry. The reason for this result is that free trade for a small country eliminates the monopolist's control over price; that is, its market power. It faces a horizontal demand curve, equal to marginal revenue, at the world price of P^W. Because the monopolist has no control over the market price, it behaves just as a competitive industry (with the same marginal costs) would behave.

This finding that free trade eliminates the Home monopolist's control over price is an extra source of gains from trade for the Home consumers because of the reduction in the monopolist's market power. We have already seen this extra gain in Chapter 6, in which we first discussed monopolistic competition. There we showed that with free trade, a monopolistically competitive firm faces more-elastic demand curves for its differentiated product, leading it to expand output and lower its prices. The same result holds in Figure 9-2, except that now we have assumed that the good produced by the Home monopolist and the imported good are homogeneous products, so they sell at exactly the same price. Because the Home good and the import are homogeneous, the demand curve X^* facing the Home monopolist in Figure 9-2 is perfectly elastic, leading the monopolist to behave in the same way under free trade as in a competitive industry.

Effect of a Home Tariff

Now suppose the Home country imposes a tariff of t dollars on imports, which increases the Home price from P^W to $P^W + t$. In Figure 9-3, the effect of the tariff is to raise the Foreign export supply curve from X^* to $X^* + t$. The Home firm can sell as much as it desires at the price of $P^W + t$ but cannot charge any more than that price. If it did, the Home consumers would import the product. Thus, the Foreign supply curve of $X^* + t$ is also the new demand curve facing the Home monopolist.

Because this new demand curve is horizontal, the new marginal revenue curve is once again the same as the demand curve, so $MR^* = X^* + t$. The reasoning for this result is similar to the reasoning under free trade: with a horizontal demand curve, there is no fall in price from selling more, so the Home firm can sell as much as it desires at the price of $P^W + t$. So the demand curve $X^* + t$ facing the Home monopolist is identical to its marginal revenue curve.

To maximize profits, the monopolist will once again set marginal revenue equal to marginal costs, which occurs at point C in Figure 9-3, with the price $P^W + t$ and

FIGURE 9-3

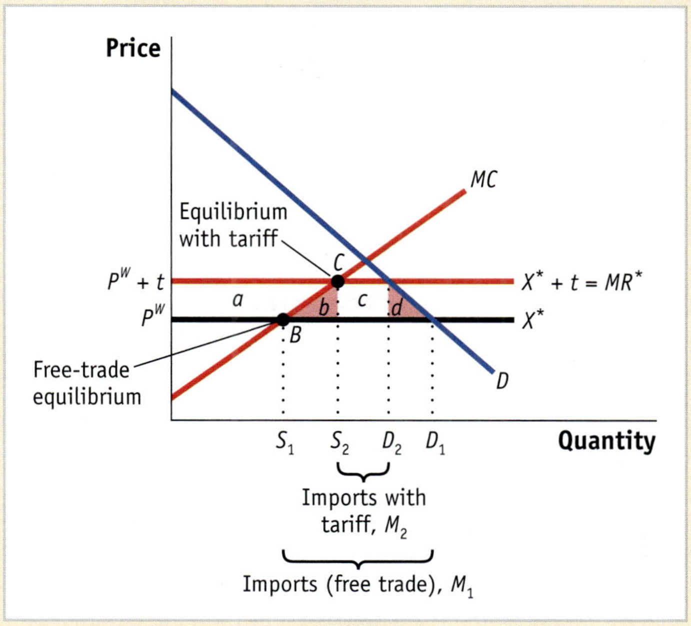

Tariff with Home Monopoly Initially, under free trade at the fixed world price P^W, the monopolist faces the horizontal demand curve (and marginal revenue curve) X^*, and profits are maximized at point B. When a tariff t is imposed, the export supply curve shifts up since Foreign firms must charge $P^W + t$ in the Home market to earn P^W. This allows the Home monopolist to increase its domestic price to $P^W + t$, but no higher, since otherwise it would lose all its customers to imports. The result is fewer imports, M_2, because Home supply S increases and Home demand D decreases. The deadweight loss of the tariff is measured by the area $(b + d)$. This result is the same as would have been obtained under perfect competition because the Home monopolist is still charging a price equal to its marginal cost.

supply of S_2. At the price $P^W + t$, Home consumers demand D_2, which is more than Home supply of S_2. The difference between demand and supply is Home imports, $M_2 = D_2 - S_2$. The effect of the tariff on the Home monopolist relative to the free-trade equilibrium is to raise its production from S_1 to S_2 and its price from P^W to $P^W + t$. The supply increase in combination with a decrease in Home demand reduces imports from M_1 to M_2.

Comparison with Perfect Competition Let us compare this monopoly equilibrium with the tariff to what would happen under perfect competition. The tariff-inclusive price facing a perfectly competitive industry is $P^W + t$, the same price faced by the monopolist. Assuming that the industry supply curve under perfect competition is the same as the monopolist's marginal cost MC, the competitive equilibrium is where price equals marginal cost, which is once again at the quantity S_2 and the price $P^W + t$. So with a tariff, a Home monopolist produces the same quantity and charges the same price as would a perfectly competitive industry. This result is similar to the result we found under free trade. This similarity occurs because the tariff still limits the monopolist's ability to raise its price: it can raise the price to $P^W + t$ but no higher because otherwise consumers will import the product. Because the monopolist has limited control over its price, it behaves in the same way a competitive industry would when facing the tariff.

Home Loss Due to the Tariff Because the tariff and free-trade equilibria are the same for a Home monopoly and a perfectly competitive industry, the deadweight loss from the tariff is also the same. As was discussed in the previous chapter, the deadweight loss under perfect competition is found by taking the total fall in consumer surplus due to the rise in price from P^W to $P^W + t$, adding the gain in producer surplus from the rise in price, and then adding the increase in government revenue due to the tariff. Summing all these components shows a net welfare loss of $(b + d)$:

Fall in consumer surplus:	$-(a + b + c + d)$
Rise in producer surplus:	$+ a$
Rise in government revenue:	$+ c$
Net effect on Home welfare:	$-(b + d)$

Under Home monopoly, the deadweight loss from the tariff is the same. Home consumers still have the loss of $(a + b + c + d)$ because of the rise in price, while the Home monopolist gains the amount a in profits because of the rise in price. With the government collecting area c in tariff revenue, the deadweight loss is still area $(b + d)$.

Effect of a Home Quota

Let us now contrast the tariff with an import quota imposed by the Home government. As we now show, the quota results in a higher price for Home consumers, and therefore a larger Home loss, than would a tariff imposed on the same equilibrium quantity of imports. The reason for the higher costs is that the quota creates a "sheltered" market for the Home firm, allowing it to exercise its monopoly power, which leads to higher prices than under a tariff. Economists and policy makers are well aware of this additional drawback to quotas, which is why the WTO has encouraged countries to replace many quotas with tariffs.

To show the difference between the quota and tariff with a Home monopoly, we use Figure 9-4, in which the free-trade equilibrium is at point B and the tariff equilibrium is at point C (the same points that appear in Figure 9-3). Now suppose that instead of the tariff, a quota is applied. We choose the quota so that it equals the imports under the tariff, which are M_2. Since imports are fixed at that level, the effective demand curve facing the Home monopolist is the demand curve D *minus* the amount M_2. We label this effective demand curve $D - M_2$. Unlike the situation under the tariff, the monopolist now retains the ability to influence its price: it can choose the optimal price and quantity along $D - M_2$. We graph the marginal revenue curve MR for the effective demand curve $D - M_2$. The profit-maximizing position for the monopolist is where marginal revenue equals marginal cost, at point E, with price P_3 and supply S_3.

Let us now compare the tariff equilibrium, at point C, with the quota equilibrium, at point E. It will definitely be the case that the price charged under the quota is higher, $P_3 > P^W + t$. The higher price under the quota reflects the ability of the monopolist to raise its price once the quota amount has been imported. The higher price occurs even though the quota equilibrium *has the same level of imports as the tariff*, M_2. Therefore, the effects of a tariff and a quota are no longer equivalent as they were under perfect competition: the quota enables a monopolist to exercise its market power and raise its price.

What about the quantity produced by the monopolist? Because the price is higher under the quota, the monopolist will definitely produce a lower quantity under the quota, $S_3 < S_2$. What is more surprising, however, is that it is even possible that the quota could lead to a fall in output as compared with free trade: in Figure 9-4, we have shown $S_3 < S_1$. This is not a necessary result, however, and instead we could have drawn the MR curve so that $S_3 > S_1$. It is surprising that the

FIGURE 9-4

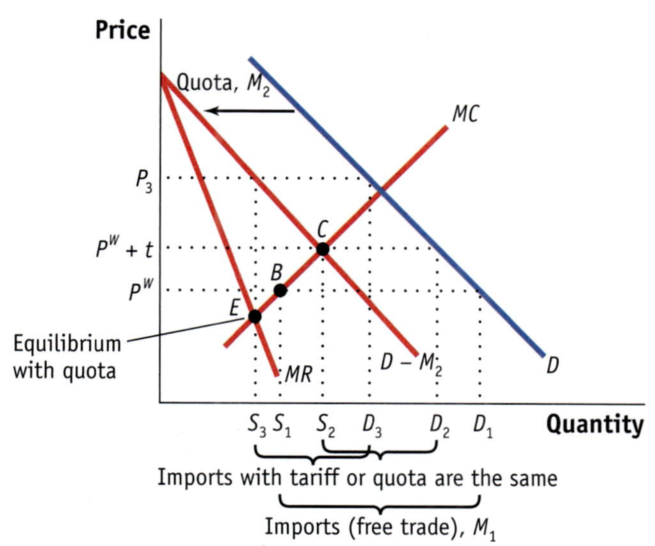

Effect of Quota with Home Monopoly Under free trade, the Home monopolist produces at point *B* and charges the world price of P^W. With a tariff of *t*, the monopolist produces at point *C* and charges the price of $P^W + t$. Imports under the tariff are $M_2 = D_2 - S_2$. Under a quota of M_2, the demand curve shifts to the left by that amount, resulting in the demand $D - M_2$ faced by the Home monopolist. That is, after M_2 units are imported, the monopolist is the only firm able to sell at Home, and so it can choose a price anywhere along the demand curve $D - M_2$. The marginal revenue curve corresponding to $D - M_2$ is *MR*, and so with a quota, the Home monopolist produces at point *E*, where *MR* equals *MC*. The price charged at point *E* is $P_3 > P^W + t$, so the quota leads to a higher Home price than the tariff.

case $S_3 < S_1$ is even possible because it suggests that workers in the industry would *fail to be protected* by the quota; that is, employment could fall because of the reduction in output under the quota. We see, then, that the quota can have undesirable effects as compared with a tariff when the Home industry is a monopoly.

Home Loss Due to the Quota Our finding that Home prices are higher with a quota than with a tariff means that Home consumers suffer a greater fall in surplus because of the quota. On the other hand, the Home monopolist earns higher profits from the quota because its price is higher. We will not make a detailed calculation of the deadweight loss from the quota with Home monopoly because it is complicated. We can say, however, that the deadweight loss will always be *higher* for a quota than for a tariff because the Home monopolist will always charge a higher price. That higher price benefits the monopolist but harms Home consumers and creates an extra deadweight loss because of the exercise of monopoly power.

Furthermore, the fact that the Home monopolist is charging a higher price also increases the quota rents, which we defined in the previous chapter as the ability to import goods at the world price and sell them at the higher Home price (in our example, this is the difference between P_3 and P^W times the amount of imports M_2). In the case of Home monopoly, the quota rents are greater than government revenue would be under a tariff. Recall that quota rents are often given to Foreign countries in the case of "voluntary" export restraints (VERs), when the government of the exporting country implements the quota, or else quota rents can even be wasted completely when rent-seeking activities occur. In either of these cases, the increase in quota rents adds to Home's losses if the rents are given away or wasted.

In the next application, we examine a quota used in the United States during the 1980s to restrict imports of Japanese cars. Because the car industry has a small number of producers, it is imperfectly competitive. So our predictions from the case of monopoly discussed previously can serve as a guide for what we expect in the case of Home oligopoly.

APPLICATION

U.S. Imports of Japanese Automobiles

A well-known case of a "voluntary" export restraint (VER) for the United States occurred during the 1980s, when the U.S. limited the imports of cars from Japan. To understand why this VER was put into place, recall that during the early 1980s, the United States suffered a deep recession. That recession led to less spending on durable goods (such as automobiles), and as a result, unemployment in the auto industry rose sharply.

In 1980 the United Automobile Workers and Ford Motor Company applied to the International Trade Commission (ITC) for protection under Article XIX of GATT and Section 201 of U.S. trade laws. As described in the previous chapter, Section 201 protection can be given when increased imports are a "substantial cause of serious injury to the domestic industry," where "substantial cause" must be "not less than any other cause." In fact, the ITC determined that the U.S. recession was a more important cause of injury to the auto industry than increased imports. Accordingly, it did not recommend that the auto industry receive protection.

With this negative determination, several members of Congress from states with auto plants continued to pursue import limits by other means. In April 1981 Senators John Danforth from Missouri and Lloyd Bentsen from Texas introduced a bill in the U.S. Senate to restrict imports. Clearly aware of this pending legislation, the Japanese government announced on May 1 that it would "voluntarily" limit Japan's export of automobiles to the U.S. market. For the period April 1981 to March 1982, this limit was set at 1.83 million autos. After March 1984 the limit was raised to 2.02 million and then to 2.51 million vehicles annually. By 1988 imports fell *below* the VER limit because Japanese companies began assembling cars in the United States.

We are interested in whether American producers were able to exercise their monopoly power and raise their prices under the quota restriction. We are also interested in how much import prices increased. To measure the increase in import prices, we need to take into account a side effect of the 1980 quota: it led to an increase in the features of Japanese cars being sold in the United States such as size, weight, horsepower, and so on, or what we call an increase in quality.[3] The overall increase in auto import prices during the 1980s needs to be broken up into the increases due to (1) the quality upgrading of Japanese cars; (2) the "pure" increase in price because of the quota, which equals the quota rents; and (3) any price increase that would have occurred anyway, even if the auto industry had not been subject to protection.

Price and Quality of Imports The impact of the VER on the price of Japanese cars is shown in Figure 9-5. Under the VER on Japanese car imports, the average price rose from $5,150 to $8,050 between 1980 and 1985. Of that $2,900 increase, $1,100 was the result of quota rents earned by Japanese producers in 1984 and

[3] The previous chapter discusses the quality effect of a U.S. import quota on Chinese textile and apparel exports to the United States.

FIGURE 9-5

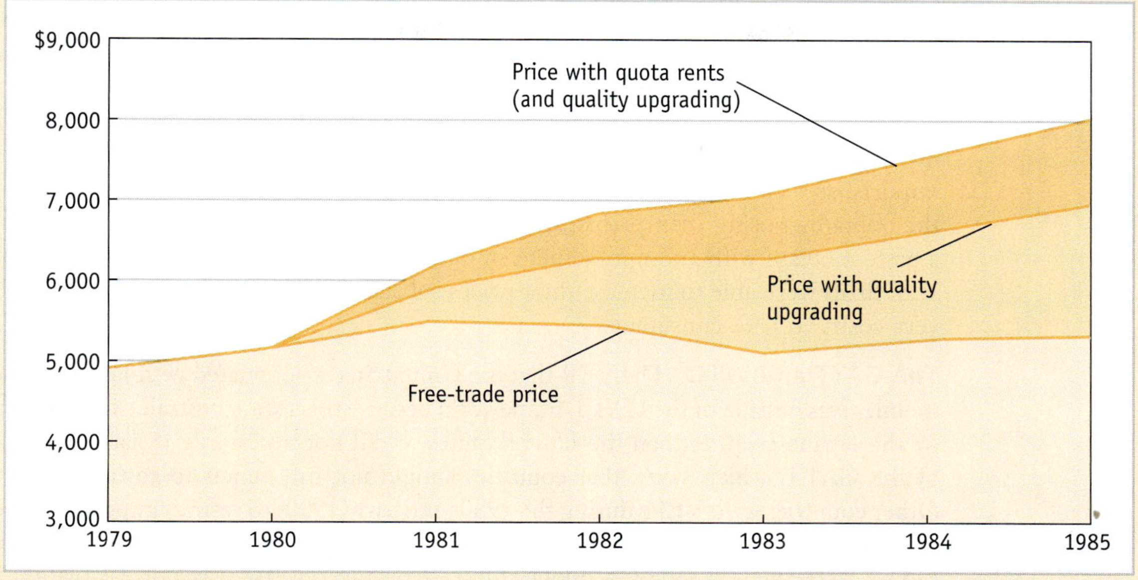

Prices of Japanese Car Imports Under the "voluntary" export restraint (VER) on Japanese car imports, the average price rose from $5,150 to $8,050 between 1980 and 1985. Of that $2,900 increase, $1,100 was the result of quota rent increases earned by Japanese producers. Another $1,650 was the result of quality improvements in the Japanese cars, which became heavier and wider, with improved horsepower, transmissions, and so on. The remaining $150 is the amount that import prices would have risen under free trade.

1985. Another $1,650 was from quality improvements in the Japanese cars, which became heavier and wider, with improved horsepower, transmissions, and so on. The remaining $150 is the amount that import prices would have risen under free trade.

Quota Rents If we multiply the quota rents of $1,100 per car by the imports of about 2 million cars, we obtain total estimated rents of $2.2 billion, which is the lower estimate of the annual cost of quota rents for automobiles. The upper estimate of $7.9 billion comes from also including the increase in price for European cars sold in the United States. Although European cars were not restricted by a quota, they did experience a significant increase in price during the quota period; that increase was due to the reduced competition from Japanese producers.

The Japanese firms benefited from the quota rents that they received. In fact, their stock prices *rose* during the VER period, though only after it became clear that the Japanese Ministry of International Trade and Industry (MITI) would administer the quotas to each producer (so that the Japanese firms would capture the rents). Moreover, because each producer was given a certain number of cars it could export to the United States, but no limit on the value of the cars, producers had a strong incentive to export more expensive models. That explains the quality upgrading that occurred during the quota, which was when Japanese producers started exporting more luxurious cars to the United States.

Price of U.S. Cars What happened to the prices of American small cars during this period? Under the VER on Japanese car imports, the average price of U.S. cars rose very rapidly when the quota was first imposed: from $4,200 in 1979 to $6,000 in 1981, a 43% increase over two years. That price increase was due to the exercise of market power by the U.S. producers, who were sheltered by the quota on their Japanese competitors. Only a small part of that price increase was explained by quality improvements since the quality of U.S. cars did not rise by as much as the quality of Japanese imports, as seen in Figure 9-6. So the American producers were able to benefit from the quota by raising their prices, and the Japanese firms also benefited by combining a price increase with an improvement in quality. The fact that both the Japanese and U.S. firms were able to increase their prices substantially indicates that the policy was very costly to U.S. consumers.

The GATT and WTO The VER that the United States negotiated with Japan in automobiles was outside of the GATT framework: because this export restraint was enforced by the Japanese rather than the United States, it did not necessarily violate Article XI of the GATT, which states that countries should not use quotas to restrict imports. Other countries used VERs during the 1980s and early 1990s to restrict imports in products such as automobiles and steel. All these cases were exploiting a loophole in the GATT agreement whereby a quota enforced by the *exporter* was not a violation of the GATT. This loophole was closed when the WTO was established in 1995. Part of the WTO agreement states that "a Member shall not seek, take or maintain any voluntary export restraints, orderly marketing arrangements or any other similar

FIGURE 9-6

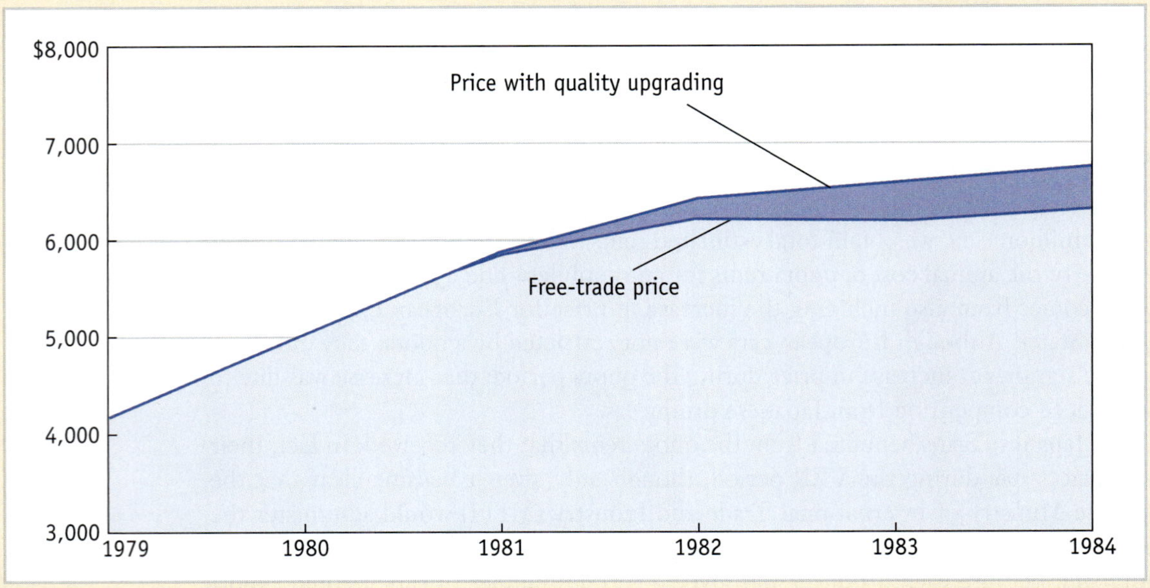

Prices of American Small Cars Under the VER on Japanese car imports, the average price of U.S. cars rose very rapidly when the quota was first imposed: from $4,200 in 1979 to $6,000 in 1981, or a 43% increase over two years. Only a very small part of that increase was explained by quality improvements, and in the later years of the quota, U.S. quality did not rise by as much as it did in the Japanese imports.

measures on the export or the import side. These include actions taken by a single Member as well as actions under agreements, arrangements and understandings entered into by two or more Members."[4] As a result of this rule, VERs can no longer be used unless they are a part of some other agreement in the WTO.[5] ■

2 Tariffs with Foreign Monopoly

So far in this chapter, we have studied the effects of a tariff or quota under Home monopoly. For simplicity, we have focused on the case in which the Home country is small, meaning that the world price is fixed. Let us now examine a different case, in which we treat the Foreign exporting firm as a monopoly. We will show that applying a tariff under a Foreign monopoly leads to an outcome similar to that of the large-country case in the previous chapter; that is, the tariff will lower the price charged by the Foreign exporter. In contrast to the small-country case, a tariff may now benefit the Home country.

Foreign Monopoly

To focus our attention on the Foreign monopolist selling to the Home market, we will assume that there is no competing Home firm, so the Home demand D in Figure 9-7 is supplied entirely by exports from the Foreign monopolist. This assumption is not very realistic because normally a tariff is being considered when there is also a Home firm. But ignoring the Home firm will simplify our analysis while still helping us to understand the effect of an imperfectly competitive Foreign exporter.

Free-Trade Equilibrium In addition to the Home demand of D in Figure 9-7, we also show Home marginal revenue of MR. Under free trade, the Foreign monopolist maximizes profits in its export market where Home marginal revenue MR equals Foreign marginal cost MC^*, at point A in Figure 9-7. It exports the amount X_1 to the Home market and charges the price of P_1.

Effect of a Tariff on Home Price If the Home country applies an import tariff of t dollars, then the marginal cost for the exporter to sell in the Home market increases to $MC^* + t$. With the increase in marginal costs, the new intersection with marginal revenue occurs at point B in Figure 9-7, and the import price rises to P_2.

Under the case we have drawn in Figure 9-7, where the MR curve is steeper than the demand curve, the increase in price from P_1 to P_2 is *less than* the amount of the tariff t. In other words, the vertical rise along the MR curve caused by the tariff (the vertical distance from point A to B, which is the tariff amount) corresponds to a smaller vertical rise moving along the demand curve (the difference between P_1 and P_2). In this case, the net-of-tariff price received by the Foreign exporter, which is $P_3 = P_2 - t$, has *fallen* from its previous level of P_1 because the price rises by less than the tariff. Since the Home country is paying a lower net-of-tariff price P_3 for its import, it has experienced a terms-of-trade gain as a result of the tariff.

---

[4] From Article 11, "Prohibition and Elimination of Certain Measures," of the WTO Agreement on Safeguards.

[5] An example is the quota in textiles that the United States negotiated with China in 2005, which was allowed under the provisions of China's entry into the WTO, as discussed in the previous chapter.

FIGURE 9-7

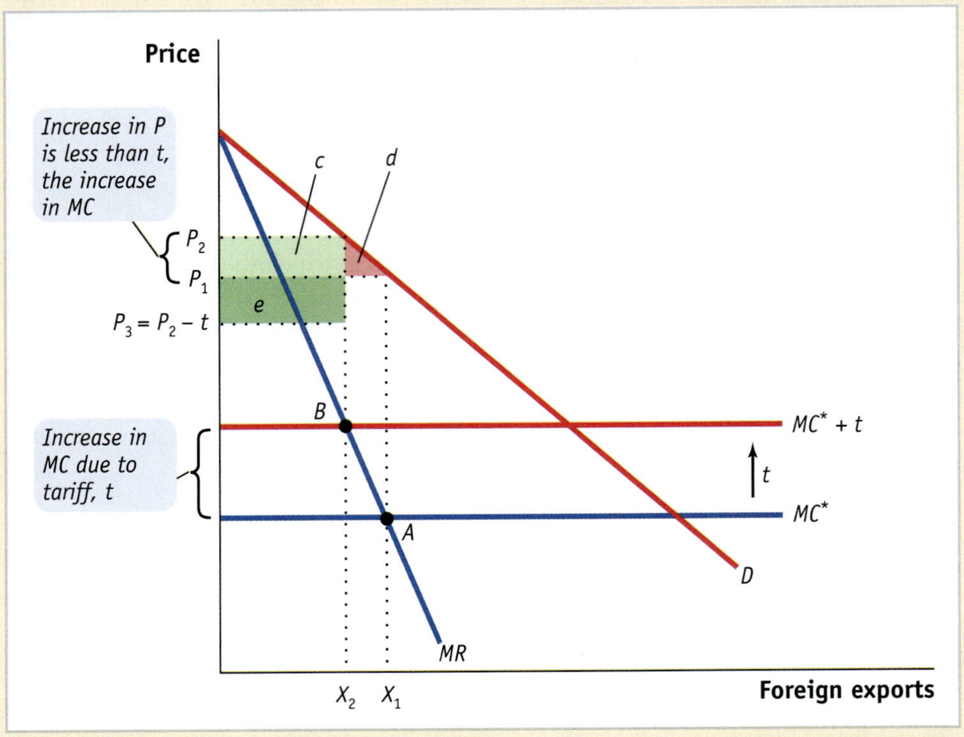

Tariff with a Foreign Monopoly Under free trade, the Foreign monopolist charges prices P_1 and exports X_1, where marginal revenue *MR* equals marginal cost MC^*. When an antidumping duty of *t* is applied, the firm's marginal cost rises to $MC^* + t$, so the exports fall to X_2 and the Home price rises to P_2. The decrease in consumer surplus is shown by the area $c + d$, of which *c* is collected as a portion of tax revenues. The net-of-tariff price that the Foreign exporter receives falls to $P_3 = P_2 - t$. Because the net-of-tariff price has fallen, the Home country has a terms-of-trade gain, area *e*. Thus, the total welfare change depends on the size of the terms-of-trade gain *e* relative to the deadweight loss *d*.

The effect of the tariff applied against a Foreign monopolist is similar to the effect of a tariff imposed by a large country (analyzed in the previous chapter). There we found that a tariff would lower the price charged by Foreign firms because the quantity of exports decreased, so Foreign marginal costs also fell. Now that we have assumed a Foreign monopoly, we get the same result but for a different reason. The marginal costs of the monopolist are constant at MC^* in Figure 9-7, or $MC^* + t$ including the tariff. The rise in marginal costs from the tariff leads to an increase in the tariff-inclusive Home price as the quantity of Home imports falls, but the monopolist chooses to increase the Home price by *less than* the full amount of the tariff. In that way, the quantity exported to Home does not fall by as much as it would if the Foreign firm increased its price by the full amount of the tariff. So, the Foreign firm is making a strategic decision to absorb part of the tariff itself (by lowering its price from P_1 to P_3) and pass through only a portion of the tariff to the Home price (which rises from P_1 to P_2).

Summary To preserve its sales to Home, the Foreign monopolist chooses to increase the Home price by less than the amount of the tariff. This result depends on having *MR* steeper than *D*, as shown in Figure 9-7. It is not necessarily the case that *MR* is steeper than D for all demand curves, but this is usually how we draw them. In the case of a straight-line demand curve such as the one drawn in Figure 9-7, for example, the marginal revenue curve is exactly twice as steep as the demand curve.[6] In this case, the Home import price rises by exactly half of the tariff amount, and the Foreign export price falls by exactly half of the tariff amount.

Effect of the Tariff on Home Welfare With the rise in the Home price from P_1 to P_2, consumers are worse off. The decline in consumer surplus equals the area between the two prices and to the left of the demand curve, which is $(c + d)$ in Figure 9-7. The increase in the Home price would in principle benefit Home firms, but we have assumed for simplicity that there is no Home producer, so we do not need to keep track of the change in Home producer surplus. We do need to take account of tariff revenue collected by the Home government, however. Tariff revenue equals the amount of the tariff t times Foreign exports X_2, which is area $(c + e)$. Therefore, the effect of the tariff on Home welfare is

Fall in Home consumer surplus:	$-(c+d)$
Rise in Home government revenue:	$+(c+e)$
Net change in Home welfare:	$+(e-d)$

We can interpret the area e as the terms-of-trade gain for the Home country, whereas the area d is the deadweight loss from the tariff. If the terms-of-trade gain exceeds the deadweight loss, $e > d$, then Home gains overall by applying a tariff, similar to the result we found for a large country in the previous chapter. As we discussed there, we can expect the terms-of-trade gain to exceed the deadweight loss when the tariff is small, so that Home welfare initially rises for small tariffs. Welfare then reaches some maximum level and then falls as the tariff is increased beyond its optimal level. The same results apply when a tariff is placed against a Foreign monopolist, provided that the marginal revenue curve is steeper than demand, as we have assumed.

To illustrate how a tariff can affect the prices charged by a Foreign monopolist in practice, we once again use the automobile industry as an example. Because there are a small number of firms in that industry, it is realistic to expect them to respond to a tariff in the way that a Foreign monopolist would.

APPLICATION

Import Tariffs on Japanese Trucks

We have found that in the case of a Foreign monopolist, Home will experience a terms-of-trade gain from a small tariff. The reason for this gain is that the Foreign firm will lower its net-of-tariff price to avoid too large an increase in the price paid by consumers in the importing country. To what extent do Foreign exporters actually behave that way?

To answer this question, we can look at the effects of the 25% tariff on imported Japanese compact trucks imposed by the United States in the early 1980s and still in place today. The history of how this tariff came to be applied is an interesting story. Recall from the application earlier in the chapter that in 1980 the United Automobile

[6] You are asked to show this result in Problem 6.

Workers and Ford Motor Company applied for a tariff under Article XIX of the GATT and Section 201 of U.S. trade law. They were turned down for the tariff, however, because the International Trade Commission determined that the U.S. recession was a more important cause of injury in the auto industry than growing imports. For cars, the voluntary export restriction (VER) with Japan was pursued. But for compact trucks imported from Japan, it turned out that another form of protection was available.

At that time, most compact trucks from Japan were imported as cab/chassis with some final assembly needed. These were classified as "parts of trucks," which carried a tariff rate of only 4%. But another category of truck—"complete or unfinished trucks"—faced a tariff rate of 25%. That unusually high tariff was a result of the "chicken war" between the United States and West Germany in 1962. At that time, Germany joined the European Economic Community (EEC) and was required to adjust its external tariffs to match those of the other EEC countries. This adjustment resulted in an increase in its tariff on imported U.S. poultry. In retaliation, the United States increased its tariffs on trucks and other products, so the 25% tariff on trucks became a permanent item in the U.S. tariff code.

That tariff created an irresistible opportunity to reclassify the Japanese imports and obtain a substantial increase in the tariff, which is exactly what the U.S. Customs Service did with prodding from the U.S. Congress. Effective August 21, 1980, imported cab/chassis "parts" were reclassified as "complete or unfinished" trucks. This reclassification raised the tariff rate on all Japanese trucks from 4 to 25%, which remains in effect today.

How did Japanese exporters respond to the tariff? According to one estimate, the tariff on trucks was only *partially* reflected in U.S. prices: of the 21% increase, only 12% (or about 60% of the increase) was passed through to U.S. consumer prices; the other 9% (or about 40% of the increase) was absorbed by Japanese producers.[7] Therefore, this tariff led to a terms-of-trade gain for the United States, as predicted by our theory: for a straight-line demand curve (as in Figure 9-7), marginal revenue is twice as steep, and the tariff will lead to an equal increase in the Home import price and decrease in the Foreign export price.[8] The evidence for Japanese trucks is not too different from what we predict in that straight-line case.

Notice that the terms-of-trade gain from the tariff applied on a Foreign monopolist is similar to the terms-of-trade gain from a tariff applied by a "large" country, as we discussed in the previous chapter. In both cases, the Foreign firm or industry absorbs part of the tariff by lowering its price, which means that the Home price rises by less than the full amount of the tariff. If the terms-of-trade gain, measured by the area e in Figure 9-7 exceed the deadweight loss d, then the Home country gains from the tariff. This is our first example of strategic trade policy that leads to a potential gain for Home.

In principle, this potential gain arises from the tariff that the United States has applied on imports of compact trucks, and that is still in place today. But some economists feel that this tariff has the undesirable side effect of encouraging the U.S. automobile industry to focus on the sales of trucks, since compact trucks have higher

---

[7] Robert Feenstra, 1989, "Symmetric Pass-Through of Tariffs and Exchange Rates under Imperfect Competition: An Empirical Test," *Journal of International Economics*, 27(1/2), 25–45.

[8] You are asked to derive this relationship numerically in Problem 7 at the end of the chapter.

prices due to the tariff.[9] That strategy by U.S. producers can work when gasoline price are low, so consumers are willing to buy trucks. At times of high prices, however, consumers instead want fuel-efficient cars, which have not been the focus of the American industry. So high fuel prices can lead to a surge in imports and fewer domestic sales, exactly what happened after the oil price increase of 1979 and again in 2008, just before the financial crisis. Some industry experts believe that these factors contributed to the losses faced by the American industry during the crisis, as explained in **HEADLINES: The Chickens Have Come Home to Roost.** ■

HEADLINES

The Chickens Have Come Home to Roost

This article discusses the history of the 25% tariff that still applies to U.S. imports of lightweight trucks. The author argues that this tariff caused some of the difficulties in the U.S. automobile industry today.

Although we call them the big three automobile companies, they have basically specialized in building trucks. This left them utterly unable to respond when high gas prices shifted the market towards hybrids and more fuel efficient cars.

One reason is that Americans like to drive SUVs, minivans and small trucks when gasoline costs $1.50 to $2.00 a gallon. But another is that the profit margins have been much higher on trucks and vans because the US protects its domestic market with a twenty-five percent tariff. By contrast, the import tariff on regular automobiles is just 2.5 percent and US duties from tariffs on all imported goods are just one percent of the overall value of merchandise imports. Since many of the inputs used to assemble trucks are not subject to tariffs anywhere near 25 percent—US tariffs on all goods average only 3.5 percent—the effective protection and subsidy equivalent of this policy has been huge.

It is no wonder much of the initial foray by Japanese transplants to the US involved setting up trucks assembly plants, no wonder that Automakers only put three doors on SUVs so they can qualify as vans and no wonder that Detroit is so opposed to the US-Korea Free Trade Agreement that would eventually allow trucks built in Korea Duty-Free access to the US market.

What accounts for this distinctive treatment of trucks? An accident of history that shows how hard it is for the government to withdraw favors even when they have no sound policy justification.

It all comes down to the long forgotten chicken wars of the 1960s. In 1962, when implementing the European Common Market, the Community denied access to US chicken producers. In response after being unable to resolve the issue diplomatically, the US responded with retaliatory tariffs that included a twenty five percent tariffs on trucks that was aimed at the German Volkswagen Combi-Bus that was enjoying brisk sales in the US.

Since the trade (GATT) rules required that retaliation be applied on a non-discriminatory basis, the tariffs were levied on all truck-type vehicles imported from all countries and have never been removed. Over time, the Germans stopped building these vehicles and today the tariffs are mainly paid on trucks coming from Asia. The tariffs have bred bad habits, steering Detroit away from building high-quality automobiles towards trucks and truck-like cars that have suddenly fallen into disfavor.

If Congress wants an explanation for why the big three have been so uncompetitive it should look first at the disguised largess it has been providing them with for years. It has taken a long time—nearly 47 years—but it seems that eventually the chickens have finally come home to roost.

Source: Robert Lawrence, guest blogger on Dani Rodrik's weblog, posted May 4, 2009. http://www.rodrik.typepad.com/dani_rodriks_weblog/2009/05/the-chickens-have-come-home-to-roost.html.

[9] Larger trucks and SUVs imported into the United States do not have this tariff, but there is another reason why U.S. firms sell many of these products: fuel-economy regulations, which apply to cars but not to trucks or SUVs. These regulations require that the fleet of cars and light trucks sold by each U.S. firms meet a certain average fuel economy, which is expensive for the firms to achieve. Since larger trucks and SUVs do not have to meet the same standard, they are cheaper to produce.

3 Dumping

With imperfect competition, firms can charge *different* prices across countries and will do so whenever that pricing strategy is profitable. Recall that we define imperfect competition as the firm's ability to influence the price of its product. With international trade, we extend this idea: not only can firms charge a price that is higher than their marginal cost, they can also choose to charge different prices in their domestic market than in their export market. This pricing strategy is called **price discrimination** because the firm is able to choose how much different groups of customers pay. To discriminate in international trade, there must be some reason that consumers in the high-price market cannot import directly from the low-cost market; for example, that reason could be transportation costs or tariffs between the markets.

Dumping occurs when a foreign firm sells a product abroad at a price that is either less than the price it charges in its local market, or less than its average cost to produce the product. Dumping is common in international trade, even though the rules of the World Trade Organization (WTO) discourage this activity. Under the rules of the WTO, an importing country is entitled to apply a tariff any time a foreign firm dumps its product on a local market. Such a tariff is called an antidumping duty. We study antidumping duties in detail in the next section. In this section, we want to ask the more general question: Why do firms dump at all? It might appear at first glance that selling abroad at prices less than local prices or less than the average costs of production must be unprofitable. Is that really the case? It turns out the answer is no. It can be profitable to sell at low prices abroad, even at prices lower than average cost.

Discriminating Monopoly To illustrate how dumping can be profitable, we use the example of a Foreign monopolist selling both to its local market and exporting to Home. As described previously, we assume that the monopolist is able to charge different prices in the two markets; this market structure is sometimes called a **discriminating monopoly.** The diagram for a Foreign discriminating monopoly is shown in Figure 9-8. The local demand curve for the monopolist is D^*, with marginal revenue MR^*. We draw these curves as downward-sloping for the monopolist because to induce additional consumers to buy its product, the monopolist lowers its price (downward-sloping D^*), which decreases the revenue received from each additional unit sold (downward-sloping MR^*).

In the export market, however, the Foreign firm will face competition from other firms selling to the Home market. Because of this competition, the firm's demand curve in the export market will be more elastic; that is, it will lose more customers by raising prices than it would in its local market. If it faces enough competition in its export market, the Foreign monopolist's export demand curve will be horizontal at the price P, meaning that it cannot charge more than the competitive market price. If the price for exports is fixed at P, selling more units does not depress the price or the extra revenue earned for each unit exported. Therefore, the marginal revenue for exports equals the price, which is labeled as P in Figure 9-8.

Equilibrium Condition We can now determine the profit-maximizing level of production for the Foreign monopolist, as well as its prices in each market. For the discriminating monopoly, profits are maximized when the following condition holds:

$$MR = MR^* = MC^*$$

FIGURE 9-8

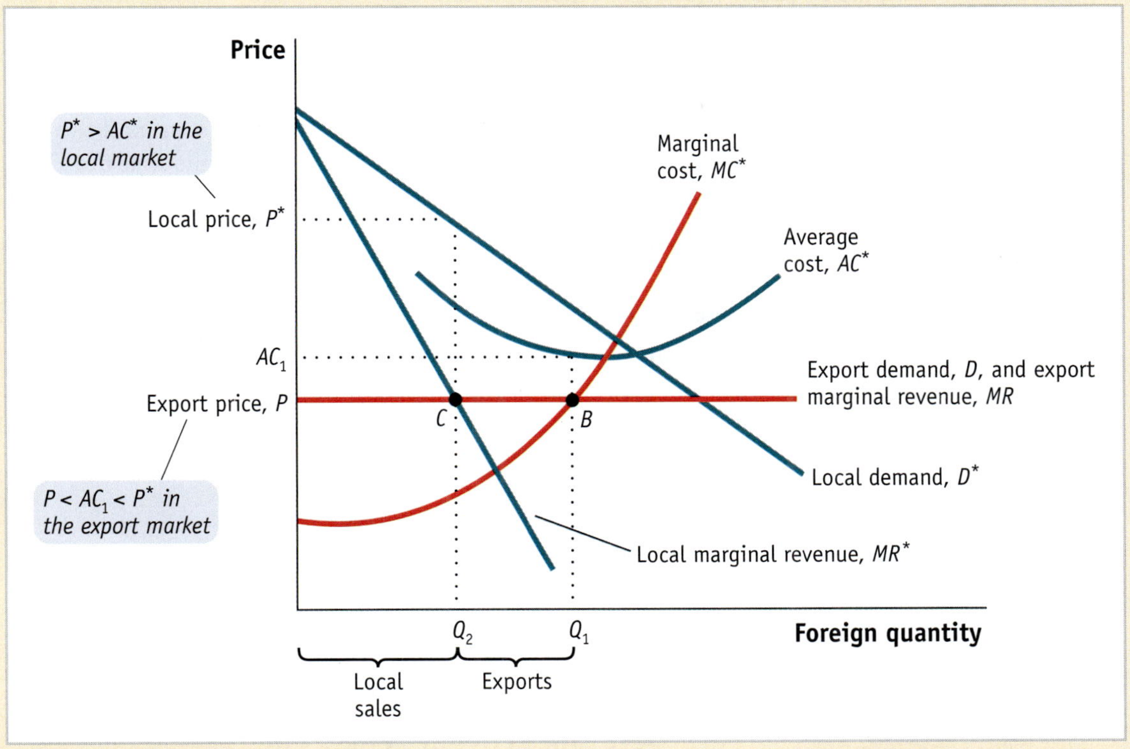

Foreign Discriminating Monopoly The Foreign monopoly faces different demand curves and charges different prices in its local and export markets. Locally, its demand curve is D^* with marginal revenue MR^*. Abroad, its demand curve is horizontal at the export price, P, which is also its marginal revenue of MR. To maximize profits, the Foreign monopolist chooses to produce the quantity Q_1 at point B, where local marginal cost equals marginal revenue in the export market, $MC^* = MR$. The quantity sold in the local market, Q_2 (at point C), is determined where local marginal revenue equals export marginal revenue, $MR^* = MR$. The Foreign monopolist sells Q_2 to its local market at P^*, and $Q_1 - Q_2$ to its export market at P. Because $P < P^*$ (or alternatively $P < AC_1$), the firm is dumping.

This equation looks similar to the condition for profit maximization for a single-market monopolist, which is marginal revenue = marginal cost, except that now the marginal revenues should also be equal in the two markets.

We illustrate this equilibrium condition in Figure 9-8. If the Foreign firm produces quantity Q_1, at point B, then the marginal cost of the last unit equals the export marginal revenue MR. But not all of the supply Q_1 is exported; some is sold locally. The amount sold locally is determined by the equality of the firm's local marginal revenue MR^* with its export marginal revenue MR (at point C), *and* the equality of its local marginal cost MC^* with MR (at point B). All three variables equal P, though the firm charges the price P^* (by tracing up the Foreign demand curve) to its local consumers. Choosing these prices, the profit-maximization equation just given is satisfied, and the discriminating monopolist is maximizing profits across both markets.

The Profitability of Dumping The Foreign firm charges P^* to sell quantity Q_2 in its local market (from Q_2, we go up to the local demand curve D^* and across to the price). The local price exceeds the price P charged in the export market. Because the

Foreign firm is selling the same product at a lower price to the export market, it is dumping its product into the export market.

What about the comparison of its export price with average costs? At total production of Q_1 at point *B*, the firm's average costs are read off the average cost curve above that point, so average costs equal AC_1, lower than the local price P^* but higher than the export price *P*. Because average costs AC_1 are above the export price *P*, the firm is also dumping according to this cost comparison. But we will argue that the Foreign firm still earns positive profits from exporting its good at the low price of *P*. To see why that is the case, we turn to a numerical example.

Numerical Example of Dumping

Suppose the Foreign firm has the following cost and demand data:

Fixed costs	=	\$100
Marginal costs	=	\$10 per unit
Local price	=	\$25
Local quantity	=	10
Export price	=	\$15
Export quantity	=	10

The profits earned from selling in its local market are

$$\underbrace{(\$25 \cdot 10)}_{\text{Revenue}} - \underbrace{\$10 \cdot 10}_{\text{Variable cost}} - \underbrace{\$100}_{\text{Fixed cost}} = \underbrace{\$50}_{\text{Profits}}$$

Notice that the average costs for the firms are

$$\text{Average costs} = \frac{\$200}{10} = \$20$$

Now suppose that this firm sells an additional 10 units abroad, at the price of \$15, which is less than its average cost of production. It is *still* worthwhile to sell these extra units because profits become

$$\underbrace{(\$25 \cdot 10 + \$15 \cdot 10)}_{\text{Revenue}} - \underbrace{\$10 \cdot 20}_{\text{Variable cost}} - \underbrace{\$100}_{\text{Fixed cost}} = \underbrace{\$100}_{\text{Profits}}$$

Profits have increased because the extra units are sold at \$15 but produced at a *marginal cost* of \$10, which is less than the price received in the export market. Therefore, each unit exported will increase profits by the difference between the price and marginal costs. Thus, even though the export price is less than average costs, profits still rise from dumping in the export market.

4 Policy Response to Dumping

In the previous section, we learned that dumping is not unusual: a Foreign monopolist that discriminates between its local and export markets by charging different prices in each can end up charging a lower price in its export market. Furthermore, the price it charges in its export market might be less than its average cost of production and still be profitable. Our interest now is in understanding the policy response in the Home importing country.

Antidumping Duties

Under the rules of the WTO, an importing country is entitled to apply an antidumping tariff any time that a foreign firm is dumping its product. An imported product is being dumped if its price is below the price that the exporter charges in its own local market; if the exporter's local price is not available, then dumping is determined by comparing the import price to (1) a price charged for the product in a third market or (2) the exporter's average costs of production.[10] If one of these criteria is satisfied, then the exporting firm is dumping and the importing country can respond with a tariff called an antidumping duty.[11] The amount of the antidumping duty is calculated as the difference between the exporter's local price and the "dumped" price in the importing country.

An example of an antidumping duty is the tariff that the European Union applies to imports of shoes from China and Vietnam. Since 2006 the European Union has applied tariffs of 10% to 16.5% on shoes imported from China and 10% on shoes imported from Vietnam. These antidumping duties were justified because of the low prices that the imported shoes are sold for in Europe. On January 3, 2010, the European Union voted to extend the duties for another 15 months, through March 2011. That decision was protested by the European Footwear Alliance, which represents major footwear firms who import shoes into Europe, and also by China, which filed an official complaint with the WTO, as described in **Headlines: China Escalates Trade Fight Over European Shoe Tariff.** The WTO will have to determine whether the European Union was entitled to extend this duty; that is, whether shoes from China and Vietnam were still being sold at prices below those in their local market, or below their costs of production.

Strategic Trade Policy? The purpose of an antidumping duty is to raise the price of the dumped good in the importing country, thereby protecting the domestic producers of that good. Because we are dealing with dumping by a Foreign monopolist, we might expect that the antidumping duty, which is a tariff, will lead to a terms-of-trade gain for the Home country. That is, we might expect that the Foreign monopolist will absorb part of the tariff through lowering its own price, as was illustrated in Figure 9-7. It follows that the rise in the consumer price in the importing country is less than the full amount of the tariff, as was illustrated in the previous application dealing with Japanese compact trucks.

Does the application of antidumping duties lead to a terms-of-trade gain for the Home country, making this another example of strategic trade policy that can potentially benefit the Home country? In the upcoming analysis, we'll find that the answer to this question is "no," and that the antidumping provisions of U.S. trade law are

---

[10] See Article VI of the GATT in Side Bar: Key Provisions of the GATT in the previous chapter.

[11] There is another type of tariff, similar to the antidumping duty, that is also used to offset low prices in the importing country, and that is the *countervailing duty*. A countervailing duty is used when the Foreign government subsidizes its own exporting firms so that they can charge lower prices for the exports. We will examine export subsidies in the next chapter.

HEADLINES

China Escalates Trade Fight Over European Shoe Tariff

This article discusses an ongoing case before the World Trade Organization dealing with European tariffs on shoes made in China, and the Chinese response.

China complained to the World Trade Organization on Thursday [February 4, 2010] about antidumping duties imposed by the European Union on Chinese-made shoes, raising tensions between the trading giants. . . . In a statement issued by its mission in Geneva, where the W.T.O. is based, the Chinese government said Europe's actions "violated various obligations under the W.T.O., and consequently caused damage to the legitimate rights and interests of Chinese exporters." It added that China "had repeatedly consulted" with the European Union but said that its concerns "had not been properly addressed or settled." In an eight-page legal complaint, the Chinese government requested consultations on both the original 2006 decision to impose the shoe duties and last year's move to extend them.

. . . While some European Union countries with footwear manufacturers, like Italy, have welcomed the antidumping duties, others support the position of large retailers that argue the duties hurt consumers by pushing up prices. As a compromise, the European Union decided late last year on a 15-month extension of charges that add 9.7 percent to 16.5 percent to the import price of Chinese shoes and 10 percent to Vietnamese shoes.

The European Footwear Alliance, which represents several big global footwear brands, including Adidas, Ecco and Timberland, opposes the duties. It said in a statement that it "shares China's view" that the European Union decision was based on flawed analysis. "Ironically the measure hurts European business and consumers the most," it said. In a letter sent last year to Catherine Ashton, then the European Union trade commissioner, the alliance said its members had paid around 800 million euros ($1.2 billion) in antidumping duties in the previous three and a half years, "and we fail to understand who has benefited."

Until recently, China had made little use of the W.T.O. procedures in trade disputes with Europe. But in 2009, when the European Union applied antidumping tariffs on imports of iron and steel fasteners from China, Beijing dragged the European Union into the W.T.O. dispute settlement process for the first time. Under W.T.O. rules, the European Union and China have 60 days to resolve the shoe dispute through bilateral consultations. If no deal is reached, China can ask the 153 members of the organization to establish a panel of three experts to examine the issue. Europe could block that once, but establishment is automatic if China makes a second request. A final decision can take 18 months or longer.

Source: Excerpted from Stephen Castle and David Jolly, "China Escalates Trade Fight Over European Shoe Tariff," The New York Times, *February 5, 2010, electronic edition.*

overused and create a much greater cost for consumers and larger deadweight losses than does the less frequent application of tariffs under the safeguard provision, Article XIX of the GATT.[12]

Comparison with Safeguard Tariff It is important to recognize that the tariff on compact trucks, discussed in the previous application, was not an antidumping duty. Rather, it was a **safeguard tariff** applied under Section 201 of the U.S. tariff code, or Article XIX of the GATT. Because the tariff on trucks was increased in the early 1980s and has not been changed since, it fits our assumption that Foreign firms treat the tariff as fixed. That assumption does not hold for antidumping duties, however, because Foreign exporting firms can *influence* the amount of an antidumping duty by their own

[12] See Article XIX of the GATT in Side Bar: Key Provisions of the GATT in the previous chapter.

choice of prices. In fact, the evidence shows that Foreign firms often change their prices and *increase* the price charged in the importing country even before an antidumping tariff is applied. To see why this occurs, let us review how the antidumping duty is calculated.

Calculation of Antidumping Duty The amount of an antidumping duty is calculated based on the Foreign firm's local price. If its local price is \$10 (after converting from Foreign's currency to U.S. dollars), and its export price to the Home market is \$6, then the antidumping tariff is calculated as the difference between these prices, \$4 in our example. This method of calculating the tariff creates an incentive for the Foreign firm to *raise* its export price even before the tariff is applied so that the duty will be lower. If the Foreign firm charges an export price of \$8 instead of \$4 but maintains its local price of \$10, then the antidumping tariff would be only \$2. Alternatively, the Foreign firm could charge \$10 in its export market (the same as its local price) and avoid the antidumping tariff altogether!

Thus, the calculation of an antidumping duty creates a strong incentive for Foreign firms to raise their export prices to reduce or avoid the duty. This increase in the import price results in a terms-of-trade *loss* for the Home country. Such an increase in the import price is illustrated in Figure 9-9 as the rise from price P_1 to P_2. This price increase leads to a gain for Home firms of area a but a loss for Home consumers of area $(a + b + c + d)$. There is no revenue collected when the duty is not imposed, so the net loss for the Home country is area $(b + c + d)$. This loss is higher than the deadweight loss from a tariff (which is area $b + d$) and illustrates the extra costs associated with the threat of an antidumping duty.

FIGURE 9-9

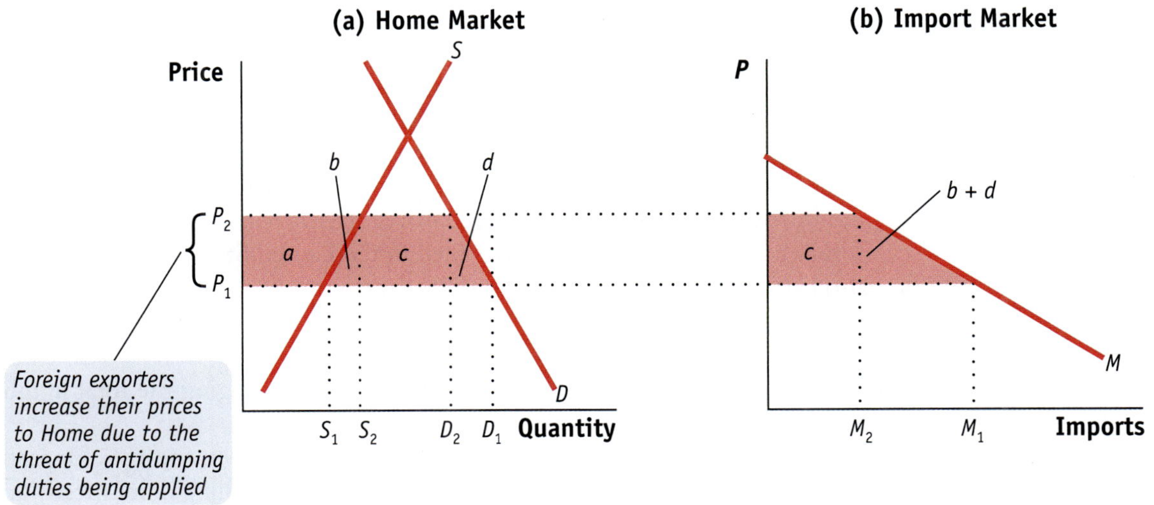

Home Loss Due to Threat of Duty A charge of dumping can sometimes lead Foreign firms to increase their prices, even without an antidumping duty being applied. In that case, there is a loss for Home consumers $(a + b + c + d)$ and a gain for Home producers (a). The net loss for the Home country is area $(b + c + d)$.

Furthermore, the fact that Foreign firms will raise their prices to reduce the potential duty gives Home firms an incentive to charge Foreign firms with dumping, even if none is occurring: just the *threat* of an antidumping duty is enough to cause Foreign firms to raise their prices and reduce competition in the market for that good. As the following application shows, these incentives lead to excessive filings of antidumping cases.

APPLICATION

Antidumping Duties Versus Safeguard Tariffs

In the previous chapter, we discussed the "safeguard" provision in Article XIX of the GATT **(Side Bar: Key Provisions of the GATT)** and Section 201 of U.S. trade law. This provision, which permits temporary tariffs to be applied, is used infrequently. As shown in Table 9-1, from 1980 to 1989, only 19 safeguard (also called "escape clause") cases were filed in the United States. In the following decade there were only nine, and from 2000 to 2009 only three such cases were filed. In each case, the U.S. International Trade Commission must determine whether rising imports are the "most important cause of serious injury, or threat thereof, to the domestic industry." Of the 31 cases filed from 1980 to 2009, the ITC made a *negative* recommendation (i.e., it did not approve the tariff requests) in 16, or about one-half the cases. One of those negative recommendations was for the tariff on Japanese compact trucks discussed in the previous application: the ITC made a negative recommendation for both cars and trucks in 1980, but trucks still obtained a tariff by reclassifying the type of trucks being imported.

The ITC made an affirmative ruling for protection in 12 cases, which then went for a final ruling to the president, who recommended import protection in only nine cases.[13] An example of a positive recommendation was the tariff on the import of steel, as discussed in the previous chapter, and the tariff imposed on heavyweight motorcycles, discussed later in this chapter. That only 31 cases were brought forward in three decades, and that tariffs were approved by the president in only nine cases, shows how infrequently this trade provision is used.

In the next panel of Table 9-1, we show the number of China-specific safeguard cases. This new trade provision, discussed in the previous chapter, took effect in 2001. Since that time, seven cases have been filed, of which two were denied by the ITC and five were approved. Of these five approved tariffs, the president also ruled in favor only once—the tariff imposed on imports of tires from China, approved by President Obama in 2009.

The infrequent use of the safeguard provision can be contrasted with the many cases of antidumping duties. The cases filed in the United States under this provision are also listed in Table 9-1, which shows that the number of antidumping cases vastly exceeds safeguard cases. From 1980 to 1989 and from 1990 to 1999, there were more than 400 antidumping cases filed in the United States. In the next 10 years, 2000 to 2009, there were another 300 or so antidumping cases, bringing the total number of antidumping cases from 1980 to 2009 to more than 1,200!

To have antidumping duties applied, a case must first go to the U.S. Department of Commerce (DOC), which rules on whether imports are selling domestically at "less

[13] In addition to the 12 affirmative ITC safeguard cases, there were two ties and one terminated case.

TABLE 9-1

Import Protection Cases in the United States, 1980–2009 This table shows the use of safeguard tariffs as compared with antidumping duties in the United States. Safeguard tariffs are used much less often.

Safeguard or Escape Clause

			TOTAL 1980–2009		
Total 1980–1989	Total 1990–1999	Total 2000–2009	Negative ITC	Affirmative ITC*	Affirmative President
19	9	3	16	12	9

China-Specific Safeguard

			TOTAL 1980–2009		
Total 1980–1989	Total 1990–1999	Total 2000–2009	Negative ITC	Affirmative ITC*	Affirmative President
NA	NA	7	2	5	1

Antidumping

			TOTAL 1980–2009		
Total 1980–1989	Total 1990–1999	Total 2000–2009	Duty Levied	Case Rejected	Withdrawn
468	428	313	545	447	148

** In addition to the 12 affirmative ITC safeguard cases, there were two ties and one terminated case.*

NA – not applicable since the China-specific safeguard began in 2001.

Sources: Wendy Hansen and Thomas J. Prusa, 1995, "The Road Most Taken: The Rise of Title VII Protection," The World Economy, *295–313. Update for 1989 to 1994, I. M. Destler, 2005,* American Trade Politics, *Washington, D.C.: Peterson Institute for International Economics, pp. 149, 165. Update for 1995 to 2009, Chad P. Bown, October 2009, "Global Antidumping Database" [Version 5.1], http://www.brandeis.edu/~cbown/global_ad/ .*

than fair value"; that is, below the price in their own market or below the average cost of making them. These rulings were positive in 93% of cases during this period. The case is then brought before the ITC, which must rule on whether imports have caused "material injury" to the domestic industry (defined as "harm that is not inconsequential, immaterial, or unimportant"). This criterion is much easier to meet than the "substantial cause of serious injury" provision for a safeguard tariff, and as a result, the ITC more frequently rules in favor of antidumping duties. Furthermore, the application of duties does not require the additional approval of the president. Of the 1,200 antidumping cases filed from 1980 to 2009, about 450 were rejected and another 550 had duties levied.

The remaining 150 antidumping cases fall into a surprising third category: those that are *withdrawn* prior to a ruling by the ITC. It turns out that the U.S. antidumping law actually permits U.S. firms to withdraw their case and, acting through an intermediary at the Department of Commerce (DOC), agree with the foreign firm on the level of prices and market shares! As we would expect, these withdrawn and settled cases result in a significant increase in market prices for the importing country.

Why do firms make claims of dumping so often? If a dumping case is successful, a duty will be applied against the Foreign competitor, and the import price will increase. If the case is withdrawn and settled, then the Foreign competitor will also raise its price. Even if the case is not successful, imports often decline during the period that the DOC or ITC is making an investigation, and the smaller quantity of imports also causes their price to rise. So regardless of the outcome of a dumping case, the increase in the price of Foreign imports benefits Home firms by allowing them to charge more for their own goods. As a result, Home producers have a strong incentive to file for protection from dumping, whether it is occurring or not. ■

5 Infant Industry Protection

We now turn to the final application of tariffs that we will study in this chapter, and that is a tariff applied to an industry that is too young to withstand foreign competition, and so will suffer losses when faced with world prices under free trade. Given time to grow and mature, the industry will be able to compete in the future. The only way that a firm in this industry could cover its losses today would be to borrow against its future profits. But if banks are not willing to lend to this firm—perhaps because it is small and inexperienced—then it will go bankrupt today unless the government steps in and offers some form of assistance, such as with a tariff or quota. This argument is called the "infant industry case" for protection. Although we include the infant industry tariff argument in this chapter on strategic trade policy, the idea of protecting a young industry dates back to the writings of John Stuart Mill (1806–1873).

To analyze this argument and make use of our results from the previous sections, we assume there is only one Home firm, so it is again a case of Home monopoly. The special feature of this Home firm is that increasing its output today will lead to lower costs in the future because it will learn how to produce its output more efficiently and at a lower cost. The question, then, is whether the Home government should intervene with a temporary protective tariff or quota today, so that the firm can survive long enough to achieve lower costs and higher profits in the future.

There are two cases in which infant industry protection is potentially justified. First, protection may be justified if a tariff today leads to an increase in Home output that, in turn, helps the firm learn better production techniques and reduce costs in the future. This is different from increasing returns to scale as discussed in Chapter 6. With increasing returns to scale, lower costs arise from producing farther down along a decreasing average cost curve; while a tariff might boost Home production and lower costs, removing the tariff would reduce production to its initial level and still leave the firm uncompetitive at world prices. For infant industry protection to be justified, the firm's learning must *shift down* the entire average cost curve to the point where it is competitive at world prices in the future, even without the tariff.

If the firm's costs are going to fall in the future, then why doesn't it simply borrow today to cover its losses and pay back the loan from future profits? Why does it need import protection to offset its current losses? The answer was already hinted at above: banks may be unwilling to lend to this firm because they don't know with certainty that the firm will achieve lower costs and be profitable enough in the future to repay the loan. In such a situation, a tariff or quota offsets an imperfection in the market for borrowing and lending (the capital market). What is most essential for the infant industry argument to be valid is not imperfect competition (a single Home firm), but rather, this imperfection in the Home capital market.

A second case in which import protection is potentially justified is when a tariff in one period leads to an increase in output and reductions in future costs *for other firms in the industry*, or even for firms in other industries. This type of **externality** occurs when firms learn from each other's successes. For instance, consider the high-tech semiconductor industry. Each firm innovates its products at a different pace, and when one firm has a technological breakthrough, other firms benefit by being able to copy the newly developed knowledge. In the semiconductor industry, it is not unusual for firms to mimic the successful innovations of other firms, and benefit from a **knowledge spillover.** In the presence of spillovers, the infant industry tariff promotes a positive externality: an increase in output for one firm lowers the costs for everyone. Because firms learn from each other, each firm on its own does not have much incentive to invest in learning by increasing its production today. In this case, a tariff is needed to offset this externality by increasing production, allowing for these spillovers to occur among firms so that there are cost reductions.

As both of these cases show, the infant industry argument supporting tariffs or quotas depends on the existence of some form of **market failure.** In our first example, the market does not provide loans to the firm to allow it to avoid bankruptcy; in the second, the firm may find it difficult to protect its intellectual knowledge through patents, which would enable it to be compensated for the spillover of knowledge to others. These market failures create a potential role for government policy. In practice, however, it can be very difficult for a government to correct market failure. If the capital market will not provide loans to a firm because it doesn't think the firm will be profitable in the future, then why would the government have better information about that firm's future prospects? Likewise, in the case of a spillover of knowledge to other firms, we cannot expect the government to know the extent of spillovers. Thus, we should be skeptical about the ability of government to distinguish the industries that deserve infant industry protection from those that do not.

Furthermore, even if either of the two conditions we have identified to potentially justify infant industry protection hold, these market failures do not guarantee that the protection will be worthwhile—we still need to compare the future benefits of protection (which are positive) with its costs today (the deadweight losses). With these warnings in mind, let's look at how infant industry protection can work when we have enough information to calculate the costs and benefits.

Free-Trade Equilibrium

In panel (a) of Figure 9-10, we show the situation a Home firm faces today, and in panel (b) we show its situation in the future. We assume that the Home country is small and therefore faces a fixed world price. As discussed earlier in the chapter, even a Home monopolist will behave in the same manner as a perfectly competitive industry under free trade, assuming that they have the same marginal costs. We also assume that any increase in the firm's output today leads to a reduction in costs in the future (i.e., a downward shift in the firm's average cost curve).

FIGURE 9-10

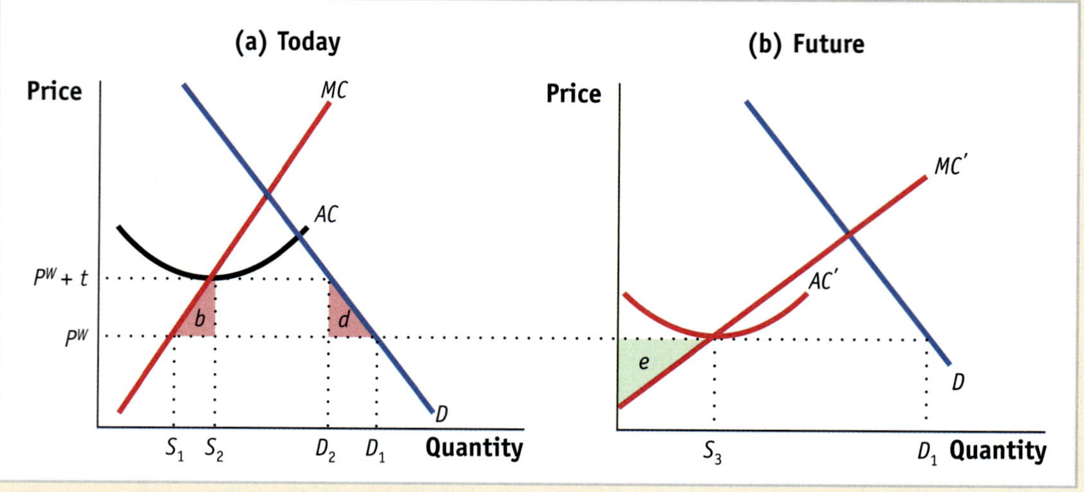

Infant Industry Protection In the situation today (panel a), the industry would produce S_1, the quantity at which $MC = P^W$. Because P^W is less than average costs at S_1, the industry would incur losses at the world price of P^W and would be forced to shut down. A tariff increases the price from P^W to $P^W + t$, allowing the industry to produce at S_2 (and survive) with the net loss in welfare of $(b + d)$. In panel (b), producing today allows the average cost curve to fall through learning to AC'. In the future, the firm can produce the quantity S_3 at the price P^W without tariff protection and earn producer surplus of e.

Equilibrium Today With free trade today, the Home firm faces the world price of P^W (which, you will recall from earlier in this chapter, is also its marginal revenue curve) and will produce to the point at which its marginal cost of production equals P^W. The Home firm therefore supplies the quantity S_1. To verify that S_1 is actually the Home supply, however, we need to check that profits are not negative at this quantity. To do so, we compare the firm's average costs with the price. The average cost curve is shown as AC in panel (a), and at the supply of S_1, average costs are much higher than the price P^W. That means the Home firm is suffering losses and would shut down today instead of producing S_1.

Tariff Equilibrium

To prevent the firm from shutting down, the Home government could apply an import tariff or quota to raise the Home price. Provided that the Home firm increases its output in response to this higher price, we assume that this increased size allows the firm to learn better production techniques so that its future costs are reduced. Given the choice of an import tariff or quota to achieve this goal, the Home government should definitely choose the tariff. The reason is that when a Home monopolist is faced with a quota rather than a tariff, it will produce *less* output under the quota so that it can further raise its price. The decrease in output leads to additional deadweight loss today, as discussed earlier in the chapter. Furthermore, because we have assumed that the firm's learning depends on how much it produces and output is lower under the quota, there would be less learning and a smaller reduction in future costs under a quota than a tariff. For both reasons, a tariff is a better policy than a quota when the goal is to nurture an infant industry.

Equilibrium Today If the government applies an import tariff of t dollars today, the Home price increases from P^W to $P^W + t$. We assume that the government sets the tariff high enough so that the new Home price, $P^W + t$, just covers the infant industry's average costs of production. At this new price, the firm produces the quantity S_2 in panel (a). As illustrated, the price $P^W + t$ exactly equals average costs, AC, at the quantity S_2, so the firm is making zero profits. Making zero profits means that the Home firm will continue to operate.

Equilibrium in the Future With the firm producing S_2 today rather than S_1, it can learn about better production methods and lower its costs in the future. The effect of learning on production costs is shown by the downward shift of the average cost curve from AC in panel (a) to AC' in panel (b).[14] The lower average costs in the future mean that the firm can produce quantity S_3 without tariff protection at the world price P^W in panel (b) and still cover its average costs. So the temporary tariff today allows the firm to operate in the future without the tariff, which is what infant industry protection is trying to achieve.

Effect of the Tariff on Welfare The application of the tariff today leads to a deadweight loss, and in panel (a), the deadweight loss is measured by the triangles $(b + d)$. But we also need to count the gain from having the firm operating in the future. In panel (b) of Figure 9-10, the producer surplus earned in the future by the firm is shown by the region e. We should think of the region e as the present value (i.e., the discounted sum over time) of the firm's future producer surplus; it is this amount that would be forgone if the firm shut down today.

To evaluate whether the tariff has been successful, we need to compare the future gain of e with the deadweight loss today of $(b + d)$. If e exceeds $(b + d)$, then the infant industry protection has been worthwhile, but if e is less than $(b + d)$, then the costs of protection today do not justify the future benefits. The challenge for government policy is to try to distinguish worthwhile cases (those for which future benefits exceed present costs) from those cases that are not. In the application that follows, we will see whether the governments of China, Brazil, and the United States have been able to distinguish between these cases.

APPLICATION

Examples of Infant Industry Protection

There are many examples of infant industry protection in practice, and we will consider three: (1) a U.S. tariff imposed to protect Harley-Davidson motorcycles in the United States during the 1980s; (2) a complete ban on imports imposed from 1977 to the early 1990s to protect the computer industry in Brazil; and (3) tariffs and quotas imposed to protect the automobile industry in China, which were reduced when China joined the WTO in 2001. The last two of these examples are for developing countries, in which we normally think of infant industry tariffs being applied. However, this is not necessarily always the case, as shown in the first example for the United States.

[14] The marginal cost curve might also shift down, from MC in panel (a) to MC' in panel (b), although that shift is not essential to our argument.

U.S. Tariff on Heavyweight Motorcycles

Harley-Davidson does not really fit the usual description of an "infant" industry: the first plant opened in 1903 in Milwaukee, Wisconsin, and it was owned and operated by William Harley and the three Davidson brothers. Until the late 1970s it did not face intense import competition from Japanese producers; but by the early 1980s, Harley-Davidson was on the verge of bankruptcy. Even though it had been around since 1903, Harley-Davidson had many of the characteristics we associate with an infant industry: the inability to compete at the international price today and (as we will see) the potential for lower costs in the future. By including this case in our discussion of infant industries, we are able to make a precise calculation of the effect of the tariffs on consumers and producers to determine whether the infant industry protection was successful.

In 1983 Harley-Davidson, the legendary U.S.-based motorcycle manufacturer, was in trouble. It was suffering losses due to a long period of lagging productivity combined with intense competition from Japanese producers. Two of these producers, Honda and Kawasaki, not only had plants in the United States but also exported Japan-made goods to the United States. Two other Japanese producers, Suzuki and Yamaha, produced and exported their products from Japan. In the early 1980s these four Japanese firms were engaged in a global price war that spilled over into the U.S. market, and inventories of imported heavyweight cycles rose dramatically in the United States. Facing this intense import competition, Harley-Davidson applied to the International Trade Commission (ITC) for Section 201 protection.

Reprinted by permission of the York Daily Record/York Sunday News

President Ronald Reagan visits the Harley-Davidson plant.

As required by law, the ITC engaged in a study to determine the source of injury to the industry, which in this case was identified as heavyweight (more than 700 cc) motorcycles. Among other factors, it studied the buildup of inventories by Japanese producers in the United States. The ITC determined that there was more than nine months' worth of inventory of Japanese motorcycles already in the United States, which could depress the prices of heavyweight cycles and threaten bankruptcy for Harley-Davidson. As a result, the ITC recommended to President Ronald Reagan that import protection be placed on imports of heavyweight motorcycles. This case is interesting because it is one of the few times that the *threat* of injury by imports has been used as a justification for tariffs under Section 201 of U.S. trade law.

President Reagan approved the recommendation from the ITC, and tariffs were imposed on imports of heavyweight motorcycles. These tariffs were initially very high, but they declined over five years. The initial tariff, imposed on April 16, 1983, was 45%; it then fell annually to 35, 20, 15, and 10% and was scheduled to end in April 1988. In fact, Harley-Davidson petitioned the ITC to end the tariff one year early, after the 15% rate expired in 1987, by which time it had cut costs and introduced new and very popular products so that profitability had been restored. Amid great fanfare, President Reagan visited the Harley-Davidson plant in Milwaukee, Wisconsin, and declared that the tariff had been a successful case of protection.

Calculation of Deadweight Loss Was the tariff on heavyweight motorcycles really successful? To answer this, we need to compare the deadweight loss of the tariff with the future gain in producer surplus. In our discussion of the steel tariff in the previous chapter, we derived a formula for the deadweight loss from using a tariff, measured relative to the import value:

$$\frac{DWL}{P \cdot M} = \frac{1}{2} \cdot \left(\frac{t}{P^W}\right) \cdot \%\Delta M$$

The information on imports of heavyweight cycles is shown in Table 9-2. Before the tariff was imposed, import sales in 1982 were $452 million and the import quantity was 164,000 motorcycles. After the tariff was imposed in April 1983, imports dropped to 139,000 in calendar year 1983, and 40,000 to 80,000 each year thereafter. The average import quantity between 1982 and 1983 was therefore (164,000 + 139,000)/2 = 151,000, so the percentage drop in import quantity between these years is calculated using a midpoint formula as (164 – 139)/151 = 0.17, or 17%. This percentage drop is reported in Table 9-2, along with the tariff of 45% in 1983.

The deadweight loss relative to import value in 1983 is measured as

$$\frac{DWL}{P \cdot M} = \tfrac{1}{2}\,(0.45 \cdot 0.17) = 0.038, \text{ or } 3.8\%$$

We can calculate the average import sales from 1982 to 1983 as (452 + 410)/2 = $431 million. Multiplying the percentage loss by average imports, we obtain the deadweight loss in 1983 of 0.038 × 431 = $16.3 million. That deadweight loss is reported in the last column of Table 9-2, along with the loss for each following year. Adding up these deadweight losses, we obtain a total loss of $112.5 million over the four years that the tariff was used.[15]

TABLE 9-2

U.S. Imports of Heavyweight Motorcycles This table shows the effects of the tariff on imports of heavyweight motorcycles in the United States.

Year	Import Sales ($ millions)	Import Quantity	% Fall in Imports (from 1982)	Tariff (%)	Net Loss/ Average Sales (%)	Deadweight Loss (% millions)
1982	452	164,000				
1983	410	139,000	17	45	3.8	16.3
1984	179	80,000	69	35	12.1	38.4
1985	191	72,000	78	20	7.8	25.2
1986	152	43,000	116	15	8.7	26.4
January–March 1987	59	14,000	98	15	7.3	6.3
Total, 1983–1987						112.5

Source: Heavy Weight Motorcycles. *Report to the President on Investigation No. TA-203-17, under Section 203 of the Trade Act of 1974. U.S. International Trade Commission, June 1987, and author's calculations.*

[15] This calculation is not quite accurate because we have used the calendar years 1983 to 1986 rather than the 12 months from April of each year to March of the next year, during which the tariff was effective.

Future Gain in Producer Surplus To judge whether the tariff was effective, we need to compare the deadweight loss of $112.5 million with the *future* gain in producer surplus (area *e* in Figure 9-10). How can we assess these future gains? We can use a technique that economists favor: we can evaluate the future gains in producer surplus by examining the stock market value of the firm around the time that the tariff was removed.

During the time that the tariff was in place, the management of Harley-Davidson reduced costs through several methods: implementing a "just-in-time" inventory system, which means producing inventory on demand rather than having excess amounts in warehouses; reducing the workforce (and its wages); and implementing "quality circles," groups of assembly workers who volunteer to meet together to discuss workplace improvements, along with a "statistical operator control system" that allowed employees to evaluate the quality of their output. Many of these production techniques were copied from Japanese firms. The company also introduced a new engine. These changes allowed Harley-Davidson to transform losses during the period from 1981 to 1982 into profits for 1983 and in following years.

In July 1986 Harley-Davidson became a public corporation and issued stock on the American Stock Exchange: 2 million shares at $11 per share, for a total offering of $22 million. It also issued debt of $70 million, which was to be repaid from future profits. In June 1987 it issued stock again: 1.23 million shares at $16.50 per share, for a total offering of $20.3 million. The sum of these stock and debt issues is $112.3 million, which we can interpret as the present discounted value of the producer surplus of the firm. This estimate of area *e* is nearly equal to the consumer surplus loss, $112.5 million, in Table 9-2. Within a month after the second stock offering, however, the stock price rose from $16.50 to $19 per share. Using that price to evaluate the outstanding stock of 3.23 million, we obtain a stock value of $61 million, plus $70 million in repaid debt, to obtain $131 million as the future producer surplus.

By this calculation, the future gain in producer surplus from tariff protection to Harley-Davidson ($131 million) exceeds the deadweight loss of the tariff ($112.5 million). Furthermore, since 1987 Harley-Davidson has become an even more successful company. Its sales and profits have grown every year, and many model changes have been introduced, so it is now the Japanese companies that copy Harley-Davidson. By March 2005 Harley-Davidson had actually surpassed General Motors in its stock market value: $17.7 billion versus $16.2 billion. Both these companies suffered losses during the financial crisis of 2008 and 2009, but Harley-Davidson continued to operate as usual (with a stock market value of $4.3 billion in mid-2009), whereas General Motors declared bankruptcy and required a government bailout (its stock market value fell to less than $0.5 billion). Although both companies can be expected to recover after the crisis, it is clear that General Motors—which once had the world's highest stock market value—has been surpassed by Harley-Davidson.

Was Protection Successful? Does this calculation mean that the infant industry protection was successful? A complete answer to that question involves knowing what would have happened if the tariff had *not* been put in place. When we say that infant industry protection is successful if the area *e* of future producer surplus gain ($131 million) exceeds the deadweight loss ($112.5 million), we are assuming that the firm would not have survived at all without the tariff protection. That assumption may be true for Harley-Davidson. It is well documented that Harley-Davidson was on the brink of bankruptcy from 1982 to 1983. Citibank had decided that it would not extend more loans to cover Harley's losses, and Harley found alternative financing on December 31, 1985, just one week before filing for bankruptcy.[16] If the tariff saved the company, then this was clearly a case of successful infant industry protection.

On the other hand, even if Harley-Davidson had not received the tariff and had filed for bankruptcy, it might still have emerged to prosper again. Bankruptcy does not mean that a firm stops producing; it just means that the firm's assets are used to repay all possible debts. Even if Harley-Davidson had gone bankrupt without the tariff, some or all of the future gains in producer surplus might have been realized. So we cannot be certain whether the turnaround of Harley-Davidson required the use of the tariff.[17]

Despite all these uncertainties, it still appears that the tariff on heavyweight motorcycles bought Harley-Davidson some breathing room. This is the view expressed by the chief economist at the ITC at that time, in the quotation at the beginning of the chapter: "If the case of heavyweight motorcycles is to be considered the only successful escape-clause [tariff], it is because it caused little harm and it helped Harley-Davidson get a bank loan so it could diversify."[18] We agree with this assessment that the harm caused by the tariff was small compared with the potential benefits of avoiding bankruptcy, which allowed Harley-Davidson to become the very successful company that it is today.

Computers in Brazil

There are many cases in which infant industry protection has not been successful. One well-known case involves the computer industry in Brazil. In 1977 the Brazilian government began a program to protect domestic firms involved in the production of personal computers (PCs). It was thought that achieving national autonomy in the computer industry was essential for strategic military reasons. Not only were imports of PCs banned, but domestic firms also had to buy from local suppliers whenever possible, and foreign producers of PCs were not allowed to operate in Brazil.

The Brazilian ban on imports lasted from 1977 to the early 1990s. This was a period of rapid innovations in PC production worldwide, with large drops in the cost of computing power. In Figure 9-11, we show the effective price of computing power in the United States and Brazil between 1982 and 1992, which fell very rapidly in both countries. The price we are graphing is "effective" because it is not just the retail price of a new PC but a price index that reflects the improvements over time in the PC's speed of calculations, storage capacity, and so on.

[16] See Peter C. Reid, 1990, *Made Well in America: Lessons from Harley-Davidson on Being the Best* (New York: McGraw-Hill).

[17] The chairman of Harley-Davidson stated in 1987 that the tariff had not actually helped the company that much because the Japanese producers were able to downsize some of their motorcycles to 699 cc engine size, and thereby avoid the tariff (*Wall Street Journal*, March 20, 1987, p. 39).

[18] John Suomela, chief economist at the U.S. International Trade Commission, as cited in Douglas A. Irwin, 2002, *Free Trade under Fire* (Princeton, NJ: Princeton University Press), pp. 136–137.

FIGURE 9-11

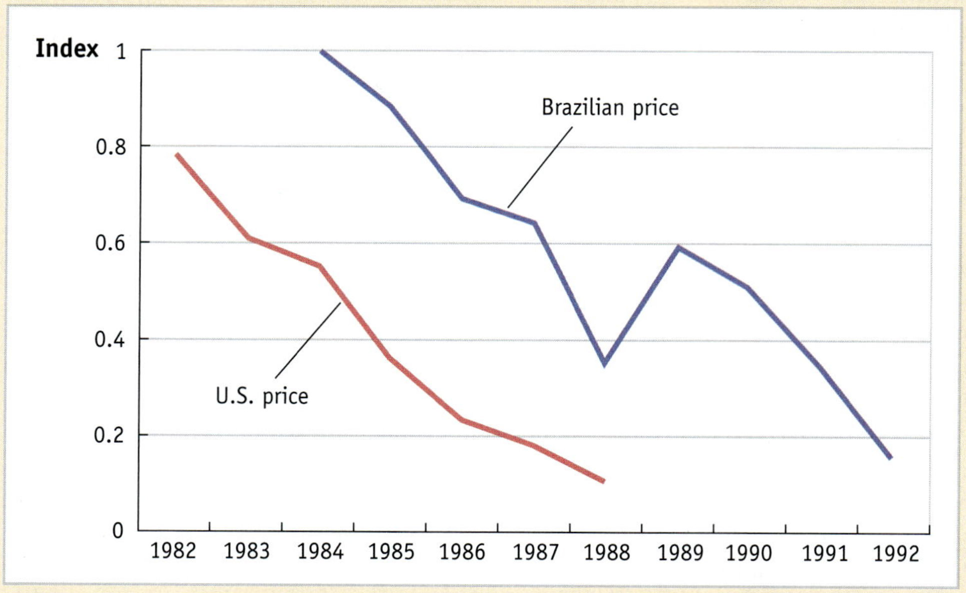

Computer Prices in the United States and Brazil, 1982–1992 This diagram shows the effective price of computer power in the United States and Brazil. Both prices fell very rapidly due to technological improvements, but the drop in the U.S. price exceeded that of the Brazilian price. The difference between the two prices is a measure of the technology gap between Brazil and the United States in the production of personal computers.

Source: Eduardo Luzio and Shane Greenstein, November 1995, "Measuring the Performance of a Protected Infant Industry: The Case of Brazilian Microcomputers," Review of Economics and Statistics, *77(4), 622–633.*

Prices in Brazil Brazilian firms were adept at reverse engineering the IBM PCs being sold from the United States. But the reverse engineering took time, and the fact that Brazilian firms were required to use local suppliers for many parts within the computers added to the costs of production. We can see from Figure 9-11 that Brazil *never achieved the same low prices* as the United States. By 1992, for example, the effective prices in Brazil were between the prices that had been achieved in the United States four or five years earlier. The persistent gap between the prices in Brazil and the United States means that Brazil was never able to produce computers at competitive prices without tariff protection. This fact alone means that the infant industry protection was not successful.

Consumer and Producer Surplus In Table 9-3, we show the welfare calculation for Brazil, as well as other details of the PC industry. Local sales peaked at about $750 million in 1986, and the following year, the Brazilian prices rose to within 20% of those in the United States. But that is as close as the Brazilian industry ever got to world prices. In 1984 prices in Brazil were nearly double those in the United States, which led to a producer surplus gain of $29 million but a consumer surplus loss in Brazil of $80 million. The net loss was therefore $80 million – $29 million = $51 million, which was 0.02% of Brazilian gross domestic product (GDP) that year. By 1986 the net loss had grown to $164 million, or 0.06% of GDP. This net loss was the deadweight loss from the tariff during the years it was in place. The industry was never able to produce in the absence of tariffs, so there are no future gains (like area *e* in Figure 9-10) that we can count against those losses.

TABLE 9-3

Brazilian Computer Industry This table shows the effects of the government ban on imports of personal computers into Brazil.

Year	Sales ($ millions)	Brazil/U.S. Price (%)	Producer Surplus Gain ($ millions)	Consumer Surplus Loss ($ millions)	Net Loss ($ millions)	Net Loss (% of GDP)
1984	126	189	29	80	51	0.02
1985	384	159	70	179	109	0.04
1986	746	143	113	277	164	0.06
1987	644	119	50	112	62	0.02
1988	279	127	29	68	39	0.01

Source: Eduardo Luzio and Shane Greenstein, November 1995, "Measuring the Performance of a Protected Infant Industry: The Case of Brazilian Microcomputers," Review of Economics and Statistics, *77(4), 622–633.*

Other Losses The higher prices in Brazil imposed costs on Brazilian industries that relied on computers in manufacturing, as well as on individual users, and they became increasingly dissatisfied with the government's policy. During his campaign in 1990, President Fernando Collor de Mello promised to abolish the infant industry protection for personal computers, which he did immediately after he was elected.

A number of reasons have been given for the failure of this policy to develop an efficient industry in Brazil: imported materials such as silicon chips were expensive to obtain, as were domestically produced parts that local firms were required to use; in addition, local regulations limited the entry of new firms into the industry. Whatever the reasons, this case illustrates how difficult it is to successfully nurture an infant industry and how difficult it is for the government to know whether temporary protection will allow an industry to survive in the future.

Protecting the Automobile Industry in China

The final example of infant industry protection that we discuss involves the automobile industry in China. In 2009 China overtook the United States as the largest automobile market in the world (measured by domestic sales plus imports). Strong competition among foreign firms located in China, local producers, and import sales have resulted in new models and falling prices so that the Chinese middle class can now afford to buy automobiles. In 2009 there were over 13 million vehicles sold in China, as compared with 10.4 million cars and light trucks sold in the United States.

Growth in automotive production and sales has been particularly strong since 2001, when China joined the World Trade Organization (WTO). With its accession to the WTO, China agreed to reduce its tariffs on foreign autos, which were as high as 260% in the early 1980s, then fell to 80 to 100% by 1996, and 25% by July 2006. The tariff on automobile parts was further cut from 25 to 10% in 2009. China has loosened its import quotas, as well. Those tariffs and quotas, in addition to restrictions at the province and city level on what type of cars could be sold, had limited China's imports and put a damper on the auto industry in that country. Prices were high and foreign producers were reluctant to sell their newest models to China. That situation has changed dramatically. Now, foreign firms scramble to compete in

AP Photo/Eugene Hoshiko

Workers at the Shanghai General Motors Plant assemble a Buick.

China with their latest designs and are even making plans to export cars from China. Is the Chinese automobile industry a successful case of infant industry protection? Are the benefits gained by the current production and export of cars greater than the costs of the tariffs and quotas imposed in the past? To answer this, we begin by briefly describing the history of the Chinese auto industry.

Production in China Beginning in the early 1980s, China permitted a number of joint ventures between foreign firms and local Chinese partners. The first of these in 1983 was Beijing Jeep, which was a joint venture between American Motors Corporation (AMC—later acquired by Chrysler Corporation) and a local firm in Beijing. The following year, Germany's Volkswagen signed a 25-year contract to make passenger cars in Shanghai, and France's Peugeot agreed to another passenger car project to make vehicles in Guangzhou.

Although joint venture agreements provided a window for foreign manufacturers to tap the China market, there were limits on their participation. Foreign manufacturers could not own a majority stake in a manufacturing plant—Volkswagen's venture took the maximum of 50% foreign ownership. The Chinese also kept control of distribution networks for the jointly produced automobiles. These various regulations, combined with high tariff duties, helped at least some of the new joint ventures achieve success. Volkswagen's Shanghai plant was by the far the winner under these rules, and it produced more than 200,000 vehicles per year by the late 1990s, more than twice as many as any other plant. Volkswagen's success was also aided by some Shanghai municipal efforts. Various restrictions on engine size, as well as incentives offered to city taxi companies that bought Volkswagens, helped ensure that only Volkswagen's models could be sold in the Shanghai market; essentially, the Shanghai Volkswagen plant had a local monopoly.

That local monopoly has been eroded by entry into the Shanghai market, however. A recent example occurred in early 2009, when General Motors opened two new plants in Shanghai, at a cost of $1.5 billion and $2.5 billion each. General Motors is a leading producer in China, and locally produced 1.8 million of the 13 million vehicles sold in China in 2009. In fact, its profits from the Chinese market were the only bright spot on its global balance sheet that year, and served to offset some of its losses in the American market, as described in **HEADLINES: Shanghai Tie-Up Drives Profits for GM.**

Cost to Consumers The tariffs and quotas used in China kept imports fairly low throughout the 1990s, ranging from a high of 222,000 cars imported in 1993 to a low of 27,500 imports in 1998 and 160,000 cars in 2005. Since tariffs were in the range of 80 to 100% by 1996, import prices were approximately doubled because of the tariffs. But the quotas imposed on auto imports probably had at least as great an impact on prices of imports *and* domestically produced cars. Our analysis earlier in the chapter showed that quotas have a particularly large impact on domestic prices when the Home firm is a monopoly. That situation applied to the sales of Volkswagen's joint venture, in Shanghai, which enjoyed a local monopoly on the sales of its vehicles.

The effect of this local monopoly was to substantially increase prices in the Shanghai market. In Figure 9-12, we show the estimated markups of price over marginal costs for autos sold in China from 1995 to 2001, by various producers. The markups for Shanghai Volkswagen are the highest, reaching a high of 54% in 1998 and then falling to 28% in 2001, for an average of 42% for the period from 1995 to 2001. In comparison, the average markup charged by Tianjin Auto was 19%, and the average markup charged by Shanghai GM was 14%. All the other producers shown in Figure 9-12 have even lower markups.

From this evidence, it is clear that Shanghai Volkswagen was able to substantially raise its prices because of the monopoly power granted by the local government. Furthermore, the Jetta and Audi models produced by Shanghai Volkswagen during the 1990s were outdated models. That plant had the highest production through 2001, despite its high prices and outdated models, so a large number of consumers in the Shanghai area and beyond bore the costs of that local protection. This example illustrates how a Home monopoly can gain from protection at the expense of consumers. The example also illustrates how protection can stifle the incentive for firms to introduce the newest models and production techniques.

Gains to Producers For the tariffs and quotas used in China to be justified as infant industry protection, they should lead to a large enough drop in future costs so that the protection is no longer needed. China has not reached that point entirely, since it still

FIGURE 9-12

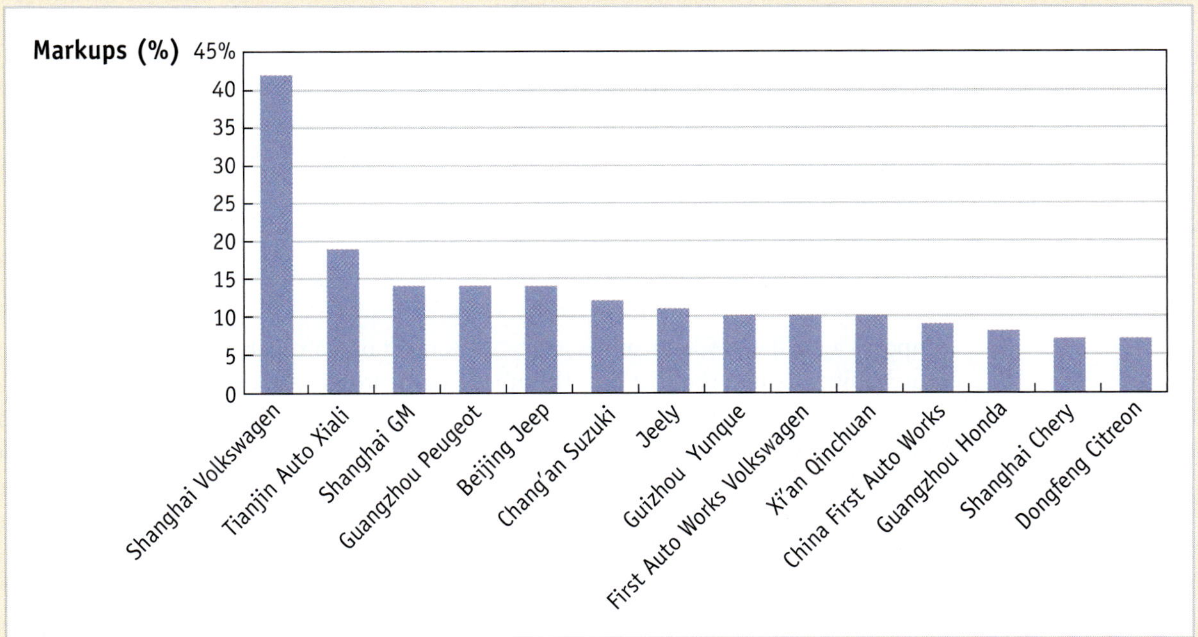

Automobile Markups by Firms in China, 1995–2001 This diagram shows the percentage markups (price over marginal cost) applied to automobiles sold in China from 1995 to 2001, by various producers. The highest markup was charged by Shanghai Volkswagen, which had a local monopoly in Shanghai.

Source: Haiyan Deng, 2006, "Market Structure and Pricing Strategy of China's Automobile Industry."

HEADLINES

Shanghai Tie-Up Drives Profits for GM

This article discusses how partnerships in China have helped GM's profits.

If General Motors believes in God, it must be thanking Him right now for China.

Mainland Chinese sales were by far the brightest spot in GM's universe last year: sales in China rose 66 per cent while US sales fell by 30 per cent. One in four GM cars is now made in China. Even those cars made in Detroit were partly designed in Shanghai. GM managed to offload distressed assets to Chinese companies: the loss-making, environment-harming Hummer was sold to a previously unknown heavy equipment manufacturer, Sichuan Tengzhong [this sale was, however, blocked by the Chinese government in February 2010], and Beijing Automotive (BAIC) took some Saab technology off GM's hands. Perhaps most importantly of all, though, China agreed last year to bankroll GM's expansion in Asia.

In exchange for a deal to sell Chinese minicommercial vehicles in India, GM agreed to give up the 50-50 ownership of its leading mainland joint venture, Shanghai General Motors, ceding 51 per cent majority control to its Chinese partner, Shanghai Automotive Industry Corp (SAIC). The Sino-American partnership said this would be only the first of many such deals. Will observers one day look back at that deal and say that was the day GM signed over its future to the Chinese? And does that deal demonstrate how China can save GM—or hint that it might gobble it up?

"The quick answer is that Chinese consumers have already saved GM," says Klaus Paur of TNS auto consultancy in Shanghai, referring to stratospheric Chinese auto sales last year. Longer term, China cannot save the US carmaker singlehandedly. "If GM cannot save itself in the US and Europe, it's not going to be saved," says one GM insider who asked not to be named.

GM does not disclose its China profits but they are estimated at . . . perhaps $500 [million] last year when the Chinese car market had such a good year. "Half a billion in profits is not going to save a company that is losing $1[billion]-plus a quarter in the US," says the GM insider. But without China, GM probably cannot be saved at all. "Take China out of the GM portfolio, then that light at the end of the GM tunnel abruptly goes dim," says Mike Dunne of Dunne & Co, an Asia-based auto consultancy.

That is a remarkable reversal from a decade ago, when the Chinese auto industry was just getting on its feet and desperately needed GM investment. In 1997, when SGM was founded, China produced only 1.3m light vehicles. Next year's Chinese sales will be more than 10 times that figure. Kevin Wale, head of GM in China, defends the decision to cede majority control to his Chinese partner: "Relationships [in a joint venture] are much stronger than numbers. If you have a bad relationship, it doesn't matter if you have 70 per cent, you have a bad relationship. We have a fantastic relationship with SAIC." Whatever role China plays in GM's future, having a symbiotic relationship with the mainland looks like the smart bet for the time being.

Source: Patti Waldmeir, "Shanghai Tie-Up Drives Profits for GM," Financial Times, *January 21, 2010.*

imposes a tariff of 25% on autos, and a 10% tariff on auto parts. These tariff rates are much lower than in the past but still substantially protect the local market. So it is premature to point to the Chinese auto industry as a successful case of infant industry protection. Still, there are some important lessons that can be learned from its experience. First, there is no doubt that past protection contributed to the inflow of foreign firms to the Chinese market. All the foreign auto companies that entered China prior to its WTO accession in 2001 did so under high levels of protection, so that acquiring a local partner was the only way to sell locally: tariffs were too high to allow significant imports to China. As a result, local costs fell as Chinese partners gained from the technology transferred to them by their foreign partners. The **Headlines: Thanks to Detroit, China Is Poised to Lead** article explains that American firms are now transferring their best technologies to China. We can conclude that tariff protection combined with the ownership restrictions for joint ventures has led to a great deal of learning and reduced costs by the Chinese partners.

HEADLINES

Thanks to Detroit, China Is Poised to Lead

This article discusses the growth in the automobile industry in China, which has benefited from the investment of multinational firms from the United States and Europe.

CHONGQING, China—Volkswagen and other carmakers used to prosper by sending outdated factory equipment to China to produce older models no longer salable in the West. But competition has become so fierce here that Honda is about to introduce its latest version of the Civic only several months after it went on sale in Europe, Japan and the United States. Toyota, meanwhile, is assembling its Prius gasoline-electric sedan only in Japan and China.

When Ford Motor opened its first production line here in western China just three years ago, it used a layout copied from a Ford factory in the Philippines to produce 20,000 sedans a year based on a small car design taken from Ford operations in India. But this winter, Ford opened a second production line next door that is practically identical to one of its most advanced factories, the Saarlouis operation in southwestern Germany. The new line produces the Focus, the same small car it builds in Germany (but different from the Focus sold in the United States). And with continuing improvements to the first line, it will bring total capacity here to 200,000 cars a year by June.

The Chinese managers here are not even satisfied with that. "I want to learn from Germany and then improve on it," said Li Jianping, the factory's vice director of manufacturing. Ford's success in rapidly expanding the scale and sophistication of its Chongqing operations illustrates how quickly the overall auto industry is expanding and modernizing in China. One requirement for a country to become an automobile exporter is to develop a highly competitive domestic market that demands excellent quality and efficiency, and China has managed to create just such a market. American and European carmakers, including Ford, General Motors, DaimlerChrysler and Volkswagen, as well as Toyota, Honda and Nissan of Japan are introducing their best technology to their plants in China, and not only to compete against one another. They also face rapidly growing competition in the Chinese market from purely local companies like Geely, Chery and Lifan.

. . . Chinese automakers are also buying modern technology and design themselves. Chery has hired some of the best-known Italian auto design firms to spruce up its cars. When the MG Rover Group of Britain entered bankruptcy proceedings last year, the Nanjing Automobile Group outbid Shanghai Automotive to take control of Rover and its fairly modern engine-producing subsidiary, Powertrain Ltd., and move it to China. The Lifan Group, a car and motorcycle maker with headquarters several miles from the Ford plant here, is bidding to buy one of the world's most advanced engine factories, a joint venture of DaimlerChrysler and BMW in southern Brazil.

Source: Excerpted from Keith Bradsher and Jeremy W. Peters, "Thanks to Detroit, China Is Poised to Lead," New York Times, *March 12, 2006.*

Second, when we look carefully at which firms in China are now beginning to export, it is not necessarily those firms that benefited the most from protection. The **Headlines** article concludes by mentioning that the Lifan Group is bidding to buy one of the world's most advanced engine factories from Brazil and move it to China. Lifan is a Chinese motorcycle manufacturer and is leapfrogging into the automobile industry by purchasing ready-made plants. It is planning to export midsize sedans costing less than $10,000 to developing countries in Asia, the Mideast, and the Caribbean and then has its sights set on the United States. Two other Chinese firms, Geely and Chery, also intend to start exporting cars, but as of 2010 have not yet been successful.

Third, at least as important as the tariffs themselves is the rapid growth of income in China, which has led to a boom in domestic sales and to additional firms entering the market, such as Lifan. It is that rapid growth in income that has led

China to overtake the United States to become the largest automobile market in the world in 2009. Tariffs have contributed to the inflow of foreign investment, but it is now the consumers in China who are forcing firms to offer the newest models built with the most efficient techniques. For now, we must leave open the question of whether the high tariffs and quotas in China are responsible for the current success of its auto industry, or whether they just resulted in high prices and lagging model designs that slowed the development of the industry. It will be some years before researchers can look back at the development of this industry and identify the specific causes of its success. ■

6 Conclusions

In the previous chapter, we discussed the use of import tariffs and quotas under perfect competition and highlighted the difference between the small-country and large-country cases. With perfect competition, a small importing country loses from a tariff (because it cannot affect world prices), but the large importing country can potentially gain from a tariff (because the tariff depresses the world price). Import quotas have effects similar to those of import tariffs under perfect competition, so we often refer to quotas and tariffs as "equivalent."

We can contrast the results obtained under perfect competition with the results we learned in this chapter, in which we assume imperfect competition—either Home or Foreign monopoly. Under Home monopoly, the effects of a tariff and quota are very different. With a tariff, the Home monopolist can increase its price by the amount of the tariff (as would a competitive industry) but cannot exercise its monopoly power. With an import quota, however, the Home firm is able to charge a higher price than it could with a tariff because it enjoys a "sheltered" market. So the import quota leads to higher costs for Home consumers than the tariff, and these two policies are no longer "equivalent," as they are under perfect competition.

Under Foreign monopoly, the results are similar to those of the large-country case analyzed in the previous chapter: the tariff leads to a fall in the price received by the Foreign monopolist, so the price paid by Home consumers rises by *less than* the full amount of the tariff. The tariff is shared between an increase in the Home price and a decrease in the Foreign price, and the Home importer obtains a terms-of-trade gain. For small tariffs, the terms-of-trade gain exceeds the deadweight loss, and the Home country gains from the tariff. So this is a case where the use of a tariff as strategic trade policy can benefit the Home country, but at the expense of the Foreign firm.

A specific example of a tariff applied against a Foreign monopoly occurs when the Foreign firm is a discriminating monopoly and it dumps its output into Home at a lower price than it charges in its own local market. When dumping occurs, the importing country is permitted by WTO rules to respond with a tariff, which is called an antidumping duty. In principle, we might expect Home to gain from the duty because the Foreign firm will lower its price (as occurs for a tariff applied against a Foreign monopolist). But we have argued that the potential for Home gains from the antidumping duty are unlikely to arise because of special features in the way these duties are applied. Instead, the expected outcome from antidumping duties is that Foreign exporters raise prices even when a duty is *not* applied, leading to Home losses. Because of these losses, the use of antidumping duties as strategic trade policy is not effective.

Another topic discussed in this chapter is the infant industry case for protection. We studied three industries as examples of infant industry protection: Harley-Davidson motorcycles in the United States, computers in Brazil, and automobiles in China. The tariff given to protect Harley-Davidson motorcycles in the United States during the 1980s appears to have been successful because Harley-Davidson survived and has become very profitable. For computers in Brazil, the ban on imports during the 1980s was not successful because the industry was never able to learn enough from the world leaders to reach the same level of efficiency and competitive prices. Finally, automobile production in China has grown rapidly and overtaken the United States, but it is still protected by a 25% tariff, so it is too early to judge whether this is a successful case of infant industry protection. In addition, the rapid growth in the domestic income of Chinese consumers has been at least as important as past tariffs to the recent growth in production and sales.

KEY POINTS

1. Free trade will lead a Home monopoly in a small country to act in the same way as a perfectly competitive industry and charge a price equal to marginal cost. Therefore, competition from imports eliminates the monopoly power of the Home firm.

2. Quotas are not equivalent to tariffs when the Home firm is a monopolist. Because a quota limits the number of imports, the Home monopolist can charge higher prices than under a tariff, which results in greater costs to consumers.

3. When a tariff is applied against a Foreign monopolist, the results are similar to those of the large-country case analyzed in the previous chapter: the Foreign monopolist increases the price in the importing country by less than the full amount of the tariff and allows its own net-of-tariff price to fall. Hence, the tariff is shared between an increase in the Home price and a decrease in the Foreign price, a terms-of-trade gain for Home.

4. Dumping is the practice of a Foreign firm exporting goods at a price that is below its own domestic price or below its average cost of production. If the price charged for the exported good is above the firm's marginal cost, then dumping is profitable. We expect to observe dumping when the Foreign firm is acting like a discriminating monopolist.

5. Countries respond to dumping by imposing antidumping duties on imports. Antidumping duties are calculated as the difference between a Foreign firm's local price (or average costs) and its export price. To reduce or avoid the antidumping duties, Foreign firms can raise their export prices. That increase in price is a terms-of-trade loss for the importer and occurs because the Foreign firm can influence the duty.

6. In the United States and other countries, the use of antidumping tariffs far exceeds the use of safeguard tariffs. It is easy for domestic firms to bring a charge of dumping, and in many cases upholding the charge results in an increase in foreign prices and a decrease in competition for the domestic firm. The excessive use of antidumping cases also invites other countries to respond with their own charges of dumping.

7. An infant industry is a firm that requires protection to compete at world prices today. When a government applies a temporary tariff, it expects that costs for the firm or the industry overall will fall due to learning, thereby allowing it to compete at world prices in the future.

KEY TERMS

strategic trade policy, p. 280
discriminating monopoly, p. 281
dumping, p. 281
antidumping duty, p. 281
infant industry, p. 281
market power, p. 281
marginal revenue, p. 282
price discrimination, p. 296
discriminating monopoly, p. 296
safeguard tariff, p. 300
externality, p. 305
knowledge spillover, p. 305
market failure, p. 305

PROBLEMS

1. Figure 9-1 shows the Home no-trade equilibrium under perfect competition (with the price P^C) and under monopoly (with the price P^M). In this problem, we compare the welfare of Home consumers in these two situations.
   a. Under perfect competition, with the price P^C, label the triangle of consumer surplus and the triangle of producer surplus. Outline the area of total Home surplus (the sum of consumer surplus and producer surplus).
   b. Under monopoly, with the price P^M, label the consumer surplus triangle.
   c. Producer surplus is the same as the profits earned by the monopolist. To measure this, label the point in Figure 9-1 where the *MR* curve intersects *MC* as point B'. For selling the units between zero and Q^M, marginal costs rise along the *MC* curve, up to B'. The monopolist earns the difference between the price P^M and *MC* for each unit sold. Label the difference between the price and the *MC* curve as producer surplus, or profits.
   d. Outline the area of total Home surplus with a Home monopoly.
   e. Compare your answer to parts (a) and (d), and outline what the difference between these two areas is. What is this difference called and why?

2. Figure 9-2 shows the free-trade equilibrium under perfect competition and under monopoly (both with the price P^W). In this problem, we compare the welfare of Home consumers in the no-trade situation and under free trade.
   a. Under perfect competition, with the price P^W, label the triangle of consumer surplus and the triangle of producer surplus. Outline the area of total Home surplus (the sum of consumer surplus and producer surplus).
   b. Based on your answer to part (a) in this problem and part (a) of the last problem, outline the area of gains from free trade under perfect competition.
   c. Under monopoly, still with the price P^W, again label the triangle of consumer surplus and the triangle of producer surplus.
   d. Based on your answer to part (c) in this problem and part (d) in the last problem, outline the area of gains from free trade under Home monopoly.
   e. Compare your answer to parts (b) and (d). That is, which area of gains from trade is higher and why?

3. Rank the following in ascending order of Home welfare and justify your answers. If two items are equivalent, indicate this accordingly.
   a. Tariff *t* in a small country with perfect competition
   b. Tariff *t* in a small country with a Home monopoly
   c. Quota with the same imports *M* in a small country, with a Home monopoly
   d. Tariff *t* in a country facing a Foreign monopoly

4. Refer to the prices of Japanese auto imports under the VER (Figure 9-5) and answer the following:
   a. What component of the price of imported automobiles from Japan rose the most over the period 1980 to 1985?
   b. Sketch how Figures 9-5 and 9-6 might have looked if the United States had applied a tariff to Japanese auto imports instead of the VER (with the same level of imports). In words, discuss how the import prices and U.S. prices might have compared under a tariff and the VER.
   c. Which policy—a tariff or the VER—would have been least costly to U.S. consumers?

5. In this problem, we analyze the effects of an import quota applied by a country facing a Foreign monopolist. In Figure 9-7, suppose that the Home country applies an import quota of X_2, meaning that the Foreign firm cannot sell any more than that amount.
   a. To achieve export sales of X_2, what is the highest price that the Foreign firm can charge?
   b. At the price you have identified in part (a), what is the Home consumer surplus?
   c. Compare the consumer surplus you identify in part (b) with the consumer surplus under free trade. Therefore, outline in Figure 9-7 the Home losses due to the quota. *Hint:* Remember that there is no Home firm, so you do not need to take into account Home producer surplus or tariff revenue. Assume that quota rents go to Foreign firms.
   d. Based on your answer to (c), which has the greater loss to the Home country—a tariff or a quota, leading to the same level of sales X_2 by the Foreign firm?

6. Suppose that the demand curve for a good is represented by the straight line

   $$P = 10 - Q$$

   Fill in the missing information in the following chart:

Quantity	Price	Total Revenue	Marginal Revenue
0			NA
1			
2			
3			
4			
5			
6			
7			
8			
9			
10			

   a. Draw a graph containing both the demand curve and marginal revenue curve.
   b. Is the marginal revenue curve a straight line as well? What is the slope of the marginal revenue curve? How does that slope compare with that of the demand curve?
   c. Does the marginal revenue curve contain negative values over the specified range of quantities? Explain why or why not.

7. Consider the case of a Foreign monopoly with no Home production, shown in Figure 9-7. Starting from free trade at point A, consider a \$10 tariff applied by the Home government.
   a. If the demand curve is linear, as in Problem 6, what is the shape of the marginal revenue curve?
   b. How much does the tariff-inclusive Home price increase because of the tariff, and how much does the net-of-tariff price received by the Foreign firm fall?
   c. Discuss the welfare effects of implementing the tariff. Use a graph to illustrate under what conditions, if any, there is an increase in Home welfare.

8. Suppose the Home firm is considering whether to enter the Foreign market. Assume that the Home firm has the following costs and demand:

Fixed costs	=	\$140
Marginal costs	=	\$10 per unit
Local price	=	\$25
Local quantity	=	20
Export price	=	\$15
Export quantity	=	10

   a. Calculate the firm's total costs from selling only in the local market.
   b. What is the firm's average cost from selling only in the local market?
   c. Calculate the firm's profit from selling only in the local market.
   d. Should the Home firm enter the Foreign market? Briefly explain why.
   e. Calculate the firm's profit from selling to both markets.
   f. Is the Home firm dumping? Briefly explain.

9. Suppose that in response to a *threatened* antidumping duty of t, the Foreign monopoly raises its price by the amount t.
   a. Illustrate the losses for the Home country.
   b. How do these losses compare with the losses from a safeguard tariff of the amount t, applied by the Home country against the Foreign monopolist?
   c. In view of your answers to (a) and (b), why are antidumping cases filed so often?

10. Why is it necessary to use a market failure to justify the use of infant industry protection?

11. What is a positive externality? Explain the argument of knowledge spillovers as a potential reason for infant industry protection.

12. If infant industry protection is justified, is it better for the Home country to use a tariff or a quota, and why?

13. Figures A, B, and C are taken from a paper by Chad Bown: "The Pattern of Antidumping and Other Types of Contingent Protection" (World Bank, PREM Notes No. 144, October 21, 2009).
   a. Figure A shows the number of newly initiated trade remedy investigations, including safeguard (SF), China safeguard (CSF), antidumping (AD), and countervailing duty (CVD) (a countervailing duty is used when foreign firms receive a subsidy from their government, and then the CVD prevents them from charging lower prices in the importing country). Each bar shows the number of new cases in each quarter of the year (Q1, Q2, etc.) for 2007 through 2009. The number of cases is graphed separately for developing countries and developed countries. What does this graph tell us about what has happened to the number of such cases since 2007? What might have caused this pattern?
   b. Figure B shows the number of safeguard (SF) tariff initiations by WTO members. Since 1995 what three years saw the largest numbers of safeguards? What might explain these increases? (Hint: Consider the U.S. business cycle over these years.)
   c. According to Figure B, year 2002 had the most safeguards actions by WTO members. How many action were started that year, and what U.S. safeguard case that year was discussed in this chapter?

FIGURE A

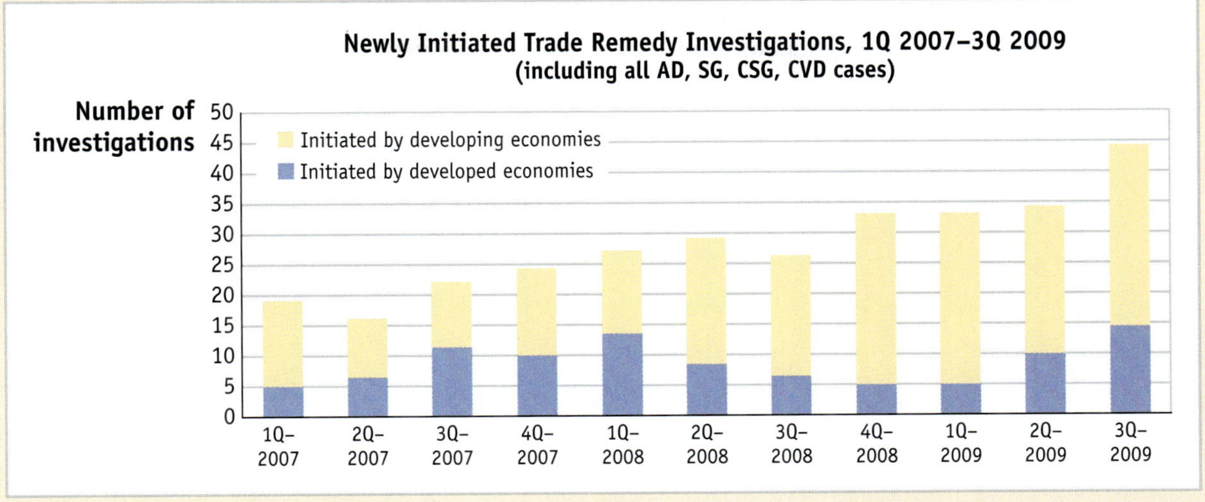

FIGURE B

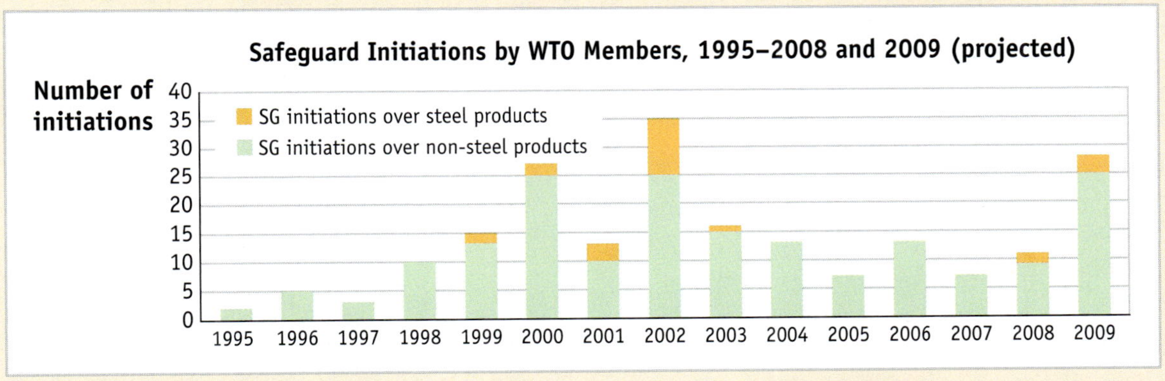

FIGURE C

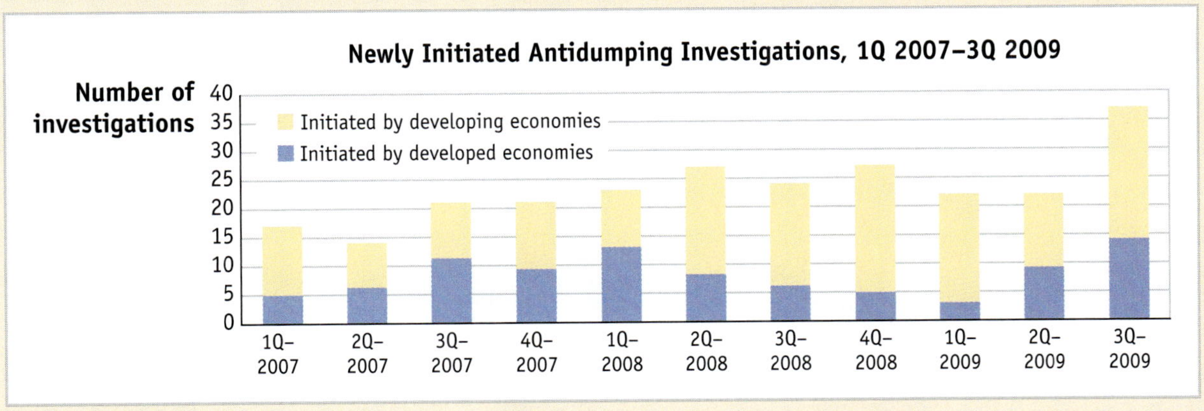

Source: Chad P. Bown, "The Pattern of Antidumping and Other Types of Contingent Protection," World Bank, PREM Notes No. 144, October 21, 2009.

http://www.web.worldbank.org/WBSITE/EXTERNAL/EXTABOUTUS/ORGANIZATION/EXTPREMNET/0,,contentMDK:22357994~pagePK:64159605~piPK:64157667~theSitePK:489961,00.html.

d. Figure C shows the number of newly initiated antidumping (AD) investigations, for quarters of the year from 2007 through 2009. Compare the number of cases in this graph with Figure A, which included safeguard (SF), China safeguard (CSF), antidumping (AD), and countervailing duty (CVD). What can you conclude about the total number of SF, CSF, and CVD cases as compared with the number of AD cases?

10

Export Subsidies in Agriculture and High-Technology Industries

At the moment, the state of Doha [negotiations] remains a riddle wrapped in a mystery inside an enigma. But one thing for sure is that the moment will come very soon when progress will have to be shown or the whole thing slung back into the deep freeze.

Financial Times, January 23, 2007[1]

The coming weeks represent the moment of truth for the Doha Round. If we are to conclude the Doha Round, we must strike a deal this month on trade in agriculture and industrial goods, provide clear signals on opening services markets and clear the decks on the remaining issues. . . .

There's no use beating around the bush; this meeting has collapsed.

Pascal Lamy, Director General or the World Trade Organization, 2008[2]

On July 21, 2008, representatives of the 152 countries belonging to the WTO met in Geneva, Switzerland, to discuss reforms of the world trading system. Like earlier meetings in Seattle (1999), Cancún, Mexico (2003), and Hong Kong (2005), this meeting was marked by large-scale protests. Groups including farmers from South Korea and fishermen from the Philippines objected to the impact that agricultural reforms could have on lowering food prices, thereby threatening their livelihoods. Farmers in South Korea, along with those in Japan, Europe, and the United States, benefit from an intricate system of tariffs (taxes on imports) and subsidies (payments to exporters) that keeps prices for their crops high but in some cases lowers prices in the rest of the world. The lower world price hurts farmers in land-rich developing countries such as Brazil, India, China, and some African nations by

[1] Alan Beattie, "The Doha Round: Riddle Wrapped in a Mystery inside an Enigma," *Financial Times*, January 23, 2007, electronic edition.
[2] Cited in Pascal Lamy, "Doha Round: The Moment of Truth," *New York Times*, July 3, 2008, and Paul Maidment, "After Doha," Forbes.com, July 29, 2008.

©Lee Jae-Won/Reuters/Corbis

Police fight rioters outside the World Trade Organization's meeting. Most of the protesters were South Korean farmers worried about rice imports.

making it harder for them to export their own agricultural products. On the other hand, the lower world prices are a benefit to land-poor developing countries that must import agricultural products. Consumers in those countries will be hurt if prices end up rising as a result of agricultural reforms in the WTO.

The first goal of this chapter is to explain agricultural subsidy policies. The primary reason that countries subsidize agricultural exports is political. Agricultural subsidies benefit a group in society (such as farmers) that the government wants to support. Such support occurs in the United States, Europe, Japan, South Korea, and many other countries. But the fact that these subsidies are costly to the governments of these countries and that they harm exporters from land-rich developing countries led to pressures in the Doha Round of WTO negotiations (2001–present) to remove them. In exchange for the removal of subsidies, it was expected that land-poor developing countries would lower their tariffs on agricultural goods. This complex negotiation involving agriculture in many countries ultimately failed, and the 2008 Geneva meeting of the Doha Round broke up without agreement, as indicated in the quote at the beginning of the chapter. We do not know at the moment whether the Doha Round will be concluded. In this chapter, we describe the tentative agreements to reduce agricultural subsidies made at the 2005 Hong Kong meeting of the WTO, and the issues that could not be resolved which led to the breakup of the 2008 Geneva meeting.

The second goal of the chapter is to examine how export subsidies can be used strategically by governments to bolster domestic companies and industries. Agriculture is not the only sector of an economy to receive subsidies—some high-technology industries also receive generous subsidies. For example, Airbus in Europe and Boeing in the United States have received various types of government assistance, which frequently leads to political friction. For high-tech industries, it is sometimes thought that the use of export subsidies will give a domestic industry a strategic advantage in international competition. That is, rather than subsidies being just politically motivated, legislators often believe that subsidies to high-tech industries might raise those industries' profits and benefit the exporting country. In this chapter, we assess these arguments by examining the effects of export subsidies on prices, the amount of trade, and welfare, for both agriculture and high-technology industries.

1 WTO Goals on Agricultural Export Subsidies

In Table 10-1, we describe the agreements made at the Hong Kong meeting of the WTO in December 2005. These agreements were never ratified by the legislatures in the countries involved, however, so it is best to think of them as goals rather than definite outcomes. Four of the items deal with agricultural subsidies and tariffs, which were the focus of that meeting.

TABLE 10-1

Agreements Made at the Hong Kong WTO Meeting, December 2005 This table shows the agreements made at the 2005 WTO meeting in Hong Kong, which had as its major focus the subsidies provided to agricultural products. This meeting was part of the Doha Round of WTO negotiations, which have not yet been concluded.

Issue	Decision Made in Hong Kong	Unresolved in Hong Kong
Agricultural export subsidies	Abolition by end of 2013, with a "substantial part" scrapped before 2011, and parallel elimination of indirect subsidies.	Must agree [on] value of indirect subsidies and detailed phase-out programs.
Domestic farm supports	Agreement to classify WTO members in three bands based on their level of domestic farm support (top—European Union, middle—United States and Japan, bottom—everyone else).	Must agree [on] size of subsidy reduction and rules to stop countries from shifting trade-distorting subsidies into categories sheltered from deep cuts.
Agricultural tariffs	Agreement on four tiers (different for rich and poor countries) and on a mechanism allowing poor nations to raise duties to counter import surges.	Must decide size of tariff cuts and number and treatment of "sensitive" and "special" products.
Cotton	Agreement to eliminate export subsidies in 2006 and grant unrestricted access for cotton exports from West African producers and other least developed countries (LDCs).	United States will have the "objective" of cutting its $4 billion subsidies to cotton growers further and faster than the still-to-be-agreed-upon overall reduction for domestic farm supports.
Industrial goods	Agreement on formula and on a "comparably high level of ambition" for tariff cuts in agriculture and industrial goods so rich nations do not demand more cuts than they give.	Must agree [on] key elements of formula, how much to cut, flexibilities for developing developing countries, and role of sectoral negotiations.
Services	Some negotiating guidelines for trade in services agreed upon . . .	The European Union is pressing for liberalization timing targets opposed by developing countries; poor nations want rich ones to accept more temporary service workers.
Development	Duty-free, quota-free access extended to 97% of product[s] . . . from least developed countries by 2008, allowing significant exclusions (e.g., U.S. textiles imports). More pledges of aid for trade.	Must agree [on] other measures to strengthen special treatment provisions for poor countries.

Source: Guy de Jonquières, "Tentative Steps Forward Seen as Better Than None at All," Financial Times, *December 19, 2005, p. 2.*

Agricultural Export Subsidies

An **export subsidy** is payment to firms for every unit exported (either a fixed amount or a fraction of the sales price). Governments give subsidies to encourage domestic firms to produce more in particular industries. As shown in Table 10-1, the member countries of the WTO agreed to abolish all export subsidies in agriculture by the end of 2013. Some agricultural exporters, such as Brazil, India, and China, had pushed for an earlier end to the subsidies but faced stiff opposition from many European countries. Europe maintains a system of agricultural subsidies known as the **Common Agricultural Policy (CAP).** For example, to help its sugar growers, the CAP pays farmers up to 50 euros per ton of harvested sugar beets, which is five times the world market price. Because of the subsidy, European farmers can afford to sell the sugar made from their sugar beets at a much lower price than the world market price. As a result, the sugar beet subsidy makes Europe a leading supplier of sugar worldwide, even though countries in more temperate or tropical climates have a natural comparative advantage. Other countries maintain agricultural subsidies that are just as generous. The United States, for example, pays cotton farmers to grow more cotton and then subsidizes agribusiness and manufacturers to buy the American cotton, so both the production *and* the sale of cotton receive subsidies. Japan allows 10% of the approximately 7 million tons of milled rice it consumes annually to enter into the country tariff-free but imposes a 500% tariff on any rice in excess of this 10% limit. There are many other examples of agricultural protection like this from countries all over the world.

Indirect Subsidies Included in the Hong Kong export subsidy agreement is the parallel elimination of **indirect subsidies** to agriculture, including food aid from developed to poor countries and other exports by state-sponsored trading companies in advanced countries. Europe has already eliminated its food aid subsidies and argues that *cash aid* to poor countries is much more effective; the United States continues to export agricultural commodities as aid. Later in the chapter, we explore the argument made by the European Union that cash aid is more effective than food aid in assisting developing countries.

Domestic Farm Supports Another item mentioned in the Hong Kong agreement is **domestic farm supports,** which refers to any assistance given to farmers, even if it is not directly tied to exports. Such domestic assistance programs can still have an indirect effect on exports by lowering the costs (and hence augmenting the competitiveness) of domestic products. The Hong Kong agreement is only a first step toward classifying the extent of such programs in each country, without any firm commitment as to when they might be eliminated.

Cotton Subsidies Finally, export subsidies in cotton received special attention because that crop is exported by many low-income African countries and is highly subsidized in the United States. The United States agreed to eliminate these export subsidies, but that action has not yet occurred because the Hong Kong agreement was never ratified. Subsidies to the cotton industry remain a contentious issue between the United States and other exporting countries, such as Brazil.

Other Matters from the Hong Kong WTO Meeting

Issues that are related to export subsidies were also discussed at the 2005 Hong Kong meeting, in addition to the elimination of the subsidies themselves. One of these issues is the use of tariffs as a response to other countries' use of subsidies. As we now explain, that issue is so contentious that it led to the breakup of the subsequent meeting in Geneva in 2008 and threatens to derail the Doha Round of negotiations.

Tariffs in Agriculture Export subsidies applied by large countries depress world prices, so that exporting countries can expect tariffs to be imposed on the subsidized products when they are imported by other countries. The agriculture-exporting developing countries pushed for a dramatic reduction in these and other agriculture-related tariffs, especially by importing industrial countries, but were not able to obtain such a commitment in Hong Kong.

These discussions continued three years later in Geneva. As indicated in **Headlines: Developing Countries Split over WTO Farm Protection,** the developing country food importers wanted two special provisions allowing them to limit the amount by which tariffs would be lowered. First, they wanted a list of "special products" that would be completely exempt from tariff reductions. Second, they wanted a "special safeguard mechanism" that could be applied to all other agricultural products. Under this mechanism, tariffs could be temporarily raised whenever imports suddenly rose or their prices suddenly fell.

Recall from Chapter 8 that Article XIX of the GATT allows for such a "safeguard tariff," and that there are specific rules allowing for its use mainly in manufactured goods (see **Side Bar: Key Provisions of the GATT in Chapter 8**). The "special safeguard mechanism" in agriculture likewise requires that countries agree on the exact conditions under which it would be used. The problem in Hong Kong was that countries could not agree on the conditions under which a "safeguard tariff" could be temporarily applied. Likewise, the negotiators at the Geneva meeting could not agree on how many agricultural products could be treated as "special" by the importing countries, and exempt from any tariff cuts. The **Headlines** article uses China as an example to show how its "special" products exempted completely from tariff cuts, or exempted temporarily under the "special safeguard mechanism," could adversely

HEADLINES

Developing Countries Split over WTO Farm Protection

This article discusses the breakup of the Geneva meeting of the WTO in 2008, over the issue of "special safeguards" for agricultural products.

GENEVA—The world's poorer countries are divided over proposals for a new global trade deal, with developing country food importers pitted against exporters pushing for greater liberalisation. The differences turn on two technical measures in the proposals on agriculture in the World Trade Organisation (WTO) Doha round talks—"special products" and the "special safeguard mechanism". . . .

Under the proposals developing countries can declare products "special" to shield them from full tariff cuts in the interests of food or livelihood security or rural development.

The discussion around special products involves the number of products that could be designated as such, and how many of those would be fully exempt from tariff cuts. . . . Speculation swirled in the WTO corridors that China—a vast potential market for rich and poor countries alike—would declare rice, cotton and sugar special products. That would hurt rice exporters like Thailand and cotton exporters from West Africa. The United States has also said it wants China to open its cotton market as a condition for making big cuts in its controversial cotton subsidies. . . .

The special safeguard mechanism would allow developing countries to hike farm tariffs temporarily—in some cases to above their current ceilings before any Doha round cuts—to counter a sudden influx of imports or collapse in prices. Exporters fear they could actually lose market access, depending on the terms, as the new [tariffs for "special" products] is taken up by countries like India who do not currently enjoy such protection.

Uruguay's WTO ambassador Guillermo Valles Galmes said current proposals for the special safeguard mechanism would have seen 82 percent of China's agricultural imports, amounting to some $26 billion, eligible for higher duties. . . .

Source: Jonathan Lynn, "Developing Countries Split over WTO Farm Protection," Reuters, July 27, 2008 (additional reporting by Laura MacInnis).

affect exporters such as Thailand, West Africa, the United States, and Uruguay. These conflicts led to the breakdown of the Geneva talks in 2008, but must eventually be resolved before the Doha Round of negotiations can be concluded.

Issues Involving Trade in Industrial Goods and Services Other issues were also discussed in Hong Kong, as listed in Table 10-1. To achieve further cuts in the tariffs on industrial goods, there was agreement in principle to use some formula for the cuts, but the exact nature of that formula was left for future negotiation. There was also an agreement to discuss opening trade in service sectors, which would benefit the industrial countries and their large service industries. The developing countries are expected to make some future offers to open their markets to trade in services, but in return they will expect wealthy countries to accept more temporary immigrant workers in their service sectors. Finally, there was agreement to allow 97% of imported products from the world's 50 least developed countries (LDCs) to enter WTO member markets tariff-free and duty-free. The United States already allows duty-free and tariff-free access for 83% of products from those 50 countries, and under this agreement, the United States would extend that access to nearly all products. Omitted from this agreement, however, are textile imports into the United States from LDCs because the United States wants to protect its domestic textile producers from low-priced imports from countries such as Bangladesh and Cambodia. This is not surprising, given our discussion of the United States' sensitivity to low-cost imports in the clothing and textiles industries, as illustrated by the history of quotas on clothing imports (see Chapter 8).

2 Agricultural Export Subsidies in a Small Home Country

To see the effect of export subsidies on prices, exports, and welfare, we begin with a small Home country that faces a fixed world price for its exports. Following that, we see how the outcomes differ when the Home country is large enough to affect world prices.

Consider a small country exporting sugar. The Home no-trade equilibrium is at point A in Figure 10-1. With free trade, Home faces the world price of sugar P^W. In panel (a) of Figure 10-1, the quantity supplied in Home at that price is S_1 and the quantity demanded is D_1 tons of sugar. Because quantity demanded is less than quantity supplied, the Home country exports $X_1 = S_1 - D_1$ tons under free trade. That quantity of exports is shown as point B in panel (b) corresponding to the free-trade price of P^W. By determining the level of exports at other prices, we can trace out the Home export supply curve X.

Impact of an Export Subsidy

Now suppose that because the government wishes to boost the exports of the domestic sugar producers, each ton of sugar exported receives a subsidy of s dollars from the government. Panel (a) of Figure 10-1 traces the effect of this subsidy on the domestic economy. With an export subsidy of s dollars per ton, exporters will receive $P^W + s$ for each ton exported rather than the lower free-trade price P^W. Because they are allowed to export any amount they want at the subsidized price, the Home firms will not accept a price less than $P^W + s$ for their domestic sales: if the domestic price was less

FIGURE 10-1

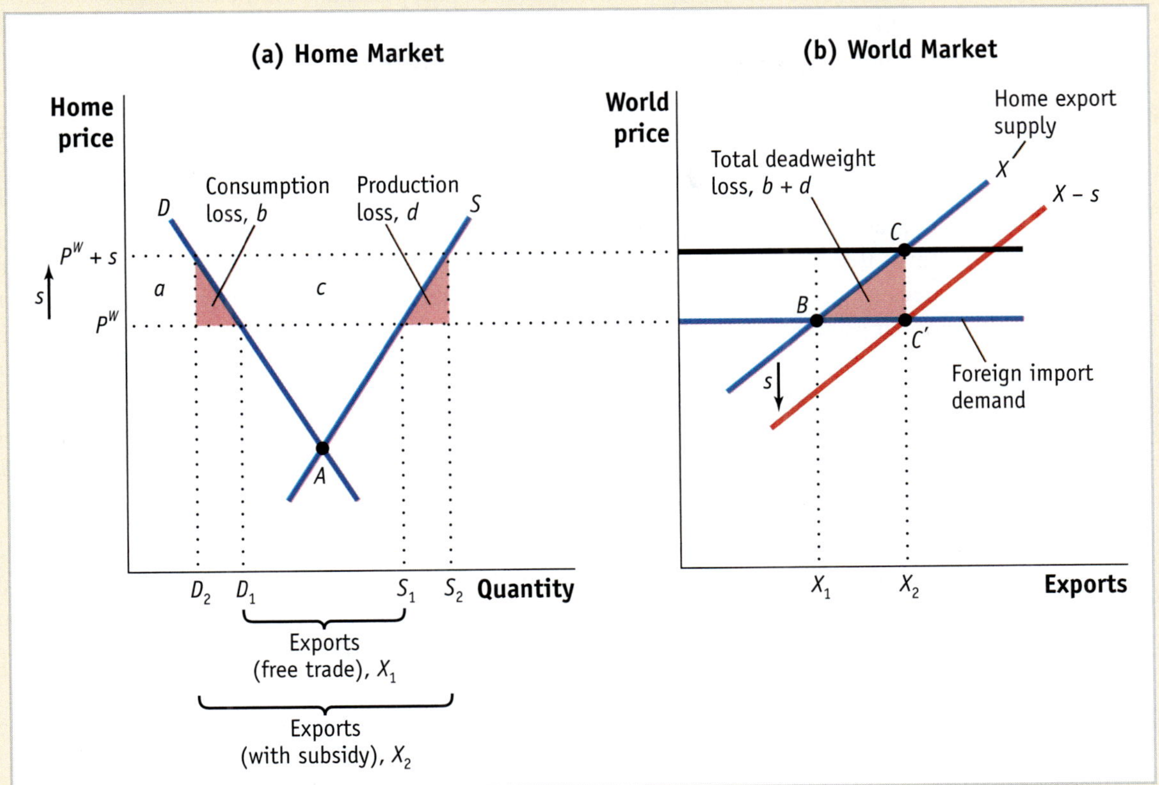

Export Subsidy for a Small Country Applying a subsidy of s dollars per unit exported will increase the price that Home exporters receive from P^W to $P^W + s$. As a result, the domestic price of the similar good will also rise by that amount. This price rise leads to an increase in Home quantity supplied from S_1 to S_2 and a decrease in Home quantity demanded from D_1 to D_2, in panel (a). Exports rise as a result of the subsidy, from X_1 to X_2 in panel (b). The Home export supply curve shifts down by exactly the amount of the subsidy since the marginal cost of a unit of exports decreases by exactly s. As in the case of a tariff, the deadweight loss as a result of the subsidy is the triangle $(b + d)$, the sum of consumer loss b and producer loss d.

than $P^W + s$, the firms would just export all their sugar at the higher price. Thus, the domestic price for sugar must rise to $P^W + s$ so that it equals the export price received by Home firms.

Notice that with the domestic sugar price rising to $P^W + s$, Home consumers could in principle *import* sugar at the price of P^W rather than buy it from local firms. To prevent imports from coming into the country, we assume that the Home government has imposed an import tariff equal to (or higher than) the amount of the export subsidy. This is a realistic assumption. Many subsidized agricultural products that are exported are also protected by an import tariff to prevent consumers from buying at lower world prices. We see that the combined effect of the export subsidy and import tariff is to raise the price paid by Home consumers and received by Home firms.

With the price rising to $P^W + s$, the quantity supplied in Home increases to S_2, while the quantity demanded falls to D_2 in panel (a). Therefore, Home exports increase to $X_2 = S_2 - D_2$. The change in the quantity of exports can be thought of in two ways as reflected by points C and C' in panel (b). On one hand, if we were to measure the *Home price* P^W on the vertical axis, point C is on the original Home export supply curve X: that is, the rise in Home price has resulted in a *movement along* Home's initial supply curve from point B to C since the quantity of exports has increased with the Home price.

On the other hand, with the vertical axis of panel (b) measuring the *world price* and given our small-country assumption that the world price is fixed at P^W, the increase in exports from X_1 to X_2 because of the subsidy can be interpreted as a *shift* of the domestic export supply curve to $X - s$, which includes point C'. Recall from Chapter 8 that the export supply curve shifts by precisely the amount of the tariff. Here, because the export subsidy is like a negative tariff, the Home export supply curve shifts down by exactly the amount s. In other words, the subsidy allows firms to sell their goods to the world market at a price exactly s dollars lower *at any point* on the export supply curve; thus, the export supply curve shifts down. According to our small-country assumption, Home is a price taker in the world market and thus always sells abroad at the world price P^W; the only difference is that with the subsidy, Home exports higher quantities.

Summary From the domestic perspective, the export subsidy increases both the price and quantity of exports, a movement along the domestic export supply curve. From the world perspective, the export subsidy results in an increase in export supply and, given an unchanged world price (due to the small-country assumption), the export supply curve shifts down by the amount of the subsidy s. As was the case with a tariff, the subsidy has driven a wedge between what domestic exporters receive ($P^W + s$ at point C) and what importers abroad pay (P^W at point C').

Impact of the Subsidy on Home Welfare Our next step is to determine the impact of the subsidy on the welfare of the exporting country. The rise in Home price lowers consumer surplus by the amount $(a + b)$ in panel (a). That is the area between the two prices (P^W and $P^W + s$) and underneath the demand curve D. On the other hand, the price increase raises producer surplus by the amount $(a + b + c)$, the area between the two prices (P^W and $P^W + s$), and above the supply curve S. Finally, we need to determine the effect on government revenue. The export subsidy costs the government s per unit exported, or $s \cdot X_2$ in total. That revenue cost is shown by the area $(b + c + d)$.

Adding up the impact on consumers, producers, and government revenue, the overall impact of the export subsidy is

Fall in consumer surplus:	$-(a + b)$
Rise in producer surplus:	$+(a + b + c)$
Fall in government revenue:	$-(b + c + d)$
Net effect on Home welfare:	$\mathbf{-(b + d)}$

The triangle $(b + d)$ in panel (b) is the net loss or **deadweight loss** due to the subsidy in a small country. The result that an export subsidy leads to a deadweight loss for the exporter is similar to the result that a tariff leads to a deadweight loss for an importing country. As with a tariff, the areas b and d can be given precise interpretations. The triangle d equals the increase in marginal costs for the extra units produced because of the subsidy and can be interpreted as the **production loss** or the *efficiency loss* for the economy. The area of the triangle b can be interpreted as the drop in consumer surplus for those individuals no longer consuming the units between D_1 and D_2, which we call the **consumption loss** for the economy. The combination of the production and consumption losses is the deadweight loss for the exporting country.

3 Agricultural Export Subsidies in a Large Home Country

Now suppose that the Home country is a large enough seller on international markets so that its subsidy affects the world price of the sugar (e.g., this occurs with European sugar subsidies and U.S. cotton subsidies). This large-country case is illustrated in Figure 10-2. In panel (b), we draw the Foreign import demand curve M^* as downward-sloping because changes in the amount exported, as will occur when Home applies a subsidy, now affect the world price.

Under free trade, the Home and world price is P^W. At this price, Home exports $X_1 = S_1 - D_1$, and the world export market is in equilibrium at the intersection of Home export supply X and Foreign import demand M^*. Home and Foreign consumers pay the same price for the good, P^W, which is the world price.

FIGURE 10-2

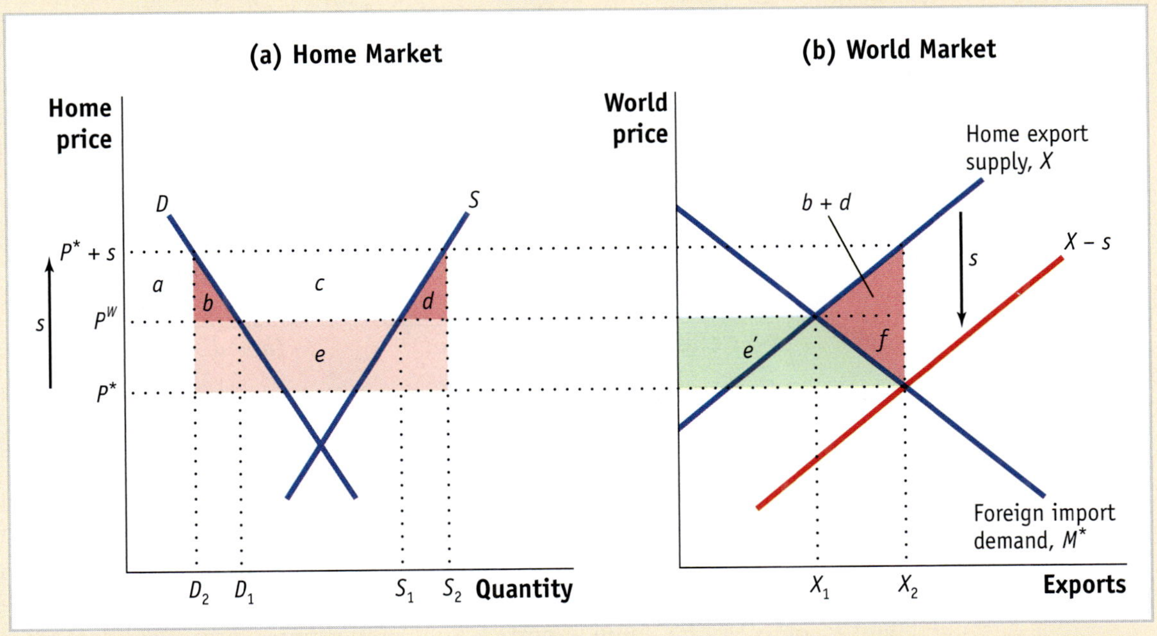

Export Subsidy for a Large Country Panel (a) shows the effects of the subsidy at Home. The Home price increases from P^W to $P^* + s$, Home quantity demanded decreases from D_1 to D_2, and Home quantity supplied increases from S_1 to S_2. The deadweight loss for Home is the area of triangle $(b + d)$, but Home also has a terms-of-trade loss of area e. In the world market, the Home subsidy shifts out the export supply curve from X to $X - s$ in panel (b). As in the small-country case, the export supply curve shifts down by the amount of the subsidy, reflecting the lower marginal cost of exports. As a result, the world price falls from P^W to P^*. The Foreign country gains the consumer surplus area e', so the world deadweight loss due to the subsidy is the area $(b + d + f)$. The extra deadweight loss f arises because only a portion of the Home terms-of-trade loss is a Foreign gain.

Effect of the Subsidy

Suppose that Home applies a subsidy of s dollars per ton of sugar exported. As we found for the small country, a subsidy to Home export production is shown as a downward shift of the Home export supply curve in panel (b) by the amount s; the vertical distance between the original export supply curve X and the new export supply curve $X - s$ is precisely the amount of the subsidy s. The new intersection of Home export supply, $X - s$, and Foreign import demand M^* corresponds to a new world price of P^*, decreased from the free-trade world price P^W, and a Home price $P^* + s$, increased from the free-trade price P^W. Furthermore, the equilibrium with the subsidy now occurs at the export quantity X_2 in panel (b), increased from X_1.

In Chapter 2, we defined the **terms of trade** for a country as the ratio of export prices to import prices. Generally, a fall in the terms of trade indicates a loss for a country because it is either receiving less for exports or paying more for imports. We have found that with the export subsidy, Foreign consumers pay a lower price for Home exports, which is therefore a fall in the Home terms of trade but a gain in the Foreign terms of trade. We should expect, therefore, that the Home country will suffer an overall loss because of the subsidy but that Foreign consumers will gain. To confirm these effects, let's investigate the impact of the subsidy on Home and Foreign welfare.

Home Welfare In panel (a) of Figure 10-2, the increase in the Home price from P^W to $P^* + s$ reduces consumer surplus by the amount $(a + b)$. In addition, the increase in the price benefits Home firms, and producer surplus rises by the amount $(a + b + c)$. We also need to take into account the cost of the subsidy. Because the amount of the subsidy is s, and the amount of Home exports (after the subsidy) is $X_2 = S_2 - D_2$, it follows that the revenue cost of the subsidy to the government is the area $(b + c + d + e)$, which equals $s \cdot X_2$ (the government pays s for every unit exported). Therefore, the overall impact of the subsidy in the large country can be summarized as follows:

Fall in consumer surplus:	$-(a + b)$
Rise in producer surplus:	$+(a + b + c)$
Fall in government revenue:	$-(b + c + d + e)$
Net effect on Home welfare:	$\mathbf{-(b + d + e)}$

In the world market, panel (b), the triangle $(b + d)$ is the deadweight loss due to the subsidy, just as it is for a small country. For the large country, however, there is an extra source of loss, the area e, which is the terms-of-trade loss to Home: $e = e' + f$ in panel (b). When we analyze Foreign and world welfare, it will be useful to divide the Home terms-of-trade loss into two sections, e' and f, but from Home's perspective, the terms-of-trade welfare loss is just their sum, area e. This loss is the decrease in export revenue because the world price has fallen to P^*; Home loses the difference between P^W and P^* on each of X_2 units exported. So a large country loses even more from a subsidy than a small country because of the reduction in the world price of its exported good.

Foreign and World Welfare While Home definitely loses from the subsidy, the Foreign importing country definitely gains. Panel (b) of Figure 10-2 illustrates the consumer surplus benefit to Foreign of the Home subsidy; the price of Foreign imports decreases and Foreign's terms of trade improves. The change in consumer surplus for Foreign is area *e′*, the area below its import demand curve M^* and between the free-trade world price P^W and the new world price (with subsidy) P^*.

When we combine the total Home consumption and production losses $(b + d)$ plus the Home terms-of-trade loss *e*, and subtract the Foreign terms-of-trade gain *e′*, there is an overall deadweight loss for the world, which is measured by the area $(b + d + f)$ in panel (b). The area *f* is the additional world deadweight loss due to the subsidy, which arises because the terms-of-trade loss in Home is not completely offset by a terms-of-trade gain in Foreign.

Because there is a transfer of terms of trade from Home to Foreign, the export subsidy might seem like a good policy tool for large wealthy countries seeking to give aid to poorer countries. However, this turns out not to be the case. The deadweight loss *f* means that using the export subsidy to increase Home production and send the excess exported goods overseas (as was the case for food aid, discussed earlier as an example of an indirect subsidy) is an inefficient way to transfer gains from trade among countries. It would be more efficient to simply give cash aid in the amount of the Home terms-of-trade loss to poor importers, a policy approach that, because it does not change the free-trade levels of production and consumption in either country, would avoid the deadweight loss $(b + d + f)$ associated with the subsidy. This argument is made by the European countries, which, several years ago, eliminated transfers of food as a form of aid and switched to cash payments. The United States has now agreed to make the same policy change, as discussed in the following application.

APPLICATION

Who Gains and Who Loses?

Now that we have studied the effect of export subsidies on world prices and trade volume in theory, we return to the agreements of the Hong Kong meeting of the WTO in December 2005 and ask: Which countries will gain and which will lose when export subsidies (including the "indirect" subsidies like food aid) are eliminated by 2013?

Gains The obvious gainers from this action will be current agricultural exporters in developing countries such as Brazil, Argentina, Indonesia, and Thailand, along with potential exporters such as India and China. These countries will gain from the rise in world prices as agricultural subsidies by the industrialized countries—especially Europe and the United States—are eliminated. These countries will gain even more when and if an agreement is reached on the elimination of agricultural tariffs in the industrial countries, including Japan and South Korea, that protect crops such as rice. Both of these actions will also benefit the industrial countries themselves, which suffer both a deadweight loss *and* a terms-of-trade loss from the combination of export subsidies and import tariffs in agriculture. Farmers in the industrial countries who lose the subsidies will be worse off, and the government might choose to offset that loss with some type of adjustment assistance. In the United States and Europe, however, it is often the largest farmers who benefit the most from subsidy programs, and they may be better able to adjust to the elimination of subsidies (through switching to other crops) than small farmers.

Losses Which countries will lose from the elimination of export subsidies? To the extent that the elimination of export subsidies leads to higher world prices, as we expect from our analysis (in Figure 10-2, the price would rise from P^* to P^W), then the food-importing countries, typically the poorer non-food-producing countries, will lose. This theoretical result is confirmed by several empirical studies. One study found that the existing pattern of agricultural supports (tariffs and subsidies) raises the per capita income of two-thirds of 77 developing nations, including most of the poorest countries, such as Burundi and Zambia.[3] This result is illustrated in Figure 10-3. Panel (a) shows net agricultural exports graphed against countries' income per capita over the period 1990 to 2000. The poorer countries (i.e., those lower on the income scale on the horizontal axis) export more agricultural products and therefore would benefit from a rise in their prices. But for *food* exports in panel (b), rather than *total agricultural* exports, it is the middle-income countries that export the most. Panel (c) shows that poor countries are *net importers* of essential food items such as corn, rice, and wheat (summarized as "cereal exports") and would be harmed by an increase in their world price. Many of the world's poorest individuals depend on cereal crops for much of their diet and would be especially hard hit by any increase in those prices.

Food Aid What about indirect subsidies such as food aid? The United States has been a principal supplier of food aid, which it uses for both humanitarian purposes and to get rid of surpluses of commodities at home. No country will argue with the need for donations in cases of starvation, as have occurred recently in the Darfur region of Sudan and in 1984 in Ethiopia, but the United States also provides food shipments to regions without shortages, an action that can depress local prices and harm local producers. European countries stopped this practice many years ago and argue that it is better to instead have United Nations relief agencies buy food from local farmers in poor regions and then distribute it to the poorest individuals in a country. In this way, the European countries boost production in the country and help to feed its poorest citizens. In the Hong Kong talks, the European Union insisted that the indirect subsidies to regions without shortages be eliminated by 2013, along with direct export subsidies, and the United States agreed to this goal.

Even though the proposals from the Hong Kong talks were never ratified, and the Doha Round of negotiations is still ongoing, some recent progress has been made toward the goal of replacing food aid with efforts to increase production. At a 2009 meeting of the Group of Eight (G8)[4] countries, pledges were made to increase funding for agricultural development by $12 billion per year, as described in **Headlines: G8 Shifts Focus from Food Aid to Farming.** This pledge represents a shift in focus away from food aid and toward agricultural sustainability in developing countries. As the **Headlines** article describes, it is a major shift in focus for the United States, where 20 times more money has been spent on food aid then on projects to increase local production.

Despite this recent announcement, however, many observers remain skeptical that the funding for agricultural development in poor countries will be forthcoming. After the G8 summit many editorials appeared challenging these countries to

[3] Margaret McMillan, Alix Peterson Zwane, and Nava Ashraf, 2007, "My Policies or Yours: Have OECD Agricultural Policies Affected Incomes in Developing Countries?" In Ann Harrison, *Globalization and Poverty* [Chicago: University of Chicago Press and National Bureau of Economic Research (NBER)], pp. 183–232.

[4] The G8 countries consist of Canada, France, Germany, Italy, Japan, Russia, the United Kingdom, and the United States. In addition, the European Union as a whole is represented at the G8.

FIGURE 10-3

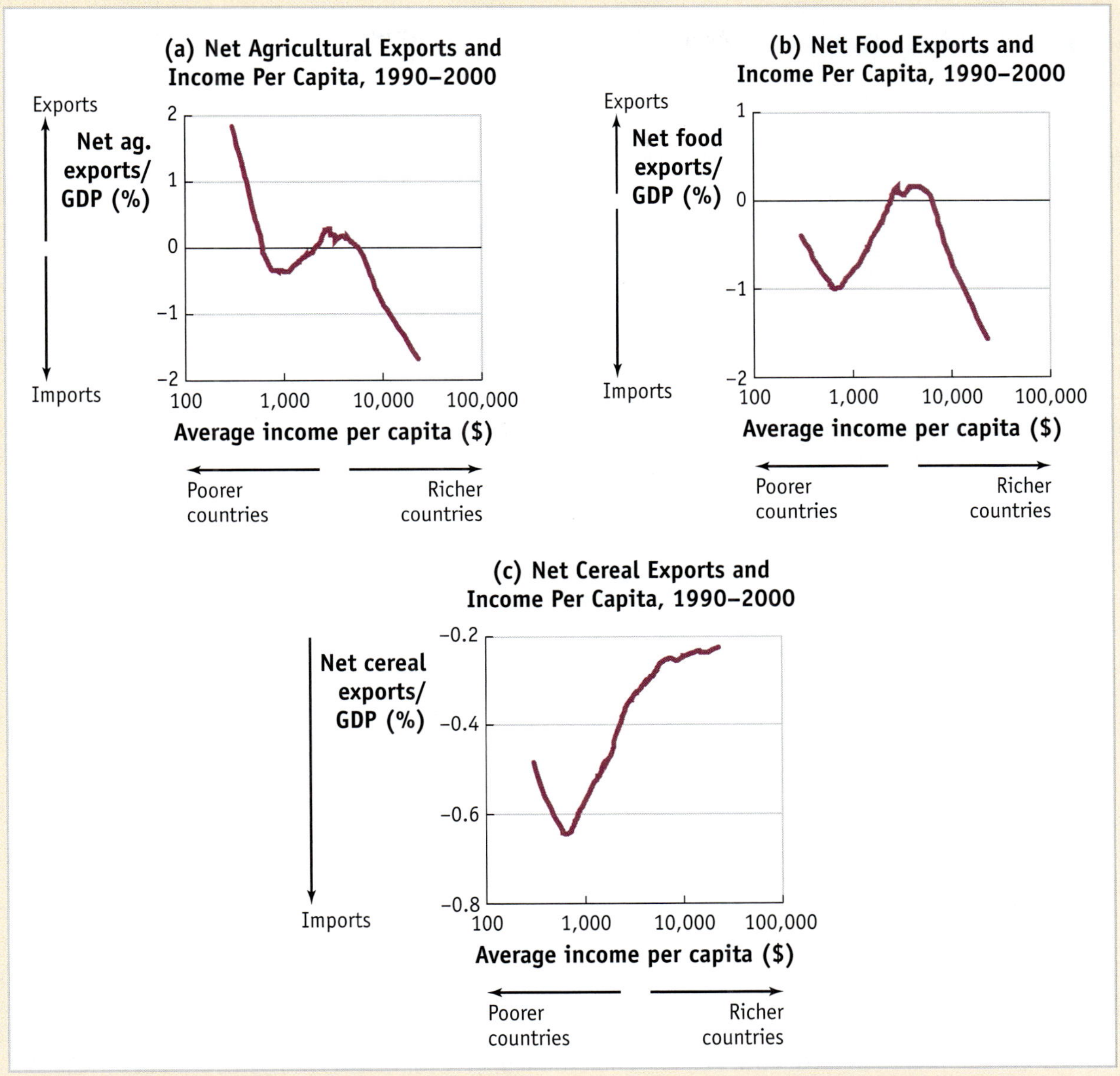

Agriculture, Food, and Cereal Exports Panel (a) shows net agricultural exports graphed against countries' income per capita. The poorer countries export more agricultural products overall and would thus benefit from a rise in the prices due to the removal of subsidies. On the other hand, panel (b) shows that it is middle-income countries that export the most food. Panel (c) shows that poor countries are net *importers* of essential food items (cereals) such as corn, rice, and wheat and would be harmed by an increase in their world price.

Source: Margaret McMillan, Alix Peterson Zwane, and Nava Ashraf, 2007, "My Policies or Yours: Have OECD Agricultural Policies Affected Incomes in Developing Countries?" In Ann Harrison, Globalization and Poverty *(Chicago: University of Chicago Press and NBER), pp. 183–232.*

follow through on their pledges. We include one of these editorials in **Headlines: Hunger and Food Security Back on Political Agenda**, written by the chairman of the European Food Security Group, a network of 40 European nongovernmental organizations (NGOs). ■

HEADLINES

G8 Shifts Focus from Food Aid to Farming

This article announces a new "food security initiative" from the G8 countries, who promised billions of dollars to assist farmers in developing countries. As the next Headlines article describes, however, not all observers believe that these funds will be forthcoming, despite the overwhelming need for the assistance.

The G8 countries will this week announce a "food security initiative," committing more than $12 [billion] for agricultural development over the next three years, in a move that signals a further shift from food aid to long-term investments in farming in the developing world. The US and Japan will provide the bulk of the funding, with $3–$4 [billion] each, with the rest coming from Europe and Canada, according to United Nations officials and Group of Eight diplomats briefed on the "L'Aquila Food Security Initiative." Officials said it would more than triple spending. . . .

The G8 initiative underscores Washington's new approach to fighting global hunger, reversing a two-decades-old policy focused almost exclusively on food aid. Hillary Clinton, US secretary of state, and Tom Vilsack, the agriculture secretary, have both highlighted the shifting emphasis in recent speeches. "For too long, our primary response [to fight hunger] has been to send emergency [food] aid when the crisis is at its worst," Ms. Clinton said last month. "This saves lives, but it doesn't address hunger's root causes. It is, at best, a short-term fix."

Washington's shift could prove contentious in the US, as its farmers are the largest exporters of several crops, including soyabean and corn. The US is the world's largest donor of food aid—mainly crops grown by US farmers, costing more than $2 [billion] last year. The Chicago Council on Global Affairs, a think-tank, estimates that Washington spends 20 times more on food aid than on long-term schemes in Africa to boost local food production. US annual spending on African farming projects topped $400 [million] in the 1980s, but by 2006 had dwindled to $60 [million], the council said in a report this year. . . .

Source: Excerpted from Javier Blas, "G8 Shifts Focus from Food Aid to Farming," Financial Times, *July 6, 2009, p. 1.*

4 Agricultural Production Subsidies

The agreements reached in Hong Kong distinguish between export subsidies in agriculture—which will be eliminated—and all other forms of domestic support that increase production (e.g., tax incentives and other types of subsidy). The reason this distinction is made is that other forms of support in agriculture are expected to have less impact on exports than direct subsidies. Therefore, there is less impact on other countries from having domestic support programs as compared with export subsidies. To illustrate this idea, let's examine the impact of a "production subsidy" in agriculture for both a small and a large country.

Suppose the government provides a subsidy of s dollars for *every unit* (e.g., ton of sugar in our example) that a Home firm produces. This is a **production subsidy** because it is a subsidy to every unit produced and not just to units that are exported. There are several ways that a government can implement such a subsidy. The government might guarantee a minimum price to the farmer, for example, and make up the difference between the minimum price and any lower price for which the farmer sells. Alternatively, the government might provide subsidies to users of the crop to purchase it, thus increasing demand and raising market prices; this would act like a subsidy to every unit produced. As mentioned earlier, the United States has used both methods to support its cotton growers.

HEADLINES

Hunger and Food Security Back on Political Agenda

This article expresses skepticism that the promises of the G8 countries for billions of dollars to assist farmers in developing countries will be forthcoming.

Global food security is a political and economic priority for the first time since the early 1970s. That should be the key message from the decision by the G8 group of leading economic nations to endorse a "food security initiative" at their meeting in Italy this week. But this welcome decision needs to be followed up by further significant policy change at national and international level if food security is to be achieved for the world's growing population over the coming decades. . . .

It is reported that the initiative will involve a commitment of $12 billion for agricultural development over the next three years. But before giving three cheers for the G8, two critical questions must be answered. Is the $12 billion additional resources or a repackaging of existing commitments? How can this initiative feed into sustained policy change aimed at increasing food security at household, national and global level?

Policy change is necessary in many countries which are currently food insecure. Investment in agricultural and rural development has been shamefully neglected over the past 30 years. Donors, including the World Bank, also bear responsibility for this. There must now be an acceptance that budget allocations to agriculture must increase and must be sustained. . . . The history of such summits is not good: the gap between the promises and subsequent actions is great. At the first such summit in 1974, Dr. Henry Kissinger made the pledge that "within 10 years, no child will go to bed hungry."

The G8 food security initiative at least provides a positive backdrop to the summit. It should provide an opportunity to many developing countries to commit to the type of policy change necessary to increase their own food security. With one billion hungry people in the world, with growing populations and with the threat that climate change presents to agricultural production capacity, such a commitment is both critical and urgent. It is good politics and good economics to do so.

Source: Excerpted from Tom Arnold, "Hunger and Food Security Back on Political Agenda," The Irish Times, *July 8, 2009, electronic edition.*

These policies all fall under Article XVI of the GATT (see **Side Bar: Key Provisions of the GATT in Chapter 8**). Article XVI states that partner countries should be notified of the extent of such subsidies, and when possible, they should be limited. In Hong Kong, the WTO members further agreed to classify countries according to the extent of such subsidies, with the European Union classified as having a high level of production subsidies, the United States and Japan having a middle level, and all other countries having low subsidies (see Table 10-1). Future discussion will determine the timing and extent of cuts in these production subsidies.

Effect of a Production Subsidy in a Small Home Country

To illustrate the effect of a production subsidy, we begin with a small country that faces a fixed world price of P^W. In Figure 10-4, panel (a), the production subsidy of s increases the price received by Home producers to $P^W + s$ and increases Home's quantity supplied from S_1 to S_2. The quantity *demanded* at Home does not change, however, because producers *continue to charge the world price* at Home. This is the case (in contrast to the export subsidy) because Home producers receive a subsidy regardless of whom they sell to (domestic consumers or Foreign consumers through exporting). So with a production subsidy, Home producers charge the world price to Foreign consumers and receive the extra subsidy from the government and likewise charge the world price to Home consumers, and again receive the extra subsidy. In contrast, for an export subsidy, Home firms receive the subsidy *only* for export sales and not for domestic sales.

Because the price for Home consumers with the production subsidy is still P^W, there is no change in the quantity demanded at Home, which remains at D_1. In panel (b), we see that the production subsidy increases the quantity of exports from $X_1 = S_1 - D_1$ to $X_2 = S_2 - D_1$. Because demand is not affected, the production subsidy increases exports by less than an export subsidy would. That result occurs because the quantity demanded decreases with an export subsidy due to higher Home prices, leading to greater Home exports. In contrast, with the production subsidy, the quantity demanded at Home is unchanged, so exports do not rise as much.

FIGURE 10-4

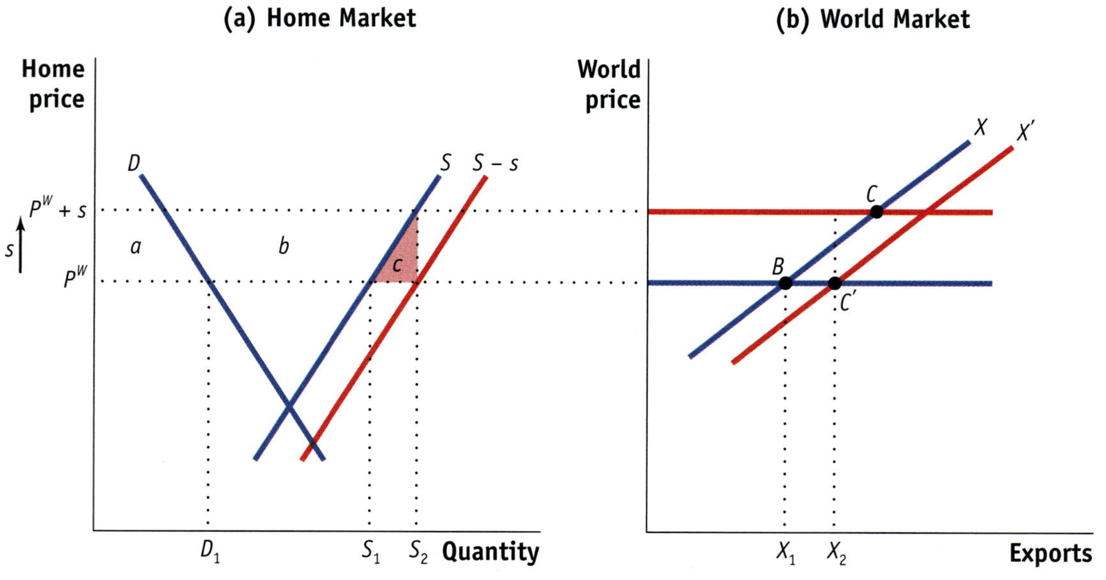

Production Subsidy for a Small Country In panel (a), applying a production subsidy of s dollars per unit produced will increase the price that Home firms receive from P^W to $P^W + s$. This price rise leads to an increase in Home quantity supplied from S_1 to S_2. The consumer price at Home is not affected because the production subsidy does not distinguish between items sold at Home or exported (firms therefore continue to charge the world price at Home), so the quantity demanded stays at D_1. The deadweight loss of the subsidy for a small country is the area c. In panel (b), exports rise as a result of the production subsidy, from X_1 to X_2, though the increase in exports is less than for the export subsidy because, for the production subsidy, quantity demanded does not change at Home.

Home Welfare With the increase in the price received by Home producers, from P^W to $P^W + s$, there is a corresponding rise in producer surplus of the amount $(a + b)$ in panel (a). The government revenue cost of the subsidy is the entire area $(a + b + c)$, which equals the amount of the subsidy s, times Home production S_2. So the overall impact of the production subsidy is

Change in consumer surplus:	*none* (because demand is not affected)
Rise in producer surplus:	$+ (a + b)$
Fall in government revenue:	$- (a + b + c)$
Net effect on Home welfare:	$- c$

The deadweight loss caused by the production subsidy in a small country, area c, is less than that caused by the export subsidy in Figure 10-1, which is area $(b + d)$. The reason that the production subsidy has a lower deadweight loss than the export subsidy is that consumer decisions have not been affected at all: Home consumers still face the price of P^W. The production subsidy increases the quantity supplied by Home producers, just as an export subsidy does, but the production subsidy does so without raising the price for Home consumers. The only deadweight loss is in production inefficiency: the higher subsidized price encourages Home producers to increase the amount of production at higher marginal costs (i.e., farther right along the supply curve) than would occur in a market equilibrium without the subsidy.

Targeting Principle Our finding that the deadweight loss is lower for the production subsidy makes it a better policy instrument than the export subsidy to achieve an increase in Home supply. This finding is an example of the **targeting principle:** *to achieve some objective, it is best to use the policy instrument that achieves the objective most directly*. If the objective of the Home government is to increase cotton supply, for example, and therefore benefit cotton growers, it is better to use a production subsidy than an export subsidy. Of course, the benefits to cotton growers come at the expense of government revenue.

There are many examples of this targeting principle in economics. To limit the consumption of cigarettes and improve public health, the best policy is a tax on cigarette purchases, as many countries use. To reduce pollution from automobiles, the best policy would be a tax on gasoline, the magnitude of which is much higher in Europe than in the United States. And, to use an example from this book, to compensate people for losses from international trade, it is better to provide trade adjustment assistance directly (discussed in Chapter 3) to those affected than to impose an import tariff or quota.

Effect of the Production Subsidy in a Large Home Country

We will not draw the large-country case in detail but will use Figure 10-4 to briefly explain the effects of a production subsidy on prices, exports, and welfare. When the price for Home producers rises from P^W to $P^W + s$, the quantity of the exported good supplied increases from S_1 to S_2. Because demand has not changed, exports increase by exactly the same amount as the quantity supplied by domestic producers. We show that increase in exports by the outward shift of the export supply curve, from X to X' in panel (b). As mentioned previously, the rise in the quantity of exports due to the production subsidy, from point B to C' in Figure 10-4, is *less than* the increase in the quantity of exports for the export subsidy, from point B to C' shown in Figure 10-1. With the export subsidy, the price for Home producers *and* consumers rose to $P^W + s$, so exports increased because of both the rise in quantity supplied and the drop in quantity demanded. As a result, the export subsidy shifted down the Home export supply curve by exactly the amount s in Figure 10-1. In contrast, with a production subsidy, exports rise only because Home quantity supplied increases so that export supply shifts down by an amount less than s in Figure 10-4.

If we drew a downward-sloping Foreign import demand curve in panel (b), then the increase in supply as a result of the production subsidy would lower the world price. But that drop in world price would be *less than* the drop that occurred with the export subsidy because the increase in exports under the production subsidy is less.

Summary Production subsidies in agriculture still lower world prices, but they lower prices by less than export subsidies. For this reason, the WTO is less concerned with eliminating production subsidies and other forms of domestic support for agriculture. These policies have a smaller impact on world prices and, as we have also shown, a smaller deadweight loss as compared with that of export subsidies.

5 High-Technology Export Subsidies

We turn now from the discussion of export subsidies in agriculture to consider an industry at the other end of the technological spectrum: high-technology products. That sector of the economy also receives substantial assistance from the government, with examples including subsidies to the aircraft industries in both the United States and Europe. In the United States, subsidies take the form of low-interest loans provided by the Export-Import Bank (a U.S. government agency that finances export-related projects) to foreign firms or governments that want to purchase aircraft from Seattle-based Boeing. On the European side, government support for research and development (R&D) and other subsidies are given to Airbus, which produces parts and assembles its finished products in a number of European countries. In Japan and South Korea, direct subsidies have been given to high-tech manufacturing firms that achieved certain targets for increasing their export sales. High-tech subsidies are given by many other countries, too.

Why do governments support their high-technology industries? In the case of agricultural products, subsidies are instituted primarily because of the political clout of those industries. Although politics also plays a role in subsidies for high-tech industries, governments also subsidize these industries because they may create benefits that spill over to other firms in the economy. That is, governments believe that high-tech industry produces a positive **externality.** This argument for a subsidy is similar to the infant industry argument used to justify protective tariffs (see Chapter 9), except that the protection is applied to an export industry rather than an import-competing industry.

"Strategic" Use of High-Tech Export Subsidies

In addition to the spillover argument for export subsidies, governments and industries also argue that export subsidies might give a **strategic advantage** to export firms that are competing with a small number of rivals in international markets. By a strategic advantage, we mean that the subsidized industry can compete more effectively with its rivals on the world market. Think of the aircraft industry, which currently has just two producers of large, wide-body airplanes: Boeing in the United States and Airbus in Europe. Each of these firms receives some type of subsidy from its government. If high-tech subsidies allow firms to compete more effectively and earn more profits in international markets, and if the extra profits are more than the amount of the subsidy, then the exporting country will obtain an overall benefit from the export subsidy, similar to the benefit when a large country applies a tariff.

To examine whether countries can use their subsidies strategically, we use the assumption of **imperfect competition.** We already used this assumption in Chapter 9, in which we considered the cases of Home monopoly and Foreign monopoly. Now we allow for two firms in the market, which is called a **duopoly.** In that case, each firm can set the price and quantity of its output (and hence maximize its profits) based on the price and quantity decisions of the other firm. When a government uses subsidies to affect this interaction between firms and to increase the profits of its own domestic firm, the government is said to be acting strategically. In this section, we examine the effects of strategic export subsidies to determine whether profits of the exporting firm will rise enough to offset the cost of the subsidy to the government.

Because we are now assuming that certain high-tech industries operate in imperfectly competitive markets, we will need to use a different set of tools to model their supply decisions than we have thus far in this chapter. To capture the strategic decision making of two firms, we use **game theory,** the modeling of strategic interactions (games) between firms as they choose actions that will maximize their returns. The main goal in this section is to model the strategic interaction of high-tech firms in Home and Foreign, and then to see the impact of export subsidies on their respective decisions and payoffs.

To examine the effect of an export subsidy, we start with the free-trade situation, before any subsidies are in place. Suppose there are two firms that are competing for sales of a new type of aircraft. For example, Airbus recently began selling the double-decker A380, and Boeing is developing a smaller aircraft called the 787 Dreamliner (discussed later in the chapter). For convenience, we focus on the decision of each firm to develop a new aircraft that competes with the other firm for sales to the rest of the world. By ignoring sales to their own countries, we will not have to keep track of consumer surplus in the United States or Europe. Instead, the measure of welfare for these countries will depend only on the profits earned by Boeing or Airbus from their sales to the rest of the world.

Payoff Matrix In Figure 10-5, we show a **payoff matrix** for Boeing and Airbus, each of which has to decide whether to produce the new aircraft. Each quadrant of the matrix shows the profit earned by Boeing in the lower-left corner and the profits of Airbus in the upper-right corner. When both firms produce (upper-left quadrant), their prices are reduced through competition, and they both end up making negative profits (i.e., losses) of \$5 million.[5]

If Airbus produces the new aircraft and Boeing does not (lower-left quadrant), then Boeing earns nothing, whereas Airbus, the only supplier, earns high profits of \$100 million. Conversely, if Boeing produces and Airbus does not (upper-right quadrant),

[5] The numbers we are using in the payoff matrix are made up for convenience, but they illustrate the idea of competition between the firms for the sale of a new aircraft.

FIGURE 10-5

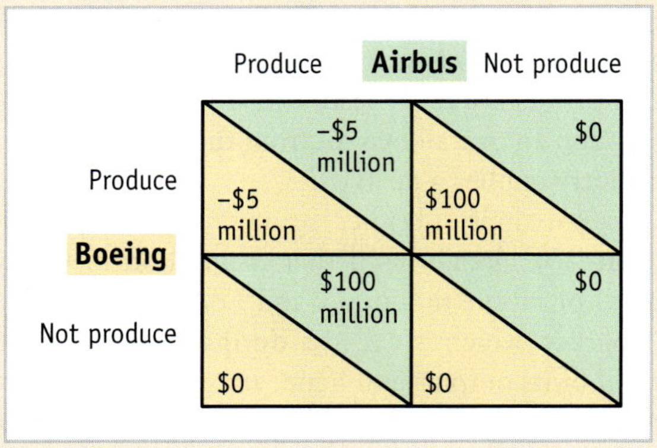

Payoff Matrix between Two Firms The lower-left number in each quadrant shows the profits of Boeing, and the upper-right number shows the profits of Airbus. Each firm must decide whether to produce a new type of aircraft. A Nash equilibrium occurs when each firm is making its best decision, given the action of the other. For this pattern of payoffs, there are two Nash equilibria, in the upper-right and lower-left quadrants, where one firm produces and the other does not.

Airbus earns nothing, and Boeing, now the only supplier, earns high profits of $100 million. Finally, if both firms choose to not produce (lower-right quadrant), then they both earn profits of 0.

Nash Equilibrium With the pattern of payoffs shown in Figure 10-5, we want to determine what the outcome of this game between the two firms will be. At first glance, this seems like a difficult problem. It is hard for each firm to decide what to do without knowing whether the other firm is going to produce. To solve this problem, we use the concept of the Nash equilibrium, named after John Nash, a winner of the Nobel Prize in economics.[6]

The idea of a **Nash equilibrium** is that each firm must make its own best decision, taking as given each possible action of the rival firm. When each firm is acting that way, the outcome of the game is a Nash equilibrium. That is, the action of each player is the best possible response to the action of the other player.

Best Strategy for Boeing To determine the Nash equilibrium, we proceed by checking each quadrant of the payoff matrix. Let us look at Boeing's possible strategies, starting with the case in which its rival, Airbus, chooses to produce. If Boeing knows that Airbus will produce, then Boeing needs to decide whether to produce or not. If Boeing produces, then it earns –$5 million (in the upper-left quadrant); if Boeing does not produce, then it earns 0 (in the lower-left quadrant). Therefore, if Airbus produces, then Boeing is better off *not* producing. This finding proves that having both firms produce is not a Nash equilibrium. Boeing would never stay in production, since it prefers to drop out of the market whenever Airbus produces.

Best Strategy for Airbus Let's continue with the case in which Boeing does not produce but Airbus does (lower-left quadrant of Figure 10-5). Is this the best strategy for Airbus? To check this, suppose that Airbus chooses instead to not produce. That would move us from the lower-left quadrant to the lower-right quadrant in Figure 10-5, meaning that Airbus's profits fall from $100 million to 0. This outcome is worse for Airbus, so it would not change its decision: it would still choose to

[6] The book and movie *A Beautiful Mind* describes the career of John Nash.

produce. We conclude that the decision illustrated in the lower-left quadrant, with Airbus producing and Boeing not producing, is a Nash equilibrium because each firm is making its best decision given what the other is doing. When Airbus produces, then Boeing's best response is to not produce, and when Boeing does not produce, then Airbus's best response is to produce. There is no reason for either firm to change its behavior from the Nash equilibrium.

Multiple Equilibria Is it possible to find more than one Nash equilibrium? To check for this, we need to check the other quadrants in Figure 10-5. Let us try the case in the upper-right quadrant, where Boeing produces but Airbus does not. Consider Airbus making the decision to produce or not, given that Boeing produces, or Boeing making the decision to produce or not, given that Airbus does not produce. Using the same logic we have already gone through, you can confirm that neither firm would want to change the decision it has made as seen in the upper-right quadrant: if either firm changed its choice, its profits would fall. If Boeing decides not to produce, then its profits fall to 0 (from the upper-right to the lower-right quadrant), whereas if Airbus decides to produce, its profits fall to –$5 million (from the upper-right to the upper-left quadrant). So we conclude that the upper-right quadrant, with Boeing producing and Airbus not producing, is *also* a Nash equilibrium. When Boeing produces, then Airbus's best response is to not produce, and when Airbus does not produce, then Boeing's best response is to produce. Finally, by applying the same logic to the other quadrants, we can confirm that there are no more Nash equilibria.

When there are two Nash equilibria, there must be some force from outside the model that determines in which equilibrium we are. An example of one such force is the **first mover advantage,** which means that one firm is able to decide whether or not to produce before the other firm. If Boeing had this advantage, it would choose to produce, and Airbus, as the second mover, would not produce, so we would be in the upper-right quadrant. Let us suppose that is the Nash equilibrium from which we start. Because Airbus is not producing, it is making zero profits. In this situation, the government in Europe might want to try to change the Nash equilibrium so that Airbus would instead earn positive profits. That is, by providing subsidies to Airbus, we want to determine whether the payoffs in the matrix change such that the Nash equilibrium also changes.

The type of subsidy we consider in our model is a cash payment to Airbus. In practice, however, subsidies are of many kinds: Boeing has benefited from U.S. military contracts, where the R&D done for those contracts has been used in its civilian aircraft, too. Airbus, on the other hand, has benefited from direct R&D subsidies to defray the "launch costs" of getting a new aircraft off the ground. Both companies have benefited from low-cost loans provided by their governments to purchasers of aircraft. Later in the chapter, we examine in more detail actual export subsidies that are used in the aircraft industry.

Effect of a Subsidy to Airbus

Suppose the European governments provide a subsidy of $25 million to Airbus. With this subsidy in place, Airbus's profits will increase by $25 million when it produces. In Figure 10-6, we add that amount to the payoffs for Airbus and check to see whether the Nash equilibria have changed. Recall that the free-trade Nash equilibria occur when one firm produces and the other does not.

FIGURE 10-6

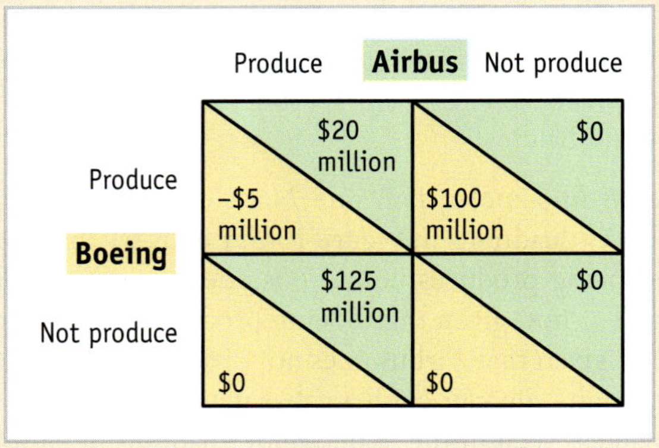

Payoff Matrix with Foreign Subsidy When the European governments provide a subsidy of $25 million to Airbus, its profits increase by that much when it produces a new aircraft. Now there is only one Nash equilibrium, in the lower-left quadrant, with Airbus producing but Boeing not producing. The profits for Airbus have increased from 0 to $125 million, while the subsidy cost only $25 million, so there is a net gain of $100 million in European welfare.

Best Strategy for Airbus Let us start with the free-trade Nash equilibrium in which Boeing produces but Airbus does not (upper-right quadrant) and see whether it changes when Airbus receives a government subsidy. After the subsidy, that option is no longer a Nash equilibrium: if Boeing is producing, then Airbus is now better off by *also* producing because then it receives a $25 million subsidy from the government. With the subsidy, it will now earn $20 million ($5 million in negative profits plus the $25 million subsidy) even when Boeing produces. Recall that in the original situation, if Boeing produced, then Airbus would not choose to produce because otherwise it would lose $5 million. With the subsidy, Airbus now earns $20 million by producing instead of losing $5 million.

Best Strategy for Boeing Is this new position a Nash equilibrium? To answer that, we need to see whether Boeing would still be making the right decision given that Airbus is producing. When Airbus produces, Boeing loses $5 million when it produces (upper-left quadrant) but loses nothing when it does not produce (lower-left quadrant). Therefore, Boeing will want to drop out of the market. Once Boeing makes the decision not to produce, Airbus's decision doesn't change. It still chooses to produce, but its payoff increases dramatically from $20 million to $125 million, and we move to the lower-left quadrant, with Airbus producing and Boeing not.

Nash Equilibrium You can readily check that the lower-left quadrant is a unique Nash equilibrium: each firm is making its best decision, given the action of the other. Furthermore, it is the *only* Nash equilibrium. The effect of the European governments' subsidy has been to shift the equilibrium from having Boeing as the only producer (where we started, in the upper right) to having Airbus as the only producer (in the lower-left quadrant).

European Welfare The European subsidy has had a big impact on the equilibrium of the game being played between the two firms. But can we necessarily conclude that Europe is better off? To evaluate that, we need to add up the welfare of the various parties involved, much as we did earlier in the chapter.

The calculation of European welfare is simplified, however, because of our assumption that production is for export to the rest of the world. From Europe's point of view, we do not need to worry about the effect of the subsidy on consumer surplus in its own market. The only two items left to evaluate, then, are the profits for Airbus from its sales to the rest of the world and the cost of the subsidy to the European government.

Airbus's profits have increased from 0 (when it was not producing but Boeing was) to \$125 million (now that Airbus is producing but Boeing is not). The revenue cost of the subsidy to Europe is \$25 million. Therefore, the net effect of the subsidy on European welfare is

Rise in producer profits:	+ 125
Fall in government revenue:	– 25
Net effect on European welfare:	**+ 100**

In this case, the subsidy led to a net gain in European welfare because the increase in profits for Airbus is more than the cost of the subsidy.[7]

Subsidy with Cost Advantage for Boeing

Our finding that the subsidy can raise European welfare depends on the numbers we assumed so far, however. Let us now consider another case in which Boeing has a cost advantage over Airbus. In this case, we assume that the cost advantage is the result not of U.S. subsidies but of U.S. comparative advantage in aircraft production.

When Boeing has a cost advantage in aircraft production, the payoff matrix is as shown in Figure 10-7. Boeing earns profits of \$5 million when both firms produce and profits of \$125 million when Airbus does not produce. There is now only one Nash equilibrium, and it is in the upper-right quadrant in which Boeing produces and Airbus does not. The alternative free-trade Nash equilibrium in Figure 10-5 (in which Airbus produces and Boeing does not) is no longer a Nash equilibrium because, with the cost advantage we are now assuming Boeing has, even if Airbus chooses to produce, it is better for Boeing to produce and earn profits of \$5 million than not produce and earn 0 profits.

FIGURE 10-7

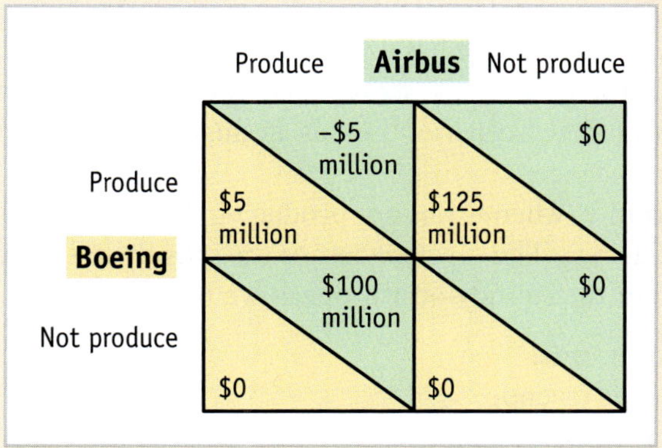

Another Payoff Matrix, with Boeing Cost Advantage If Boeing has a cost advantage in the production of aircraft, the payoffs are as shown here. Boeing earns profits of \$5 million when both firms are producing and profits of \$125 million when Airbus does not produce. Now there is only one Nash equilibrium, in the upper-right quadrant, where Boeing produces and Airbus does not.

[7] Notice that if the initial equilibrium was one in which Airbus produced and Boeing did not, then the only effect of the subsidy would be to make this equilibrium unique; it would not change the decision of either firm. Moreover, the effect on total European welfare would be zero because the subsidy would be just a transfer from the European government to Airbus.

FIGURE 10-8

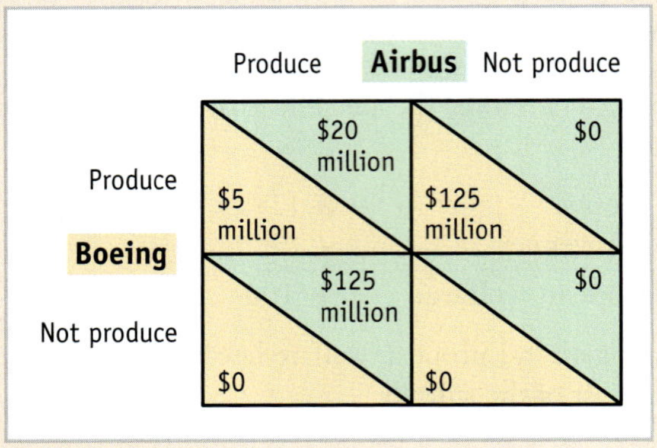

Another Payoff Matrix with Foreign Subsidy When the European governments provide a subsidy of $25 million to Airbus, its profits increase by that much when it produces. Now the only Nash equilibrium is in the upper-left quadrant, where both firms produce. The profits for Airbus have increased from 0 to $20 million, but the subsidy costs $25 million, so there is a net loss of $5 million in European welfare.

Now suppose, once again, that the European governments provide a $25 million subsidy to Airbus. We add that amount to the payoffs of Airbus when it produces (still assuming that Boeing has a cost advantage over Airbus), as shown in Figure 10-8.

Best Strategy for Airbus Let's see how the subsidy has affected the previous Nash equilibrium in which Boeing produces and Airbus does not (upper-right quadrant). Given that Boeing produces, the decision to not produce is no longer the best one for Airbus: with the subsidy now in place and Boeing producing, Airbus's best decision is to produce and to earn profits of $20 million (upper-left quadrant) rather than 0.

Best Strategy for Boeing

Is this new position a Nash equilibrium? Once again, we need to check to see whether, given Airbus's new postsubsidy decision to produce, Boeing is still making the right decision. Given that Airbus produces, then Boeing earns profits of $5 million when it produces and 0 when it does not. Therefore, Boeing will stay in the market, and we have proved that having both firms produce is a Nash equilibrium.

European Welfare Once Again When Boeing has a cost advantage, the European subsidy allows Airbus to enter the market, but it *has not* resulted in the exit of Boeing as it did in the earlier no-cost-advantage scenario. Let us evaluate the effect on European welfare under these circumstances.

Airbus's profits have increased from 0 (when it was not producing, but Boeing was) to 20 (now that both firms are producing). The revenue cost of the subsidy to Europe is still 25. Therefore, the net effect of the subsidy on European welfare is

Rise in producer profits:	+ 20
Fall in government revenue:	– 25
Net effect on European welfare:	**– 5**

When Boeing has a cost advantage, then, the subsidy leads to a *net loss* in European welfare because the increase in profits for Airbus is less than the cost of the subsidy.

Summary The lessons that we should draw from these various examples is that under conditions of imperfect competition, a subsidy by one government to its exporting firm might increase welfare for its nation, but it might not. Although profits for the exporting firm certainly rise, there is an increase in welfare only if profits rise by more than the cost of the subsidy. This condition is more likely to be satisfied if the subsidy leads to the *exit* of the other firm from the market. In that case, the profits earned by the single firm could very well exceed the cost of the subsidy. When both firms remain in the market after the subsidy, however, it is unlikely that the increase in profits for the subsidized firm will exceed the subsidy cost. In the following application, we are especially interested in whether subsidies in the aircraft industry have kept one firm out of a market segment in which another produces.

APPLICATION

Subsidies to Commercial Aircraft

In the large passenger aircraft industry, there have been just three competitors: Boeing and McDonnell-Douglas in the United States and Airbus in Europe. The former two companies merged on August 1, 1997, so the industry effectively became a duopoly. The United States and Europe have used various types of subsidies to support their respective firms. First, there are indirect subsidies that arise because in the production of civilian and military aircraft, the research and development (R&D) for the military versions effectively subsidize R&D for the civilian aircraft. These indirect subsidies have benefited both McDonnell-Douglas and Boeing in the United States. Second, the government might directly subsidize the R&D costs of a new aircraft, as Europe subsidizes R&D at Airbus. Third, the government can subsidize the interest rates that aircraft buyers pay when they borrow money to purchase aircraft. Europe and the United States both provide such low-interest loans, for instance, through the Export-Import Bank in the United States as mentioned previously.

1992 Agreement Recognizing that these subsidies are ultimately costly, the United States and the European Community reached an agreement to limit them in 1992. The main features of this agreement are summarized in Table 10-2. Development subsidies are limited to 33% of the total development costs of a new aircraft, and it is expected that the aircraft manufacturers will repay these subsidies at the government interest rate. In addition, the agreement limits indirect (military) subsidies to not more than 4% of any firm's annual sales, prohibits production subsidies, and limits the ability of government agencies to subsidize the interest rate on purchases of aircraft. According to one estimate, this agreement reduced subsidies by between 7.5 and 12.5% of the costs of production. As a result of the reduction in subsidies, prices for aircraft rose by somewhere between 3.1 and 8.8%. This agreement between the United States and Europe benefited the countries' governments because they no longer had to spend the money on the subsidies, and most likely also benefited the aircraft companies because prices rose, but the higher prices led to welfare losses for the purchasing countries.

The Superjumbo There are recent claims that the terms of the 1992 agreement were violated by Airbus as it launched its newest aircraft: the double-decker A380, which is even larger than the Boeing 747 and will compete directly with the 747 in long flights. This "superjumbo" aircraft carries up to 555 passengers and consists of two passenger decks for its entire length. Its first test flight in Europe took place in April 2005, and its first commercial flight to the United States was in March 2007.

The expenditures to develop the A380 are estimated to have been $12 billion, one-third of which the governments of France, Germany, the Netherlands, Belgium,

TABLE 10-2

Provisions of the 1992 Agreement between the United States and the European Community on Trade in Civil Aircraft This table shows the major provisions of a 1992 agreement between the United States and Europe that limited the subsidies provided to the development and production of civilian aircraft.

Aircraft Covered
- All aircraft of 100 seats or larger are subject to the provisions of the agreement.

Direct Support Levels
- Funds advanced by governments for aircraft development may not exceed 33 percent of total development costs and are to be provided only to programs in which there is a reasonable expectation of recoupment within 17 years.

Interest Rates
- Airbus will repay the first 25 percent of total development costs at the government cost of borrowing within 17 years of first disbursement; the remaining 8 percent will be repaid at the government cost of borrowing plus 1 percent within 17 years of first disbursement.

Indirect Supports
- Both sides agree that indirect (i.e., military) supports should neither confer unfair advantage on manufacturers of civil aircraft nor lead to distortions in international trade in such aircraft.
- Identifiable benefits from indirect support are limited to 3 percent of the value of industry-wide turnover in each signatory and 4 percent of the value of each firm's annual sales. Benefits will primarily be calculated as cost reductions in the development of a civil aircraft program realized from technology acquired through government R&D programs.

Escape Clause on Emergency Aid
- Either side can temporarily derogate from the agreement, with the exception of the development support provisions, if survival and financial viability of an aircraft manufacturer are in jeopardy. Any such withdrawal would require consultations with representatives of the other side, full disclosure of information to justify the withdrawal, and full explanation of the remedy to be used.

Production Supports
- No further production subsidies are allowed.

Dispute Settlement Mechanisms
- Both sides will consult at least twice a year to ensure the functioning of the agreement. Either side may request consultations related to the agreement at any time. Such consultations must be held no later than 30 days after they are requested.

Source: Excerpted from Laura D'Andrea Tyson, 1992, Who's Bashing Whom? Trade Conflict in High Technology Industries *(Washington, D.C.: Peterson Institute for International Economics).*

Spain, Finland, and the United Kingdom are expected to pay. The European governments provided some $3.5 billion in low-interest loans to cover development costs. In 2005 both the United States and the EU filed countercomplaints at the WTO regarding illegal subsidies by the other party to their respective aircraft producers. Europe was accused of "illegally" subsidizing the A380, while the United States was accused of subsidizing the development of Boeing's 787 commercial jet. The complaints charged that these subsidies violate the 1992 agreement, with the United States going so far as to call for the termination of that agreement because of Europe's noncompliance.

Headlines: W.T.O. Says Aid to Airbus for A380 Was Illegal describes the results of a preliminary report from the World Trade Organization in September 2009. The WTO ruled in favor of Boeing's claim that the roughly $4 billion in low-interest loans to cover the development costs of the A380 did not meet the terms of the 1992 agreement. Under that agreement, the loans should be repaid at government rates (or the government rate plus 1 percent), which are close to commercial interest rates. If this preliminary ruling is upheld, then Airbus will have to refinance the loans at commercial rates.

HEADLINES

W.T.O. Says Aid to Airbus for A380 Was Illegal

A recent report from the WTO has found that some of the subsidies provided by European countries to launch the A380 aircraft violated the terms of a 1992 agreement with the United States. At the request of the European Union, the WTO has launched a similar investigation against the U.S. for its indirect subsidies to Boeing.

A preliminary report by the World Trade Organization has found that Airbus received illegal subsidies for the $13 billion A380 superjumbo jet and several other airplanes, hurting Boeing in the battle for sales, American and European officials said Friday. But the European Union was not determined to have systematically abused global trade rules, several people with knowledge of the report said. Both American and European Union officials declared victory after the 1,000-page confidential finding was given to trade agencies. It is the first round of an acrimonious trade dispute that began almost five years ago. . . .

The report is a response to a complaint filed by the United States on behalf of Boeing, which argues that the European Union and its governments funneled billions of dollars in illegal subsidies to Airbus from 1970 to 2004. . . . The most critical charge, experts said, involved about $15 billion in low-cost government loans to develop Airbus planes. Roughly $4 billion of the loans in question went to the twin-deck A380 jet, which entered service in 2007.

Boeing lawyers had said that a ruling against Airbus could mean that it will be required to either refinance those loans on commercial terms or otherwise restructure them. Under the current terms of the loans, Airbus makes its repayments as its planes are delivered to customers. Airbus has delivered 18 of 200 orders for the A380.

A counterclaim by the European Union, meanwhile, is being reviewed by a separate W.T.O. panel. That suit contends that Boeing has received at least $24 billion in backdoor subsidies through generous contracts with the United States military and space programs, as well as significant tax breaks from Washington State. An interim report on the Boeing case is expected in six to nine months and would be subject to the same comment and appeals process.

Source: Excerpted from Nicola Clark and Christopher Drew, "W.T.O. Says Aid to Airbus for A380 Was Illegal," The New York Times, *September 5, 2009, p. B1.*

Meanwhile, Airbus has filed a case at the WTO charging that Boeing received illegal subsidies through military contracts. An example is the $35 billion contract to build a new aerial refueling tanker for the U.S. Air Force, which was initially won by Airbus in 2008 but later overturned. The WTO will rule on Airbus's case in 2010.

National Welfare Will the development subsidies provided by the European governments to the Airbus A380 increase their national welfare? From the theory presented previously, that outcome is more likely to happen if Airbus is the only firm producing in that market. And such is the case, because Boeing has announced that it will not try to produce a double-decker aircraft to compete with the A380. Instead, it will modify its current 747 model and will focus its R&D on its new 787 Dreamliner aircraft, a midsize, 250-passenger aircraft.

Because Boeing will not enter the market with its own double-decker aircraft, it is possible that the profits earned by Airbus will be large enough to cover the subsidy costs, the criterion for an increase in national welfare. But that outcome is certainly not guaranteed. The profits earned by Airbus on the A380 will depend on how many aircraft are sold and at what price. Airbus has stated that it needs to produce at least 250 planes to cover its development costs but that it expects to sell 1,500 A380s over the next 20 years. As of January 2010, it had delivered only 25 of 202 aircraft ordered and was experiencing significant delays in production. Boeing, on the other hand,

Kyodo/AP Images

Boeing 787 Dreamliner's first take-off on December 15, 2009.

believes that market demand for such a superjumbo will not exceed 700 aircraft over the next 20 years. It remains to be seen whether the subsidies provided by the European Union for the A380 will ultimately pay off.

Boeing has its own share of difficulties with the production of the 787 Dreamliner, which was initially scheduled for delivery in 2008, but did not make its first flight until December 15, 2009. The article **Headlines: Dreamliner Production Gets Closer Monitoring** describes how Boeing outsourced many of the components of the 787 to firms in other countries, but then had difficulty in assembling these components back in the United States. Boeing has had to invest in new equipment and means of communication with its suppliers abroad to overcome the complexities in managing all the stages of production in an aircraft.

Finally, note that Airbus will produce a competitor for the 787 Dreamliner, and that is the A350 wide-body jet. France, Germany, and Britain have pledged $4.1 billion in launch funding for the A350, which is still in the early design phase and is not expected to be delivered until 2013. After that time, Boeing and Airbus will be in direct competition for customers. The fact that both firms are producing a new mid-size wide-body aircraft makes it less likely that either country will recoup the subsidies provided and experience a rise in national welfare from the subsidies. ■

6 Conclusions

Countries use export subsidies in a wide range of industries, including agriculture and high technology. For agriculture, the underlying motivation for the export subsidies is to prop up food prices, thereby raising the real incomes of farmers. This motivation was also discussed at the end of Chapter 3 using the specific-factors model. In this chapter, we used supply and demand curves to analyze the effect of export subsidies, but obtain the same result as in the specific-factors model: export subsidies raise prices for producers, thereby increasing their real income (in the specific-factors model) and their producer surplus (using supply curves).

Shifting income toward farmers comes with a cost to consumers, however, because of the higher food prices in the exporting country. When we add up the loss in consumer surplus, the gain in producer surplus, and the revenue cost of the subsidy, we obtain a net loss for the exporting country as a result of the subsidy. This deadweight loss is similar to that from a tariff in a small country. On the other hand, for a large country, an import tariff and an export subsidy have different welfare implications. Both policies lead to a rise in domestic prices (of either the import good or the export good) and a fall in world prices. For an export subsidy, however, the fall in world prices is a terms-of-trade loss for the exporting country. This means that applying an export subsidy in a large exporting country leads to even greater losses than applying it to a small country: there is no possibility of gain, as we found for a large-country import tariff.

The losses arising from an export subsidy, for either a small or a large country, are less severe when we instead consider production subsidies. A production subsidy

HEADLINES

Dreamliner Production Gets Closer Monitoring

This article describes the delays that Boeing has experienced in producing the new 787 aircraft, due to the offshoring of its components.

EVERETT, Wash.—To get the troubled 787 Dreamliner back on track after more than two years of delays, officials at Boeing Co. are counting on interpreters who can handle 28 languages, earthquake detectors and high-resolution video cameras.

The features are core to a major overhaul of production methods that Boeing hopes will tighten control, provide more information and speed work in its belated effort to get the Dreamliner off the ground. The U.S. aerospace giant is playing catch-up because it overreached six years ago, when it set out to make the world's most high-tech passenger jet but didn't prepare sufficiently for the project's complexity.

At the time, Boeing took the unprecedented step of outsourcing most of the Dreamliner's manufacturing. Boeing had previously designed and built its planes in-house, bearing the whole expense. But early this decade, when air traffic plunged after the Sept. 11 terrorist attacks, top Boeing executives balked at investing more than $10 billion to develop a new plane.

Instead, suppliers would independently bankroll their parts of the project, sharing costs and risk. Investors liked the idea, lifting Boeing's stock price from a low around $31 per share in August 2003 to a high above $107 in July 2007.

But when factory workers here started assembling the first Dreamliner around the time the stock hit its high, the system's flaws became clear as quality suffered and major components weren't completed. Many suppliers were accustomed only to manufacturing from blueprints supplied by Boeing—they weren't ready to manage sub-contractors or get designs approved by safety authorities. Others couldn't increase production fast enough. Boeing, which had earlier culled its own engineers to cut costs, was stretched too thin to monitor and fix blunders.

"The initial plan outran our ability to execute it," said Boeing Chief Executive Jim McNerney. "I think we got the balance wrong at the beginning of this program." In recent months Boeing has been trying to draw a line under the Dreamliner's problems by improving communication, taking major production lines back in-house and adding engineers to oversee work. . . .

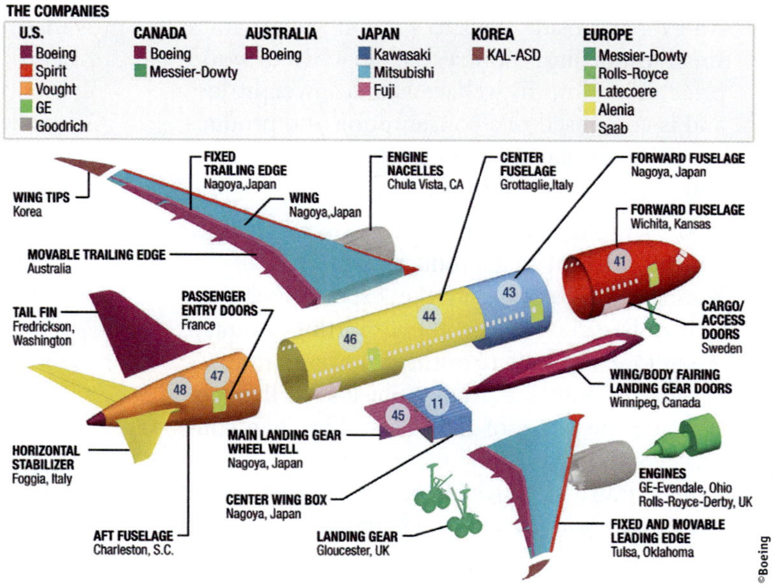

Source: Text excerpted from Daniel Michaels and Peter Sanders, "Dreamliner Production Gets Closer Monitoring," The Wall Street Journal, *October 8, 2009, electronic edition.*

provides a farmer with an extra payment for every unit produced, regardless of whether it is sold at home or abroad. So consumer prices do not change from their world level. Since consumer prices are not affected, exports increase only because domestic supply increases. In other words, the excess supply in response to production subsidies will indirectly spill over into international markets but production subsidies do not exclusively subsidize those exports (as export subsidies do). For these reasons, the losses arising from production subsidies in an exporting country are less severe than the losses arising from export subsidies. At the Hong Kong meeting of the WTO in December 2005, countries agreed to eliminate export subsidies in agriculture by 2013 but made a much weaker agreement for production subsidies and other domestic farm supports.

The losses experienced by an export country due to subsidies potentially change when we consider high-technology industries. In this chapter, we have examined an international duopoly (two firms) producing a good for sale in the rest of the world: Boeing and Airbus, competing for sales of a new aircraft. We have shown that it is *possible* for an export subsidy to lead to gains for the exporting country, by increasing the profits earned by the exporting firms by more than the cost of the subsidy. But that result often requires the subsidy to force the other firm out of the market, which does not necessarily occur. If both firms stay in the market and are subsidized by their governments, then it is unlikely that the subsidies are in the national interest of either the United States or the European Union; instead, the countries purchasing the aircraft gain because of the lower price, while the United States and Europe lose as a result of the costs of the subsidies.

KEY POINTS

1. An export subsidy leads to a fall in welfare for a small exporting country facing a fixed world price. The drop in welfare is a deadweight loss and is composed of a consumption and production loss, similar to an import tariff for a small country.
2. In the large-country case, an export subsidy lowers the price of that product in the rest of the world. The decrease in the export price is a terms-of-trade loss for the exporting country. Therefore, the welfare of the exporters decreases because of both the deadweight loss of the subsidy and the terms-of-trade loss. This is in contrast to the effects of an import tariff in the large-country case, which generates a terms-of-trade gain for the importing country.
3. Export subsidies applied by a large country create a benefit for importing countries in the rest of the world, by lowering their import prices. Therefore, the removal of these subsidy programs has an adverse affect on those countries. In fact, many of the poorest countries are net food importers that will face higher prices as agricultural subsidies in the European Union and the United States are removed.
4. Production subsidies to domestic producers also have the effect of increasing domestic production. However, consumers are unaffected by these subsidies. As a result, the deadweight loss of a production subsidy is less than that for an equal export subsidy, and the terms-of-trade loss is also smaller.
5. It is common for countries to provide subsidies to their high-technology industries because governments believe that these subsidies can create a strategic advantage for their firms on international markets. Because these industries often have only a few global competitors, we use game theory (the study of strategic interactions) to determine how firms make their decisions under imperfect competition.
6. A Nash equilibrium in a game is a situation in which each player is making the best response to the action of the other player. In a game with multiple Nash equilibria, the outcome can depend on an external factor, such as the ability of one player to make the first move.
7. Export subsidies can affect the Nash equilibrium of a game by altering the profits of the firms. If a subsidy increases the profits to a firm by more than the subsidy cost, then it is worthwhile for a government to undertake the subsidy. As we have seen, though, subsidies are not always worthwhile unless they can induce the competing firm to exit the market altogether, which may not occur.

KEY TERMS

export subsidy, p. 327
Common Agricultural Policy (CAP), p. 327
indirect subsidies, p. 328
domestic farm supports, p. 328
deadweight loss, p. 332
production loss, p. 332
consumption loss, p. 333
terms of trade, p. 334
production subsidy, p. 338
targeting principle, p. 341
externality, p. 342
strategic advantage, p. 342
imperfect competition, p. 343
duopoly, p. 343
game theory, p. 343
payoff matrix, p. 343
Nash equilibrium, p. 344
first mover advantage, p. 345

PROBLEMS

1. Describe the impact of each of the following goals from the Hong Kong WTO meeting on (i) domestic prices and welfare of the country taking the action and (ii) world prices and welfare for the partner countries.
   a. Elimination of agriculture export subsidies
   b. Reduction of agricultural tariffs
   c. Duty-free, quota-free access for 97% of goods originating in the world's least developed countries
2. Consider a large country with export subsidies in place for agriculture. Suppose the country changes its policy and decides to cut its subsidies in half.
   a. Are there gains or losses to the large country, or is it ambiguous? What is the impact on domestic prices for agriculture and on the world price?
   b. Suppose a small food-importing country abroad responds to the lowered subsidies by lowering its tariffs on agriculture by the same amount. Are there gains or losses to the small country, or is it ambiguous? Explain.
   c. Suppose a large food-importing country abroad reciprocates by lowering its tariffs on agricultural goods by the same amount. Are there gains or losses to this large country, or is it ambiguous? Explain.
3. Suppose Home is a small exporter of wheat. At the world price of $100 per ton, Home growers export 20 tons. Now suppose the Home government decides to support its domestic producer with an export subsidy of $40 per ton. Use the following figure to answer these questions.

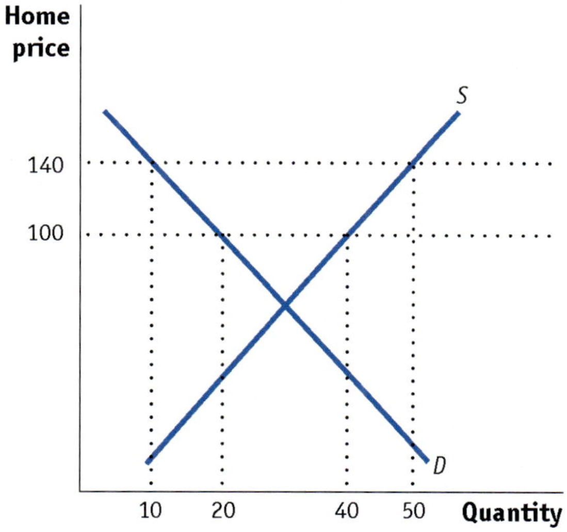

   a. What is the quantity exported under free trade and with the export subsidy?
   b. Calculate the effect of the export subsidy on consumer surplus, producer surplus, and government revenue.
   c. Calculate the overall net effect of the export subsidy on Home welfare.
4. Refer to Problem 3. Rather than a small exporter of wheat, suppose that Home is a large country. Continue to assume that the free-trade world price is $100 per ton and that the Home government provides the domestic producer with an export subsidy in

the amount of $40 per ton. Because of the export subsidy, the local price increases to $120, while the foreign market price declines to $80 per ton. Use the following figure to answer these questions.

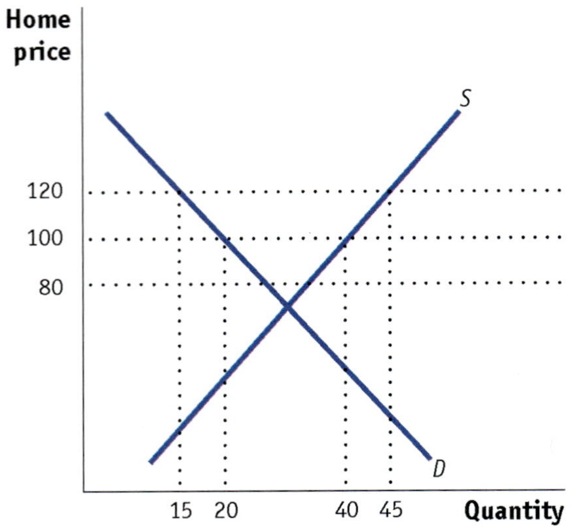

a. Relative to the small-country case, why does the new domestic price increase by less than the amount of the subsidy?
b. Calculate the effect of the export subsidy on consumer surplus, producer surplus, and government revenue.
c. Calculate the overall net effect of the export subsidy on Home welfare. Is the large country better or worse off as compared to the small country with the export subsidy? Explain.

5. Refer to Problem 3. Suppose Home is a small exporter of wheat. At the world price of $100 per ton, Home growers export 20 tons. But rather than an export subsidy, suppose the Home government provides its domestic producer with a production subsidy of $40 per ton. Use the following figure to answer these questions.

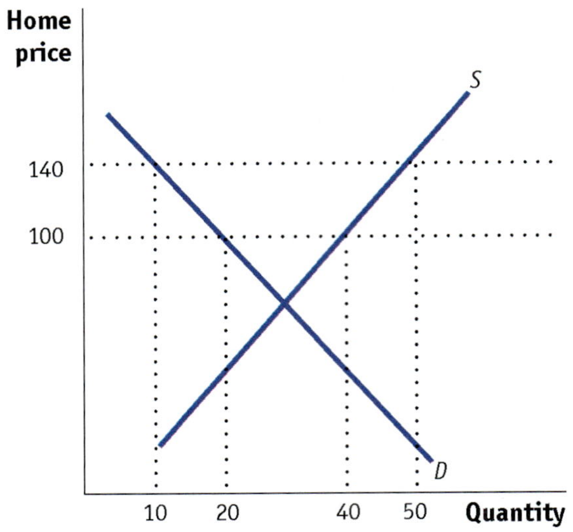

a. What is the quantity exported with the production subsidy?
b. Calculate the effect of the production subsidy on consumer surplus, producer surplus, and government revenue.
c. Calculate the overall net effect of the production subsidy on Home welfare. Is the cost of the production subsidy more or less than the cost of the export subsidy for the small country? Explain.

6. As mentioned in **Headlines: Developing Countries Split over WTO Farm Protection,** the failure of the WTO talks in Geneva in 2008 was, in part, due to disagreement between developing countries over agricultural subsidies and tariffs. Explain how two developing countries, such as Uruguay and China, can have such different interests when it comes to agricultural subsidies and tariffs. Then explain how the interests of a poor nation like Zambia differ from those of Uruguay and China.

7. Explain why the WTO is more concerned with the use of direct export subsidies than production subsidies in achieving the same level of domestic support.

8. Boeing and Airbus are the world's only major producers of large, wide-bodied aircrafts. But with the cost of fuel increasing and changing demand in the airline industry, the need for smaller regional jets has increased. Suppose that both firms must decide whether they will produce a smaller plane. We will assume that Boeing has a slight cost advantage over Airbus in both large and small planes, as shown in the payoff matrix below (in millions of U.S. dollars). Assume that each producer chooses to produce only large, only small, or no planes at all.
   a. What is the Nash equilibrium of this game?
   b. Are there multiple equilibria? If so, explain why. Hint: Guess at an equilibrium and then check whether either firm would want to change its action, given the action of the other firm. Remember that Boeing can change only its own action, which means moving up or down a column, and likewise, Airbus can change only its own action, which means moving back or forth on a row.

9. Refer to Problem 8. Now suppose the European government wants Airbus to be the sole producer in the lucrative small-aircraft market. Then answer the following:
   a. What is the minimum amount of subsidy that Airbus must receive when it produces small aircraft to ensure that outcome as the unique Nash equilibrium?
   b. It is worthwhile for the European government to undertake this subsidy?

10. Here we examine the effects of domestic sales taxes on the market for exports, as an example of the "targeting principle." For example, in the domestic market, there are heavy taxes on the purchase of cigarettes. Meanwhile, the United States has several very large cigarette companies that export their products abroad.
   a. What is the effect of the sales tax on the quantity of cigarette exports from the United States? *Hint:* Your answer should parallel the case of production subsidies but for a consumption tax instead.
   b. How does the change in exports, if any, due to the sales tax compare with the effect of an export subsidy on cigarettes?

		Airbus		
		Large planes	Small planes	Not produce
Boeing	Large planes	Boeing 10, Airbus −5	Boeing 115, Airbus 125	Boeing 115, Airbus 0
	Small planes	Boeing 150, Airbus 100	Boeing 15, Airbus 0	Boeing 150, Airbus 0
	Not produce	Boeing 0, Airbus 100	Boeing 0, Airbus 125	Boeing 0, Airbus 0

11. Refer to Problem 10. Based on your answer there, would foreign countries have a reason to object to the use of a sales tax on cigarettes by the United States? Based on your knowledge of the GATT/WTO provisions (see **Side Bar: Key Provisions of the GATT** in Chapter 8), are foreign countries entitled to object to the use of such a tax?

12. To improve national welfare, a large country would do better to implement an export subsidy rather than an import tariff. Is this true or false? Explain why.

13. Who gains and who loses when governments in Europe and the United States provide subsidies to Airbus and Boeing?

14. Provide motivations for the use of export subsidies. Does your answer depend on whether firms compete under perfect or imperfect competition?

11

International Agreements: Trade, Labor, and the Environment

Seattle was a riot, they tried to pin on us.
But we didn't show up, with gas and billy clubs
An un-armed mass of thousands, just trying to be heard.
But there are no world leaders that want to hear our words.

Lyrics from "Seattle Was a Riot" by the punk-rock band Anti-Flag, 1999

We now have a Copenhagen Accord which I think contains a number of very significant elements. . . . But not an accord that is legally binding. Not an accord that, at this moment, pins down industrialised countries to individual targets. Not an accord that at this stage specifies what major developing countries will do.

Yvo de Boer, Executive Secretary of the United Nations Framework Convention on Climate Change, December 19, 2009

In 1999 policy makers from around the world met in Seattle, Washington, to discuss the next round of trade negotiations under the World Trade Organization (WTO). But the meeting never achieved that goal because it was disrupted by large groups of protesters who filled the streets. The protest at times turned violent (as described in the lyrics above from "Seattle Was a Riot"). The scale of these protests took many people by surprise; after all, discussions about trade reform had been occurring since the General Agreement on Trade and Tariffs (GATT) was formed in 1947, but never before had there been such an organized protest against it. What explains this grassroots movement against the WTO?

In past rounds of negotiations, the GATT and now the WTO have been successful in lowering tariffs in most sectors of its members' economies. The barriers to trade remaining for the WTO to address now go beyond tariffs and involve issues of national interest that are indirectly related to trade. One of those issues is the environment. Most countries have national laws governing environmental

©Hagerty Patrick/Corbis Sygma

In protests at the 1999 meeting of the World Trade Organization in Seattle, Washington, environmentalists dressed as turtles and other endangered species that had been affected by recent WTO rulings.

issues, such as the use of pesticides or genetically modified organisms, the protection of endangered species, the extent to which firms can release pollutants into the atmosphere, the harvesting of renewable and nonrenewable resources, and so on. Inevitably, some of these rules will also affect international trade, and that is where the WTO comes in. Under the Uruguay Round of negotiations (1986–1994), the WTO toughened its own rules governing the extent to which national laws can affect international trade. Countries that believed they were excluded from a foreign market because of unreasonable environmental standards there could bring a dispute before the WTO, where a panel of judges in Geneva would rule on the case. In principle, the panel's ruling would be binding on the countries involved.

The new WTO rules governing environmental regulations infuriated grassroots groups in the United States and abroad. Just before the Seattle meeting, these environmental groups formed a coalition with union leaders, religious groups, third-world activists, and others who believed that the WTO might threaten the interests of those whom they represent. In addition, a wide range of political groups—from conservatives to anarchists—believed it was undesirable for a WTO panel in Geneva to make rulings that would affect U.S. regulations. Members of all these groups gathered in Seattle to voice their dissatisfaction with the WTO. The environmentalists dressed as dolphins, turtles, and other endangered species that had been affected by recent WTO rulings. The scenes of these costumed creatures marching arm in arm with steelworkers gave an entirely new image to protests against the WTO.

Press Association via AP Images

Protesters at the U.N. climate change conference, Copenhagen, December 2009.

Protests over the environment were also evident at a meeting 10 years later, in December 2009, held in Copenhagen, Denmark. Called the Copenhagen Climate Summit, this international meeting was supposed to establish binding reductions for countries' emissions of greenhouse gases. Hundreds of protesters were arrested and thousands more attended rallies, some dressed as polar bears and panda bears to highlight the threat of gobal warming to the habitat of those animals. Although expectations for the summit were high, the meeting unfortunately broke up without any binding commitments from countries to reduce their greenhouse gas emissions, as indicated in the quotation at the beginning of the chapter from Yvo de Boer, Executive Secretary of the United Nations Framework Convention on Climate Change.[1]

The goal of this chapter is to examine why international agreements like those negotiated under the WTO for trade, and those negotiated for environmental reasons like the Copenhagen Climate Summit, are needed. We begin by reviewing the reasons why international agreements dealing with tariffs

[1] Two months after the Copenhagen Climate Summit, Mr. Yvo de Boer resigned his position.

are needed. As we discussed in an earlier chapter, countries that are large can influence the price they pay for imports by applying an import tariff: the tariff increases the import price for consumers in the large country but lowers the price received by foreign exporting firms. The reduction in the price received by exporters is a **terms-of-trade gain** for the importing country. We show in this chapter that when two or more countries apply tariffs against each other in an attempt to capture this terms-of-trade gain, they both end up losing. The terms-of-trade gain for one country is canceled by the use of a tariff in another country, so both countries wind up losing as a result of the tariffs.

To avoid such losses, international agreements to reduce tariffs and move toward free trade are needed. These international agreements take several forms. The WTO is a **multilateral agreement,** involving many countries, with agreement to lower tariffs between all the members. There are also smaller **regional trade agreements,** involving several countries, often located near each other. The North American Free Trade Agreement (NAFTA) and the European Union are both examples of regional trade agreements, which lead to free trade among the countries who are parties to the agreement. A very recent example is an agreement between China and the Association of Southest Asian Nations (ASEAN) for the China-ASEAN free-trade area. That agreement eliminated tariffs on 90% of products traded between China and six members of ASEAN—Brunei, Indonesia, Malaysia, Philippines, Singapore, and Thailand—on January 1, 2010, with the remaining four countries of the association (Cambodia, Laos, Myanmar, and Vietnam) added by 2015. This Asian free-trade area covers nearly 1.9 billion people, or more than one-quarter of the world's population. In economic terms, it is the third largest free-trade area in the world, after the European Union and NAFTA.

Besides eliminating tariffs on trade, the NAFTA agreement had two other "side agreements": one involved the rights of workers in each country, and the other involved the environment. In this chapter, we discuss the extent to which NAFTA and other labor agreements protect the rights of workers, then we discuss international agreements on the environment. Rulings at the WTO have an indirect impact on the environment, which is what concerned many protesters in Seattle. But other international agreements, such as that attempted at the Copenhagen Climate Summit and its precursor, the Kyoto Protocol, have a more direct impact. Both of these agreements were intended to reduce carbon dioxide emissions worldwide and therefore slow global warming. We argue that for "global" pollutants such as carbon dioxide, countries do not fully recognize the environmental costs of their economic activity. International agreements are needed to ensure that countries recognize these environmental costs, and such agreements are in the best interests of the world community, even though they are hard to achieve.

1 International Trade Agreements

When countries seek to reduce trade barriers between themselves, they enter into a **trade agreement**—a pact to reduce or eliminate trade restrictions. Multilateral trade agreements occur among a large set of countries, such as the members of the WTO, that have negotiated many "rounds" of trade agreements. Under the **most favored nation principle** of the WTO, the lower tariffs agreed to in multilateral negotiations must be extended *equally* to all WTO members (see Article I in **Side Bar: Key Provisions of the GATT,** in a previous chapter). Countries joining the

WTO enjoy the low tariffs extended to all member countries but must also agree to lower their own tariffs.

The WTO is an example of a multilateral trade agreement, which we analyze first in this section. To demonstrate the logic of multilateral agreements, we assume for simplicity that there are only two countries in the world that enter into an agreement; however, the theoretical results that we obtain also apply when there are many countries. The important feature of multilateral agreements is that no countries are *left out* of the agreement.

Following our discussion of multilateral agreements, we analyze regional trade agreements that occur between smaller groups of countries and find that the implications of regional trade agreements differ from those of multilateral trade agreements. When entering into a regional trade agreement, countries agree to eliminate tariffs between themselves but do not reduce tariffs against the countries left out of the agreement. For example, the United States has many regional trade agreements, including those with Israel, Jordan, Chile, with the countries of Central America and the Dominican Republic (through an agreement called CAFTA-DR), and new agreements being planned with South Korea, Panama, and Colombia, which have not been ratified.[2] In South America, the countries of Argentina, Brazil, Paraguay, Uruguay, and Venezuela belong to a free-trade area called Mercosur. In fact, there are more than 200 free-trade agreements worldwide, which some economists feel threaten the WTO as the major forum for multilateral trade liberalization.

The Logic of Multilateral Trade Agreements

Before we begin our analysis of the effects of multilateral trade agreements, let's review the effects of tariffs imposed by large countries under perfect competition.

Tariffs for a Large Country In Figure 11-1, we show the effects of a large-country (Home) tariff, repeated from an earlier chapter. We previously found that a tariff leads to a deadweight loss for Home, which is the sum of consumption and production losses, of area $(b + d)$ in Figure 11-1. In addition, the tariff leads to a terms-of-trade gain for Home, which is area e, equal to the reduction in Foreign price due to the tariff, $(P^W - P^*)$, multiplied by the amount of Home imports under the tariff, $(D_2 - S_2)$. If Home applies an optimal tariff, then its terms-of-trade gain exceeds its deadweight loss, so that $e > (b + d)$. Panel (b) shows that for the rest of the world (which in our two-country case is just Foreign), the tariff leads to a deadweight loss f from producing an inefficiently low level of exports relative to free trade, and a terms-of-trade loss e due to the reduction in its export prices. That is, the Home terms-of-trade gain comes at the expense of an equal terms-of-trade loss e for Foreign, plus a Foreign deadweight loss f.

Payoff Matrix This quick review of the welfare effects of a large-country tariff under perfect competition can be used to derive some new results. Although our earlier analysis indicated that it is optimal for large countries to impose small positive tariffs, that rationale ignored the strategic interaction among *multiple* large countries. If every country imposes even a small positive tariff, is it still optimal behavior for each country individually? We can use game theory to model the strategic choice of whether or

[2] The free-trade agreements with these three countries were negotiated by President George W. Bush before leaving office in January 2009, but not ratified by Congress. President Obama mentioned these agreements in his State of the Union address on January 27, 2010, saying that: "we will strengthen our trade relations in Asia and with key partners like South Korea and Panama and Colombia."

FIGURE 11-1

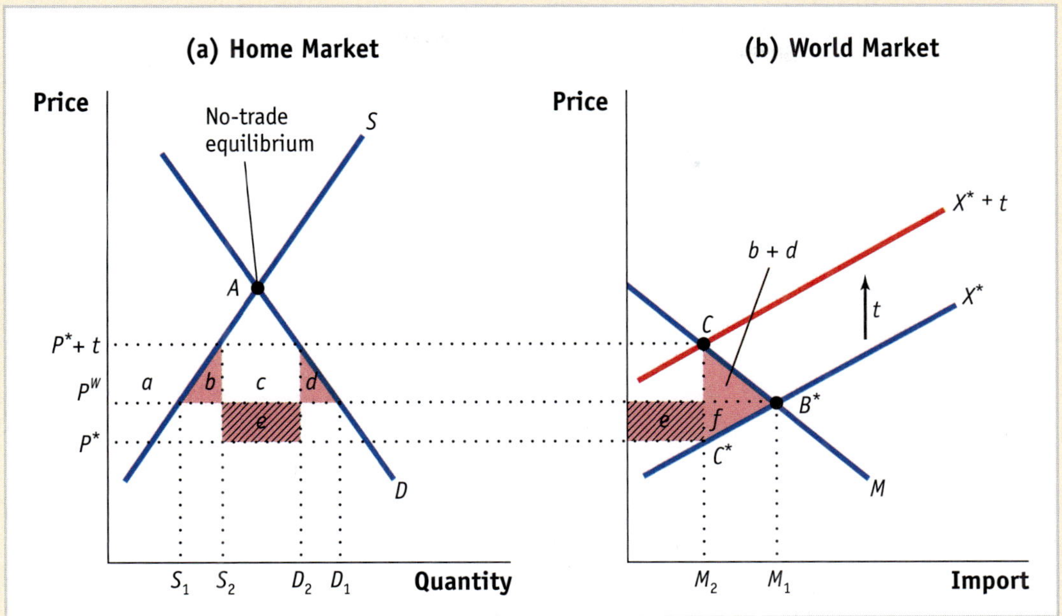

Tariff for a Large Country The tariff shifts up the export supply curve from X^* to $X^* + t$. As a result, the Home price increases from P^W to $P^* + t$, and the Foreign price falls from P^W to P^*. The deadweight loss at Home is the area of the triangle $(b + d)$, and Home also has a terms-of-trade gain of area e. Foreign loses the area $(e + f)$, so the net loss in world welfare is the triangle $(b + d + f)$.

not to apply a tariff, and use a payoff matrix to determine the Nash equilibrium outcome for each country's tariff level. A Nash equilibrium occurs when each player is taking the action that is the best response (i.e., yielding the highest payoff) to the action of the other player.

In Figure 11-2, we show a payoff matrix between the Home and Foreign countries (both large), each of which has to decide whether to impose a tariff against the other country. Each quadrant of the matrix includes Home's payoff in the lower-left corner and Foreign's payoff in the upper-right corner. We will start with a situation of free trade and then measure the change in welfare for Home or Foreign by applying a tariff. For convenience, we will also assume that the two countries are exactly the same size, so their payoffs are symmetric.

Free Trade When both countries do not impose tariffs, we are in a free-trade situation, shown in the upper-left quadrant. For convenience, let us write the payoffs for the two countries under free trade as zero, which means that we will measure the payoffs in any other situation as *relative to* free trade.

Tariffs First, suppose that Home imposes a tariff but Foreign does not. Then the Home payoff as compared with free trade is $e - (b + d)$ (which is positive for an optimal tariff), and the Foreign payoff is $-(e + f)$, the terms-of-trade and deadweight losses described previously. These payoffs are shown in the lower-left quadrant of the matrix. Now suppose that Foreign imposes a tariff but Home does not. Because we have assumed that the Home and Foreign countries are the same size, they have the same potential payoffs from using a tariff. Under these circumstances, the Foreign

FIGURE 11-2

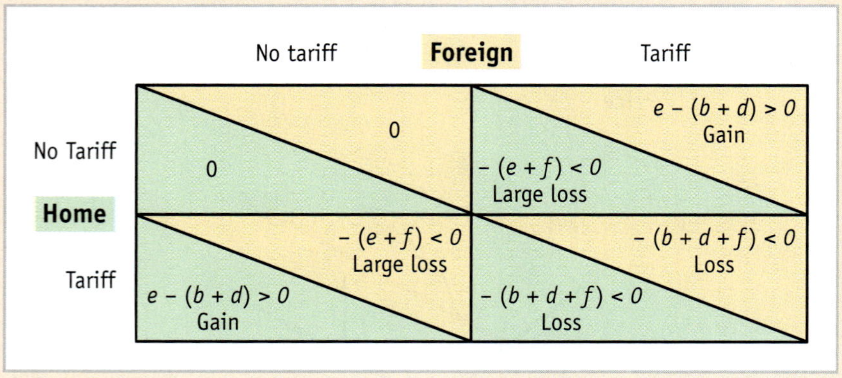

Payoffs in a Tariff Game This payoff matrix shows the welfare of the Home and Foreign countries as compared with free trade (upper-left quadrant in which neither country applies a tariff). Welfare depends on whether one or both countries apply a tariff. The structure of payoffs is similar to the "prisoner's dilemma" because both countries suffer a loss when they both apply tariffs, and yet this is the unique Nash equilibrium.

payoff from its own tariff is $e - (b + d) > 0$, and the Home payoff is the loss $-(e + f)$. These two payoffs are shown in the upper-right quadrant of the matrix.

Finally, suppose that *both* countries impose optimal tariffs and that the tariffs are the same size. Then the terms-of-trade gain that each country gets from its own tariff is canceled out by the terms-of-trade loss it suffers because of the other country's tariff. In that case, neither country gets any terms-of-trade gain but both countries still suffer a deadweight loss. That deadweight loss is $(b + d)$ from each country's own tariffs plus area f, the deadweight loss from the other country's tariff. The total deadweight loss for each country is $-(b + d + f)$, as shown in the lower-right quadrant of the matrix.

Prisoner's Dilemma The pattern of payoffs in Figure 11-2 has a special structure called the **prisoner's dilemma.** The "prisoner's dilemma" refers to a game in which two accomplices are caught for a crime that they committed, and each has to decide whether to confess. They are kept in separate cells, so they cannot communicate with each other. If one confesses and the other does not, then the person confessing will get a much lighter jail sentence and is better off than taking the chance of being found guilty in a trial. But if they both confess, then they both go to jail for the full sentence. This is like the pattern in Figure 11-2, in which each country acting on its own has an incentive to apply a tariff, but if they both apply tariffs, they will both be worse off.

Nash Equilibrium The only Nash equilibrium in Figure 11-2 is for both countries to apply a tariff (lower-right quadrant). Starting at that point, if either country eliminates its tariff, then it loses $(e + f)$ as compared with free trade, rather than $(b + d + f)$. Because we know that $e > (b + d)$ for an optimal tariff, it follows that each country acting on its own is worse off by moving to free trade (i.e., removing its tariff). That is, the loss $(e + f)$ is greater than the loss $(b + d + f)$. As a result, the Nash equilibrium is for both countries to apply a tariff.

But, like having both prisoners confess, the outcome for both countries when each country applies a tariff is quite bad. They both suffer the deadweight losses that arise from their own tariff and their partner's tariff, without any terms-of-trade gain. The Nash equilibrium in this case leads to an outcome that is undesirable for both countries even though it is the best outcome for each country given that the other country is imposing a tariff.

Trade Agreement This bad outcome can be avoided if the countries enter into some kind of trade agreement. In an earlier chapter, for example, we saw how the WTO dispute-settlement mechanism came into play when the steel tariffs applied by President Bush became problematic for the United States' trading partners. The EU filed a case at the WTO objecting to these tariffs, and it was ruled that the tariffs did not meet the criterion for a safeguard tariff. As a result, the WTO ruled that European countries could *retaliate* by imposing tariffs of their own against U.S. exports. The threat of these tariffs led President Bush to eliminate the steel tariffs ahead of schedule, and the outcome moved from both countries potentially applying tariffs to both countries having zero tariffs. Likewise, China has requested that the WTO launch an investigation to determine whether the tariff on tires applied by President Obama meets the criterion of the relevant trade laws. If not, then China would be entitled to retaliate, and this threat could possibly lead to the removal of the tariff on tires before its three-year expiration date.

Thus, the WTO mechanism eliminated the prisoner's dilemma by providing an incentive to remove tariffs; the outcome was in the preferred upper-left quadrant of the payoff matrix in Figure 11-2, rather than the original Nash equilibrium in the lower-right quadrant. The same logic comes into play when countries agree to join the WTO. They are required to reduce their own tariffs, but in return, they are also assured of receiving lower tariffs from other WTO members. That assurance enables countries to mutually reduce their tariffs and move closer to free trade.

Regional Trade Agreements

Under regional trade agreements, several countries eliminate tariffs among themselves but maintain tariffs against countries outside the region. Such regional trade agreements are permitted under Article XXIV of the GATT (see **Side Bar: Key Provisions of the GATT,** in an earlier chapter). That article states that countries can enter into such agreements provided they do not jointly increase their tariffs against outside countries.

Although they are authorized by the GATT, regional trade agreements contradict the most favored nation principle, which states that every country belonging to the GATT/WTO should be treated equally. The countries included in a regional trade agreement are treated better (since they face zero tariffs) than the countries excluded. For this reason, regional trade agreements are sometimes called **preferential trade agreements,** to emphasize that the member countries are favored over other countries. Despite this violation of the most favored nation principle, regional trade agreements are permitted because it is thought that the removal of trade barriers among expanding groups of countries is one way to achieve freer trade worldwide.

Regional trade agreements can be classified into two basic types: free-trade areas and customs unions.

Free-Trade Area A **free-trade area** is a group of countries agreeing to eliminate tariffs (and other barriers to trade) among themselves but keeping whatever tariffs they formerly had with the rest of the world. In 1989 Canada entered into a free-trade agreement with the United States under which tariffs between the two countries were eliminated over the next decade. Known as the Canada-U.S. Free Trade Agreement, it was signed five years before the agreement with Mexico, in 1994, that created free trade among all three countries under the North American Free Trade Agreement (NAFTA). Each of these countries has its own tariffs with all other countries of the world.

Customs Union A **customs union** is similar to a free-trade area, except that in addition to eliminating tariffs among countries in the union, the countries within a customs union also agree to a *common* schedule of tariffs with each country outside the union. Examples of customs unions include the countries in the European Union (EU) and the signatory countries of Mercosur in South America. All countries in the EU have identical tariffs with respect to each outside country; the same holds for the countries in Mercosur.[3]

Rules of Origin The fact that the countries in a free-trade area do not have common tariffs for outside countries, as do countries within a customs union, leads to an obvious problem with free-trade areas: if China, for example, wants to sell a good to Canada, what would prevent it from first exporting the good to the United States or Mexico, whichever has the lowest tariff, and then shipping it to Canada? The answer is that free-trade areas have complex **rules of origin** that specify what type of goods can be shipped duty-free within the free-trade area.

A good entering Mexico from China, for example, is not granted duty-free access to the United States or Canada, unless that good is first incorporated into another product in Mexico, giving the new product enough "North American content" to qualify for duty-free access. So China or any other outside country cannot just choose the lowest-tariff country through which to enter North America. Rather, products can be shipped duty-free between countries only if most of their production occurred within North America. To determine whether this criterion has been satisfied, the rules of origin must specify—for each and every product—how much of its production (as determined by value-added or the use of some key inputs) took place in North America. As you can imagine, it takes many pages to specify these rules for each and every product, and it is said that the rules of origin for NAFTA take up more space in the agreement than all other considerations combined!

Notice that these rules are not needed in a customs union because in that case the tariffs on outside members are the same for all countries in the union: there is no incentive to import a good into the lowest-tariff country. So why don't countries just create a customs union, making the rules of origin irrelevant? The answer is that modifying the tariffs applied against an outside country is a politically sensitive issue. The United States, for example, might want a higher tariff on textiles than Canada or Mexico, and Mexico might want a higher tariff on corn. NAFTA allows each of these three countries to have its own tariffs for each commodity on outside countries. So despite the complexity of rules of origin, they allow countries to enter into a free-trade agreement without modifying their tariffs on outside countries.

Now that we understand the difference between free-trade areas and customs unions, let us set that difference aside and focus on the main economic effects of regional trade agreements, by which we mean free-trade areas or customs unions.

---

[3] When new countries enter the EU or Mercosur, they must adjust their outside tariffs to the customs union level. Sometimes that will mean *increasing* a tariff on an outside member, as occurred when West Germany joined the European Economic Community in 1962. Germany increased the tariff that it charged on imported U.S. poultry, to be in accordance with the tariffs charged by the European Economic Community on U.S. imports, and in retaliation, the United States increased its tariffs on trucks and other products imported from Germany. This episode became known as the "chicken war." The tariff of 25% on trucks applied by the United States became a permanent item in the U.S. tariff code and today applies to compact trucks imported by the United States from Japan (see Application: Import Tariffs on Japanese Trucks in an earlier chapter).

Trade Creation and Trade Diversion

When a regional trade agreement is formed and trade increases between member countries, the increase in trade can be of two types. The first type of trade increase, **trade creation,** occurs when a member country imports a product from another member country that formerly it produced for itself. In this case, there is a gain in consumer surplus for the importing country (by importing greater amounts of goods at lower prices) and a gain in producer surplus for the exporting country (from increased sales). These gains from trade are analogous to those that occur from the opening of trade in the Ricardian or Heckscher–Ohlin models. No other country inside or outside the trade agreement is affected because the product was not traded before. Therefore, trade creation brings welfare gains for both countries involved.

The second reason for trade to increase within a regional agreement is due to **trade diversion,** which occurs when a member country imports a product from another member country that it formerly imported *from a country outside of the new trade region.* The article **Headlines: China-ASEAN Treaty Threatens Indian Exporters** gives an example of trade diversion that could result from the free-trade agreement between the China and the ASEAN countries, implemented on January 1, 2010.

HEADLINES

China-ASEAN Treaty Threatens Indian Exporters

This article discusses the China-ASEAN free-trade area, implemented on January 1, 2010. By eliminating tariffs between China and the ASEAN countries, this free-trade area will make it more difficult for India to export to those countries, which is an example of trade diversion.

BEIJING—Indian exporters are faced with a new challenge as the free trade agreement between China and members of the Association of Southeast Asian Nations became operational on Friday. It will mean nearly zero duty trade between several Asian nations making it difficult for Indian businesses to sell a range of products.

India has been planning to enlarge its trade basket to include several commodities that are now supplied to China by ASEAN countries. These products include fruits, vegetables and grains. Indian products, which will face 10–12 per cent import duty [tariff], may find it extremely difficult to survive the competition from ASEAN nations. China is cutting tariffs on imports from ASEAN nations from an average of 9.8 per cent to about 0.1 per cent. The original members of ASEAN—Brunei, Indonesia, Malaysia, the Philippines, Singapore and Thailand—have also agreed to dramatically cut import duty on Chinese products from an average of 12.8 per cent to just 0.6 per cent. The newly created free trade area involves 11 countries will a total population of 1.9 billion and having a combined gross domestic product of $6 trillion.

The successful implementation of the FTA is bound to force New Delhi to expatiate similar trade agreements with countries in the ASEAN region besides China. India is in the process of discussing trade agreements with several countries including China. New Delhi has also inked agreements with Beijing on the supply of fruits, vegetables and Basmati rice. But they remain to be implemented. At present, 58 per cent of Indian exports to China consists of iron ore with very little component of value added goods. India has been trying to widen the trade basket to include manufactured goods, fruits and vegetables. This effort might be severely hit because goods from ASEAN nations will now cost much less to the Chinese consumer. . . .

Source: Excerpted from Saibal Dasgupta, "China-ASEAN Treaty Threatens Indian Exporters," The Times of India, *January 3, 2010.*

Numerical Example of Trade Creation and Diversion

To illustrate the potential for trade diversion, we use an example from NAFTA, in which the United States might import auto parts from Mexico that it formerly imported from Asia.[4] Let us keep track of the gains and losses for the countries involved. Asia will lose export sales to North America, so it suffers a loss in producer surplus in its exporting industry. Mexico gains producer surplus by selling the auto parts. The problem with this outcome is that Mexico is not the most efficient (lowest cost) producer of auto parts: we know that Asia is more efficient because that is where the United States initially purchased its auto parts. Because the United States is importing from a less efficient producer, there is some potential loss for the United States due to trade diversion. We can determine whether this is indeed the case by numerically analyzing the cases of trade creation and trade diversion.

Suppose that the costs to the United States of importing an auto part from Mexico or from Asia are as shown in Table 11-1. The rightmost columns show the total costs of the part under free trade (zero tariff), with a 10% tariff and 20% tariff, respectively. Under free trade, the auto part can be produced in Mexico for \$20 or in Asia for \$19. Thus, Asia is the most efficient producer. If the United States purchased the part from an American supplier, it would cost \$22, as shown in the last row of the table. With a tariff of 10%, the costs of importing from Mexico or Asia are increased to \$22 and \$20.90, respectively. Similarly, a 20% tariff would increase the cost of importing to \$24 and \$22.80, respectively. Under NAFTA, however, the cost of importing from Mexico is \$20 regardless of the tariff.

With the data shown in Table 11-1, we can examine the effect of NAFTA on each country's welfare. First, suppose that the tariff applied by the United States is 20%, as shown in the last column. Before NAFTA, it would have cost \$24 to import the auto part from Mexico, \$22.80 to import it from Asia, and \$22 to produce it locally in the United States. Before NAFTA, then, producing the part in the United States for \$22 is the cheapest option. With the tariff of 20%, therefore, there are no imports of this auto part into the United States.

TABLE 11-1

Cost of Importing an Automobile Part This table shows the cost to the United States of purchasing an automobile part from various source countries, with and without tariffs. If there is a 20% tariff on all countries, then it would be cheapest for the United States to buy the auto part from itself (for \$22). But when the tariff is eliminated on Mexico after NAFTA, then the United States would instead buy from that country (for \$20), which illustrates the idea of trade creation. If instead we start with a 10% tariff on all countries, then it would be cheapest for the United States to buy from Asia (for \$20.90). When the tariff on Mexico is eliminated under NAFTA, then the United States would instead buy there (for \$20), illustrating the idea of trade diversion.

	U.S. Tariff		
	0%	10%	20%
From Mexico, before NAFTA	\$20	\$22	\$24
From Asia, before NAFTA	\$19	\$20.90	\$22.80
From Mexico, after NAFTA	\$20	\$20	\$20
From Asia, after NAFTA	\$19	\$20.90	\$22.80
From the United States	\$22	\$22	\$22

Trade Creation When Mexico joins NAFTA, it pays no tariff to the United States, whereas Asia continues to have a 20% tariff applied against it. After NAFTA, the United States will import the part from Mexico for \$20 because the price is less than the U.S. cost of \$22. Therefore, all the auto parts will be imported from Mexico. This is an example of trade creation. The United States clearly gains from the

[4] The largest exporters of auto parts to the United States currently are Canada, Mexico, and Japan. So the Asian country in this example can be thought of as Japan. In the future, however, China is expected to become a major exporter of auto parts, especially for the labor-intensive parts now produced in Mexico.

lower cost of the auto part; Mexico gains from being able to export to the United States; and Asia neither gains nor loses, because it never sold the auto part to the United States to begin with.

Trade Diversion Now suppose instead that the U.S. tariff on auto parts is 10% (the middle column of Table 11-1). Before NAFTA, the United States can import the auto part from Mexico for $22 or from Asia for $20.90. It still costs $22 to produce the part at home. In this case, the least-cost option is for the United States to import the auto part from Asia. When Mexico joins NAFTA, however, this outcome changes. It will cost $20 to import the auto part from Mexico duty-free, $20.90 to import it from Asia subject to the 10% tariff, and $22 to produce it at home. The least-cost option is to import the auto part from Mexico. Because of the establishment of NAFTA, the United States *switches* the source of its imports from Asia to Mexico, an example of trade diversion.

Producer surplus in Asia falls because it loses its export sales to the United States, whereas producer surplus in Mexico rises. What about the United States? Before NAFTA, it imported from Asia at a price of $20.90, of which 10% (or $1.90 per unit) consisted of the tariff. The net-of-tariff price that Asia received for the auto parts was $19. After NAFTA the United States instead imports from Mexico, at the price of $20, but it does not collect any tariff revenue at all. So the United States gains 90¢ on each unit from paying a lower price, but it also loses $1.90 in tariff revenue from not purchasing from Asia. From this example, it seems that importing the auto part from Mexico is not a very good idea for the United States because it no longer collects tariff revenue. To determine the overall impact on U.S. welfare, we can analyze the same example in a graph.

Trade Diversion in a Graph

In Figure 11-3, we show the free-trade price of the auto part from Asia as P_{asia}, and the free-trade export supply curve from Asia is the horizontal line labeled S_{asia}. By treating this price as fixed, we are supposing that the United States is a small country relative to the potential supply from Asia. Inclusive of the tariff, the cost of imported parts from Asia becomes $P_{asia} + t$, and the supply curve is $S_{asia} + t$. The free-trade supply from Mexico is shown as the upward-sloping curve labeled S_{mex}; inclusive of the tariff, the supply curve is $S_{mex} + t$.

Before NAFTA, both Mexico and Asia face the same tariff of t. So the equilibrium imports occur at point A, where the quantity imported is Q_1 and the tariff-inclusive price to the United States is $P_{asia} + t$. Of the total imports Q_1, the amount Q_2 comes from Mexico at point B, since under perfect competition these imports have the same tariff-inclusive price as those from Asia. Thus, tariff revenue is collected on imports from both Mexico and Asia, so the total tariff revenue is the area $(a + b + c + d)$ in Figure 11-3.

After Mexico joins NAFTA, it is able to sell to the United States duty-free. In that case, the relevant supply curve is S_{mex}, and imports from Mexico expand to Q_3 at point C. Notice that the price charged by Mexico at point C still equals the tariff-inclusive price from Asia, which is $P_{asia} + t$, even though Mexican imports do not have any tariff. Mexico charges that price because its marginal costs have risen along its supply curve, so even though the tariff has been removed, the price of its imports to the United States has not changed.

FIGURE 11-3

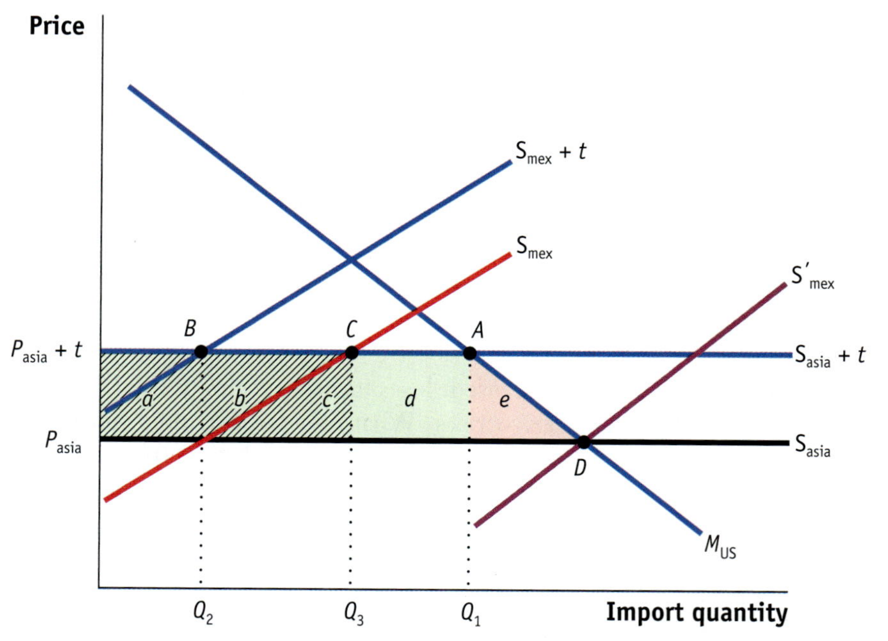

Trade Diversion With Mexico and Asia facing the same tariff of t for sales into the United States, the equilibrium is at A with the quantity Q_2 exported by Mexico and the remainder exported by Asia at a price of $P_{asia} + t$. U.S. tariff revenue is the area $(a + b + c + d)$. Eliminating the tariff with Mexico under NAFTA leads to an expansion of Mexican exports to Q_3. The United States loses the tariff revenue $(a + b + c)$, which is the U.S. loss as a result of trade diversion from Asia to Mexico.

Because the imports from Mexico enter the United States duty-free, the United States loses tariff revenue of $t \cdot Q_3$, which is the area $(a + b + c)$ in Figure 11-3. The price of imports to the United States has not changed, so the United States is worse off due to NAFTA by the loss in its tariff revenue. Mexico is better off because of the increase in its producer surplus from charging the price $P_{asia} + t$, without paying any tariff on its expanded amount of exports. Mexico's producer surplus rises by $(a + b)$, the area to the left of the supply curve S_{mex}. If we add together the changes in U.S. and Mexican welfare, the combined change in their welfare is

Loss in U.S. tariff revenue:	$-(a + b + c)$
Gain in Mexico's producer surplus:	$+(a + b)$
Combined effect due to NAFTA:	$\boldsymbol{-c}$

So we see that the combined welfare of the United States and Mexico actually *falls* as a result of NAFTA. This is a very counterintuitive result because we normally expect that countries will be better off when they move toward free trade. Instead, in this example, we see that one of the countries within the regional agreement is worse off (the United States), and so much so that its fall in welfare exceeds the gains for Mexico, so that their combined welfare falls!

Interpretation of the Loss This is one of the few instances in this textbook in which a country's movement toward free trade makes that country worse off. What is the reason for this result? Asia is the most efficient producer of auto parts in this example for units $Q_3 - Q_2$: its marginal costs equal P_{asia} (not including the tariff). By diverting production to Mexico, the marginal costs of Mexico's extra exports to the United States rise from P_{asia} (which is the marginal cost at quantity Q_2, not including the tariff) to $P_{asia} + t$ (which is Mexico's marginal cost at quantity Q_3). Therefore, the United States necessarily loses from trade diversion, and by more than Mexico's gain.

The combined loss to the United States and Mexico of area c can be interpreted as the average difference between Mexico's marginal cost (rising from P_{asia} to $P_{asia} + t$) and Asia's marginal cost (P_{asia}), multiplied by the extra imports from Mexico. This interpretation of the net loss area c is similar to the "production loss" or "efficiency loss" due to a tariff for a small country. However, in this case, the net loss comes from *removing* a tariff among the member countries of a regional agreement rather than from adding a tariff.

What you should keep in mind in this example of the adverse effects of trade diversion is that the tariff between the United States and Mexico was removed, but the tariff against imports of auto parts from Asia was maintained. So it is really only a halfway step toward free trade. We have shown that this halfway step can be bad for the countries involved rather than good. This effect of trade diversion explains why some economists oppose regional trade agreements but support multilateral agreements under the WTO.

Not All Trade Diversion Creates a Loss We should stress that the loss due to a regional trade agreement in this example is not a *necessary* result, but a *possible* result, depending on our assumptions of Mexico's marginal costs. There could also be a gain to the importing country. In Figure 11-3, for example, suppose that after joining NAFTA, Mexico has considerable investment in the auto parts industry, and its supply curve shifts to S'_{mex} rather than S_{mex}. Then equilibrium imports to the United States will occur at point D, at the price P_{asia}, and Mexico will *fully* replace Asia as a supplier of auto parts. As compared with the initial situation with the tariff, the United States will lose all tariff revenue of area $(a + b + c + d)$. But the import price drops to P_{asia}, so it has a gain in consumer surplus of area $(a + b + c + d + e)$. Therefore, the net change in U.S. welfare is

Gain in consumer surplus:	$+ (a + b + c + d + e)$
Loss in tariff revenue:	$- (a + b + c + d)$
Net effect on U.S. welfare:	$+ e$

The United States experiences a net gain in consumer surplus in this case, and Mexico's producer surplus rises because it is exporting more.

This case combines elements of trade diversion (Mexico has replaced Asia) and trade creation (Mexico is exporting more to the United States than total U.S. imports before NAFTA). Thus, we conclude that NAFTA and other regional trade agreements have the potential to create gains among their members, but only if the amount of trade creation exceeds the amount of trade diversion. In the following application we look at what happened to Canada and the United States when free trade opened between them, to see whether the extent of trade creation for Canada exceeded the amount of trade diversion.

APPLICATION

Trade Creation and Diversion for Canada

In 1989 Canada formed a free-trade agreement with the United States and, five years later, entered into the North American Free Trade Agreement with the United States and Mexico. Research by Professor Daniel Trefler at the University of Toronto has analyzed the effect of these free-trade agreements on Canadian manufacturing industries. As summarized in Chapter 6, initially there was unemployment in Canada, but that was a short-term result. A decade after the free-trade agreement with the United States, employment in Canadian manufacturing had recovered and that sector also enjoyed a boom in productivity.

In his research, Trefler also estimated the amount of trade creation versus trade diversion for Canada in its trade with the United States. He found that the reduction in Canadian tariffs on U.S. goods increased imports of those goods by 54%. This increase was trade creation. However, since Canada was now buying more tariff-free goods from the United States, those tariff reductions reduced Canadian imports from the rest of the world by 40% (trade diversion). To compare these amounts, keep in mind that imports from the United States make up 80% of all Canadian imports, whereas imports from the rest of the world make up the remaining 20%. So the 54% increase in imports from the United States should be multiplied (or weighted) by its 80% share in overall Canadian imports to get the amount of trade creation. Likewise, the 40% reduction in imports from the rest of the world should be multiplied by its 20% share in Canadian imports to get trade diversion. Taking the difference between the trade created and diverted, we obtain

$$\underbrace{80\%}_{\substack{\text{Share of} \\ \text{U.S. imports}}} \times \underbrace{54\%}_{\substack{\text{Increase in} \\ \text{U.S. imports}}} - \underbrace{20\%}_{\substack{\text{Share of} \\ \text{other imports}}} \times \underbrace{40\%}_{\substack{\text{Decrease in} \\ \text{other imports}}} \approx 35\% > 0$$

Because this calculation gives a positive number, Trefler concludes that trade creation exceeded trade diversion when Canada and the United States entered into the free-trade agreement. Therefore, Canada definitely gained from the free-trade agreement with the United States. ■

2 International Agreements on Labor Issues

Regional agreements often include issues other than tariffs and trade. For example, the NAFTA agreement included two side agreements that were negotiated by President Clinton to help ensure its passage through the U.S. Congress. One side agreement dealt with the environment (discussed later in this chapter), and the other dealt with labor issues.

We use the term **labor standards** to refer to all issues that directly affect workers, including occupational health and safety, child labor, minimum wages, and so on. Labor standards were included in NAFTA to satisfy several groups. First, consumers and policy makers are often concerned with the working conditions in factories abroad and want to avoid "sweat shop" conditions that exploit workers. Second, unions in the industrial countries are also concerned with these conditions, partly because of solidarity with foreign workers and partly because of the concern that poor labor standards abroad will create more competition for U.S. workers (imports will be cheaper because manufacturers don't have to spend as much on safer working conditions and other labor standards).

Economists are sometimes skeptical about such concerns for foreign workers, however, and view attempts to enforce minimum labor standards as a form of "disguised protection" in the industrial countries. For example, the Indian economist T. N. Srinivasan of Yale University states, "The demand for linkage between trading rights and observance of standards with respect to the environment and labor would seem to arise largely from protectionist motives."[5] Likewise, the World Bank writes, "The real danger of using trade sanctions as an instrument for promoting basic rights is that the trade-standards linkage could become highjacked by protectionist interests attempting to preserve activities rendered uncompetitive by cheaper imports."[6] The former prime minister of Malaysia, Mahathir bin Mohammed, goes even further: "Western countries openly propose to eliminate the competitive edge of East Asia. . . . [T]he professed concern about workers welfare is motivated by selfish interest . . . to put as many obstacles as possible in the way of anyone attempting to catch up and compete with the West."[7] Whether you agree with these sentiments or not, economics teaches that we need to be careful that enforcing labor standards abroad does not worsen the situation for foreign workers by leading to unemployment. We will discuss some examples in which such an outcome has occurred.

Labor Side Agreement under NAFTA

The labor side agreement negotiated under NAFTA does not change the existing labor laws in these countries but is meant to improve the *enforcement* of such laws. If one country believes that another is failing to enforce its own laws in these areas, then a complaint can be brought before a commission of the North American Agreement on Labor Cooperation (NAALC), which includes representatives from each country and which attempts to resolve the dispute through consultation and cooperation. Although many cases deal with conditions in the *maquiladora* plants in Mexico, operating just south of the Mexico-U.S. border, complaints have also been brought against the United States, as with a case in 1998 involving farm workers picking apples in the State of Washington, for example.[8] In that case, the petitioners in Mexico charged that the United States failed to protect the rights of workers, especially migrant labor. The resolution of this case, reached in 2000, called for "planned outreach sessions at which these issues were to be discussed with migrant workers as well as a public forum for workers, unions, employers, and government officials."[9]

---

[5] T. N. Srinivasan, 1994, "International Labor Standards Once Again." In U.S. Department of Labor, Bureau of International Affairs, *International Labor Standards and Global Economic Integration: Proceedings of a Symposium* (Washington, D.C.), p. 36. All quotations in this paragraph are cited in Richard B. Freeman, 1996, "International Labor Standards and World Trade: Friends or Foes?" In Jeffrey J. Schott, ed., *The World Trading System: Challenges Ahead* (Washington, D.C.: Peterson Institute for International Economics), Chap. 5.

[6] World Bank, *World Development Report*, 1995, p. 79.

[7] *International Herald Tribune*, May 17, 1994, p. 6.

[8] The annual reports of the North American Commission for Labor Cooperation are available at http://www.naalc.org; choose "Publications" and then "Annual Reports."

[9] See the summary of this and other NAALC cases in Joel Solomon, 2001, "Trading Away Rights: The Unfulfilled Promise of NAFTA's Labor Side Agreement," http://www.hrw.org.

Critics of the NAALC agreement have argued that the procedures for resolving disputes are slow and include major exceptions that render them ineffective. For example, a study at the University of California, Los Angeles, concluded, "The NAALC has failed to protect workers' rights to safe jobs and is in danger of fading into oblivion."[10] Others argue that the agreement has created an institutional forum in which unions and labor activists from the three countries can build solidarity and that even the review of cases alone can lead firms to modify their practices.

Other Labor Agreements

Besides the labor side agreement in NAFTA, there are many other examples of international agreements that monitor the conditions of workers in foreign countries. Unions and other organizations are concerned with issues such as job safety, the right of workers to unionize, workers' entitlement to breaks and not being forced to work overtime, and so on. In some cases, the pressure from unions and grassroots organizations can lead to positive changes in the situation faced by workers in other countries. Consumers also have an important role to play through their purchasing power: if consumers are more likely to buy a product that has been produced using methods that respect the rights of workers, then companies will implement such methods more quickly.

Consumer Responsibility How much do consumers value the idea that the clothing they purchase is made under conditions that do not exploit foreign workers? A survey conducted by the National Bureau of Economic Research asked people to respond to this question, with the results shown in Table 11-2.[11]

Individuals in the first group, Sample *A*, were asked whether they cared about "the condition of workers who make the clothing they buy," and 84% responded that they care a lot or somewhat. Then they were asked, "How much more would you be willing to pay for items made under good working conditions," for items worth $10 and $100. The premium they were willing to pay was $2.80 for a $10 item and $15 for a $100 item.

Individuals in the second group, Sample *B*, were asked about the premium they would pay for a T-shirt made under "good" conditions, but also about the discount needed to buy a T-shirt made under "bad" conditions. In this group, 84% said that they would choose an identically priced alternative to a T-shirt "with a nice logo" if local students told them that the one with the nice logo was made under poor working conditions. Furthermore, 65% said they would not buy the T-shirt made under poor working conditions at all. Among the 35% who were willing to consider buying it, the average discount to buy it was $4.30, whereas the premium they were willing to pay if assured the T-shirt was made under good conditions was $1.83.

The results of this survey highlight several interesting observations about people's attitudes toward labor standards. One such observation is that consumers have a downward-sloping demand curve for labor standards; that is, many people are willing

[10] "NAFTA's Labor Side Agreement: Fading into Oblivion? An Assessment of Workplace Health and Safety Cases," March 2004, UCLA Center for Labor Research and Education.

[11] See Kimberly Ann Elliott and Richard B. Freeman, 2003, "White Hats or Don Quixotes: Human Rights Vigilantes in the Global Economy." In Richard B. Freeman, Joni Hersch, and Lawrence Mishel, eds., *Emerging Labor Market Institutions for the 21st Century* [Chicago: University of Chicago Press for the National Bureau of Economic Research (NBER)]; and Kimberly Ann Elliott and Richard B. Freeman, 2003, *Can Labor Standards Improve under Globalization?* (Washington, D.C.: Peterson Institute for International Economics), Chap. 2.

TABLE 11-2

Survey Responses This table summarizes the responses from a survey conducted by the National Bureau of Economic Research that asked individuals their attitudes toward an item made under good working conditions and under poor working conditions.

Sample A	
Consumers who say they care about the condition of workers who make the clothing they buy:	
A lot	46%
Somewhat	38%
Only a little	8%
Not at all (or no response)	8%
Consumers willing to pay more for an item if assured it was made under good working conditions:	81%
Additional amount willing to pay for $10 item	$2.80
Additional amount willing to pay for $100 item	$15
Sample B	
Would choose an alternative to a T-shirt "with a nice logo" that local students say is made under poor working conditions if alternative is the same price	84%
Would not buy T-shirt made under poor working conditions at all	65%
Would buy T-shirt made under poor working conditions at average discount of	$4.30
Would pay more for T-shirt if came with assurance it was made under good conditions	78%
Average additional amount would pay (including as zeros those who did not offer to pay more or were inconsistent)	$1.83

Source: Kimberly Ann Elliott and Richard B. Freeman, 2003, Can Labor Standards Improve under Globalization? *(Washington, D.C: Peterson Institute for International Economics), Chap. 2, Table 2.1, Sample A.*

to pay at least a small amount to ensure good labor standards (or simply switch to an alternative with the same price), though relatively few are willing to pay a lot. For example, for a higher-priced good, consumers were willing to pay a smaller percentage of its value to ensure good labor conditions. A second observation is that individuals had to receive a higher discount to purchase a shirt made under poor conditions than they were willing to pay for a shirt made under good conditions. This finding indicates that consumers are more worried about potential losses (paying more) than potential gains (the discount), which is a commonly observed characteristic of consumer behavior. Results similar to those reported in Table 11-2 have also been found in larger-scale surveys of consumers in the United States and the United Kingdom. We conclude that a sizable number of consumers are willing to adjust their shopping patterns in response to the conditions faced by foreign workers.

Corporate Responsibility Because of the pressure from consumers and unions, corporations have started to monitor and improve the conditions in their overseas plants and the plants of their overseas subcontractors. One example of this monitoring is reported in **Headlines: Wal-Mart Orders Chinese Suppliers to Lift Standards.** Wal-Mart insisted that its factories in China meet strict guidelines on both labor and environmental standards, or lose its business.

Country Responsibility Beyond the actions of consumers, unions, and corporations, should national governments monitor and enforce labor regulations in foreign countries? Several U.S. trade laws give the president the power to withhold trade privileges from countries that do not give their workers basic rights, including the right to organize. One study showed that these provisions have been used by the president

HEADLINES

Wal-Mart Orders Chinese Suppliers to Lift Standards

In response to criticism from activists in the United States, Wal-Mart has established strict labor and environmental standards that its overseas suppliers must follow. This article reports on these standards for factories in China.

Wal-Mart, the world's biggest retailer, yesterday told its Chinese suppliers to meet strict environmental and social standards or risk losing its business. "Meeting social and environmental standards is not optional," Lee Scott, Wal-Mart's chief executive, told a gathering of more than 1,000 suppliers in Beijing. "A company that cheats on overtime and on the age of its labour, that dumps its scraps and its chemicals in our rivers, that does not pay its taxes or honour its contracts will ultimately cheat on the quality of its products."

Wal-Mart has been pursuing a drive to improve its reputation on environmental and social issues over the past three years in response to growing criticism in the US over issues that include labour conditions in its supplier factories. . . . The requirements include a clear demonstration of compliance with Chinese environmental laws, an improvement of 20 per cent in energy efficiency at the company's 200 largest China suppliers and disclosure of the names and addresses of every factory involved in the production process. The company will require a 25 per cent rise in the efficiency of energy-intensive products such as flat-screen TVs by 2011.

Source: Excerpted from Tom Mitchell and Jonathan Birchall, "Wal-Mart Orders Chinese Suppliers to Lift Standards," The Financial Times, *October 23, 2008, p. 19.*

32 times from 1985 to 1994, but only one-half of the cases are judged to have been effective in improving workers' rights.[12]

There are two problems with trying to withhold trade privileges. First, denying preferences to a foreign country across all industries is a very broad foreign policy action, when the problems may occur only in particular companies. Second, these laws involve a comparison of U.S. labor standards with those found abroad and the judgment that foreign practices are inadequate. Many people believe that countries should choose their own domestic policies, even when they conflict with established norms abroad, and that countries should not impose their preferences on each other.[13]

An alternative approach to government sanctions is for nongovernmental organizations (NGOs) to take actions that limit undesirable sweatshop activities. According to one research study focusing on Indonesia, actions by NGOs are actually more effective than government action.[14] This study showed that when the U.S. government threatened to withdraw tariff privileges for Indonesia, the minimum wage was doubled in real terms. That increase in the wage reduced the employment of unskilled workers by as much as 10%, so these workers were harmed. The anti-sweatshop activism by NGOs targeted at textile, apparel, and footwear plants raised real wages as well, by ensuring that plants paid the minimum wage. But this activism did not

[12] Kimberly Ann Elliott and Richard B. Freeman, 2003, *Can Labor Standards Improve under Globalization?* (Washington, D.C.: Peterson Institute for International Economics), p. 79.

[13] An important example here is child labor, which is avoided in industrial countries but may be necessary for families' survival in developing countries.

[14] Ann Harrison and Jason Scorse, May 2004, "Moving Up or Moving Out? Anti-Sweatshop Activists and Labor Market Outcomes," NBER Working Paper No. 10492.

reduce employment to the same extent. Plants targeted by activists were more likely to close, but those losses were offset by employment gains at surviving plants, which benefited from the growth in exports in these industries. So there was no significant decline in employment from the pressure exerted by NGOs.

The message of this study is that pressure from the U.S. government to raise wages was too blunt a tool to be effective, whereas the actions of NGOs, which were better targeted at particular plants, resulted in higher wages with little or no net loss in employment. In addition, the pressure from activists can sometimes make U.S. companies more willing to reveal their foreign plants, as Nike has done, thereby making them open to monitoring.

Living Wage The final question we can ask about labor issues is whether it is fair to expect foreign firms to pay a **living wage** to their workers; that is, a wage above the norm in the developing country. This issue is perhaps the most controversial part of labor standards because it involves a difficult judgment: How high should foreign wages be to make them acceptable to activists in industrial countries? Economists have a ready answer: the wages should be as high as the market will allow, and not any higher. Raising wages above their equilibrium level will very likely lead to unemployment. In extreme cases, workers laid off from manufacturing jobs in developing countries might be forced into prostitution or other illegal activities that are far worse than the low-wage factory positions they held.

These types of concerns lead many economists and policy makers to reject calls for a "living wage." But this rejection *does not* mean that we should abandon other types of labor standards. Workers in all countries are entitled to conditions that are safe and clean, honesty in payment, the right to unionize, and so on. Consumers, corporations, and unions all play an important role in advocating for such conditions in foreign countries, and that advocacy needs to continue. The enforcement of labor standards can ensure that workers benefit from trade without being exploited in the workplace.

3 International Agreements on the Environment

Many of the protesters at the 1999 Seattle meeting of the WTO, shown in the photo at the start of this chapter, were concerned about how WTO rulings affect the environment. The WTO does not directly address environmental issues; other international agreements, called **multilateral environmental agreements,** deal specifically with the environment. There are some 200 multilateral environmental agreements, including the Convention on International Trade in Endangered Species (CITES) and the Montreal Protocol on Substances that Deplete the Ozone Layer (which has eliminated the use of chlorofluorocarbons, CFCs, which deplete the ozone layer). But the WTO still indirectly affects the environment as the protesters in Seattle were well aware. We begin by clarifying the role of the GATT and WTO in environmental issues.

Environmental Issues in the GATT and WTO

In an earlier chapter (see **Side Bar: Key Provisions of the GATT**), we summarized some of the founding articles of the GATT. Not mentioned there was Article XX, known as the "green provision." Article XX allows countries to adopt their own laws in relation to environmental issues, provided that these laws are applied uniformly to domestic and foreign producers so that the laws do not discriminate against imports.

In its full text, Article XX of the GATT states that "subject to the requirement that such measures are not applied in a manner which would constitute a . . . disguised restriction on international trade, nothing in this Agreement shall be construed to prevent the adoption or enforcement by any contracting party of measures: . . . (b) necessary to protect human, animal or plant life or health; . . . (g) relating to the conservation of exhaustible natural resources if such measures are made effective in conjunction with restrictions on domestic production or consumption."

If the provisions of the GATT and WTO permit countries to apply their own environmental regulations, why were people dressed as turtles and dolphins protesting WTO rulings at the 1999 Seattle meetings? To understand the concerns of these protesters, we need to dig into the details of some specific GATT/WTO cases, summarized in Table 11-3.[15]

Tuna-Dolphin Case In 1991, before the WTO was formed, Mexico brought a GATT case against the United States. The reason for the case was that the United States had banned imports of tuna from Mexico because Mexican fishermen did not catch tuna using nets that safeguarded against the accidental capture of dolphins. The U.S. Marine Mammal Protection Act requires that U.S. tuna fishermen use nets that are safe for dolphins, and by Article XX(g) of the GATT, the United States reasoned that the same requirement could be extended to Mexican fishermen. But the U.S. ban on imports of tuna from Mexico ran afoul of the GATT.

GATT concluded that the United States could not ban the import of tuna because the United States applied the import restriction to the *production process method* and not the product itself. The idea that the production process could not be a basis for a trade restriction was a principle of GATT that was upheld in this case. In addition, the GATT panel ruled that "GATT rules did not allow one country to take trade action for the purpose of attempting to enforce its own domestic laws in another country—even to protect animal health or exhaustible natural resources." Both of these conclusions were a blow to environmentalists interested in protecting the dolphins, and this is the reason that some of the Seattle protesters were dressed as dolphins.

Even though the GATT panel ruled in favor of Mexico and against the United States in this case, the strong consumer response led to the dolphins being protected. Interested parties in the United States and Mexico worked out a system of labeling that now appears on cans of tuna in the United States, declaring the product to be "dolphin-safe." Since 1990 the major companies have sold only this "dolphin friendly" product from Mexico, and the labeling procedure was found to be consistent with GATT. So despite the initial ruling against the United States, the outcome of this case has had the desired effect of protecting dolphins in Mexican waters (in addition to the protection they already received in U.S. waters).

---

[15] These cases are drawn from Jeffrey A. Frankel, November 2003, "The Environment and Globalization," NBER Working Paper No. 10090. Environmental cases are summarized on the WTO webpage at http://www.wto.org/English/tratop_e/envir_e/edis00_e.htm, and details are also provided at the Trade and Environmental Database at the American University, http://www.american.edu/TED/ted.htm.

TABLE 11-3

Environmental Cases at the GATT and WTO This table shows the outcome of environmental cases ruled upon by the GATT and WTO.

Case	Issue	Outcome
Tuna-Dolphin		
In 1991 Mexico appealed to the GATT against a U.S. ban on Mexican tuna imports.	The United States put a ban on imports of tuna from Mexico that were not caught with nets which were safe for dolphins (as required in the United States under the Marine Mammal Protection Act).	In 1992 the GATT ruled in favor of Mexico that the U.S. import ban violated GATT rules. But the strong consumer response led to labeling of imported tuna as "dolphin friendly."
Shrimp-Turtle		
In 1996 India, Malaysia, Pakistan, and Thailand appealed to the WTO against a U.S. ban on shrimp imports.	The United States put a ban on imports of shrimp from India, Malaysia, Pakistan, and Thailand that were not caught with nets safe for sea turtles (as required in the United States under the Endangered Species Act).	In 1998 the WTO ruled in favor of India, Malaysia, Pakistan, and Thailand that the U.S. import ban violated WTO rules. But the United States could still require these countries to use turtle-safe nets, provided that adequate notice and consultation were pursued.
Gasoline		
In 1994 Venezuela and Brazil appealed to the GATT against a U.S. ban on gasoline imports.	The United States put a ban on imports of gasoline from Venezuela and Brazil because the gas exceeded the maximum amount allowed of a smog-causing chemical (under the U.S. Clean Air Act).	In 1996 the WTO ruled in favor of Venezuela and Brazil that the U.S. import restriction violated equal treatment of domestic and foreign producers. The United States adjusted the rules to be consistent with the WTO and still pursued its own clean air goals.
Biotech Food		
In 2003 the United States appealed to the WTO that Europe was keeping out genetically modified food and crops.	Since 1998 no imports of genetically modified food or crops had been approved in the European Union.	In 2006 the WTO ruled that the European actions violated the principle that import restrictions must be based on "scientific risk assessments." Labeling and consumer concerns in Europe will still limit such imports.

Source: Updated from Jeffrey A. Frankel, 2005, "The Environment and Globalization." In Michael Weinstein, ed., Globalization: What's New, *(New York: Columbia University Press), pp. 129–169. Reprinted in R. Stavins, ed., 2005,* Economics of the Environment *(New York: W. W. Norton), pp. 361–398.*

Shrimp-Turtle Case In 1996, just after the WTO was formed, a second closely related case arose involving shrimp and sea turtles. In this case, India, Malaysia, Pakistan, and Thailand appealed to the WTO against a U.S. ban on shrimp imports. The United States had banned imports of shrimp from these countries because they were not caught with nets that were safe for sea turtles, as required in the United States under the Endangered Species Act of 1987. Again, by Article XX(g) of the GATT, the United States reasoned that the same requirement could be extended against fishermen from these Asian countries.

Although this case has a number of similarities to the earlier tuna-dolphin case, the outcome at the WTO was different. The WTO still ruled against the United States, but in this case it *did not rule* against the principle that one country could restrict imports based on the production process method used in another country. On the contrary, the WTO ruled that the United States was consistently applying its laws to American and Asian producers in requiring that turtle-safe nets be used. The problem with the U.S. import ban was that it was applied without due notice and consultation with the exporting countries involved, which did not allow the countries sufficient time to employ turtle-safe devices. In other words, the WTO ruling against the United States was on narrow, technical grounds and not on the principle of protecting endangered species in foreign waters.

In many ways, this WTO ruling was more favorable to environmentalists than the earlier tuna-dolphin ruling at the GATT. The WTO panel explicitly recognized that "the conservation of exhaustible natural resources" referred to in Article XX(g) applies to living resources, especially if they are threatened with extinction. After the United States allowed more flexibility in its regulations and made good-faith efforts to develop an agreement with the Asian producers, the laws requiring the use of turtle-safe nets for exporters were found to be consistent with the WTO in a 2001 ruling.

Gasoline from Venezuela and Brazil A third GATT/WTO case that involves environmental issues was brought against the United States by Venezuela and Brazil in 1994. The United States had restricted imports of gasoline from these countries because the gas did not meet the requirements of the U.S. Clean Air Act (which mandates a maximum amount of certain smog-causing chemicals). In this case, the WTO ruled in 1996 that the United States violated the principle that national and foreign producers should be treated equally. The issue was that refineries in the United States were given a three-year grace period to meet the Clean Air Act goals, whereas that grace period was not extended to refineries abroad. So the U.S. import restriction discriminated against the refineries in Venezuela and Brazil.

This gasoline case is often seen as a loss for environmentalists, but economists would argue that U.S. regulations were in fact acting like "disguised protection" against the import of Venezuelan gasoline. From the perspective of promoting free trade and treating foreign producers fairly, the WTO was correct in ruling against the United States. The United States was not blocked by the WTO in pursuing clean air goals, but it had to modify its requirements so that they were applied equally to U.S. and foreign producers.

Biotech Food in Europe A final, ongoing case concerns whether food that has been genetically modified can be imported into Europe. In 2003 the United States (joined by Argentina and Canada) appealed to the WTO that the European Union was keeping out genetically modified food and crops. Since 1998 no such imports had been approved in the European Union, though it denied that there was any "moratorium" on these imports. Rather, Europe claimed that it needed more time to study the health effects of genetically modified organisms and was not approving such imports for precautionary reasons.

The WTO ruled in 2006 that the European actions violated the principle that import restrictions must be based on "scientific risk assessments." That is, countries cannot keep out imports based on precautionary reasons but must have some scientific evidence to back up the import restriction. Despite this ruling, Europe can use consumer labeling to allow the buyers to decide whether to purchase foods that have been genetically modified. As in our earlier discussion of the labeling of U.S. tuna imports from Mexico, it is expected that the labeling of genetically modified organisms in Europe will allow consumers to exert their power in limiting purchases of these foods if they so choose.

Summary of GATT/WTO Cases The cases in Table 11-3 show that WTO rulings have not adversely affected the environment: in the tuna-dolphin case, the reaction of consumers in the United States was enough to ensure that dolphin-safe nets were used in Mexico; in the shrimp-turtle case, the WTO did not object to the principle of requiring foreign countries to use turtle-friendly nets, as do U.S. companies; in the gasoline case, the imports from Venezuela and Brazil had to meet the requirements of the Clean Air Act, after the same grace period given to U.S. firms; and in the case of biotech foods, labeling in Europe is expected to limit such imports if consumers so choose.

These outcomes have led some observers to conclude that even though environmentalists have lost some specific cases at the WTO, they have gained the upper hand in ensuring that environmental concerns are respected: environmentalists may have lost some battles, but they have won the war! This conclusion does not mean that environmental concerns can now be dropped. On the contrary, the lobbying activity of environmental groups, including the costumed protesters at the Seattle meetings, has been important in shifting public opinion and WTO rulings in directions that support the environment, and such lobbying activities should continue to be pursued.

Does Trade Help or Harm the Environment?

Having clarified the role of the WTO in resolving specific cases brought between particular countries, let us turn to the more general question of whether trade helps or harms the environment. Some of the protesters at the 1999 WTO meetings in Seattle believe that trade is bad for the environment and have examples to support that belief. But there are other examples to support the claim that trade is good for the environment. So the answer to the question of whether trade helps or harms the environment is that *either* outcome is possible, depending on the case being considered. Let us turn to some examples to see the possible outcomes.

U.S. Sugar Quota The United States maintains an import quota on sugar. The import quota leads to higher prices for American buyers, both consumers and firms, who pay domestic prices that can be as high as twice the world price. One source of demand for imported sugarcane comes from firms that are producing ethanol, an alternative (or additive) to gasoline that can be produced from sugar or corn. Because of the high import price for sugarcane, however, these firms instead purchase corn from American farmers, who are themselves subsidized by the U.S. government. As a result of the quota for sugar imports and the subsidies for corn production, much more corn than sugar is used to produce ethanol.

The problem with this arrangement is that producing ethanol from corn is much less energy-efficient than producing it from sugarcane. As described in the article **Headlines: The Power of Big Corn,** corn depletes the soil and requires fertilizers to grow, which themselves use energy in their production. Because the net energy savings by making ethanol from corn and using it as a gasoline substitute are poor, it would be better to use sugarcane to produce ethanol, *if* it could be purchased at world prices. This example shows how the U.S. quota on sugar has an indirect and negative

HEADLINES

The Power of Big Corn

Because of the U.S. import quota on imports of sugarcane, corn is used instead to produce ethanol. This editorial argues that the corn-based ethanol does not save energy, and it would be better to use sugarcane.

The nation's growing appetite for ethanol as an alternative motor fuel is so great that one environmental group warns of a corn shortage, which could raise prices for the many corn-based food and drink products the nation consumes. This competition for corn, though, could be easily avoided if Congress would do away with the tariffs and import restrictions that keep the United States from making greater use of sugar-based ethanol, which requires much less energy than the corn-based version. . . .

The country is relying on corn for ethanol even though it is far from ideal for the purpose. The ratio of energy gained versus the energy needed to plant, fertilize, and harvest the crop is poor, and corn crops are notoriously hard on soil. With technological advances, scientists hope to be able to replace corn with agricultural waste or a non-food plant like switchgrass.

In the meantime, sugar cane could be used to produce ethanol with much less investment in energy. But domestic sugar growers get such a high price for their product due to government price-fixing, tariffs, and import restrictions that it would be uneconomic for them to turn to ethanol production. Those same tariffs and import limits make it impossible to import any of the world's abundant supply of sugar and turn it into ethanol. And just to make sure that no one imports cheap Brazilian sugar-based ethanol, Congress has protected the Corn Belt with a 51 cent per gallon tariff on foreign ethanol.

The result is that ethanol in the United States uses more energy and costs more than it has to, and American drivers use less of it than they would with a freer market. The Earth Policy Institute report points to a further cost to corn farmers' grip on Congress: excessive use of the crop for ethanol could drive up food prices. The country would benefit if Congress would get out of the way and let sugar-based ethanol compete on a level playing field.

Source: Excerpted from "The Power of Big Corn," Boston Globe, *January 15, 2007, editorial.*

impact on the environment. Eliminating the quota, and allowing free trade in sugar, would benefit the environment because it would allow more sugarcane to be used to produce ethanol, rather than corn.

U.S. Automobile VER The sugar quota example is not the only case in which a U.S. trade restriction has worked to harm the environment. In an earlier chapter, we discussed the "voluntary" export restraint (VER) on exports of Japanese cars to the United States, which began in 1981. The VER limited the number of cars that Japanese firms could export each year, but not their value, so there was an incentive for the Japanese firms to export larger and/or more luxurious models. As the quality of the Japanese cars rose, so did the engine size and weight of the vehicles; as a result, the average gas mileage of the imported cars fell.

The impact of the VER on gas mileage is shown in Figure 11-4, where we use data on the Japanese imported cars from 1979 to 1982, before and after the VER began. The horizontal axis shows the change in the quantity sold (in percent) between these years, and the vertical axis shows the gas mileage of each model. The data show that the luxury models with the lowest gas mileage—such as the Maxima, Cressida, and Mazda 626—experienced the greatest increase in sales between these years. Sales went up despite the limit on total imports because the prices of these more luxurious models did not rise as much as the prices of the economy models. U.S. consumers shifted

FIGURE 11-4

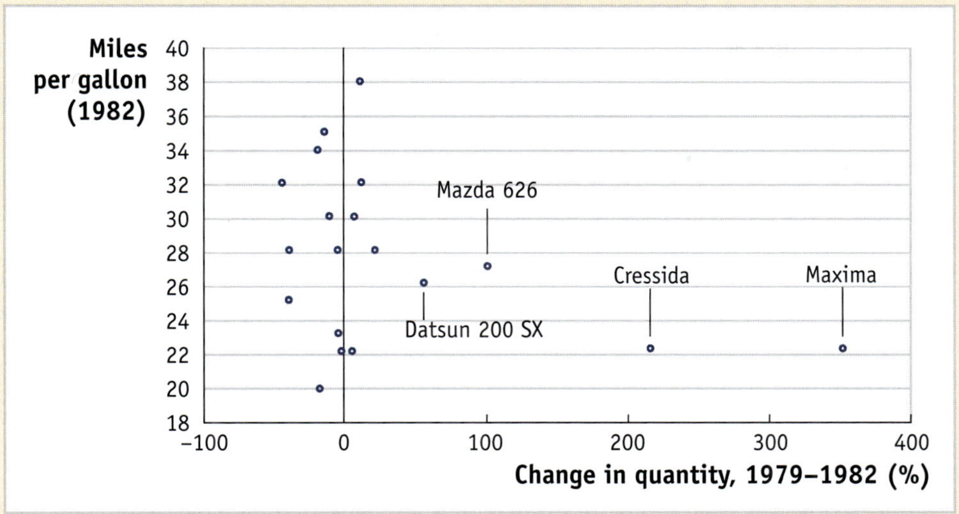

U.S. Imports of Japanese Autos This figure uses data on Japanese imported cars from 1979 to 1982, before and after the "voluntary" export restraint with Japan began. The horizontal axis shows the change in the quantity sold (in percent) between these years, and the vertical axis shows the gas mileage of each model. The models with the lowest mileage—such as the Maxima, Cressida, and Mazda 626—experienced the greatest increase in sales between these years.

their purchases toward the luxury models, and because those models had worse gas mileage, the VER increased the use of energy and led to greater carbon dioxide emissions from the vehicles, therefore harming the environment. Conversely, a free-trade policy would have allowed consumers to continue to import more fuel-efficient cars from Japan during the 1980s and would have been better for the environment.

The Tragedy of the Commons

The two previous examples, dealing with trade in sugar and automobiles, illustrate how free trade can be good for the environment. We now turn to two other cases in which free trade has harmed the environment by threatening endangered species.

Trade in Fish Because of overharvesting, many species of fish are no longer commercially viable and, in some extreme cases, are close to extinction. Examples include the Atlantic cod, tuna in the Mediterranean, and sturgeon in European and Asian waters. According to one scientific study, 29% of fish and seafood species have collapsed; that is, their catch has declined by 90% or more between 1950 and 2003. The same authors writing in 2009 find that the "exploitation rates" of some species were reduced, but that "63% of assessed fish stocks worldwide still require rebuilding, and even lower exploitation rates are needed to reverse the collapse of vulnerable species."[16]

[16] Juliet Eilperin, "World's Fish Supply Running Out, Researchers Warn," *Washington Post*, November 3, 2006, p. A01, citing an article from *Science*; and Boris Worm, et al., "Rebuilding Global Fisheries," *Science* 2009, 325, pp. 578–585.

What has led to this overharvesting of fish? Economists believe that this outcome occurs whenever people are competing for the same resource stock (fish, in this case) and refer to this phenomena as the **tragedy of the commons.** When a resource such as fish is treated as **common property** that anyone can harvest, it will be subject to overfishing and its stocks will diminish rapidly over time as each producer seeks to maximize its own share of the resource. International trade can exacerbate the tragedy of the commons by directing global demand toward the resources of a particular country or region so that there is even more overharvesting of fish under free trade.[17]

The Solution to the Tragedy of the Commons The fundamental cause of the tragedy is not that the resource is traded internationally but that the resource is treated as common property by the people who are harvesting it. If instead there was a system of rules that assigned property rights to the resource and limited the harvest of each person, then the overharvesting could be avoided. When a resource is truly global in nature, however, then it is not enough to assign property rights within a country; instead, an international agreement is needed to prevent overharvesting of the resource. One country acting on its own does not have enough incentive to control its harvest if other countries do not also enact controls. In the absence of international controls, international trade will make the tragedy of the commons and overharvesting worse, as has occurred for some species of fish.

International agreements for fish and other endangered species are arranged through the Convention on International Trade in Endangered Species (CITES). The article **Headlines: Europe Leans Toward Bluefin Trade Ban** describes recent action taken by European officials under CITES to limit international trade in bluefin tuna (which is prized for sushi) from European waters. If the bluefin tuna is listed as endangered under CITES, then international trade in this species would have to stop not only for Europe but also for American fishermen. The fishing industry is opposed to this ban, as is Japan as the principal consuming nation.

Trade in Buffalo The example of trade in fish is not the only case in which international trade has interacted with the tragedy of the commons to result in the near extinction of a species. A historical case from America occurred with the slaughter of the Great Plains buffalo in a 10-year period from 1870 to 1880. Various reasons are often given for the slaughter: the railroad allowed hunters to reach the Great Plains easier; the buffalo were killed by the U.S. military in its fight against Native Americans; and climate change on the Great Plains, which had a wet period up to the 1850s followed by 30 years of drought, combined with overhunting by Native Americans. But recent research has uncovered a new reason that dominates all others for the slaughter of the buffalo: an invention in London circa 1871 that allowed the buffalo hides to be tanned for industrial use (such as for belts), creating a huge demand from Europe for the hides.[18] As a result, the price of hides increased in

[17] See James A. Brander and M. Scott Taylor, April 1998, "Open Access Renewable Resources: Trade and Trade Policy in a Two-Country World," *Journal of International Economics*, 44(2), 181–210, for a theoretical model in which international trade interacts with the tragedy of the commons to result in losses from trade for the exporter.

[18] See M. Scott Taylor, March 2007, "Buffalo Hunt: International Trade and the Virtual Extinction of the North American Bison," NBER Working Paper No. 12969.

America, and the vast majority of untanned hides were exported to Europe for use in industry.

An estimate of the import of untanned hides from the United States to the United Kingdom and France is shown in Figure 11-5. These estimates come from comparing import demand in the United Kingdom and France with demand in Canada, where the invention allowing buffalo hides to be tanned for industrial use was not known. We are therefore looking at the *extra* demand in the United Kingdom and France after the invention was put to use. We can see from Figure 11-5 that the amount of imports into these countries (in excess of imports into Canada) was small or negative before 1871, but then grew rapidly and peaked in 1875. That year the United Kingdom and France combined imported more than 1 million hides and, over the entire period from 1871 to 1878, imported some 3.5 million hides, which can plausibly account for the slaughter of the entire Great Plains herd.[19] A further slight increase in imports in the 1880s likely reflects hides from the Northern herd of buffalo in the United States.

FIGURE 11-5

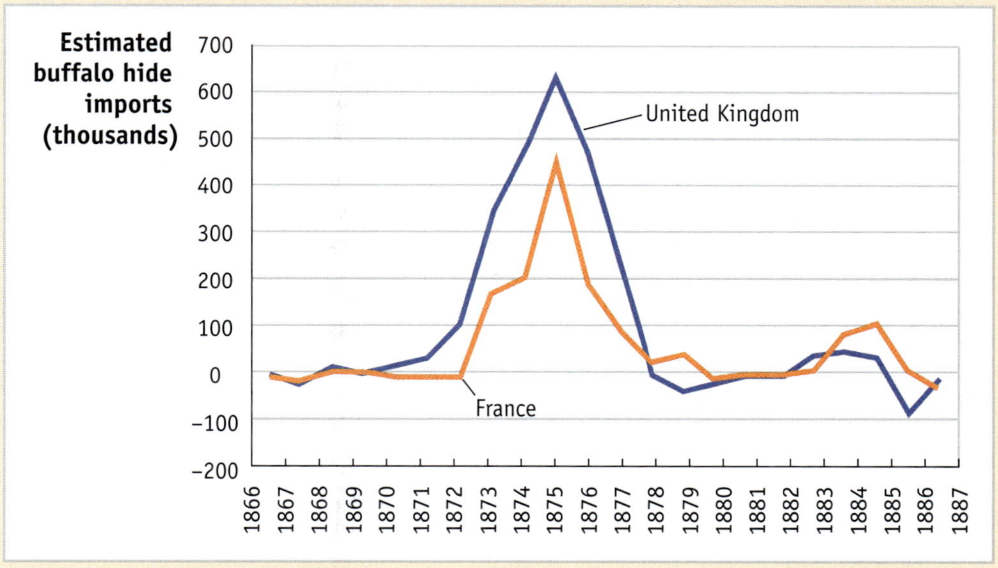

Buffalo Hide Imports This figure shows estimates of the imports to the United Kingdom and France of buffalo hides from the United States. The amount of imports into these countries (in excess of imports to Canada) was small or negative before 1871, but then grew rapidly and peaked in 1875. That year the United Kingdom and France combined imported more than 1 million hides and over the entire period from 1871 to 1878 imported some 3.5 million hides. Much of this trade volume can be attributed to an invention in London in 1871 that allowed buffalo hides to be tanned for industrial use.

Source: M. Scott Taylor, March 2007, "Buffalo Hunt: International Trade and the Virtual Extinction of the North American Bison," NBER Working Paper No. 12969.

---

[19] The import data for the United Kingdom and France are in pounds, so these estimates of imports assume that each four hides weigh 112 pounds.

HEADLINES

Europe Leans Toward Bluefin Trade Ban

This article reports on actions taken by European officials to classify the bluefin tuna as an endangered species, which would ban international trade in this species.

PARIS—European officials are increasing pressure for an international ban on the commercial fishing of bluefin tuna, a threatened species whose fatty belly is prized for sushi. But they are facing a delicate balancing act as they try to weigh economic interests of a Mediterranean fishing industry, a sushi-loving Japan, and a species that some experts say is on the verge of extinction. . . .

In July [2009], Monaco proposed that bluefin tuna be listed as an "Appendix 1" endangered species under the Convention on International Trade in Endangered Species of Wild Fauna and Flora. Such a listing would provide the same level of protection accorded pandas and some whales, effectively banning international trade in the fish. A panel of the United Nations Food and Agriculture Organization concluded in December that the species met the criteria for an Appendix 1 listing. Monaco's proposal will be lodged officially when the 175 nations that are parties to the treaty meet [in March 2010] in Doha, Qatar. . . .

The fishing industry was quick to voice its disapproval. Mourad Kahoul, president of an association representing industrial fishing fleets in France, Italy and Spain, said that his group "is doing everything it can to change the government's mind on this," and that there were differing scientific views on the outlook for the fish. . . . The United States fishing industry is "strongly opposed" to listing the fish under the endangered species convention, said Rich Ruais, executive director of the American Bluefin Tuna Association, who said the trade ban "would create a huge black market" . . . .

Japan has not yet made its own position official, though it is widely expected to fight the proposal, as was the case in 1992 when Sweden sought to have the bluefin listed. The United States initially said it supported Monaco, but it has not made clear its position.

Source: Excerpted from David Jolly, "Europe Leans Toward Bluefin Trade Ban," New York Times, *February 4, 2010.*

Figure 11-5 shows convincingly that international trade, combined with the innovation in tanning technology in London and the absence of any property rights over the buffalo, was responsible for the slaughter of the buffalo. That is a sad result of market forces and one that we want to avoid today through agreements such as CITES. Multilateral environmental agreements are needed to prevent international trade from exacerbating the tragedy of the commons. We now turn to a final case in which this problem can occur, and that is with global pollution.

International Agreements on Pollution

Pollution is a by-product of many manufacturing activities. The tragedy of the commons applies to pollution, too, because companies and countries can treat the air and water as a common-property resource, allowing pollutants to enter it without regard for where these pollutants end up. Pollution is an international issue because it can often cross borders in the water or atmosphere. We will use the term "global pollutants" for substances that cross country borders. Examples include chlorofluorocarbons (CFCs), which result in a depletion of the ozone layer in the atmosphere, and carbon dioxide (CO_2), which contributes to global warming. In contrast, we use the term "local pollutants" for substances that, for the most part, stay within a country. An example is smog, which is caused by the carbon monoxide (CO) in factory emissions and automobile exhaust.

Global Pollutants For global pollutants, a prisoner's dilemma similar to that illustrated in Figure 11-2 for tariffs again applies. Because the pollution crosses international borders, each country does not face the full cost of its own pollution. It follows that there is little incentive to regulate global pollutants. In the absence of regulation, however, countries will end up with the bad outcome of having too much global pollution, so international agreements are needed to control the amount.

Payoff Matrix To make this argument more carefully, in Figure 11-6 we show the payoff matrix for two countries, each of which decides whether to regulate the emissions of a pollutant. The regulations could take the form of limits on how much of the pollutant an industry can emit, which means that the industry must install special equipment to reduce its emissions, at its own expense. Each quadrant of the matrix includes Home's payoff in the lower-left corner and Foreign's payoff in the upper-right corner. We start with a situation of regulation and then measure the change in welfare for Home or Foreign when there are no pollution regulations (or when pollution regulations are not enforced).

Starting in the upper-left cell, when both countries regulate emissions of the pollutant, consumers are better off as compared with no regulations, while producers are worse off because of the expense of the regulations. If one country—say, Home—decides to not regulate, then its producers would gain because they no longer have to install the extra equipment to reduce emissions, but consumers in Home and Foreign would lose if regulations are not used because of the extra pollution. The outcome is similar if Foreign decides to not regulate: its producers gain, and consumers in both countries lose. Finally, if neither country regulates, then there is a large loss for consumers from the extra pollution and a small gain for producers due to the cost savings from not installing the equipment (this gain is small because neither producer is subject to the regulations, so competition can eliminate most of their gains).

Nash Equilibrium Let us use the structure of payoffs in Figure 11-6 to determine the Nash equilibrium. Start in the upper-left quadrant, where both countries regulate their pollution emissions. If either country deviates from this position and does not

FIGURE 11-6

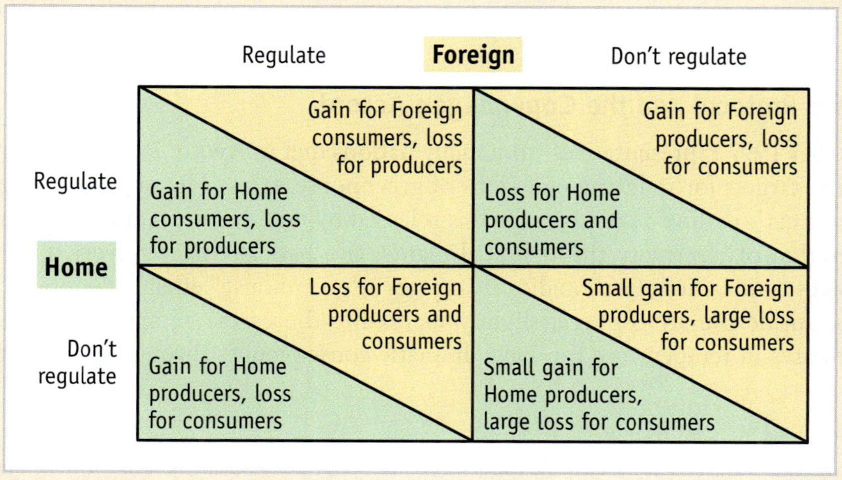

Payoffs in an Environmental Game This payoff matrix shows the gains and losses for Home and Foreign countries, depending on whether they adopt environmental regulations. If governments weigh producer surplus more than consumer surplus, then the structure of payoffs is similar to the prisoner's dilemma because the Nash equilibrium is to have both countries not adopt regulations. That outcome can occur with "global" pollutants.

regulate, it will experience a gain for producers and a loss for consumers. If pollution is local, then the country might realize that the costs to consumers outweigh the gains to producers. That is why the Environmental Protection Agency (EPA) in the United States regulates the pollution from factories and from cars: the gains to consumers from reducing pollution outweigh the costs to producers.

In the case of global pollution, however, this calculation changes. If a country's pollution crosses international borders, as with CO_2 emissions, then the perceived gains to a country's *own* consumers from regulating the pollution may be less than the costs to producers. In that case, neither country will want to stay in the regulated quadrant in the upper left of Figure 11-6 and will have an incentive to *not* regulate its global pollution. Given that one country does not regulate its global pollution, the other country will have an even greater incentive to not regulate: if Home does not regulate in Figure 11-6 so that we are in the bottom row, then Foreign's best decision will likely be to not regulate either because the additional loss to its consumers will be offset by a gain to producers.[20]

Thus, the payoffs shown in Figure 11-6 can lead us to a situation in which neither country regulates pollution, in the lower-right quadrant, despite the large losses to consumers. That outcome is similar to the prisoner's dilemma that we discussed for the tariff game (Figure 11-2): both countries can end up with a bad outcome (with high tariffs or high pollution), even though they are individually making their best decisions. Just like the tariff game, multilateral agreements are needed to ensure that countries end up instead in the upper-left quadrant, with both countries regulating the global pollution.

Multilateral Agreements One example of an international agreement is the Montreal Protocol on Substances that Deplete the Ozone Layer, which has successfully eliminated the use of chlorofluorocarbons (CFCs). In that case, the scientific evidence showing that CFCs were creating a "hole" in the ozone layer above Australia and New Zealand was conclusive. In addition, the CFCs that were used in refrigerators, air conditioners, and other appliances could be replaced with alternative chemicals at relatively low cost. So it was not that difficult to get all countries to agree to a ban on the use of CFCs, which began in 1989 and has already reduced the damage to the ozone layer. A more difficult case is that of global warming, which is regulated by an agreement known as the Kyoto Protocol, and more recently by the Copenhagen Accord, as discussed in our final application.

APPLICATION

The Kyoto Protocol and the Copenhagen Accord

In December 1997 representatives from many nations met in Kyoto, Japan, to discuss nonbinding targets for reducing emissions of greenhouse gases. The principal greenhouse gas is carbon dioxide (CO_2), which is released by cars, factories, home heating, the generation of electricity through coal plants, and basically nearly every activity that involves combustion. Carbon dioxide creates a "greenhouse" effect, whereby heat is trapped inside the atmosphere, slightly increasing the earth's temperature. Even small increases in temperature can have dramatic consequences through the melting

[20] In the problems at the end of the chapter, you are asked to work through examples using specific numbers for the gains and losses in Figure 11-6, to determine the Nash equilibrium.

of ice caps, which raises the level of oceans; changes weather patterns; affects agriculture, tourism, and other economic activities; endangers species; and may have even worse consequences.

The **Kyoto Protocol** built on the United Nations' 1992 treaty on climate change, which was ratified by 189 countries, including the United States. Five years later, in 1997, the Kyoto Protocol established specific targets for reduction in greenhouse gas emissions: the industrial countries should cut their emissions of greenhouse gases by a collective 5.2% less than their 1990 levels (which is estimated to be a reduction of 29% from what 2010 levels are predicted to occur without the agreement). Targets for individual countries range from an 8% reduction for the European Union, 7% for the United States, 6% for Japan, 0% for Russia, and permitted increases for Australia and Iceland. In addition, a market for emissions targets was established so that Russia, for example, could sell its credits to other countries if it produces less than its 1990 level of greenhouse gases.

More than 160 have countries ratified this agreement, including about 40 industrial countries. Russia ratified the treaty on November 18, 2004, bringing the amount of greenhouse gases accounted for by the members to more than 55% of the world total. The treaty then took effect three months later, on February 16, 2005. However, the United States did not ratify this treaty and is the only large industrial country to not join the effort. Why did the United States refuse to join, and what actions can be taken instead to reduce global emissions?

There are four reasons often given to explain why the United States did not join the Kyoto Protocol:[21] (1) although the evidence toward global warming is strong, we still do not understand all the consequences of policy actions; (2) while the United States is the largest emitter of greenhouse gases, meeting the Kyoto targets would negatively affect its economy; (3) Kyoto failed to include the developing countries, especially China and India; (4) there are other ways to pursue reductions in greenhouse gas emissions.

The first point has become less plausible over time, as the evidence for and consequences of global warming become more apparent. The second point is true: the United States is the largest emitter of greenhouse gases (because of its very large economy), and meeting the Kyoto goals would certainly impose significant costs on the economy. The costs to the United States would probably be higher than the costs to Germany, for example, because East Germany had plants that were highly polluting in 1990 that have now been shut down. The percentage reduction in German pollution is calculated from a baseline that includes the highly polluting plants, whereas the percentage reduction in the United States is calculated from a baseline using plants that were already polluting less in 1990, due to U.S. regulations.

Nevertheless, the fact that costs are high should not prevent countries from trying to reduce greenhouse gas emissions. A 2006 report by the Stern Commission in the United Kingdom argues that the costs of *not* reducing greenhouse gas emissions are unacceptably high: as high as "the great wars and the economic depression of the first half of the twentieth century" and damage from climate change that is potentially irreversible.[22]

[21] These reasons are all mentioned in a speech given by President George W. Bush to the United Nations in 2001. See "In the President's Words: 'A Leadership Role on the Issue of Climate Change,'" *New York Times*, June 12, 2001, electronic edition.

[22] "The Economics of Climate Change," available at http://www.hm-treasury.gov.uk, as cited in Martin Wolf, "A Compelling Case for Action to Avoid a Climatic Catastrophe," *Financial Times*, November 1, 2006, p. 13.

The third point—that the Kyoto Protocol leaves out developing countries such as China and India—is perhaps the major reason why the United States did not ratify the treaty. Just as in the prisoner's dilemma game illustrated in Figure 11-6, if one player does not regulate its emissions, then there is less incentive for the other player to also regulate. For this reason, the Copenhagen Climate Summit, held in Copenhagen in December 2009, brought together all the major countries with an interest in climate change—119 nations in total—to try and hammer out a new agreement. Unfortunately, the meeting ended with only modest goals, called the **Copenhagen Accord:** a recognition that further increases in global average temperature should be kept below 2 degrees centigrade; an agreement that industrialized countries will submit goals for greenhouse gas emissions reductions, while developing countries will communicate their efforts in this regard; and the establishment of a fund to finance the needs of developing countries in fighting the effect of climate change. But as indicated in **Headlines: Dismal Outcome at Copenhagen Fiasco,** these goals come without any firm means to enforce them.

HEADLINES

Dismal Outcome at Copenhagen Fiasco

In the introduction to the chapter, we discussed the Copenhagen Climate Summit, held in December 2009, which was intended to establish new guidelines for reductions in greenhouse gas emissions. The summit did not achieve that goal, unfortunately, and this article discusses possible next steps.

The [Copenhagen Accord] agreement cobbled together by the US, China, India, Brazil and South Africa is merely an expression of aims. It recognises the scientific case for keeping the rise in global temperatures to 2°C. It calls on developed countries to provide $100 [billion] a year in support of poor nations' efforts by 2020, but without saying who pays what to whom. It appears to commit none of the signatories to anything.

. . . Climate change requires global co-operation, to be sure, because the global stock of greenhouse gases is the driver. Collective action is essential. The free-rider problem is obvious and has to be addressed. But the maximalist approach to this, a global treaty with binding caps on emissions, is going to be extraordinarily difficult to achieve. Even if the will were there, enforcing the caps would be a problem, as the Kyoto Protocol amply attests. If the maximalist model can be revived in time for next December's [2010] scheduled conference in Mexico, well and good: the key thing, though, is that progress should not be held hostage to it. The need is for greater pragmatism and flexibility.

The US and China can take the lead. In Copenhagen, friction between the two was evident, with the US calling for independent verification of emissions reductions, and China resisting infringements of its sovereignty. In fact the two countries are not so far apart: the US Congress is as jealous of national sovereignty, and as wary of international obligations, as China. Both countries should lead by example, with unilateral low-cost carbon-abatement policies already announced or under consideration: cap and trade in the US, measures to reduce carbon intensity in China. The international framework need not insist on lock-step agreement. Above all, it should not obstruct policies that push the right way. . . .

Generous aid to developing countries for greenhouse gas abatement is warranted, but should be negotiated separately. Again, the need is to unpack the problem into manageable pieces. Copenhagen has shown the limits to the current approach. Reviving international co-operation is of paramount importance. This can best be done by asking less of it.

Source: Excerpted from "Dismal Outcome at Copenhagen Fiasco," Financial Times, *December 21, 2009, p. 8.*

The **Headlines** article recognizes that action on global climate change requires global cooperation. But the multilateral deal that was attempted at Copenhagen is not the only way to go. Countries can and should pursue domestic policies that limit greenhouse gas emmissions. Europe already has a well-functioning market for carbon emissions, which allows companies and countries to buy and sell credits for such emissions. The United States is considering the same type of market under a "cap and trade" system, which puts a cap (upper limit) on the carbon emissions of each firm, but allows them to trade credits with other firms. Although China does not yet envisage such a system, it is making another type of contribution by focusing on alternative energy, becoming the world's largest producer and exporter of solar panel cells and wind turbines. Furthermore, in March 2010, China and India agreed to join the Copenhagen Accord, as has the United States and more than 100 other countries. These actions show that the modest goals of the Copenhagen Accord have made it easier for countries to join that agreement than the earlier, binding limits of the Kyoto Protocol. Even though this accord does not include a means of enforcement, it could form the basis for future international cooperation on climate change. ■

4 Conclusions

Throughout this book, we have referred to international agreements on trade, including multilateral agreements such as the GATT and WTO and regional agreements such as NAFTA. In this chapter, we have explored the rationale for these agreements more carefully, and we also discussed the areas other than trade—such as labor standards and the environment—that these agreements encompass.

The first issue we addressed is why international agreements are needed at all. The answer is that there are strong temptations for countries to use tariffs for their own benefit, or to avoid adopting environmental regulations, as occurs when countries do not face the costs of their own global pollutants. In these situations, countries have an incentive to use tariffs or not regulate, but when all countries act in this manner, they end up losing: the outcome can be high tariffs or high pollution. This outcome can occur because the countries are in a "prisoner's dilemma" type of game in which the Nash equilibrium leads both parties to act in ways that seem right taken on their own but result in a poor outcome (i.e., both use tariffs or pollute). International agreements are needed to avoid these bad equilibria and restore a free-trade or low-pollution outcome.

A second issue we have addressed is that *halfway* steps toward the complete use of markets (as with complete free trade) can also have bad results. We found that such an outcome was a possibility with regional trade agreements, also called "preferential trade agreements," if the amount of trade diversion caused by the agreement is more than the amount of trade creation. Because preferential trade agreements provide zero tariffs only to the countries included in the agreement but maintain tariffs against all outside countries, they are a halfway step toward free trade. Countries that are not members of the agreement are worse off from being excluded. We have also shown that such agreements *might* make the member countries worse off, too, because the lowest-cost producers can be excluded from the agreement.

Another case in which a halfway step toward open markets can make countries worse off is with the overharvesting of resources. We have argued that in the absence of property rights for an exhaustible resource such as fish, opening countries to free trade can lead to even more harvesting of the resource, to the point of near extinction or extinction. That outcome is bad for the exporting country, at least. So free trade *in the absence of well-defined property rights* can lead to losses. Economists think of this case as opening one market (i.e., free trade between countries) without having a properly functioning market for the resource (i.e., no property rights). Viewed in that way, the overharvesting of an exhaustible resource is similar to trade diversion in a regional trade agreement, since the trade agreement also opens one market (i.e., free trade between member countries) without having complete free trade (i.e., tariffs are applied against the nonmember countries). Both overharvesting and trade diversion are bad outcomes that arise in settings in which markets are not functioning properly.

Finally, we have argued that actions by consumers, unions, and firms to improve labor standards and the environment are important. Such actions, including the protests at the 1999 WTO meetings, *have* made a difference in the rulings of the WTO in environmental cases: although environmentalists have lost some battles at the WTO, some observers believe they have won the war. We can also expect that such actions make a difference to the labor standards enjoyed by workers and the environmental safeguards used by firms.

KEY POINTS

1. There are two primary types of free-trade agreements: multilateral and regional. Multilateral agreements are negotiated among large groups of countries (such as all countries in the WTO) to reduce trade barriers among them, whereas regional agreements operate among a smaller group of countries, often in the same region.

2. Under perfect competition, we can analyze the benefits of multilateral agreements by considering the Nash equilibrium of a two-country game in which the countries are deciding whether to apply a tariff. The unique Nash equilibrium for two large countries is to apply tariffs against each other, which is an example of a "prisoner's dilemma." By using an agreement to remove tariffs, both countries become better off by eliminating the deadweight losses of the tariffs.

3. Regional trade agreements are also known as "preferential trade agreements," because they give preferential treatment (i.e., free trade) to the countries included within the agreement, but maintain tariffs against outside countries. There are two types of regional trade agreements: free-trade areas (such as NAFTA) and customs unions (such as the European Union).

4. The welfare gains and losses that arise from regional trade agreements are more complex than those that arise from multilateral trade agreements because only the countries included within the agreement have zero tariffs, while tariffs are maintained against the countries outside the agreement. Under a free-trade area, the countries within the regional trade agreement each have their own tariffs against outside countries; whereas under a customs union, the countries within the regional trade agreement have the same tariffs against outside countries.

5. Trade creation occurs when a country within a regional agreement imports a product from another member country that formerly it produced for itself. In this case, there is a welfare gain for both the buying and the selling country.

6. Trade diversion occurs when a member country imports a product from another member country that it formerly imported from a country outside of the new trade region. Trade diversion leads to losses for the former exporting country and possibly for the importing country and the new trading region as a whole.

7. Labor standards refer to all issues that directly affect workers, including occupational health and safety, child labor, minimum wages, the right to unionize, and so on. The enforcement of labor standards is sometimes included within trade agreements and is an issue on which consumer groups and unions often demand action.

8. The WTO does not deal directly with the environment, but environmental issues come up as the WTO is asked to rule on specific cases. A review of these cases shows that the WTO has become more friendly to environmental considerations in its rulings.

9. International agreements on the environment are needed for the same reasons that agreements on tariffs are needed—to avoid a prisoner's dilemma type of outcome, which is bad for all countries. The Kyoto Protocol of 2005 had only limited success because the United States did not agree to participate, and developing countries such as China and India were excluded. The Copenhagen Accord of 2009 also did not achieve international commitments with firm enforcement, but at least the United States, China, India, and more than 100 other countries have agreed to participate.

KEY TERMS

terms-of-trade gain, p. 361
multilateral agreement, p. 361
regional trade agreement, p. 361
trade agreement, p. 361
most favored nation principle, p. 361
prisoner's dilemma, p. 364
preferential trade agreements, p. 365
free-trade area, p. 365
customs union, p. 366
rules of origin, p. 366
trade creation, p. 367
trade diversion, p. 367
labor standards, p. 372
living wage, p. 377
multilateral environmental agreements, p. 377
tragedy of the commons, p. 384
common property, p. 384
Kyoto Protocol, p. 389
Copenhagen Accord, p. 390

PROBLEMS

1. a. How is a customs union different from a free-trade area? Provide examples of each.
   b. Why do some economists prefer multilateral trade agreements over regional trade agreements?

2. Figure 11-2 shows the tariff game among large countries.
   a. Redraw the payoff matrix for a game between a large and small country.
   b. What is/are the Nash equilibrium/equilibria, assuming that the large country applies an optimal tariff?
   c. What does your answer to (b) tell you about the role of the WTO in a situation like this?

3. Consider the following variation of Table 11-1 for the U.S. semiconductor market:

	U.S. TARIFF		
	0%	10%	20%
From Canada, before NAFTA	$46	$*W*	$55.2
From Asia, before NAFTA	$42	$*X*	$*Y*
From Canada, after NAFTA	$46	$*Z*	$*Z*
From Asia, after NAFTA	$42	$*X*	$*Y*
From the United States	$47	$47	$47

a. Fill in the values for *W*, *X*, *Y*, and *Z*.

b. Suppose that before NAFTA, the United States had a 20% tariff on imported semiconductors. Which country supplied the U.S. market? Is it the lowest-cost producer?

c. After NAFTA, who supplies the U.S. market? Has either trade creation or diversion occurred because of NAFTA? Explain.

d. Now suppose that before NAFTA, the United States had a 10% tariff on imported semiconductors. Then repeat parts (b) and (c).

e. In addition to the assumptions made in (d), consider the effect of an increase in high-technology investment in Canada due to NAFTA, allowing Canadian firms to develop better technology. As a result, *three years after the initiation of NAFTA*, Canadian firms can begin to sell their products to the United States for $46. What happens to the U.S. trade pattern three years after NAFTA? Has either trade creation or diversion occurred because of NAFTA? Explain.

4. Assume that Thailand and India are potential trading partners of China. Thailand is a member of ASEAN but India is not. Suppose the import price of textiles from India (P_{India}) is 50 per unit under free trade and is subject to a 20% tariff. As of January 1st 2010, China and Thailand entered into the China-ASEAN free-trade area, eliminating tariffs on Thai imports. Use the following figure to answer these questions:

a. Before the China-ASEAN free-trade area, how much does China import from each trading partner? What is the import price? Calculate the tariff revenue.

b. After the China-ASEAN free-trade area, how much does China import from each trade partner? What is the import price? What is the total tariff revenue of China?

c. Based on your answer to part (b), what is the impact of the China-ASEAN free-trade area on the welfare of China?

d. What is the effect of the China-ASEAN free-trade area on the welfare of Thailand and India?

e. As mentioned in the **Headlines: China-ASEAN Treaty Threatens Indian Exporters,** the China-ASEAN agreement may lead to a similar one between China and India. How would this affect China's imports from each country? What would be the effect on welfare in China, Thailand, and India if such an agreement was signed?

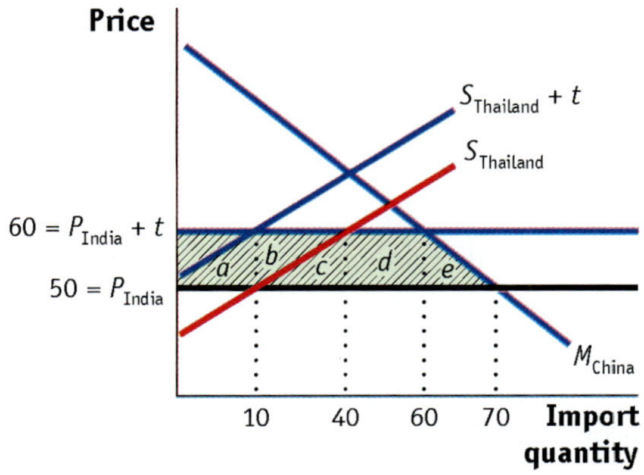

5. Redraw the graph of trade diversion (Figure 11-3) with the S'_{mex} curve intersecting the M_{US} curve *between* points *A* and *D*.

a. When the United States and Mexico join NAFTA, who supplies auto parts to the United States? Does the United States import a larger quantity of auto parts after NAFTA; that is, does trade creation occur?

b. What is the change in government revenue compared to before NAFTA?

c. Is the United States better off for joining NAFTA?

6. Refer to the survey in Table 11-2 regarding consumers' attitudes toward working conditions.

a. Fill in the survey questions for yourself and at least five friends.

b. Average your results, and compare them with those in Table 11-2. Are there any consistent differences in the answers from your friends and those in Table 11-2?

c. Do the answers from your friends show the following two characteristics?
   i. Many people are willing to pay at least a small amount to ensure good labor standards (or simply switch to an alternative with the same price), though relatively few are willing to pay a lot.
   ii. Individuals had to receive a higher discount to purchase a T-shirt made under poor conditions than they were willing to pay for a T-shirt made under good conditions.

   Explain whether these characteristics apply to your friends or not.

7. Using Table 11-3, explain why environmentalists have "lost the battle but won the war" in their dealings with the WTO. Refer to specific WTO cases in your answer.

8. Refer to following variations of the payoff matrix for the environmental game shown in Figure 11-6. In this problem, a number is assigned to represent the welfare level of each outcome for Home and Foreign.

   a. First, consider the case of global pollution in which the government puts more weight on producer profits than consumer well-being when calculating welfare (this is so since a portion of consumer costs are borne by the other country). How can you tell that the government favors producers over consumers from the following payoff matrix? What is the Nash equilibrium for this environmental game? Is it a prisoner's dilemma? Briefly explain.

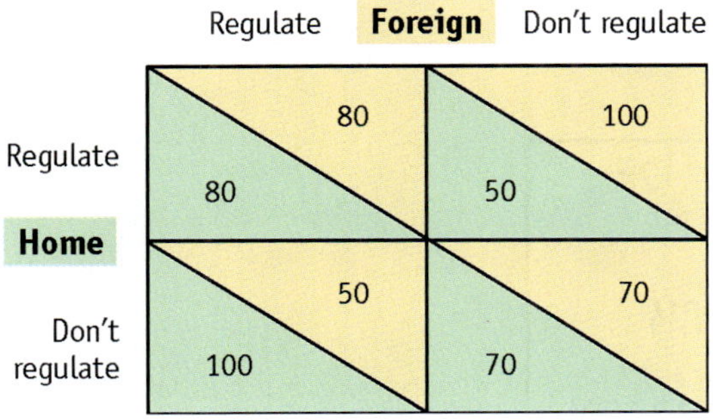

   b. Next, consider the case of local pollution in which the government puts more weight on consumer well-being than producer profits when calculating welfare. How can you tell that the government favors consumers over producers from the following payoff matrix? What is the Nash equilibrium for this environmental game? Is it a prisoner's dilemma? Briefly explain.

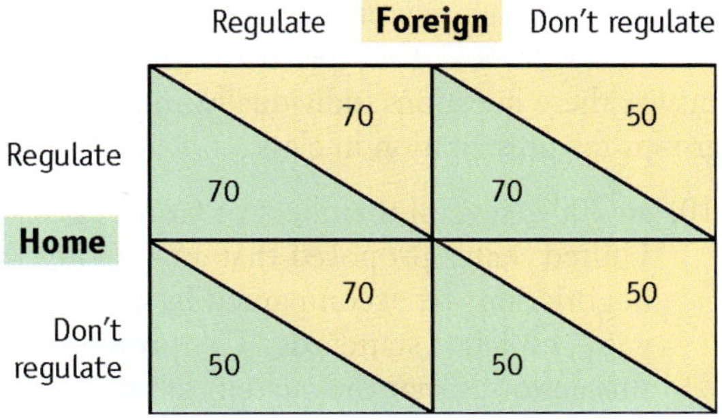

9. Consider the case of protecting the bluefin tuna discussed in **Headlines: Europe Leans Toward Bluefin Trade Ban.** Refer to question 8, and relate this real-world example to the payoff matrices in parts (a) and (b), assuming that Home and Foreign are the United States and Europe. "Regulate" means that the bluefin tuna is classified as endangered, so there is no international trade in this species, whereas "don't regulate" means that it is not classified as endangered.

   a. Which of the two payoff matrices corresponds with both the United States and Europe being more concerned with the fishing industry than with the well-being of the bluefin tuna? What is the Nash equilibrium of that game?
   b. Which of the two payoff matrices corresponds with both the United States and Europe being more concerned with the bluefin species itself than with the fishing industry? What is the Nash equilibrium of that game?
   c. Suppose that Europe is more concerned with the continuation of the bluefin species, and the United States is more concerned with the fishing industry. Draw a payoff matrix for this case and solve for the Nash equilibrium of the game.

Longer study questions: The following questions ask you to consider a real-life situation involving international trade agreements, dealing with trade, labor, or the environment. For each question, you are asked to develop an "agree" or "disagree" position on each situation. These situations are drawn from recent press reports, which are available in the instructor's manual. You can research the issues on the Web and also rely on any relevant information from this textbook. Your instructor might ask you to answer these questions individually, in pairs, or in groups for presentation in class.

10. In 2007, several members of Congress in the United States proposed that any further trade negotiations be accompanied by a "grand bargain" on labor standards. The problem with this action is that the current labor practices of the United States sometimes run afoul of the guidelines of the International Labour Organization (ILO), which would open up the United States to criticism and potentially sanctions from that agency. The article "Why a 'Grand Deal' on Labour Could End Trade Talks" describes these concerns and argues that such a "grand deal" would be a mistake for the United States. A full text of this article is available at http://www.iie.com/publications/opeds/oped.cfm?ResearchID=716.

    Answer the following: Do you agree or disagree with the proposal for the United States to pursue a "grand deal" on labor standards, bringing its own laws into line with those of the International Labour Organization?

11. In March 2007 it was announced that several restaurants in the greater San Francisco area would no longer provide bottled water to their patrons to save on the environmental costs of transporting that water: do a web search for the phrase "bottled water backlash" to find articles about the San Francisco restaurants and other companies taking this action. Instead, these companies would install filtering equipment that would allow them to serve local water. Although these actions are intended to be more environmentally friendly, they will affect firms and countries that sell bottled water. One of these countries is Fiji, which obtains a major portion of its export earnings from bottled water.

    Answer the following: Do you agree or disagree with the actions taken by the restaurants in San Francisco?

NET WORK

Google "corporate responsibility" to find an example, other than Nike, of a corporation or group of companies that is adopting procedures to protect workers' rights or the environment. Briefly describe the procedures being adopted.

Index

Note: Page numbers followed by f indicate figures; page numbers followed by n indicate notes; page numbers followed by t indicate tables; key terms are in **boldface** type.

A

B

J

K

L

Q

R

U

V

W

International Economics is available in four versions: a two-semester, twenty-two chapter hardcover edition, paperback split editions of *International Trade* and *International Macroeconomics*, and a shorter one-semester *Essentials of International Economics* edition. See inside front cover for a chapter correlation guide.

The following annotated table of contents for the full two-semester version of the text describes the main goal for each chapter and notes what makes each chapter unique.